PLAYFAIR
FOOTBALL ANNUAL
2002–2003

55th edition

Editors: Glenda Rollin and
Jack Rollin

D0242659

headline

Copyright © 2002 HEADLINE BOOK PUBLISHING

First published in 2002
by HEADLINE BOOK PUBLISHING

10 9 8 7 6 5 4 3 2 1

Cover photographs Front and spine: Steven Gerrard (Liverpool); back: Craig Bellamy (Newcastle United) – both *Actionimages*.

ISBN 0 7553 1109 4

Typeset by Wearset Ltd, Boldon, Tyne and Wear

Printed and bound in Great Britain by
Clays Ltd, St Ives plc

HEADLINE BOOK PUBLISHING
A division of Hodder Headline
338 Euston Road
London NW1 3BH

www.headline.co.uk
www.hodderheadline.com

CONTENTS

European and International Football

Other Football

Information and Records

EDITORIAL

There was understandable disappointment over England's defeat in the World Cup, given the scale of the expectations of success before the finals. But just how sound the basis was for this optimism is another matter.

From a position where qualification seemed unlikely, the new manager Sven Goran Eriksson achieved his first goal of ensuring England a place in the Asian tournament, without the necessity for the play-offs, but it was too close to be considered comfortable. David Beckham's last minute free-kick against Greece ensuring the draw which was enough, but only because of Germany's failure to beat Finland.

No, the cornerstone of our hopes came from that 5-1 win over the Germans in Munich, the most humiliating result suffered by Germany since England's 6-3 win in 1938. By the time it came to head off to South Korea and Japan in the summer, media hype had reached a stage where it seemed the wagon was rolling along in an unstoppable fashion.

Came the infamous Group of Death game with Argentina and almost the entire nation was at a standstill either watching a TV screen or listening to the radio. Beckham duly exacted revenge for his controversial dismissal against the Argentines four years earlier and when Brazil were faced in the quarter-finals, there was something akin to gridlock on the nation's interest in anything but the match. We lost against ten men and appeared to have neither the tactical know-how nor fitness to combat a superior football team.

In the aftermath there were calls for a winter break and a reduction in League matches to enable players to do justice to themselves at international level and fresh enough to face opponents whose domestic commitments are fewer. However, the reality is that it is the growth of European matches which cause the problem. In 1966 when England won the World Cup, the English champions would have needed to play just eight games to reach the European Cup Final. As it was Liverpool were knocked out in the second round, while in 2000–01 they competed in 12 matches to even get to the UEFA Cup Final. Had they been in the European Champions League a minimum of 16 would have been required for a similar position going into the final.

Undoubtedly further success in the World Cup would have erased the memory of many problems faced by the game during the season. There was a real threat of a players strike over money the Professional Footballers Association considered necessary to provide for players no longer able to function because of injury and in their view owed to them by television agreement.

Ironically settlement over the issue was completed before the crash of ITV Digital which seriously affected the finances of football clubs in the Nationwide Football League. A partial deal when a consortium of BSkyB and the BBC which took over the franchise only scratched at the surface of such lost revenue.

Moreover the continued spiral of wages had even the wealthiest of top clubs finding it more and more difficult to balance the books as the clamour for success grew and grew. To underline the necessity to chase the elusive in honours, more than half the 92 first class clubs in the FA Premier League and Nationwide Football League changed managers during the season.

While there seemed at last to have been a concerted effort on the part of the authorities to prevent known troublemakers from visiting the World Cup final in Asia, pockets of hooliganism still plagued the domestic game from time to time. Discipline both on and off the field was to be found wanting on occasions. And as a society we cannot dismiss such a situation as the times we live in.

What then of the future? By 2006 it will be 40 years since we last won the World Cup and the finals will be held in Germany, our defeated opponents in the 1966 finale. While we can point to more than 100 players with English clubs who featured throughout the finals last summer, the greater proportion of these were of course foreign imports who have helped to raise the standard of football in our Premier League. But it has left a question mark on the improvement at top international level of our own talent.

The next four years could be crucial ones for the game in this country, while it continues to thrive at domestic level, the need for advancement in competing with the best in the world is paramount if we wish to have any chance of recapturing the glory which is still a memory around England's 1966 World Cup triumph.

STOP PRESS

Summer transfers completed and pending: **Aston Villa:** Marcus Allback (Heerenveen) £2m; Stefan Postma (De Graafschap) £1.5m. **Birmingham C:** Robbie Savage (Leicester C) £2.5m. **Blackburn R:** Marc Sebastian Pelzer (Kaiserslautern) undisclosed; Andy Todd (Charlton Ath) £750,000. **Bolton W:** Bulent Akin (Galatasaray) undisclosed; Delroy Facey (Huddersfield T) Free; Jay-Jay Okocha (Paris St Germain) Free. **Chelsea:** Enrique De Lucas (Espanyol) Free. **Fulham:** Martin Herrera (Alaves) Free; Facundo Sava (Gimnasia) undisclosed. **Liverpool:** El-Hadji Diouf (Lens) £10m; Bruno Cheyrou (Lille) £3.7m; Salif Diao (Sedan) undisclosed. **Manchester C:** Sylvain Distin (Paris St Germain) £4m; Mikkel Bischoff (AB Copenhagen) £750,000; Marc Vivien Foe (Lyon) £550,000; Nicolas Anelka (Paris St Germain) £13m; Vicente Matias Vuoso (Independiente) £3.5m; Tyrone Loran (Volendam) undisclosed; Peter Schmeichel (Aston Villa) Free. **Middlesbrough:** Massimo Maccarone (Empoli) £8.15m; Franck Queudrue (Lens) £2.5m. **Newcastle U:** Hugo Viana (Sporting Lisbon) £8.5m. **Southampton:** Michael Svensson (Troyes) £2m. **Sunderland:** Phil Babb (Sporting Lisbon) Free. **WBA:** Ronnie Wallwork (Manchester U) Free. **West Ham U:** Youssef Soufiane (Auxerre) Free; Raimond Van der Gouw (Manchester U) Free.

Other moves: Ricardo Fuller, Tivoli Gardens to Preston NE £500,000; Hayden Foxe, West Ham U to Portsmouth £400,000; Tyrone Mears, Manchester C to Preston NE £200,000; Richard Hughes, Bournemouth to Portsmouth £100,000; Steve Robinson, Preston NE to Luton T £50,000; Paul Edwards, Swindon T to Wrexham Free; Ian Breckin, Chesterfield to Wigan Ath Free; Lee Hardy, Oldham Ath to Macclesfield T Free; Rod Wallace, Bolton W to Gillingham Free; David Zdrillic, Unterhaching to Walsall Free; Ian Stevens, Carlisle U to Shrewsbury T Free; Rigobert Song, West Ham U to Lens; Matthew Robinson, Reading to Oxford U Free; Alex Nyarko, Everton to Paris St Germain Loan; Daniel Maye, Port Vale to Southend U; Scott McNiven, Oldham Ath to Oxford U Free; John Anderson, Livingston to Hull C Free; Ritchie Appleby, Kidderminster H to Hull C Free; Gunnar Halle, Bradford C to Lillestrom Free; Paul Harsley, Halifax T to Northampton T; Greg Lincoln, Margate to Northampton T Free; Matt Murphy, Bury to Swansea C Free; Paul Reid, Bury to Swansea C; Greg Shields, Charlton Ath to Kilmarnock Free; Allan Smart, Oldham Ath to Dundee U; David Smith, Grimsby T to Swansea C; Tony Thorpe Bristol C to Luton T Free; David Robertson, Leeds U to Montrose; Patrick Suffo, Sheffield U to Numancia; Matthew Taylor, Luton T to Portsmouth; Jon Beswetherick, Plymouth Arg to Sheffield W; Mark Boyd, Newcastle U to Port Vale Free; Tom Cowan, Cambridge U to York C Free; Dean Cropper, Sheffield W to Lincoln C Free; Andy Dibble, Stockport Co to Wrexham; Craig Faulconbridge, Wrexham to Wycombe W Free; James Goodwin, Celtic to Stockport Co Free; Bradley Hughes, Watford to Grimsby T Free; Damien Lynch, Nottingham F to Bohemians, Free; Kesiena Metitiri, West Ham U to Bristol C Free; Neil Moore, Telford U to Mansfield T Free; Carl Muggleton, Cheltenham T to Chesterfield Free; Kevin Muscat, Wolverhampton W to Rangers Free; George O'Callaghan, Port Vale to Cork T; Dion Scott, Walsall to Mansfield T Free; Gareth Sheldon, Scunthorpe U to Exeter C; Greg Strong, Motherwell to Hull C; James Thomas, Blackburn R to Swansea C Free; Martin Thomas, Oxford U to Exeter C Free; Simon Weaver, Nuneaton B to Lincoln C Free; Dean Gordon, Middlesbrough to Coventry C; Danny Butterfield, Grimsby T to Crystal Palace Free; Paul Heckingbottom, Darlington to Norwich C Free; Shaka Hislop, West Ham U to Portsmouth Free; Steve Yates, Tranmere R to Sheffield U Free; Stuart McCall, Bradford C to Sheffield U; Iffy Onuora, Gillingham to Sheffield U; Karl Colley, Newcastle U to Sheffield U Free; Lloyd Owusu, Brentford to Sheffield W Free; Chris Greenacre, Mansfield T to Stoke C Free; Dani Rodrigues, Southampton to Walsall Free; Ivar Ingimarsson, Brentford to Wolverhampton W Free; Chris Brandon, Torquay U to Chesterfield Free; Paul Rickers, Oldham Ath to Northampton T; Marc Bircham, Millwall to QPR; Kevin Gray, Huddersfield T to Tranmere R Free; Alan Connell, Ipswich T to Bournemouth Free; Adam Barrett, Mansfield T to Bristol R; Anwar U'ddin, Sheffield W to Bristol R; Kevin Austin, Cambridge U to Bristol R; Guiliano Grazioli, Swindon T to Bristol R; Danny Boxall, Brentford to Bristol R; Paul Tait, Crewe Alex to Bristol R, Matt Clarke, Halifax T to Darlington; James Coppinger, Newcastle U to Exeter C; Ian Ashbee, Cambridge U to Hull C; Sean Parrish, Chesterfield to Kidderminster H Free; Lee Steele, Brighton & HA to Oxford U Free; James Hunt, Northampton T to Oxford U Free; Chris Beech, Huddersfield T to Rochdale Free; David Moss, Falkirk to Swansea C Free; Sam Collins, Bury to Port Vale Free; Omer Riza, West Ham U to Cambridge U; Lee Grant, York C to Aston Villa.

Loans: Gary Caldwell, Newcastle U to Coventry C; Leon Knight, Chelsea to Sheffield W; Vincent Pericard, Juventus to Portsmouth.

LEAGUE REVIEW AND CLUB SECTION

The records went tumbling down as Arsenal wrested the FA Premier League title in 2001–02, courtesy of a splendid run in the second half of the season which saw them unbeaten in 21 matches after 18 December and finishing with 13 consecutive wins. Additionally they scored in every League game and were unbeaten away from Highbury, a feat only previously achieved in the Football League's inaugural season by Preston North End who only had to play 11 times on travel.

Arsenal had beaten their own record of ten consecutive wins established in 1998 and Manchester United's run of 11 two years ago. United's feat of 17 unbeaten away games was also overtaken as well as the achievement of Liverpool in scoring in 25 successive Premier League matches, the Gunners taking their total to 39 overall.

When Arsenal won 2-0 at Bolton Wanderers on 29 April they were five points ahead of Manchester United, both with two matches still to play. Four days after their FA Cup final triumph, Arsenal sealed their season with double success by winning 1-0 at Old Trafford against the champions Manchester United, thus taking the crown they had lost to them in 1999.

Liverpool even denied United of runners-up position in what had proved a disappointing season for the previous champions. With the uncertainty of whether Sir Alex Ferguson was to renew a contract with the club after stating his intention of resigning plus indifferent form, United were as low as ninth by early December and despite a recovery it was too much to expect them to regain such lost ground.

Arsenal called upon the services of 25 different players in the League campaign, none of them ever-present. In fact Patrick Vieira, with 36 appearances including one as a substitute, was the nearest to a full complement. Thierry Henry was leading scorer with 24 goals.

Liverpool apart from one or two costly lapses had another fine season and yet again managed to beat Manchester United home and away. Newcastle United did well to finish fourth and at times in December and January had topped the table. So, too, in the early stages had Bolton Wanderers, whose subsequent experience proved one of avoiding relegation.

Leeds United understandably seemed distracted at times by off-the-field problems and could not improve on fifth place and Chelsea's notorious inconsistent tendencies left them a position lower than that. At the other end of the scale, Sunderland survived at the death, but less fortunate were Ipswich Town, Derby County and Leicester City who found themselves going down to be replaced by Manchester City, West Bromwich Albion and Birmingham City after a dramatic penalty shoot-out success in the play-offs against Norwich City. Sadly Birmingham's previous tie at Millwall had ended in disturbing scenes of rioting.

Attendances in the FA Premier League totalled 13,043,118 compared with 12,472,094 in 2000–01, representing an increase of 4.58% on the previous season, easily the highest in the ten year history of the competition. In addition the Football League reported gates aggregating at 14,716,162 for the three divisions, again their best return during the period of the Premier League's existence.

Thus the overall total for the four professional leagues reached 27,188,256 last topped in the 1971–72 season, a figure which must be a comfort to both bodies, even allowing for the problems which exist over the escalation of financial burdens currently affecting the game.

Down from the First Division went Crewe Alexandra, Barnsley and Stockport County with Brighton & Hove Albion, Reading and Stoke City via the play-offs taking over from them.

The quartet relegated from Division Two were Bournemouth, Bury, Wrexham and Cambridge United, while up from Division Three come Plymouth Argyle, Luton Town and Mansfield Town automatically plus relative newcomers Cheltenham Town who beat the newest entries Rushden & Diamonds in the play-offs.

Out of the League for the second time in their history have gone Halifax Town to be replaced by Boston United who had a titanic struggle with Dagenham & Redbridge for the Nationwide Conference title. Such two-club duels may be a feature of the past as plans to increase the number of non-league clubs into the Football League and vice-versa are ratified to two each season. However Boston faced serious charges brought by the FA in the summer.

FA Barclaycard Premiership

			Home		Goals		Away			Goals			
		P	W	D	L	F	A	W	D	L	F	A	GD	Pts
1	Arsenal	38	12	4	3	42	25	14	5	0	37	11	43	87
2	Liverpool	38	12	5	2	33	14	12	3	4	34	16	37	80
3	Manchester U	38	11	2	6	40	17	13	3	3	47	28	42	77
4	Newcastle U	38	12	3	4	40	23	9	5	5	34	29	22	71
5	Leeds U	38	9	6	4	31	21	9	6	4	22	16	16	66
6	Chelsea	38	11	4	4	43	21	6	9	4	23	17	28	64
7	West Ham U	38	12	4	3	32	14	3	4	12	16	43	–9	53
8	Aston Villa	38	8	7	4	22	17	4	7	8	24	30	–1	50
9	Tottenham H	38	10	4	5	32	24	4	4	11	17	29	–4	50
10	Blackburn R	38	8	6	5	33	20	4	4	11	22	31	4	46
11	Southampton	38	7	5	7	23	22	5	4	10	23	32	–8	45
12	Middlesbrough	38	7	5	7	23	26	5	4	10	12	21	–12	45
13	Fulham	38	7	7	5	21	16	3	7	9	15	28	–8	44
14	Charlton Ath	38	5	6	8	23	30	5	8	6	15	19	–11	44
15	Everton	38	8	4	7	26	23	3	6	10	19	34	–12	43
16	Bolton W	38	5	7	7	20	31	4	6	9	24	31	–18	40
17	Sunderland	38	7	7	5	18	16	3	3	13	11	35	–22	40
18	Ipswich T	38	6	4	9	20	24	3	5	11	21	40	–23	36
19	Derby Co	38	5	4	10	20	26	3	2	14	13	37	–30	30
20	Leicester C	38	3	7	9	15	34	2	6	11	15	30	–34	28

LEADING GOALSCORERS 2001-02

FA BARCLAYCARD PREMIERSHIP

	League	FA Cup	Worthington Cup	Other	Total
Thierry Henry (*Arsenal*)	24	1	0	7	32
Ruud Van Nistelrooy (*Manchester U*)	23	2	0	11	36
Jimmy Floyd Hasselbaink (*Chelsea*)	23	3	3	0	29
Alan Shearer (*Newcastle U*)	23	2	2	0	27
Michael Owen (*Liverpool*)	19	2	0	6	27
Ole Gunnar Solskjaer (*Manchester U*)	17	1	0	7	25
Robbie Fowler (*Leeds U*)	15	0	0	1	16
(*including 3 League goals and 1 European Cup goal for Liverpool*)					
Eidur Gudjohnsen (*Chelsea*)	14	3	3	3	23
Marian Pahars (*Southampton*)	14	1	1	0	16
Frederik Ljungberg (*Arsenal*)	12	2	0	3	17
Michael Ricketts (*Bolton W*)	12	1	2	0	15
Juan Angel (*Aston Villa*)	12	0	0	2	14
James Beattie (*Southampton*)	12	0	2	0	14
Darius Vassell (*Aston Villa*)	12	0	0	0	12
Mark Viduka (*Leeds U*)	11	1	1	3	16
David Beckham (*Manchester U*)	11	0	0	5	16
Jason Euell (*Charlton Ath*)	11	1	1	0	13
Kevin Phillips (*Sunderland*)	11	1	1	0	13
Frederic Kanoute (*West Ham U*)	11	1	0	0	12

Other matches consist of European games, LDV Vans Trophy, Charity Shield and Football League play-offs. Only goals scored in the respective divisions count in the table. Players listed in order of League goals total.

Nationwide Football League Division 1

			Home		Goals			Away			Goals			
		P	W	D	L	F	A	W	D	L	F	A	GD	Pts
1	Manchester C	46	19	3	1	63	19	12	3	8	45	33	56	99
2	WBA	46	15	4	4	36	11	12	4	7	25	18	32	89
3	Wolverhampton W	46	13	4	6	33	18	12	7	4	43	25	33	86
4	Millwall	46	15	3	5	43	22	7	8	8	26	26	21	77
5	Birmingham C	46	14	4	5	44	20	7	9	7	26	29	21	76
6	Norwich C	46	15	6	2	36	16	7	3	13	24	35	9	75
7	Burnley	46	11	7	5	39	29	10	5	8	31	33	8	75
8	Preston NE	46	13	7	3	45	21	7	5	11	26	38	12	72
9	Wimbledon	46	9	8	6	30	22	9	5	9	33	35	6	67
10	Crystal Palace	46	13	3	7	42	22	7	3	13	28	40	8	66
11	Coventry C	46	12	4	7	33	19	8	2	13	26	34	6	66
12	Gillingham	46	12	5	6	38	26	6	5	12	26	41	–3	64
13	Sheffield U	46	8	8	7	34	30	7	7	9	19	24	–1	60
14	Watford	46	10	5	8	38	30	6	6	11	24	26	6	59
15	Bradford C	46	10	1	12	41	39	5	9	9	28	37	–7	55
16	Nottingham F	46	7	11	5	26	21	5	7	11	24	30	–1	54
17	Portsmouth	46	9	6	8	36	31	4	8	11	24	41	–12	53
18	Walsall	46	10	6	7	29	27	3	6	14	22	44	–20	51
19	Grimsby T	46	9	7	7	34	28	3	7	13	16	44	–22	50
20	Sheffield W	46	6	7	10	28	37	6	7	10	21	34	–22	50
21	Rotherham U	46	7	13	3	32	29	3	6	14	20	37	–14	49
22	Crewe Alex	46	8	8	7	23	32	4	5	14	24	44	–29	49
23	Barnsley	46	9	9	5	37	33	2	6	15	22	53	–27	48
24	Stockport Co	46	5	1	17	19	44	1	7	15	23	58	–60	26

NATIONWIDE DIVISION 1

	League	FA Cup	Worthington Cup	Other	Total
Shaun Goater (Manchester C)	28	2	2	0	32
Clint Morrison (Crystal Palace)	22	0	2	0	24
Darren Huckerby (Manchester C)	20	1	5	0	26
Stern John (Birmingham C)	20	0	1	1	22
(Including 13 League goals and 1 Worthington Cup goal for Nottingham F)					
Doug Freedman (Crystal Palace)	20	0	1	0	21
Dean Sturridge (Wolverhampton W)	20	0	0	1	21
Peter Crouch (Portsmouth)	18	0	1	0	19
David Connolly (Wimbledon)	18	0	0	0	18
Marlon King (Gillingham)	17	1	2	0	20
Steve Claridge (Millwall)	17	0	1	0	18
Gareth Taylor (Burnley)	16	0	0	0	16
Mark Robins (Rotherham U)	15	0	1	0	16
Bruce Dyer (Barnsley)	14	1	3	0	18
Richard Sadlier (Millwall)	14	2	1	0	17
Lee Hughes (Coventry C)	14	0	0	0	14
Eoin Jess (Bradford C)	14	0	0	0	14
Richard Cresswell (Preston NE)	13	2	1	0	16
Tommy Mooney (Birmingham C)	13	0	2	0	15
Iwan Roberts (Norwich C)	13	0	0	1	14
Tim Cahill (Millwall)	13	0	0	0	13
Marcelo (Walsall)	13	0	0	0	13
(including 12 League goals for Birmingham C)					

Nationwide Football League Division 2

		P	Home W	D	L	Goals F	A	Away W	D	L	Goals F	A	GD	Pts
1	Brighton & HA	46	17	5	1	42	16	8	10	5	24	26	24	90
2	Reading	46	12	7	4	36	20	11	8	4	34	23	27	84
3	Brentford	46	17	5	1	48	12	7	6	10	29	31	34	83
4	Cardiff C	46	12	8	3	39	25	11	6	6	36	25	25	83
5	Stoke C	46	16	4	3	43	12	7	7	9	24	28	27	80
6	Huddersfield T	46	13	7	3	35	19	8	8	7	30	28	18	78
7	Bristol C	46	13	6	4	38	21	8	4	11	30	32	15	73
8	QPR	46	11	10	2	35	18	8	4	11	25	31	11	71
9	Oldham Ath	46	14	6	3	47	27	4	10	9	30	38	12	70
10	Wigan Ath	46	9	6	8	36	23	7	10	6	30	28	15	64
11	Wycombe W	46	13	5	5	38	26	4	8	11	20	38	−6	64
12	Tranmere R	46	10	9	4	39	19	6	6	11	24	41	3	63
13	Swindon T	46	10	7	6	26	21	5	7	11	20	35	−10	59
14	Port Vale	46	11	6	6	35	24	5	4	14	16	38	−11	58
15	Colchester U	46	9	6	8	35	33	6	6	11	30	43	−11	57
16	Blackpool	46	8	9	6	39	31	6	5	12	27	38	−3	56
17	Peterborough U	46	11	5	7	46	26	4	5	14	18	33	5	55
18	Chesterfield	46	9	3	11	35	36	4	10	9	18	29	−12	52
19	Notts Co	46	8	7	8	28	29	5	4	14	31	42	−12	50
20	Northampton T	46	9	4	10	30	33	5	3	15	24	46	−25	49
21	Bournemouth	46	9	4	10	36	33	1	10	12	20	38	−15	44
22	Bury	46	6	9	8	26	32	5	2	16	17	43	−32	44
23	Wrexham	46	7	7	9	29	32	4	3	16	27	57	−33	43
24	Cambridge U	46	7	7	9	29	34	0	6	17	18	59	−46	34

NATIONWIDE DIVISION 2

	League	FA Cup	Worthington Cup	Other	Total
Bobby Zamora (Brighton & HA)	28	2	2	0	32
Andy Thomson (QPR)	21	0	0	0	21
Lloyd Owusu (Brentford)	20	0	1	1	22
Danny Allsopp (Notts Co)	19	2	4	3	28
Nicky Forster (Reading)	19	0	0	0	19
Leon McKenzie (Peterborough U)	18	1	0	1	20
Andy Liddell (Wigan Ath)	18	0	0	0	18
Ben Burgess (Brentford)	17	1	0	0	18
Jamie Forrester (Northampton T)	17	0	1	0	18
Tony Thorpe (Bristol C)	16	0	1	1	18
Leon Knight (Huddersfield T (on loan))	16	1	0	0	17
Lee Peacock (Bristol C)	15	0	0	2	17
Jamie Cureton (Reading)	15	1	0	0	16
Scott McGleish (Colchester U)	15	1	0	0	16
Simon Haworth (Tranmere R)	15	0	1	0	16
(including 10 League goals and 1 Worthington Cup goal for Wigan Ath)					
Stuart Barlow (Tranmere R)	14	1	2	0	17
Paul Evans (Brentford)	14	0	0	0	14

Nationwide Football League Division 3

			Home		Goals		Away			Goals			
		P	W	D	L	F	A	W	D	L	F	A	GD	Pts
1	Plymouth Arg	46	19	2	2	41	11	12	7	4	30	17	43	102
2	Luton T	46	15	5	3	50	18	15	2	6	46	30	48	97
3	Mansfield T	46	17	3	3	49	24	7	4	12	23	36	12	79
4	Cheltenham T	46	11	11	1	40	20	10	4	9	26	29	17	78
5	Rochdale	46	13	8	2	41	22	8	7	8	24	30	13	78
6	Rushden & Diamonds	46	14	5	4	40	20	6	8	9	29	33	16	73
7	Hartlepool U	46	12	6	5	53	23	8	5	10	21	25	26	71
8	Scunthorpe U	46	14	5	4	43	22	5	9	9	31	34	18	71
9	Shrewsbury T	46	13	4	6	36	19	7	6	10	28	34	11	70
10	Kidderminster H	46	13	6	4	35	17	6	3	14	21	30	9	66
11	Hull C	46	12	6	5	38	18	4	7	12	19	33	6	61
12	Southend U	46	12	5	6	36	22	3	8	12	15	32	−3	58
13	Macclesfield T	46	7	7	9	23	25	8	6	9	18	27	−11	58
14	York C	46	11	5	7	26	20	5	4	14	28	47	−13	57
15	Darlington	46	11	6	6	37	25	4	5	14	23	46	−11	56
16	Exeter C	46	7	9	7	25	32	7	4	12	23	41	−25	55
17	Carlisle U	46	11	5	7	31	21	1	11	11	18	35	−7	52
18	Leyton Orient	46	10	4	9	37	25	3	6	14	18	46	−16	52
19	Torquay U	46	8	6	9	27	31	4	9	10	19	32	−17	51
20	Swansea C	46	7	8	8	26	26	6	4	13	27	51	−24	51
21	Oxford U	46	8	7	8	34	28	3	7	13	19	34	−9	47
22	Lincoln C	46	8	4	11	25	27	2	12	9	19	35	−18	46
23	Bristol R	46	8	7	8	28	28	3	5	15	12	32	−20	45
24	Halifax T	46	5	9	9	24	28	3	3	17	15	56	−45	36

NATIONWIDE DIVISION 3

	League	FA Cup	Worthington Cup	Other	Total
Steve Howard (*Luton T*)	24	0	0	0	24
Luke Rodgers (*Shrewsbury T*)	22	0	0	0	22
Chris Greenacre (*Mansfield T*)	21	5	2	0	28
Julian Alsop (*Cheltenham T*)	20	4	0	2	26
Onandi Lowe (*Rushden & D*)	19	0	0	1	20
Gordon Watson (*Hartlepool U*)	18	0	0	0	18
Gary Alexander (*Hull C*)	17	2	1	3	23
Nathan Ellington (*Bristol R*)	15	4	0	2	21
Ian Clark (*Darlington*)	15	0	0	0	15
(including 2 League goals for Hartlepool U)					
Dean Crowe (*Luton T*)	15	0	0	0	15
Richie Foran (*Carlisle U*)	14	1	0	1	16
Kevin Townson (*Rochdale*)	14	0	0	1	15
Michael Proctor (*York C (on loan)*)	14	0	0	0	14
Martin Carruthers (*Scunthorpe U*)	13	3	0	1	17
Steve Torpey (*Scunthorpe U*)	13	0	0	2	15
Paul Moody (*Oxford U*)	13	0	0	0	13
Lee Nogan (*York C*)	13	0	0	0	13
Lee Thorpe (*Lincoln C*)	13	0	0	0	13

FA BARCLAYCARD PREMIERSHIP

HOME TEAM	Arsenal	Aston Villa	Blackburn R	Bolton W	Charlton Ath	Chelsea	Derby Co	Everton	Fulham	Ipswich T
Arsenal	—	3-2	3-3	1-1	2-4	2-1	1-0	4-3	4-1	2-0
Aston Villa	1-2	—	2-0	3-2	1-0	1-1	2-1	0-0	2-0	2-1
Blackburn R	2-3	3-0	—	1-1	4-1	0-0	0-1	1-0	3-0	2-1
Bolton W	0-2	3-2	1-1	—	0-0	2-2	1-3	2-2	0-0	4-1
Charlton Ath	0-3	1-2	0-2	1-2	—	2-1	1-0	1-2	1-1	3-2
Chelsea	1-1	1-3	0-0	5-1	0-1	—	2-1	3-0	3-2	2-1
Derby Co	0-2	3-1	2-1	1-0	1-1	1-1	—	3-4	0-1	1-3
Everton	0-1	3-2	1-2	3-1	0-3	0-0	1-0	—	2-1	1-2
Fulham	1-3	0-0	2-0	3-0	0-0	1-1	0-0	2-0	—	1-1
Ipswich T	0-2	0-0	1-1	1-2	0-1	0-0	3-1	0-0	1-0	—
Leeds U	1-1	1-1	3-1	0-0	0-0	0-0	3-0	3-2	0-1	2-0
Leicester C	1-3	2-2	2-1	0-5	1-1	2-3	0-3	0-0	0-0	1-1
Liverpool	1-2	1-3	4-3	1-1	2-0	1-0	2-0	1-1	0-0	5-0
Manchester U	0-1	1-0	2-1	1-2	0-0	0-3	5-0	4-1	3-2	4-0
Middlesbrough	0-4	2-1	1-3	1-1	0-0	0-2	5-1	1-0	2-1	0-0
Newcastle U	0-2	3-0	2-1	3-2	3-0	1-2	1-0	6-2	1-1	2-2
Southampton	0-2	1-3	1-2	0-0	1-0	0-2	2-0	0-1	1-1	3-3
Sunderland	1-1	1-1	1-0	1-0	2-2	0-0	1-1	1-0	1-1	1-0
Tottenham H	1-1	0-0	1-0	3-2	0-1	2-3	3-1	1-1	4-0	1-2
West Ham U	1-1	1-1	2-0	2-1	2-0	2-1	4-0	1-0	0-2	3-1

2001–2002 RESULTS

Leeds U	Leicester C	Liverpool	Manchester U	Middlesbrough	Newcastle U	Southampton	Sunderland	Tottenham H	West Ham U
1-2	4-0	1-1	3-1	2-1	1-3	1-1	3-0	2-1	2-0
0-1	0-2	1-2	1-1	0-0	1-1	2-1	0-0	1-1	2-1
1-2	0-0	1-1	2-2	0-1	2-2	2-0	0-3	2-1	7-1
0-3	2-2	2-1	0-4	1-0	0-4	0-1	0-2	1-1	1-0
0-2	2-0	0-2	0-2	0-0	1-1	1-1	2-2	3-1	4-4
2-0	2-0	4-0	0-3	2-2	1-1	2-4	4-0	4-0	5-1
0-1	2-3	0-1	2-2	0-1	2-3	1-0	0-1	1-0	0-0
0-0	2-2	1-3	0-2	2-0	1-3	2-0	1-0	1-1	5-0
0-0	0-0	0-2	2-3	2-1	3-1	2-1	2-0	0-2	0-1
1-2	2-0	0-6	0-1	1-0	0-1	1-3	5-0	2-1	2-3
—	2-2	0-4	3-4	1-0	3-4	2-0	2-0	2-1	3-0
0-2	—	1-4	0-1	1-2	0-0	0-4	1-0	2-1	1-1
1-1	1-0	—	3-1	2-0	3-0	1-1	1-0	1-0	2-1
1-1	2-0	0-1	—	0-1	3-1	6-1	4-1	4-0	0-1
2-2	1-0	1-2	0-1	—	1-4	1-3	2-0	1-1	2-0
3-1	1-0	0-2	4-3	3-0	—	3-1	1-1	0-2	3-1
0-1	2-2	2-0	1-3	1-1	3-1	—	2-0	1-0	2-0
2-0	2-1	0-1	1-3	0-1	0-1	1-1	—	1-2	1-0
2-1	2-1	1-0	3-5	2-1	1-3	2-0	2-1	—	1-1
0-0	1-0	1-1	3-5	1-0	3-0	2-0	3-0	0-1	—

NATIONWIDE FOOTBALL LEAGUE

HOME TEAM	Barnsley	Birmingham C	Bradford C	Burnley	Coventry C	Crewe Alex	Crystal Palace	Gillingham	Grimsby T	Manchester C
Barnsley	—	1-3	3-3	1-1	1-1	2-0	1-4	4-1	0-0	0-3
Birmingham C	1-0	—	4-0	2-3	2-0	3-1	1-0	2-1	4-0	1-2
Bradford C	4-0	1-3	—	2-3	2-1	2-0	1-2	5-1	3-2	0-2
Burnley	3-3	0-1	1-1	—	1-0	3-3	1-0	2-0	1-0	2-4
Coventry C	4-0	1-1	4-0	0-2	—	1-0	2-0	1-2	0-1	4-3
Crewe Alex	2-0	0-0	2-2	1-2	1-6	—	0-0	0-0	2-0	1-3
Crystal Palace	1-0	0-0	2-0	1-2	1-3	4-1	—	3-1	5-0	2-1
Gillingham	3-0	1-1	0-4	2-2	1-2	1-0	3-0	—	2-1	1-3
Grimsby T	1-0	3-1	0-1	3-1	0-1	1-0	5-2	1-2	—	0-2
Manchester C	5-1	3-0	3-1	5-1	4-2	5-2	1-0	4-1	4-0	—
Millwall	3-1	1-1	3-1	0-2	3-2	2-0	3-0	1-2	3-1	2-3
Norwich C	2-1	0-1	1-4	2-1	2-0	2-2	2-1	2-1	1-1	2-0
Nottingham F	0-0	0-0	1-0	1-0	2-1	2-2	4-2	2-2	0-0	1-1
Portsmouth	4-4	1-1	0-1	1-1	1-0	2-4	4-2	2-1	4-2	2-1
Preston NE	2-2	1-0	1-1	2-3	4-0	2-2	2-1	0-2	0-0	2-1
Rotherham U	1-1	2-2	1-1	1-1	0-0	2-2	2-3	3-2	1-1	1-1
Sheffield U	1-1	4-0	2-2	3-0	0-1	1-0	1-3	0-0	3-1	1-3
Sheffield W	3-1	0-1	1-1	0-2	2-1	1-0	1-3	0-0	0-0	2-6
Stockport C	1-3	0-3	1-0	0-2	0-2	0-1	0-1	0-2	3-3	2-1
Walsall	2-1	1-2	2-2	1 0	0-1	2-1	2-2	1-1	4-0	0-0
Watford	3-0	3-3	0-0	1-2	3-0	0-1	1-0	2-3	2-0	1-2
WBA	3-1	1-0	1-0	1-0	1-0	4-1	2-0	1-0	0-1	4-0
Wimbledon	0-1	3-1	1-2	0-0	0-1	2-0	1-1	3-1	2-1	2-1
Wolverhampton W	4-1	2-1	3-1	3-0	3-1	0-1	0-1	2-0	0-1	0-2

DIVISION 1 2001–2002 RESULTS

Millwall	Norwich C	Nottingham F	Portsmouth	Preston NE	Rotherham U	Sheffield U	Sheffield W	Stockport Co	Walsall	Watford	WBA	Wimbledon	Wolverhampton W
1-1	0-2	2-1	1-4	2-1	1-1	1-1	3-0	2-2	4-1	2-0	3-2	1-1	1-0
4-0	4-0	1-1	1-1	0-1	2-2	2-0	2-0	2-1	1-0	3-2	0-1	0-2	2-2
1-2	0-1	2-1	3-1	0-1	3-1	1-2	0-2	2-4	2-0	4-3	0-1	3-3	0-3
0-0	1-1	1-1	1-1	2-1	3-0	2-0	1-2	3-2	5-2	1-0	0-2	3-2	2-3
0-1	2-1	0-0	2-0	2-2	2-0	1-0	2-0	0-0	2-1	0-2	0-1	3-1	0-1
1-0	1-0	0-3	1-1	2-1	2-0	2-2	0-2	0-0	2-1	1-0	1-1	0-4	1-4
1-3	3-2	1-1	0-0	2-0	2-0	0-1	4-1	4-1	2-0	0-2	0-1	4-0	0-2
1-0	0-2	3-1	2-0	5-0	2-1	0-1	2-1	3-3	2-0	0-0	2-1	0-0	2-3
2-2	0-2	0-0	3-1	2-2	0-2	1-0	0-0	3-1	2-2	0-3	0-0	6-2	1-1
2-0	3-1	3-0	3-1	3-2	2-1	0-0	4-0	2-2	3-0	3-0	0-0	0-4	1-0
—	4-0	3-3	1-0	2-1	1-0	2-0	1-2	3-0	2-2	1-0	1-0	0-1	1-0
0-0	—	1-0	0-0	3-0	0-0	2-1	2-0	2-0	1-1	3-1	2-0	2-1	2-0
1-2	2-0	—	0-1	1-1	2-0	1-1	0-1	2-1	2-3	0-0	0-1	0-0	2-2
3-0	1-2	3-2	—	0-1	0-0	1-0	0-0	2-0	1-1	0-1	1-2	1-2	2-3
1-0	4-0	2-1	2-0	—	2-1	3-0	4-2	6-0	1-1	1-1	1-0	1-1	1-2
0-0	1-1	1-2	2-1	1-0	—	1-1	1-1	3-2	2-0	1-1	2-1	3-2	0-3
3-2	2-1	0-0	4-3	2-2	2-2	—	0-0	3-0	0-1	0-2	0-3	0-1	2-2
1-1	0-5	0-2	2-3	1-2	1-2	0-0	—	5-0	2-1	2-1	1-1	1-2	2-2
0-4	2-1	1-3	0-1	0-2	0-1	1-2	3-1	—	0-2	2-1	1-2	1-2	1-4
0-0	2-0	2-0	0-0	1-2	3-2	1-2	0-3	1-0	—	0-3	2-1	2-1	0-3
1-4	2-1	1-2	3-0	1-1	3-2	0-3	3-1	1-1	2-1	—	1-2	3-0	1-1
0-2	1-0	1-0	5-0	2-0	1-1	0-1	1-1	4-0	1-0	1-1	—	0-1	1-1
2-2	0-1	1-0	3-3	2-0	1-0	1-1	1-1	3-1	2-2	0-0	0-1	—	0-1
1-0	0-0	1-0	2-2	2-3	2-1	1-0	0-0	2-2	3-0	1-0	0-1	1-0	—

NATIONWIDE FOOTBALL LEAGUE

HOME TEAM	Blackpool	AFC Bournemouth	Brentford	Brighton & HA	Bristol C	Bury	Cambridge U	Cardiff C	Chesterfield	Colchester U
Blackpool	—	4-3	1-3	2-2	5-1	0-1	1-1	1-1	1-0	2-1
AFC Bournemouth	0-1	—	0-2	1-1	1-3	3-2	2-2	1-3	3-1	0-1
Brentford	2-0	1-0	—	4-0	2-2	5-1	2-1	2-1	0-0	4-1
Brighton & HA	4-0	2-1	1-2	—	2-1	2-1	4-3	1-0	2-2	1-0
Bristol C	2-1	1-0	0-2	0-1	—	2-0	2-0	1-1	3-0	3-1
Bury	1-1	2-1	2-0	0-2	2-2	—	2-2	3-0	2-1	1-3
Cambridge U	0-3	2-2	2-1	0-0	0-3	3-1	—	2-1	4-1	1-2
Cardiff City	2-2	2-2	3-1	1-1	1-3	1-0	2-0	—	2-1	1-1
Chesterfield	2-1	2-1	0-1	1-2	2-1	2-0	2-0	0-2	—	3-6
Colchester U	1-1	1-2	1-1	1-4	0-0	0-1	3-1	0-1	1-2	—
Huddersfield T	2-4	1-0	1-1	1-2	1-0	2-0	2-1	2-2	0-0	2-1
Northampton T	1-3	1-0	1-0	2-0	0-3	1-0	2-2	1-2	0-2	2-3
Notts Co	1-0	2-0	0-0	2-2	2-0	1-2	2-1	0-0	1-1	1-1
Oldham Ath	2-1	3-3	3-2	2-0	0-1	4-0	2-2	1-7	1-1	4-1
Peterborough U	3-2	6-0	1-1	0-1	4-1	2-1	1-0	1-1	1-1	3-1
Port Vale	1-1	0-0	2-1	0-1	1-0	1-0	5-0	0-2	4-1	3-1
QPR	2-0	1-1	0-0	0-0	0-0	3-0	1-0	2-1	0-0	2-2
Reading	3-0	2-2	1-2	0-0	3-2	1-1	1-0	1-2	0-1	3-0
Stoke C	2-0	2-0	3-2	3-1	1-0	4-0	5-0	1-1	1-0	3-0
Swindon T	1-0	0-0	2-0	1-1	1-2	3-1	2-0	0-3	2-1	1-0
Tranmere R	4-0	0-0	1-0	0-0	1-0	1-2	6-1	0-1	0-0	0-0
Wigan Ath	0-1	0-0	1-1	3-0	1-2	1-1	4-1	4-0	1-1	2-3
Wrexham	1-1	2-1	0-3	1-2	0-1	1-0	5-0	1-3	0-1	1-1
Wycombe W	1-4	1-1	5-3	1-1	2-1	0-2	2-0	0-1	0-0	0-0

DIVISION 2 2001–2002 RESULTS

Huddersfield T	Northampton T	Notts Co	Oldham Ath	Peterborough U	Port Vale	QPR	Reading	Stoke C	Swindon T	Tranmere R	Wigan Ath	Wrexham	Wycombe W
1-2	1-2	0-0	0-2	2-2	4-0	2-2	0-2	2-2	1-0	1-1	3-1	3-0	2-2
2-3	5-1	4-2	3-2	0-2	0-0	1-2	1-0	3-1	0-0	0-2	2-0	3-0	1-2
3-0	3-0	2-1	2-2	2-1	2-0	0-0	1-1	1-0	2-0	4-0	0-1	3-0	1-0
1-0	2-0	2-2	3-0	1-1	1-0	2-1	3-1	1-0	0-0	1-0	2-1	0-0	4-0
1-1	1-3	3-2	3-0	1-0	1-1	2-0	3-3	1-1	3-1	2-0	2-2	1-0	0-1
0-0	2-1	0-4	1-1	2-0	1-1	1-2	1-1	0-1	0-3	0-1	0-2	2-2	1-1
0-1	3-3	0-2	1-1	0-0	0-1	2-1	2-2	0-2	1-2	2-1	2-2	0-2	2-0
1-2	2-0	2-1	3-1	0-2	1-0	1-1	2-2	2-0	3-0	1-2	1-2	3-2	1-0
1-1	2-2	2-1	4-2	0-1	1-1	2-3	0-2	1-2	4-0	0-2	1-2	3-2	0-1
3-3	3-1	0-1	2-1	2-1	2-0	3-1	2-0	1-3	1-3	2-1	2-2	2-1	2-2
—	2-0	2-2	0-0	3-1	2-1	1-0	0-1	0-0	2-0	2-1	0-0	5-1	2-1
0-3	—	0-2	0-1	2-1	1-0	2-2	0-2	1-1	1-1	4-1	0-2	4-1	4-1
2-1	0-3	—	0-2	1-0	1-3	0-2	3-4	0-0	3-1	3-0	1-3	2-2	0-1
1-1	4-2	4-1	—	2-0	2-0	1-0	0-1	2-1	2-0	1-1	1-1	3-1	2-0
1-2	2-0	0-1	2-2	—	3-0	4-1	1-2	1-2	1-1	5-0	0-2	2-3	2-1
1-1	0-1	4-2	3-2	4-1	—	1-0	0-2	1-1	0-2	1-1	1-0	1-3	1-1
3-2	0-1	3-2	1-1	1-0	4-1	—	0-0	1-0	4-0	1-2	1-1	2-1	4-3
1-0	0-0	2-1	2-2	2-2	2-0	1-0	—	1-0	1-3	4-1	1-1	2-0	2-0
1-1	2-0	1-0	0-0	1-0	0-1	0-1	2-0	—	2-0	1-2	2-2	1-0	5-1
0-1	2-1	1-0	0-2	0-0	3-0	0-1	0-0	0-3	—	2-2	1-1	3-1	1-1
1-0	2-0	4-2	2-2	1-0	3-1	2-3	2-2	2-2	0-0	—	1-2	5-0	1-1
1-0	3-0	1-1	1-0	2-1	0-1	1-2	0-2	6-1	1-0	1-2	—	2-3	0-0
1-1	3-2	2-1	3-3	1-2	1-3	1-0	0-2	0-1	2-2	1-1	2-0	—	0-0
2-4	2-1	3-0	2-1	3-0	3-1	1-0	0-2	1-0	1-1	2-1	1-0	5-2	—

NATIONWIDE FOOTBALL LEAGUE

HOME TEAM	Bristol R	Carlisle U	Cheltenham T	Darlington	Exeter C	Halifax T	Hartlepool U	Hull C	Kidderminster H	Leyton Orient
Bristol R	—	0-0	1-2	1-0	0-0	2-0	0-1	1-1	2-1	5-3
Carlisle U	1-0	—	0-0	1-3	1-0	0-0	0-2	0-0	1-0	6-1
Cheltenham T	0-0	2-0	—	0-0	3-1	2-1	3-0	1-0	2-1	1-1
Darlington	1-0	2-2	0-2	—	4-0	5-0	1-1	0-1	2-0	3-0
Exeter C	1-0	1-0	0-2	4-2	—	0-0	0-2	1-3	2-1	0-0
Halifax T	0-0	2-2	4-1	2-2	1-1	—	0-2	0-1	1-0	0-0
Hartlepool U	1-1	3-1	0-1	1-2	2-0	3-0	—	4-0	1-1	3-1
Hull C	0-0	0-1	5-1	1-2	2-0	3-0	1-1	—	2-1	1-1
Kidderminster H	2-0	2-2	0-0	1-0	3-1	2-0	3-2	3-0	—	0-1
Leyton Orient	3-1	0-0	0-2	0-0	1-1	3-1	2-0	0-0	1-3	—
Lincoln C	0-1	3-1	0-1	1-1	0-0	1-2	2-0	2-1	0-1	2-0
Luton T	3-0	1-1	2-1	5-2	3-0	5-0	2-2	0-1	1-0	3-0
Macclesfield T	2-1	1-1	1-0	1-1	1-2	1-1	0-1	0-0	0-1	2-1
Mansfield T	2-0	2-0	2-1	4-2	0-1	2-1	3-0	4-2	1-1	3-2
Oxford U	0-0	1-1	3-0	1-2	1-2	6-1	1-2	1-0	1-1	1-1
Plymouth Arg	1-0	3-0	2-0	1-0	3-0	3-0	1-0	1-0	2-1	3-0
Rochdale	2-1	1-1	2-2	3-1	2-0	2-0	0-0	3-2	2-0	3-0
Rushden & Diamonds	3-1	3-1	1-0	2-1	2-1	2-1	2-1	3-3	0-2	1-0
Scunthorpe U	1-2	2-1	1-2	7-1	3-4	4-0	1-0	2-1	1-0	4-1
Shrewsbury T	0-1	1-0	2-1	3-0	0-1	3-0	1-3	1-1	4-0	1-0
Southend U	2-1	3-2	0-1	1-0	3-1	4-1	0-0	2-0	1-0	1-2
Swansea C	2-1	0-0	2-2	2-0	4-2	0-2	0-1	1-0	2-1	0-1
Torquay U	2-1	2-1	0-1	2-1	0-2	2-4	1-0	1-1	1-4	1-1
York C	3-0	0-0	1-3	2-0	2-3	1-0	1-0	2-1	0-1	2-1

DIVISION 3 2001–2002 RESULTS

Lincoln C	Luton T	Macclesfield T	Mansfield T	Oxford U	Plymouth Arg	Rochdale	Rushden & Diamonds	Scunthorpe U	Shrewsbury T	Southend U	Swansea C	Torquay U	York C
1-2	3-2	0-2	0-1	1-1	1-2	0-2	0-3	1-1	0-0	2-1	4-1	1-0	2-2
2-2	0-2	3-2	0-1	2-1	0-2	1-2	3-0	3-0	0-1	0-0	3-1	2-0	2-1
2-1	1-1	4-1	2-3	2-0	0-0	1-1	1-1	3-3	1-0	1-1	2-2	2-2	4-0
2-1	3-2	0-1	0-1	1-0	1-4	1-0	0-0	2-1	3-3	2-2	0-0	1-3	3-1
1-1	2-2	0-0	0-1	3-2	2-3	1-1	1-1	0-4	2-2	2-1	0-3	0-0	2-1
3-0	2-4	0-0	1-0	0-2	0-2	1-2	2-4	0-0	1-2	1-1	0-1	2-0	1-1
1-1	1-2	1-2	1-1	0-1	1-0	1-1	5-1	3-2	2-2	5-1	7-1	4-1	3-0
1-1	0-4	0-1	4-1	3-0	0-0	3-1	2-1	0-1	3-0	0-0	2-1	1-0	4-0
1-1	1-4	0-1	1-1	0-0	0-0	4-1	3-0	1-0	1-0	2-0	0-2	1-0	4-1
5-0	1-3	2-0	2-0	3-0	0-0	4-2	2-1	0-0	2-4	2-1	2-2	1-2	1-2
—	0-1	1-0	1-4	1-0	0-1	1-1	2-4	3-2	1-2	0-1	3-0	0-0	1-3
1-1	—	0-0	5-3	1-1	2-0	0-1	1-0	2-3	1-0	2-0	3-0	5-1	2-1
0-1	4-1	—	0-1	0-1	1-1	0-1	0-0	4-3	2-1	0-0	1-3	0-2	2-1
2-1	4-1	4-0	—	2-1	0-3	3-1	1-4	2-1	2-1	0-0	3-0	2-0	1-1
2-1	1-2	0-2	3-2	—	1-1	1-2	3-2	0-1	0-1	2-0	2-1	1-1	2-2
2-0	2-1	2-0	1-0	4-2	—	1-2	1-0	2-1	0-1	0-0	3-1	2-2	1-0
2-2	1-0	1-1	3-1	1-1	1-3	—	0-0	2-2	1-0	0-1	2-0	2-0	5-4
0-0	1-2	2-0	3-1	2-1	2-3	1-1	—	0-0	3-0	0-1	4-0	0-0	3-0
1-1	0-2	1-1	0-0	1-0	2-1	2-1	1-1	—	3-1	2-0	2-2	1-0	1-0
1-1	0-2	1-1	3-0	1-0	3-1	1-0	0-2	2-2	—	2-0	3-0	0-1	3-2
1-1	1-2	3-0	1-0	2-2	0-1	0-0	4-2	2-0	0-2	—	4-2	1-1	0-1
0-0	1-3	0-1	2-0	0-0	0-1	0-1	0-0	2-2	3-3	3-2	—	2-2	0-1
2-0	0-1	1-2	0-0	3-3	0-1	3-0	1-1	0-0	2-1	2-1	1-2	—	0-3
2-0	1-2	1-0	3-1	1-0	0-0	0-0	0-1	0-2	1-1	2-1	0-2	1-1	—

ARSENAL FA PREMIERSHIP

Name	Ht	Wt	Birthplace	D.O.B.	Previous Club
Adams Tony (D)	6 3	13 02	Romford	10 10 66	Apprentice
Aliadiere Jeremie (F)	6 0	11 00	Rambouillet	30 3 83	Scholar
Bailey Alex (D)	5 9	10 07	Newham	21 9 83	Scholar
Barrett Graham (F)	5 10	11 07	Dublin	6 10 81	Trainee
Bentley David (F)	5 10	10 07	Peterborough	27 8 84	Scholar
Bergkamp Dennis (F)	6 0	12 05	Amsterdam	18 5 69	Internazionale
Bradley Stephen (M)	5 8	9 07	Dublin	19 11 84	Scholar
Brown Jermaine (F)	5 11	11 00	Lambeth	12 1 83	Scholar
Campbell Sol (D)	6 2	14 02	Newham	18 9 74	Tottenham H
Chilvers Liam (D)	6 0	12 04	Chelmsford	6 10 81	
Chorley Ben (D)	6 3	13 02	Sidcup	30 9 82	Scholar
Cole Ashley (D)	5 8	10 10	Stepney	20 12 80	Trainee
Edu (M)	6 1	12 04	Sao Paulo	15 5 78	Corinthians
Garry Ryan (D)	6 2	13 00	Hornchurch	29 9 83	Scholar
Grondin David (D)	5 9	11 11	Paris	8 5 80	St Etienne
Halls John (D)	6 0	11 00	Islington	14 2 82	Scholar
Henry Thierry (F)	6 2	13 01	Paris	17 8 77	Juventus
Jeffers Francis (F)	5 10	10 07	Liverpool	25 1 81	Everton
Juan (D)	5 6	9 07	Sao Paulo	6 2 82	Sao Paulo
Kanu Nwankwo (F)	6 5	12 01	Owerri	1 8 76	Internazionale
Keown Martin (D)	6 1	12 04	Oxford	24 7 66	Everton
Lauren Etame-Mayer (M)	5 11	11 03	Londi Keisi	19 1 77	Mallorca
Ljungberg Frederik (M)	5 9	10 13	Halmstad	16 4 77	Halmstad
Luzhny Oleg (D)	5 10	12 01	Ukraine	5 8 68	Dynamo Kiev
Manninger Alex (G)	6 2	13 03	Salzburg	4 6 77	Graz
Mendez Alberto (M)	5 11	11 09	Nuremberg	24 10 74	FC Feucht
Noble David (M)	6 0	12 04	Hitchin	2 2 82	Scholar
Parlour Ray (M)	5 10	11 12	Romford	7 3 73	Trainee
Paulinho (M)	5 7	10 04	Sao Paulo	2 3 83	Sao Paulo
Pennant Jermaine (M)	5 8	10 01	Nottingham	15 1 83	
Pires Robert (M)	6 1	11 09	Reims	29 10 73	Marseille
Ricketts Rohan (M)	5 9	11 00	Clapham	22 12 82	Scholar
Seaman David (G)	6 4	13 00	Rotherham	19 9 63	QPR
Sidwell Steven (M)	5 10	11 02	Wandsworth	14 12 82	Scholar
Skulason Olafur-Ingi (M)	6 0	11 10	Reykjavik	1 4 83	Fylkir
Spicer John (M)	5 11	11 07	Romford	13 9 83	Scholar
Stack Graham (G)	6 2	12 06	Hampstead	26 9 81	Scholar
Stepanovs Igor (D)	6 4	13 05	Ogre	21 1 76	Skonto Riga
Svard Sebastian (D)	6 1	12 02	Hvidovre	15 1 83	
Tavlaridis Efstathios (D)	6 2	12 11	Serres	25 1 80	Iraklis
Taylor Stuart (G)	6 5	13 06	Romford	28 11 80	Trainee
Thomas Jerome (M)	5 10	11 10	Brent	23 3 83	Scholar
Toure Kolo (M)	5 10	11 09	Ivory Coast	19 3 81	ASEC Mimosas
Upson Matthew (D)	6 1	11 04	Hartismere	18 4 79	Luton T
Van Bronckhorst Giovanni (M)	5 9	11 03	Rotterdam	5 2 75	Rangers
Vieira Patrick (M)	6 4	13 00	Dakar	23 6 76	AC Milan
Volz Moritz (D)	5 10	12 06	Siegen	21 1 83	
Wiltord Sylvain (F)	5 9	12 04	Neuilly-sur-Mame	10 5 74	Bordeaux
Wright Richard (G)	6 2	14 04	Ipswich	5 11 77	Ipswich T

League Appearances: Adams, T. 10; Aliadiere, J. (1); Bergkamp, D. 22(11); Campbell, S. 29(2); Cole, A. 29; Dixon, L. 3(10); Edu 8(6); Grimandi, G. 11(15); Henry, T. 31(2); Jeffers, F. 2(4); Kanu, N. 9(14); Keown, M. 21(1); Lauren, E. 27; Ljungberg, F. 24(1); Luzhny, O. 15(3); Parlour, R. 25(2); Pires, R. 27(1); Seaman, D. 17; Stepanovs, I. 6; Taylor, S. 9(1); Upson, M. 10(4); Van Bronckhorst, G. 13(8);

Vieira, P. 35(1); Wiltord, S. 23(10); Wright, R. 12.
Goals – League (79): Henry 24 (4 pens), Ljungberg 12, Wiltord 10, Bergkamp 9, Pires 9 (1 pen), Kanu 3, Campbell 2, Cole 2, Jeffers 2, Lauren 2 (1 pen), Vieira 2, Edu 1, Van Bronckhorst 1.
Worthington Cup (6): Wiltord 4 (1 pen), Edu 1, Kanu 1 (pen).
FA Cup (17): Bergkamp 3, Kanu 2, Ljungberg 2, Parlour 2, Wiltord 2, Adams 1, Campbell 1, Edu 1, Henry 1, Pires 1, own goal 1.
Ground: Arsenal Stadium, Highbury, London N5 1BU. Telephone (020) 7704 4000.
Record attendance: 73,295 v Sunderland, Div 1, 9 March 1935. **Capacity:** 38,500.
Manager: Arsène Wenger.
Secretary: David Miles.
Most League Goals: 127, Division 1, 1930–31.
Highest League Scorer in Season: Ted Drake, 42, 1934–35.
Most League Goals in Total Aggregate: Cliff Bastin, 150, 1930–47.
Most Capped Player: Kenny Sansom, 77 (86), England, 1981–1988.
Most League Appearances: David O'Leary, 558, 1975–93.
Honours – FA Premier League: Champions – 1997–98, 2001–02. **Football League:** Division 1 Champions – 1930–31, 1932–33, 1933–34, 1934–35, 1937–38, 1947–48, 1952–53, 1970–71, 1988–89, 1990–91. **FA Cup winners** 1929–30, 1935–36, 1949–50, 1970–71, 1978–79, 1992–93, 1997–98, 2001–02. **Football League Cup winners** 1986–87, 1992–93. **European Competitions: European Cup-Winners' Cup winners:** 1993–94. **Fairs Cup winners:** 1969–70.
Colours: Red shirts with white sleeves, white shorts, white stockings with red trim.

ASTON VILLA   FA PREMIERSHIP

Player						
Alpay Ozalan (D)	6 2	14 00	Izmir	29	5 73	Fenerbahce
Amoo Ryan (M)	5 10	9 12	Leicester	11	10 83	Scholar
Angel Juan Pablo (F)	6 0	12 10	Medellin	24	10 75	River Plate
Balaban Bosko (F)	5 10	11 10	Rijeka	15	10 78	Dynamo Zagreb
Barry Gareth (D)	5 11	12 06	Hastings	23	2 81	Trainee
Bewers Jonathan (D)	5 8	9 13	Kettering	10	9 82	Trainee
Boateng George (M)	5 9	10 12	Nkawkaw	5	9 75	Coventry C
Cooke Stephen (M)	5 7	9 00	Walsall	15	2 83	
Crouch Peter (F)	6 7	11 12	Macclesfield	30	1 81	Portsmouth
Davis Steven (M)	3 7	9 07	Ballymena	1	1 85	Scholar
Delaney Mark (D)	6 1	11 07	Haverfordwest	13	5 76	Carmarthen T
Dublin Dion (F)	6 2	12 04	Leicester	22	4 69	Coventry C
Edwards Rob (D)	6 1	11 10	Telford	25	12 82	Trainee
Enckelman Peter (G)	6 2	12 05	Turku	10	3 77	TPS Turku
Ennis Pierre (D)	5 10	12 03	Dublin	25	2 84	Scholar
Fahey Keith (M)	5 10	12 07	Dublin	15	1 83	
Hadji Mustapha (M)	5 11	11 12	Ifrane	16	11 71	Coventry C
Henderson Wayne (G)	5 11	12 02	Dublin	16	9 83	Scholar
Hendrie Lee (M)	5 10	11 00	Birmingham	18	5 77	Trainee
Hitzlsperger Thomas (D)	6 0	11 12	Germany	5	4 82	Bayern Munich
Husbands Michael (F)	5 9	9 13	Birmingham	13	11 83	Scholar
Hylton Leon (D)	5 9	11 00	Birmingham	27	1 83	
Hynes Peter (F)	5 9	11 12	Dublin	28	11 83	
Jackman Daniel (D)	5 4	9 08	Worcester	3	1 83	Scholar
Kachloul Hassan (M)	6 1	12 01	Agadir	19	2 73	Southampton
McGrath John (F)	5 10	10 04	Limerick	27	3 80	Belvedere
Melaugh Gavin (M)	5 7	9 07	Derry	9	7 81	Trainee
Mellberg Olof (D)	6 1	12 10	Amncharad	3	9 77	Santander
Merson Paul (F)	6 0	13 02	Northolt	20	3 68	Middlesbrough
Moore Stefan (F)	5 10	10 12	Birmingham	28	9 83	Scholar
Myhill Boaz (G)	6 3	14 06	California	9	11 82	Scholar
Ridgewell Liam (M)	5 10	10 03	London	21	7 84	Scholar

Samuel J Lloyd (D)	5 11	11 04	Trinidad	29 3 81	Charlton Ath
Scullion David (F)	5 8	10 03	Craigavon	27 4 84	
Smith Jay (M)	5 7	10 00	London	24 9 81	Scholar
Staunton Steve (D)	6 0	12 12	Drogheda	19 1 69	Liverpool
Stone Steve (M)	5 8	12 07	Gateshead	20 8 71	Nottingham F
Stuart Cameron (D)	5 6	10 08	York	9 1 84	Scholar
Taylor Ian (M)	6 1	12 00	Birmingham	4 6 68	Sheffield W
Vassell Darius (F)	5 7	12 00	Birmingham	13 6 80	Trainee
Willetts Ben (D)	5 9	11 05	West Bromwich	10 2 83	
Wright Alan (D)	5 4	9 09	Ashton-under-Lyme	28 9 71	Blackburn R

League Appearances: Alpay, O. 14; Angel, J. 26(3); Balaban, B. (8); Barry, G. 16(4); Boateng, G. 37; Crouch, P. 7; Delaney, M. 30; Dublin, D. 9(12); Enckelman, P. 9; Ginola, D. (5); Hadji, M. 17(6); Hendrie, L. 25(4); Hitzisperger, T. 11(1); Kachloul, H. 17(5); Mellberg, O. 32; Merson, P. 18(3); Samuel, J. 17(6); Schmeichel, P. 29; Staunton, S. 30(3); Stone, S. 14(8); Taylor, I. 7(9); Vassell, D. 30(6); Wright, A. 23.

Goals – League (46): Angel 12 (2 pens), Vassell 12, Dublin 4, Taylor 3, Crouch 2, Hadji 2, Hendrie 2, Kachloul 2, Merson 2, Boateng 1, Hitzisperger 1, Schmeichel 1, Stone 1, own goal 1.

Worthington Cup (1): Dublin 1.

FA Cup (2): Taylor 1, own goal 1.

Ground: Villa Park, Trinity Rd, Birmingham B6 6HE. Telephone (0121) 327 2299.

Record attendance: 76,588 v Derby Co, FA Cup 6th rd, 2 March 1946.

Capacity: 42,584.

Manager: Graham Taylor.

Secretary: Steven Stride.

Most League Goals: 128, Division 1, 1930–31.

Highest League Scorer in Season: 'Pongo' Waring, 49, Division 1, 1930–31.

Most League Goals in Total Aggregate: Harry Hampton, 215, 1904–15.

Most Capped Player: Steve Staunton 64 (102), Republic of Ireland.

Most League Appearances: Charlie Aitken, 561, 1961–76.

Honours – Football League: Division 1 Champions – 1893–94, 1895–96, 1896–97, 1898–99, 1899–1900, 1909–10, 1980–81. Division 2 Champions – 1937–38, 1959–60. Division 3 Champions – 1971–72. **FA Cup:** Winners 1887, 1895, 1897, 1905, 1913, 1920, 1957. **Football League Cup:** Winners 1961, 1975, 1977, 1994, 1996. **European Competitions: European Cup winners:** 1981–82, **European Super Cup winners:** 1982–83.

Colours: Claret shirts with blue and yellow trim, white shorts with claret and blue trim, sky blue and claret stockings with white turnover.

BARNSLEY   DIV. 2

Austin Neil (F)	5 10	11 09	Barnsley	26 4 83	Trainee
Barker Christopher (D)	6 0	11 11	Sheffield	2 3 80	Alfreton
Barrowclough Carl (F)	5 7	9 08	Doncaster	25 9 81	Scholar
Bertos Leo (M)	5 8	12 08	Wellington	20 12 81	
Betsy Kevin (M)	6 1	12 03	Seychelles	20 3 78	Fulham
Crooks Lee (D)	6 2	13 12	Wakefield	14 1 78	Manchester C
Dixon Kevin (D)	5 8	12 08	Easington	27 6 80	Leeds U
Donovan Kevin (M)	5 10	11 12	Halifax	17 12 71	Grimsby T
Dudgeon James (D)	6 2	12 04	Newcastle	19 3 81	Trainee
Dyer Bruce (F)	5 11	12 08	Ilford	13 4 75	Crystal Palace
Fallon Rory (F)	6 2	12 02	Gisbourne	20 3 82	North Shore U
Flynn Mike (D)	6 1	13 05	Oldham	23 2 69	Stockport Co
Ghent Matthew (G)	6 3	14 09	Burton	5 10 80	Lincoln C
Gibbs Paul (D)	5 11	11 07	Great Yarmouth	26 10 72	Brentford
Gorre Dean (M)	5 7	11 09	Surinam	10 9 70	Huddersfield T
Hayward Steve (M)	5 11	12 13	Walsall	8 9 71	Fulham

Name			Birthplace		Previous Club
Jones Gary (M)	5 11	12 06	Birkenhead	3 6 77	Rochdale
Kay Antony (F)	5 11	11 07	Barnsley	21 10 82	Trainee
Lumsdon Chris (M)	5 11	10 02	Newcastle	15 12 79	Sunderland
Marriott Andy (G)	6 0	12 05	Sutton-in-Ashfield	11 10 70	Sunderland
Miller Christopher (D)	5 8	11 09	Paisley	19 11 82	Scholar
Morgan Chris (D)	6 1	12 13	Barnsley	9 11 77	Trainee
Mulligan David (M)	5 5	9 12	Fazakerley	24 3 82	Scholar
Neil Alex (M)	5 9	11 02	Bellshill	9 6 81	Dunfermline Ath
O'Callaghan Brian (D)	6 1	12 03	Limerick	24 2 81	Pike Rovers
Oldham Adam (M)			Sheffield	26 1 85	
Parry Craig (G)	5 11	12 04	Barnsley	15 3 84	Scholar
Rankin Isiah (F)	5 10	11 00	London	22 5 78	Bradford C
Regan Carl (D)	6 0	11 03	Liverpool	14 1 80	Everton
Salli Janne (D)	6 2	12 08	Seinajoki	14 12 77	
Sheron Mike (F)	5 10	12 08	Liverpool	11 1 72	QPR
Ward Mitch (M)	5 8	11 08	Sheffield	19 6 71	Everton

League Appearances: Barker, C. 43(1); Barnard, D. 34(4); Bedeau, A. (3); Bertos, L. 2(2); Betsy, K. 10; Chettle, S. 31(1); Christie, J. (1); Corbo, M. (1); Crooks, L. 20(6); Donovan, K. 28(4); Dyer, B. 42(2); Fallon, R. 2(7); Flynn, M. 7; Gallen, K. 8(1); Ghent, M. 1; Gibbs, P. 4; Gorre, D. 14(5); Jones, G. 25; Jones, L. 2(11); Kay, A. (1); Lumsdon, C. 32; Marriott, A. 17(1); McSwegan, G. 1(4); Miller, K. 28; Morgan, C. 42; Mulligan, D. 27(1); Naylor, R. 7(1); Neil, A. 17(8); O'Callaghan, B. 1(5); Oster, J. 2; Parkin, J. 4; Rankin, I. 2(7); Regan, C. 6(4); Sand, P. 4(2); Scothern, A. (1); Sheron, M. 23(10); Tinkler, E. 8(8); Ward, M. 12(3).
Goals – League (59): Dyer 14, Sheron 12, Barnard 7 (3 pens), Lumsdon 7 (5 pens), Morgan 4, Barker 3, Gallen 2, Gorre 2, Neil 2, Donovan 1, Jones G 1, Rankin 1, Sand 1, own goals 2.
Worthington Cup (5): Dyer 3, Jones G 1, Tinkler 1.
FA Cup (2): Barnard 1, Dyer 1.
Ground: Oakwell Ground, Grove St, Barnsley S71 1ET. Telephone (01226) 211211.
Record attendance: 40,255 v Stoke C, FA Cup 5th rd, 15 February 1936. **Capacity:** 23,186.
Manager: Steve Parkin.
Secretary: Michael Spinks.
Most League Goals: 118, Division 3 (N), 1933–34.
Highest League Scorer in Season: Cecil McCormack, 33, Division 2, 1950–51.
Most League Goals in Total Aggregate: Ernest Hine, 123, 1921–26 and 1934–30.
Most Capped Player: Gerry Taggart, 35 (50), Northern Ireland.
Most League Appearances: Barry Murphy, 514, 1962–78.
Honours – Football League: Division 3 (N) Champions – 1933–34, 1938–39, 1954–55. **FA Cup:** Winners 1912.
Colours: Red shirts, white shorts, red stockings.

BIRMINGHAM CITY   FA PREMIERSHIP

Name			Birthplace		Previous Club
Barrowman Andrew (F)	5 11	11 06	Wishaw	27 11 84	Scholar
Bennett Ian (G)	6 0	13 01	Worksop	10 10 71	Peterborough U
Capaldi Tony (D)	6 0	11 06	Porsgrunn	12 8 81	Trainee
Carter Darren (M)	6 2	12 11	Solihull	18 12 83	Scholar
Devlin Paul (F)	5 8	11 08	Birmingham	14 4 72	Sheffield U
Eaden Nicky (D)	5 9	12 04	Sheffield	12 12 72	Barnsley
Fagan Craig (F)	5 11	11 09	Birmingham	11 12 82	Scholar
Furlong Paul (F)	6 0	13 11	London	1 10 68	Chelsea
Gill Jeremy (D)	5 11	11 12	Clevedon	8 9 70	Yeovil T
Grainger Martin (D)	5 10	12 11	Enfield	23 8 72	Brentford
Grondin Christophe (M)			Toulouse	2 9 83	Toulouse
Holdsworth David (D)	6 1	13 02	Walthamstow	8 11 68	Sheffield U

Horsfield Geoff (F)	6 0	11 07	Barnsley	1 11 73	Fulham
Hughes Bryan (M)	5 9	11 03	Liverpool	19 6 76	Wrexham
Hutchinson Jonathan (D)	5 11	11 11	Middlesbrough	2 4 82	Scholar
Hyde Graham (M)	5 7	11 09	Doncaster	10 11 70	Sheffield W
John Stern (M)	6 0	12 11	Trinidad	30 10 76	Nottingham F
Johnson Andrew (F)	5 7	10 09	Bedford	10 2 81	Trainee
Johnson Damien (M)	5 9	11 09	Lisburn	18 11 78	Blackburn R
Johnson Michael (D)	5 11	12 08	Nottingham	4 7 73	Notts Co
Kenna Jeff (D)	5 11	12 04	Dublin	27 8 70	Blackburn R
Lazaridis Stan (M)	5 9	11 12	Perth	16 8 72	West Ham U
Luntala Tresor (M)	5 9	10 11	Dreux	31 5 82	
Mooney Tommy (F)	5 11	13 08	Teeside North	11 8 71	Watford
Parker Sonny (M)			Middlesbrough	28 2 83	Trainee
Purse Darren (D)	6 2	13 01	Stepney	14 2 76	Oxford U
Sadler Matthew (D)	5 11	11 05	Birmingham	26 2 85	Scholar
Tebily Oliver (D)	6 0	13 05	Abidjan	19 12 75	Celtic
Vaesen Nico (G)	6 3	12 13	Hasselt	28 9 69	Huddersfield T
Vickers Steve (D)	6 2	12 10	Bishop Auckland	13 10 67	Middlesbrough
Ward Christopher (F)	4 81	11 00	Preston	28 4 81	Lancaster C
Williams Tom (M)	6 0	11 13	Carshalton	8 7 80	Peterborough U
Woodhouse Curtis (M)	5 7	12 02	Driffield	17 4 80	Sheffield U

League Appearances: Bak, A. 2(2); Bennett, I. 18; Bragstad, B. 3; Burrows, D. 9(3); Carter, D. 12(1); Devlin, P. 11(2); Eaden, N. 24(5); Ferrari, C. (4); Fleming, C. 6; Furlong, P. 2(9); Gill, J. 14; Grainger, M. 39(1); Holdsworth, D. 3(1); Horsfield, G. 33(7); Hughes, B. 27(4); Hughes, M. 3; Hutchinson, J. (3); Hyde, G. 1(4); John, S. 15; Johnson, A. 9(14); Johnson, D. 5(3); Johnson, M. 30(2); Kelly, A. 6; Kenna, J. 21; Lazaridis, S. 22(10); Luntala, T. 9(6); Marcelo 17(4); McCarthy, J. 3(1); Mooney, T. 29(4); O'Connor, M. 24; Purse, D. 35(1); Sonner, D. 10(5); Tebily, O. 7; Vaesen, N. 22(1); Vickers, S. 13(1); Williams, T. 4; Woodhouse, C. 18(10).

Goals – League (70): Mooney 13 (4 pens), Marcelo 12, Horsfield 11, Hughes B 7, John 7, Grainger 4, Johnson A 3, Purse 3 (1 pen), Carter 1, Devlin 1, Eaden 1, Furlong 1, Johnson D 1, Johnson M 1, Sonner 1, Vickers 1, own goals 2.

Worthington Cup (6): Mooney 2 (1 pen), Hughes B 1, Johnson A 1, Johnson M 1, own goal 1.

FA Cup (0).

Ground: St Andrews, Birmingham B9 4NH. Telephone (0121) 772 0101.

Record attendance: 66,844 v Everton, FA Cup 5th rd,11 February 1939. **Capacity:** 30,009.

Manager: Steve Bruce.

Secretary: Alan Jones BA, MBA

Most League Goals: 103, Division 2, 1893–94 (only 28 games).

Highest League Scorer in Season: Joe Bradford, 29, Division 1, 1927–28.

Most League Goals in Total Aggregate: Joe Bradford, 249, 1920–35.

Most Capped Player: Malcolm Page, 28, Wales.

Most League Appearances: Frank Womack, 491, 1908–28.

Honours – Football League: Division 2 Champions – 1892–93, 1920–21, 1947–48, 1954–55, 1994–95. **Football League Cup:** Winners 1963. **Leyland Daf Cup:** Winners 1991. **Auto Windscreens Shield:** Winners 1995.

Colours: Blue shirts, blue shorts, blue and white stockings.

BLACKBURN ROVERS   FA PREMIERSHIP

Bell Andrew (F)			Blackburn	12 2 84	Scholar
Bjornebye Stig Inge (D)	5 10	11 09	Elverum	11 12 69	Brondby
Burgess Ben (F)	6 4	14 05	Buxton	9 11 81	Trainee
Cole Andy (F)	5 11	12 04	Nottingham	15 10 71	Manchester U

Corbett Jimmy (F)	5 10	12 00	Hackney	6 7 80	Trainee
Cumming Stuart (M)			Aberdeen	30 1 85	
Curtis John (D)	5 10	11 07	Nuneaton	3 9 78	Manchester U
Danns Neil (F)			Liverpool	23 11 82	Scholar
Donnelly Ciaran (M)			Blackpool	2 4 84	Scholar
Douglas Jonathan (M)	6 0	12 07	Monaghan	22 11 81	Trainee
Duff Damien (F)	5 10	12 00	Ballyboden	3 3 79	Lourdes Celtic
Dunn David (M)	5 10	12 05	Blackburn	27 12 79	Trainee
Dunning Darren (M)	5 7	11 08	Scarborough	8 1 81	Trainee
Fitzgerald John (M)			Dublin	10 2 84	Scholar
Flitcroft Garry (M)	6 1	12 11	Bolton	6 11 72	Manchester C
Friedel Brad (G)	6 3	14 00	Lakewood	18 5 71	Liverpool
Gillespie Keith (F)	5 10	11 12	Larne	18 2 75	Newcastle U
Grabbi Corrado (F)	5 11	12 13	Turin	29 7 75	Ternana
Greer Gordon (D)	6 2	12 05	Glasgow	14 12 80	Port Glasgow
Hignett Craig (M)	5 9	11 10	Whiston	12 1 70	Barnsley
Jansen Matt (F)	5 11	12 04	Carlisle	20 10 77	Crystal Palace
Johansson Nils-Eric (D)	6 2	13 03	Stockholm	13 1 80	Nuremberg
Johnson Jemal (M)			New Jersey	3 5 84	
Kelly Alan (G)	6 2	14 05	Preston	1 8 68	Sheffield U
Mahon Alan (M)	5 8	11 10	Dublin	4 4 78	Sporting Lisbon
Martin Anthony (M)			Dublin	20 9 83	Scholar
McNamee David (D)	5 11	11 02	Glasgow	10 10 80	St Mirren BC
Miller Alan (G)	6 4	14 12	Epping	29 3 70	WBA
Morgan Alan (M)			Edinburgh	27 11 83	Scholar
Neill Lucas (M)	6 1	12 07	Sydney	9 3 78	Millwall
O'Brien Burton (F)	5 10	10 12	South Africa	10 6 81	S Form
Ostenstad Egil (F)	6 0	12 11	Haugesund	2 1 72	Southampton
Renton Keiron (G)			Edinburgh	13 2 84	Scholar
Richards Marc (F)	5 11	12 12	Wolverhampton	8 7 82	Trainee
Robinson Ryan (G)	6 2	13 02	Cumbria	13 10 82	Scholar
Short Craig (D)	6 3	13 12	Bridlington	25 6 68	Everton
Taylor Martin (D)	6 4	15 00	Ashington	9 11 79	Trainee
Taylor Michael (M)			Liverpool	21 11 82	Scholar
Tugay Kerimoglu (M)	5 9	11 00	Istanbul	24 8 70	Rangers
Unsal Hakan (M)	5 10	13 01	Sinop	14 5 73	Galatasaray
Watt Jerome (M)			Preston	20 10 84	Scholar

League Appearances: Bent, M. 1(8); Berg, H. 34; Bjornebye, S. 23; Blake, N. (3); Cole, A. 15; Curtis, J. 10; Duff, D. 31(1); Dunn, D. 26(3); Flitcroft, G. 26(3); Friedel, B. 36; Gillespie, K. 21(11); Grabbi, C. 10(4); Hignett, C. 4(16); Hughes, M. 4(17); Jansen, M. 34(1); Johansson, N. 14(6); Johnson, D. 6(1); Kelly, A. 2; Mahon, A. 10(3); McAteer, J. 1(3); Neill, L. 31; Ostenstad, E. 2(2); Short, C. 21(1); Taylor, M. 12(7); Tugay, K. 32(1); Unsal, H. 7(1); Yordi 5(3).
Goals – League (55): Jansen 10, Cole 9, Duff 7, Dunn 7 (1 pen), Hignett 4, Tugay 3, Gillespie 2, Yordi 2, Berg 1, Blake 1, Flitcroft 1, Grabbi 1, Hughes 1, Johnson 1, Mahon 1, Neill 1, own goals 3.
Worthington Cup (18): Jansen 6, Cole 3, Hignett 3, Duff 1, Dunning 1, Hughes 1, Johansson 1, Johnson 1, Short 1.
FA Cup (5): Cole 1, Dunn 1 (pen), Grabbi 1, Hignett 1, Johansson 1.
Ground: Ewood Park, Blackburn BB2 4JF. Telephone (01254) 698888.
Record attendance: 61,783 v Bolton W, FA Cup 6th rd, 2 March, 1929. **Capacity:** 31,367.
Manager: Graeme Souness.
Secretary: Tom Finn.
Most League Goals: 114, Division 2, 1954–55.
Highest League Scorer in Season: Ted Harper, 43, Division 1, 1925–26.
Most League Goals in Total Aggregate: Simon Garner, 168, 1978–92.
Most Capped Player: Henning Berg, 52 (90), Norway.

Most League Appearances: Derek Fazackerley, 596, 1970–86.
Honours – FA Premier League: Champions – 1994–95. Football League:
Division 1 Champions – 1911–12, 1913–14. Division 2 Champions – 1938–39.
Division 3 Champions – 1974–75. **FA Cup:** Winners 1884, 1885, 1886, 1890, 1891,
1928. **Football League Cup:** Winners 2002. **Full Members' Cup:** Winners 1986–87.
Colours: Blue and white halved shirts, white shorts with navy blue strip, white
stockings with navy blue trim.

BLACKPOOL   DIV. 2

Barnes Phil (G)	6 1	11 01	Sheffield	2 3 79	Trainee
Bullock Martin (M)	5 5	10 07	Derby	5 3 75	Barnsley
Clarke Chris (D)	6 3	12 02	Leeds	18 12 80	Halifax T
Coid Danny (M)	5 11	11 07	Liverpool	3 10 81	Trainee
Collins Lee (M)	5 8	11 06	Bellshill	3 2 74	Swindon T
Fenton Graham (F)	5 10	12 10	Wallsend	22 5 74	St Mirren
Hills John (M)	5 9	11 02	St Annes-on-Sea	22 4 78	Everton
Hughes Ian (D)	5 10	12 08	Bangor	2 8 74	Bury
Jaszczun Tommy (D)	5 10	10 10	Kettering	16 9 77	Aston Villa
MacKenzie Neil (M)	6 2	12 12	Birmingham	15 4 76	Kidderminster H
Milligan Jamie (M)	5 6	9 12	Blackpool	3 1 80	Everton
Murphy John (F)	6 2	14 00	Whiston	18 10 76	Chester C
O'Kane John (D)	5 10	12 02	Nottingham	15 11 74	Bolton W
Reid Brian (D)	6 2	11 12	Paisley	15 6 70	Dunfermline Ath
Taylor Scott (F)	5 10	11 06	Chertsey	5 5 76	Stockport Co
Walker Richard (F)	6 0	12 00	Sutton Coldfield	8 11 77	Aston Villa
Wellens Richard (M)	5 9	11 06	Manchester	26 3 80	Manchester U

League Appearances: Barnes, P. 30; Blinkhorn, M. (3); Bullock, M. 37(6); Cald-
well, S. 6; Clarke, C. 10(1); Clarkson, P. 1(1); Coid, D. 24(3); Collins, L. 24(8); Day,
R. 4(5); Dunning, D. 5; Fenton, G. 6(9); Hills, J. 30(7); Hughes, I. 13(7); Jaszczun,
T. 36(4); MacKenzie, N. 6(8); Marshall, I. 21; Milligan, J. 9(8); Milligan, M. 1(1);
Murphy, J. 33(4); Murphy, N. 1; O'Kane, J. 34(4); Ormerod, B. 21; Parkinson, G.
13(2); Payton, A. 4; Pullen, J. 16; Reid, B. 26; Simpson, P. 25(7); Taylor, S. 13(4);
Thompson, P. 10(3); Walker, R. 16(5); Wellens, R. 31(5).
Goals – League (66): Murphy J 13, Ormerod 13, Walker 8, Fenton 5, Hills 5 (1
pen), O'Kane 4, Coid 3, Bullock 2, Collins 2, Taylor 2, Hughes 1, MacKenzie 1,
Marshall 1, Payton 1, Simpson 1 (pen), Thompson 1, Wellens 1, own goals 2.
Worthington Cup (3): Ormerod 3.
FA Cup (9): Murphy J 2, Ormerod 2, Hills 1, Jaszczun 1, McKenzie 1 (pen), Simp-
son 1, own goal 1.
Ground: Bloomfield Rd Ground, Blackpool FY1 6JJ. Telephone (01253) 404331.
Record attendance: 38,098 v Wolverhampton W, Division 1, 17 September 1955.
Capacity: 11,000.
Manager: Steve McMahon.
Secretary: Petra Collins.
Most League Goals: 98, Division 2, 1929–30.
Highest League Scorer in Season: Jimmy Hampson, 45, Division 2, 1929–30.
Most League Goals in Total Aggregate: Jimmy Hampson, 246, 1927–38.
Most Capped Player: Jimmy Armfield, 43, England.
Most League Appearances: Jimmy Armfield, 568, 1952–71.
Honours – Football League: Division 2 Champions – 1929–30. **FA Cup:** Winners
1953. **Anglo-Italian Cup:** Winners 1971. **LDV Vans Trophy:** Winners 2002.
Colours: Tangerine shirts, white shorts, tangerine stockings.

BOLTON WANDERERS   FA PREMIERSHIP

Name (Pos)	Ht		DOB			Birthplace	Previous club
Baldacchino Ryan (M)	5	9	12 03	Leicester	13 1 81		Blackburn R
Banks Steve (G)	6	0	13 12	Hillingdon	9 2 72		Blackpool
Barness Anthony (D)	5	11	11 10	Lewisham	25 3 73		Charlton Ath
Bon Jeremy (G)				Begles	21 10 84		Bordeaux
Buchanan Wayne (D)				Bambridge	12 1 82		Scholar
Charlton Simon (D)	5	8	11 00	Huddersfield	25 10 71		Birmingham C
Downey Chris (F)	5	10	9 11	Warrington	19 4 83		Scholar
Farrelly Gareth (M)	6	1	13 07	Dublin	28 8 75		Everton
Forschelet Gerald (D)				Papeete	19 9 81		Cannes
Frandsen Per (M)	5	11	12 10	Copenhagen	6 2 70		Blackburn R
Gardner Ricardo (M)	5	9	11 01	St Andrews	25 9 78		Harbour View
Hansen Bo (M)	6	1	12 02	Jutland	16 6 72		Brondby
Hendry Colin (D)	6	1	12 07	Keith	7 12 65		Coventry C
Holden Dean (D)	6	0	12 03	Salford	15 9 79		
Holdsworth Dean (F)	5	11	13 06	Walthamstow	8 11 68		Wimbledon
Hunt Nicky (D)	6	1	10 06	Westhoughton	3 9 83		Scholar
Jaaskelainen Jussi (G)	6	3	13 05	Mikkeli	19 4 75		VPS
Johnson Jermaine (M)				Jamaica	25 6 80		
Morini Emmanuelle (F)	5	8	10 07	Rome	31 1 82		Roma
N'Gotty Bruno (D)	6	1	13 08	Lyon	10 6 71		Marseille
Niven Derek (M)	6	1	11 02	Falkirk	12 12 83		Stenhousemuir
Nolan Kevin (M)	6	0	14 00	Liverpool	24 6 82		Scholar
Norris David (M)	5	7	11 06	Peterborough	22 2 81		Boston U
O'Hare Alan (D)				Dundalk	31 7 82		
Pedersen Henrik (F)	6	1	13 08	Denmark	10 6 75		Silkeborg
Poole Kevin (G)	5	10	11 11	Bromsgrove	21 7 63		Birmingham C
Richardson Leam (D)	5	8	11 04	Leeds	19 11 79		Blackburn R
Ricketts Michael (F)	6	2	11 12	Birmingham	4 12 78		Walsall
Ryan Ciaran (D)				Dublin	27 2 83		Scholar
Smith Jeff (M)	5	10	11 01	Middlesbrough	28 6 80		Hartlepool U
Southall Nicky (M)	5	10	12 12	Stockton	28 1 72		Gillingham
Taylor Cleveland (F)				Leicester	9 9 83		Scholar
Tofting Stig (M)	5	9	12 08	Aarhus	14 8 69		Hamburg
Walters Jonathan (F)				Birkenhead	20 9 83		Blackburn R
Whitlow Mike (D)	6	1	13 03	Northwich	13 1 68		Leicester C

League Appearances: Banks, S. 1; Barness, A. 19(6); Bergsson, G. 30; Bobic, F. 14(2); Charlton, S. 35(1); Diawara, D. 4(5); Djorkaeff, Y. 12; Espartero, M. (3); Farrelly, G. 11(7); Frandsen, P. 25(4); Gardner, R. 29(2); Hansen, B. 10(7); Hendry, C. 3; Holdsworth, D. 9(22); Jaaskelainen, J. 34; Johnson, J. 4(6); Konstantinidis, K. 3; Marshall, I. (2); N'Gotty, B. 24(2); Nolan, K. 34(1); Pedersen, H. 5(6); Poole, K. 3; Richardson, L. (1); Ricketts, M. 26(11); Smith, J. (1); Southall, N. 10(8); Tofting, S. 6; Wallace, R. 14(5); Warhurst, P. 25; Whitlow, M. 28(1).

Goals – League (44): Ricketts 12, Nolan 8, Bobic 4, Djorkaeff 4, Frandsen 3, Gardner 3, Wallace 3, Holdsworth 2, Bergsson 1, Hansen 1, N'Gotty 1, Southall 1, own goal 1.

Worthington Cup (7): Holdsworth 2 (1 pen), Ricketts 2, Nishizawa 1, Pedersen 1, Wallace 1.

FA Cup (4): Bergsson 1, Norris 1, Pedersen 1, Ricketts 1.

Ground: Reebok Stadium, Burnden Way, Lostock, Bolton BL6 6JW. Telephone Bolton (01204) 673673.

Record attendance: 69,912 v Manchester C, FA Cup 5th rd, 18 February 1933.

Capacity: 27,879.

Manager: Sam Allardyce.

Secretary: Simon Marland.

Most League Goals: 100, Division 1, 1996–97.

Highest League Scorer in Season: Joe Smith, 38, Division 1, 1920–21.

Most League Goals in Total Aggregate: Nat Lofthouse, 255, 1946–61.
Most Capped Player: Mark Fish, 34 (60), South Africa.
Most League Appearances: Eddie Hopkinson, 519, 1956–70.
Honours – Football League: Division 1 Champions – 1996–97. Division 2 Champions – 1908–09, 1977–78. Division 3 Champions – 1972–73. **FA Cup winners** 1923, 1926, 1929, 1958. **Sherpa Van Trophy:** Winners 1989.
Colours: White shirts, navy blue shorts, blue stockings.

BOSTON UNITED   DIV. 3

Nationwide Conference Appearances: Angel, 26(8); Bastock, 41; Beesley, 3(3); Brabin, 1; Brown, 21(5); Charlery, 12; Clare, 39(1); Clifford, 40; Cook, 11(21); Costello, 17(9); Elding, 12(7); Ellender, 36; Evans, 1; Gould, 26(6); Gray, 3; Lodge, 19(3); Marsh, 7; McGarry, 2(4); Monington, 25; Murphy, 4(14); Rodwell, 16; Rusk, 23(4); Scott, 7; Tarrant, 4(6); Thompson, 4; Town, 5(18); Warburton, 5(1); Weatherstone, R. 19(5); Weatherstone, S. 33(1).
Goals – League (84): Clare 24 (7 pens), Weatherstone S 12, Charlery 8, Elding 6, Angel 4, Town 4, Brown 3, Cook 3, Gould 3, Ellender 2, Murphy 2, Rodwell 2, Rusk 2, Costello 1, Marsh 1, Scott 1, Tarrant 1, Warburton 1, Weatherstone R 1, own goals 3.
Ground capacity: 8781
Record attendance: 10,086 v Corby Town, Friendly, 1955.
Manager: To be appointed.
General Manager/Secretary: John Blackwell
Honours – Nationwide Conference: Champions 2001–02. **Dr. Martens:** Champions – 1999–2000. Runners-up – 1998–99. **Unibond League:** Runners-up – 1995–96, 1997–98. **Unibond Challenge Cup:** Runners-up – 1996–97. **FA Trophy:** Runners-up – 1984–85. **Northern Premier League:** Champions – 1972–73, 1973–74, 1976–77, 1977–78. **Northern Premier League Cup:** Winners – 1974, 1976. **Northern Premier League Challenge Shield:** Winners – 1974, 1975, 1977, 1978. **Lincolnshire Senior Cup:** Winners – 1935, 1937, 1938, 1946, 1950, 1955, 1956, 1960, 1977, 1979, 1986, 1988, 1989. **Non-League Champions of Champions Cup:** Winners – 1973, 1977. **East Anglian Cup:** – Winners 1961. **Central Alliance League:** Champions – 1961–62. **United Counties League:** Champions – 1965–66. **West Midlands League:** Champions – 1966–67, 1967–68. **Eastern Professional Floodlit Cup:** Winners – 1972.
Colours: Amber and black striped shirts, black shorts with amber stripe, black stockings with yellow top.

AFC BOURNEMOUTH   DIV. 3

Bernard Narada (M)	5 7	10 07	Bristol	30 1 81	Trainee
Broadhurst Karl (D)	6 1	11 07	Portsmouth	18 3 80	Trainee
Elliott Wade (M)	5 10	11 01	Southampton	14 12 78	
Eribenne Chukkie (F)	5 10	11 12	London	2 11 80	Coventry C
Feeney Warren (F)	5 10	11 05	Belfast	17 1 81	Leeds U
Fletcher Carl (M)	5 10	11 07	Camberley	7 4 80	Trainee
Fletcher Steve (F)	6 2	14 09	Hartlepool	26 7 72	Hartlepool U
Foyewa Amos (F)	5 8	12 00	Nigeria	26 12 81	
Grant Peter (M)	5 8	11 07	Bellshill	30 8 65	Reading
Hayter James (F)	5 9	10 13	Newport (IW)	9 4 79	Trainee
Holmes Derek (F)	6 2	13 07	Lanark	18 10 78	Ross Co
Hughes Richard (M)	6 2	12 00	Glasgow	25 6 79	Atalanta
Kandol Tresor (F)	6 0	13 07	Banga	30 8 81	Luton T
Maher Shaun (D)	6 1	13 02	Dublin	20 6 78	Bohemians
Menetrier Michael (G)	6 0	13 02	Reims	23 9 78	Metz

O'Connor Gareth (F)	5 10	11 00	Dublin	10 11 78	Bohemians
Purches Stephen (M)	5 11	11 09	Ilford	14 1 80	West Ham U
Stewart Gareth (G)	6 0	12 08	Preston	3 2 80	Blackburn R
Stock Brian (M)	5 11	11 02	Winchester	24 12 81	Trainee
Thomas Danny (M)	5 7	10 10	Leamington Spa	1 5 81	Leicester C
Tindall Jason (M)	6 1	12 01	Stepney	15 11 77	Charlton Ath

League Appearances: Bernard, N. 4(4); Birmingham, D. 3(1); Broadhurst, K. 22(1); Cooke, S. 6(1); Elliott, W. 40(6); Eribenne, C. 6(18); Feeney, W. 35(2); Fletcher, C. 35; Fletcher, S. 1(1); Ford, J. 5(2); Foyewa, A. 1(7); Hayter, J. 43(1); Holmes, D. 34(3); Howe, E. 38; Huck, W. (7); Hughes, R. 16(6); Kandol, T. 3(9); Maher, S. 28(3); McAnespie, K. 3(4); Melligan, J. 7(1); Menetrier, M. 1; O'Connor, G. 12(16); Purches, S. 41; Smith, D. 1(2); Stewart, G. 45; Stock, B. 19(7); Thomas, D. 3(9); Tindall, J. 44; Young, N. 10(1).
Goals – League (56): Feeney 13 (3 pens), Holmes 9, Elliott 8 (4 pens), Hayter 7, Fletcher C 5, Howe 4, Tindall 3, Hughes 2, Purches 2, Stock 2, McAnespie 1.
Worthington Cup (0).
FA Cup (3): Fletcher S 1, Hayter 1, Hughes 1.
Ground: The Fitness First Stadium at Dean Court, Bournemouth BH7 7AF. Telephone (01202) 726300.
Record attendance: 28,799 v Manchester U, FA Cup 6th rd, 2 March 1957.
Capacity: 9600 rising to 12,000.
Manager: Sean O'Driscoll.
Secretary: K. R. J. MacAlister.
Most League Goals: 88, Division 3 (S), 1956–57.
Highest League Scorer in Season: Ted MacDougall, 42, 1970–71.
Most League Goals in Total Aggregate: Ron Eyre, 202, 1924–33.
Most Capped Player: Gerry Peyton, 7 (33), Republic of Ireland.
Most League Appearances: Sean O'Driscoll, 423, 1984–95.
Honours – Football League: Division 3 Champions – 1986–87. **Associate Members' Cup:** Winners 1984.
Colours: Red and black striped shirts, black shorts, black stockings.

BRADFORD CITY   DIV. 1

Atherton Peter (D)	5 11	13 12	Wigan	6 4 70	Sheffield W
Bower Mark (D)	5 10	11 00	Bradford	23 1 80	Trainee
Cadamarteri Danny (F)	5 9	12 10	Bradford	12 10 79	Everton
Carbone Benito (F)	5 7	10 10	Begnara	14 8 71	Aston Villa
Combe Alan (G)	6 1	12 02	Edinburgh	3 4 74	Dundee U
Davison Aidan (G)	6 1	13 12	Sedgefield	11 5 68	Sheffield U
Emanuel Lewis (D)	5 8	12 01	Bradford	14 10 83	Scholar
Jacobs Wayne (D)	5 9	11 02	Sheffield	3 2 69	Rotherham U
Jess Eoin (F)	5 10	11 09	Aberdeen	13 12 70	Aberdeen
Jorgensen Claus (M)	5 11	11 00	Holstebro	27 4 76	Bournemouth
Juanjo (F)	5 9	10 08	Barcelona	4 5 77	Hearts
Kearney Tom (M)	5 11	10 08	Liverpool	7 10 81	Everton
Lawrence Jamie (M)	5 9	12 10	Balham	8 3 70	Leicester C
Lee Andrew (F)	5 7	9 07	Bradford	18 8 82	Scholar
Locke Gary (M)	6 0	11 13	Edinburgh	16 6 75	Hearts
Molenaar Robert (D)	6 2	14 04	Zaandam	27 2 69	Leeds U
Myers Andy (D)	5 10	13 12	Hounslow	3 11 73	Chelsea
Standing Michael (M)	5 10	10 05	Shoreham	20 3 81	Aston Villa
Tod Andrew (D)	5 10	11 13	Dunfermline	4 11 71	Dunfermline Ath
Walsh Gary (G)	6 3	14 13	Wigan	21 3 68	Middlesbrough
Ward Ashley (F)	6 0	11 00	Manchester	24 11 70	Blackburn R
Wetherall David (D)	6 3	13 12	Sheffield	14 3 71	Leeds U

League Appearances: Atherton, P. 1; Blake, R. 19(7); Bower, M. 9(1); Cadamarteri, D. 14; Caldwell, S. 9; Carbone, B. 10(1); Combe, A. 16; Davison, A. 9; Emanuel, L. 8(1); Etherington, M. 12(1); Grant, G. 4(6); Grayson, S. 7; Halle, G. 31(1); Jacobs, W. 37(1); Jess, E. 43(2); Jorgensen, C. 13(5); Juanjo 5(12); Kearney, T. 5; Lawrence, J. 13(8); Lee, A. (1); Locke, G. 26(5); Makel, L. 2(11); McCall, S. 42(1); Molenaar, R. 21; Muggleton, C. 4; Myers, A. 28(4); Sharpe, L. 11(7); Tod, A. 25(5); Walsh, G. 17(1); Ward, A. 27; Wetherall, D. 17(2); Whalley, G. 21(2).
Goals – League (69): Jess 14, Blake 10 (2 pens), Ward 10 (2 pens), Carbone 5, Tod 4, McCall 3, Bower 2, Cadamarteri 2, Lawrence 2, Locke 2, Myers 2, Sharpe 2 (1 pen), Wetherall 2, Etherington 1, Grant 1, Halle 1, Jacobs 1, Jorgensen 1, Juanjo 1, own goals 3.
Worthington Cup (7): Blake 2 (1 pen), Tod 2, Lawrence 1, McCall 1, Ward 1 (pen).
FA Cup (0).
Ground: Valley Parade, Bradford BD8 7DY. Telephone (01274) 773355.
Record attendance: 39,146 v Burnley, FA Cup 4th rd, 11 March 1911. **Capacity:** 25,000.
Manager: Nicky Law.
Secretary: Jon Pollard.
Most League Goals: 128, Division 3 (N), 1928–29.
Highest League Scorer in Season: David Layne, 34, Division 4, 1961–62.
Most League Goals in Total Aggregate: Bobby Campbell, 121, 1981–84, 1984–86.
Most Capped Player: Jamie Lawrence, 12, Jamaica.
Most League Appearances: Cec Podd, 502, 1970–84.
Honours – Football League: Division 2 Champions – 1907–08. Division 3 Champions – 1984–85. Division 3 (N) Champions – 1928–29. **FA Cup:** Winners 1911.
Colours: Claret and amber shirts, black shorts, amber stockings.

BRENTFORD   DIV. 2

Name					
Anderson Ijah (D)	5 9	11 09	Hackney	30 12 75	Tottenham H
Dobson Michael (D)	6 0	13 05	Isleworth	9 4 81	Trainee
Evans Stephen (M)	5 11	11 02	Caerphilly	25 9 80	Crystal Palace
Fieldwick Lee (D)	5 11	11 09	Croydon	6 9 82	Trainee
Gottskalksson Olafur (G)	6 3	13 12	Keflavik	12 3 68	Hibernian
Hunt Steve (F)	5 8	10 12	Waterford	1 8 80	Crystal Palace
Hutchinson Eddie (M)	6 2	13 01	Kingston	23 2 82	Sutton U
Julian Alan (G)	6 2	13 05	Ashford	11 3 83	Trainee
Lovett Jay (D)	6 2	12 04	Brighton	22 1 78	Crawley T
Marshall Scott (D)	6 1	12 13	Edinburgh	1 5 73	Southampton
McCammon Mark (F)	6 3	15 00	Barnet	7 8 78	Charlton Ath
O'Connor Kevin (F)	5 11	12 02	Blackburn	24 2 82	Trainee
Peters Mark (F)	5 8	10 08	Frimley	4 10 83	Southampton
Powell Darren (D)	6 4	13 03	Hammersmith	10 3 76	Hampton
Rowlands Martin (F)	5 8	11 07	Hammersmith	8 2 79	Farnborough T
Smith Jay (D)	5 11	11 11	Lambeth	29 12 81	Trainee
Smith Paul (G)	6 4	14 00	Epsom	17 12 79	Charlton Ath
Somner Matt (D)	6 0	13 01	Isleworth	8 12 82	Trainee
Tabb Jay (M)	5 7	11 03	Tooting	21 2 84	Trainee
Williams Mark (F)	5 9	11 03	Chatham	19 10 81	Scholar

League Appearances: Anderson, I. 33(2); Boxall, D. (5); Bryan, D. (1); Burgess, B. 43; Caceres, A. 5; Dobson, M. 38(1); Evans, P. 40; Gibbs, P. 23(4); Gottskalksson, O. 28; Hunt, S. 34(1); Hutchinson, E. 2(7); Ingimarsson, I. 46; Lovett, J. 2; Mahon, G. 34(1); McCammon, M. 1(13); O'Connor, K. 13(12); Owusu, L. 43(1); Partridge, S. (1); Powell, D. 41; Price, J. 15; Rowlands, M. 13(10); Sidwell, S. 29(1); Smith, P. 18; Tabb, J. (3); Theobald, D. 5(1); Williams, M. (20).
Goals – League (77): Owusu 20, Burgess 17, Evans 14 (6 pens), Rowlands 7, Ingimarsson 6, Hunt 4, Sidwell 4, Gibbs 2 (2 pens), Powell 1, Price 1, Williams 1.

Worthington Cup (2): O'Connor 1, Owusu 1.
FA Cup (3): Burgess 1, Dobson 1, Gibbs 1.
Ground: Griffin Park, Braemar Rd, Brentford, Middlesex TW8 0NT. Telephone (020) 8847 2511.
Record attendance: 39,626 v Preston NE, FA Cup 6th rd, 5 March 1938. **Capacity:** 12,500.
Manager: Wally Downes.
Secretary: Polly Kates.
Most League Goals: 98, Division 4, 1962–63.
Highest League Scorer in Season: Jack Holliday, 38, Division 3 (S), 1932–33.
Most League Goals in Total Aggregate: Jim Towers, 153, 1954–61.
Most Capped Player: John Buttigieg, 22 (98), Malta.
Most League Appearances: Ken Coote, 514, 1949–64.
Honours – Football League: Division 2 Champions – 1934–35. Division 3 Champions – 1991–92, 1998–99. Division 3 (S) Champions – 1932–33. Division 4 Champions – 1962–63.
Colours: Red and white vertical striped shirts, black shorts, black stockings.

BRIGHTON & HOVE ALBION   DIV. 1

Brooker Paul (F)	5 8	10 04	Hammersmith	25 11 76	Fulham
Carpenter Richard (M)	6 0	13 00	Sheppey	30 9 72	Cardiff C
Cullip Danny (D)	6 0	13 04	Ascot	17 9 76	Brentford
Hart Gary (F)	5 9	12 07	Harlow	21 9 76	Stansted
Jones Nathan (M)	5 6	10 10	Rhondda	28 5 73	Southend U
Kuipers Michels (G)	6 2	14 09	Amsterdam	26 6 74	Bristol R
Lee David (M)	5 10	12 07	Basildon	28 3 80	Hull C
Marney Daniel (F)	5 9	10 12	Sidcup	2 10 81	Scholar
Mayo Kerry (D)	5 9	13 05	Cuckfield	21 9 77	Trainee
McArthur Duncan (M)	5 9	12 06	Brighton	6 5 81	Trainee
Melton Steve (M)	5 11	12 03	Lincoln	3 10 78	Stoke C
Oatway Charlie (M)	5 7	11 11	Hammersmith	28 11 73	Brentford
Packham Will (G)	6 2	13 02	Brighton	13 1 81	Trainee
Pethick Robbie (D)	5 10	12 02	Tavistock	8 9 70	Bristol R
Pitcher Geoff (M)	5 7	11 11	Sutton	15 8 75	Colchester U
Rogers Paul (M)	6 0	12 12	Portsmouth	21 3 65	Wigan Ath
Virgo Adam (D)	6 2	13 12	Brighton	25 1 83	
Watson Paul (D)	5 8	11 05	Hastings	4 1 75	Brentford
Wilkinson Shaun (D)	5 6	10 08	Portsmouth	12 9 81	Scholar
Zamora Bobby (F)	6 1	11 11	Barking	16 1 81	Trainee

League Appearances: Brooker, P. 30(11); Carpenter, R. 45; Crosby, A. (2); Cullip, D. 44; Gray, W. 3(1); Hadland, P. (2); Hart, G. 34(5); Jones, N. 29(7); Kuipers, M. 39; Lee, D. (2); Lehmann, D. 3(4); Lewis, J. 14(1) Mayo, K. 30(3); McPhee, C. 2; Melton, S. 5(5); Morgan, S. 42; Oatway, C. 27(5); Packham, W. 1; Pethick, R. 13(11); Pitcher, G. 2(8); Rogers, P. 19(6); Royce, S. 6; Steele, L. 20(17); Virgo, A. 4(2); Watson, P. 45; Webb, D. 7(5); Wicks, M. 2; Zamora, B. 40(1).
Goals – League (66): Zamora 28 (6 pens), Steele 9, Watson 5, Brooker 4, Hart 4, Carpenter 3, Lewis 3, Jones 2, Gray 1, Melton 1, Morgan 1, Oatway 1, Rogers 1, Webb 1, own goals 2.
Worthington Cup (2): Zamora 2.
FA Cup (3): Zamora 2, Cullip 1.
Offices: Hanover House, 118 Queens Road, Brighton BN1 3XG. Telephone: (01273) 778855. **Ground:** Withdean Stadium, Tongdean Lane, Brighton.
Record attendance: 36,747 v Fulham, Division 2, 27 December 1958.
Capacity: 6960.
Manager: To be appointed.
Secretary: Derek Allan.

Most League Goals: 112, Division 3 (S), 1955–56.
Highest League Scorer in Season: Peter Ward, 32, Division 3, 1976–77.
Most League Goals in Total Aggregate: Tommy Cook, 114, 1922–29.
Most Capped Player: Steve Penney, 17, Northern Ireland.
Most League Appearances: 'Tug' Wilson, 509, 1922–36.
Honours – Football League: Division 2 Champions – 2001–02. Division 3 Champions – 2000–01. Division 3 (S) Champions – 1957–58. Division 4 Champions – 1964–65.
Colours: Blue and white striped shirts, white shorts, white stockings.

BRISTOL CITY   DIV. 2

Amankwaah Kevin (D)	6 1	12 10	London	19 5 82	Scholar	
Anyinsah Joseph (M)			Bristol	8 10 84	Scholar	
Beadle Peter (F)	6 2	15 00	Lambeth	13 5 72	Notts Co	
Bell Mickey (D)	5 8	12 09	Newcastle	15 11 71	Wycombe W	
Brown Aaron (M)	5 10	13 01	Bristol	14 3 80	Trainee	
Brown Marvin (F)	5 8	11 12	Bristol	6 7 83		
Burke Andrew (M)			Camden	9 1 83		
Burnell Joe (D)	5 9	11 13	Bristol	10 10 80	Trainee	
Burns John (M)	5 10	11 04	Dublin	4 12 77	Nottingham F	
Carey Louis (D)	5 10	12 06	Bristol	20 1 77	Trainee	
Cleverley Benjamin (M)	5 9	10 00	Bristol	12 9 81	Scholar	
Clist Simon (M)	5 9	11 05	Bournemouth	13 6 81	Tottenham H	
Coles Daniel (D)	6 0	12 08	Bristol	31 10 81	Scholar	
Correia Albano (F)	6 2	12 13	Guinea Bissau	18 10 81		
Doherty Tom (M)	5 8	11 07	Bristol	17 3 79	Trainee	
Fortune Clayton (D)	6 3	13 10	Forest Gate	10 11 82	Tottenham H	
Hill Matt (D)	5 8	11 10	Bristol	26 3 81	Trainee	
Hulbert Robin (M)	5 10	11 10	Plymouth	14 3 80	Swindon T	
Jones Darren (D)	6 1	14 00	Newport	28 8 83	Scholar	
Jones Steve (F)	6 1	13 04	Cambridge	17 3 70	Charlton Ath	
Lever Mark (D)	6 1	13 12	Beverley	29 3 70	Grimsby T	
Loxton Craig (M)			Bath	14 9 84	Scholar	
Matthews Lee (F)	5 9	13 04	Middlesbrough	16 1 79	Leeds U	
Mercer Billy (G)	6 1	13 02	Liverpool	22 5 69	Chesterfield	
Murray Scott (M)	5 8	11 02	Aberdeen	26 5 74	Aston Villa	
Peacock Lee (F)	5 9	14 05	Paisley	9 10 76	Manchester C	
Phillips Steve (G)	6 1	13 02	Bath	6 5 78	Paulton R	
Roberts Chris (F)	5 11	14 02	Cardiff	22 10 79	Exeter C	
Rosenior Liam (F)			London	9 7 84	Scholar	
Shanahan Aaron (M)			Coventry	10 9 82	Coventry C	
Sheppard Kyle (D)			Cardiff	4 12 82	Chelsea	
Stowell Mike (G)	6 2	14 01	Preston	19 4 65	Wolverhampton W	
Tinnion Brian (M)	6 2	13 01	Stanley	23 3 68	Bradford C	
Woodman Craig (D)	5 9	10 11	Tiverton	22 12 82	Trainee	

League Appearances: Amankwaah, K. 18(6); Bell, M. 41(1); Brown, A. 34(2); Brown, M. 1(9); Burnell, J. 26(4); Carey, L. 34(1); Clist, S. 9(11); Coles, D. 20(3); Doherty, T. 27(7); Fortune, C. 1(1); Goodridge, G. (2); Hill, M. 40; Hulbert, R. 4(7); Jones, D. 1(1); Jones, S. 17(6); Lever, M. 26(3); Matthews, L. 6(16); Murray, S. 34(3); Peacock, L. 28(3); Phillips, S. 21(1); Roberts, C. 4; Robinson, S. 6; Rodrigues, D. (4); Rosenior, L. (1); Singh, H. 3; Stowell, M. 25; Summerbell, M. 5; Thorpe, T. 36(6); Tinnion, B. 35(3); Woodman, C. 5(1).
Goals – League (68): Thorpe 16 (2 pens), Peacock 15 (2 pens), Murray 8, Bell 7 (3 pens), Jones S 5, Matthews 3, Tinnion 3, Amankwaah 1, Brown A 1, Clist 1, Doherty 1, Hill 1, Lever 1, Robinson 1, own goals 4.
Worthington Cup (4): Amankwaah 1, Clist 1, Jones 1, Thorpe 1.

FA Cup (0).
Ground: Ashton Gate, Bristol BS3 2EJ. Telephone (0117) 9630630.
Record attendance: 43,335 v Preston NE, FA Cup 5th rd, 16 February 1935.
Capacity: 21,479.
Manager: Danny Wilson.
Secretary: Michelle McDonald.
Most League Goals: 104, Division 3 (S), 1926–27.
Highest League Scorer in Season: Don Clark, 36, Division 3 (S), 1946–47.
Most League Goals in Total Aggregate: John Atyeo, 314, 1951–66.
Most Capped Player: Billy Wedlock, 26, England.
Most League Appearances: John Atyeo, 597, 1951–66.
Honours – Football League: Division 2 Champions – 1905–06. Division 3 (S)
Champions – 1922–23, 1926–27, 1954–55. **Welsh Cup winners** 1934. **Anglo-Scottish
Cup:** Winners 1977–78. **Freight Rover Trophy winners** 1985–86.
Colours: Red shirts, red shorts, white stockings.

BRISTOL ROVERS   DIV. 3

Andreasson Marcus (D)	6 4	13 04	Liberia	13 7 78	Osters
Astafjevs Vitalijs (M)	5 11	12 04	Riga	3 4 71	Skonto Riga
Bryant Simon (M)	5 11	12 11	Bristol	22 11 82	Scholar
Cameron Martin (F)	6 2	14 01	Dunfermline	16 6 78	
Challis Trevor (D)	5 8	11 13	Paddington	23 10 75	QPR
Clarke Ryan (G)	6 3	12 13	Bristol	30 4 82	Scholar
Gall Kevin (M)	5 9	10 08	Merthyr	4 2 82	Newcastle U
Hogg Lewis (M)	5 9	11 04	Bristol	13 9 82	Trainee
Howie Scott (G)	6 4	14 04	Motherwell	4 1 72	Reading
Jones Scott (D)	5 10	12 01	Sheffield	1 5 75	Barnsley
Lopez Carlos (D)	5 11	12 07	Madrid	22 7 79	
McKeever Mark (M)	5 11	12 00	Derry	16 11 78	Sheffield W
Ommel Sergio (F)	6 2	12 06	The Hague	2 9 77	Groningen
Plummer Dwayne (M)	5 9	11 00	Bristol	12 5 78	Bristol C
Richards Justin (F)	6 0	13 11	Sandwell	16 10 80	WBA
Shore Jamie (M)	5 9	12 05	Bristol	1 9 77	Norwich C

League Appearances: Arndale, N. (1); Astafjevs, V. 14(5); Bryant, S. 8; Bubb, A.
3(10); Cameron, M. 10(15); Carlisle, W. 5; Challis, T. 28(1); Clarke, R. (1); Ellington, N. 27; Foran, M. 30(1); Foster, S. 33; Gall, K. 25(6); Gilroy, D. 2(2); Ham-
mond, E. 3(4); Hillier, D. 27, Hogg, L. 22(1); Howie, S. 46; Jones, S. 14(5); Lopez,
C. 6; Lopez, R. 5(2); Mauge, R. 14(1); McKeever, M. 6(2); Ommel, S. 18(5); Plum-
mer, D. 12(3); Pritchard, D. 1(4); Quinn, J. 6; Richards, J. (1); Ross, N. 2(3); Shore,
D. 9; Smith, M. 17(2); Thomas, J. 7; Thomson, A. 29(2); Toner, C. 6; Trought, M.
17(3); Walters, M. 7(19); Weare, R. 9(1); Wilson, C. 38.
Goals – League (40): Ellington 15 (1 pen), Ommel 8, Cameron 4 (1 pen), Gall 3,
Foran 2, Astafjevs 1, Foster 1, Hillier 1, Quinn 1 (pen), Thomas 1, Thomson 1,
Weare 1, own goal 1.
Worthington Cup (1): Hiller 1.
FA Cup (8): Ellington 4, Astafjevs 1, Hogg 1, Ommel 1, Walters 1.
Ground: The Memorial Ground, Filton Avenue, Horfield, Bristol BS7 0BF.
Record attendance: 9464 v Liverpool, FA Cup 4th rd, 8 February 1992
(Twerton Park). 38,472 v Preston NE, FA Cup 4th rd, 30 January 1960 (Eastville).
11,433 v Sunderland, League Cup 3rd rd, 31 October 2000 (Memorial Ground).
Capacity: 11,976.
Director of Football/Team Manager: Ray Graydon.
Secretary: Roger Brinsford.
Most League Goals: 92, Division 3 (S), 1952–53.
Highest League Scorer in Season: Geoff Bradford, 33, Division 3 (S), 1952–53.
Most League Goals in Total Aggregate: Geoff Bradford, 242, 1949–64.

Most Capped Player: Vitalijs Astafjevs, 16 (79), Latvia.
Most League Appearances: Stuart Taylor, 546, 1966–80.
Honours – Football League: Division 3 (S) Champions – 1952–53. Division 3 Champions – 1989–90.
Colours: Blue and white quartered shirts, white shorts, blue stockings.

BURNLEY   DIV. 1

Blake Robbie (F)	5 9	12 06	Middlesbrough	4 3 76	Bradford C
Branch Graham (F)	6 2	12 02	Liverpool	12 2 72	Stockport Co
Briscoe Lee (D)	5 11	11 12	Pontefract	30 9 75	Sheffield W
Cook Paul (M)	5 11	11 00	Liverpool	22 6 67	Stockport Co
Cox Ian (D)	6 0	12 00	Croydon	25 3 71	Bournemouth
Davis Steve (D)	6 2	14 07	Hexham	30 10 68	Luton T
Gnohere Arthur (D)	6 0	13 00	Yamoussoukro	20 11 78	
Grant Tony (M)	5 11	10 10	Liverpool	14 11 74	Manchester C
Little Glen (M)	6 3	13 00	Wimbledon	15 10 75	Glentoran
Maylett Brad (M)	5 8	10 07	Manchester	24 12 80	Trainee
McGregor Mark (D)	5 9	12 08	Chester	16 2 77	Wrexham
Michopoulos Nick (G)	6 3	14 00	Karditsa	20 2 70	PAOK Salonika
Moore Alan (M)	5 10	11 11	Dublin	25 11 74	Middlesbrough
Moore Ian (F)	5 11	12 02	Birkenhead	26 8 76	Stockport Co
Papadopoulos Dimitri (F)	5 8	11 04	Kazakhstan	20 9 81	Akratitos
Payton Andy (F)	5 9	11 13	Whalley	23 10 67	Huddersfield T
Rasmussen Mark (M)	5 6	10 10	Newcastle	28 11 83	
Shandran Anthony (F)	5 9	12 10	North Shields	17 9 81	Scholar
Taylor Gareth (F)	6 2	13 07	Weston-Super-Mare	25 2 73	Manchester C
Weller Paul (M)	5 8	11 02	Brighton	6 3 75	Trainee

League Appearances: Armstrong, G. 11(7); Ball, K. 37(5); Beresford, M. 13; Blake, R. 1(9); Branch, G. 8(2); Briscoe, L. 43(1); Cook, P. 25(3); Cox, I. 32(2); Davis, S. 22(1); Ellis, T. (11); Gascoigne, P. 3(3); Gnohere, A. 31(3); Grant, T. 26(2); Johnrose, L. (6); Johnson, D. 8; Little, G. 31(6); Maylett, B. (10); McGregor, M. 1; Michopoulos, N. 33; Moore, A. 23(6); Moore, I. 41(5); Mullin, J. (4); Papadopoulos, D. (6); Payton, A. (15); Taylor, G. 35(5); Thomas, M. 10(2); Weller, P. 29(9); West, D. 43(1).
Goals – League (70): Taylor 16 (2 pens), Moore I 11, Little 9 (2 pens), Briscoe 5, Cook 5 (2 pens), Johnson 5, Payton 4 (3 pens), Gnohere 3, Moore A 3, Armstrong 2, Cox 2, Weller 2, Davis 1, Ellis 1, own goal 1.
Worthington Cup (2): McGregor 1, Moore A 1.
FA Cup (5): Moore I 3, Little 1, Moore A 1.
Ground: Turf Moor, Burnley BB10 4BX. Telephone (01282) 700000.
Record attendance: 54,775 v Huddersfield T, FA Cup 3rd rd, 23 February 1924.
Capacity: 22,619.
Manager: Stan Ternent.
Secretary: Cathy Pickup.
Most League Goals: 102, Division 1, 1960–61.
Highest League Scorer in Season: George Beel, 35, Division 1, 1927–28.
Most League Goals in Total Aggregate: George Beel, 178, 1923–32.
Most Capped Player: Jimmy McIlroy, 51 (55), Northern Ireland.
Most League Appearances: Jerry Dawson, 522, 1907–28.
Honours – Football League: Division 1 Champions – 1920–21, 1959–60. Division 2 Champions – 1897–98, 1972–73. Division 3 Champions – 1981–82. Division 4 Champions – 1991–92. **FA Cup winners** 1913–14. **Anglo-Scottish Cup:** Winners 1978–79.
Colours: Claret and blue shirts, white shorts, white stockings.

Barrass Matt (D)	5 10	12 05	Bury	28	2 81	Trainee
Billy Chris (M)	6 0	12 13	Huddersfield	2	1 73	Notts Co
Borley David (M)	5 9	12 08	Newcastle	17	4 83	Scholar
Bullock Darren (M)	5 9	12 10	Worcester	12	2 69	Swindon T
Clegg George (M)	5 10	12 00	Manchester	16	11 80	Manchester U
Connell Lee (D)	6 1	13 01	Bury	24	6 81	Trainee
Evans Gary (D)	5 9	12 03	Doncaster	13	9 82	Scholar
Forrest Martyn (M)	5 9	11 07	Bury	2	1 79	Trainee
Garner Glyn (G)	6 2	13 04	Pontypool	9	12 76	Llanelli
Hill Nicky (D)	6 0	13 07	Accrington	26	2 81	Trainee
Kenny Paddy (G)	6 1	15 00	Halifax	15	5 78	Bradford PA
Lawson Ian (F)	5 11	12 08	Huddersfield	4	11 77	Stockport Co
Nelson Michael (D)	6 2	13 03	Gateshead	15	3 82	
Newby Jon (F)	5 11	11 00	Warrington	28	11 78	Liverpool
Nugent Dave (F)	5 11	12 00	Liverpool	2	5 85	Scholar
O'Shaughnessy Paul (M)	5 10	11 10	Bury	3	10 81	Scholar
Preece Andy (F)	6 2	13 06	Evesham	27	3 67	Blackpool
Redmond Steve (D)	5 11	13 02	Liverpool	2	11 67	Oldham Ath
Seddon Gareth (F)	5 9	12 04	Burnley	23	5 80	Atherstone U
Stuart Jamie (D)	5 10	11 02	Southwark	5	10 76	Millwall
Swailes Danny (D)	6 3	13 03	Bolton	1	4 79	Trainee
Tarsuslugil Edward (D)	5 9	11 07	Leeds	3	11 82	Doncaster R
Unsworth Lee (D)	5 11	11 09	Eccles	25	2 73	Crewe Alex

League Appearances: Armstrong, C. 11; Barrass, M. 6(1); Bhutia, B. 3; Billy, C. 19(2); Borley, D. 16(5); Bullock, D. 2(2); Clarkson, P. 4; Clegg, G. 25(6); Collins, S. 26(3); Connell, L. 9(4); Evans, G. 1; Forrest, M. 31(3); Garner, G. 5(2); Gunby, S. (1); Hill, N. 3(2); Jarrett, J. 32(5); Kenny, P. 41; Lawson, I. 12(12); Murphy, M. 5(4); Nelson, M. 28(3); Newby, J. 46; Nugent, D. 1(4); O'Shaughnessy, P. (2); Preece, A. 4(9); Redmond, S. 26; Reid, P. 23(5); Seddon, G. 23(12); Singh, H. 11(1); Stuart, J. 24; Swailes, D. 26(2); Syros, G. 9; Unsworth, L. 34(1).
Goals – League (43): Newby 6 (1 pen), Seddon 6, Clegg 4, Lawson 4, Billy 3, Borley 3 (1 pen), Reid 3 (1 pen), Jarrett 2, Nelson 2, Singh 2, Forrest 1, Preece 1, Redmond 1, Stuart 1, Swailes 1, Syros 1, Unsworth 1, own goal 1.
Worthington Cup (1): Reid 1 (pen).
FA Cup (2): Seddon 1, Singh 1.
Ground: Gigg Lane, Bury BL9 9HR. Telephone (0161) 764 4881.
Record attendance: 35,000 v Bolton W, FA Cup 3rd rd, 9 January 1960. **Capacity:** 11,669.
Manager: Andy Preece.
Secretary: Jill Neville.
Most League Goals: 108, Division 3, 1960–61.
Highest League Scorer in Season: Craig Madden, 35, Division 4, 1981–82.
Most League Goals in Total Aggregate: Craig Madden, 129, 1978–86.
Most Capped Player: Bill Gorman, 11 (13), Republic of Ireland and (4), Northern Ireland.
Most League Appearances: Norman Bullock, 506, 1920–35.
Honours – Football League: Division 2 Champions – 1894–95, 1996–97. Division 3 Champions – 1960–61. **FA Cup winners** 1900, 1903. **Auto Windscreens Shield winners** 1997.
Colours: White shirts, royal blue shorts, royal blue stockings.

Player			Birthplace			
Alcide Colin (F)	6 2	13 11	Huddersfield	14	4 72	York C
Angus Stevland (D)	6 0	12 00	Essex	16	9 80	West Ham U
Bourgeois Daryl (D)			Newham	22	9 82	Southend U
Bridges David (M)	6 0	12 00	Huntingdon	22	9 82	Scholar
Chillingworth Daniel (F)	6 0	12 06	Cambridge	13	9 81	Scholar
Fleming Terry (M)	5 9	10 01	Marston Green	1	5 73	Plymouth Arg
Goodhind Warren (D)	5 11	11 02	Johannesburg	16	8 77	Barnet
Guttridge Luke (M)	5 5	8 06	Barnstaple	27	3 82	Torquay U
Kitson Dave (F)	6 3	13 00	Hitchin	21	1 80	Arlesey
Marshall Shaun (G)	6 1	13 03	Fakenham	3	10 78	Trainee
Murray Fred (D)	5 10	11 12	Tipperary	22	5 82	Blackburn R
Nacca Franco (D)	5 6	10 00	Venezuela	9	11 82	Scholar
One Armand (F)	6 4	14 00	Paris	15	3 83	
Paynter Owen (M)			Newmarket	22	10 82	Scholar
Prokas Richard (M)	5 9	11 05	Penrith	22	1 76	Carlisle U
Revell Alex (F)	6 3	13 00	Cambridge	7	7 83	Scholar
Scully Tony (M)	5 7	11 06	Dublin	12	6 76	QPR
Tann Adam (D)	6 0	11 05	Fakenham	12	5 82	Scholar
Taylor John (F)	6 2	15 00	Norwich	24	10 64	Luton T
Tudor Shane (M)	5 8	11 00	Wolverhampton	10	2 82	Wolverhampton W
Wanless Paul (M)	6 1	14 08	Banbury	14	12 73	Lincoln C
Warner Phil (D)	5 10	11 12	Southampton	2	2 79	Southampton
Youngs Tom (F)	5 9	11 01	Bury St Edmunds	31	8 79	Trainee

League Appearances: Alcide, C. 7(1); Angus, S. 41; Ashbee, I. 38; Austin, K. 4(2); Bridges, D. 1(6); Byrne, D. 3(1); Chillingworth, D. 10(2); Clements, M. (1); Cowan, T. 3(2); Duncan, A. 20(4); Fleming, T. 28(6); Goodhind, W. 11(3); Guttridge, L. 27(2); Jackman, D. 5(2); Kandol, T. 2(2); Kelly, L. 1(1); Kitson, D. 30(3); Marshall, S. 4(3); McAnespie, S. (1); Murray, F. 21; Mustoe, N. (5); One, A. 18(14); Perez, L. 42; Prokas, R. 8(1); Revell, A. 7(17); Richardson, M. 4(2); Scully, T. 19(6); Tann, A. 24(1); Taylor, S. (3); Traore, D. 2(5); Tudor, S. 31(1); Walling, D. 20; Wanless, P. 28(1); Warner, P. 11(1); Youngs, T. 36(6).
Goals – League (47): Youngs 11 (1 pen), Kitson 9, Wanless 6 (1 pen), One 4, Tudor 3, Ashbee 2 (1 pen), Chillingworth 2, Guttridge 2 (1 pen), Revell 2, Scully 2, Bridges 1, Cowan 1, Jackman 1, Prokas 1.
Worthington Cup (1): Alcide 1.
FA Cup (1): Tudor 1.
Ground: Abbey Stadium, Newmarket Rd, Cambridge CB5 8LN. Telephone (01223) 566500. **Capacity:** 9247.
Record attendance; 14,000 v Chelsea, Friendly, 1 May 1970.
Manager: John Taylor.
Secretary: Andrew Pincher.
Most League Goals: 87, Division 4, 1976–77.
Highest League Scorer in Season: David Crown, 24, Division 4, 1985–86.
Most League Goals in Total Aggregate: John Taylor, 86, 1988–92; 1996–01.
Most Capped Player: Tom Finney, 7 (15), Northern Ireland.
Most League Appearances: Steve Spriggs, 416, 1975–87.
Honours – Football League: Division 3 Champions – 1990–91. Division 4 Champions – 1976–77.
Colours: Amber shirts with black trim, black shorts, amber stockings.

Player			Birthplace			
Alexander Neil (G)	6 0	11 11	Edinburgh	10	3 78	Livingston
Boland Willie (M)	5 9	12 02	Ennis	6	8 74	Coventry C

Name	Height	Weight	Birthplace	Date	Previous club
Bonner Mark (M)	5 10	11 00	Ormskirk	7 7 74	Blackpool
Bowen Jason (F)	5 7	11 02	Merthyr	24 8 72	Reading
Campbell Andy (F)	5 11	11 07	Middlesbrough	18 4 79	Middlesbrough
Collins James (F)	6 2	13 01	Newport	23 4 83	Scholar
Dimond Kristian (M)			Cardiff	1 2 83	Crystal Palace
Earnshaw Robert (F)	5 8	10 07	Zambia	6 4 81	Trainee
Evans Kevin (M)	6 2	12 01	Carmarthen	16 12 80	Leeds U
Fish Nicholas (M)			Cardiff	15 9 84	Scholar
Fortune-West Leo (F)	6 3	14 01	Stratford	9 4 71	Rotherham U
Gabbidon Daniel (D)	5 10	12 01	Cwmbran	8 8 79	WBA
Giles Martyn (D)	6 0	11 04	Cardiff	10 4 83	Scholar
Gordon Gavin (F)	6 1	12 00	Manchester	24 6 79	Lincoln C
Hamilton Des (M)	5 11	14 04	Bradford	15 8 76	Newcastle U
Heal Simon (M)			Barnstaple	10 11 82	Scholar
Hughes David (D)	6 4	14 01	Wrexham	1 2 79	Shrewsbury T
Ingram Richard (M)			Merthyr	15 2 85	Scholar
Jeanne Leon (M)	5 10	11 01	Cardiff	17 1 80	QPR
Jones Gethin (D)	5 11	12 00	Carmarthen	8 8 81	Carmarthen T
Jordan Andrew (D)	6 1	13 01	Manchester	14 12 79	Bristol C
Kavanagh Graham (M)	5 10	12 01	Dublin	2 12 73	Stoke C
Kendall Lee (G)	5 11	14 04	Newport	8 1 81	Crystal Palace
Legg Andy (M)	5 8	10 01	Neath	28 7 66	Reading
Low Josh (M)	6 1	14 03	Bristol	15 2 79	Leyton Orient
Maxwell Leyton (M)	5 8	12 01	Rhyl	3 10 79	Liverpool
Parkins Michael (M)			Cardiff	12 1 85	Scholar
Prior Spencer (D)	6 3	13 01	Rochford	22 4 71	Manchester C
Simpkins Mike (D)	6 1	12 00	Sheffield	28 11 78	Chesterfield
Thorne Peter (F)	6 0	12 09	Manchester	21 6 73	Stoke C
Wallis Tony (M)			Portsmouth	9 10 82	Scholar
Walton Mark (G)	6 4	16 03	Merthyr	1 6 69	Brighton & HA
Weston Rhys (D)	6 0	12 09	Kingston	27 10 80	Arsenal
Young Scott (D)	6 2	13 01	Pontypridd	14 1 76	Trainee

League Appearances: Alexander, N. 46; Boland, W. 40(2); Bonner, M. 25(4); Bowen, J. 21(4); Brayson, P. 16(19); Campbell, A. 8; Collins, J. 2(5); Croft, G. 3(3); Earnshaw, R. 28(2); Fortune-West, L. 18(18); Gabbidon, D. 44; Gordon, D. 7; Gordon, G. 12(3); Hamilton, D. 14(5); Hughes, D. 1(1); Jeanne, L. (2); Jones, G. (1); Kavanagh, G. 43; Legg, A. 27(8); Low, J. 11(11); Maxwell, L. 5(12); Nugent, K. 1; Prior, S. 33(4); Simpkins, M. 13(4); Thorne, P. 23(3); Weston, R. 35(2); Young, S. 30(3).
Goals – League (75): Kavanagh 13 (3 pens), Earnshaw 11 (2 pens), Fortune-West 9, Thorne 8, Campbell 7, Bowen 5, Young 4, Brayson 3 (1 pen), Gabbidon 3, Gordon D 2, Legg 2, Prior 2, Boland 1, Collins 1, Croft 1, Gordon G 1, Maxwell 1, own goal 1.
Worthington Cup (1): Earnshaw 1.
FA Cup (9): Earnshaw 2, Kavanagh 2 (1 pen), Brayson 1, Fortune-West 1, Gordon G 1, Hamilton 1, Young 1.
Ground: Ninian Park, Cardiff CF11 8SX. Telephone (029) 2022 1001.
Record attendance: 61,566, Wales v England, 14 October 1961. **Capacity:** 15,585.
Manager: Lennie Lawrence
Secretary: Jason Turner.
Most League Goals: 95, Division 3, 2000–01.
Highest League Scorer in Season: Stan Richards, 30, Division 3 (S), 1946–47.
Most League Goals in Total Aggregate: Len Davies, 128, 1920–31.
Most Capped Player: Alf Sherwood, 39 (41), Wales.
Most League Appearances: Phil Dwyer, 471, 1972–85.
Honours – Football League: Division 3 (S) Champions – 1946–47. **FA Cup winners** 1926–27 (the only occasion the Cup has been won by a club outside England). **Welsh Cup winners** 21 times.
Colours: Blue shirts, blue shorts, blue stockings.

Player			Birthplace			Previous club
Andrews Lee (D)	6 0	10 11	Carlisle	23	4 83	Scholar
Birch Mark (D)	5 10	11 08	Stoke	5	1 77	Trainee
Foran Richie (F)	6 1	12 10	Dublin	16	6 80	
Galloway Mick (M)	5 11	11 05	Nottingham	13 10 74		Chesterfield
Maddison Lee (D)	5 11	11 00	Bristol	5 10 72		Dundee
McDonagh Will (D)	6 1	12 01	Dublin	14	3 83	Bohemians
Murphy Peter (D)	5 11	12 07	Dublin	27 10 80		Blackburn R
Thurston Mark (D)	6 2	11 08	Carlisle	10	2 80	Trainee
Thwaites Adam (D)	5 10	11 10	Carlisle	18 12 81		Trainee
Wake Brian (M)			Stockton	13	8 82	
Weaver Luke (G)	6 1	13 02	Woolwich	26	6 79	Sunderland
Whitehead Stuart (D)	6 0	12 02	Bromsgrove	17	7 77	Bolton W

League Appearances: Allan, J. 10(19); Andrews, L. 37(2); Bell, S. 3(2); Berkley, A. 2(3); Birch, M. 42; Dickinson, M. (1); Elliott, S. 6; Foran, R. 37; Friars, S. (1); Green, S. 16; Haddow, A. 4; Hadland, P. 4; Halliday, S. 28(15); Harkin, M. 2(2); Hews, C. 4(1); Hopper, T. 20(9); Hore, J. (3); Jack, M. 16(16); Keen, P. 36; Maddison, L. 5(2); McAughtrie, C. 2(3); McDonagh, W. 7(5); McGill, B. 27(1); Morley, D. 14(4); Murphy, P. 39(1); Rogers, D. 26(1); Rooke, S. (1); Skinner, S. 1(5); Slaven, J. (2); Soley, S. 19(2); Stevens, I. 23(3); Thurston, M. 1; Thwaites, A. (1); Weaver, L. 10; Whitehead, S. 29(3); Willis, S. (1); Winstanley, M. 36.
Goals – League (49): Foran 14 (5 pens), Stevens 8, Halliday 7, Soley 4, Green 3, Allan 2, Hews 2, McGill 2, Hadland 1, Hopper 1, McAughtrie 1, McDonagh 1, Rogers 1, Whitehead 1, Winstanley 1.
Worthington Cup (0).
FA Cup (2): Foran 1, Soley 1.
Ground: Brunton Park, Carlisle CA1 1LL. Telephone (01228) 526237.
Record attendance: 27,500 v Birmingham C, FA Cup 3rd rd, 5 January 1957 and v Middlesbrough, FA Cup 5th rd, 7 February 1970. **Capacity:** 16,651.
Manager: Billy Barr.
Secretary: Sarah McKnight.
Most League Goals: 113, Division 4, 1963–64.
Highest League Scorer in Season: Jimmy McConnell, 42, Division 3 (N), 1928–29.
Most League Goals in Total Aggregate: Jimmy McConnell, 126, 1928–32.
Most Capped Player: Eric Welsh, 4, Northern Ireland.
Most League Appearances: Allan Ross, 466, 1963–79.
Honours – Football League: Division 3 Champions – 1964–65, 1994–95. **Auto Windscreens Shield winners:** 1997
Colours: Blue shirts, blue shorts, blue stockings.

CHARLTON ATHLETIC   FA PREMIERSHIP

Player			Birthplace			Previous club
Bart-Williams Chris (M)	5 11	12 07	Freetown	16	6 74	Nottingham F
Bartlett Shaun (F)	6 0	12 06	Cape Town	31 10 72		Zurich
Brown Steve (D)	6 1	14 10	Brighton	13	5 72	Trainee
De Bolla Mark (F)	5 7	11 09	London	1	1 83	Trainee
Deane Adrian (M)	5 10	10 00	London	24	2 83	
Dincer Fatih (D)	5 8	11 00	Stockholm	13	7 83	
Euell Jason (F)	5 11	11 13	Lambeth	6	2 77	Wimbledon
Fish Mark (D)	6 4	12 11	Cape Town	14	3 74	Bolton W
Fortune Jon (D)	6 2	12 12	Islington	23	8 80	Trainee
Jensen Claus (M)	6 1	13 04	Nykobing	29	4 77	Bolton W
Johansson Jonatan (F)	6 1	12 08	Stockholm	16	8 75	Rangers
Kiely Dean (G)	6 0	12 13	Salford	10 10 70		Bury
Kinsella Mark (M)	5 8	12 01	Dublin	12	8 72	Colchester U

Kishishev Radostin (D)	5 10	12 08	Bourgas	30	7 74	Litets Lovech
Konchesky Paul (D)	5 8	11 07	Barking	15	5 81	Trainee
Lisbie Kevin (F)	5 10	11 01	Hackney	17	10 78	Trainee
Long Stacy (F)	5 8	10 00	Bromley	11	1 85	Scholar
McCafferty Neil (M)	5 7	10 00	Derry	19	7 84	Scholar
Parker Scott (M)	5 8	11 02	Lambeth	13	10 80	Trainee
Powell Chris (D)	5 10	11 13	Lambeth	8	9 69	Derby Co
Pringle Martin (F)	6 2	12 03	Gothenburg	18	11 70	Benfica
Rachubka Paul (G)	6 1	13 01	San Luis Opispo	21	5 81	Manchester U
Roberts Ben (G)	6 2	13 00	Bishop Auckland	22	6 75	Middlesbrough
Robinson John (M)	5 10	12 01	Bulawayo	29	8 71	Brighton & HA
Robson Paul (D)	5 9	11 05	Hull	4	8 83	Doncaster R
Rowett Gary (D)	6 0	12 10	Bromsgrove	6	3 74	Leicester C
Rufus Richard (D)	6 1	12 12	Lewisham	12	1 75	Trainee
Shields Greg (D)	5 10	11 04	Falkirk	21	8 76	Dunfermline Ath
Stuart Graham (M)	5 8	12 00	Tooting	24	10 70	Sheffield U
Svensson Mathias (F)	6 1	12 08	Boras	24	9 74	Crystal Palace
Todd Andy (D)	5 11	13 04	Derby	21	9 74	Bolton W
Turner Michael (D)	6 4	12 06	Lewisham	9	11 83	Scholar
Young Luke (D)	5 11	12 06	Harlow	19	7 79	Tottenham H

League Appearances: Bart-Williams, C. 10(6); Bartlett, S. 10(4); Brown, S. 11(3); Costa, J. 22(2); Euell, J. 31(5); Fish, M. 25; Fortune, J. 14(5); Jensen, C. 16(2); Johansson, J. 21(9); Kiely, D. 38; Kinsella, M. 14(3); Kishishev, R. (3); Konchesky, P. 22(12); Lisbie, K. 10(12); MacDonald, C. (2); Parker, S. 36(2); Peacock, G. 1(4); Powell, C. 35(1); Robinson, J. 16(12); Rufus, R. 10; Salako, J. 2(1); Stuart, G. 31; Svensson, M. 6(6); Todd, A. 3(2); Young, L. 34.

Goals – League (38): Euell 11, Johansson 5, Lisbie 5, Stuart 3, Brown 2, Bart-Williams 1, Bartlett 1, Jensen 1, Konchesky 1, MacDonald 1, Parker 1, Powell 1, Robinson 1, Rufus 1, own goals 3.

Worthington Cup (5): Brown 1, Euell 1 (pen), Fortune 1, Konchesky 1, Robinson 1.

FA Cup (3): Stuart 2 (1 pen), Euell 1.

Ground: The Valley, Floyd Road, Charlton, London SE7 8BL. Telephone (020) 8333 4000.

Record attendance: 75,031 v Aston Villa, FA Cup 5th rd, 12 February 1938 (at The Valley). **Capacity:** 20,043 rising to 26,500.

Manager: Alan Curbishley.

Secretary: Chris Parkes.

Most League Goals: 107, Division 2, 1957–58.

Highest League Scorer in Season: Ralph Allen, 32, Division 3 (S), 1934–35

Most League Goals in Total Aggregate: Stuart Leary, 153, 1953–62.

Most Capped Player: John Robinson, 30, Wales.

Most League Appearances: Sam Bartram, 583, 1934–56.

Honours – Football League: Division 1 Champions – 1999–2000. Division 3 (S) Champions – 1928–29, 1934–35. **FA Cup winners** 1947.

Colours: Red shirts, white shorts, red stockings.

CHELSEA FA PREMIERSHIP

Aleksidze Rati (F)	6 0	12 02	Georgia	3	8 78	Dynamo Tbilisi
Ambrosetti Gabriele (M)	5 11	11 05	Varese	7	8 73	Vicenza
Babayaro Celestine (D)	5 9	11 09	Kaduna	29	8 78	Anderlecht
Bogarde Winston (D)	6 3	14 02	Rotterdam	22	10 70	Barcelona
Bosnich Mark (G)	6 2	14 10	Fairfield	13	1 72	Manchester U
Cole Carlton (F)	6 3	12 13	Surrey	12	11 83	Scholar
Cudicini Carlo (G)	6 1	12 02	Milan	6	9 73	Castel di Sangro
Cummings Warren (D)	5 9	11 05	Aberdeen	15	10 80	Trainee
Dalla Bona Samuele (F)	6 0	13 03	San Dona di Piave	6	2 81	

De Goey Ed (G)	6 6	14 05	Gouda	20 12 66	Feyenoord
De Oliveira Filipe (F)	5 10	10 12	Braga	27 5 84	
Desailly Marcel (D)	6 0	13 05	Accra	7 9 68	AC Milan
Di Cesare Valerio (D)	6 2	11 13	Rome	23 5 83	
Evans Rhys (G)	6 1	11 12	Swindon	27 1 82	Trainee
Ferrer Albert (D)	5 6	12 02	Barcelona	6 6 70	Barcelona
Forssell Mikael (F)	6 0	12 08	Steinfurt	15 3 81	HJK Helsinki
Gallas William (D)	6 0	11 13	Asnieres	17 8 77	Marseille
Gronkjaer Jesper (M)	6 2	13 03	Nuuk	12 8 77	Ajax
Gudjohnsen Eidur (F)	6 1	14 01	Reykjavik	15 9 78	Bolton W
Hasselbaink					
Jimmy Floyd (F)	5 10	13 10	Paramaribo	27 3 72	Atletico Madrid
Huth Robert (D)	6 2	12 12	Berlin	18 8 84	
Jeffreys Danny (M)	5 7	9 04	Hammersmith	21 1 85	Scholar
Keenan Joe (M)	5 8	9 12	Southampton	14 10 82	Trainee
Kitamirike Joel (D)	5 11	12 08	Uganda	5 4 84	Scholar
Kneissl Sebastian (F)	5 11	11 05	Germany	13 1 83	
Knight Leon (F)	5 4	9 04	Hackney	16 9 82	Trainee
Lampard Frank (M)	6 0	14 00	Romford	21 6 78	West Ham U
Le Saux Graeme (D)	5 10	11 09	Jersey	17 10 68	Blackburn R
Melchiot Mario (D)	6 2	11 11	Amsterdam	4 11 76	Ajax
Morris Jody (M)	5 5	10 04	Hammersmith	22 12 78	Trainee
Nicolas Alexis (M)	5 10	9 12	London	13 2 83	Aston Villa
Parkin Sam (F)	6 2	13 03	Roehampton	14 3 81	School
Petit Emmanuel (M)	6 1	13 03	Dieppe	22 9 70	Barcelona
Stanic Mario (M)	6 2	13 07	Zagreb	10 4 72	Parma
Terry John (D)	6 1	12 13	Barking	7 12 80	Trainee
Thornton Paul (D)	5 8	11 00	Surrey	7 1 83	Trainee
Wolleaston Robert (M)	5 11	11 07	Perivale	21 12 79	Trainee
Zenden Boudewijn (F)	5 8	11 09	Maastricht	15 8 76	Barcelona
Zola Gianfranco (F)	5 6	10 08	Oliena	5 7 66	Parma

League Appearances: Babayaro, C. 18; Bosnich, M. 5; Cole, C. 2(1); Cudicini, C. 27(1); Dalla Bona, S. 16(8); De Goey, E. 6; Desailly, M. 24; Ferrer, A. 2(2); Forssell, M. 2(20); Gallas, W. 27(3); Gronkjaer, J. 11(2); Gudjohnsen, E. 26(6); Hasselbaink, J. 35; Huth, R. (1); Jokanovic, S. 12(8); Keenan, J. (1); Lampard, F. 34(3); Le Saux, G. 26(1); Melchiot, M. 35(2); Morris, J. 2(3); Petit, E. 26(1); Stanic, M. 18(9); Terry, J. 32(1); Zenden, B. 13(9); Zola, G. 19(16).

Goals – League (66): Hasselbaink 23 (3 pens), Gudjohnsen 14 (1 pen), Lampard 5, Dalla Bona 4, Forssell 4, Zenden 3, Zola 3, Melchiot 2, Cole 1, Desailly 1, Gallas 1, Le Saux 1, Petit 1, Stanic 1, Terry 1, own goal 1.

Worthington Cup (8): Gudjohnsen 3, Hasselbaink 3, Forssell 2.

FA Cup (16): Forssell 3, Gudjohnsen 3, Hasselbaink 3, Terry 2, Gallas 1, Lampard 1, Le Saux 1, Stanic 1, Zola 1.

Ground: Stamford Bridge, London SW6 1HS. Telephone (020) 7385 5545.

Record attendance: 82,905 v Arsenal, Division 1, 12 October 1935.

Capacity: 42,449.

Manager: Claudio Ranieri.

Secretary: Alan Shaw.

Most League Goals: 98, Division 1, 1960–61.

Highest League Scorer in Season: Jimmy Greaves, 41, 1960–61.

Most League Goals in Total Aggregate: Bobby Tambling, 164, 1958–70.

Most Capped Player: Dan Petrescu, 43 (95), Romania.

Most League Appearances: Ron Harris, 655, 1962–80.

Honours – Football League: Division 1 Champions – 1954–55. **FA Cup winners** 1970, 1997, 2000. **Football League Cup winners** 1964–65, 1997–98. **Full Members' Cup winners** 1985–86. **Zenith Data Systems Cup winners** 1989–90. **European Cup-Winners' Cup winners** 1970–71, 1997–98. **Super Cup Winners:** 1999.

Colours: Royal blue shirts and shorts with white trim, white stockings with royal blue trim.

CHELTENHAM TOWN   DIV. 2

Alsop Julian (F)	6 5	14 04	Nuneaton	28 5 73	Swansea C
Bird David (M)	5 8	12 00	Gloucester	26 12 84	Cinderford T
Book Steve (G)	5 11	11 08	Bournemouth	7 7 69	Lincoln C
Devaney Martin (F)	5 11	12 05	Cheltenham	1 6 80	Coventry C
Duff Michael (D)	6 1	12 05	Belfast	11 1 78	Trainee
Duff Shane (D)	6 1	12 10	Wroughton	2 4 82	
Griffin Anthony (D)	5 11	11 07	Bournemouth	22 3 79	Bournemouth
Hill Keith (D)	6 0	12 12	Bolton	17 5 69	Rochdale
Howells Lee (M)	5 11	11 12	Fremantle	14 10 68	Apprentice
Jones Steve (D)	5 10	12 00	Bristol	25 12 70	Swansea C
Kear Richard (F)	5 9	11 00	Gloucester	5 11 83	Trainee
Naylor Tony (F)	5 4	10 13	Manchester	29 3 67	Port Vale
Victory Jamie (D)	5 11	12 13	London	14 11 75	Bournemouth
Walker Richard (D)	5 10	13 00	Derby	9 11 71	Notts Co
Yates Mark (M)	5 11	13 01	Birmingham	24 1 70	Doncaster R

League Appearances: Alsop, J. 38(3); Banks, C. 38; Book, S. 39; Brough, J. 9(12); Devaney, M. 8(17); Duff, M. 45; Finnigan, J. 12; Grayson, N. 13(21); Griffin, A. 21(3); Higgs, S. (1); Hill, K. 2(3); Hopkins, G. (3); Howarth, N. 18(8); Howells, L. 31; Jackson, M. (1); Jones, S. 2(3); Lee, M. 2(3); McAuley, H. 3(4); Milton, R. 37(2); Muggleton, C. 7; Naylor, T. 43(1); Tyson, N. 1(7); Victory, J. 45(1); Walker, R. 11(1); White, J. (4); Williams, L. 36(2); Yates, M. 45.
Goals – League (66): Alsop 20, Naylor 12, Victory 7, Yates 7 (1 pen), Duff 3, Williams 3, Finnigan 2, Howells 2, Milton 2, Brough 1, Devaney 1, Grayson 1 (pen), Howarth 1, Tyson 1, Walker 1, White 1, own goal 1.
Worthington Cup (1): Grayson 1.
FA Cup (12): Naylor 5, Allsop 4, Devaney 1, Howells 1, Milton 1.
Ground: Whaddon Road, Cheltenham, Gloucester GL52 5NA. Telephone (01242) 573558.
Record attendance: at Whaddon Road: 8326 v Reading, FA Cup 1st rd, 17 November 1956; at Cheltenham Athletic Ground: 10,389 v Blackpool, FA Cup 3rd rd, 13 January 1934.
Capacity: 7407.
Manager: Graham Allner.
Secretary: Paul Godfrey.
Most League Goals: 115, Southern League, 1957–58.
Highest League Scorer in Season: Dave Lewis, 33 (53 in all competitions), Southern League Division 1, 1974–75.
Most League Goals in Total Aggregate: Dave Lewis, 205 (290 in all competitions), 1970–83.
Most League Appearances: Roger Thorndale, 523 (702 in all competitions), 1958–76.
Most Capped Player: Michael Duff, 1, Northern Ireland.
Honours – Football League: Promoted from Division 3 (play-offs) 2001–02.
Football Conference: Champions – 1998–99. **FA Trophy winners** 1997–98.
Colours: Red and white striped shirts, white shorts, white stockings.

CHESTERFIELD   DIV. 2

Allott Mark (F)	5 11	10 12	Middleton	16 3 78	Oldham Ath
Blatherwick Steve (D)	6 1	15 00	Nottingham	20 9 73	Burnley
Booty Martyn (D)	5 8	12 03	Kirby Muxloe	30 5 71	Southend U
Breckin Ian (D)	5 11	11 07	Rotherham	24 2 75	Rotherham U
Burt Jamie (F)			Ashington	29 9 79	Whitby T

D'Auria David (M)	5 9	11 11	Swansea	26 3 70	Hull C
Davies Gareth (D)	6 1	11 12	Hereford	11 12 73	Swindon T
Ebdon Marcus (M)	5 10	11 02	Pontypool	17 10 70	Peterborough U
Edwards Rob (M)	5 9	12 04	Manchester	23 2 70	Huddersfield T
Howson Stuart (M)	6 1	12 13	Chorley	30 9 81	Blackburn R
Hurst Glynn (F)	5 10	11 06	Barnsley	17 1 76	Stockport Co
Innes Mark (D)	5 10	12 04	Bellshill	27 9 78	Oldham Ath
Rowland Keith (M)	5 10	10 07	Portadown	1 9 71	QPR
Tutill Steve (D)	5 10	12 06	Derwent	1 10 69	Darlington

League Appearances: Abbey, N. 46; Allott, M. 19(2); Beckett, L. 20(1); Blatherwick, S. 4(1); Booty, M. 40; Breckin, I. 42; Buchanan, W. 3; Burt, J. 18(6); D'Auria, D. 10(4); Ebdon, M. 29(2); Edwards, R. 30(1); Hewitt, J. 1; Hitzisperger, T. 5; Howard, J. 12(8); Howson, S. 13; Hurst, G. 22(1); Hyde, G. 8(1); Ingledow, J. 12(5); Innes, M. 22(1); Jones, M. 1(5); Moore, S. 1(1); O'Hare, A. 19; Parrish, S. 11(9); Payne, S. 44; Pearce, G. 5(2); Reeves, D. 20(2); Richardson, L. 13(1); Rowland, K. 6(3); Rushbury, A. (3); Walsh, D. (1); Williams, D. 19(5); Willis, R. 11(13).
Goals – League (53): Hurst 9, Burt 7, Beckett 6, Howard 5, Allott 4 (1 pen). Reeves 4 (2 pens), Willis 4, Booty 2, Ebdon 2, Innes 2, Breckin 1, D'Auria 1, Edwards 1, Howson 1, Hyde 1, Parrish 1, Payne 1, Richardson 1.
Worthington Cup (1): Rowland 1.
FA Cup (4): Beckett 2, D'Auria 1, own goal 1.
Ground: Recreation Ground, Chesterfield S40 4SX. Telephone (01246) 209765.
Record attendance: 30,968 v Newcastle U, Division 2, 7 April 1939. **Capacity:** 6879.
Manager: Dave Rushbury.
Secretary: Alan Walters.
Most League Goals: 102, Division 3 (N), 1930–31.
Highest League Scorer in Season: Jimmy Cookson, 44, Division 3 (N), 1925–26.
Most League Goals in Total Aggregate: Ernie Moss, 161, 1969–76, 1979–81 and 1984–86.
Most Capped Player: Walter McMillen, 4 (7), Northern Ireland; Mark Williams, 4 (17), Northern Ireland.
Most League Appearances: Dave Blakey, 613, 1948–67.
Honours – Football League: Division 3 (N) Champions – 1930–31, 1935–36. Division 4 Champions – 1969–70, 1984–85. **Anglo-Scottish Cup winners** 1980–81.
Colours: Blue shirts, blue shorts, blue stockings.

COLCHESTER UNITED   DIV. 2

Brown Simon (G)	6 2	15 00	Chelmsford	3 12 76	Tottenham H
Coote Adrian (F)	6 2	12 10	Gt Yarmouth	30 9 78	Norwich C
Duguid Karl (F)	5 11	11 07	Hitchin	21 3 78	Trainee
Fitzgerald Scott (D)	6 1	13 00	Westminster	13 8 69	Millwall
Izzet Kem (M)	5 7	11 00	Whitechapel	29 9 80	Charlton Ath
Keeble Chris (M)	5 10	10 12	Colchester	17 9 78	Ipswich T
Keith Joe (D)	5 7	11 00	London	1 10 78	West Ham U
McGleish Scott (F)	5 9	11 12	Camden Town	10 2 74	Barnet
Morgan Dean (F)	6 0	12 01	Enfield	3 10 83	Scholar
Pinault Thomas (M)	5 9	11 10	Grasse	4 12 81	Cannes
Rapley Kevin (F)	5 10	12 02	Reading	21 9 77	Notts Co

League Appearances: Barrett, G. 19(1); Blatsis, C. 7; Bowry, B. 27(9); Brown, S. 19; Canham, M. (1); Chambers, T. (1); Clark, S. 19(2); Coote, A. 5(14); Duguid, K. 36(5); Dunne, J. 6(2); Fitzgerald, S. 36(1); Gregory, D. 15(1); Halls, J. 6; Izzet, K. 36(4); Johnson, G. 19(1); Johnson, R. 13(3); Keith, J. 33(8); Knight, R. 1; MacDonald, C. 2(2); McGleish, S. 44(2); Morgan, D. 1(29); Opara, L. (1); Pinault, T. 37(5); Rapley, K. 26(9); Stockwell, M. 45(1); White, A. 28(5); Woodman, A. 26.

Goals – League (65): McGleish 15 (1 pen), Rapley 9, Stockwell 9, Barrett 4, Coote 4, Duguid 4, Keith 4 (2 pens), Izzet 3, White 3, Dunne 2, Bowry 1, Johnson G 1, Johnson R 1, MacDonald 1, own goals 4.
Worthington Cup (3): Izzet 1, Keith 1, Stockwell 1.
FA Cup (2): Duguid 1, McGleish 1.
Ground: Layer Rd Ground, Colchester CO2 7JJ. Telephone (01206) 508800.
Record attendance: 19,072 v Reading, FA Cup 1st rd, 27 Nov, 1948. **Capacity:** 7341.
Manager: Steve Whitton.
Secretary: Miss Sonya Constantine.
Most League Goals: 104, Division 4, 1961–62.
Highest League Scorer in Season: Bobby Hunt, 38, Division 4, 1961–62.
Most League Goals in Total Aggregate: Martyn King, 130, 1956–64.
Most Capped Player: None.
Most League Appearances: Micky Cook, 613, 1969–84.
Honours – GM Vauxhall Conference winners 1991–92. **FA Trophy winners** 1991–92.
Colours: Blue and white striped shirts, navy shorts, white stockings.

COVENTRY CITY   DIV. 1

Betts Robert (D)	5 10	11 00	Doncaster	21 12 81	School
Bothroyd Jay (F)	6 3	13 00	Islington	7 5 82	Trainee
Brancati Marco (M)	5 10	11 05	Rome	16 4 83	
Chippo Youssef (M)	5 11	12 00	Rabat	10 5 73	Porto
Dahl Andreas (M)	5 11	12 10	Sweden	6 6 84	IFK Hassleholm
Davenport Calum (D)	6 4	14 00	Bedford	1 1 83	Trainee
Delorge Laurent (M)	5 10	11 12	Leuven	21 7 79	
Eustace John (M)	5 11	11 12	Solihull	3 11 79	Dundee U
Fahlman Per (G)	6 0	12 07	Sweden	26 4 84	
Ford Brian (D)	5 11	12 00	Edinburgh	23 9 82	Trainee
Fowler Lee (M)	5 7	10 00	Cardiff	10 6 83	Scholar
Gallieri Antonio (F)	5 8	11 00	Rome	5 7 83	
Grant Stephen (D)	5 7	10 12	Kirkcaldy	28 7 84	Scholar
Guerrero Ivan (D)	5 7	10 00	Comayagua	30 11 77	Motagua
Hedman Magnus (G)	6 3	14 00	Stockholm	19 3 73	AIK Stockholm
Higgins Ruaidhri (M)	5 10	12 00	Derry	23 10 84	Scholar
Hughes Lee (F)	6 0	11 06	Birmingham	22 5 76	WBA
Hyldgaard Morten (G)	6 6	14 00	Herning	26 1 78	Ikast
Joachim Julian (F)	5 6	12 00	Boston	20 9 74	Aston Villa
Kenna Conor (D)	5 10	12 00	Dublin	21 11 84	Scholar
Konjic Muhamed (D)	6 3	13 00	Bosnia	14 5 70	Monaco
Martinez Jairo (F)	5 9	11 08	Honduras	14 5 78	
McSheffrey Gary (F)	5 8	10 06	Coventry	13 8 82	Trainee
Miller Kirk (D)	5 10	11 10	Coventry	15 9 83	Scholar
Mills Lee (F)	6 4	12 09	Mexborough	10 7 70	Portsmouth
Montgomery Gary (G)	6 1	13 07	Leamington Spa	8 10 82	Scholar
Noon Mark (M)	5 10	12 00	Leamington Spa	23 9 83	Scholar
Normann Runar (M)	5 11	12 00	Harstad	1 3 78	Lillestrom
O'Neill Keith (M)	6 1	13 03	Dublin	16 12 76	Middlesbrough
Pead Craig (M)	5 9	11 06	Bromsgrove	15 9 81	Trainee
Pipe David (M)	5 9	12 01	Caerphilly	5 11 83	Scholar
Quigley Stephen (D)			Dublin	13 1 85	Scholar
Quinn Barry (M)	6 0	12 02	Dublin	9 5 79	Trainee
Regan Martin (D)			Tralee	29 1 85	Scholar
Rice Stephen (M)	5 9	10 10	Dublin	6 10 84	Scholar
Safri Youseff (M)	5 8	10 12	Casablanca	13 1 77	Raja
Shaw Richard (D)	5 9	12 08	Brentford	11 9 68	Crystal Palace

Spong Richard (D)	5 11	11 09	Falun	23 9 83	Scholar
Strachan Gavin (M)	5 10	11 07	Aberdeen	23 12 78	Trainee
Thompson David (M)	5 7	10 00	Birkenhead	12 9 77	Liverpool
Thornton Barry (F)			Dublin	21 1 85	Scholar
Yazdani Hussain (M)			Dublin	6 1 85	Scholar
Zuniga Ysrael (F)	5 9	11 00	Lima	27 8 76	

League Appearances: Antonelius, T. 3(2); Betts, R. 4(5); Bothroyd, J. 24(7); Breen, G. 30; Carbonari, H. 5; Carsley, L. 25(1); Chippo, Y. 29(5); Davenport, C. 1(2); Delorge, L. 21(7); Edworthy, M. 18(2); Eustace, J. 5(1); Flowers, T. 5; Fowler, L. 5(8); Goram, A. 6(1); Guerrero, I. 3(1); Hall, M. 27(2); Healy, C. 17; Hedman, M. 34; Hughes, L. 35(3); Joachim, J. 4(12); Kirkland, C. 1; Konjic, M. 38; Martinez, J. 5(6); McSheffrey, G. 1(7); Mills, L. 19(1); Nilsson, R. 9; Normann, R. (2); O'Neill, K. 7(4); Pead, C. 1; Quinn, B. 18(4); Safri, Y. 32(1); Shaw, R. 29(3); Strachan, G. (1); Thompson, D. 35(2); Trollope, P. 5(1); Williams, P. 4(1); Zuniga, Y. 1(6).

Goals – League (59): Hughes 14 (4 pens), Thompson 12, Bothroyd 6, Mills 5, Chippo 4, Delorge 4, Martinez 3, Carsley 2, Healy 2, Konjic 2, Hall M 1, Joachim 1, McSheffrey 1, Safri 1, own goal 1.

Worthington Cup (2): Carsley 1, Thompson 1.

FA Cup (0).

Ground: Highfield Road Stadium, King Richard Street, Coventry CV2 4FW. Telephone (024) 7623 4000.

Record attendance: 51,455 v Wolverhampton W, Division 2, 29 April 1967.

Capacity: 23,633.

Manager: Gary McAllister.

Secretary: Graham Hover.

Most League Goals: 108, Division 3 (S), 1931–32.

Highest League Scorer in Season: Clarrie Bourton, 49, Division 3 (S), 1931–32.

Most League Goals in Total Aggregate: Clarrie Bourton, 171, 1931–37.

Most Capped Player: Magnus Hedman, 44 (49), Sweden.

Most League Appearances: Steve Ogrizovic, 507, 1984–2000.

Honours – Football League: Division 2 Champions – 1966–67. Division 3 Champions – 1963–64. Division 3 (S) Champions 1935–36. **FA Cup winners** 1986–87.

Colours: Sky blue shirts with navy mesh panels and navy collar, navy shorts with sky blue stitching, sky blue stockings with navy piping.

CREWE ALEXANDRA   DIV. 2

Ashton Dean (F)	6 2	12 08	Swindon	24 11 83	Schoolboy
Bankole Ademola (G)	6 3	14 08	Lagos	9 9 69	QPR
Bell Lee (M)	5 11	11 05	Crewe	26 1 83	Scholar
Betts Tom (D)	6 0	12 00	Stone	3 12 82	Scholar
Brammer Dave (M)	5 11	12 00	Bromborough	28 2 75	Port Vale
Collins Wayne (M)	5 10	12 02	Manchester	4 3 69	Fulham
Edwards Paul (F)	6 0	10 09	Derby	10 11 82	
Foster Stephen (D)	5 11	11 00	Warrington	10 9 80	Trainee
Frost Carl (M)	5 9	10 07	Chester	19 7 83	Scholar
Higdon Michael (M) -	6 1	11 03	Liverpool	2 9 83	School
Hulse Rob (F)	6 1	12 08	Crewe	25 10 79	Trainee
Ince Clayton (G)	6 3	13 00	Trinidad	13 7 72	Defence Force
Jack Rodney (F)	5 7	10 07	Kingston, Jamaica	28 9 72	Torquay U
Jeffs Ian (M)	5 7	10 02	Chester	12 10 82	Scholar
Jones Steve (F)	5 10	10 05	Derry	25 10 76	Leigh RMI
Liddle Gareth (D)	6 0	12 05	Manchester	10 8 82	Scholar
Little Colin (F)	5 10	11 00	Wythenshaw	4 11 72	Hyde U
Lunt Kenny (M)	5 10	10 02	Runcorn	20 11 79	Trainee

44

McCready Chris (D)	6 1	12 05	Chester	5 9 81	Scholar
Morris Alexander (M)			Stoke	5 10 82	Scholar
Rix Ben (M)	5 9	11 05	Wolverhampton	11 12 82	Scholar
Robinson James (M)	5 10	11 03	Whiston	18 9 82	Scholar
Sodje Efetobar (D)	6 1	12 00	Greenwich	5 10 72	Colchester U
Sorvel Neil (M)	6 0	12 05	Widnes	2 3 73	Macclesfield T
Vaughan David (M)	5 7	11 00	St Asaph	18 2 83	Scholar
Walker Richard (D)	6 2	12 09	Stafford	17 9 80	Trainee
Walton David (D)	6 2	13 09	Bellingham	10 4 73	Shrewsbury T
Wright David (D)	5 11	10 09	Warrington	1 5 80	Trainee
Yates Adam (D)	5 10	10 07	Stoke	28 5 83	Scholar

League Appearances: Ashton, D. 29(2); Bankole, A. 28; Barrett, G. 2(1); Brammer, D. 29(1); Charnock, P. 21(2); Collins, W. 13(7); Foster, S. 29(5); Grant, J. 1; Hulse, R. 40(1); Ince, C. 18(1); Jack, R. 24(9); Jones, S. 1(5); Little, C. 8(9); Lunt, K. 45; Macauley, S. 9; McCready, C. (1); Navarro, A. 7; Richards, M. 1(3); Rix, B. 6(15); Smith, S. 41(1); Sodje, E. 34(2); Sorvel, N. 31(7); Street, K. 2(7); Tait, P. 3(9); Thomas, G. 8(6); Vaughan, D. 11(2); Walker, R. (1); Walton, D. 29(2); Whalley, G. 7; Wright, D. 29(1).
Goals – League (47): Hulse 12, Ashton 7, Jack 7, Foster 5, Lunt 5, Brammer 2, Sodje 2, Thomas 2, Charnock 1, Little 1, Smith S 1 (pen), Street 1, Walton 1.
Worthington Cup (6): Brammer 1, Hulse 1, Little 1, Richards 1, Smith 1 (pen), Watson 1.
FA Cup (7): Ashton 3, Foster 1, Rix 1, Thomas 1, Vaughan 1.
Ground: Football Ground, Gresty Rd, Crewe CW2 6EB. Telephone (01270) 213014.
Record attendance: 20,000 v Tottenham H, FA Cup 4th rd, 30 January 1960.
Capacity: 10,046.
Manager: Dario Gradi MBE.
Secretary: Mrs Gill Palin.
Most League Goals: 95, Division 3 (N), 1931–32.
Highest League Scorer in Season: Terry Harkin, 35, Division 4, 1964–65.
Most League Goals in Total Aggregate: Bert Swindells, 126, 1928–37.
Most Capped Player: Clayton Ince, Trinidad & Tobago.
Most League Appearances: Tommy Lowry, 436, 1966–78.
Honours – Welsh Cup: Winners 1936, 1937.
Colours: Red shirts, white shorts, red stockings.

CRYSTAL PALACE   DIV. 1

Akinbiyi Ade (F)	6 1	12 08	Hackney	10 10 74	Leicester C
Berhalter Gregg (D)	6 1	12 05	Englewood	1 8 73	Cambuur
Black Tommy (M)	5 7	11 10	Chigwell	26 11 79	Arsenal
Carasso Cedric (G)	6 3	13 12	Avignon	30 12 81	Avignon
Clarke Matt (G)	6 4	13 08	Sheffield	3 11 73	Bradford C
Fleming Curtis (D)	5 10	12 09	Manchester	8 10 68	Middlesbrough
Frampton Andrew (D)	5 11	10 10	Wimbledon	3 9 79	Trainee
Freedman Dougie (F)	5 9	12 05	Glasgow	21 1 74	Nottingham F
Granville Danny (D)	6 0	12 00	Islington	19 1 75	Manchester C
Gray Julian (M)	6 1	11 08	Lewisham	21 9 79	Arsenal
Harrison Craig (D)	6 0	11 08	Middlesbrough	10 11 77	Middlesbrough
Heeroo Gavin (M)			London	2 9 84	
Hopkin David (M)	6 1	13 13	Greenock	21 8 70	Bradford C
Kabba Steven (F)	5 10	11 07	Lambeth	7 3 81	Trainee
Kolinko Aleksandrs (G)	6 2	14 02	Latvia	18 6 75	Skonto Riga
Morrison Clinton (F)	6 1	11 02	Tooting	14 5 79	Trainee
Mullins Hayden (D)	6 0	11 12	Reading	27 3 79	Trainee
Pollock Jamie (M)	6 0	13 03	Stockton	16 2 74	Manchester C
Popovic Tony (D)	6 5	13 01	Australia	7 4 73	Shimizu S-Pulse

Riihilahti Aki (M)	5 11	12 06	Helsinki	9 9 76	
Rubins Andrejs (M)	5 8	10 13	Latvia	26 11 78	Skonto Riga
Smith Jamie (D)	5 8	11 02	Birmingham	17 9 74	Wolverhampton W
Symons Kit (D)	6 1	13 00	Basingstoke	8 3 71	Fulham
Thomson Steve (M)	5 8	10 04	Glasgow	23 1 78	Trainee

League Appearances: Akinbiyi, A. 9(5); Austin, D. 27(8); Benjamin, T. 5(1); Berhalter, G. 6(8); Black, T. 5(20); Carasso, C. (1); Clarke, M. 28; Edwards, C. 9; Fleming, C. 17; Frampton, A. 1(1); Freedman, D. 39(1); Gooding, S. (1); Granville, D. 16; Gray, J. 35(8); Harrison, C. 4(2); Hopkin, D. 13(7); Kabba, S. 1(3); Kirovski, J. 25(11); Kolinko, A. 18(1); Morrison, C. 45; Mullins, H. 43; Murphy, S. 11; Popovic, T. 20; Riihilahti, A. 45; Rodger, S. 29(7); Routledge, W. (2); Rubins, A. (7); Smith, J. 28(4); Symons, K. 9; Thomson, S. 10(13); Vickers, S. 6; Zhiyi, F. 2.
Goals – League (70): Morrison 22, Freedman 20 (3 pens), Kirovski 5, Riihilahti 5, Smith 4, Hopkin 3, Akinbiyi 2, Gray 2, Popovic 2, Benjamin 1, Berhalter 1, Rodger 1, own goals 2.
Worthington Cup (7): Black 2, Morrison 2, Freedman 1 (pen), Riihilahiti 1, Rodger 1.
FA Cup (0).
Ground: Selhurst Park, London SE25 6PU. Telephone (0181) 768 6000.
Record attendance: 51,482 v Burnley, Division 2, 11 May 1979. **Capacity:** 26,400.
Manager: Trevor Francis.
Club Secretary: Mike Hurst.
Most League Goals: 110, Division 4, 1960–61.
Highest League Scorer in Season: Peter Simpson, 46, Division 3 (S), 1930–31.
Most League Goals in Total Aggregate: Peter Simpson, 153, 1930–36.
Most Capped Player: Eric Young, 19 (21), Wales.
Most League Appearances: Jim Cannon, 571, 1973–88.
Honours – Football League: Division 1 – Champions 1993–94. Division 2 Champions – 1978–79. Division 3 (S) 1920–21. **Zenith Data Systems Cup winners** 1991.
Colours: Red and blue vertical striped shirts, red shorts, red stockings with blue tops.

DARLINGTON   DIV. 3

Atkinson Brian (M)	5 10	12 05	Darlington	19 1 71	Sunderland
Betts Simon (M)	5 8	11 00	Middlesbrough	3 3 73	Colchester U
Brightwell David (D)	6 2	12 09	Lutterworth	7 1 71	Hull C
Brumwell Phil (M)	5 8	11 00	Darlington	8 8 75	Hull C
Campbell Paul (M)	6 0	11 05	Middlesbrough	29 1 80	Trainee
Clark Ian (M)	5 11	11 07	Stockton	23 10 74	Hartlepool U
Collett Andy (G)	6 0	12 01	Middlesbrough	28 10 73	Bristol R
Conlon Barry (F)	6 3	13 07	Drogheda	1 10 78	York C
Convery Mark (M)	5 6	10 05	Newcastle	29 5 81	Sunderland
Ford Mark (M)	5 8	10 01	Pontefract	10 10 75	Torquay U
Hodgson Richard (M)	5 10	11 08	Sunderland	1 10 79	Scunthorpe U
Keltie Clark (M)	5 11	11 05	Gateshead	31 8 83	Shildon
Kilty Mark (D)	5 11	12 05	Sunderland	24 6 81	Trainee
Liddle Craig (D)	5 11	12 07	Newcastle	21 10 71	Middlesbrough
Maddison Neil (M)	5 10	12 00	Darlington	2 10 69	Middlesbrough
Mellanby Danny (F)	5 10	11 09	Bishop Auckland	17 7 79	Bishop Auckland
Naylor Glenn (F)	6 0	11 08	Goole	11 8 72	York C
Pearson Gary (D)	6 0	12 04	Easington	7 12 76	Sheffield U
Reed Adam (D)	6 0	12 00	Bishop Auckland	18 2 75	Blackburn R
Wainwright Neil (M)	6 1	12 00	Warrington	4 11 77	Sunderland
Waller Russell (M)			Adelaide	6 2 84	

League Appearances: Atkinson, B. 35; Betts, S. 29; Brightwell, D. 22; Brumwell, P. 16(6); Caldwell, G. 4; Campbell, P. 8(8); Chillingworth, D. 2(2); Clark, I. 28; Collett, A. 28; Conlon, B. 35; Convery, M. 6(11); Finch, K. 11(1); Ford, M. 34(1); Harper, S. 15(8); Healy, B. 1(1); Heckingbottom, P. 40(2); Hodgson, R. 24(12); Jackson, K. 1(10); Jeannin, A. 11; Keltie, C. (1); Kilty, M. 1; Liddle, C. 31; Maddison, N. 24(6); Marcelle, C. (3); Marsh, A. 1; McGurk, D. 10(2); Mellanby, D. 22(2); Naylor, G. 6; Pearson, G. 9; Porter, C. 7; Reed, A. 7; Rundle, A. 5(7); Sheeran, M. 1(21); Wainwright, N. 32(3).

Goals – League (60): Clark 13 (5 pens), Conlon 10, Ford 7 (3 pens), Sheeran 6, Mellanby 4, Wainwright 4, Heckingbottom 3, Hodgson 2, Liddle 2, Atkinson 1, Campbell 1, Chillingworth 1, Convery 1, Harper 1, Healy 1, Maddison 1, Naylor 1, Pearson 1.

Worthington Cup (0).

FA Cup (5): Wainwright 2, Campbell 1, Chillingworth 1, Conlon 1.

Ground: Feethams Ground, Darlington DL1 5JB. Telephone (01325) 240240.

Record attendance: 21,023 v Bolton W, League Cup 3rd rd, 14 November 1960.

Capacity: 8500.

Manager: Tommy Taylor.

Secretary: Lisa Charlton.

Most League Goals: 108, Division 3 (N), 1929–30.

Highest League Scorer in Season: David Brown, 39, Division 3 (N), 1924–25.

Most League Goals in Total Aggregate: Alan Walsh, 90, 1978–84.

Most Capped Player: Jason Devos, 3, Canada.

Most League Appearances: Ron Greener, 442, 1955–68.

Honours – Football League: Division 3 (N) Champions – 1924–25. Division 4 Champions – 1990–91.

Colours: White and black with red piping.

DERBY COUNTY   DIV. 1

Bannister Patrick (M)			Walsall	3 12 83	Scholar
Barton Warren (D)	6 3	11 13	Islington	19 3 69	Newcastle U
Boertien Paul (D)	5 11	11 11	Carlisle	21 1 79	Carlisle U
Bolder Adam (M)	5 8	11 13	Hull	25 10 80	Hull C
Bragstad Bjorn (D)	6 3	14 06	Trondheim	5 1 71	Rosenborg
Burley Craig (M)	6 1	13 03	Ayr	24 9 71	Celtic
Burton Deon (F)	5 9	12 08	Reading	25 10 77	Portsmouth
Carbonari Horace Angel (D)	6 3	14 08	Rosario	2 5 71	Rosario Central
Christie Malcolm (F)	6 0	12 06	Peterborough	11 4 79	Nuneaton B
Elliott Steve (D)	6 2	14 08	Derby	29 10 78	Trainee
Evatt Ian (D)	6 3	14 04	Coventry	23 11 81	Trainee
Flanagan Martin (M)			Omagh	13 1 84	Scholar
Grant Lee (G)	6 2	13 00	Watford	27 1 83	Scholar
Grenet Francois (D)	5 10	11 06	Bordeaux	8 3 75	
Higginbotham Danny (D)	6 1	13 03	Manchester	29 12 78	Manchester U
Hunt Lewis (D)	5 11	12 08	Birmingham	25 8 82	Scholar
Jackson Richard (D)	5 7	11 02	Whitby	18 4 80	Scarborough
Kinkladze Georgiou (M)	5 6	11 05	Tbilisi	6 7 73	Ajax
Lee Robert (M)	5 10	11 10	Plaistow	1 2 66	Newcastle U
Mawene Youl (D)	6 1	13 05	Caen	16 7 79	
McArdle Fiachra (M)			Newry	18 8 83	Scholar
Morris Lee (F)	5 9	11 02	Driffield	30 4 80	Sheffield U
Moukoko Tonton (M)			Congo	22 12 83	Scholar
Murray Adam (M)	5 9	11 11	Birmingham	30 9 81	Trainee
O'Neil Brian (M)	6 0	13 10	Paisley	6 9 72	Wolfsburg
Oakes Andy (G)	6 1	12 04	Crewe	11 1 77	Hull C

Poom Mart (G)	6 4	14 03	Tallinn	3 2 72	Flora Tallinn
Powell Darryl (M)	6 1	13 03	Lambeth	15 11 71	Portsmouth
Ravanelli Fabrizio (F)	6 2	13 04	Perugia	11 12 68	Lazio
Riggott Chris (D)	6 2	13 09	Derby	1 9 80	Trainee
Robinson Marvin (F)	6 0	13 05	Crewe	11 4 80	Trainee
Strupar Branko (F)	6 3	14 06	Zagreb	9 2 70	Genk
Twigg Gary (F)	6 0	11 02	Glasgow	19 3 84	Scholar
Valakari Simo (M)	5 11	12 08	Helsinki	24 4 73	Motherwell
Weckstrom Kristoffer (F)			Helsinki	26 5 83	IFK Mariehamn
Zavagno Luciano (D)	5 11	11 07	Rosario	6 8 77	Troyes

League Appearances: Barton, W. 14; Boertien, P. 23(9); Bolder, A. 2(9); Burley, C. 11; Burton, D. 8(9); Carbonari, H. 3; Carbone, B. 13; Christie, M. 27(8); Daino, D. 2; Ducrocq, P. 19; Elliott, S. 2(4); Evatt, I. 1(2); Feuer, I. 2; Foletti, P. 1(1); Grenet, F. 12(3); Higginbotham, D. 37; Jackson, R. 6(1); Johnson, S. 7; Kinkladze, G. 13(11); Lee, R. 13; Mawene, Y. 17; Morris, L. 9(6); Murray, A. 3(3); O'Neil, B. 8(2); Oakes, A. 20; Poom, M. 15; Powell, D. 23; Ravanelli, F. 30(1); Riggott, C. 37; Robinson, M. (2); Strupar, B. 8(4); Twigg, G. (1); Valakari, S. 6(3); Zavagno, L. 26.
Goals – League (33): Christie 9, Ravanelli 9 (1 pen), Morris 4, Strupar 4, Burton 1, Carbone 1, Higginbotham 1 (pen), Kinkladze 1, Mawene 1, Powell 1, Robinson 1.
Worthington Cup (5): Burton 2, Burley 1, Kinkladze 1, Ravanelli 1.
FA Cup (1): Ravanelli 1.
Ground: Pride Park Stadium, Derby DE24 8XL. Telephone: (01332) 202202.
Record attendance: 41,826 v Tottenham H, Division 1, 20 September 1969.
Capacity: 33,597.
Manager: John Gregory.
Secretary: Keith Pearson ACIS.
Most League Goals: 111, Division 3 (N), 1956–57.
Highest League Scorer in Season: Jack Bowers, 37, Division 1, 1930–31; Ray Straw, 37 Division 3 (N), 1956–57.
Most League Goals in Total Aggregate: Steve Bloomer, 292, 1892–1906 and 1910–14.
Most Capped Player: Deon Burton, 39, Jamaica.
Most League Appearances: Kevin Hector, 486, 1966–78 and 1980–82.
Honours – Football League: Division 1 Champions – 1971–72, 1974–75. Division 2 Champions – 1911–12, 1914–15, 1968–69, 1986–87. Division 3 (N) 1956–57. **FA Cup winners** 1945–46.
Colours: White shirts with black piping, black shorts, white stockings.

EVERTON   FA PREMIERSHIP

Alexandersson Niclas (M)	5 9	11 08	Halmstad	29 12 71	Sheffield W
Beck Steven (M)			Liverpool	4 6 84	Scholar
Brown Scott (M)			Chester	8 5 85	Scholar
Campbell Kevin (F)	6 0	13 13	Lambeth	4 2 70	Trabzonspor
Carney David (M)			Sydney	30 11 83	Scholar
Carsley Lee (M)	5 10	12 04	Birmingham	28 2 74	Coventry C
Chadwick Nick (F)	5 11	10 09	Stoke	26 10 82	
Clarke Peter (D)	6 0	12 00	Southport	3 1 82	Trainee
Crowder Martin (D)			Liverpool	11 4 84	Scholar
Ferguson Duncan (F)	6 4	13 07	Stirling	27 12 71	Newcastle U
Garside Craig (D)	5 11	13 00	Chester	11 1 85	Scholar
Gemmill Scot (M)	5 10	11 08	Paisley	2 1 71	Nottingham F
Gerrard Paul (G)	6 2	13 11	Heywood	22 1 73	Oldham Ath
Gravesen Thomas (M)	5 9	13 06	Vejle	11 3 76	Hamburg
Hibbert Tony (D)	5 9	11 05	Liverpool	20 2 81	Trainee
Linderoth Tobias (M)	5 10	11 08	Marseille	21 4 79	Stabaek
McLeod Kevin (M)	5 11	12 00	Liverpool	12 9 80	Trainee

Moogan Alan (M)			Liverpool	22 2 84	Scholar
Moogan Brian (D)			Liverpool	22 2 84	Scholar
Moore Joe-Max (F)	5 8	11 06	USA	23 2 71	New England Rev
Naysmith Gary (D)	5 9	12 01	Edinburgh	16 11 78	Hearts
Nyarko Alex (M)	6 0	13 00	Accra	15 10 73	Lens
O'Hanlon Sean (D)	6 1	12 05	Southport	2 1 83	
Osman Leon (F)	5 8	10 09	Billinge	17 5 81	Trainee
Pembridge Mark (M)	5 7	11 09	Merthyr	29 11 70	Benfica
Pettinger Andrew (G)			Scunthorpe	21 4 84	Scunthorpe U
Pilkington George (D)	5 11	11 00	Rugeley	7 11 81	Trainee
Pistone Alessandro (D)	5 11	11 08	Milan	27 7 75	Newcastle U
Radzinski Tomasz (F)	5 7	11 10	Poznan	14 12 73	Anderlecht
Schumacher Steven (M)			Liverpool	30 4 84	Scholar
Simonsen Steve (G)	6 2	14 00	South Shields	3 4 79	Tranmere R
Southern Keith (M)	5 10	12 04	Gateshead	24 4 81	Trainee
Southern Robert (M)			Gateshead	24 9 83	Scholar
Stubbs Alan (D)	6 2	13 12	Kirkby	6 10 71	Celtic
Symes Michael (F)	6 2	12 00	Gt Yarmouth	31 10 83	Scholar
Tal Idan (M)	5 10	10 13	Petah Tikva	13 9 75	Maccabi Petah Tikva
Unsworth Dave (D)	6 1	15 02	Chorley	16 10 73	Aston Villa
Watson Steve (D)	6 0	12 07	North Shields	1 4 74	Aston Villa
Weir David (D)	6 5	14 03	Falkirk	10 5 70	Hearts

League Appearances: Alexandersson, N. 28(3); Blomqvist, J. 10(5); Cadamarteri, D. 2(1); Campbell, K. 21(2); Carsley, L. 8; Chadwick, N. 2(7); Clarke, P. 5(2); Cleland, A. (3); Ferguson, D. 17(5); Gascoigne, P. 8(10); Gemmill, S. 31(1); Gerrard, P. 13; Ginola, D. 2(3); Gravesen, T. 22(3); Hibbert, T. 7(3); Linderoth, T. 4(4); Moore, J. 3(13); Naysmith, G. 23(1); Pembridge, M. 10(4); Pistone, A. 25; Radzinski, T. 23(4); Simonsen, S. 25; Stubbs, A. 29(2); Tal, I. 1(6); Unsworth, D. 28(5); Watson, S. 24(1); Weir, D. 36; Xavier, A. 11(1).

Goals – League (45): Ferguson 6 (2 pens), Radzinski 6, Campbell 4, Watson 4, Weir 4, Chadwick 3, Unsworth 3 (1 pen), Alexandersson 2, Gravesen 2, Moore 2, Stubbs 2, Blomqvist 1, Carsley 1, Gascoigne 1, Gemmill 1, Pembridge 1, Pistone 1, own goal 1.

Worthington Cup (1): Ferguson 1 (pen).

FA Cup (7): Campbell 3, Ferguson 1, Radzinski 1, Stubbs 1, own goal 1.

Ground: Goodison Park, Liverpool L4 4EL. Telephone (0151) 330 2200.

Record attendance: 78,299 v Liverpool, Division 1, 18 September 1948. **Capacity:** 40,170.

Manager: David Moyes.

Secretary: David Harrison.

Most League Goals: 121, Division 2, 1930–31.

Highest League Scorer in Season: William Ralph 'Dixie' Dean, 60, Division 1, 1927–28   (All-time League record).

Most League Goals in Total Aggregate: William Ralph 'Dixie' Dean, 349, 1925–37.

Most Capped Player: Neville Southall, 92, Wales.

Most League Appearances: Neville Southall, 578, 1981–98.

Honours – Football League: Division 1 Champions – 1890–91, 1914–15, 1927–28, 1931–32, 1938–39, 1962–63, 1969–70, 1984–85, 1986–87. Division 2 Champions – 1930–31. **FA Cup:** Winners 1906, 1933, 1966, 1984, 1995. **European Competitions: European Cup-Winners' Cup winners:** 1984–85.

Colours: Royal blue shirts with white panels, white shorts with blue trim, blue stockings with white trim.

Ampadu Kwame (M)	5 10	11 10	Bradford	20 12 70	Leyton Orient
Breslan Geoff (M)	5 9	10 05	Torbay	4 6 80	Trainee
Buckle Paul (M)	5 8	11 08	Welwyn	16 12 70	Colchester U
Burrows Mark (D)	6 3	12 08	Kettering	14 8 80	Coventry C
Cronin Glenn (M)	5 8	10 11	Dublin	14 9 81	Trainee
Flack Steve (F)	6 1	14 07	Cambridge	29 5 71	Cardiff C
Fraser Stuart (G)	6 0	12 00	Cheltenham	1 8 78	Stoke C
McCarthy Sean (F)	6 1	12 05	Bridgend	12 9 67	Plymouth Arg
McConnell Barry (D)	5 11	10 10	Exeter	1 1 77	Trainee
Mudge James (F)	5 11	11 09	Exeter	25 3 83	Scholar
Power Graeme (D)	5 11	11 07	Northwick Park	7 8 77	Bristol R
Richardson Jay (M)	5 9	11 09	Kenton	14 11 79	Chelsea
Roscoe Andy (M)	5 9	12 00	Liverpool	4 6 73	Mansfield T
Watson Alex (D)	6 1	12 00	Liverpool	5 4 68	Torquay U
Whitworth Neil (D)	6 0	12 13	Ince	12 4 72	Hull C

League Appearances: Afful, L. (2); Ampadu, K. 33(3); Barlow, M. 26(4); Birch, G. 5(10); Breslan, G. 21(12); Buckle, P. 19(6); Burrows, M. 6(3); Campbell, J. 14(2); Cronin, G. 24(6); Curran, C. 35(2); Diallo, C. (2); Elliott, S. (1); Flack, S. 27(9); Fraser, S. 10(2); Goff, S. 2; Gregg, M. 2; Gross, M. 1; Kerr, D. 5; McCarthy, S. 18(8); McConnell, B. 30(2); Moor, R. (2); Power, G. 36(1); Read, P. 3(12); Richardson, J. 5(13); Roberts, C. 34(3); Roscoe, A. 35(3); Tomlinson, G. 25(7); Van Heusden, A. 33; Walker, A. 1; Watson, A. 42(1); Whitworth, N. 12(3); Zabek, L. 2.
Goals – League (48): Roberts 11, Roscoe 7, Flack 6, McCarthy 6, Tomlinson 5, McConnell 3 (2 pens), Breslan 2, Buckle 1 (pen), Campbell 1, Curran 1, Kerr 1, Power 1, Watson 1, own goals 2.
Worthington Cup (0).
FA Cup (3): Curran 1, Roscoe 1, Tomlinson 1.
Ground: St James Park, Exeter EX4 6PX. Telephone (01392) 411243.
Record attendance: 20,984 v Sunderland, FA Cup 6th rd (replay), 4 March 1931.
Capacity: 9036.
Manager: John Cornforth.
Secretary: Stuart Brailey.
Most League Goals: 88, Division 3 (S), 1932–33.
Highest League Scorer in Season: Fred Whitlow, 33, Division 3 (S), 1932–33.
Most League Goals in Total Aggregate: Tony Kellow, 129, 1976–78, 1980–83, 1985–88.
Most Capped Player: Dermot Curtis, 1 (17), Eire.
Most League Appearances: Arnold Mitchell, 495, 1952–66.
Honours – Football League: Division 4 Champions – 1989–90. **Division 3 (S) Cup:** Winners 1934.
Colours: Red and white shirts, white shorts and stockings.

FULHAM FA PREMIERSHIP

Boa Morte Luis (F)	5 10	11 10	Lisbon	4 8 77	Southampton
Brevett Rufus (D)	5 8	11 13	Derby	24 9 69	QPR
Clark Lee (M)	5 8	11 10	Wallsend	27 10 72	Sunderland
Coleman Chris (D)	6 2	14 07	Swansea	10 6 70	Blackburn R
Collins John (M)	5 8	10 10	Galashiels	31 1 68	Everton
Cornwall Luke (F)	5 10	10 02	Lambeth	23 7 80	Trainee
Davis Sean (M)	5 9	12 00	Lambeth	20 9 79	Trainee
Doherty Sean (M)	5 8	10 00	Basingstoke	10 5 85	Scholar
Finnan Steve (D)	5 10	12 04	Limerick	20 4 76	Notts Co
Goldbaek Bjarne (M)	5 10	12 04	Denmark	6 10 68	Chelsea

Goma Alain (D)	6 0	13 05	Sault	15 10 72	Newcastle U
Hammond Elvis (F)	5 10	11 06	Accra	6 10 80	Trainee
Harley Jon (D)	5 9	11 05	Maidstone	26 9 79	Chelsea
Hayles Barry (F)	5 10	12 11	Lambeth	17 5 72	Bristol R
Hudson Mark (D)	6 3	12 06	Guildford	30 3 82	Trainee
Hutchinson Tom (D)	6 1	12 06	Kingston	23 2 82	
Knight Zat (D)	6 6	14 06	Solihull	2 5 80	
Legwinski Sylvain (M)	6 1	11 10	Clermont-Ferrand	6 10 73	Bordeaux
Lewis Eddie (M)	5 10	10 13	California	17 5 74	San Jose Clash
Malbranque Steed (M)	5 8	11 10	Mouscron	6 1 80	Lyon
Marlet Steve (F)	5 11	11 10	Pithiviers	1 10 74	Lyon
McAnespie Kieran (D)	5 8	11 06	Gosport	11 9 79	St Johnstone
Melville Andy (D)	6 1	12 13	Swansea	29 11 68	Sunderland
Ouaddou Abdes (D)	6 4	12 03	Ksar-Askour	1 11 78	Nancy
Pratley Darren (F)	6 0	10 13	Barking	22 4 85	Scholar
Rehman Zesh (M)	6 2	12 09	Birmingham	14 10 83	Scholar
Saha Louis (F)	6 1	12 06	Paris	8 8 78	Metz
Shevel David (M)	5 8	9 10	Croydon	14 9 83	Scholar
Stolcers Andrejs (M)	5 11	11 00	Latvia	8 7 74	Spartak Moscow
Taylor Maik (G)	6 3	14 02	Hildeshein	4 9 71	Southampton
Thompson Glyn (G)	6 2	13 01	Telford	24 2 81	Shrewsbury T
Van der Sar Edwin (G)	6 5	14 08	Voorhout	29 10 70	Juventus
Willock Calum (F)	6 0	12 09	London	29 10 81	Scholar

League Appearances: Betsy, K. (1); Boa Morte, L. 15(8); Brevett, R. 34(1); Clark, L. 5(4); Collins, J. 29(5); Davis, S. 25(5); Finnan, S. 38; Goldbaek, B. 8(5); Goma, A. 32(1); Harley, J. 5(5); Hayles, B. 27(8); Knight, Z. 8(2); Legwinski, S. 30(3); Lewis, E. 1; Malbranque, S. 33(4); Marlet, S. 21(5); Melville, A. 35; Ouaddou, A. 4(4); Saha, L. 28(8); Stolcers, A. (5); Symons, K. 2(2); Taylor, M. 1; Van der Sar, E. 37; Willock, C. (2).
Goals – League (36): Hayles 8, Malbranque 8, Saha 8 (1 pen), Marlet 6, Legwinski 3, Boa Morte 1, Goldbaek 1, own goal 1.
Worthington Cup (8): Hayles 2, Boa Morte 1, Brevett 1, Collins 1, Legwinski 1, Malbranque 1 (pen), Saha 1.
FA Cup (8): Marlet 3, Hayles 2, Legwinski 1, Malbranque 1, own goal 1.
Ground: South Africa Road, London W12 7PA. (QPR). Telephone (020) 7893 8383.
Record attendance: 49,335 v Millwall, Division 2, 8 October 1938. **Capacity:** 19,148.
Manager: Jean Tigana.
Secretary: Lee Hoos.
Most League Goals: 111, Division 3 (S), 1931–32.
Highest League Scorer in Season: Frank Newton, 43, Division 3 (S), 1931–32.
Most League Goals in Total Aggregate: Gordon Davies, 159, 1978–84, 1986–91.
Most Capped Player: Johnny Haynes, 56, England.
Most League Appearances: Johnny Haynes, 594, 1952–70.
Honours – Football League: Division 1 Champions – 2000–01. Division 2 Champions – 1948–49, 1998–99. Division 3 (S) Champions – 1931–32.
Colours: White shirts, black trim, black shorts, white stockings red and black trim.

GILLINGHAM   DIV. 1

Ashby Barry (D)	6 1	14 04	London	2 11 70	Brentford
Bartram Vince (G)	6 2	15 04	Birmingham	7 8 68	Arsenal
Brown Jason (G)	6 0	15 05	Southwark	18 5 82	Charlton Ath
Butters Guy (D)	6 2	16 04	Hillingdon	30 10 69	Portsmouth
Edge Roland (D)	5 9	12 09	Gillingham	25 11 78	Trainee
Gooden Ty (M)	5 8	12 08	Canvey Island	23 10 72	Swindon T
Hessenthaler Andy (M)	5 7	11 10	Gravesend	17 6 65	Watford

Hope Chris (D)	6 1	12 11	Sheffield	14 11 72	Scunthorpe U
Ipoua Guy (F)	6 0	13 13	Douala	14 1 76	Scunthorpe U
James Kevin (F)	5 7	11 12	Southwark	3 1 80	Charlton Ath
King Marlon (F)	6 0	12 10	Dulwich	26 4 80	Barnet
Nosworthy Nayron (D)	6 1	12 10	London	11 10 80	Trainee
Osborn Simon (M)	5 8	11 08	New Addington	19 1 72	Port Vale
Patterson Mark (D)	5 8	12 08	Leeds	13 9 68	Plymouth Arg
Pennock Adrian (D)	6 1	14 03	Ipswich	27 3 71	Bournemouth
Perpetuini David (M)	5 10	12 01	Hitchin	26 9 79	Watford
Phillips Michael (M)	5 10	10 00	Camberwell	22 1 83	Trainee
Rose Richard (D)	6 0	11 07	Pembury	8 9 82	Trainee
Shaw Paul (F)	5 11	13 03	Burnham	4 9 73	Millwall
Smith Paul (M)	6 0	14 00	East Ham	18 9 71	Brentford
Spiller Daniel (M)	5 7	11 01	Maidstone	10 10 81	Trainee
White Ben (D)	6 0	14 01	Hastings	2 6 82	Trainee

League Appearances: Ashby, B. 28; Bartram, V. 36; Brown, J. 10; Browning, M. 38(4); Butters, G. 21(2); Edge, R. 14; Gooden, T. 20(5); Hessenthaler, A. 10(7); Hope, C. 46; Ipoua, G. 20(20); James, K. (10); King, M. 38(4); Nosworthy, N. 29; Onuora, I. 31(2); Osborn, S. 23(5); Patterson, M. 17(3); Pennock, A. 9(1); Perpetuini, D. 25(9); Rose, R. 2(1); Samuel, J. 7(1); Saunders, M. 6(13); Shaw, P. 27(10); Smith, P. 46; Spiller, D. (1); Taylor, R. 3(8).
Goals – League (64): King 17 (3 pens), Onuora 11, Ipoua 8, Shaw 7, Hope 4, Osborn 4, Browning 3, Smith 2, Ashby 1, Butters 1, Gooden 1, Perpetuini 1, Saunders 1, own goals 3.
Worthington Cup (4): King 2 (1 pen), Onuora 1, own goal 1.
FA Cup (4): Gooden 1, King 1, Shaw 1, own goal 1.
Ground: Priestfield Stadium, Gillingham ME7 4DD. Telephone (01634) 851854, 576828.
Record attendance: 23,002 v QPR, FA Cup 3rd rd 10 January 1948. **Capacity:** 10,600.
Player-Manager: Andy Hessenthaler.
Secretary: Mrs G. E. Poynter.
Most League Goals: 90, Division 4, 1973–74.
Highest Scorer in Season: Ernie Morgan, 31, Division 3 (S), 1954–55; Brian Yeo, 31, Division 4, 1973–74.
Most League Goals in Total Aggregate: Brian Yeo, 135, 1963–75.
Most Capped Player: Tony Cascarino, 3 (88), Republic of Ireland.
Most League Appearances: John Simpson, 571, 1957–72.
Honours – Football League: Division 4 Champions – 1963–64.
Colours: Blue.

GRIMSBY TOWN   DIV. 1

Bolder Chris (M)	5 11	12 00	Hull	19 8 82	Hull C
Campbell Stuart (M)	5 10	10 13	Corby	9 12 77	Leicester C
Coldicott Stacy (M)	5 8	12 08	Worcester	29 4 74	WBA
Cooke Terry (M)	5 7	10 08	Marston Green	5 8 76	Manchester C
Coyne Danny (G)	6 0	13 04	Prestatyn	27 8 73	Tranmere R
Croudson Steve (G)	6 0	11 12	Grimsby	14 9 79	Trainee
Ford Simon (D)	6 1	12 04	Lincoln	17 11 81	Charlton Ath
Gallimore Tony (D)	5 11	13 04	Crewe	21 2 72	Carlisle U
Groves Paul (M)	5 11	13 04	Derby	28 2 66	WBA
Jevons Phil (F)	5 11	12 00	Liverpool	1 8 79	Everton
Livingstone Steve (F)	6 1	15 03	Middlesbrough	8 9 68	Chelsea
McDermott John (D)	5 7	10 13	Middlesbrough	3 2 69	Trainee
Murray Neil (M)	5 9	10 10	Bellshill	21 2 73	Dundee U
Pouton Alan (M)	6 0	12 10	Newcastle	1 2 77	York C
Raven Paul (D)	6 1	12 11	Salisbury	28 7 70	WBA

Rowan Jonathan (F)	5 10	11 00	Grimsby	29 11 81	
Thompson Chris (F)	5 10	11 12	Warrington	7 2 82	Liverpool
Ward Iain (D)	6 0	10 10	Cleethorpes	13 5 83	
Willems Menno (M)	6 0	11 13	Amsterdam	10 3 77	Vitesse

League Appearances: Allen, B. 19(9); Beharall, D. 13(1); Boulding, M. 24(11); Broomes, M. 13(2); Burnett, W. 18(14); Busscher, R. (1); Butterfield, D. 43(3); Campbell, S. 32(1); Chapman, B. 12(5); Coldicott, S. 19(7); Cooke, T. 3; Coyne, D. 45; Croudson, S. 1; Falconer, W. 1(1); Ford, S. 8(5); Gallimore, T. 38; Groves, P. 43; Jeffrey, M. 4(14); Jevons, P. 25(6); Livingstone, S. (3); McDermott, J. 24; Neilson, A. 8(2); Pouton, A. 35; Pringle, M. 2; Raven, P. 4(5); Robinson, P. 1(4); Rowan, J. 19(5); Smith, D. 4; Taylor, R. 4; Thompson, C. 4(4); Todd, A. 12; Ward, I. 1; Willems, M. 27(3).
Goals – League (50): Boulding 11, Jevons 6 (1 pen), Pouton 5 (4 pens), Allen 4, Rowan 4, Campbell 3, Todd 3, Burnett 2, Butterfield 2, Groves 2, Cooke 1, Ford 1, Jeffrey 1, Smith D 1, Taylor 1, Willems 1, own goals 2.
Worthington Cup (7): Broomes 2, Jevons 2, Allen 1, Jeffrey 1, Rowan 1.
FA Cup (0).
Ground: Blundell Park, Cleethorpes, North-East Lincolnshire DN35 7PY. Telephone (01472) 605050.
Record attendance: 31,651 v Wolverhampton W, FA Cup 5th rd, 20 February 1937.
Capacity: 10,033.
Manager: Paul Groves.
Secretary: Ian Fleming.
Most League Goals: 103, Division 2, 1933–34.
Highest League Scorer in Season: Pat Glover, 42, Division 2, 1933–34.
Most League Goals in Total Aggregate: Pat Glover, 180, 1930–39.
Most Capped Player: Pat Glover, 7, Wales.
Most League Appearances: John McDermott, 497, 1987–.
Honours – Football League: Division 2 Champions – 1900–01, 1933–34. Division 3 (N) Champions – 1925–26, 1955–56. Division 3 Champions – 1979–80. Division 4 Champions – 1971-72. **League Group Cup:** Winners 1981–82. **Auto Windscreens Shield:** Winners 1997–98.
Colours: Black and white striped shirts, black shorts, black stockings with red turnover.

HALIFAX TOWN   NATIONWIDE CONFERENCE

Clarke Matthew (F)	6 3	13 00	Leeds	18 12 80	Wolverhampton W
Harsley Paul (M)	5 10	11 11	Scunthorpe	29 5 78	Scunthorpe U
Herbert Robert (M)	5 10	12 04	Durham	29 8 83	Scholar
Kerrigan Steve (F)	6 1	12 01	Bailleston	9 10 72	Shrewsbury T
Ludden Dominic (D)	5 7	10 09	Basildon	30 3 74	Preston NE
Midgley Craig (F)	5 7	11 06	Hartlepool	24 5 76	Hartlepool U
Oleksewycz Stephen (F)	5 8	11 00	Halifax	24 2 83	
Redfearn Neil (M)	5 11	13 01	Dewsbury	20 6 65	Wigan Ath
Rezai Carl (D)	5 9	11 00	Manchester	16 10 82	
Smith Craig (M)	5 8	10 10	Bradford	8 6 84	Scholar
Woodward Andy (D)	6 0	13 08	Stockport	23 9 73	Sheffield U

League Appearances: Bushell, S. 25; Butler, L. 21(1); Clarke, C. 24; Clarke, M. 22(9); Crookes, P. 1; Farrell, A. 7(2); Fitzpatrick, I. 26(3); Harsley, P. 45; Heinemann, N. 3; Herbert, R. 11(1); Houghton, S. 7; Jones, G. 20(15); Jules, M. 34(1); Kerrigan, S. 23(7); Ludden, D. 2; Mcdonald, C. 21(8); Midgley, C. 12(12); Mitchell, G. 41(2); Oleksewycz, S. (2); Redfearn, N. 27(3); Reilly, A. (2); Richards, M. 5; Richardson, B. 24; Smith, C. (2); Smith, G. 11; Stoneman, P. 32; Swales, S. 20(4); Winder, N. (1); Wood, J. 10(6); Woodward, A. 29(1); Wright, P. 3(11).

Goals – League (39): Harsley 11 (2 pens), Fitzpatrick 8, Redfearn 6 (1 pen), Jones 4, Midgley 3, Middleton 2, Bushell 1, Clarke M 1, Stoneman 1, Swales 1, Woodward 1.
Worthington Cup (0).
FA Cup (3): Harsley 1, Middleton 1, Wood 1.
Ground: The Shay Stadium, Shaw Hill, Halifax HX1 2YS. Telephone Halifax (01422) 345543.
Record attendance: 36,885 v Tottenham H, FA Cup 5th rd, 15 February 1953.
Capacity: 9900.
Manager: Chris Wilder.
Acting Secretary: Jenna Helliwell.
Most League Goals: 83, Division 3 (N), 1957–58.
Highest League Scorer in Season: Albert Valentine, 34, Division 3 (N), 1934–35.
Most League Goals in Total Aggregate: Ernest Dixon, 129, 1922–30.
Most Capped Player: None.
Most League Appearances: John Pickering, 367, 1965–74.
Honours – Football League: Division 3 (N)—Runners-up 1934–35; Division 4: Runners-up 1968–69. **Vauxhall Conference:** Champions 1997–98.
Colours: Blue shirts, blue shorts, blue stockings with white band.

HARTLEPOOL UNITED   DIV. 3

Barron Micky (D)	5 11	11 10	Lumley	22 12 74	Middlesbrough
Bass Jonathan (D)	6 0	12 02	Weston-Super-Mare	1 1 76	Birmingham C
Boyd Adam (F)	5 9	10 12	Hartlepool	25 5 82	Scholar
Clarke Darrell (M)	5 10	11 06	Mansfield	16 12 77	Mansfield T
Easter Jermaine (F)	5 10	12 03	Cardiff	15 1 82	Trainee
Henderson Kevin (F)	5 11	13 12	Ashington	8 6 74	Burnley
Humphreys Richie (M)	5 11	12 07	Sheffield	30 11 77	Cambridge U
Lee Graeme (D)	6 2	13 08	Middlesbrough	31 5 78	Trainee
Provett Jim (G)	5 11	11 12	Stockton	22 12 82	Trainee
Robinson Mark (D)	5 9	11 00	Guisborough	24 7 81	Trainee
Ross Brian (M)	5 6	10 02	Hartlepool	21 8 83	
Sharp James (D)	6 2	14 06	Reading	2 1 76	Andover T
Simms Gordon (D)	6 3	12 03	Larne	23 3 81	Wolverhampton W
Smith Paul (M)	6 0	13 03	Easington	22 1 76	Torquay U
Stephenson Paul (M)	5 10	12 12	Wallsend	2 1 68	York C
Sweeney Anthony (M)	6 0	11 07	Stockton	5 9 83	Scholar
Tinkler Mark (M)	6 2	13 00	Bishop Auckland	24 10 74	Southend U
Widdrington Tommy (M)	5 9	11 12	Newcastle	1 10 71	Port Vale
Williams Anthony (G)	6 2	13 08	Ogwr	20 9 77	Blackburn R
Williams Eifion (F)	5 11	11 02	Bangor	15 11 75	Torquay U

League Appearances: Arnison, P. 11(8); Barron, M. 39; Bass, J. 19(1); Boyd, A. 10(19); Clark, I. 5(2); Clarke, D. 24(9); Coppinger, J. 14; Easter, J. (12); Henderson, K. 13(10); Hollund, M. 3; Humphreys, R. 42(4); Lee, G. 38(1); Lormor, T. 4(13); Ormerod, A. 2; Parkin, J. 1); Robinson, M. 33(4); Sharp, J. 13(2); Simms, G. 6(4); Smith, P. 30(1); Stephenson, P. 23(6); Sweeney, A. (2); Tinkler, M. 39(1); Watson, G. 31(1); Westwood, C. 35; Widdrington, T. 24; Williams, A. 43; Williams, E. 5(3).
Goals – League (74): Watson 18 (1 pen), Boyd 9, Tinkler 9, Clarke 7, Humphreys 5, Lee 4, Smith 4, Williams E 4, Clark 2 (1 pen), Coppinger 2, Easter 2, Henderson 2, Widdrington 2, Barron 1, Bass 1, Lormor 1, Westwood 1.
Worthington Cup (0).
FA Cup (1): Clarke 1.
Ground: Victoria Park, Clarence Road, Hartlepool TS24 8BZ. Telephone (01429) 272584.
Record attendance: 17,426 v Manchester U, FA Cup 3rd rd, 5 January 1957.

Capacity: 7629.
Manager: Chris Turner.
Secretary: Maureen Smith.
Most League Goals: 90, Division 3 (N), 1956–57.
Highest League Scorer in Season: William Robinson, 28, Division 3 (N), 1927–28;
Joe Allon, 28, Division 4, 1990–91.
Most League Goals in Total Aggregate: Ken Johnson, 98, 1949–64.
Most Capped Player: Ambrose Fogarty, 1 (11), Republic of Ireland.
Most League Appearances: Wattie Moore, 447, 1948–64.
Honours – Nil.
Colours: Royal blue and white stripes.

HUDDERSFIELD TOWN   DIV. 2

Baldry Simon (M)	5 10	12 11	Huddersfield	12 2 76	Trainee
Booth Andy (F)	6 0	12 04	Huddersfield	6 12 73	Sheffield W
Brown Nathaniel (F)	6 2	12 05	Sheffield	15 6 81	Trainee
Clarke Doni (M)	5 8	10 11	Burnley	18 9 81	Scholar
Clarke Nathan (D)	6 2	11 11	Halifax	30 7 83	Scholar
Evans Gareth (D)	5 10	12 01	Leeds	10 4 81	Leeds U
Facey Delroy (F)	6 0	14 12	Huddersfield	22 4 80	Trainee
Fowler Adam (M)	5 9	10 10	Huddersfield	11 9 81	Scholar
Hay Nathan (D)	5 7	10 07	Leeds	5 10 81	Scholar
Heary Thomas (D)	5 10	12 06	Dublin	14 2 79	Trainee
Holland Chris (M)	6 1	12 10	Clitheroe	11 9 75	Birmingham C
Irons Kenny (M)	5 10	12 06	Liverpool	4 11 70	Tranmere R
Jenkins Steve (D)	5 11	12 12	Merthyr	16 7 72	Swansea C
Macari Paul (F)	5 6	12 02	Manchester	23 8 76	Sheffield U
Mattis Dwayne (M)	6 0	12 03	Huddersfield	31 7 81	Trainee
Moses Adi (D)	5 10	12 12	Doncaster	4 5 75	Barnsley
Schofield Danny (F)	5 10	11 09	Doncaster	10 4 80	Brodsworth
Scott Paul (M)	5 11	12 08	Wakefield	5 11 79	Trainee
Senior Chris (F)	5 6	9 01	Huddersfield	18 11 81	Scholar
Senior Michael (M)	5 9	10 07	Huddersfield	3 3 81	Trainee
Senior Philip (G)	5 11	10 12	Huddersfield	30 10 82	Trainee
Simpson Neil (M)	5 7	10 00	Bradford	2 12 81	Scholar
Smith Martin (F)	5 11	11 13	Sunderland	13 11 74	Sheffield U
Stead Jonathan (M)			Huddersfield	7 4 83	Scholar
Thorrington John (M)	5 8	10 06	Johannesburg	10 7 79	Manchester U
Worthington Jonathan (M)			Dewsbury	16 4 83	Scholar

League Appearances: Armstrong, C. 7(4); Baldry, S. 3(1); Beech, C. 6(3); Booth,
A. 30(6); Clarke, N. 36; Delaney, D. 1(1); Evans, G. 35; Facey, D. 11(2); Gray, K.
44; Hay, C. 19(12); Heary, T. 21(11); Holland, C. 35(2); Ifil, J. 1(1); Irons, K. 34(7);
Jenkins, S. 40; Knight, L. 31; Lucketti, C. 2; Macari, P. (6); Margetson, M. 46; Mat-
tis, D. 21(8); Moses, A. 13(4); Schofield, D. 39(1); Thorrington, J. 29(2); Wijnhard,
C. 2(11).
Goals – League (65): Knight 16, Booth 11, Schofield 8, Irons 7 (2 pens), Thorring-
ton 6 (1 pen), Hay 5, Facey 2, Armstrong 1, Beech 1, Clarke 1, Gray 1, Holland 1,
Jenkins 1, Mattis 1, Wijnhard 1, own goals 2.
Worthington Cup (0).
FA Cup (2): Knight 1, Moses 1.
Ground: The Alfred McAlpine Stadium, Leeds Road, Huddersfield HD1 6PX.
Telephone (01484) 484100.
Record attendance: 67,037 v Arsenal, FA Cup 6th rd, 27 February 1932. **Capacity:**
24,500.
Manager: Mick Wadsworth.
Secretary: Ann Hough.

Most League Goals: 101, Division 4, 1979–80.
Highest League Scorer in Season: Sam Taylor, 35, Division 2, 1919–20; George Brown, 35, Division 1, 1925–26.
Most League Goals in Total Aggregate: George Brown, 142, 1921–29; Jimmy Glazzard, 142, 1946–56.
Most Capped Player: Jimmy Nicholson, 31 (41), Northern Ireland.
Most League Appearances: Billy Smith, 520, 1914–34.
Honours – Football League: Division 1 Champions – 1923–24, 1924–25, 1925–26. Division 2 Champions – 1969–70. Division 4 Champions – 1969–70. **FA Cup winners** 1922.
Colours: Blue and white striped shirts, white shorts, white stockings with blue trim.

HULL CITY   DIV. 3

Alexander Gary (F)	5 11	13 00	Lambeth	15 8 79	Swindon T
Beresford David (M)	5 5	11 04	Middleton	11 11 76	Huddersfield T
Bloomer Matt (D)	6 1	13 00	Cleethorpes	3 11 78	Grimsby T
Bradshaw Gary (F)	5 6	10 06	Hull	30 12 82	Scholar
Dudfield Lawrie (F)	6 1	13 09	Southwark	7 5 80	Leicester C
Edwards Mike (D)	6 0	12 10	North Ferriby	25 4 80	Trainee
Glennon Matt (G)	6 2	14 09	Stockport	8 10 78	Bolton W
Greaves Mark (D)	6 1	13 00	Hull	22 1 75	Brigg Town
Holt Andy (D)	6 1	12 07	Stockport	21 5 78	Oldham Ath
Johnsson Julian (M)	6 1	12 08	Denmark	24 2 75	
Kerr Scott (M)	5 9	10 08	Leeds	11 12 81	Scholar
Mann Neil (M)	5 10	12 01	Nottingham	19 11 72	Grantham T
Matthews Rob (M)	6 0	13 00	Slough	14 10 70	Stockport Co
Mohan Nicky (D)	6 1	14 00	Middlesbrough	6 10 70	Stoke C
Musselwhite Paul (G)	6 2	14 02	Portsmouth	22 12 68	Sheffield W
Petty Ben (D)	6 0	12 05	Solihull	22 3 77	Stoke C
Philpott Lee (M)	5 10	11 08	Barnet	21 2 70	Lincoln C
Price Mike (D)	5 9	11 01	Wrexham	29 4 82	Everton
Whittle Justin (D)	6 1	13 00	Derby	18 3 71	Stoke C
Wicks Matt (D)	6 2	13 05	Reading	8 9 78	Brighton & HA
Williams Ryan (F)	5 4	11 04	Sutton-in-Ashfield	31 8 78	Chesterfield

League Appearances: Alexander, G. 43; Beresford, D. 33(8); Bloomer, M. (3); Bradshaw, G. 3; Caceres, A. 1(3); Dudfield, L. 32(6); Edwards, M. 38(1); Folan, C. (1); Glennon, M. 26; Goodison, I. 14(2); Greaves, M. 25(1); Holt, A. 24(6); Johnsson, J. 38(2); Lee, D. 2(9); Lightbourne, K. 3(1); Matthews, R. 9(6); Mohan, N. 26(1); Morley, B. 1(2); Musselwhite, P. 20; Norris, D. 3(3); Petty, B. 22(5); Philpott, L. 9(2); Price, M. (1); Reddy, M. 1(4); Roberts, N. 3(3); Rowe, R. 5(9); Sneekes, R. 17(5); Tait, P. (2); Van Blerk, J. 10; Whitmore, T. 23(11); Whittle, J. 35(1); Wicks, M. 14; Williams, R. 26(3).
Goals – League (57): Alexander 17 (1 pen), Dudfield 12 (1 pen), Johnsson 4, Reddy 4, Matthews 3, Rowe 2 (1 pen), Whitmore 2, Williams R 2 (1 pen), Beresford 1, Bradshaw 1, Edwards 1, Greaves 1, Lee 1, Mohan 1, Norris 1, Philpott 1, Van Blerk 1, own goals 2.
Worthington Cup (3): Alexander 1, Greaves 1, Whitmore 1.
FA Cup (7): Alexander 2, Dudfield 2, Johnsson 1, Matthews 1, own goal 1.
Ground: Boothferry Park, Hull HU4 6EU. Telephone (01482) 575263.
Record attendance: 55,019 v Manchester U, FA Cup 6th rd, 26 February 1949.
Capacity: 15,756.
Manager: Jan Molby.
Assistant Secretary: Phil Hough.
Most League Goals: 109, Division 3, 1965–66.
Highest League Scorer in Season: Bill McNaughton, 39, Division 3 (N), 1932–33.
Most League Goals in Total Aggregate: Chris Chilton, 195, 1960–71.

Most Capped Player: Terry Neill, 15 (59), Northern Ireland.
Most League Appearances: Andy Davidson, 520, 1952–67.
Honours – Football League: Division 3 (N) Champions – 1932–33, 1948–49.
Division 3 Champions – 1965–66.
Colours: Black, amber and white shirts, black shorts, black stockings.

IPSWICH TOWN   DIV. 1

Abidallah Nabil (M)	5 7	9 00	Amsterdam	5 8 82	
Ambrose Darren (M)	6 0	11 07	Harlow	29 2 84	Scholar
Armstrong Alun (F)	6 0	13 08	Gateshead	22 2 75	Middlesbrough
Artun Erdem (D)			London	11 11 82	Trainee
Beevers Lee (D)	6 1	12 07	Doncaster	4 12 83	Scholar
Bent Darren (F)	5 11	11 07	Tooting	6 2 84	Scholar
Bent Marcus (F)	6 2	12 04	Hammersmith	19 5 78	Blackburn R
Bloomfield Matt (M)	5 8	11 00	Ipswich	8 2 84	Scholar
Bramble Titus (D)	6 2	14 10	Ipswich	31 7 81	Trainee
Branagan Keith (G)	6 0	14 00	Fulham	10 7 66	Bolton W
Brown Wayne (D)	6 0	12 06	Barking	20 8 77	Trainee
Clapham Jamie (M)	5 9	11 05	Lincoln	7 12 75	Tottenham H
Counago Pablo (F)	5 11	11 06	Pontevedra	9 8 79	Celta Vigo
Croft Gary (D)	5 8	11 08	Stafford	17 2 74	Blackburn R
Dickinson Robert (M)	5 9	10 00	Leeds	27 11 83	Scholar
Gaardsoe Thomas (M)	6 2	12 06	Denmark	23 11 79	Aalborg
George Finidi (F)	6 0	12 04	Port Harcourt	15 4 71	Mallorca
Holland Matt (M)	5 9	12 07	Bury	11 4 74	Bournemouth
Heidarsson Hermann (D)	6 3	13 01	Iceland	11 7 74	Wimbledon
Karic Amir (D)	5 11	12 08	Oramovica Ponja	31 12 73	Maribor
Kelly Darren (G)			Dublin	30 5 84	Scholar
Le Pen Ulrich (M)	5 7	9 09	Auray	21 1 74	Rennes
Logan Richard (F)	6 0	12 05	Bury St Edmunds	4 1 82	Trainee
Magilton Jim (M)	6 0	13 10	Belfast	6 5 69	Sheffield W
Makin Chris (D)	5 10	11 02	Manchester	8 5 73	Sunderland
Marshall Andy (G)	6 2	13 07	Bury	14 4 75	Norwich C
McGreal John (D)	5 11	13 00	Birkenhead	2 6 72	Tranmere R
Miller Justin (D)	6 0	11 07	Johannesburg	16 12 80	Academy
Miller Tommy (M)	6 1	11 12	Easington	8 1 79	Hartlepool U
Naylor Richard (F)	6 1	13 07	Leeds	28 2 77	Trainee
Pullen James (G)	6 2	14 00	Chelmsford	18 3 82	Heybridge S
Reuser Martijn (M)	5 7	12 10	Amsterdam	1 2 75	Vitesse
Richards Matthew (D)			Harlow	26 12 84	Scholar
Sereni Matteo (G)	6 1	12 07	Parma	11 2 75	Sampdoria
Stewart Marcus (F)	5 10	11 08	Bristol	7 11 72	Huddersfield T
Venus Mark (D)	6 0	13 02	Hartlepool	6 4 67	Wolverhampton W
Wilnis Fabian (D)	5 8	12 06	Paramaribo	23 8 70	De Graafschap
Wright Jermaine (M)	5 10	12 07	Greenwich	21 10 75	Crewe Alex

League Appearances: Ambrose, D. (1); Armstrong, A. 21(11); Bent, D. 2(3); Bent, M. 22(3); Bramble, T. 16(2); Branagan, K. (1); Clapham, J. 22(10); Counago, P. 1(12); Gaardsoe, T. 3(1); George, F. 21(4); Holland, M. 38; Hreidarsson, H. 38; Le Pen, U. 1(3); Magilton, J. 16(8); Makin, C. 37; Marshall, A. 13; McGreal, J. 27; Miller, T. 5(3); Naylor, R. 5(9); Peralta, S. 16(6); Reuser, M. 18(6); Sereni, M. 25; Stewart, M. 20(8); Venus, M. 29; Wilnis, F. 6(8); Wright, J. 24(5).
Goals – League (41): Bent M 9, George 6, Stewart 6 (1 pen), Armstrong 4, Holland 3, Peralta 3, Clapham 2, Bent D 1, Gaardsoe 1, Hreidarsson 1, McGreal 1, Naylor 1, Reuser 1, Venus 1, Wright 1.
Worthington Cup (4): Reuser 2, Armstrong 1, Bent M 1.

FA Cup (5): Peralta 2, Bent M 1, Muggleton 1, Stewart 1.
Ground: Portman Road, Ipswich, Suffolk IP1 2DA. Telephone (01473) 400500.
Record attendance: 38,010 v Leeds U, FA Cup 6th rd, 8 March 1975.
Capacity: 30,250.
Manager: George Burley.
Secretary: David C. Rose.
Most League Goals: 106, Division 3 (S), 1955–56.
Highest League Scorer in Season: Ted Phillips, 41, Division 3 (S), 1956–57.
Most League Goals in Total Aggregate: Ray Crawford, 203, 1958–63 and 1966–69.
Most Capped Player: Allan Hunter, 47 (53), Northern Ireland.
Most League Appearances: Mick Mills, 591, 1966–82.
Honours – Football League: Division 1 Champions – 1961–62. Division 2 Champions – 1960–61, 1967–68, 1991–92. Division 3 (S) Champions – 1953–54, 1956–57. **FA Cup:** Winners 1977–78. **European Competitions: UEFA Cup winners:** 1980–81.
Colours: Blue shirts, white shorts, blue stockings.

KIDDERMINSTER HARRIERS   DIV. 3

Ayres Lee (D)	6 1	11 00	Birmingham	28 8 82	
Bennett Dean (M)	5 10	11 00	Wolverhampton	13 12 77	WBA
Blake Mark (M)	5 11	13 05	Nottingham	16 12 70	Mansfield T
Brock Stuart (G)	6 1	13 03	Sandwell	26 9 76	Northampton T
Broughton Drewe (F)	6 3	12 04	Hitchin	25 10 78	Peterborough U
Corbett Andy (F)	6 0	11 04	Worcester	20 2 82	
Danby John (G)			Stoke	20 9 83	
Doyle Daire (M)	5 10	11 06	Dublin	18 10 80	Coventry C
Ducros Andy (F)	5 6	9 08	Evesham	16 9 77	Coventry C
Foster Ian (F)	5 7	10 07	Merseyside	11 11 76	Liverpool
Hadley Stewart (F)	5 11	13 05	Stourbridge	30 12 73	Mansfield T
Henriksen Bo (F)	5 11	11 11	Roskilde	7 2 75	Herfolge
Hinton Craig (D)	5 11	11 00	Wolverhampton	26 11 77	Birmingham C
Joy Ian (D)	5 10	11 00	San Diego	14 7 81	Montrose
Lewis Matt (F)			Coventry	20 3 84	Marconi
Sall Abdou (D)	6 3	12 13	Senegal	1 11 80	Toulouse
Shilton Sam (M)	5 11	11 06	Nottingham	21 7 78	Hartlepool U
Smith Adie (D)	5 10	12 00	Birmingham	11 8 73	Bromsgrove R
Stamps Scott (D)	5 11	11 09	Edgbaston	20 3 75	Colchester U
Williams Danny (M)	6 2	13 01	Wrexham	12 7 79	Wrexham

League Appearances: Appleby, R. 18(1); Ayres, L. 5(1); Bennett, D. 39(3); Bird, T. 14(12); Blake, M. 23(1); Brock, S. 42; Broughton, D. 23(15); Clarkson, I. 36(3); Corbett, A. 2; Danby, J. (2); Davies, B. 9; Doyle, D. (1); Ducros, A. 7(7); Foster, I. 21(12); Hadley, S. 5(5); Henriksen, B. 24(1); Hinton, C. 41; Joy, I. 13(3); Larkin, C. 31(2); Lewis, M. (2); Medou-Otye, P. 2; Montgomery, G. 2; Nixon, E. 2; Sall, A. 27; Shail, M. 4; Shilton, S. 12(12); Smith, A. 33(3); Stamps, S. 36(1); Williams, D. 37(1).
Goals – League (56): Bennett 8, Broughton 8, Foster 8 (1 pen), Henriksen 8, Larkin 6, Appleby 4, Blake 4, Bird 2 (2 pens), Ducros 2, Sall 2, Smith 2, Williams 1, own goal 1.
Worthington Cup (2): Bird 2.
FA Cup (0).
Ground: Aggborough Stadium, Hoo Road, Kidderminster DY10 1NB. Telephone (01562) 823 931.
Record attendance: 9,155 v Hereford U, 27 November 1948.
Capacity: 6229.
Manager: Ian Britton.
Football Secretary: Roger Barlow.

Honours – Conference: Champions 1993–94, 1999–2000; Runners-up 1996–97. **FA Trophy:** 1986–87 (winners); 1990–91 (runners-up), 1994–95 (runners-up). **League Cup:** 1996–97 (winners). **Welsh FA Cup:** 1985–86 (runners-up), 1988–89 (runners-up). **Southern League Cup:** 1979–80 (winners). **Worcester Senior Cup:** (21). **Birmingham Senior Cup:** (7). **Staffordshire Senior Cup:** (4). **West Midland League Champions:** (6), Runners-up (3). **Southern Premier:** Runners-up (1). **West Midland League Cup:** Winners (7). **Keys Cup:** Winners (7). **Border Counties Floodlit League Champions:** (3). **Camkin Floodlit Cup:** Winners (3). **Bass County Vase:** Winners (1). **Conference Fair Play Trophy:** (5)

Colours: Red shirts with white flash, red shorts and stockings with white trim.

LEEDS UNITED   FA PREMIERSHIP

Allaway Shaun (G)	6 2	12 00	Reading	16 2 83	Trainee
Armstrong Chris (F)	6 1	13 02	Durham	8 11 84	Scholar
Bakke Eirik (M)	5 11	12 05	Sogndal	13 9 77	Sogndal
Batty David (M)	5 8	12 00	Leeds	2 12 68	Newcastle U
Bowyer Lee (M)	5 9	10 04	London	3 1 77	Charlton Ath
Breen Gerard (M)	5 11	13 01	County Louth	.29 3 84	Scholar
Bridges Michael (F)	6 1	12 05	North Shields	5 8 78	Sunderland
Burns Jacob (M)	5 10	11 11	Sydney	21 4 78	Paramatta Power
Cansdell-Sheriff					
Shane (D)	6 0	11 12	Sydney	10 11 82	NSW Academy
Corr Barry (F)	6 2	11 06	Co Wicklow	2 4 85	Scholar
Cousins Andrew (M)	5 6	10 08	Dublin	30 1 85	Scholar
Coyles William (G)	6 0	11 09	Co Antrim	20 12 84	Scholar
Cronin Kevin (M)			Dublin	18 5 85	Scholar
Dacourt Olivier (M)	5 9	11 07	Montreuil	25 9 74	Lens
Duberry Michael (D)	6 0	14 00	Enfield	14 10 75	Chelsea
Edwards Stewart (D)	5 9	11 00	Swansea	1 10 84	Scholar
Farrell Craig (F)	6 0	12 11	Middlesbrough	5 12 82	Trainee
Farren Larry (D)	6 0	11 11	Donegal	29 7 83	Scholar
Ferdinand Rio (D)	6 2	13 12	Peckham	7 11 78	West Ham U
Ferguson Steven (M)	5 7	9 13	Newry	25 2 83	St Andrew's
Folan Caleb (F)	6 2	13 00	Leeds	26 10 82	Trainee
Fowler Robbie (F)	5 8	11 06	Liverpool	9 4 75	Liverpool
Harte Ian (D)	5 9	12 06	Drogheda	31 8 77	Trainee
Johnson Seth (M)	5 8	12 04	Birmingham	12 3 79	Derby Co
Johnson Simon (F)	5 9	11 12	West Bromwich	9 3 83	Scholar
Keane Robbie (F)	5 9	12 06	Dublin	8 7 80	Internazionale
Keegan Paul (M)	5 11	11 11	Dublin	5 7 84	Scholar
Kelly Gary (D)	5 8	11 00	Drogheda	9 7 74	Home Farm
Kewell Harry (F)	5 11	13 04	Sydney	22 9 78	NSW Academy
Keyes Edward (D)	5 7	9 05	Dublin	2 5 85	Scholar
Kilgallon Matthew (D)	6 1	12 04	York	8 1 84	Scholar
Kinsella Alan (F)	5 8	11 00	Dublin	2 2 84	Scholar
Krief Domonique (M)	5 9	10 02	Leeds	15 9 83	Scholar
Lavery Sean (M)	5 7	11 12	Lurgan	16 11 83	Scholar
Martyn Nigel (G)	6 1	14 00	St Austell	11 8 66	Crystal Palace
Matteo Dominic (D)	6 1	12 08	Dumfries	28 4 74	Liverpool
McMaster Jamie (M)	5 10	11 11	Sydney	29 11 82	NSW Academy
McPhail Stephen (M)	5 8	12 05	London	9 12 79	Trainee
McStay Henry (D)	5 9	11 03	Co Armagh	6 3 85	Scholar
Mills Danny (D)	5 10	12 05	Norwich	18 5 77	Charlton Ath
Milosevic Danny (G)	6 3	14 12	Carlton	26 6 78	Perth Glory
Mitchell Peter (D)	5 8	11 00	Londonderry	10 4 84	Scholar
Newey Tom (D)	5 10	10 02	Sheffield	31 10 82	Scholar

Radebe Lucas (D)	6 1	12 04	Johannesburg	12 4 69	Kaiser Chiefs
Richardson Frazer (D)	5 11	11 11	Rotherham	29 10 82	Trainee
Robinson Paul (G)	6 4	15 09	Beverley	15 10 79	Trainee
Shields Robbie (M)	5 6	9 03	Dublin	1 5 84	Scholar
Singh Harpal (F)	5 7	10 09	Bradford	15 9 81	Trainee
Smith Alan (F)	5 10	11 11	Leeds	28 10 80	Trainee
Stiens Craig (F)	5 8	12 04	Swansea	31 7 84	Scholar
Tyrrell Derek (F)	6 0	11 02	Dublin	14 4 85	Scholar
Viduka Mark (F)	6 2	14 11	Melbourne	9 10 75	Celtic
Ward Michael (F)	5 8	11 00	Omagh	17 4 84	Scholar
Wilcox Jason (M)	6 0	11 11	Bolton	15 7 71	Blackburn R
Woodgate Jonathan (D)	6 2	13 00	Middlesbrough	22 1 80	Trainee

League Appearances: Bakke, E. 20(7); Batty, D. 30(6); Bowyer, L. 24(1); Dacourt, O. 16(1); Duberry, M. 3; Ferdinand, R. 31; Fowler, R. 22; Harte, I. 34(2); Johnson, S. 12(2); Keane, R. 16(9); Kelly, G. 19(1); Kewell, H. 26(1); Martyn, N. 38; Matteo, D. 32; Maybury, A. (1); McPhail, S. (1); Mills, D. 28; Smith, A. 19(4); Viduka, M. 33; Wilcox, J. 4(9); Woodgate, J. 11(2).
Goals – League (53): Fowler 12, Viduka 11, Kewell 8, Bowyer 5, Harte 5 (1 pen), Smith 4, Keane 3, Bakke 2, Mills 1, own goals 2.
Worthington Cup (6): Keane 3, Bakke 1, Kewell 1, Viduka 1.
FA Cup (1): Viduka 1.
Ground: Elland Road, Leeds LS11 0ES. Telephone (0113) 2266000.
Record attendance: 57,892 v Sunderland, FA Cup 5th rd (replay), 15 March 1967.
Capacity: 40,296.
Manager: Terry Venables.
Secretary: Ian Silvester.
Most League Goals: 98, Division 2, 1927–28.
Highest League Scorer in Season: John Charles, 42, Division 2, 1953–54.
Most League Goals in Total Aggregate: Peter Lorimer, 168, 1965–79 and 1983–86.
Most Capped Player: Billy Bremner, 54, Scotland.
Most League Appearances: Jack Charlton, 629, 1953–73.
Honours – Football League: Division 1 Champions – 1968–69, 1973–74, 1991–92. Division 2 Champions – 1923–24, 1963–64, 1989–90. **FA Cup:** Winners 1972. **Football League Cup:** Winners 1967–68. **European Competitions:** European Fairs Cup winners: 1967–68, 1970–71.
Colours: All white with royal blue trim.

LEICESTER CITY   DIV. 1

Ashton Jon (D)	6 2	13 05	Nuneaton	4 10 82	Scholar
Benjamin Trevor (F)	6 2	14 02	Kettering	8 2 79	Cambridge U
Darby Brett (F)	5 8	11 09	Leicester	10 11 83	Scholar
Davidson Callum (D)	5 10	12 10	Stirling	25 6 76	Blackburn R
Deane Brian (F)	6 3	14 03	Leeds	7 2 68	Middlesbrough
Delaney Damien (D)			Cork	20 7 81	Cork C
Dickov Paul (F)	5 8	10 13	Glasgow	1 11 72	Manchester C
Eadie Darren (F)	5 7	10 09	Chippenham	10 6 75	Norwich C
Elliott Matt (D)	6 3	15 01	Roehampton	1 11 68	Oxford U
Flowers Tim (G)	6 2	15 01	Kenilworth	3 2 67	Blackburn R
Heath Matthew (D)	6 4	14 03	Leicester	1 11 81	Scholar
Impey Andrew (M)	5 8	11 08	Hammersmith	30 9 71	West Ham U
Izzet Muzzy (M)	5 10	10 11	Hackney	31 10 74	Chelsea
Jones Matthew (M)	5 11	12 09	Llanelli	1 9 80	Leeds U
Laursen Jacob (D)	6 0	12 13	Vejle	6 10 71	FC Copenhagen
Lewis Junior (F)	6 2	11 08	Wembley	9 10 73	Gillingham
Lyth Ashley (D)	5 10	11 00	Whitby	14 6 83	
Marshall Lee (D)	6 2	12 12	Islington	21 1 79	Norwich C

McSweeney Leon (F)	5 10	10 05	Cork	19 2 83	Cork C
Mortimer Alex (M)	5 10	10 06	Manchester	28 11 82	Trainee
Noble Karl (M)	5 10	11 12	Leicester	5 9 82	Scholar
Oakes Stefan (M)	5 11	12 12	Leicester	6 9 78	Trainee
Piper Matt (F)	6 1	12 09	Leicester	29 9 81	Trainee
Price Michael (G)	6 3	13 11	Ashington	3 4 83	Scholar
Reeves Martin (M)	6 1	11 09	Birmingham	7 9 81	Scholar
Rogers Alan (M)	5 10	12 08	Liverpool	3 1 77	Nottingham F
Royce Simon (G)	6 2	12 10	Newham	9 9 71	Charlton Ath
Savage Robbie (M)	5 11	11 01	Wrexham	18 10 74	Crewe Alex
Scowcroft James (F)	6 1	14 08	Bury St Edmunds	15 11 75	Ipswich T
Sherman David (D)	5 9	12 07	Wegberg	19 5 83	Scholar
Sinclair Frank (D)	5 10	12 03	Lambeth	3 12 71	Chelsea
Stevenson Jon (F)	5 6	11 06	Leicester	13 10 82	Scholar
Stewart Jordan (M)	6 0	11 09	Birmingham	3 3 82	Trainee
Taggart Gerry (D)	6 2	14 03	Belfast	18 10 70	Bolton W
Walker Ian (G)	6 2	13 04	Watford	31 10 71	Tottenham H
Williamson Tom (M)			Leicester	24 12 84	Scholar
Wise Dennis (M)	5 6	10 07	Kensington	15 12 66	Chelsea
Wright Thomas (M)			Leicester	28 9 84	Scholar
Zayed Eamon (F)	6 0	12 07	Dublin	4 10 83	St Josephs

League Appearances: Akinbiyi, A. 16(5); Ashton, J. 3(4); Benjamin, T. 4(7); Davidson, C. 29(1); Deane, B. 13(2); Delaney, D. 2(1); Dickov, P. 11(1); Elliott, M. 31; Flowers, T. 3(1); Gunnlaugsson, A. (2); Heath, M. 3(2); Impey, A. 20(7); Izzet, M. 29(2); Jones, M. 6(4); Laursen, J. 10; Lewis, J. 4(2); Marshall, L. 29(6); Oakes, S. 16(5); Piper, M. 14(2); Reeves, M. 1(4); Rogers, A. 9(4); Rowett, G. 9(2); Savage, R. 35; Scowcroft, J. 21(3); Sinclair, F. 33(2); Stevenson, J. (6); Stewart, J. 9(3); Sturridge, D. 8(1); Taggart, G. (1); Walker, I. 35; Williamson, T. (1); Wise, D. 15(2); Wright, T. (1).
Goals – League (30): Deane 6, Scowcroft 5, Dickov 4, Izzet 4 (2 pens), Sturridge 3, Akinbiyi 2, Jones 1, Oakes 1, Piper 1, Stevenson 1, Wise 1, own goal 1.
Worthington Cup (1): Akinbiyi 1.
FA Cup (2): Scowcroft 2.
Ground: The Walkers Stadium, Filbert Way, Leicester LE2 7GL
Record attendance: 47,298 v Tottenham H, FA Cup 5th rd, 18 February 1928.
Capacity: 32,500.
Manager: Micky Adams.
Secretary: Andrew Neville.
Most League Goals: 109, Division 2, 1956–57.
Highest League Scorer in Season: Arthur Rowley, 44, Division 2, 1956–57.
Most League Goals in Total Aggregate: Arthur Chandler, 259, 1923–35.
Most Capped Player: John O'Neill, 39, Northern Ireland.
Most League Appearances: Adam Black, 528, 1920–35.
Honours – Football League: Division 2 Champions – 1924–25, 1936–37, 1953–54, 1956–57, 1970–71, 1979–80. **Football League Cup:** Winners 1964, 1997, 2000.
Colours: Royal blue shirts, royal blue shorts, blue stockings.

LEYTON ORIENT   DIV. 3

Barrett Scott (G)	5 11	14 06	Ilkeston	2 4 63	Cambridge U
Brazier Matt (M)	5 10	10 10	Whipps Cross	2 7 76	Cardiff C
Downer Simon (D)	6 1	13 02	Romford	19 10 81	Trainee
Fletcher Gary (F)	5 11	12 06	Liverpool	4 6 81	Northwich Vic
Harris Andy (D)	5 11	12 05	Springs	26 2 77	Southend U
Hutchings Carl (M)	6 0	11 06	Hammersmith	24 9 74	Southend U
Ibehre Jabo (F)	6 2	13 00	Islington	28 1 83	Trainee
Jones Billy (D)	6 1	11 04	Chatham	26 6 83	Trainee

Joseph Matt (D)	5 5	10 07	Bethnal Green	30 9 72	Cambridge U
Lockwood Matt (D)	5 10	11 07	Rochford	17 10 76	Bristol R
Martin John (M)	5 8	10 03	Bethnal Green	15 7 81	Trainee
McGhee Dave (D)	6 0	13 07	Worthing	19 6 76	Brentford
McLean Aaron (F)	5 9	10 10	Hammersmith	25 5 83	Trainee
Nugent Kevin (F)	6 1	13 07	Edmonton	10 4 69	Cardiff C
Smith Dean (D)	6 0	13 03	West Bromwich	19 3 71	Hereford U
Tate Chris (F)	6 0	12 08	York	27 12 77	Halifax T
Thorpe Lee (F)	6 0	11 13	Wolverhampton	14 12 75	Lincoln C
Toner Ciaran (M)	6 1	12 02	Craigavon	30 6 81	Bristol R
Watts Steve (F)	6 0	14 02	Lambeth	11 7 76	Fisher Ath

League Appearances: Barnard, D. 6(4); Barrett, S. 32; Bayes, A. 12(1); Beall, B. 7(4); Brazier, M. 8; Canham, S. 23(1); Castle, S. (1); Christie, I. 9(6); Constantine, L. 9(1); Dorrian, C. 2(1); Downer, S. 11(1); Fletcher, G. 3(6); Gough, N. 1(10); Gray, W. 13(2); Hadland, P. (5); Harris, A. 45; Hatcher, D. 2(6); Herrera, R. 2; Houghton, S. 10(11); Hutchings, C. 9(1); Ibehre, J. 21(7); Jones, B. 16; Joseph, M. 29(1); Leigertwood, M. 8; Lockwood, M. 20(4); Martin, J. 29(2); McElholm, B. (2); McGhee, D. 39(1); McLean, A. 4(23); Minton, J. 32(1); Morris, G. 2; Newton, A. 10; Nugent, K. 7(2); Oakes, S. 11; Partridge, D. 6(1); Smith, D. 45; Tate, C. 1(6); Watts, S. 22(8).

Goals – League (55): Watts 9, Gray 5, Houghton 5 (2 pens), Minton 5, Canham 4, Ibehre 4, Christie 3, Constantine 3, Lockwood 2 (1 pen) Martin 2, McGhee 2, Smith 2, Gough 1, Hadland 1, Harris 1, Hutchings 1, Joseph 1, McLean 1, Newton 1, Nugent 1, own goal 1.

Worthington Cup (2): Houghton 1, Minton 1.

FA Cup (8): Watts 3, Canham 1, Christie 1, Gray 1, Ibehre 1, Smith 1.

Ground: Leyton Stadium, Brisbane Road, Leyton, London E10 5NE. Telephone (020) 8926 1111.

Record attendance: 34,345 v West Ham U, FA Cup 4th rd, 25 January 1964.

Capacity: 11,127.

Manager: Paul Brush.

Secretary: Kirstine Nicholson.

Most League Goals: 106, Division 3 (S), 1955–56.

Highest League Scorer in Season: Tom Johnston, 35, Division 2, 1957–58.

Most League Goals in Total Aggregate: Tom Johnston, 121, 1956–58, 1959–61.

Most Capped Players: Tunji Banjo, 7 (7), Nigeria; John Chiedozie, 7 (9), Nigeria; Tony Grealish, 7 (45), Eire.

Most League Appearances: Peter Allen, 432, 1965–78.

Honours – Football League: Division 3 Champions – 1969–70. Division 3 (S) Champions – 1955–56.

Colours: Red shirts with white chest panel, red shorts, white stockings.

LINCOLN CITY   DIV. 3

Bailey Mark (D)	5 8	11 07	Stoke	12 8 76	Rochdale
Battersby Tony (F)	6 0	13 07	Doncaster	30 8 75	Bury
Bimson Stuart (D)	5 11	11 06	Liverpool	29 9 69	Bury
Black Kingsley (M)	5 10	12 00	Luton	22 6 68	Grimsby T
Buckley Adam (M)	5 9	11 07	Nottingham	2 8 79	Grimsby T
Camm Mark (D)	5 8	11 05	Mansfield	1 10 80	Trainee
Gain Peter (M)	5 9	11 07	Hammersmith	2 11 76	Tottenham H
Hamilton Ian (M)	5 10	12 07	Stevenage	14 12 67	Notts Co
Logan Richard (D)	6 0	13 03	Barnsley	24 5 69	Scunthorpe U
Marriott Alan (G)	5 11	12 01	Bedford	3 9 78	Tottenham H
Mayo Paul (D)	5 11	11 08	Lincoln	13 10 81	Scholar
Morgan Paul (D)	6 0	11 05	Belfast	23 10 78	Preston NE

Pettinger Paul (G)	6 0	13 00	Sheffield	1 10 75	Rotherham U
Sedgemore Ben (M)	5 10	12 13	Wolverhampton	5 8 75	Macclesfield T
Smith Paul (M)	5 11	11 10	Hastings	25 1 76	Nottingham F

League Appearances: Bailey, M. 18; Barnett, J. 23(3); Battersby, T. 28(11); Betts, R. 1(2); Bimson, S. 34(1); Black, K. 30(1); Bloomer, M. 4(1); Brown, G. 32(4); Buckley, A. 19(12); Cameron, D. 23(21); Camm, M. 5(11); Finnigan, J. 21(2); Gain, P. 35(7); Hamilton, I. 26; Holmes, S. 18(2); Horrigan, D. (1); Logan, R. (2); Marriott, A. 43; Mayo, P. 11(3); Morgan, P. 32(2); Pettinger, P. 3; Sedgemore, B. 33(10); Smith, P. 6(2); Thorpe, L. 37; Walker, J. 24(7).
Goals – League (44): Thorpe 13, Cameron 6, Battersby 5 (1 pen), Black 5, Holmes 4 (3 pens), Walker 3, Barnett J 2, Gain 2, Sedgemore 2, Morgan 1, own goal 1.
Worthington Cup (1): Battersby 1.
FA Cup (3): Cameron 1, Hamilton 1, Holmes 1.
Ground: Sincil Bank, Lincoln LN5 8LD. Telephone (01522) 880011.
Record attendance: 23,196 v Derby Co, League Cup 4th rd, 15 November 1967.
Capacity: 10,147.
Manager: Keith Alexander.
Secretary: F. J. Martin.
Most League Goals: 121, Division 3 (N), 1951–52.
Highest League Scorer in Season: Allan Hall, 42, Division 3 (N), 1931–32.
Most League Goals in Total Aggregate: Andy Graver, 144, 1950–55 and 1958–61.
Most Capped Player: David Pugh, 3 (7), Wales; George Moulson, 3, Republic of Ireland.
Most League Appearances: Grant Brown, 407, 1989–2002.
Honours – Football League: Division 3 (N) Champions – 1931–32, 1947–48, 1951–52. Division 4 Champions – 1975–76.
Colours: Red and white striped shirts, red shorts and stockings.

LIVERPOOL   FA PREMIERSHIP

Anelka Nicolas (F)	6 1	12 04	Versailles	14 3 79	Paris St Germain
Arphcxad Pcgguy (G)	6 2	13 07	Abymes	18 5 73	Leicester C
Babbel Markus (D)	6 0	13 03	Munich	8 9 72	Bayern Munich
Barmby Nick (M)	5 6	11 04	Hull	11 2 74	Everton
Baros Milan (F)	6 0	13 02	Valassake Mezirici	28 10 81	Banik Ostrava
Berger Patrik (M)	6 1	13 00	Prague	10 11 73	Borussia Dortmund
Biscan Igor (M)	6 3	12 08	Zagreb	4 5 78	Dynamo Zagreb
Carragher Jamie (M)	6 1	12 05	Liverpool	28 1 78	Trainee
Diomede Bernard (M)	5 9	12 04	Bourges	23 1 74	Auxerre
Dudek Jerzy (G)	6 2	12 08	Ribnek	23 3 73	Feyenoord
Foley-Sheridan Michael (M)			Dublin	9 3 83	
Gerrard Steven (M)	6 1	12 03	Whiston	30 5 80	Trainee
Hamann Dietmar (M)	6 2	12 01	Waldasson	27 8 73	Newcastle U
Heggem Vegard (D)	5 11	12 04	Trondheim	13 7 75	Rosenborg
Henchoz Stephane (D)	6 1	12 13	Billens	7 9 74	Blackburn R
Heskey Emile (F)	6 1	14 04	Leicester	11 1 78	Leicester C
Hyypia Sami (D)	6 4	13 11	Porvoo	7 10 73	Willem II
Kirkland Christopher (G)	6 6	14 12	Leicester	2 5 81	Coventry C
Litmanen Jari (F)	6 0	12 10	Lahti	20 2 71	Barcelona
Massie Jason (M)			Whiston	13 9 84	
McAllister Gary (M)	6 1	11 11	Motherwell	25 12 64	Coventry C
McNulty Stephen (M)			Liverpool	26 9 83	Scholar
Mellor Neil (M)			Sheffield	4 11 82	Scholar
Murphy Danny (M)	5 9	12 08	Chester	18 3 77	Crewe Alex
Otsemobor John (D)			Liverpool	23 3 83	Trainee
Owen Michael (F)	5 8	10 13	Chester	14 12 79	Trainee

Partridge Richie (M)	5 8	10 07	Dublin	12 9 80	Trainee
Peers Mark (M)			St Helens	14 5 84	
Potter Darren (M)			Liverpool	21 12 84	Scholar
Raven David (M)			Wirral	10 3 85	Scholar
Riise John Arne (M)	6 1	12 08	Molde	24 9 80	Monaco
Sjolund Danny (F)	5 11	12 00	Mariehamn	22 4 83	West Ham U
Smicer Vladimir (M)	5 10	12 02	Degin	24 5 73	Lens
Smyth Mark (M)			Liverpool	9 1 85	Scholar
Traore Djimi (D)	6 1	12 06	Saint-Ouen	1 3 80	Laval
Vaughan Stephen (M)			Liverpool	22 1 85	Scholar
Vignal Gregory (D)	5 11	12 03	Montpellier	19 7 81	
Warnock Stephen (M)			Ormskirk	12 12 81	Trainee
Welsh John (D)			Liverpool	10 1 84	Scholar
Wright Andrew (M)			Southport	15 1 85	Scholar
Wright Stephen (D)	6 0	11 11	Liverpool	8 2 80	Trainee
Xavier Abel (D)	6 3	12 07	Mozambique	30 11 72	Everton

League Appearances: Anelka, N. 13(7); Arphexad, P. 1(1); Babbel, M. 2; Barmby, N. 2(4); Berger, P. 12(9); Biscan, I. 4(1); Carragher, J. 33; Dudek, J. 35; Fowler, R. 8(2); Gerrard, S. 26(2); Hamann, D. 31; Henchoz, S. 37; Heskey, E. 26(9); Hyypia, S. 37; Kirkland, C. 1; Litmanen, J. 8(13); McAllister, G. 14(11); Murphy, D. 31(5); Owen, M. 25(4); Redknapp, J. 2(2); Riise, J. 34(4); Smicer, V. 13(9); Vignal, G. 3(1); Westerveld, S. 1; Wright, S. 10(2); Xavier, A. 9(1).
Goals – League (67): Owen 19 (1 pen), Heskey 9, Riise 7, Murphy 6, Anelka 4, Litmanen 4, Smicer 4, Fowler 3, Gerrard 3, Hyypia 3, Berger 1, Hamann 1, Redknapp 1, Xavier 1, own goal 1.
Worthington Cup (1): McAllister 1 (pen).
FA Cup (3): Owen 2, Anelka 1.
Ground: Anfield Road, Liverpool L4 0TH. Telephone (0151) 263 2361.
Record attendance: 61,905 v Wolverhampton W, FA Cup 4th rd, 2 February 1952.
Capacity: 45,362.
Manager: Gerard Houllier.
Secretary: Bryce Morrison.
Most League Goals: 106, Division 2, 1895–96.
Highest League Scorer in Season: Roger Hunt, 41, Division 2, 1961–62.
Most League Goals in Total Aggregate: Roger Hunt, 245, 1959–69.
Most Capped Player: Ian Rush, 67 (73), Wales.
Most League Appearances: Ian Callaghan, 640, 1960–78.
Honours – Football League: Division 1 – Champions 1900–01, 1905–06, 1921–22, 1922–23, 1946–47, 1963–64, 1965–66, 1972–73, 1975–76, 1976–77, 1978–79, 1979–80, 1981–82, 1982–83, 1983–84, 1985–86, 1987–88, 1989–90 (Liverpool have a record number of 18 League Championship wins). Division 2 Champions – 1893–94, 1895–96, 1904–05, 1961–62. **FA Cup:** Winners 1965, 1974, 1986, 1989, 1992, 2001. **League Cup:** Winners 1981, 1982, 1983, 1984, 1995, 2001. Super Cup: Winners 1985–86. **European Competitions: European Cup winners:** 1976–77, 1977–78, 1980–81, 1983–84. **UEFA Cup winners:** 1972–73, 1975–76, 2001. **Super Cup winners:** 1977.
Colours: All red.

LUTON TOWN   DIV. 2

Bayliss Dave (D)	6 0	12 08	Liverpool	8 6 76	Rochdale
Boyce Emmerson (D)	6 0	12 03	Aylesbury	24 9 79	Trainee
Coyne Chris (D)	6 1	13 08	Brisbane	20 12 78	Dundee
Crowe Dean (F)	5 6	11 07	Stockport	6 6 79	Stoke C
Emberson Carl (G)	6 2	15 00	Epsom	13 7 73	Walsall
Forbes Adrian (M)	5 7	11 12	Greenford	23 1 79	Norwich C
Fotiadis Andrew (F)	6 0	12 13	Hitchin	6 9 77	School

Griffiths Carl (F)	5 11	12 04	Oswestry	15 7 71	Leyton Orient
Hillier Ian (D)	6 1	11 12	Neath	26 12 79	Tottenham H
Holmes Peter (M)	5 11	11 05	Bishop Auckland	18 11 80	Sheffield W
Howard Steve (F)	6 3	15 00	Durham	10 5 76	Northampton T
Leary Michael (M)	5 11	12 03	Ealing	17 4 83	Scholar
Mansell Lee (M)	5 9	10 12	Gloucester	28 10 82	Scholar
Neilson Alan (D)	5 11	12 08	Wegburg	26 9 72	Fulham
Nicholls Kevin (M)	5 10	12 02	Newham	2 1 79	Wigan Ath
Ovendale Mark (G)	6 2	14 00	Leicester	22 11 73	Bournemouth
Perrett Russell (D)	6 1	12 09	Barton-on-Sea	18 6 73	Cardiff C
Skelton Aaron (M)	5 11	12 09	Welwyn	22 11 74	Colchester U
Spring Matthew (M)	6 0	12 08	Harlow	17 11 79	Trainee
Taylor Matthew (D)	5 11	11 08	Oxford	27 11 81	Trainee

League Appearances: Bayliss, D. 15(3); Boyce, E. 30(7); Brkovic, A. 17(4); Coyne, C. 29(2); Crowe, D. 32(2); Douglas, S. 2(7); Dryden, R. 2(1); Emberson, C. 33; Forbes, A. 15(25); Fotiadis, A. (8); George, L. 2(2); Griffiths, C. 10; Hillier, I. 11(12); Holmes, P. 4(3); Howard, S. 42; Hughes, P. 12(10); Johnson, M. 11(7); Kabba, S. (3); Locke, A. 1(2); Mansell, L. 6(5); McSwegan, G. 2(1); Neilson, A. 8; Nicholls, K. 42; Ovendale, M. 13; Perrett, R. 39(1); Skelton, A. 9; Spring, M. 42; Stirling, J. 1; Street, K. 1(1); Taylor, M. 43; Valois, J. 32(2).
Goals – League (96): Howard 24, Crowe 15, Taylor 11, Griffiths 7, Nicholls 7 (4 pens), Spring 6, Valois 6, Forbes 4, Coyne 3, Perrett 3, Hughes 2, Brkovic 1, Fotiadis 1, Hillier 1, Holmes 1, Johnson 1, Mansell 1, Skelton 1, own goal 1.
Worthington Cup (0).
FA Cup (2): Brkovic 1, Forbes 1.
Ground: Kenilworth Road Stadium, 1 Maple Rd, Luton, Beds. LU4 8AW. Telephone (01582) 411622.
Record attendance: 30,069 v Blackpool, FA Cup 6th rd replay, 4 March 1959.
Capacity: 9975.
Manager: Joe Kinnear.
Secretary: Cherry Newbery.
Most League Goals: 103, Division 3 (S), 1936–37.
Highest League Scorer in Season: Joe Payne, 55, Division 3 (S), 1936–37.
Most League Goals in Total Aggregate: Gordon Turner, 243, 1949–64.
Most Capped Player: Mal Donaghy, 58 (91), Northern Ireland.
Most League Appearances: Bob Morton, 494, 1948–64.
Honours – Football League: Division 2 Champions – 1981–82. Division 4 Champions – 1967–68. Division 3 (S) Champions – 1936–37. **Football League Cup winners** 1987–88.
Colours: White shirts with orange and black trim, black shorts with orange and white trim, black stockings with two white hoops.

MACCLESFIELD TOWN   DIV. 3

Abbey George (D)	5 8	10 08	Port Harcourt	20 10 78	Sharks
Adams Daniel (D)	5 8	13 08	Manchester	3 1 76	Altrincham
Byrne Chris (M)	5 9	10 00	Hulme	9 2 75	Stockport Co
Came Shaun (D)	6 3	13 00	Crewe	15 6 83	Trainee
Hitchen Steve (D)	5 8	11 07	Salford	28 11 76	Blackburn R
Lightbourne Kyle (F)	6 2	12 02	Bermuda	29 9 68	Stoke C
Martin Lee (G)	6 0	13 07	Huddersfield	9 9 68	Halifax T
O'Neill Paul (D)	5 11	11 02	Bolton	17 6 82	Trainee
Priest Chris (M)	5 10	12 00	Leigh	18 10 73	Chester C
Ridler Dave (D)	6 0	12 00	Liverpool	12 3 76	Wrexham
Tinson Darren (D)	6 0	13 07	Birmingham	15 11 69	Northwich V
Tipton Matthew (F)	5 10	11 02	Bridgend	29 6 80	Oldham Ath

Welch Michael (D)   Crewe   11 1 82 Barnsley
Whittaker Dan (M)   5 10   11 00   Manchester   14 11 80

League Appearances: Abbey, G. 15(2); Adams, D. 38(1); Askey, J. 1(17); Bullock, M. 2(1); Byrne, C. 26(6); Came, S. 1; Eyre, R. 12(2); Glover, L. 38(5); Hitchen, S. 28(2); Keen, K. 29(1); Lambert, R. 32(3); Lightbourne, K. 22(7); Macauley, S. 12; Martin, L. 8(1); McAvoy, A. 4(6); Munroe, K. 19(11); O'Neill, P. 7(4); Priest, C. 32(1); Ridler, D. 37(2); Shuttleworth, B. (3); Smith, D. 8; Smith, J. 7(1); Tinson, D. 46; Tipton, M. 12(1); Tracey, R. 10(10); Welch, M. 6; Whitehead, D. 1(1); Whittaker, D. 15(1); Wilson, S. 38; Woolley, M. (3).
Goals – League (41): Glover 9 (4 pens), Lambert 8, Byrne 6, Lightbourne 4, Tipton 3, Smith J 2, Tracey 2, Whittaker 2, Askey 1, Hitchen 1, Priest 1, Tinson 1, own goal 1.
Worthington Cup (1): Glover 1.
FA Cup (7): Byrne 2, Glover 2, Lambert 2, Keen 1.
Ground: The Moss Rose Ground, London Road, Macclesfield, Cheshire SK11 7SP. Telephone: (01625) 264686.
Record attendance: 9008 v Winsford U, Cheshire Senior Cup 2nd rd, 4 February 1948. **Capacity:** 6235 (seated 2537, standing 3698).
Manager: David Moss.
Secretary: Colin Garlick.
Most League Goals: 66, Division 3, 1999–2000.
Highest League Scorer in Season: Richard Barker, 16, Division 3, 1999–2000.
Most League Goals in Total Aggregate: John Askey, 29, 1997–2002.
Most League Appearances: Darren Tinson, 218, 1997–2002.
Honours – Nil.
Colours: Royal blue shirts, white shorts, blue stockings.

MANCHESTER CITY   FA PREMIERSHIP

Almond James (F)			Northallerton	5 10 83	Scholar
Barton Joey (M)	5 9	11 00	Huyton	2 9 82	Scholar
Benarbia Ali (M)	5 8	10 08	Oran	8 10 68	Paris St Germain
Berkovic Eyal (M)	5 7	10 12	Haifa	2 4 72	Blackburn R
Browne Gary (F)	5 10	10 10	Dundonald	17 1 83	Scholar
Charvet Laurent (D)	5 11	13 07	Beziers	8 5 73	Newcastle U
Day Rhys (D)	6 2	12 10	Bridgend	31 8 82	Scholar
Dunfield Terry (M)	5 10	11 02	Canada	20 2 82	Trainee
Dunne Richard (D)	6 1	16 05	Dublin	21 9 79	Everton
Ellegaard Kevin Stuhr (G)	6 5	14 00	Denmark	23 5 83	Farum
Elliott Stephen (F)			Dublin	6 1 84	School
Flood William (M)			Dublin	10 4 85	
Goater Shaun (F)	6 0	12 06	Bermuda	25 2 70	Bristol C
Haaland Alf-Inge (D)	6 1	12 02	Bryne	23 11 72	Leeds U
Hodgson David (M)			Billinge	2 9 83	
Horlock Kevin (M)	5 11	12 12	Erith	1 11 72	Swindon T
Howey Steve (D)	6 1	13 05	Sunderland	26 10 71	Newcastle U
Huckerby Darren (F)	5 10	12 05	Nottingham	23 4 76	Leeds U
James William (M)			Swansea	11 1 84	Scholar
Jensen Niclas (D)	6 0	12 00	Copenhagen	17 8 74	FC Copenhagen
Jihai Sun (D)	5 10	10 07	Dalian	30 9 77	Dalian Wanda
Jordan Stephen (D)	6 0	11 13	Warrington	6 3 82	Scholar
Joyce Damien (M)	5 8	12 03	Dublin	8 3 83	Scholar
Kilheeney Ciaran (F)			Stockport	9 1 84	
Killen Chris (F)	6 0	12 11	Wellington	8 10 81	Miramar R
Macken Jonathan (F)	5 10	12 00	Manchester	7 9 77	Preston NE
McCarthy Patrick (D)	6 1	12 08	Dublin	31 5 83	Scholar

McDowall Ryan (M)			Knowsley	30 3 84	School
McTaggart Daniel (M)			St Asaph	1 12 83	Scholar
Mears Tyrone (D)	5 11	11 11	Stockport	18 2 83	
Mettomo Lucien (D)	6 0	12 00	Douala	19 4 77	St Etienne
Murphy Brian (G)	6 0	13 01	Waterford	7 5 83	
Nash Carlo (G)	6 4	15 04	Bolton	13 9 73	Stockport Co
Negouai Christian (M)	6 4	13 00	Martinique	20 1 75	
Paisley Stephen (D)	6 1	12 08	Dublin	28 7 83	Scholar
Ritchie Paul (D)	5 11	12 10	Kirkcaldy	21 8 75	Bolton W
Shuker Chris (F)	5 4	9 06	Liverpool	9 5 82	Scholar
Tiatto Danny (D)	5 7	11 06	Melbourne	22 5 73	Stoke C
Tickle David (M)			Billinge	3 9 83	
Toure Alioune (F)	5 8	11 05	Saint-Denis	9 9 78	Nantes
Wanchope Paulo (F)	6 3	13 08	Heredia	31 7 76	West Ham U
Weaver Nick (G)	6 4	14 05	Sheffield	2 3 79	Mansfield T
Westwood Keiren (G)			Manchester	23 10 84	
Whelan Glenn (M)	5 10	11 13	Dublin	13 1 84	Scholar
Whitley Jeff (M)	5 8	11 00	Zambia	28 1 79	Trainee
Wiekens Gerard (D)	6 1	13 06	Tolhuiswyk	25 2 73	
Wright-Phillips Shaun (F)	5 4	9 10	London	25 10 81	

League Appearances: Benarbia, A. 38; Berkovic, E. 20(5); Charvet, L. 3; Colosimo, S. (6); Dickov, P. (7); Dunne, R. 41(2); Edghill, R. 9(2); Etuhu, D. 11(1); Goater, S. 42; Grant, T. 2(1); Granville, D. 12(4); Haaland, A. (3); Horlock, K. 33(9); Howey, S. 34; Huckerby, D. 30(10); Jensen, N. 16(2); Jihai, S. 2(5); Killen, C. (3); Macken, J. 4(4); Mears, T. (1); Mettomo, L. 17(6); Mike, L. 1(1); Nash, C. 22(1); Negouai, C. 2(3); Pearce, S. 38; Ritchie, P. (8); Shuker, C. (2); Tiatto, D. 36(1); Toure, A. (1); Wanchope, P. 14(1); Weaver, N. 24(1); Whitley, J. (2); Wiekens, G. 24(5); Wright-Phillips, S. 31(4).
Goals – League (108): Goater 28, Huckerby 20 (2 pens), Wanchope 12 (3 pens), Benarbia 8, Wright-Phillips 8, Horlock 7, Berkovic 6, Macken 5, Howey 3, Pearce 3 (1 pen), Dunne 1, Granville 1, Jensen 1, Mettomo 1, Negouai 1, Tiatto 1, own goals 2.
Worthington Cup (10): Huckerby 5, Goater 2, Dickov 1, Shuker 1, own goal 1.
FA Cup (6): Goater 2, Berkovic 1, Horlock 1, Huckerby 1, Wanchope 1.
Ground: Maine Road, Moss Side, Manchester M14 7WN. Telephone (0161) 232 3000.
Record attendance: 84,569 v Stoke C, FA Cup 6th rd, 3 March 1934 (British record for any game outside London or Glasgow). **Capacity:** 34,026.
Manager: Kevin Keegan.
General Secretary: J. B. Halford.
Most League Goals: 108, Division 2, 1926–27, 108, Division 1, 2001–02.
Highest League Scorer in Season: Tommy Johnson, 38, Division 1, 1928–29.
Most League Goals in Total Aggregate: Tommy Johnson, 158, 1919–30.
Most Capped Player: Colin Bell, 48, England.
Most League Appearances: Alan Oakes, 565, 1959–76.
Honours – Football League: Division 1 Champions – 1936–37, 1967–68, 2001–02. Division 2 Champions – 1898–99, 1902–03, 1909–10, 1927–28, 1946–47, 1965–66.
FA Cup winners 1904, 1934, 1956, 1969. **Football League Cup winners** 1970, 1976.
European Competitions: European Cup-Winners' Cup winners: 1969–70.
Colours: Lazer blue shirts, white shorts, lazer blue and navy stockings.

MANCHESTER UNITED   FA PREMIERSHIP

Barthez Fabien (G)	5 11	12 08	Lavelanet	28 6 71	Monaco
Beckham David (M)	6 0	11 13	Leytonstone	2 5 75	Trainee
Brown Wes (D)	6 1	13 11	Manchester	13 10 79	Trainee
Butt Nicky (M)	5 10	11 11	Manchester	21 1 75	Trainee
Carroll Roy (G)	6 2	13 12	Enniskillen	30 9 77	Wigan Ath

Chadwick Luke (F)	5 11	11 08	Cambridge	18 11 80	Trainee
Cogger John (D)	5 10	13 05	Waltham Forest	12 9 83	Scholar
Culkin Nick (G)	6 2	13 09	York	6 7 78	York C
Davis Jimmy (F)	5 8	11 05	Bromsgrove	6 2 82	Trainee
Djordjic Bojan (F)	5 10	11 01	Belgrade	6 2 82	
Fletcher Darren (M)	6 0	13 01	Edinburgh	1 2 84	Scholar
Forlan Diego (F)	5 8	11 11	Montevideo	19 5 79	Independiente
Fortune Quinton (F)	5 9	11 09	Cape Town	21 5 77	Atletico Madrid B
Fox David (M)	5 9	12 02	Stoke	13 12 83	Scholar
Giggs Ryan (F)	5 11	11 00	Cardiff	29 11 73	School
Heath Colin (F)	6 0	13 01	Chesterfield	31 12 83	Scholar
Hilton Kirk (D)	5 7	10 01	Flixton	2 4 81	Trainee
Humphreys Chris (F)	5 9	13 05	Manchester	22 9 83	Scholar
Johnson Eddie (F)	5 10	13 05	Chester	20 9 84	Scholar
Jowsey James (G)	6 0	12 04	Scarborough	24 11 83	Scholar
Keane Roy (M)	5 11	11 10	Cork	10 8 71	Nottingham F
Lynch Mark (D)	5 11	11 03	Manchester	2 9 81	Trainee
May David (D)	6 0	13 05	Oldham	24 6 70	Blackburn R
Mooniaruck Kalam (F)	5 8	11 09	Yeovil	22 11 83	Scholar
Muirhead Ben (F)	5 9	10 05	Doncaster	5 1 83	Trainee
Nardiello Daniel (F)	5 11	11 04	Coventry	22 10 82	Trainee
Neville Gary (D)	5 11	12 04	Bury	18 2 75	Trainee
Neville Phil (D)	5 11	12 00	Bury	21 1 77	Trainee
O'Shea John (D)	6 3	12 10	Waterford	30 4 81	Waterford
Pugh Danny (M)	6 0	12 10	Manchester	19 10 82	Scholar
Rankin John (M)	5 8	12 08	Bellshill	27 6 83	Scholar
Roche Lee (D)	5 10	10 10	Bolton	28 10 80	Trainee
Scholes Paul (M)	5 7	11 00	Salford	16 11 74	Trainee
Silvestre Mikael (D)	6 0	13 01	Chambray les Tours	9 8 77	Internazionale
Solskjaer Ole Gunnar (F)	5 10	11 11	Kristiansund	26 2 73	Molde
Steele Luke (G)	6 2	12 00	Peterborough	24 9 84	Scholar
Stewart Michael (M)	5 11	11 11	Edinburgh	26 2 81	Trainee
Tate Alan (D)	6 1	13 05	Easington	2 9 82	Scholar
Taylor Kris (M)	5 9	13 05	Stafford	12 1 84	Scholar
Tierney Paul (M)	5 10	12 10	Salford	15 9 82	Scholar
Timm Mads (F)	5 9	12 10	Odense	31 10 84	Scholar
Van Nistelrooy Ruud (F)	6 2	12 13	Oss	1 7 76	PSV Eindhoven
Veron Juan Sebastian (F)	6 1	12 08	Buenos Aires	9 3 75	Lazio
Wallwork Ronnie (D)	5 10	13 01	Manchester	10 9 77	Trainee
Webber Danny (F)	5 9	10 08	Manchester	28 12 81	Trainee
Williams Ben (G)	6 0	13 01	Manchester	27 8 82	Scholar
Williams Matthew (F)	5 8	9 11	St Asaph	5 11 82	
Wood Neil (F)	5 10	13 02	Manchester	4 1 83	Trainee
Yorke Dwight (F)	5 10	12 03	Canaan	3 11 71	Aston Villa

League Appearances: Barthez, F. 32; Beckham, D. 23(5); Blanc, L. 29; Brown, W. 15(2); Butt, N. 20(5); Carroll, R. 6(1); Chadwick, L. 5(3); Cole, A. 7(4); Forlan, D. 6(7); Fortune, Q. 8(6); Giggs, R. 18(7); Irwin, D. 10(2); Johnsen, R. 9(1); Keane, R. 28; May, D. 2; Neville, G. 31(3); Neville, P. 21(7); O'Shea, J. 4(5); Scholes, P. 30(5); Silvestre, M. 31(4); Solskjaer, O. 23(7); Stam, J. 1; Stewart, M. 2(1); Van Nistelrooy, R. 29(3); Van der Gouw, R. (1); Veron, J. 24(2); Wallwork, R. (1); Yorke, D. 4(6).

Goals – League (87): Van Nistelrooy 23 (4 pens), Solskjaer 17, Beckham 11 (1 pen), Scholes 8, Giggs 7, Veron 5, Cole 4, Keane 3, Neville P 2, Blanc 1, Butt 1, Fortune 1, Johnsen 1, Yorke 1, own goals 2.

Worthington Cup (0).

FA Cup (3): Van Nistelrooy 2, Solskjaer 1.

Ground: Old Trafford, Sir Matt Busby Way, Manchester M16 0RA. Telephone (0161) 868 8000.

Record attendance: 76,962 Wolverhampton W v Grimsby T, FA Cup semi-final. 25 March 1939. **Capacity:** 68,210.
Manager: Sir Alex Ferguson CBE.
Secretary: Kenneth Merrett.
Most League Goals: 103, Division 1, 1956–57 and 1958–59.
Highest League Scorer in Season: Dennis Viollet, 32, 1959–60.
Most League Goals in Total Aggregate: Bobby Charlton, 199, 1956–73.
Most Capped Player: Bobby Charlton, 106, England.
Most League Appearances: Bobby Charlton, 606, 1956–73.
Honours – FA Premier League: Champions – 1992–93, 1993–94, 1995–96, 1996–97, 1998–99, 1999–2000, 2000–01. **Football League:** Division 1 Champions – 1907–8, 1910–11, 1951–52, 1955–56, 1956–57, 1964–65, 1966–67. Division 2 Champions – 1935–36, 1974–75. **FA Cup winners** 1909, 1948, 1963, 1977, 1983, 1985, 1990, 1994, 1996, 1999. **Football League Cup winners** 1991–92. **European Competitions: European Cup winners:** 1967–68, 1998–99. **European Cup-Winners' Cup winners:** 1990–91. **Super Cup winners:** 1991. **Inter-Continental Cup winners:** 1999.
Colours: Red shirts, white shorts, black stockings.

MANSFIELD TOWN   DIV. 2

Bacon Danny (F)	5 10	10 12	Mansfield	20 9 80	Trainee
Bingham Michael (G)	6 0	12 07	Preston	21 5 81	Blackburn R
Bradley Shayne (F)	5 11	13 02	Gloucester	8 12 79	Southampton
Disley Craig (M)	5 10	11 00	Worksop	24 8 81	Trainee
Hassell Bobby (D)	5 9	12 06	Derby	4 6 80	Trainee
Jervis David (D)	5 10	11 00	Worksop	18 1 82	Trainee
Lawrence Liam (M)	5 10	11 03	Retford	14 12 81	Trainee
Pilkington Kevin (G)	6 1	13 00	Hitchin	8 3 74	Wigan Ath
Reddington Stuart (D)	6 4	13 07	Lincoln	21 2 78	Chelsea
Robinson Les (D)	5 9	12 04	Shirebrook	1 3 67	Oxford U
Sisson Michael (M)	5 9	10 10	Sutton-in-Ashfield	24 11 78	Trainee
White Andy (F)	6 4	14 03	Derby	6 11 81	Hucknall T
Williamson Lee (M)	5 10	10 04	Derby	7 6 82	Trainee

League Appearances: Asher, A. 1(9); Bacon, D. 1(7); Barrett, A. 26(3); Bingham, M. 1(1); Bradley, S. 7(9); Clarke, J. 1; Corden, W. 46; Disley, C. 31(5); Greenacre, C. 43(1); Harris, R. (6); Hassell, B. 43; Jervis, D. (3); Kelly, D. 11(6); Lawrence, L. 32; Murray, A. 13; Pemberton, M. 33(5); Pilkington, K. 45; Piper, M. 8; Reddington, S. 34(4); Robinson, L. 36; Sellars, S. 5(1); Tankard, A. 22(8); Wheatcroft, P. 1(1); White, A. 16(6); White, J. 6(1); Williams, L. (2); Williamson, L. 44(2).
Goals – League (72): Greenacre 21, Corden 8 (2 pens), Disley 7, Murray 7, Kelly 4, Pemberton 4, White A 4, Bradley 3, Williamson 3, Lawrence 2, Tankard 2, Bacon 1, Hassell 1, Piper 1, Reddington 1, Sellars 1, own goals 2.
Worthington Cup (3): Greenacre 2, White 1.
FA Cup (6): Greenacre 5, Corden 1.
Ground: Field Mill Ground, Quarry Lane, Mansfield NG18 5DA. Telephone (0870) 756 3160.
Record attendance: 24,467 v Nottingham F, FA Cup 3rd rd, 10 January 1953.
Capacity: 9990.
Manager: Stuart Watkiss.
Secretary: Christine Reynolds.
Most League Goals: 108, Division 4, 1962–63.
Highest League Scorer in Season: Ted Harston, 55, Division 3 (N), 1936–37.
Most League Goals in Total Aggregate: Harry Johnson, 104, 1931–36.
Most Capped Player: John McClelland, 6 (53), Northern Ireland.
Most League Appearances: Rod Arnold, 440, 1970–83.

Honours – Football League: Division 3 Champions – 1976–77. Division 4 Champions – 1974–75. Freight Rover Trophy winners 1986–87.
Colours: Amber shirts with royal blue trim, royal blue shorts with amber trim, amber stockings with blue trim.

MIDDLESBROUGH   FA PREMIERSHIP

Bernhardt Arthur (F)	6 1	12 00	Santa Catarina	27 8 82	Nova Hamburgo
Boksic Alen (F)	6 1	14 01	Niakarska	21 1 70	Lazio
Cade Jamie (F)	5 8	10 10	Durham	15 1 84	Scholar
Close Brian (D)	5 10	12 03	Belfast	27 1 82	
Cooper Colin (D)	5 11	11 11	Sedgefield	28 2 67	Nottingham F
Crossley Mark (G)	6 0	15 09	Barnsley	16 6 69	Nottingham F
Dove Craig (M)	5 8	11 00	Hartlepool	6 8 83	Scholar
Downing Stewart (M)	6 0	11 00	Middlesbrough	22 7 84	Scholar
Ehiogu Ugo (D)	6 2	14 10	Hackney	3 11 72	Aston Villa
Festa Gianluca (D)	5 11	13 00	Cagliari	15 3 69	Internazionale
Gavin Jason (D)	6 0	11 12	Dublin	14 3 80	Trainee
Gilroy Keith (M)	5 10	10 13	Sligo	8 7 83	
Greening Jonathan (M)	6 0	11 13	Scarborough	2 1 79	Manchester U
Gulliver Philip (D)	6 2	13 05	Bishop Auckland	12 9 82	Scholar
Hudson Mark (M)	5 10	11 03	Bishop Auckland	24 10 80	Trainee
Job Joseph-Desire (F)	5 11	11 00	Venissieux	1 12 77	Lens
Johnston Allan (M)	5 10	11 12	Glasgow	14 12 73	Rangers
Jones Brad	6.3	11 07	Armadale	19 3 82	Trainee
Marinelli Carlos (M)	5 8	11 06	Buenos Aires	4 3 82	Boca Juniors
Murphy David (D)	6 1	12 03	Hartlepool	1 3 84	Scholar
Nemeth Szilard (F)	5 11	11 04	Komarno	8 8 77	Inter Bratislava
Parnaby Stuart (M)	5 11	11 00	Durham City	19 7 82	Trainee
Queudrue Franck (D)	6 1	12 07	Paris	27 8 78	Lens
Russell Sam (G)	6 0	10 13	Middlesbrough	4 10 82	Scholar
Schwarzer Mark (G)	6 5	15 01	Sydney	6 10 72	Bradford C
Southgate Gareth (D)	6 0	12 03	Watford	3 9 70	Aston Villa
Stamp Phil (M)	5 11	14 09	Middlesbrough	12 12 75	Trainee
Stockdale Robbie (D)	6 0	12 03	Redcar	30 11 79	Trainee
Summerbell Mark (M)	5 9	11 01	Durham	30 10 76	Trainee
Whelan Noel (F)	6 2	12 03	Leeds	30 12 74	Coventry C
Wilkshire Luke (M)	5 8	11 00	Wollongong	2 10 81	
Wilson Mark (M)	5 10	12 07	Scunthorpe	9 2 79	Manchester U
Windass Dean (F)	5 10	12 06	North Ferriby	1 4 69	Bradford C

League Appearances: Beresford, M. (1); Boksic, A. 20(2); Campbell, A. (4); Carbone, B. 13; Cooper, C. 14(4); Crossley, M. 17(1); Deane, B. 6(1); Debeve, M. 1(3); Downing, S. 2(1); Ehiogu, U. 29; Festa, G. 8; Fleming, C. 8; Gavin, J. 5(4); Gordon, D. (1); Greening, J. 36; Hudson, M. (2); Ince, P. 31; Job, J. 3(1); Johnston, A. 13(4); Marinelli, C. 12(8); Murphy, D. (5); Mustoe, R. 31(5); Nemeth, S. 11(10); Okon, P. 1(3); Queudrue, F. 28; Ricard, H. 6(3); Schwarzer, M. 21; Southgate, G. 37; Stamp, P. 3(3); Stockdale, R. 26(2); Vickers, S. 2; Whelan, N. 18(1); Wilkshire, L. 6(1); Wilson, M. 2(8); Windass, D. 8(19).
Goals – League (35): Boksic 8 (2 pens), Whelan 4, Nemeth 3, Cooper 2, Ince 2, Marinelli 2, Mustoe 2, Queudrue 2, Carbone 1, Deane 1, Ehiogu 1, Festa 1, Greening 1, Johnston 1, Southgate 1, Stockdale 1, Windass 1, own goal 1.
Worthington Cup (4): Nemeth 2, Murphy 1, Wilson 1.
FA Cup (8): Whelan 3, Campbell 1, Ehiogu 1, Ince 1, Nemeth 1, own goal 1.
Ground: Riverside Stadium, Middlesbrough, Cleveland TS3 6RS. Telephone (01642) 877700
Record attendance: 53,596 v Newcastle U, Division 1, 27 December 1949 (at Ayresome Park) and 34,800 v Leeds U, Premier League, 26 February 2000.

Capacity: 35,049.
Manager: Steve McClaren.
Secretary: Karen Nelson.
Most League Goals: 122, Division 2, 1926–27.
Highest League Scorer in Season: George Camsell, 59, Division 2, 1926–27 (Second Division record).
Most League Goals in Total Aggregate: George Camsell, 325, 1925–39.
Most Capped Player: Wilf Mannion, 26, England.
Most League Appearances: Tim Williamson, 563, 1902–23.
Honours – Football League: Division 1 Champions 1994–95. Division 2 Champions 1926–27, 1928–29, 1973–74. Amateur Cup winners 1895, 1898, Anglo-Scottish Cup: Winners 1975–76.
Colours: All red with white facing.

MILLWALL   DIV. 1

Booth Stuart (M)	5 11	11 11	Roehampton	7 12 83	School
Braniff Kevin (F)	5 11	10 03	Belfast	4 3 83	Scholar
Bull Ronnie (D)	5 7	10 10	Hackney	26 12 80	Trainee
Cahill Tim (M)	5 10	10 10	Sydney	6 12 79	Sydney U
Claridge Steve (F)	6 0	12 07	Portsmouth	10 4 66	Portsmouth
Cogan Barry (M)	5 9	9 0	Sligo	4 11 84	Scholar
Dolan Joe (D)	6 3	13 02	Harrow	27 5 80	Chelsea
Dunne Alan (D)	5 10	10 13	Dublin	23 8 82	Scholar
Elliott Marvin (M)			Wandsworth	15 9 84	Scholar
Gueret Willy (G)	6 1	13 05	Saint Claude	3 8 73	
Harpur Chad (G)	5 10	12 11	Johannesburg	3 9 82	
Harris Neil (F)	5 11	12 00	Orsett	12 7 77	Cambridge C
Hearn Charley (M)	5 10	12 00	Ashford	5 11 83	School
Ifill Paul (M)	6 0	12 01	Brighton	20 10 79	Trainee
Kinet Christophe (M)	5 8	10 12	Huy	31 12 74	Strasbourg
Lambu Goma (M)	5 3	9 0	London	10 11 84	Scholar
Lawrence Matthew (D)	6 1	12 08	Northampton	19 6 74	Wycombe W
Livermore David (M)	5 11	12 03	Edmonton	20 5 80	Trainee
May Ben (F)	6 1	12 06	Gravesend	10 3 84	
Nethercott Stuart (D)	6 1	13 08	Ilford	21 3 73	Tottenham H
Odunsi Leke (M)	5 9	11 07	Walworth	5 12 80	Trainee
Phillips Mark (D)	6 1	11 00	Lambeth	27 1 82	Scholar
Rees Matthew (M)	6 2	12 00	Swansea	2 9 82	Trainee
Reid Steven (M)	6 0	12 02	Kingston	10 3 81	Trainee
Robinson Paul (D)	6 1	11 09	Barnet	7 1 82	Scholar
Ryan Robbie (D)	5 10	12 01	Dublin	16 5 77	Huddersfield T
Sadlier Richard (F)	6 2	13 02	Dublin	14 1 79	Belvedere
Samba Cherno (M)	5 10	10 01	Gambia	10 1 85	Scholar
Sweeney Peter (F)	6 0	12 01	Glasgow	25 9 84	Scholar
Tuttle David (D)	6 2	15 00	Reading	6 2 72	Barnsley
Ward Darren (D)	6 4	11 04	Kenton	13 9 78	Watford
Warner Tony (G)	6 4	15 07	Liverpool	11 5 74	Liverpool

League Appearances: Bircham, M. 22(2); Braniff, K. (1); Bull, R. 20(6); Cahill, T. 43; Claridge, S. 39(2); Dublin, D. 5; Dunne, A. (1); Dyche, S. 35; Green, R. 12(1); Gueret, W. (1); Harris, N. 9(12); Hearn, C. (2); Ifill, P. 27(13); Kinet, C. 11(6); Lawrence, M. 24(2); Livermore, D. 43; McPhail, S. 3; Moody, P. (1); Naylor, R. 2(1); Neill, L. 2(1); Nethercott, S. 46; Odunsi, L. (2); Phillips, M. 1; Reid, S. 33(2); Ryan, R. 32(5); Sadlier, R. 36(1); Savarese, G. (1); Stamp, P. (1); Sweeney, P. (1); Tuttle, D. 5; Ward, D. 10(4); Warner, T. 46.
Goals – League (69): Claridge 17 (4 pens), Sadlier 14, Cahill 13, Reid 5, Harris 4 (1 pen), Ifill 4, Dyche 3, Kinet 3, Nethercott 3, Dublin 2, Neill 1.

Worthington Cup (3): Claridge 1 (pen), Moody 1, Sadlier 1.
FA Cup (2): Sadlier 2.
Ground: The Den, Zampa Road, Bermondsey SE16 3LN. Telephone (020) 7232 1222.
Record attendance: 20,093 v Arsenal, FA Cup 3rd rd, 10 January 1994. **Capacity:** 20,146.
Manager: Mark McGhee.
Secretary: Yvonne Haines.
Most League Goals: 127, Division 3 (S), 1927–28.
Highest League Scorer in Season: Richard Parker, 37, Division 3 (S), 1926–27.
Most League Goals in Total Aggregate: Teddy Sheringham, 93, 1984–91.
Most Capped Player: Eamonn Dunphy, 22 (23), Republic of Ireland.
Most League Appearances: Barry Kitchener, 523, 1967–82.
Honours – Football League: Division 2 Champions – 1987–88, 2000–01. Division 3 (S) Champions – 1927–28, 1937–38. Division 4 Champions – 1961–62. **Football League Trophy winners** 1982–83.
Colours: Blue shirts, white shorts.

NEWCASTLE UNITED   FA PREMIERSHIP

Acuna Clarence (M)	5 10	12 00	Rancagua	8	2 75	Univ de Chile
Ameobi Foluwashola (F)	6 3	12 03	Zaria	12 10 81		Trainee
Bassedas Christian (M)	5 8	11 09	Buenos Aires	16	2 73	Velez Sarsfield
Beaumont James (M)	5 7	10 10	Stockton	11 12 84		Scholar
Bellamy Craig (F)	5 10	11 00	Cardiff	13	7 79	Coventry C
Bernard Olivier (D)	5 7	10 11	Lyon	14 10 79		
Brennan Stephen (D)	5 8	11 10	Dublin	26	3 83	
Caldwell Gary (D)	5 11	11 10	Stirling	12	4 82	Trainee
Caldwell Steven (D)	6 0	11 05	Stirling	12	9 80	Trainee
Chopra Michael (F)	5 8	9 06	Newcastle	23 12 83		Scholar
Colley Karl (D)	6 1	12 06	Sheffield	13 10 83		Sheffield W
Coppinger James (F)	5 7	10 03	Middlesbrough	18	1 81	Darlington
Cort Carl (F)	6 4	12 07	Southwark	1 11 77		Wimbledon
Dabizas Nikos (D)	6 1	12 07	Amindeo	3	8 73	Olympiakos
Distin Sylvain (D)	6 3	13 12	Bagnolet	16 12 77		Paris St Germain
Dyer Kieron (M)	5 7	9 07	Ipswich	29 12 78		Ipswich T
Elliott Robbie (D)	5 8	12 03	Gosforth	25 12 73		Bolton W
Gardner Ross (M)	5 8	10 06	South Shields	15 12 85		Scholar
Gavilan Diego (M)	5 8	10 07	Asuncion	1	3 80	Cerro Porteno
Given Shay (G)	6 1	13 04	Lifford	20	4 76	Blackburn R
Green Stuart (M)	5 10	11 00	Carlisle	15	6 81	Trainee
Griffin Andy (D)	5 9	10 10	Billinge	7	3 79	Stoke C
Harper Steve (G)	6 2	13 00	Easington	14	3 75	Seaham Red Star
Hogg Ryan (D)	6 2	13 00	Ashington	20 11 82		Scholar
Hughes Aaron (D)	6 1	11 02	Cookstown	8 11 79		Trainee
Jenas Jermaine (M)	5 10	12 00	Nottingham	18	2 83	Nottingham F
Karelse John (G)	6 3	13 07	Kapelle	17	5 70	NAC Breda
Kendrick Joseph (D)	6 0	11 05	Dublin	26	6 83	Scholar
Kerr Brian (M)	5 10	10 11	Motherwell	12 10 81		Trainee
Lua-Lua Lomano (F)	5 8	12 00	Kinshasa	28 12 80		Colchester U
Makongo Calvin (F)	6 1	12 00	Kinshasha	31 12 84		Scholar
Marcelino Elena (D)	6 2	13 00	Gijon	26	9 71	Mallorca
McClen Jamie (M)	5 8	10 07	Newcastle	13	5 79	Trainee
McDermott Neale (M)	5 9	10 11	Newcastle	8	3 85	Scholar
O'Brien Alan (M)	5 9	11 00	Dublin	20	2 85	Scholar
O'Brien Andy (D)	6 3	11 05	Harrogate	29	6 79	Bradford C
Offiong Richard (F)	5 11	12 00	South Shields	17 12 83		Scholar
Orr Bradley (M)	6 0	11 11	Liverpool	1 11 82		Scholar

Quinn Wayne (D)	5 10	11 12	Truro	19 11 76	Sheffield U
Robert Laurent (F)	5 8	10 13	Saint-Benoit	21 5 75	Paris St Germain
Robson Damon (M)	5 7	13 06	Co Durham	19 9 83	Scholar
Shearer Alan (F)	6 0	12 06	Newcastle	13 8 70	Blackburn R
Solano Nolberto (M)	5 9	11 02	Callao	12 12 74	Boca Juniors
Speed Gary (M)	5 10	10 12	Deeside	8 9 69	Everton

League Appearances: Acuna, C. 10(6); Ameobi, F. 4(11); Barton, W. 4(1); Bassedas, C. 1(1); Bellamy, C. 26(1); Bernard, O. 4(12); Cort, C. 6(2); Dabizas, N. 33(2); Distin, S. 20(8); Dyer, K. 15(3); Elliott, R. 26(1); Given, S. 38; Griffin, A. 3(1); Hughes, A. 34; Jenas, J. 6(6); Lee, R. 15(1); Lua-Lua, L. 4(16); McClen, J. 3; O'Brien, A. 31(3); Robert, L. 34(2); Shearer, A. 36(1); Solano, N. 37; Speed, G. 28(1).

Goals – League (74): Shearer 23 (5 pens), Bellamy 9, Robert 8, Solano 7, Speed 5, Acuna 3, Bernard 3, Dabizas 3, Dyer 3, Lua-Lua 3, O'Brien 2, Cort 1, Elliott 1, Lee 1, own goals 2.

Worthington Cup (9): Bellamy 4, Ameobi 2, Shearer 2, Robert 1.
FA Cup (8): Shearer 2 (1 pen), Acuna 1, Hughes 1, McClen 1, O'Brien 1, Robert 1, Solano 1.
Ground: St James' Park, Newcastle-upon-Tyne NE1 4ST. Telephone (0191) 201 8400.
Record attendance: 68,386 v Chelsea, Division 1, 3 Sept 1930. **Capacity:** 52,193.
Manager: Sir Bobby Robson CBE.
Secretary: Russell Cushing.
Most League Goals: 98, Division 1, 1951–52.
Highest League Scorer in Season: Hughie Gallacher, 36, Division 1, 1926–27.
Most League Goals in Total Aggregate: Jackie Milburn, 177, 1946–57.
Most Capped Player: Alf McMichael, 40, Northern Ireland.
Most League Appearances: Jim Lawrence, 432, 1904–22.
Honours – Football League: Division 1 – Champions 1904–05, 1906–07, 1908–09, 1926–27, 1992–93. Division 2 Champions – 1964–65. **FA Cup winners** 1910, 1924, 1932, 1951, 1952, 1955. **Texaco Cup winners** 1973–74, 1974–75. **European Competitions:** European Fairs Cup winners: 1968–69. **Anglo-Italian Cup winners:** 1973.
Colours: Black and white striped shirts, black shorts and stockings.

NORTHAMPTON TOWN   DIV. 2

Asamoah Derek (F)	5 6	10 04	Ghana	1 5 81	Slough T
Burgess Daryl (D)	5 11	11 04	Birmingham	24 1 71	WBA
Carruthers Chris (M)	6 1	12 03	Kettering	19 8 83	Scholar
Forrester Jamie (F)	5 6	11 00	Bradford	1 11 74	Walsall
Frain John (D)	5 10	12 04	Birmingham	8 10 68	Birmingham C
Gabbiadini Marco (F)	5 10	13 04	Nottingham	20 1 68	Darlington
Hope Richard (D)	6 3	13 05	Middlesbrough	22 6 78	Darlington
Lavin Gerard (D)	5 10	11 10	Corby	5 2 74	Bristol C
Marsh Chris (D)	5 11	13 02	Sedgley	14 1 70	Wycombe W
McGregor Paul (M)	5 10	11 06	Liverpool	17 12 74	Plymouth Arg
Spedding Duncan (D)	6 2	11 01	Frimley	7 9 77	Southampton

League Appearances: Asamoah, D. 3(37); Burgess, D. 36; Carruthers, C. 6(7); Cavill, A. (1); Dempsey, P. 13(7); Evatt, I. 10(1); Forrester, J. 40(3); Frain, J. 25(2); Gabbiadini, M. 30(5); Hargreaves, C. 38(1); Hodge, J. 4(15); Hope, R. 35(8); Hunt, J. 38; Hunter, R. 38(2); Lavin, G. 2; Marsh, C. 26; McGregor, P. 37(2); Morison, S. (1); Parkin, S. 31(9); Sampson, I. 24(3); Sollitt, A. 8(2); Spedding, D. 22(1); Welch, K. 38; Wolleaston, R. 2(5).

Goals – League (54): Forrester 17 (6 pens), Gabbiadini 7, Hope 6, Hunt 4, Hunter 4 (2 pens), Parkin 4, Asamoah 3, Hargreaves 3, McGregor 3, Burgess 1, Carruthers

1, Hodge 1.
Worthington Cup (3): Forrester 1, McGregor 1, Parkin 1.
FA Cup (2): Gabbiadini 2.
Ground: Sixfields Stadium, Upton Way, Northampton NN5 5QA. Telephone (01604) 757773.
Record attendance: 24,523 v Fulham, Division 1, 23 April 1966. **Capacity:** 7653.
Manager: Kevan Broadhurst.
Secretary: Norman Howells.
Most League Goals: 109, Division 3, 1962–63 and Division 3 (S), 1952–53.
Highest League Scorer in Season: Cliff Holton, 36, Division 3, 1961–62.
Most League Goals in Total Aggregate: Jack English, 135, 1947–60.
Most Capped Player: E. Lloyd Davies, 12 (16), Wales.
Most League Appearances: Tommy Fowler, 521, 1946–61.
Honours – Football League: Division 3 Champions – 1962–63. Division 4 Champions – 1986–87.
Colours: Claret shirts with thin white piping, white shorts, claret stockings.

NORWICH CITY   DIV. 1

Abbey Zema (F)	6 1	12 09	Luton	17 4 77	Cambridge U
Crichton Paul (G)	6 1	13 05	Pontefract	3 10 68	Burnley
Drury Adam (D)	5 10	11 06	Cottenham	29 8 78	Peterborough U
Easton Clint (M)	5 11	10 09	Barking	1 11 77	Watford
Emblen Neil (M)	6 1	13 08	Bromley	19 6 71	Wolverhampton W
Fleming Craig (D)	5 11	12 09	Halifax	6 10 71	Oldham Ath
Green Robert (G)	6 3	13 00	Chertsey	18 1 80	Trainee
Holt Gary (M)	6 1	11 13	Irvine	9 3 73	Kilmarnock
Kenton Darren (D)	5 11	12 00	Wandsworth	13 9 78	Trainee
Libbra Marc (F)	6 2	12 06	Toulon	5 8 72	Hibernian
Llewellyn Chris (M)	6 0	11 10	Merthyr	29 8 79	Trainee
MacKay Malky (D)	6 3	13 01	Bellshill	19 2 72	Celtic
McGovern Brian (D)	6 3	12 07	Dublin	28 4 80	Arsenal
McVeigh Paul (M)	5 6	10 07	Belfast	6 12 77	Tottenham H
Nedergaard Steen (M)	6 1	11 11	Odense	25 2 70	Odense
Nielsen David (F)	6 0	12 00	Sonderborg	1 12 76	Wimbledon
Notman Alex (F)	5 7	10 13	Edinburgh	10 12 79	Manchester U
Rivers Mark (F)	5 10	11 00	Crewe	26 11 75	Crewe Alex
Roberts Iwan (F)	6 3	13 01	Bangor	26 6 68	Wolverhampton W
Russell Darel (M)	6 0	12 04	Mile End	22 10 80	Trainee
Sutch Daryl (D)	5 11	12 05	Lowestoft	11 9 71	Trainee

League Appearances: Abbey, Z. 6; Benjamin, T. 3(3); Crichton, P. 5(1); Drury, A. 35; Easton, C. 10(4); Emblen, N. 1(1); Fleming, C. 46; Green, R. 41; Holt, G. 46; Kenton, D. 30(3); Libbra, M. 17(17); Llewellyn, C. 5(8); MacKay, M. 44; McGovern, B. 5(4); McVeigh, P. 37(5); Mulryne, P. 39(1); Nedergaard, S. 37(3); Nielsen, D. 22(1); Notman, A. 6(24); Rivers, M. 19(13); Roberts, A. 4(1); Roberts, I. 29(1); Russell, D. 13(10); Sutch, D. 6(13).
Goals – League (60): Roberts I 13 (2 pens), McVeigh 8, Nielsen 8, Libbra 7, Mulryne 6, Kenton 4, MacKay 3, Holt 2, Nedergaard 2, Rivers 2, Abbey 1, Easton 1, own goals 3.
Worthington Cup (0).
FA Cup (0).
Ground: Carrow Road, Norwich NR1 1JE. Telephone (01603) 760760.
Record attendance: 43,984 v Leicester C, FA Cup 6th rd, 30 March 1963. **Capacity:** 21,468.
Manager: Nigel Worthington.
Secretary: Kevan Platt.
Most League Goals: 99, Division 3 (S), 1952–53.

Highest League Scorer in Season: Ralph Hunt, 31, Division 3 (S), 1955–56.
Most League Goals in Total Aggregate: Johnny Gavin, 122, 1945–54, 1955–58.
Most Capped Player: Mark Bowen, 35 (41), Wales.
Most League Appearances: Ron Ashman, 592, 1947–64.
Honours – Football League: Division 2 Champions – 1971–72, 1985–86. Division 3
(S) Champions – 1933–34. **Football League Cup:** Winners 1962, 1985.
Colours: Yellow shirts, green shorts, yellow stockings.

NOTTINGHAM FOREST   DIV. 1

Antoine-Curier Mickael (F)	6 0	12 00	Orsay	5 3 83	
Birch Jay (F)			Barnsley	23 11 83	Scholar
Bopp Eugene (M)	5 11	12 03	Kiev	5 9 83	Bayern Munich
Brennan Jim (D)	5 11	13 01	Toronto	8 5 77	Bristol C
Cash Brian (M)	5 9	11 01	Dublin	24 11 82	Trainee
Dawson Michael (D)	6 2	12 02	Northallerton	18 11 83	School
Doig Chris (D)	6 2	13 07	Dumfries	13 2 81	Trainee
Edwards Christian (D)	6 2	12 03	Caerphilly	23 11 75	Swansea C
Formann Pascal (G)	6 1	11 07	Werne	16 11 82	
Foy Keith (D)	5 10	13 01	Crumlin	30 12 81	Trainee
Harewood Marlon (F)	6 1	13 07	Hampstead	25 8 79	Trainee
Haskins Andy (M)			York	30 4 84	School
Hjelde Jon Olav (D)	6 3	13 07	Levanger	30 7 72	Rosenborg
Jeffrey Richard (F)	5 9	11 00	Derby	4 11 83	Scholar
Johnson David (F)	5 6	12 00	Kingston, Jamaica	15 8 76	Ipswich T
Jones Gary (F)	6 3	14 07	Chester	10 5 75	Tranmere R
Kearney Liam (M)	5 7	10 12	Dublin	10 1 83	Scholar
Lester Jack (F)	5 11	11 06	Sheffield	8 10 75	Grimsby T
Louis-Jean Mathieu (D)	5 9	11 03	Mont-St-Aignan	22 2 76	Le Havre
Peyton Emmet (G)			Castlebar	26 10 83	
Prutton David (M)	6 0	12 00	Hull	12 9 81	Trainee
Reid Andrew (G)			Aberdeen	3 6 85	Scholar
Reid Andy (F)	5 8	11 02	Dublin	29 7 82	Trainee
Robertson Gregor (D)			Edinburgh	19 1 84	
Roche Barry (G)	6 5	14 00	Dublin	6 4 82	Trainee
Scimeca Riccardo (D)	6 1	13 05	Leamington Spa	13 6 75	Aston Villa
Thompson John (D)	6 0	12 01	Dublin	12 10 81	
Tynan Scott (M)			Knowsley	27 11 83	Wigan Ath
Vaughan Tony (D)	6 1	13 04	Manchester	11 10 75	Manchester C
Ward Darren (G)	6 0	13 02	Worksop	11 5 74	Notts Co
Webb Steven (M)			Macclesfield	13 9 84	Academy
Westcarr Craig (F)	5 11	11 04	Nottingham	29 1 85	Scholar
Williams Gareth (M)	6 1	12 03	Glasgow	16 12 81	Trainee

League Appearances: Bart-Williams, C. 17; Bopp, E. 12(7); Brennan, J. 41; Cash,
B. (5); Dawson, K. 3; Dawson, M. 1; Doig, C. 8; Edds, G. (1); Edwards, C. 2(4);
Foy, K. 2; Gray, A. 8(8); Harewood, M. 20(8); Hjelde, J. 42; Jenas, J. 28; John, S.
20(6); Johnson, A. (1); Johnson, D. 17(5); Jones, G. 2(3); Lester, J. 23(9); Louis-
Jean, M. 37(1); Proudlock, A. 3; Prutton, D. 43; Reid, A. 19(10); Rogers, A. 3;
Scimeca, R. 35(2); Summerbee, N. 17; Thompson, J. 8; Vaughan, T. 5(3); Ward, D.
46; Westcarr, C. (8); Williams, G. 44.
Goals – League (50): John 13 (1 pen), Harewood 11 (3 pens), Lester 5, Jenas 4 (1
pen), Bart-Williams 3 (1 pen), Johnson D 3, Prutton 3, Summerbee 2, Bopp 1,
Doig 1, Gray 1, Jones 1, Louis-Jean 1, own goal 1.
Worthington Cup (3): Bart-Williams 1, John 1, Lester 1.
FA Cup (0).
Ground: City Ground, Nottingham NG2 5FJ. Telephone (0115) 9824444.

Record attendance: 49,945 v Manchester U, Division 1, 28 October 1967. **Capacity:** 30,602.
Manager: Paul Hart.
Secretary: Paul White.
Most League Goals: 110, Division 3 (S), 1950–51.
Highest League Scorer in Season: Wally Ardron, 36, Division 3 (S), 1950–51.
Most League Goals in Total Aggregate: Grenville Morris, 199, 1898–1913.
Most Capped Player: Stuart Pearce, 76 (78), England.
Most League Appearances: Bob McKinlay, 614, 1951–70.
Honours – Football League: Division 1 – Champions 1977–78, 1997–98. Division 2 Champions – 1906–07, 1921–22. Division 3 (S) Champions – 1950–51. **FA Cup:** Winners 1898, 1959. **Football League Cup:** Winners 1977–78, 1978–79, 1988–89, 1989–90. **Anglo-Scottish Cup:** Winners 1976–77. **Simod Cup:** Winners 1989. **Zenith Data Systems Cup:** Winners 1991–92. **European Competitions: European Cup winners:** 1978–79, 1979–80. **Super Cup winners:** 1979–80.
Colours: Red shirts, white shorts, red stockings.

NOTTS COUNTY   DIV. 2

Allsopp Danny (F)	6 1	14 00	Melbourne	10 8 78	Manchester C
Baraclough Ian (D)	6 1	12 11	Leicester	4 12 70	QPR
Bolland Paul (M)	5 11	12 10	Bradford	23 12 79	Bradford C
Brough Michael (M)	6 0	12 05	Nottingham	1 8 81	Trainee
Cas Marcel (M)	6 1	12 10	Breda	30 4 72	RBC
Caskey Darren (M)	5 8	12 04	Basildon	21 8 74	Reading
Deeney Saul (G)	6 1	12 07	Londonderry	12 3 83	Scholar
Fenton Nick (D)	6 0	12 04	Preston	23 11 79	Manchester C
Garden Stuart (G)	6 0	12 06	Dundee	10 2 72	
Hackworth Tony (F)	6 1	13 07	Durham	19 5 80	Leeds U
Heffernan Paul (F)	5 10	11 05	Dublin	29 12 81	Newton
Holmes Richard (D)	5 11	11 08	Grantham	7 11 80	Trainee
Ireland Craig (D)	6 3	13 09	Dundee	29 11 75	Airdrieonians
Liburd Richard (D)	5 9	11 08	Nottingham	26 9 73	Carlisle U
Mildenhall Steve (G)	6 4	15 01	Swindon	13 5 78	Swindon T
Nicholson Kevin (M)	5 8	12 01	Derby	2 10 80	Northampton T
Riley Paul (D)	5 9	10 07	Nottingham	29 9 82	Scholar
Stallard Mark (F)	6 0	13 09	Derby	24 10 74	Wycombe W
Stone Danny (D)	6 0	12 03	Liverpool	14 9 82	Blackburn R

League Appearances: Allsopp, D. 43; Baraclough, I. 30(3); Bolland, P. 16(3); Brough, M. 14(7); Cas, M. 39(1); Caskey, D. 39(3); Chilvers, L. 9; Fenton, N. 41(1); Garden, S. 21; Grayson, S. 10; Hackworth, T. 9(24); Hamilton, I. 6(3); Heffernan, P. 18(5); Holmes, R. 1; Ireland, C. 26(1); Jorgensen, H. (2); Liburd, R. 22(3); McNamara, N. (4); Mildenhall, S. 25(1); Nicholson, K. 15(9); Owers, G. 26(4); Quinn, J. 6; Richardson, I. 21(3); Richardson, L. 20(1); Riley, P. 3(3); Stallard, M. 21(5); Stone, D. 5(1); Warren, M. 12(5); Whitley, J. 6; Wilkie, L. 2.
Goals – League (59): Allsopp 19 (3 pens), Cas 6, Heffernan 6, Caskey 5, Stallard 4, Baraclough 3, Fenton 3, Quinn 3, Liburd 2, Richardson I 2, Chilvers 1, Grayson 1, Hackworth 1, Ireland 1, Nicholson 1, Owers 1.
Worthington Cup (6): Allsopp 4 (1 pen), Mildenhall 1, Stallard 1.
FA Cup (3): Allsopp 2, Owers 1.
Ground: County Ground, Meadow Lane, Nottingham NG2 3HJ. Telephone (0115) 952 9000.
Record attendance: 47,310 v York C, FA Cup 6th rd, 12 March 1955. **Capacity:** 20,300.
Manager: Billy Dearden.
Secretary: Tony Cuthbert.
Most League Goals: 107, Division 4, 1959–60.
Highest League Scorer in Season: Tom Keetley, 39, Division 3 (S), 1930–31.

Most League Goals in Total Aggregate: Les Bradd, 124, 1967–78.
Most Capped Player: Kevin Wilson, 15 (42), Northern Ireland.
Most League Appearances: Albert Iremonger, 564, 1904–26.
Honours – Football League: Division 2 Champions – 1896–97, 1913–14, 1922–23.
Division 3 Champions – 1997–98. Division 3 (S) Champions –1930–31, 1949–50.
Division 4 Champions – 1970–71. **FA Cup:** Winners 1893–94. **Anglo-Italian Cup:**
Winners 1995.
Colours: Black and white striped shirts, black shorts, black stockings.

OLDHAM ATHLETIC   DIV. 2

Andrews Wayne (F)	5 10	11 09	Paddington	25 11 77	Watford
Appleby Matty (M)	5 10	11 10	Middlesbrough	16 4 72	Barnsley
Armstrong Chris (D)	5 9	11 00	Newcastle	5 8 82	Bury
Balmer Stuart (D)	6 0	13 02	Falkirk	20 9 69	Wigan Ath
Baudet Julien (D)	6 3	12 08	St Martin D'heres	13 1 79	Toulouse
Beharall David (D)	6 2	11 12	Newcastle	8 3 79	Grimsby T
Boshell Daniel (M)	5 11	11 11	Bradford	30 5 81	Trainee
Carss Tony (M)	5 10	11 09	Alnwick	31 3 76	Carlisle U
Clegg Michael (D)	5 8	11 11	Ashton-under-Lyne	3 7 77	Manchester U
Corazzin Carlo (F)	5 10	12 07	Canada	25 12 71	Northampton T
Dudley Craig (F)	5 11	10 02	Ollerton	12 9 79	Notts Co
Duxbury Lee (M)	5 10	10 07	Keighley	7 10 69	Bradford C
Eyre John (F)	6 0	12 06	Hull	9 10 74	Hull C
Eyres David (M)	5 11	11 06	Liverpool	26 2 64	Preston NE
Garnett Shaun (D)	6 2	13 01	Wallasey	22 11 69	Swansea C
Gill Wayne (M)	5 9	11 00	Chorley	28 11 75	Tranmere R
Hall Fitz (D)	6 4	12 01	Walthamstow	20 12 80	Chesham U
Kelly Gary (G)	5 11	12 08	Fulwood	3 8 66	Bury
Miskelly David (G)	6 0	12 02	Ards	.3 9 79	Trainee
Murray Paul (M)	5 8	10 05	Carlisle	31 8 76	Southampton
Reeves David (F)	6 0	12 06	Birkenhead	19 11 67	Chesterfield
Sheridan Darren (M)	5 6	11 04	Manchester	8 12 67	Wigan Ath
Sheridan John (M)	5 10	11 12	Stretford	1 10 64	Bolton W
Smart Allan (F)	6 2	12 04	Perth	8 7 74	Watford

League Appearances: Adebola, D. 5; Allott, M. 9(6); Appleby, M. 16(1); Armstrong, C. 31(1); Balmer, S. 35(1); Baudet, J. 13(7); Beharall, D. 18; Boshell, D. 2(2); Carss, T. 7(7); Clegg, M. 5(1); Colusso, C. 6(7); Corazzin, C. 24(9); Dudley, C. 6(3); Duxbury, L. 34(6); Eyre, J. 11(9); Eyres, D. 40(5); Garnett, S. 4(4); Gill, W. 3; Goram, A. 4; Griffin, A. (1); Haining, W. 1(3); Hall, F. 4; Hardy, L. (1); Holden, D. 20(3); Innes, M. (5); Kelly, G. 22(1); McNiven, S. 32(3); Miskelly, D. 4; Murray, P. 23(1); Prenderville, B. 10(2); Rachubka, P. 16; Reeves, D. 11(2); Richards, M. 3(2); Rickers, P. 13(11); Sheridan, D. 25(3); Sheridan, J. 24(3); Smart, A. 14(7); Tipton, M. 11(11).
Goals – League (77): Corazzin 9 (1 pen), Eyres 9 (1 pen), Balmer 6, Smart 6 (1 pen), Eyre 5, Murray 5, Tipton 5 (1 pen), Allott 4, Duxbury 4, Reeves 3 (1 pen), Appleby 2, Colusso 2, Holden 2, Rickers 2, Sheridan D 2, Sheridan J 2 (1 pen), Baudet 1, Beharall 1, Carss 1, Dudley 1, Hall 1, own goals 4.
Worthington Cup (0).
FA Cup (6): Eyres 3, Duxbury 2, Sheridan J 1.
Ground: Boundary Park, Oldham OL1 2PA. Telephone (0870) 753 2000.
Record attendance: 46,471 v Sheffield W, FA Cup 4th rd. 25 January 1930.
Capacity: 13,559 (all seated).
Manager: Iain Dowie.
Secretary: Alan Hardy.
Most League Goals: 95, Division 4, 1962–63.
Highest League Scorer in Season: Tom Davis, 33, Division 3 (N), 1936–37.

Most League Goals in Total Aggregate: Roger Palmer, 141, 1980–94.
Most Capped Player: Gunnar Halle, 24 (64), Norway.
Most League Appearances: Ian Wood, 525, 1966–80.
Honours – Football League: Division 2 Champions – 1990–91, Division 3 (N) Champions – 1952–53. Division 3 Champions – 1973–74.
Colours: Blue shirts, blue shorts, blue stockings.

OXFORD UNITED   DIV. 3

Player					
Alexis Michael (M)			Oxford	2 1 85	
Bound Matt (D)	6 2	14 06	Bradford-on-Avon	9 11 72	Swansea C
Brooks Jamie (F)	5 9	10 08	Oxford	12 8 83	Scholar
Crosby Andy (D)	6 2	13 13	Rotherham	3 3 73	Brighton & HA
Guyett Scott (D)	6 2	12 09	Ascot	20 1 76	
Hackett Chris (M)	6 0	11 09	Oxford	1 3 83	Scholar
King Simon (D)	6 0	12 08	Oxford	11 4 83	Scholar
Louis Jefferson (F)	6 2	14 12	Harrow	22 2 79	Thame U
McCaldon Ian (G)	6 5	16 00	Liverpool	14 9 74	Livingston
Moody Paul (F)	6 3	16 00	Portsmouth	13 6 67	Millwall
Omoyinmi Emmanuel (M)	5 7	10 11	Nigeria	28 12 77	West Ham U
Powell Paul (M)	5 8	12 02	Wallingford	30 6 78	Trainee
Ricketts Sam (D)	6 1	11 09	Wendover	11 10 81	Trainee
Savage David (M)	6 2	13 06	Dublin	30 7 73	Northampton T
Scott Andy (F)	6 1	12 03	Epsom	2 8 72	Brentford
Stockley Sam (D)	6 0	12 08	Tiverton	5 9 77	Barnet
Sylla Norman (M)			Bondy	27 9 82	
Waterman David (M)	5 11	11 13	Guernsey	16 5 77	Portsmouth
Whitehead Dean (M)	6 0	12 07	Oxford	12 1 82	Trainee
Woodman Andy (G)	6 2	14 08	Camberwell	11 8 71	Colchester U

League Appearances: Beauchamp, J. 2(1); Bolland, P. 20; Bound, M. 22; Brooks, J. 18(7); Crosby, A. 22(1); Douglas, S. 1(3); Folland, R. (10); Gray, P. 14(7); Guyett, S. 20(2); Hackett, C. 5(10); Hatswell, W. 21; King, S. 1(1); Knight, R. 3; Louis, J. (1); Maddison, L. 11; McCaldon, I. 28; Moody, P. 29(6); Morley, D. 16(2); Omoyinmi, E. 11(12); Patterson, D. 2; Powell, P. 33(3); Quinn, R. 11(5); Richardson, J. 16(2); Ricketts, S. 19(10); Savage, D. 42; Scott, A. 25(5); Stockley, S. 39(2); Tait, P. 13(1); Thomas, M. 13(1); Waterman, D. 4(1); Whitehead, D. 30(10); Woodman, A. 15.
Goals – League (53): Moody 13 (4 pens), Brooks 10, Scott 8 (1 pen), Gray 4, Powell 4 (1 pen), Morley 3, Omoyinmi 3, Thomas 2 (1 pen), Beauchamp 1, Bolland 1, Crosby 1, Ricketts 1, Savage 1, Whitehead 1.
Worthington Cup (1): Scott 1.
FA Cup (0).
Ground: The Kassam Stadium, Grenoble Road, Oxford OX4 4XP. Telephone (01865) 337500.
Record attendance: 22,750 (at Manor Ground) v Preston NE, FA Cup 6th rd, 29 February 1964. Capacity: 12,450.
Manager: Ian Atkins.
Secretary: Mick Brown.
Most League Goals: 91, Division 3, 1983–84.
Highest League Scorer in Season: John Aldridge, 30, Division 2, 1984–85.
Most League Goals in Total Aggregate: Graham Atkinson, 77, 1962–73.
Most Capped Player: Jim Magilton, 18 (52), Northern Ireland.
Most League Appearances: John Shuker, 478, 1962–77.
Honours – Football League: Division 2 Champions – 1984–85. Division 3 Champions – 1967–68, 1983–84. Football League Cup: Winners 1985–86.
Colours: Yellow shirts with navy trim, navy shorts and stockings.

Bullard Jimmy (M)	5 9	10 00	Newham	23 10 78	West Ham U
Clarke Lee (F)	5 11	10 08	Peterborough	28 7 83	Yaxley
Connor Dan (G)	6 2	13 04	Dublin	31 1 81	Trainee
Cullen Jon (M)	6 0	13 00	Durham	10 1 73	Sheffield U
Danielsson Helgi (M)	6 0	12 00	Reykjavik	13 7 81	Fylkir
Edwards Andy (D)	6 2	12 13	Epping	17 9 71	Birmingham C
Farrell Dave (M)	5 11	11 08	Birmingham	11 11 71	Wycombe W
Fenn Neale (F)	5 9	10 12	Edmonton	18 1 77	Tottenham H
Forinton Howard (F)	5 11	12 04	Boston	18 9 75	Birmingham C
Forsyth Richard (M)	5 11	13 00	Dudley	3 10 70	Blackpool
French Daniel (M)	5 11	11 00	Peterborough	25 11 79	Trainee
Gill Matthew (M)	5 11	11 07	Cambridge	8 11 80	Trainee
Green Francis (F)	5 9	11 04	Derby	23 4 80	Ilkeston T
Jelleyman Gareth (D)	5 10	10 03	Holywell	14 11 80	Trainee
Joseph Marc (D)	6 2	10 07	Leicester	10 11 76	Cambridge U
Laurie Steve (D)	6 3	13 00	Melbourne	30 10 82	West Ham U
Lee Jason (F)	6 3	13 03	Newham	9 5 71	Chesterfield
MacDonald Gary (M)	6 1	12 00	Germany	25 10 79	Portsmouth
McKenzie Leon (F)	5 10	10 03	Croydon	17 5 78	Crystal Palace
Murray Dan (D)	6 2	12 12	Cambridge	16 5 82	Scholar
Pearce Dennis (D)	6 0	11 07	Wolverhampton	10 9 74	Notts Co
Rea Simon (D)	6 1	13 00	Coventry	20 9 76	Birmingham C
Shields Tony (M)	5 8	10 01	Derry	4 6 80	Trainee
Showler Paul (M)	5 10	11 00	Doncaster	10 10 66	Luton T
Tolley Shane (F)	5 8	10 00	Devon	18 2 85	Scholar
Tyler Mark (G)	5 11	12 00	Norwich	2 4 77	Trainee

League Appearances: Bullard, J. 36(4); Clarke, A. 19(9); Clarke, L. (1); Connor, D. (1); Cowan, T. 4(1); Cullen, J. 10(3); Danielsson, H. 20(11); Edwards, A. 44; Farrell, D. 35(3); Fenn, N. 25(11); Forinton, H. 13(4); Forsyth, R. 30(2); French, D. 1(9); Gill, M. 11(1); Green, F. 12(11); Hanlon, R. (1); Hooper, D. 7(6); Jelleyman, G. 6(4); Joseph, M. 44; Kimble, A. 3; MacDonald, G. 7(1); McKenzie, L. 28(2); Oldfield, D. 27(3); Pearce, D. 8(1); Rea, S. 27(3); Shields, T. 6(9); Steele, L. 2; Toner, C. 6; Tyler, M. 44; Williams, T. 31(3).
Goals – League (64): McKenzie 18 (1 pen), Bullard 8 (2 pens), Farrell 6, Fenn 6, Clarke A 5, Green 3, Danielsson 2, Edwards 2, Forinton 2, Gill 2, Joseph 2, Williams T 2, Cowan 1, Cullen 1, French 1, MacDonald 1, Oldfield 1, Rea 1.
Worthington Cup (4): Clarke A 1, Fenn 1, Forsyth 1, own goal 1.
FA Cup (9): Clarke A 2, Farrell 2, Bullard 1 (pen), Danielsson 1, Fenn 1, McKenzie 1, own goal 1.
Ground: London Road Ground, Peterborough PE2 8AL. Telephone (08700) 550 442.
Record attendance: 30,096 v Swansea T, FA Cup 5th rd, 20 February 1965.
Capacity: 15,314.
Manager: Barry Fry.
Secretary: Julie Etherington.
Most League Goals: 134, Division 4, 1960–61.
Highest League Scorer in Season: Terry Bly, 52, Division 4, 1960–61.
Most League Goals in Total Aggregate: Jim Hall, 122, 1967–75.
Most Capped Player: Tony Millington, 8 (21), Wales.
Most League Appearances: Tommy Robson, 482, 1968–81.
Honours – Football League: Division 4 Champions – 1960–61, 1973–74.
Colours: Royal blue shirts, white shorts, blue stockings with white tops.

Adams Steve (M)	6 0	12 01	Plymouth	25 9 80	Trainee
Bastow Darren (M)	5 11	12 00	Torquay	22 12 81	Trainee
Bent Jason (M)	5 9	11 11	Toronto	8 3 77	Colorado Rapids
Broad Joseph (M)			Bristol	24 8 82	Trainee
Connolly Paul (D)	6 0	11 09	Liverpool	29 9 83	Scholar
Coughlan Graham (D)	6 2	13 04	Dublin	18 11 74	Livingston
Evans Micky (F)	6 0	13 00	Plymouth	1 1 73	Bristol R
Evers Sean (M)	5 10	9 07	Hitchin	10 10 77	Reading
Friio David (M)	6 0	11 07	Thionville	17 2 73	ASOA Valence
Gritton Martin (F)	6 1	12 02	Glasgow	1 6 78	Porthleven
Heaney Neil (F)	5 9	11 06	Middlesbrough	3 11 71	Dundee U
Hodges Lee (M)	6 0	12 01	Epping	4 9 73	Reading
Keith Marino (F)	5 10	12 12	Peterhead	16 12 74	Livingston
Larrieu Romain (G)	6 2	13 00	Mont-de-Marsan	31 8 76	ASOA Valence
McGlinchey Brian (D)	5 6	10 02	Derry	26 10 77	Gillingham
Phillips Martin (M)	5 6	12 08	Exeter	13 3 76	Portsmouth
Stonebridge Ian (F)	6 0	11 04	Lewisham	30 8 81	Tottenham H
Sturrock Blair (M)			Dundee	25 8 81	Dundee U
Taylor Craig (D)	6 1	13 02	Plymouth	24 1 74	Swindon T
Trudgian Ryan (M)	6 0	12 01	Truro	15 9 83	Scholar
Wills Kevin (M)	5 9	10 04	Torbay	15 10 80	Trainee
Worrell David (D)	5 11	11 08	Dublin	12 1 78	Dundee U
Wotton Paul (D)	5 11	11 01	Plymouth	17 8 77	Trainee

League Appearances: Adams, S. 40(6); Adamson, C. 1; Banger, N. 3(7); Bent, J. 16(5); Beswetherick, J. 27(5); Broad, J. 1(6); Coughlan, G. 46; Crowe, D. (1); Evans, M. 30(8); Evers, S. 3(4); Friio, D. 41; Gritton, M. (2); Heaney, N. 1(7); Hodges, L. 42(3); Keith, M. 13(10); Larrieu, R. 45; McGlinchey, B. 26(3); Phillips, M. 37(2); Stonebridge, I. 29(13); Sturrock, B. 4(15); Taylor, C. (1); Wills, K. 13(5); Worrell, D. 42; Wotton, P. 46.
Goals – League (71): Coughlan 11, Keith 9, Friio 8, Stonebridge 8, Evans 7, Hodges L 6, Phillips M 6, Wotton 5 (4 pens), Bent 3, Adams 2, Banger 2, McGlinchey 1, Sturrock 1, own goals 2.
Worthington Cup (0).
FA Cup (7): Friio 2, Phillips 2, Bent 1, Stonebridge 1, Wotton 1.
Ground: Home Park, Plymouth, Devon PL2 3DQ. Telephone (01752) 562561.
Record attendance: 43,596 v Aston Villa, Division 2, 10 October 1936.
Capacity: 20,134.
Manager: Paul Sturrock.
Secretary: Carole Rowntree.
Most League Goals: 107, Division 3 (S), 1925–26 and 1951–52.
Highest League Scorer in Season: Jack Cock, 32, Division 3 (S), 1925–26.
Most League Goals in Total Aggregate: Sammy Black, 180, 1924–38.
Most Capped Player: Moses Russell, 20 (23), Wales.
Most League Appearances: Kevin Hodges, 530, 1978–92.
Honours – Football League: Division 3 (S) Champions – 1929–30, 1951–52. Division 3 Champions – 1958–59, 2001–02.
Colours: Green shirts, green shorts, green stockings.

PORTSMOUTH   DIV. 1

Allen Rory (F)	5 11	11 10	Beckenham	17 10 77	Tottenham H
Barrett Neil (M)	5 10	11 00	Tooting	24 12 81	Chelsea
Bradbury Lee (F)	6 2	13 10	Isle of Wight	3 7 75	Crystal Palace

Name			Birthplace	Date	Status
Bradshaw Craig (M)			Chertsey	31 7 84	Scholar
Burchill Mark (F)	5 8	11 09	Broxburn	18 8 80	Ipswich T
Buxton Lewis (D)	6 1	13 10	Newport (IW)	10 12 83	School
Casey Mark (M)			Glasgow	9 10 82	
Cooper Shaun (D)	5 10	10 07	Isle of Wight	5 10 83	School
Courville Uliano (M)	6 0	12 06	Mantes La Jolie	8 8 78	Ajaccio
Crowe Jason (D)	5 9	11 02	Sidcup	30 9 78	Arsenal
Curtis Tom (M)	5 10	12 10	Exeter	1 3 73	Chesterfield
Derry Shaun (M)	5 10	13 02	Nottingham	6 12 77	Sheffield U
Harper Kevin (F)	5 7	12 00	Oldham	15 1 76	Derby Co
Hiley Scott (D)	5 8	11 08	Plymouth	27 9 68	Southampton
Howe Eddie (D)	5 9	11 02	Amersham	29 11 77	Bournemouth
Hunt Warren (M)			Portsmouth	2 3 84	Scholar
Kawaguchi Yoshikatsu (G)	5 10	12 03	Shizuoka	15 8 75	Yokohama Marinos
Lovell Stephen (F)	5 11	11 08	Amersham	6 12 80	Bournemouth
Molyneaux Lee (M)			Portsmouth	16 1 83	Scholar
Nightingale Luke (F)	5 11	11 07	Portsmouth	22 12 80	Trainee
O'Neil Gary (M)	5 10	11 00	Beckenham	18 5 83	Trainee
Pettefer Carl (M)	5 7	10 02	Taplow	22 3 81	Trainee
Pitt Courtney (M)	5 7	10 08	London	17 12 81	Scholar
Primus Linvoy (D)	6 0	12 04	Forest Gate	14 9 73	Reading
Quashie Nigel (M)	5 9	12 08	Nunhead	20 7 78	Nottingham F
Tardif Chris (G)	5 11	12 07	Guernsey	10 9 79	Trainee
Tiler Carl (D)	6 2	14 03	Sheffield	11 2 70	Charlton Ath
Todorov Svetoslav (F)	6 0	12 02	Dobrich	30 8 78	West Ham U
Vincent Jamie (D)	5 10	11 09	London	18 6 75	Huddersfield T
Vine Rowan (F)	6 1	11 12	Basingstoke	21 9 82	Scholar
White Tom (M)			Chichester	30 10 81	Trainee
Zamperini Alessandro (D)	6 2	12 08	Rome	15 8 82	

League Appearances: Barrett, N. 23(3); Beasant, D. 27; Biagini, L. 6(2); Bradbury, L. 17(5); Brady, G. 1(5); Burchill, M. 5(1); Buxton, L. 27(2); Cooper, S. 3(4); Crouch, P. 37; Crowe, J. 18(4); Curtis, T. 3(6); Derry, S. 12; Edinburgh, J. 7; Harper, K. 37(2); Hiley, S. 28(5); Howe, E. 1; Ilic, S. 7; Kawaguchi, Y. 11; Lovell, S. 8(12); Miglioranzi, S. 1(2); Mills, L. 2; Moore, D. 2; O'Neil, G. 27(6); Panopoulos, M. 1(1); Pettefer, C. 1(1); Pitt, C. 29(10); Primus, L. 21(1); Prosinecki, R. 30(3); Quashie, N. 33(2); Rudonja, M. 2(1); Summerbell, M. 5; Tardif, C. 1; Thogersen, T. 2(3); Tiler, C. 7(1); Todorov, S. 3; Vincent, J. 29(5); Vine, R. 3(8); Waterman, D. 8(1); Wilson, S. 5; Zamperini, A. 16.

Goals – League (60): Crouch 18, Prosinecki 9 (3 pens), Bradbury 7 (3 pens), Burchill 4 (1 pen), Pitt 3, Barrett 2, Biagini 2, Lovell 2, Primus 2, Quashie 2, Zamperini 2, Crowe 1, Edinburgh 1, Harper 1, O'Neil 1, Todorov 1, Vincent 1, own goal 1.

Worthington Cup (1): Crouch 1.

FA Cup (1): own goal 1.

Ground: Fratton Park, Frogmore Rd, Portsmouth PO4 8RA. Telephone (01705) 731204.

Record attendance: 51,385 v Derby Co, FA Cup 6th rd, 26 February 1949.

Capacity: 19,179.

Manager: Harry Redknapp.

Secretary: Paul Weld.

Most League Goals: 91, Division 4, 1979–80.

Highest League Scorer in Season: Guy Whittingham, 42, Division 1, 1992–93.

Most League Goals in Total Aggregate: Peter Harris, 194, 1946–60.

Most Capped Player: Jimmy Dickinson, 48, England.

Most League Appearances: Jimmy Dickinson, 764, 1946–65.

Honours – Football League: Division 1 Champions – 1948–49, 1949–50. Division 3 (S) Champions – 1923–24. Division 3 Champions – 1961–62, 1982–83. **FA Cup:** Winners 1939.
Colours: Blue shirts, white shorts, red stockings.

PORT VALE   DIV. 2

Armstrong Ian (M)	5 7	10 01	Liverpool	16 11 81	Liverpool
Bridge-Wilkinson Marc (M)	5 6	11 03	Coventry	16 3 79	Derby Co
Brisco Neil (M)	6 0	13 02	Billinge	26 1 78	Manchester C
Brooker Stephen (F)	6 0	13 13	Newport Pagnell	21 5 81	Watford
Burns Liam (D)	6 0	13 06	Belfast	30 10 78	Trainee
Carragher Matthew (D)	5 9	11 08	Liverpool	14 1 76	Wigan Ath
Cummins Michael (M)	6 0	12 13	Dublin	1 6 78	Middlesbrough
Delany Dean (G)	6 0	13 02	Dublin	15 9 80	Everton
Goodlad Mark (G)	6 1	14 02	Barnsley	9 9 79	Nottingham F
Ingram Rae (D)	5 11	13 02	Manchester	6 12 74	Macclesfield T
McClare Sean (M)	5 11	12 10	Rotherham	12 1 78	Barnsley
McPhee Stephen (F)	5 7	11 08	Glasgow	5 6 81	Coventry C
Rowland Stephen (D)	5 10	12 01	Wrexham	2 11 81	Scholar

League Appearances: Armstrong, I. 20(11); Atangana, M. 1(1); Birchall, C. (1); Bridge-Wilkinson, M. 15(4); Brisco, N. 34(3); Brooker, S. 41; Burgess, R. 1(1); Burns, L. 30(3); Burton, S. 33(4); Byrne, P. 1(1); Carragher, M. 41; Cummins, M. 46; Delany, D. 3(1); Dodd, A. 5(4); Donnelly, P. 1(5); Durnin, J. 18(1); Gibson, A. 1; Goodlad, M. 43; Hardy, P. 8; Ingram, R. 22(2); Killen, C. 8(1); Maye, D. (2); McClare, S. 19(4); McPhee, S. 44; O'Callaghan, G. 8(3); Osborn, S. 7; Paynter, B. 2(5); Rowland, S. 25; Torpey, S. (1); Walsh, M. 27(1); Webber, D. 2(2).
Goals – League (51): McPhee 11 (2 pens), Brooker 9, Cummins 8, Bridge-Wilkinson 6, Killen 6, Armstrong 3, O'Callaghan 3, Dodd 1, Durnin 1, Hardy 1, McClare 1, Rowland 1.
Worthington Cup (2): McPhee 2.
FA Cup (3): Brooker 1, Burgess 1, Cummins 1.
Ground: Vale Park, Burslem, Stoke-on-Trent ST6 1AW. Telephone (01782) 655 800.
Record attendance: 50,000 v Aston Villa, FA Cup 5th rd, 20 February 1960.
Capacity: 17,677
Manager: Brian Horton.
Secretary: F. W. Lodey.
Most League Goals: 110, Division 4, 1958–59.
Highest League Scorer in Season: Wilf Kirkham 38, Division 2, 1926–27.
Most League Goals in Total Aggregate: Wilf Kirkham, 154, 1923–29, 1931–33.
Most Capped Player: Tony Rougier, Trinidad and Tobago.
Most League Appearances: Roy Sproson, 761, 1950–72.
Honours – Football League: Division 3 (N) Champions – 1929–30, 1953–54. Division 4 Champions – 1958–59. **LDV Vans Trophy winners:** 2001
Colours: White shirts, black shorts, black and white stockings.

PRESTON NORTH END   DIV. 1

Abbott Pawel (F)	6 1	11 07	York	2 12 81	LKS Lodz
Alexander Graham (D)	5 11	12 04	Coventry	10 10 71	Luton T
Anderson Iain (F)	5 5	12 04	Glasgow	23 7 77	Toulouse
Bailey John (M)	5 5	10 05	Manchester	2 7 84	Scholar
Barry-Murphy Brian (M)	5 11	13 03	Cork	27 7 78	Cork City
Cartwright Lee (M)	5 8	11 05	Rossendale	19 9 72	Trainee

Cresswell Richard (F)	6 0	12 04	Bridlington	20 9 77	Leicester C
Eaton Adam (D)	5 10	12 00	Liverpool	2 5 80	Everton
Edwards Rob (D)	6 0	13 03	Kendal	1 7 73	Bristol C
Etuhu Dixon (M)	6 2	13 00	Kano	8 6 82	Manchester C
Gregan Sean (M)	6 2	14 11	Stockton	29 3 74	Darlington
Healy David (F)	5 7	10 09	Downpatrick	5 8 79	Manchester U
Jackson Michael (D)	6 0	13 07	Chester	4 12 73	Bury
Keane Michael (M)	5 6	11 05	Dublin	29 12 82	Scholar
Lonergan Andrew (G)	6 2	13 10	Preston	19 10 83	Scholar
Lucas David (G)	6 0	12 04	Preston	23 11 77	Trainee
Lucketti Chris (D)	6 1	13 04	Littleborough	28 9 71	Huddersfield T
McKenna Paul (M)	5 5	13 03	Eccleston	29 10 77	Trainee
Moilanen Teuvo (G)	6 3	13 00	Oulu	12 12 73	Jaro
Murdock Colin (D)	6 3	13 05	Belfast	12 7 76	Manchester U
Rankine Mark (M)	5 7	12 01	Doncaster	30 9 69	Wolverhampton W
Robinson Steve (M)	5 7	11 03	Lisburn	10 12 74	Trainee
Skora Eric (M)	5 11	12 05	France	20 8 81	
Wright Mark (F)	5 10	12 07	Chorley	4 9 81	Schoolboy

League Appearances: Ainsworth, G. 3(2); Alexander, G. 45; Anderson, I. 16(15); Barry-Murphy, B. 2(2); Basham, S. (16); Cartwright, L. 34(2); Cresswell, R. 27(13); Eaton, A. 6(6); Edwards, R. 36; Etuhu, D. 16; Gallacher, K. 1(4); Gregan, S. 40(1); Gudjonsson, T. 4(3); Healy, D. 35(9); Hendry, C. 2; Jackson, M. 12(1); Keane, M. 17(3); Kidd, R. 5(1); Lucas, D. 23(1); Lucketti, C. 40; Macken, J. 28(3); McKenna, P. 37(1); Moilanen, T. 23(1); Murdock, C. 22(1); Rankine, M. 24(2); Reid, P. (1); Robinson, S. (2); Skora, E. 2(2); Wijnhard, C. 6.

Goals – League (71): Cresswell 13, Healy 10, Macken 8, Alexander 6 (5 pens), Anderson 5, McKenna 4, Rankine 4, Etuhu 3, Wijnhard 3, Edwards 2, Keane 2, Lucketti 2, Murdock 2, Ainsworth 1, Basham 1, Cartwright 1, Gallacher 1, Gregan 1, Reid 1, own goal 1.

Worthington Cup (4): Cresswell 1, Gallacher 1, Jackson 1, Macken 1.

FA Cup (5): Cresswell 2, Alexander 1 (pen), Macken 1, Skora 1.

Ground: Deepdale, Preston PR1 6RU. Telephone (01772) 902020.

Record attendance: 42,684 v Arsenal, Division 1, 23 April 1938. **Capacity:** 22,226.

Manager: Craig Brown.

Secretary: G. E. Harrison.

Most League Goals: 100, Division 2, 1927–28 and Division 1, 1957–58.

Highest League Scorer in Season: Ted Harper, 37, Division 2, 1932–33.

Most League Goals in Total Aggregate: Tom Finney, 187, 1946–60.

Most Capped Player: Tom Finney, 76, England.

Most League Appearances: Alan Kelly, 447, 1961–75.

Honours – Football League: Division 1 Champions – 1888–89 (first champions), 1889–90. Division 2 Champions – 1903–04, 1912–13, 1950–51, 1999–2000. Division 3 Champions –1970–71, 1995–96. **FA Cup winners** 1889, 1938.

Colours: White shirts, navy shorts, white stockings.

QUEENS PARK RANGERS   DIV. 2

Brady Richard (F)	5 8	10 04	Dartford	17 9 82	Trainee
Carlisle Clarke (D)	6 3	12 07	Preston	14 10 79	Blackpool
Connolly Karl (F)	5 10	11 08	Prescot	9 2 70	Wrexham
D'Austin Ryan (M)	5 9	10 13	Edgware	29 11 82	Trainee
Day Chris (G)	6 2	13 06	Whipps Cross	28 7 75	Watford
Dodou Ebeli M'bombo (F)	5 5	9 11	Kinshasa	11 9 80	
Duncan Lyndon (D)	5 8	11 02	Ealing	12 1 83	Trainee
Fitzgerald Brian (M)	5 9	12 00	Perivale	23 10 83	School
Forbes Terrell (D)	6 0	12 05	Southwark	17 8 81	West Ham U

Gallen Kevin (F)	5 11	13 05	Hammersmith	21 9 75	Barnsley
Gradley Patrick (M)			London	1 6 83	Scholar
Griffiths Leroy (F)	5 11	13 05	London	30 12 76	Hampton & Richmond B
Langley Richard (M)	6 0	12 06	London	27 12 79	Trainee
Murphy Danny (D)	5 6	10 04	London	4 12 82	Trainee
Pacquette Richard (F)	5 11	13 12	Paddington	28 1 83	Trainee
Palmer Steve (D)	6 1	12 13	Brighton	31 3 68	Watford
Peacock Gavin (M)	5 9	11 08	Eltham	18 11 67	Chelsea
Plummer Chris (D)	6 2	13 08	Isleworth	12 10 76	Trainee
Shittu Dan (D)	6 2	16 03	Lagos	2 9 80	Charlton Ath
Walshe Ben (M)	5 11	12 12	Hammersmith	24 5 83	Scholar
Wattley David (M)			Enfield	5 9 83	School

League Appearances: Agogo, M. (2); Ben Askar, A. 18; Bignot, M. 41(4); Bonnot, A. 17(5); Bruce, P. 13; Burgess, O. 4; Connolly, K. 24(9); Daly, W. 1; Day, C. 16; De Ornelas, F. 1(1); Digby, F. 19; Dodou, E. 20(16); Evans, R. 11; Fitzgerald, B. (1); Foley, D. 3(2); Forbes, T. 43; Gallen, K. 25; Griffiths, L. 23(7); Koejoe, S. (2); Langley, R. 15(3); Leaburn, C. (1); McEwen, R. 2(3); Murphy, D. 10(2); Oli, D. (2); Pacquette, R. 8(8); Palmer, S. 46; Peacock, G. 19(1); Perry, M. 13(3); Plummer, C. 1; Rose, M. 37(2); Shittu, D. 27; Taylor, R. 3(1); Thomas, J. 4; Thomson, A. 29(9); Wardley, S. 5(5); Warren, C. 8(6).
Goals – League (60): Thomson 21 (6 pens), Gallen 7, Connolly 4 (1 pen), Palmer 4, Dodou 3, Griffiths 3, Langley 3, Rose 3, Pacquette 2, Peacock 2, Shittu 2, Bonnot 1, Bruce 1, Burgess 1, Foley 1, Thomas 1, own goal 1.
Worthington Cup (1): own goal 1.
FA Cup (0).
Ground: South Africa Road, W12 7PA. Telephone (020) 8743 0262.
Record attendance: 35,353 v Leeds U, Division 1, 27 April 1974. **Capacity:** 19,148.
Manager: Ian Holloway.
Secretary: Sheila Marson.
Most League Goals: 111, Division 3, 1961–62.
Highest League Scorer in Season: George Goddard, 37, Division 3 (S), 1929–30.
Most League Goals in Total Aggregate: George Goddard, 172, 1926–34.
Most Capped Player: Alan McDonald, 52, Northern Ireland.
Most League Appearances: Tony Ingham, 519, 1950–63.
Honours – Football League: Division 2 Champions – 1982–83. Division 3 (S) Champions – 1947–48. Division 3 Champions – 1966–67. **Football League Cup winners** 1966–67.
Colours: Blue and white hooped shirts, white shorts, white stockings.

READING   DIV. 1

Allaway Ricky (D)	6 2	12 05	Reading	16 2 83	Trainee
Ashdown Jamie (G)	6 1	13 05	Reading	30 11 80	
Boucaud Andre (M)			Enfield	9 10 84	Scholar
Butler Martin (F)	5 11	12 00	Dudley	15 9 74	Cambridge U
Cureton Jamie (F)	5 8	10 07	Bristol	28 8 75	Bristol R
Forster Nicky (F)	5 8	11 05	Caterham	8 9 73	Birmingham C
Gamble Joe (M)	5 6	11 02	Cork	14 1 82	Cork C
Harper James (M)	5 9	11 10	Chelmsford	9 11 80	Arsenal
Henderson Darius (F)	6 1	13 08	Doncaster	7 9 81	Trainee
Hughes Andy (M)	6 0	12 10	Manchester	2 1 78	Notts Co
Igoe Sammy (M)	5 6	10 00	Spelthorne	30 9 75	Portsmouth
Mackie John (D)	6 1	13 00	London	5 7 76	Sutton U
Murty Graeme (M)	5 10	11 10	Saltburn	13 11 74	York C
Newman Ricky (D)	5 10	12 06	Guildford	5 8 70	Millwall
Parkinson Phil (M)	6 0	12 08	Chorley	1 12 67	Bury

Rougier Tony (F)	6 0	14 01	Trinidad	17	7 71	Port Vale
Salako John (F)	5 9	11 12	Nigeria	11	2 69	Charlton Ath
Savage Bas (F)	6 3	13 08	London	7	1 82	Walton & Hersham
Shorey Nicky (D)	5 9	10 10	Romford	19	2 81	Leyton Orient
Smith Alex (M)	5 8	10 06	Liverpool	15	2 76	Port Vale
Tyson Nathan (F)	6 0	10 01	Reading	4	5 82	Trainee
Viveash Adrian (D)	6 2	12 13	Swindon	30	9 69	Walsall
Warren Steven (M)			London	27	9 83	Crystal Palace
Watson Kevin (M)	5 10	12 08	Hackney	3	1 74	Rotherham U
Whitbread Adrian (D)	6 0	12 12	Epping	22	10 71	Portsmouth
Whitehead Phil (G)	6 3	15 10	Halifax	17	12 69	WBA
Williams Adrian (D)	6 2	13 02	Reading	16	8 71	Wolverhampton W

League Appearances: Ashdown, J. 1; Branch, M. (2); Butler, M. 14(3); Cureton, J. 24(14); Forster, N. 36(6); Gamble, J. 2(4); Hahnemann, M. 6; Harper, J. 19(7); Henderson, D. 2(36); Hughes, A. 34(5); Igoe, S. 27(8); Jones, K. 10(6); Mackie, J. 27; Murty, G. 43; Parkinson, P. 32(1); Roberts, B. 6; Robinson, M. 14; Roget, L. 1; Rougier, T. 20(13); Salako, J. 31; Savage, B. (1); Shorey, N. 32; Smith, A. 12(1); Smith, N. 3(11); Tyson, N. (1); Viveash, A. 18; Watson, K. 12; Whitbread, A. 14; Whitehead, P. 33; Williams, A. 33(2).
Goals – League (70): Forster 19 (2 pens), Cureton 15 (1 pen), Henderson 7, Hughes 6, Salako 6, Butler 2 (1 pen) Mackie 2, Parkinson 2, Smith A 2, Harper 1, Igoe 1, Rougier 1, Smith N 1, Viveash 1, Watson 1, Williams 1, own goals 2.
Worthington Cup (4): Henderson 2, Parkinson 1, Smith A 1.
FA Cup (1): Cureton 1.
Ground: Madejski Stadium, Junction 11, M4, Reading, Berks RG2 0FL. Telephone (0118) 968 1100.
Record attendance: 33,042 v Brentford, FA Cup 5th rd, 19 February 1927.
Capacity: 24,200.
Manager: Alan Pardew.
Secretary: Sue Hewett.
Most League Goals: 112, Division 3 (S), 1951–52.
Highest League Scorer in Season: Ronnie Blackman, 39, Division 3 (S), 1951–52.
Most League Goals in Total Aggregate: Ronnie Blackman, 158, 1947–54.
Most Capped Player: Jimmy Quinn, 17 (46), Northern Ireland.
Most League Appearances: Martin Hicks, 500, 1978–91.
Honours – Football League: Division 2 Champions – 1993–94. Division 3 Champions – 1985–86. Division 3 (S) Champions – 1925–26. Division 4 Champions – 1978–79. **Simod Cup winners** 1987–88.
Colours: Blue and white hooped shirts, white shorts, white stockings with blue bands.

ROCHDALE   DIV. 3

Connor Paul (F)	6 2	11 08	Bishop Auckland	12	1 79	Stoke C
Doughty Matt (D)	5 8	11 00	Warrington	2	11 81	Scholar
Duffy Lee (D)	5 7	10 07	Oldham	24	7 82	Scholar
Durkan Kieron (F)	5 10	12 09	Chester	1	12 73	Macclesfield T
Edwards Neil (G)	5 8	11 02	Aberdare	8	12 70	Stockport Co
Evans Wayne (D)	5 10	12 03	Welshpool	25	8 71	Walsall
Flitcroft David (M)	5 11	13 05	Bolton	14	1 74	Chester C
Gilks Matthew (G)	6 0	12 10	Rochdale	4	6 82	Scholar
Griffiths Gareth (D)	6 4	14 00	Winsford	10	4 70	Wigan Ath
McCourt Patrick (F)	5 10	11 00	Derry	16	12 83	Scholar
McEvilly Lee (F)	6 0	13 00	Liverpool	15	4 82	Burscough
Oliver Michael (M)	5 10	11 04	Middlesbrough	2	8 75	Darlington
Platt Clive (F)	6 3	13 04	Wolverhampton	27	10 77	Walsall
Simpson Paul (F)	5 7	11 03	Carlisle	26	7 66	Blackpool
Townson Kevin (F)	5 6	10 07	Liverpool	19	4 83	

League Appearances: Atkinson, G. 8(3); Banks, S. 15; Bayliss, D. 9; Coleman, S. 8(3); Connor, P. 11(6); Doughty, M. 32(4); Duffy, L. 1(5); Dunning, D. 4(1); Durkan, K. 16(14); Edwards, N. 7; Evans, W. 43; Flitcroft, D. 21(14); Ford, T. 17; Gilks, M. 19; Griffiths, G. 41; Hahnemann, M. 5; Jobson, R. 34(1); Jones, G. 20; Jones, S. 6(3); McAuley, S. 23; McCourt, P. 10(13); McEvilly, L. 13(5); McLoughlin, A. 15(3); Oliver, M. 45; Platt, C. 41(2); Simpson, P. 7; Todd, L. 8(2); Townson, K. 17(24); Ware, P. 4(4); Wheatcroft, P. 6.
Goals – League (65): Townson 14 (1 pen), Oliver 7, Platt 7, Jones G 5 (2 pens), Simpson 5, Griffiths 4, McCourt 4, McEvilly 4, Jobson 3, Wheatcroft 3, Ford 2, Coleman 1, Connor 1, Doughty 1, Durkan 1, Jones S 1, McLoughlin 1 (pen), own goal 1.
Worthington Cup (1): Ford 1.
FA Cup (2): Doughty 1, Oliver 1.
Ground: Spotland, Sandy Lane, Rochdale OL11 5DS. Telephone (01706) 644648.
Record attendance: 24,231 v Notts Co, FA Cup 2nd rd, 10 December 1949.
Capacity: 10,208.
Manager: Paul Simpson.
Secretary: Hilary Molyneux Dearden.
Most League Goals: 105, Division 3 (N), 1926–27.
Highest League Scorer in Season: Albert Whitehurst, 44, Division 3 (N), 1926–27.
Most League Goals in Total Aggregate: Reg Jenkins, 119, 1964–73.
Most Capped Players: Patrick McCourt, 1, Northern Ireland and Lee McEvilly, 1, Northern Ireland.
Most League Appearances: Graham Smith, 317, 1966–74.
Honours – Nil.
Colours: Blue shirts with white trim, blue shorts, blue stockings with white hoop on turnover.

ROTHERHAM UNITED   DIV. 1

Artell David (D)	6 3	13 10	Rotherham	22 11 80	Trainee
Barker Richard (F)	6 0	13 12	Sheffield	30 5 75	Macclesfield T
Beech Chris (D)	5 9	11 13	Congleton	5 11 75	Cardiff C
Branston Guy (D)	6 1	14 13	Leicester	9 1 79	Leicester C
Bryan Marvin (D)	5 11	12 13	Paddington	2 8 75	Bury
Byfield Darren (F)	5 11	13 06	Sutton Coldfield	29 9 76	Walsall
Daws Nick (M)	5 11	13 07	Salford	15 3 70	Bury
Garner Darren (M)	5 10	12 01	Plymouth	10 12 71	Plymouth Arg
Gray Ian (G)	6 2	13 13	Manchester	25 2 75	Stockport Co
Hudson Danny (M)	5 9	11 00	Mexborough	25 6 79	Trainee
Hurst Paul (D)	5 5	9 12	Sheffield	25 9 74	Trainee
Jones Rhodri (D)	5 11	12 05	Cardiff	19 1 82	Manchester U
Lee Alan (F)	6 2	13 09	Galway	21 8 78	Burnley
McIntosh Martin (D)	6 2	13 04	East Kilbride	19 3 71	Hibernian
Miranda Jose (M)	5 7	9 12	Lisbon	20 4 74	
Monkhouse Andy (M)	6 2	12 05	Leeds	23 10 80	Trainee
Mullin John (M)	5 9	12 09	Bury	11 8 75	Burnley
Pollitt Mike (G)	6 3	14 10	Farnworth	29 2 72	Chesterfield
Robins Mark (F)	5 8	11 10	Ashton-under-Lyne	22 12 69	Walsall
Scott Rob (D)	6 1	12 06	Epsom	15 8 73	Fulham
Sedgwick Chris (M)	6 0	12 03	Sheffield	28 4 80	Trainee
Swailes Chris (D)	6 2	12 07	Gateshead	19 10 70	Bury
Talbot Stuart (M)	6 0	13 10	Birmingham	14 6 73	Port Vale
Warne Paul (F)	5 9	11 09	Norwich	8 5 73	Wigan Ath

League Appearances: Barker, R. 11(24); Beech, C. 2(6); Branston, G. 10; Bryan, M. 19; Byfield, D. 3; Daws, N. 21(14); Gray, I. (1); Hurst, P. 45; Lee, A. 37(1); Lowndes, N. 2; McIntosh, M. 39; Miranda, J. 2; Monkhouse, A. 21(17); Mullin, J. 27(7); Pollitt, M. 46; Robins, M. 34(7); Scott, R. 35(3); Sedgwick, C. 39(5); Swailes, C. 44; Talbot, S. 36(2); Warne, P. 14(11); Watson, K. 19.

Goals – League (52): Robins 15 (5 pens), Lee 9 (1 pen), Swailes 6, McIntosh 4, Barker 3, Scott R 3, Byfield 2, Monkhouse 2, Mullin 2, Beech 1, Branston 1, Daws 1, Sedgwick 1, Talbot 1, Watson 1.
Worthington Cup (2): Lee 1, Robins 1.
FA Cup (4): Mullin 2, Barker 1, Warne 1.
Ground: Millmoor Ground, Rotherham S60 1HR. Telephone (01709) 512434.
Record attendance: 25,137 v Sheffield U, Division 2, 13 December 1952. **Capacity:** 11,486.
Manager: Ronnie Moore.
Most League Goals: 114, Division 3 (N), 1946–47.
Highest League Scorer in Season: Wally Ardron, 38, Division 3 (N), 1946–47.
Most League Goals in Total Aggregate: Gladstone Guest, 130, 1946–56.
Most Capped Player: Shaun Goater, 19, Bermuda.
Most League Appearances: Danny Williams, 459, 1946–62.
Honours – Football League: Division 3 Champions – 1980–81. Division 3 (N) Champions – 1950–51. Division 4 Champions – 1988–89. **Auto Windscreens Shield:** Winners 1996
Colours: Red shirts, white shorts, red stockings.

RUSHDEN & DIAMONDS   DIV. 3

Bell David (M)	5 10	11 06	Kettering	21 1 84	Trainee
Burgess Andy (M)	6 2	11 11	Bedford	10 8 81	
Darby Duane (F)	5 11	14 00	Birmingham	17 10 73	Notts Co
Dempster John (D)	6 0	11 06	Kettering	1 4 83	Trainee
Dowell Adam (G)	6 1	12 10	Gateshead	6 12 82	Sunderland
Duffy Robert (F)	6 1	12 01	Swansea	2 12 82	
Gray Stuart (D)	5 10	13 05	Harrogate	18 12 73	Reading
Hall Paul (M)	5 8	10 02	Manchester	3 7 72	Walsall
Hanlon Ritchie (M)	6 1	12 13	Kenton	25 5 78	Peterborough U
Lowe Onandi (F)	6 3	14 07	Kingston, Jamaica	2 12 74	Rochester Rhinos
McElhatton Mike (M)	5 11	13 03	Killarney	16 4 75	Scarborough
Mills Gary (M)	5 9	11 04	Sheppey	20 5 81	
Mustafa Tarkan (D)	5 11	11 11	Islington	28 8 73	Kettering T
Partridge Scott (F)	5 9	11 02	Leicester	13 10 74	Brentford
Pennock Tony (G)	6 1	12 10	Swansea	10 4 71	
Sambrook Andrew (D)	5 10	11 08	Chatham	13 7 79	Gillingham
Solkhon Brett (D)	5 11	12 03	Canvey Island	12 9 82	
Talbot Daniel (D)	5 9	10 07	Enfield	30 1 84	
Turley Billy (G)	6 3	15 06	Wolverhampton	15 7 73	Northampton T
Underwood Paul (D)	5 11	12 08	Wimbledon	16 8 73	Enfield
Wardley Stuart (M)	6 1	13 11	Cambridge	10 9 75	QPR

League Appearances: Angell, B. 3(2); Bell Jnr, D. (1); Brady, J. 9(13); Burgess, A. 28(4); Butterworth, G. 28(1); Carey, S. 7(1); Carr, D. 1; Darby, D. 17(13); Dempster, J. (2); Douglas, S. 4(5); Duffy, R. 1(7); Folan, C. 1(5); Gray, S. 12; Hall, P. 34; Hanlon, R. 33(2); Hunter, B. 23; Jackson, J. 5; Lee, C. 1; Lowe, O. 25; McElhatton, M. 4(3); Mills, G. 3(6); Mustafa, T. 21(2); Partridge, S. 26(11); Patmore, W. 4; Pennock, T. 3(2); Peters, M. 40; Rodwell, J. 8(1); Sambrook, A. 25(1); Setchell, G. 13(9); Sigere, J. 4(3); Solkhon, B. (1); Talbot, D. 2(1); Thomson, P. 1(1); Tillson, A. 14; Turley, B. 43; Underwood, P. 40; Warburton, R. 1; Wardley, S. 18; Wormull, S. 4(1).
Goals – League (69): Lowe 19, Hall 8, Darby 7, Hanlon 6 (3 pens), Partridge 5, Burgess 4, Wardley 4, Angell 2, Brady 1, Butterworth 1, Duffy 1, Hunter 1, McElhatton 1, Mustafa 1, Patmore 1, Setchell 1, Sigere 1, Thomson 1, own goals 4.
Worthington Cup (3): Darby 1, Mustafa 1, Peters 1.
FA Cup (2): Hanlon 2 (1 pen).
Ground: Nene Park, Diamond Way, Irthlingborough, Northants NN9 5QF. Telephone (01933) 652 000.

Record Attendance: 6431 v Leeds U, F.A. Cup 3rd rd, 2 January 1999.
Ground Capacity: 6441
Manager: Brian Talbot.
Secretary: David Joyce.
Most League Goals: 109, Southern League Midland Division, 1993–94.
Honours – Conference: Champions 2000–01. **Southern League Midland Division:** Champions 1993–94. **Premier Division:** Champions 1995–96. **FA Trophy:** Semi-finalists 1994. **Northants FA Hillier Senior Cup:** Winners 1993–94, 1998–99. **Maunsell Premier Cup:** Winners 1994–95, 1998–99.
Colours: White shirts with blue trim and red piping, blue shorts, white stockings.

SCUNTHORPE UNITED   DIV. 3

Beagrie Peter (M)	5 9	12 04	Middlesbrough	28 11 65	Wigan Ath
Brough Scott (M)	5 5	9 11	Doncaster	10 2 83	
Carruthers Martin (F)	5 10	11 13	Nottingham	7 8 72	Southend U
Cotterill James (D)	5 11	12 04	Barnsley	3 8 82	Scholar
Dawson Andy (D)	5 9	11 12	Northallerton	20 10 78	Nottingham F
Evans Tom (G)	6 1	13 11	Doncaster	31 12 76	Crystal Palace
Graves Wayne (M)	5 7	11 01	Scunthorpe	18 9 80	Trainee
Jackson Mark (D)	5 11	12 13	Leeds	30 9 77	Leeds U
Kell Richard (M)	6 1	10 13	Bishop Auckland	15 9 79	Torquay U
McCombe Jamie (D)	6 5	12 05	Pontefract	1 1 83	Scholar
Pepper Nigel (M)	5 10	13 12	Rotherham	5 4 68	Southend U
Ridley Lee (D)	5 9	11 10	Scunthorpe	5 12 81	Scholar
Sparrow Matthew (M)	5 11	10 06	London	3 10 81	Scholar
Stanton Nathan (D)	5 9	12 07	Nottingham	6 5 81	Trainee
Torpey Steve (F)	6 3	13 06	Islington	8 12 70	Bristol C
Wilcox Russ (D)	6 0	13 01	Hemsworth	25 3 64	Preston NE

League Appearances: Anderson, M. (1); Barwick, T. 7(3); Beagrie, P. 39(1); Bradshaw, C. 18(3); Brough, S. 5(14); Calvo-Garcia, A. 33(1); Carruthers, M. 30(3); Cotterill, J. 8(2); Croudson, S. 4; Dawson, A. 44; Dudley, C. 1(3); Evans, T. 42; Grant, K. 3(1); Graves, W. 16(1); Hodges, L. 26(9); Jackson, M. 45; Jeffrey, M. 4(2); Kell, R. 16; McCombe, J. 11(6); McGibbon, P. 6; Parton, A. 1; Pepper, N. (1); Quailey, B. 15(15); Ridley, L. 2(2); Sheldon, G. 6(8); Sparrow, M. 20(4); Stanton, N. 39(3); Thom, S. 17(3); Torpey, S. 37(2); Vaughan, T. 5; Wilcox, R. 6(3).
Goals – League (74): Carruthers 13, Torpey 13, Beagrie 11 (5 pens), Quailey 8, Calvo-Garcia 6, Hodges 6, Graves 3, Jackson 3, Sheldon 2, Thom 2, Bradshaw 1, Brough 1, Grant 1, Jeffrey 1, Kell 1, Sparrow 1, own goal 1.
Worthington Cup (0).
FA Cup (7): Carruthers 3, Calvo-Garcia 2, Hodges 1, McCombe 1.
Ground: Glanford Park, Scunthorpe, South Humberside DN15 8TD. Telephone (01724) 848077.
Record attendance: Old Showground: 23,935 v Portsmouth, FA Cup 4th rd, 30 January 1954. Glanford Park: 8775 v Rotherham U, Division 4, 1 May 1989.
Capacity: 9183.
Manager: Brian Laws.
Secretary: A. D. Rowing.
Most League Goals: 88, Division 3 (N), 1957–58.
Highest League Scorer In Season: Barrie Thomas, 31, Division 2, 1961 62.
Most League Goals in Total Aggregate: Steve Cammack, 110, 1979–81, 1981–86.
Most Capped Player: None.
Most League Appearances: Jack Brownsword, 595, 1950–65.
Honours – Division 3 (N) Champions – 1957–58.
Colours: White shirt with claret and blue trim, white shorts and stockings with claret and blue trim.

Asaba Carl (F)	6 2	13 04	London	28 1 73	Gillingham
Brown Michael R (M)	5 9	12 04	Hartlepool	25 1 77	Manchester C
Croissant Benoit (D)	6 0	12 06	Vitriy le Francois	9 8 80	Troyes
Cryan Colin (D)	5 10	13 00	Dublin	23 3 81	Scholar
De Vogt Wilko (G)	6 1	12 08	Breda	17 9 75	
Doane Ben (D)	5 10	11 00	Sheffield	22 12 79	Trainee
Featherstone Lee (M)			Chesterfield	20 7 83	Scholar
Jagielka Philip (M)	5 11	13 01	Manchester	17 8 82	Scholar
Javary Jean-Philippe (M)	5 10	11 13	Montpellier	10 1 78	Plymouth Arg
Killeen Lewis (F)			Peterborough	23 9 82	Scholar
Kozluk Robert (D)	5 8	11 05	Sutton-in-Ashfield	5 8 77	Derby Co
Mallon Ryan (F)	5 9	11 08	Sheffield	22 3 83	Schoolboy
Montgomery Nick (M)	5 9	11 08	Leeds	28 10 81	Scholar
Murphy Shaun (D)	6 1	13 10	Sydney	5 11 70	WBA
Ndlovu Peter (F)	5 8	10 02	Bulawayo	25 2 73	Birmingham C
Nicholson Shane (D)	5 10	12 02	Newark	3 6 70	Stockport Co
Nugent Robert (D)			Manchester	27 12 82	Scholar
Page Robert (D)	6 0	13 00	Tylorstown	3 9 74	Watford
Peschisolido Paul (F)	5 7	10 12	Canada	25 5 71	Fulham
Purkiss Ben (D)			Sheffield	1 4 84	
Quinn Gerry (M)			Dublin	16 9 83	
Sandford Lee (D)	6 0	14 02	Basingstoke	22 4 68	Stoke C
Scott Ben (G)			Doncaster	16 11 83	Schoolboy
Smith Grant (M)	5 11	12 08	Irvine	5 5 80	Reading
Thompson Lee (M)	5 7	10 10	Sheffield	25 3 83	
Thompson Tyrone (F)	5 9	11 02	Sheffield	8 5 82	Scholar
Tonge Michael (M)	5 11	12 04	Manchester	7 4 83	Scholar
Tracey Simon (G)		14 01	Woolwich	9 12 67	Wimbledon
Ullathorne Robert (D)	5 8	11 03	Wakefield	11 10 71	Leicester C

League Appearances: Asaba, C. 26(3); Brown, M. 36; Cryan, C. (1); Curle, K. 30(2); D'Jaffo, L. 23(9); De Vogt, W. 5(1); Devlin, P. 14(5); Doane, B. 14; Ford, B. 20(6); Furlong, P. 4; Jagielka, P. 14(9); Javary, J. 6(1); Killeen, L. (1); Kozluk, R. 6(2); Littlejohn, A. 1(2); Lovell, S. 3(2); Mallon, R. (1); Montgomery, N. 14(17); Murphy, S. 27; Ndlovu, P. 41(4); Nicholson, S. 21(4); Page, R. 43; Peschisolido, P. 19(10); Phelan, T. 8; Sandford, L. 5(1); Santos, G. 14(16); Smith, G. 1(6); Suffo, P. 10(10); Tonge, M. 27(3); Tracey, S. 41; Uhlenbeek, G. 19(1); Ullathorne, R. 14; Ward, M. (1).
Goals – League (53): Asaba 7, Peschisolido 6, Brown 5, D'Jaffo 5 (2 pens), Ndlovu 4, Suffo 4, Jagielka 3, Nicholson 3 (2 pens), Tonge 3, Devlin 2, Furlong 2 (1 pen), Montgomery 2, Santos 2, Curle 1, Doane 1, Javary 1, Lovell 1, own goal 1.
Worthington Cup (4): Devlin 1, D'Jaffo 1, Ndlovu 1, Suffo 1.
FA Cup (1): Brown 1.
Ground: Bramall Lane Ground, Sheffield S2 4SU. Telephone (0114) 2215757
Record attendance: 68,287 v Leeds U, FA Cup 5th rd, 15 February 1936.
Capacity: 30,945.
Manager: Neil Warnock.
Secretary: J. Howarth.
Most League Goals: 102, Division 1, 1925–26.
Highest League Scorer in Season: Jimmy Dunne, 41, Division 1, 1930–31.
Most League Goals in Total Aggregate: Harry Johnson, 205, 1919–30.
Most Capped Player: Billy Gillespie, 25, Northern Ireland.
Most League Appearances: Joe Shaw, 629, 1948–66.
Honours – Football League: Division 1 Champions – 1897–98. Division 2 Champions – 1952–53. Division 4 Champions – 1981–82. **FA Cup:** Winners 1899, 1902, 1915, 1925.
Colours: Red and white striped shirts with white trim, white shorts and white stockings.

SHEFFIELD WEDNESDAY   DIV. 1

Armstrong Craig (D)	5 11	12 10	South Shields	23 5 75	Huddersfield T
Bromby Leigh (D)	5 11	11 06	Dewsbury	2 6 80	
Byrne Michael (M)			Dublin	14 2 84	Nottingham F
Connolly Calem (F)	5 8	11 10	Leeds	12 2 82	
Crane Tony (M)	6 1	12 06	Liverpool	8 9 82	Trainee
Di Piedi Michaelli (F)	6 6	13 05	Palermo	4 12 80	
Donnelly Simon (M)	5 9	10 06	Glasgow	1 12 74	Celtic
Ekoku Efan (F)	6 2	12 00	Manchester	8 6 67	Grasshoppers
Geary Derek (D)	5 6	10 08	Dublin	19 6 80	
Hamshaw Matthew (M)	5 9	11 09	Rotherham	1 1 82	Trainee
Haslam Steven (D)	5 11	10 10	Sheffield	6 9 79	Trainee
Hendon Ian (D)	6 1	13 08	Ilford	5 12 71	Northampton T
Kuqi Shefki (F)	6 2	13 13	Kosovo	11 11 76	Stockport Co
McLaren Paul (M)	6 1	13 00	High Wycombe	17 11 76	Luton T
Morrison Owen (M)	5 8	11 12	Derry	8 12 81	Trainee
O'Donnell Phil (M)	5 10	11 07	Bellshill	25 3 72	Celtic
Pressman Kevin (G)	6 1	15 05	Fareham	6 11 67	Apprentice
Quinn Alan (M)	5 9	10 02	Dublin	13 6 79	Cherry Orchard
Shaw Matthew (M)			Blackpool	7 5 84	
Sibon Gerald (F)	6 3	13 04	Emmen	19 4 74	Ajax
Soltvedt Trond Egil (M)	6 1	12 09	Voss	15 2 67	Southampton
Stringer Chris (G)	6 6	12 00	Grimsby	16 6 83	Scholar
Westwood Ashley (D)	5 11	11 02	Bridgnorth	31 8 76	Bradford C

League Appearances: Armstrong, C. 7(1); Bonvin, P. 7(16); Bromby, L. 26; Broomes, M. 18(1); Burrows, D. 8; Crane, T. 4(11); Di Piedi, M. 2(10); Djordjic, B. 4(1); Donnelly, S. 14(9); Ekoku, E. 21(6); Gallacher, K. (4); Geary, D. 29(3); Hamshaw, M. 13(8); Haslam, S. 39(2); Heald, P. 5; Hendon, I. 9; Hinchcliffe, A. 1; Johnson, D. 7; Johnson, T. 8; Kuqi, S. 17; Lescott, A. 2(5); Maddix, D. 33(3); McCarthy, J. 4; McLaren, P. 29(6); Morrison, O. 11(13); O'Donnell, P. 6(2); Palmer, C. 10; Pressman, K. 40; Quinn, A. 35(3); Roberts, S. (1); Sibon, G. 31(4); Soltvedt, T. 38; Stringer, C. 1; Westwood, A. 25(1); Windass, D. 2.
Goals – League (49): Sibon 12 (3 pens), Ekoku 7 (2 pens), Kuqi 6, Bonvin 4, Donnelly 4, Johnson T 3, Johnson D 2, McLaren 2, Morrison 2, Quinn 2, Bromby 1, Di Piedi 1, Maddix 1, Soltvedt 1, Westwood 1.
Worthington Cup (17): Ekoku 5 (1 pen), Soltvedt 2, Bonvin 1, Crane 1, Di Piedi 1, Hamshaw 1, McLaren 1, Maddix 1, Morrison 1 (pen), O'Donnell 1, Sibon 1, Westwood 1.
FA Cup (1): Hamshaw 1.
Ground: Hillsborough, Sheffield, S6 1SW. Telephone (0114) 2212121
Record attendance: 72,841 v Manchester C, FA Cup 5th rd, 17 February 1934.
Capacity: 39,859.
Manager: Terry Yorath.
Chief Executive: Alan D. Sykes.
Most League Goals: 106, Division 2, 1958–59.
Highest League Scorer in Season: Derek Dooley, 46, Division 2, 1951–52.
Most League Goals in Total Aggregate: Andy Wilson, 199, 1900 20.
Most Capped Player: Nigel Worthington, 50 (66), Northern Ireland.
Most League Appearances: Andy Wilson, 501, 1900–20.
Honours – Football League: Division 1 Champions – 1902–03, 1903–04, 1928–29, 1929–30. Division 2 Champions – 1899–1900, 1925–26, 1951–52, 1955–56, 1958–59.
FA Cup winners 1896, 1907, 1935. **Football League Cup winners** 1990–91.
Colours: Blue and white striped shirts, black shorts, blue stockings.

Aiston Sam (F)	6 1	12 00	Newcastle	21 11 76	Sunderland
Drysdale Leon (D)	5 9	10 12	London	3 2 81	Trainee
Dunbavin Ian (G)	6 1	13 00	Knowsley	27 5 80	Liverpool
Heathcote Mick (D)	6 2	12 05	Durham	10 9 65	Plymouth Arg
Jagielka Steve (F)	5 8	11 03	Manchester	10 3 78	Trainee
Jemson Nigel (F)	5 11	13 00	Preston	10 8 69	Oxford U
Lowe Ryan (F)	5 11	11 05	Liverpool	18 9 78	Burscough
Moss Darren (D)	5 10	11 00	Wrexham	24 5 81	Chester C
Murray Karl (M)	5 10	11 12	Islington	24 6 82	Trainee
Redmile Matt (D)	6 3	14 10	Nottingham	12 11 76	Notts Co
Rodgers Luke (F)	5 8	10 00	Birmingham	1 1 82	Trainee
Tolley Jamie (M)	6 1	10 08	Shrewsbury	12 5 83	Scholar

League Appearances: Aiston, S. 22(13); Atkins, M. 42; Cartwright, M. 14; Drysdale, L. 22(4); Dunbavin, I. 32(2); Fallon, R. 8(3); Freestone, C. 3(4); Guinan, S. 4(1); Heathcote, M. 33(1); Jagielka, S. 25(6); Jemson, N. 28; Jenkins, I. 3(2); Lormor, T. 7; Lowe, R. 22(16); Moss, D. 23(8); Murphy, C. (4); Murray, K. 25(9); Redmile, M. 44; Rioch, G. 38; Rodgers, L. 38; Thompson, A. 13(1); Tolley, J. 19(4); Tretton, A. 15(4); Walker, J. (3); Wilding, P. 12(10); Woan, I. 14.
Goals – League (64): Rodgers 22, Jemson 10 (2 pens), Lowe 7, Jagielka 5, Woan 3, Aiston 2, Atkins 2 (1 pen), Heathcote 2, Lormor 2, Moss 2, Murray 2, Redmile 2, Rioch 2, Tolley 1.
Worthington Cup (1): Jemson 1.
FA Cup (0).
Ground: Gay Meadow, Shrewsbury SY2 6AB. Telephone (01743) 360111.
Record attendance: 18,917 v Walsall, Division 3, 26 April 1961. **Capacity:** 8000.
Manager: Kevin Ratcliffe.
Secretary: Mrs J. Shone.
Most League Goals: 101, Division 4, 1958–59.
Highest League Scorer in Season: Arthur Rowley, 38, Division 4, 1958–59.
Most League Goals in Total Aggregate: Arthur Rowley, 152, 1958–65 (completing his League record of 434 goals).
Most Capped Player: Jimmy McLaughlin, 5 (12), Northern Ireland; Bernard McNally, 5, Northern Ireland.
Most League Appearances: Mickey Brown, 418, 1986–91, 1992–94; 1996–2001.
Honours – Football League: Division 3 Champions – 1978–79, 1993–94. **Welsh Cup** winners 1891, 1938, 1977, 1979, 1984, 1985.
Colours: Amber and blue shirts, blue shorts, blue stockings with amber trim.

SOUTHAMPTON   FA PREMIERSHIP

Baird Chris (D)	5 10	11 11	Ballymoney	25 2 82	Scholar
Beattie James (F)	6 1	13 06	Lancaster	27 2 78	Blackburn R
Benali Francis (D)	5 9	11 04	Southampton	30 12 68	Apprentice
Bevan Scott (G)	6 6	15 10	Southampton	16 9 79	Trainee
Blayney Alan (G)	6 2	13 12	Belfast	9 10 81	Scholar
Bleidelis Imants (M)	5 10	12 01	Latvia	16 8 75	Skonto Riga
Bridge Wayne (D)	5 10	12 05	Southampton	5 8 80	Trainee
Byles Clive (D)	5 11	12 00	Southampton	8 1 84	Scholar
Chala Kleber (M)	5 10	12 07	Ibarra	29 6 71	Nacional
Crowell Matt (M)	5 9	10 09	Bridgend	3 7 84	Scholar
Davies Kevin (F)	6 0	14 08	Sheffield	26 5 77	Blackburn R
Delap Rory (M)	6 3	13 00	Sutton Coldfield	6 7 76	Derby Co
Delgado Agustin (F)	6 3	13 08	Ibarra	23 12 74	Necaxa
Dodd Jason (D)	5 10	12 11	Bath	2 11 70	Bath C

Draper Mark (M)	5 10	12 02	Long Eaton	11 11 70	Aston Villa
El Khalej Tahar (D)	6 2	13 10	Morocco	16 6 68	Benfica
Eyene Jacinto (M)	5 7	10 02	Equatorial Guinea	2 5 82	
Fernandes Fabrice (F)	5 8	10 07	Aubervilliers	29 10 79	Rangers
Gray Steven (D)	6 2	12 11	Dublin	17 10 81	
Howard Brian (M)	5 8	11 01	Winchester	23 1 83	Trainee
Huxley Matthew (M)			Bristol	27 5 82	Scholar
Jones Paul (G)	6 3	15 02	Chirk	18 4 67	Stockport Co
Jones Richard (M)	5 10	10 01	Swansea	6 1 85	Scholar
Lucas Jay (M)	6 1	13 03	Wollongong	14 1 85	Scholar
Lundekvam Claus (D)	6 3	13 05	Austevoll	22 2 73	Brann
Marsden Chris (M)	5 11	12 08	Sheffield	3 1 69	Birmingham C
McDonald Scott (F)	5 7	12 07	Dandenorg	21 8 83	
Mills Jonathan (M)	5 9	11 03	Swindon	8 9 83	Oxford U
Monk Garry (D)	6 1	13 10	Bedford	6 3 79	Trainee
Moss Neil (G)	5 10	14 03	New Milton	10 5 75	Bournemouth
Oakley Matthew (M)	5 10	12 06	Peterborough	17 8 77	Trainee
Ormerod Brett (F)	5 11	11 12	Blackburn	18 10 76	Blackpool
Pahars Marian (F)	5 8	10 08	Latvia	5 8 76	Skonto Riga
Petrescu Dan (D)	5 10	11 06	Bucharest	22 12 67	Bradford C
Svensson Anders (M)	5 10	12 10	Gothenburg	17 7 76	Elfsborg
Telfer Paul (M)	5 10	11 13	Edinburgh	21 10 71	Coventry C
Tessem Jo (M)	6 2	13 01	Norway	28 2 72	Molde
Williams Gareth (G)	6 1	12 05	Pontypool	18 3 85	Scholar
Williams Paul (D)	5 11	14 04	Burton	26 3 71	Coventry C
Williamson Mike (D)	6 4	13 03	Stoke	8 11 83	Trainee

League Appearances: Beattie, J. 24(4); Benali, F. (3); Bleidelis, I. (1); Bridge, W. 38; Davies, K. 18(5); Delap, R. 24(4); Delgado, A. (1); Dodd, J. 26(3); Draper, M. 1(1); El Khalej, T. 12(2); Fernandes, F. 6(5); Jones, P. 36; Le Tissier, M. (4); Lundekvam, C. 34; Marsden, C. 27(1); McDonald, S. (2); Monk, G. 1(1); Moss, N. 2; Murray, P. (1); Oakley, M. 26(1); Ormerod, B. 8(10); Pahars, M. 33(3); Petrescu, D. (2); Richards, D. 4; Ripley, S. 1(4); Rosler, U. 3(1); Svensson, A. 33(1); Telfer, P. 27(1); Tessem, J. 7(15); Williams, P. 27(1).

Goals – League (46): Pahars 14 (2 pens), Beattie 12 (2 pens), Svensson 4, Marsden 3, Davies 2, Delap 2, Tessem 2, El Khalej 1, Fernandes 1, Oakley 1, Ormerod 1, Telfer 1, own goals 2.

Worthington Cup (7): Beattie 2 (1 pen), Svensson 2, Davies 1, El-Khalej 1, Pahars 1.

FA Cup (1): Pahars 1 (pen).

Ground: The Friends Provident St Mary's Stadium, Britannia Road, Southampton SO14 5FP. Telephone (0870) 220 0000.

Record attendance: 31,973 v Newcastle U, FA Premier League, 11 May 2002.

Capacity: 32,551.

Manager: Gordon Strachan.

Secretary: Brian Truscott.

Most League Goals: 112, Division 3 (S), 1957–58.

Highest League Scorer in Season: Derek Reeves, 39, Division 3, 1959–60.

Most League Goals in Total Aggregate: Mike Channon, 185, 1966–77, 1979–82.

Most Capped Player: Peter Shilton, 49 (125), England.

Most League Appearances: Terry Paine, 713, 1956–74.

Honours – Football League: Division 3 (S) Champions – 1921–22. Division 3 Champions – 1959–60. **FA Cup:** Winners 1975–76.

Colours: Red and white striped shirts, black shorts, white stockings with black and red trim.

Belgrave Barrington (F)	5 9	13 00	Bedford	16 9 80	Plymouth Arg
Bramble Tesfaye (F)	6 2	13 07	Ipswich	20 7 80	Cambridge C
Broad Stephen (D)	6 0	12 00	Epsom	10 6 80	Chelsea
Byrne Paul (M)	5 11	13 00	Dublin	30 6 72	Celtic
Clark Steve (M)	6 0	12 09	Mile End	10 2 82	Scholar
Cort Leon (D)	6 4	13 00	Southwark	11 9 79	Millwall
Gay Daniel (G)	6 0	12 13	Kings Lynn	5 8 82	Norwich C
Hunter Leon (M)	5 7	11 06	London	27 8 81	Scholar
Maher Kevin (M)	6 0	12 13	Ilford	17 10 76	Tottenham H
McSweeney Dave (D)	5 9	12 00	Basildon	28 12 81	Scholar
Rawle Mark (F)	5 11	12 04	Leicester	27 4 79	Boston U
Richards Tony (F)	6 1	13 05	Newham	17 9 73	Barnet
Searle Damon (D)	5 10	11 07	Cardiff	26 10 71	Carlisle U
Smith Ben (M)	5 10	12 13	Chelmsford	23 11 78	Yeovil T
Thurgood Stuart (M)	5 8	11 10	Enfield	4 11 81	Shimizu S-Pulse
Webb Daniel (F)	6 1	12 03	Poole	2 7 83	
Whelan Phil (D)	6 4	14 05	Stockport	7 3 72	Oxford U

League Appearances: Alderton, R. (2); Barry-Murphy, B. 8; Beard, M. 5(9); Belgrave, B. 32(2); Bramble, T. 32(3); Broad, S. 30(2); Clark, A. (2); Clark, S. 9(3); Cort, L. 43(2); Dsane, R. 1(1); Flahavan, D. 41; Forbes, S. 3(10); Gay, D. 5(1); Harris, J. 2(3); Holness, D. 1(1); Hutchings, C. 28(1); Johnson, L. 24(4); Kerrigan, D. 6(5); Lunan, D. (1); Maher, K. 36; McSweeney, D. 13(8); Newman, R. 10(1); Rawle, M. 25(5); Richards, T. 9(8); Risbridger, G. (1); Searle, D. 41(2); Selley, I. 14; Smith, B. (1); Szmid, M. 1(1); Thurgood, S. 34(5); Wallace, A. (2); Webb, D. 10(6); Whelan, P. 43(1).
Goals – League (51): Bramble 9 (2 pens), Belgrave 5, Maher 5 (2 pens), Rawle 5, Whelan 5, Cort 4, Hutchings 4 (1 pen), Broad 2, Johnson 2, Newman 2, Richards 2, Webb 2, Barry-Murphy 1, Clark S 1, Searle 1, own goal 1.
Worthington Cup (0).
FA Cup (7): Bramble 3, Belgrave 2, Rawle 1, Whelan 1.
Ground: Roots Hall Football Ground, Victoria Avenue, Southend-on-Sea SS2 6NQ. Telephone (01702) 304050
Record attendance: 31,090 v Liverpool FA Cup 3rd rd, 10 January 1979. **Capacity:** 12,392.
Manager: Rob Newman.
Secretary: Miss Helen Giles.
Most League Goals: 92, Division 3 (S), 1950–51.
Highest League Scorer in Season: Jim Shankly, 31, 1928–29; Sammy McCrory, 1957–58, both in Division 3 (S).
Most League Goals in Total Aggregate: Roy Hollis, 122, 1953–60.
Most Capped Player: George Mackenzie, 9, Eire.
Most League Appearances: Sandy Anderson, 452, 1950–63.
Honours – Football League: Division 4 Champions – 1980–81.
Colours: Navy blue.

STOCKPORT COUNTY DIV. 2

Beckett Luke (F)	5 11	11 06	Sheffield	25 11 76	Chesterfield
Briggs Keith (M)	6 0	11 00	Glossop	11 12 81	Trainee
Byrne Mark (F)	5 10	11 00	Billinge	8 5 83	Blackburn R
Challinor Dave (D)	6 1	12 00	Chester	2 10 75	Tranmere R
Clare Robert (D)	6 2	13 00	Belper	28 2 83	Trainee
Clark Peter (D)	6 1	12 04	Romford	10 12 79	Carlisle U
Daly Jon (F)	6 3	12 00	Dublin	8 1 83	Trainee

Ellison Kevin (F)	6 0	12 00	Liverpool	23	2 79	Leicester C
Fradin Karim (M)	5 11	12 00	Ste Martin d'Hyeres	2	2 72	Nice
Gibb Ali (M)	5 9	11 07	Salisbury	17	2 76	Northampton T
Hancock Glynn (D)	6 0	12 02	Biddulph	24	5 82	Trainee
Hardiker John (D)	5 11	11 01	Preston	7	7 82	Morecambe
Helin Petri (D)	5 10	13 00	Helsinki	13	12 69	Luton T
Holt David (F)			Gorton	18	11 84	Trainee
Jones Lee (G)	6 3	14 10	Pontypridd	9	8 70	Bristol R
Kielty Anthony (D)	6 0	12 07	Manchester	6	4 83	Trainee
Lambert Ricky (M)	6 2	12 01	Liverpool	16	2 82	Macclesfield T
Lescott Aaron (M)	5 8	10 10	Birmingham	2	12 78	Sheffield W
Palmer Carlton (M)	6 3	13 00	Oldbury	5	12 65	Coventry C
Pemberton Martin (M)	5 11	11 08	Bradford	1	2 76	Mansfield T
Ross Neil (F)	6 1	12 02	West Bromwich	10	8 82	Trainee
Spencer James (G)	6 3	15 04	Stockport	11	4 85	Trainee
Thomas Andy (D)	5 7	10 00	Stockport	2	12 82	Trainee
Welsh Andy (F)	5 8	9 06	Manchester	24	11 83	Scholar
Wilbraham Aaron (F)	6 3	12 04	Knutsford	21	10 79	Trainee
Wild Peter (F)	5 9	11 10	Bramhall	12	10 82	Trainee
Williams Chris (F)	5 7	9 00	Manchester	2	2 85	Scholar
Woodthorpe Colin (D)	6 0	11 08	Ellesmere Pt	13	1 69	Aberdeen

League Appearances: Arphexad, P. 3; Beckett, L. 17(2); Briggs, K. 30(2); Bryngelsson, F. 3; Byrne, M. 1(4); Carratt, P. (2); Challinor, D. 18; Clare, R. 21(2); Clark, P. 12(2); Daly, J. 11(2); Delaney, D. 10(2); Dibble, A. 13; Ellison, K. 6(5); Flowers, T. 4; Flynn, M. 26; Fradin, K. 18(2); Gibb, A. 40(1); Hancock, G. (1); Hardiker, J. 11(1); Hardy, N. 4(6); Helin, P. 10(3); Holt, D. (1); Hurst, G. 12(3); Jones, L. 21(3); Kuqi, S. 15(3); Lescott, A. 17; McLachlan, F. 11; McSheffrey, G. 3(2); Palmer, C. 20(1); Roget, L. 20(2); Ross, N. 2(1); Sandford, L. 7; Smith, D. 9(2); Sneekes, R. 8(1); Spencer, J. 1(1); Taylor, S. 19(9); Thomas, A. 7(3); Turner, S. 4(2); Van Blerk, J. 13; Welsh, A. 9(6); Wilbraham, A. 19(2); Wild, P. 1; Williams, C. 1(4); Wiss, J. 7(4); Woodthorpe, C. 22(12).
Goals – League (42): Beckett 7, Kuqi 5 (3 pens), Hurst 4, Taylor 4, Hardiker 3, Palmer 3, Wilbraham 3, Flynn 2, Fradin 2, Hardy 2, Daly 1, Delaney 1, McLachlan 1, McSheffrey 1, Roget 1 (pen), Ross 1, own goal 1.
Worthington Cup (4): Taylor 3, Kuqi 1.
FA Cup (1): Daly 1 (pen).
Ground: Edgeley Park, Hardcastle Road, Stockport, Cheshire SK3 9DD. Telephone (0161) 286 8888.
Record attendance: 27,833 v Liverpool, FA Cup 5th rd, 11 February 1950.
Capacity: 10,817.
Manager: Carlton Palmer.
Secretary: Gary Glendenning BA (HONS) FCCA.
Most League Goals: 115, Division 3 (N), 1933–34.
Highest League Scorer in Season: Alf Lythgoe, 46, Division 3 (N), 1933–34.
Most League Goals in Total Aggregate: Jack Connor, 132, 1951–56.
Most Capped Player: Jarkko Wiss, 9 (36), Finland.
Most League Appearances: Andy Thorpe, 489, 1978–86, 1988–92.
Honours – Football League: Division 3 (N) Champions – 1921–22, 1936–37. Division 4 Champions – 1966–67.
Colours: Royal blue shirts with white trim, royal blue shorts with white trim, white stockings with blue trim.

STOKE CITY   DIV. 1

Clarke Clive (D)	6 1	12 02	Dublin	14	1 80	Trainee
Commons Kris (D)	5 6	9 08	Nottingham	30	8 83	Scholar
Cooke Andy (F)	6 0	12 07	Shrewsbury	20	1 74	Burnley

Cutler Neil (G)	6 1	12 00	Birmingham	3	9 76	Aston Villa
Dadason Rikhardur (F)	6 4	12 00	Reykjavik	26	4 72	Viking
Foster Ben (G)			Leamington	3	4 83	Racing Club Warwick
Goodfellow Marc (F)	5 10	11 00	Swadlincote	20	9 81	
Gudjonsson Bjarni (M)	5 8	11 02	Reykjavik	26	2 79	Genk
Gunnarsson Brynjar (D)	6 1	12 01	Reykjavik	16	10 75	Moss
Handyside Peter (D)	6 2	13 09	Dumfries	31	7 74	Grimsby T
Henry Karl (M)	6 0	11 04	Wolverhampton	26	11 82	Trainee
Hoekstra Peter (M)	6 3	12 03	Asser	4	4 73	
Iwelumo Chris (F)	6 4	13 00	Coatbridge	1	8 79	Aarhus Fremad
Marteinsson Petur (M)	6 1	12 02	Reykjavik	14	7 73	Stabaek
Neal Lewis (M)	5 11	10 11	Leicester	14	7 81	
O'Connor James (M)	5 8	11 00	Dublin	1	9 79	Trainee
Oulare Souleymane (F)	5 11	12 09	Guinea	16	10 72	
Owen Gareth (D)	6 1	11 07	Staffordshire	21	9 82	Scholar
Rowson David (M)	5 10	11 09	Aberdeen	14	9 76	Aberdeen
Shtanyuk Sergei (D)	6 3	12 12	Minsk	11	1 72	Moscow Dynamo
Thomas Wayne (D)	5 11	11 02	Gloucester	17	5 79	Torquay U
Thordarson Stefan (F)	6 1	12 02	Reykjavik	27	3 75	
Van Deurzen Jurgen (M)	5 7	11 00	Genk	26	1 74	
Viander Jani (G)	6 4	13 04	Tuusula	18	8 75	
Wilson Brian (D)	5 10	11 00	Manchester	9	5 83	Scholar

League Appearances: Brightwell, I. 3(1); Burton, D. 11(1); Clarke, C. 42(1); Cooke, A. 26(9); Cutler, N. 36; Dadason, R. 6(5); Dinning, T. 5; Flynn, M. 11(2); Goodfellow, M. 11(12); Gudjonsson, B. 46; Gunnarsson, B. 21(2); Gunnlaugsson, A. 9; Handyside, P. 34; Henry, K. 9(15); Hoekstra, P. 20(4); Iwelumo, C. 22(16); Marteinsson, P. 2(1); Miles, J. (1); Neal, L. 6(5); O'Connor, J. 43; Oulare, S. (1); Rowson, D. 8(5); Shtanyuk, S. 40; Smart, A. (2); Thomas, W. 40; Thordarson, S. 3(18); Thorne, P. 5; Van Deurzen, J. 37(3); Ward, G. 10; Wilson, B. (1).
Goals – League (67): Iwelumo 10, Cooke 9, Goodfellow 5, Gunnarsson 5, Dadason 4 (3 pens), Thordarson 4, Thorne 4 (1 pen), Van Deurzen 4, Gudjonsson 3, Gunnlaugsson 3 (1 pen), Hoekstra 3 (2 pens), Burton 2, O'Connor 2, Shtanyuk 2, Thomas 2, Clarke 1, own goals 4.
Worthington Cup (0).
FA Cup (6): Gunnarsson 2, Cooke 1, Gudjohnson 1, Handyside 1, Iwelumo 1.
Ground: Britannia Stadium, Stoke-on-Trent ST4 4EG. Telephone: (01782) 592222.
Record attendance: 51,380 v Arsenal, Division 1, 29 March 1937. **Capacity:** 28,218.
Manager: Steve Cotterill.
Most League Goals: 92, Division 3 (N), 1926–27.
Highest League Scorer in Season: Freddie Steele, 33, Division 1, 1936–37.
Most League Goals in Total Aggregate: Freddie Steele, 142, 1934–49.
Most Capped Player: Gordon Banks, 36 (73), England.
Most League Appearances: Eric Skeels, 506, 1958–76.
Honours – Football League: Division 2 Champions – 1932–33, 1962–63, 1992–93. Division 3 (N) Champions – 1926–27. **Football League Cup:** Winners 1971–72. **Autoglass Trophy winners** 1992. **Auto Windscreens Shield winners** 2000.
Colours: Red and white striped shirts, white shorts, red and white hooped stockings.

SUNDERLAND   FA PREMIERSHIP

Arca Julio (M)	6 2	11 00	Quilmes	31	1 81	
Bellion David (F)	6 0	11 09	Paris	27	11 82	Cannes
Bjorklund Joachim (D)	6 0	12 06	Vaxjo	12	2 71	Venezia
Black Christopher (M)			Ashington	7	9 82	Scholar
Butler Thomas (M)	5 7	10 06	Ballymena	25	4 81	Trainee

Name	Ht	Wt	Birthplace	Birthdate	Previous Club
Byrne Cliff (D)	6 0	12 11	Dublin	27 4 82	
Capper Stephen (F)			Dublin	28 2 83	Scholar
Clark Ben (D)	6 2	12 06	Shotley Bridge	24 1 83	Manchester U
Collins Patrick (M)			Oman	4 2 85	Scholar
Craddock Jody (D)	6 2	12 00	Bromsgrove	25 7 75	Cambridge U
Dickman Jonjo (M)	5 8	10 05	Hexham	22 9 81	
Emerson (D)	6 2	13 04	Porto Alegre	30 3 72	Chelsea
Gray Michael (D)	5 9	10 07	Sunderland	3 8 74	Trainee
Graydon Keith (F)			Dublin	10 2 83	
Haas Bernt (D)	6 1	12 08	Vienna	8 4 78	Grasshoppers
Ingham Michael (G)	6 4	13 10	Preston	7 9 80	Malachians
James Craig (D)			Middlesbrough	15 11 82	Scholar
Kennedy Jon (G)	6 1	14 03	Rotherham	30 11 80	Worksop T
Kilbane Kevin (M)	6 0	12 07	Preston	1 2 77	WBA
Kyle Kevin (F)	6 3	13 00	Stranraer	7 6 81	
Laslandes Lilian (F)	6 1	13 05	Pauillac	4 9 71	Bordeaux
Macho Jurgen (G)	6 4	13 12	Vienna	24 8 77	First Vienna
Maley Mark (D)	6 0	13 00	Newcastle	26 1 81	Trainee
McAteer Jason (M)	5 10	11 12	Birkenhead	18 6 71	Blackburn R
McCann Gavin (M)	6 1	12 08	Blackpool	10 1 78	Everton
McCartney George (D)	5 11	10 10	Belfast	29 4 81	Trainee
McGill Brendan (M)	5 8	9 02	Dublin	22 3 81	
Medina Nicolas (M)	5 9	10 04	Buenos Aires	17 2 82	Argentinos Jun
Mercimek Baki (D)	6 1	11 11	Amsterdam	17 9 82	Haarlem
Oster John (M)	5 9	10 09	Boston	8 12 78	Everton
Peeters Tom (M)	5 10	11 00	Bornem	25 9 78	Ekeren
Phillips Kevin (F)	5 8	11 05	Hitchin	25 7 73	Watford
Proctor Michael (F)	6 0	11 08	Sunderland	3 10 80	Trainee
Quinn Niall (F)	6 5	14 08	Dublin	6 10 66	Manchester C
Ramsden Simon (M)	6 0	12 04	Bishop Auckland	17 12 81	Scholar
Reddy Michael (F)	6 1	11 07	Graignamanagh	24 3 80	Kilkenny C
Reyna Claudio (M)	5 9	11 09	New Jersey	20 7 73	Rangers
Rossiter Mark (M)			Sligo	27 5 83	Scholar
Ryan Richard (M)			Kilkenny	6 1 85	Scholar
Schwarz Stefan (M)	6 0	12 00	Malmo	18 4 69	Valencia
Shields Dene (F)	5 9	12 00	Edinburgh	16 9 82	Raith R
Shippen Carl (M)			Bishop Auckland	2 3 84	Scholar
Sorensen Thomas (G)	6 4	13 08	Odense	12 6 76	Odense
Straker Philip (M)			Middlesbrough	9 11 83	Scholar
Sullivan David (M)			Glasgow	7 9 76	
Teggart Neil (F)			Downpatrick	16 9 84	Scholar
Thirlwell Paul (M)	5 11	11 04	Springwell Village	13 2 79	Trainee
Turns Craig (G)			Easington	4 11 82	Scholar
Varga Stanislav (D)	6 5	14 09	Lipany	8 10 72	Slovan Bratislava
Williams Darren (D)	5 11	12 00	Middlesbrough	28 4 77	York C

League Appearances: Arca, J. 20(2); Bellion, D. (9); Bjorklund, J. 11(1); Butler, T. 2(5); Craddock, J. 30; Emerson 12; Gray, M. 35; Haas, B. 27; Hutchison, D. 2; Kilbane, K. 24(4); Kyle, K. (6); Laslandes, L. 5(7); Macho, J. 4; Mboma, P. 5(4); McAteer, J. 26; McCann, G. 29; McCartney, G. 12(6); Phillips, K. 37; Quinn, N. 24(14); Rae, A. 1(2); Reyna, C. 17; Schwarz, S. 18(2); Sorensen, T. 34; Thirlwell, P. 11(3); Varga, S. 9; Williams, D. 23(5).

Goals – League (29): Phillips 11 (1 pen), Quinn 6, Reyna 3, Kilbane 2, McAteer 2, Arca 1, Craddock 1, Emerson 1, Mboma 1, Schwarz 1.

Worthington Cup (2): Laslandes 1, Phillips 1.

FA Cup (1): Phillips 1.

Ground: Sunderland Stadium of Light, Sunderland, Tyne and Wear SR5 1SU. Telephone: (0191) 551 5000.

Record attendance: 75,118 v Derby Co, FA Cup 6th rd replay, 8 March 1933 (Roker Park). 48,353 v Liverpool, FA Premier League, 13 April 2002 (Stadium of Light). **Capacity:** 48,353.
Manager: Peter Reid.
Secretary: Jane Purdon.
Most League Goals: 109, Division 1, 1935–36.
Highest League Scorer in Season: Dave Halliday, 43, Division 1, 1928–29.
Most League Goals in Total Aggregate: Charlie Buchan, 209, 1911–25.
Most Capped Player: Charlie Hurley, 38 (40), Republic of Ireland.
Most League Appearances: Jim Montgomery, 537, 1962–77.
Honours – Football League: Division 1 Champions – 1891–92, 1892–93, 1894–95, 1901–02, 1912–13, 1935–36, 1995–96, 1998–99. Division 2 Champions – 1975–76. Division 3 Champions – 1987–88. **FA Cup:** Winners 1937, 1973.
Colours: Red and white striped shirts, black shorts, black stockings.

SWANSEA CITY   DIV. 3

Cusack Nick (M)	6 0	11 13	Maltby	24 12 65	Fulham
De-Vulgt Leigh (M)	5 9	11 02	Swansea	17 3 81	Trainee
Evans Terry (D)	5 7	11 08	Pontypridd	8 1 76	Cardiff C
Freestone Roger (G)	6 2	12 02	Newport	19 8 68	Chelsea
Howard Mike (D)	5 7	10 07	Birkenhead	2 12 78	Tranmere R
Jenkins Lee (M)	5 9	11 00	Pontypool	28 6 79	Trainee
Lacey Damien (M)	5 9	11 03	Bridgend	3 8 77	Trainee
Mumford Andrew (M)	6 1	12 03	Neath	18 6 81	Llanelli
O'Leary Kristian (D)	5 11	12 09	Port Talbot	30 8 77	Trainee
Phillips Gareth (M)	5 8	9 08	Pontypridd	19 8 79	Trainee
Romo David (M)	5 11	12 06	Nimes	7 8 78	Guingamp
Sidibe Mamady (F)	6 4	12 02	Mali	18 12 79	
Smith Jason (D)	6 3	14 00	Bromsgrove	6 9 74	Coventry C
Watkin Steve (F)	5 10	11 10	Wrexham	16 6 71	Wrexham
Williams John (F)	6 1	13 12	Birmingham	11 5 68	Darlington

League Appearances: Appleby, R. 3(7); Bound, M. 18; Brodie, S. 21(5); Casey, R. 6(10); Coates, J. 44(1); Cusack, N. 33(2); De-Vulgt, L. 7(3); Draper, C. (2); Evans, S. 4; Evans, T. 16; Freestone, R. 43; Howard, M. 42; Jenkins, L. 14(1); Jones, J. 3; Keegan, M. (2); Lacey, D. 5(11); Mazzina, N. 3; Mumford, A. 28(4); O'Leary, K. 30(1); Phillips, G. 29(6); Roberts, S. 13; Romo, D. 3(7); Sharp, N. 22(3); Sidibe, M. 26(5); Smith, J. 7(1); Todd, C. 28(4); Tyson, N. 7(4); Watkin, S. 25(6); Williams, J. 26(15)
Goals – League (53): Watkin 8 (3 pens), Sidibe 7, Coates 5, Mumford 5, Roberts 5, Williams 4, Todd 3, Bound 2 (2 pens), Brodie 2, Cusack 2, O'Leary 2, Phillips 2, Howard 1, Jenkins 1, Lacey 1, Romo 1, Sharp 1, Tyson 1.
Worthington Cup (0).
FA Cup (5): Cusack 2, Sidibie 1, Watkin 1, Williams 1.
Ground: Vetch Field, Swansea SA1 3SU. Telephone (01792) 474114.
Record attendance: 32,796 v Arsenal, FA Cup 4th rd, 17 February 1968. **Capacity:** 10,402.
Player-coach: Nick Cusack.
Secretary: Jackie Rockey.
Most League Goals: 90, Division 2, 1956–57.
Highest League Scorer in Season: Cyril Pearce, 35, Division 2, 1931–32.
Most League Goals in Total Aggregate: Ivor Allchurch, 166, 1949–58, 1965–68.
Most Capped Player: Ivor Allchurch, 42 (68), Wales.
Most League Appearances: Wilfred Milne, 585, 1919–37.
Honours – Football League: Division 3 Champions – 1999–2000. Division 3 (S) Champions – 1924–25, 1948–49. **Autoglass Trophy:** Winners 1994. **Welsh Cup:** Winners 9 times.
Colours: All white with black trim.

SWINDON TOWN DIV. 2

Name			Birthplace		Previous
Cobian Juan (D)	5 6	10 10	Buenos Aires	11 9 75	Aberdeen
Collins Christopher (M)			Merthyr	6 8 83	Scholar
Davis Sol (D)	5 8	11 00	Cheltenham	4 9 79	Trainee
Duke David (M)	5 10	11 01	Inverness	7 11 78	Sunderland
Edwards Paul (M)			Manchester	1 1 80	Altrincham
Gurney Andy (D)	5 8	10 08	Bristol	25 1 74	Reading
Heywood Matthew (D)	6 3	14 00	Chatham	26 8 79	Burnley
Invincible Danny (M)	6 0	12 02	Australia	31 3 79	Marconi Stallions
O'Halloran Keith (D)	5 9	11 06	Ireland	10 11 75	St Johnstone
Robinson Steve (M)	5 9	11 00	Nottingham	17 10 75	Birmingham C
Ruddock Neil (D)	6 2	12 12	Wandsworth	9 5 68	Crystal Palace
Sabin Eric (F)	6 0	12 00	Sarcelles	22 1 75	
Walton Graeme (M)			Newcastle	9 12 83	Scholar
Young Alan (F)	5 6	12 00	Swindon	12 8 83	Scholar

League Appearances: Brayley, B. (7); Carlisle, W. 10(1); Cobian, J. (1); Davies, G. (2); Davis, S. 15(6); Duke, D. 36(6); Edwards, N. 2(5); Edwards, P. 14(6); Foley, D. 5(2); Grazioli, G. 24(7); Griemink, B. 45; Gurney, A. 43; Herring, I. (1); Hewlett, M. 38(1); Heywood, M. 42(2); Howe, B. 33(6); Invincible, D. 40(4); McAreavey, P. 8(11); McKinney, R. 1; O'Halloran, K. 6; Osei-Kuffour, J. 4(7); Reeves, A. 24(1); Robinson, M. 6(2); Robinson, S. 37(3); Ruddock, N. 14(1); Sabin, E. 33(1); Williams, J. (1); Willis, A. 19(3); Young, A. 7(7).
Goals – League (46): Grazioli 8, Gurney 6 (1 pen), Invincible 6, Sabin 5, Heywood 3, Carlisle 2, Duke 2, O'Halloran 2 (2 pens), Osei-Kuffour 2, Reeves 2, Foley 1, Hewlett 1, Howe 1, Ruddock 1, Willis 1, Young 1, own goals 2.
Worthington Cup (2): Howe 1, O'Halloran 1 (pen).
FA Cup (6): Invincible 2, Edwards P 1, Haywood 1, Howe 1, Ruddock 1 (pen).
Ground: County Ground, Swindon, Wiltshire SN1 2ED. Telephone (01793) 333 700.
Record attendance: 32,000 v Arsenal, FA Cup 3rd rd, 15 January 1972. **Capacity:** 15,728.
Manager: Andy King.
Secretary: Mike Squires.
Most League Goals: 100, Division 3 (S), 1926–27.
Highest League Scorer in Season: Harry Morris, 47, Division 3 (S), 1926–27.
Most League Goals in Total Aggregate: Harry Morris, 216, 1926–33.
Most Capped Player: Rod Thomas, 30 (50), Wales.
Most League Appearances: John Trollope, 770, 1960–80.
Honours – Football League: Division 2 Champions – 1995–96. Division 4 Champions – 1985–86. **Football League Cup:** Winners 1968–69. **Anglo-Italian Cup:** Winners 1970.
Colours: Red shirts, white shorts, red stockings.

TORQUAY UNITED DIV. 3

Name			Birthplace		Previous
Ashington Ryan (F)	5 10	12 06	Torbay	28 3 83	Scholar
Bedeau Anthony (F)	5 10	12 03	Hammersmith	24 3 79	Trainee
Benefield Jimmy (F)	5 11	11 05	Bristol	6 5 83	Scholar
Canoville Lee (F)	6 0	11 04	Ealing	14 3 81	Arsenal
Dearden Kevin (G)	5 11	14 02	Luton	8 3 70	Wrexham
Douglin Troy (D)	6 0	12 03	Coventry	7 5 82	Trainee
Fowler Jason (M)	6 3	12 07	Bristol	20 8 74	Cardiff C
Graham David (F)	5 11	12 01	Edinburgh	6 10 78	Dunfermline Ath
Hankin Sean (M)	5 11	12 04	Camberley	28 2 81	Crystal Palace
Hazell Reuben (D)	5 11	11 11	Birmingham	24 4 79	Tranmere R

Hill Kevin (M)	5 8	10 06	Exeter	6	3 76	Torrington
Hockley Matthew (D)	5 10	11 11	Paignton	5	6 82	Trainee
Holmes Paul (D)	5 10	12 05	Stocksbridge	18	2 68	WBA
James John (D)			Plymouth	3	8 84	Topsham T
Morris Jason (D)	6 0	12 07	Torquay	7	5 83	Buckland Ath
Northmore Ryan (G)	6 2	13 00	Plymouth	5	9 80	Trainee
Rees Jason (M)	5 6	10 11	Aberdare	22	12 69	Exeter C
Russell Alex (M)	5 10	12 00	Crosby	17	3 73	Cambridge U
Stephens Nicholas (M)	6 2	12 00	Plymouth	30	5 83	Scholar
Woods Steve (D)	6 0	13 00	Northwich	15	12 76	Chesterfield
Woozley David (D)	6 0	12 10	Berkshire	6	12 79	Crystal Palace

League Appearances: Aggrey, J. 2; Ashford, R. 1(1); Banger, N. 1; Bedeau, A. 9(12); Benefield, J. 3(5); Brabin, G. 6; Brandon, C. 22(5); Brown, D. 2; Canoville, L. 10(2); Dearden, K. 46; Douglin, T. 5(1); Fowler, J. 14; Goodridge, G. 9(8); Graham, D. 31(5); Greyling, A. (2); Hankin, S. 27; Hanson, C. 6; Hazell, R. 19; Healy, B. 2; Herrera, R. 2(1); Hill, K. 40(4); Hockley, M. 12; Holmes, P. 17(1); Law, G. (5); Logan, R. 16; MacDonald, G. 5; Martin, A. 5; McNeil, M. 16; Nicholls, M. 4(5); O'Brien, M. (1); Parker, K. 2; Preece, D. 4(2); Rees, J. 26(7); Richardson, M. 18(12); Roach, N. 5(7); Russell, A. 33; Russell, L. 7(4); Tully, S. 17(1); Williams, E. 8(17); Williamson, M. 3; Woods, S. 38; Woozley, D. 15(1).
Goals – League (46): Graham 8, Russell A 7 (2 pens), Richardson 6, Bedeau 4, Logan 4 (1 pen), Brandon 3, Hill 2, Woods 2, Ashford 1, Canoville 1, Fowler 1, Goodridge 1, Nicholls 1, Roach 1, Williams 1, own goals 3.
Worthington Cup (2): Brandon 1, Graham 1.
FA Cup (1): Hill 1.
Ground: Plainmoor Ground, Torquay, Devon TQ1 3PS. Telephone (01803) 328666.
Record attendance: 21,908 v Huddersfield T, FA Cup 4th rd, 29 January 1955.
Capacity: 6283.
First Team Coach: Leroy Rosenior.
Secretary: Mrs H. Kindeleit-Badcock.
Most League Goals: 89, Division 3 (S), 1956–57.
Highest League Scorer in Season: Sammy Collins, 40, Division 3 (S), 1955–56.
Most League Goals in Total Aggregate: Sammy Collins, 204, 1948–58.
Most Capped Player: Rodney Jack, St Vincent.
Most League Appearances: Dennis Lewis, 443, 1947–59.
Honours – Nil
Colours: Yellow shirts with navy and white inserts under arm and white V. neck, yellow shorts, yellow stockings.

TOTTENHAM HOTSPUR   FA PREMIERSHIP

Acimovic Milenko (M)	6 1	12 08	Ljubljana	15	2 77	Red Star Belgrade
Anderton Darren (M)	6 1	12 11	Southampton	3	3 72	Portsmouth
Bowditch Ben (D)			Harlow	19	2 84	Scholar
Bunjevcevic Goran (D)	6 1	11 11	Karlovac	17	2 73	Red Star Belgrade
Carr Stephen (D)	5 9	12 04	Dublin	29	8 76	Trainee
Clemence Stephen (M)	6 0	12 04	Liverpool	31	3 78	Trainee
Davies Simon (M)	5 10	11 07	Haverfordwest	23	10 79	Peterborough U
Doherty Gary (D)	6 1	13 06	Carndonagh	31	1 80	Luton T
Etherington Matthew (F)	5 9	10 12	Truro	14	8 81	Peterborough U
Ferdinand Les (F)	5 11	13 02	Paddington	8	12 66	Newcastle U
Ferguson Steven (F)	5 10	11 02	Dunfermline	1	4 82	Musselburgh Windsor
Freund Steffen (M)	5 11	12 08	Brandenburg	19	1 70	Borussia Dortmund
Gardner Anthony (D)	6 3	14 00	Stafford	19	9 80	Port Vale
Hughes Mark (M)			Dungannon	16	9 83	Scholar

Iversen Steffen (F)	6 1	12 07	Oslo	10 11 76	
Jackson Johnnie (M)	6 1	12 11	Camden	15 8 82	Trainee
Jalal Shwan (G)			Baghdad	14 8 83	Hastings T
Keller Kasey (G)	6 2	13 12	Washington	27 11 69	Rayo Vallecano
Kelly Gavin (G)	6 0	13 07	Hammersmith	3 6 81	Trainee
Kelly Stephen (D)			Dublin	6 9 83	
King Ledley (D)	6 2	14 05	Bow	12 10 80	Trainee
Leonhardsen Oyvind (M)	5 10	11 07	Kristiansund	17 8 70	Liverpool
McKie Marcel (D)			Edmonton	22 9 84	Scholar
O'Donoghue Paul (D)			Lewisham	14 12 83	Scholar
Perry Chris (D)	5 8	10 12	Carshalton	26 4 73	Wimbledon
Piercy John (M)	5 9	11 13	Forest Gate	18 9 79	Trainee
Poyet Gustavo (M)	6 2	13 00	Montevideo	15 11 67	Chelsea
Rebrov Sergei (F)	5 7	11 00	Gorlovka	3 6 74	Dynamo Kiev
Redknapp Jamie (M)	6 0	13 04	Barton-on-Sea	25 6 73	Liverpool
Richards Dean (D)	6 2	13 12	Bradford	9 6 74	Southampton
Sheringham Teddy (F)	5 11	12 05	Highams Park	2 4 66	Manchester U
Sherwood Tim (M)	6 1	13 03	St Albans	2 2 69	Blackburn R
Slabber Jamie (F)			Enfield	31 12 84	Scholar
Snee George (F)			Dublin	26 1 83	Scholar
Sullivan Neil (G)	6 2	15 02	Sutton	24 2 70	Wimbledon
Sutton John (F)			Norwich	26 12 83	Scholar
Taricco Mauricio (D)	5 8	11 07	Buenos Aires	10 3 73	Ipswich T
Thatcher Ben (D)	5 10	12 06	Swindon	30 11 75	Wimbledon
Thelwell Alton (D)	5 10	12 02	Holloway	5 9 80	Trainee
Thomas Walter (M)			Sierra Leone	19 11 83	Scholar
Ziege Christian (D)	6 1	12 13	Berlin	1 2 72	Liverpool

League Appearances: Anderton, D. 33(2); Bunjevcevic, G. 5(1); Clemence, S. 4(2); Davies, S. 22(9); Doherty, G. 4(3); Etherington, M. 3(8); Ferdinand, L. 22(3); Freund, S. 19(1); Gardner, A. 11(4); Iversen, S. 12(6); Keller, K. 9; King, L. 32; Leonhardsen, O. 2(5); Perry, C. 30(3); Poyet, G. 32(2); Rebrov, S. 9(21); Richards, D. 24; Sheringham, T. 33(1); Sherwood, T. 15(4); Sullivan, N. 29; Taricco, M. 30; Thatcher, B. 11(1); Thelwell, A. (2); Ziege, C. 27.

Goals – League (49): Poyet 10, Sheringham 10 (3 pens), Ferdinand 9, Ziege 5, Davies 4, Iversen 4, Anderton 3, Richards 2, Rebrov 1, own goal 1.

Worthington Cup (21): Ferdinand 5, Davies 3, Rebrov 3, Iversen 2, Sheringham 2 (1 pen), Anderton 1, King 1, Poyet 1, Sherwood 1, Ziege 1, own goal 1.

FA Cup (10): Poyet 3, Anderton 1 (pen), Etherington 1, Ferdinand 1, Iversen 1, Sheringham 1, Ziege 1, own goal 1.

Ground: 748 High Rd, Tottenham, London N17 0AP. Telephone (020) 8365 5000.

Record attendance: 75,038 v Sunderland, FA Cup 6th rd, 5 March 1938.

Capacity: 36,236.

Manager: Glenn Hoddle.

Secretary: John Alexander.

Most League Goals: 115, Division 1, 1960–61.

Highest League Scorer in Season: Jimmy Greaves, 37, Division 1, 1962–63.

Most League Goals in Total Aggregate: Jimmy Greaves, 220, 1961–70.

Most Capped Player: Pat Jennings, 74 (119), Northern Ireland.

Most League Appearances: Steve Perryman, 655, 1969–86.

Honours – Football League: Division 1 Champions – 1950–51, 1960–61. Division 2 Champions – 1919–20, 1949–50. **FA Cup:** Winners 1901 (as non-**League** club), 1921, 1961, 1962, 1967, 1981, 1982, 1991. **Football League Cup:** Winners 1970–71, 1972–73, 1998–99. **European Competitions: European Cup-Winners' Cup winners:** 1962–63. **UEFA Cup winners:** 1971–72, 1983–84.

Colours: White shirts, navy blue shorts, white stockings.

Name		Ht	Wt	From			To
Achterberg John (G)	6 1	13 00	Utrecht	8	7 71	Eindhoven
Allen Graham (D)	6 0	12 00	Bolton	8	4 77	Everton
Baker Phillip (D)	6 0	11 10	Birkenhead	4 11 82	Scholar
Barlow Stuart (A)	5 10	11 03	Liverpool	16	7 68	Wigan Ath
Harrison Danny (M)	5 10	12 03	Liverpool	4 11 82	Scholar
Haworth Simon (F)	6 1	14 02	Cardiff	30	3 77	Wigan Ath
Hay Alexander (F)	5 10	11 05	Birkenhead	14 10 81	Scholar
Hill Clint (D)	6 0	11 06	Liverpool	19 10 78	Trainee
Hinds Richard (D)	6 2	12 00	Sheffield	22	8 80	Schoolboy
Hume Iain (F)	5 7	11 02	Edinburgh	31 10 83	
Koumas Jason (M)	5 10	11 06	Wrexham	25	9 79	Trainee
Linwood Paul (M)			Birkenhead	24 10 83	Scholar
McGuire Jamie (M)			Birkenhead	13 11 83	Scholar
Mellon Micky (M)	5 10	12 11	Paisley	18	3 72	Burnley
Murphy Joe (G)	6 2	13 06	Dublin	21	8 81	Trainee
N'Diaye Seyni (F)	6 2	13 06	Dakar	1	6 73	Caen
Navarro Alan (D)	5 10	11 07	Liverpool	31	5 81	Liverpool
Olsen James (D)	5 10	12 00	Bootle	23 10 81	Liverpool
Parkinson Andy (F)	5 8	10 12	Liverpool	27	5 79	Liverpool
Price Jason (M)	6 2	11 05	Pontypridd	12	4 77	Brentford
Sharps Ian (D)	6 3	13 05	Warrington	23 10 80	Trainee
Taylor Ryan (D)			Liverpool	19	8 84	Scholar

League Appearances: Achterberg, J. 25; Allen, G. 30(1); Allison, W. 13(14); Barlow, S. 31(7); Challinor, D. 6; Flynn, S. 30(1); Harrison, D. 1; Haworth, S. 12; Hay, A. 2(1); Hazell, R. 6; Henry, N. 39; Hill, C. 30; Hinds, R. 6(4); Hume, I. 1(13); Jobson, R. 1; Koumas, J. 38; Mellon, M. 23(4); Morgan, A. 1(1); Murphy, J. 21(1); N'Diaye, S. 6(5); Navarro, A. 21; Nixon, E. 1(1); Parkinson, A. 14(17); Price, J. 20(4); Rideout, P. 14(1); Roberts, G. 45; Sharps, I. 25(4), Thornton, S. 9(2); Yates, S. 36(1).

Goals – League (63): Barlow 14 (2 pens), Koumas 8, Price 7, Flynn 5, Haworth 5, Allison 4, Rideout 4, Yates 3, Hill 2, N'Diaye 2, Parkinson 2, Roberts 2, Allen 1, Henry 1, Mellon 1, Navarro 1, Thornton 1.

Worthington Cup (7): Barlow 2, Flynn 2, Henry 1, Koumas 1, Mellon 1.

FA Cup (16): Koumas 4, Price 4, Flynn 3, Allison 1, Barlow 1 (pen), Navarro 1, Rideout 1, Yates 1.

Ground: Prenton Park, Prenton Road West, Prenton, Wirral L42 9PN. Telephone (0151) 608 4194.

Record attendance: 24,424 v Stoke C, FA Cup 4th rd, 5 February 1972.

Capacity: 16,587.

Manager: Dave Watson.

Secretary: Mick Horton.

Most League Goals: 111, Division 3 (N), 1930–31.

Highest League Scorer in Season: Bunny Bell, 35, Division 3 (N), 1933–34.

Most League Goals in Total Aggregate: Ian Muir, 142, 1985–95.

Most Capped Player: John Aldridge, 30 (69), Republic of Ireland.

Most League Appearances: Harold Bell, 595, 1946–64 (incl. League record 401 consecutive appearances).

Honours – Football League Division 3 (N) Champions – 1937–38. **Welsh Cup:** Winners 1935. **Leyland Daf Cup:** Winners 1990.

Colours: White shirts, white shorts with blue trim.

WALSALL   DIV. 1

Barras Tony (D)	6 0	13 00	Billingham	29 3 71	Reading	
Biancalani Frederic (D)	5 11	12 01	France	21 7 74	Nancy	
Birch Gary (F)	6 0	12 03	Birmingham	8 10 81	Trainee	
Carbon Matt (D)	6 2	12 05	Nottingham	8 6 75	WBA	
Gadsby Matt (D)	6 1	11 12	Sutton Coldfield	6 9 79	Trainee	
Harper Lee (G)	6 1	13 11	Chelsea	30 10 71	QPR	
Hawley Karl (F)	5 8	12 02	Walsall	6 12 81	Scholar	
Herivelto Harry (M)	5 10	11 06	Brazil	23 8 75	Cruzeiro	
Leitao Jorge (F)	5 11	13 05	Oporto	14 1 74	Feirense	
Matias Pedro (M)	6 0	12 00	Madrid	11 10 73	Tranmere R	
Roper Ian (D)	6 3	13 04	Nuneaton	20 6 77	Trainee	
Wright Mark (M)	5 11	11 00	Wolverhampton	24 2 82	Scholar	

League Appearances: Andre, C. 5; Angell, B. 13(7); Aranalde, Z. 43(2); Barras, T. 25(1); Bennett, T. 34(6); Biancalani, F. 13(5); Birch, G. (1); Brightwell, I. 25(2); Byfield, D. 24(13); Carbon, M. 22; Chettle, S. 6; Corica, S. 13; Curtis, T. 31(5); Gadsby, M. 17(5); Garrocho, C. 2(2); Goodman, D. 7(10); Harper, L. 3; Hawley, K. (1); Herivelto, H. 11(13); Holdsworth, D. 9; Keates, D. 6(7); Leitao, J. 24(14); Marcelo 9; Matias, P. 25(5); O'Connor, M. 12(1); Ofodile, A. (1); Roper, I. 24(3); Scott, D. (1); Shields, G. 7; Simpson, F. 21(7); Thogersen, T. 7; Tillson, A. 8(1); Uhlenbeek, G. 5; Walker, J. 43; Wrack, D. 40(3).
Goals – League (51): Leitao 8, Matias 5, Barras 4, Byfield 4, Herivelto 4, Wrack 4, Angell 3, Corica 3, Aranalde 2, Biancalani 2, Simpson 2, Thogersen 2, Carbon 1, Goodman 1, Holdsworth 1, Keates 1 (pen), Marcelo 1, O'Connor 1, Tillson 1, own goal 1.
Worthington Cup (4): Barras 1, Byfield 1, Herivelto 1, Wrack 1.
FA Cup (5): Leitao 2, Angell 1, Bennett 1, Byfield 1.
Ground: Bescot Stadium, Bescot Cresent, Walsall WS1 4SA. Telephone (01922) 622791.
Record attendance: 10,628 B International, England v Switzerland, 20 May 1991.
Capacity: 6700 until December 2002, then 10,700.
Manager: Colin Lee.
Secretary/Commercial Manager: Roy Whalley.
Most League Goals: 102, Division 4, 1959–60.
Highest League Scorer in Season: Gilbert Alsop, 40, Division 3 (N), 1933–34 and 1934–35.
Most League Goals in Total Aggregate: Tony Richards, 184, 1954–63; Colin Taylor, 184, 1958–63, 1964–68, 1969–73.
Most Capped Player: Mick Kearns, 15 (18), Republic of Ireland.
Most League Appearances: Colin Harrison, 467, 1964–82.
Honours – Football League: Division 4 Champions – 1959–60.
Colours: Red shirts, red shorts, red stockings with black and white trim.

WATFORD   DIV. 1

Baardsen Espen (G)	6 5	13 03	San Rafael	7 12 77	Tottenham H	
Blizzard Dominic (M)			High Wycombe	2 9 83	Scholar	
Blondeau Patrick (D)	5 9	11 06	Marseille	27 1 68	Marseille	
Chamberlain Alec (G)	6 2	13 10	March	20 6 64	Sunderland	
Cook Lee (M)	5 9	11 04	Hammersmith	3 8 82	Aylesbury U	
Cox Neil (D)	6 0	12 01	Scunthorpe	8 10 71	Bolton W	
Doyley Lloyd (D)	5 10	11 04	London	1 12 82	Scholar	
Fisken Gary (M)	5 10	12 08	Watford	27 10 81	Scholar	
Foley Dominic (F)	6 1	12 08	Cork	7 7 76	Wolverhampton W	
Forde Fabian (F)	5 11	12 10	London	26 10 81	Scholar	

Gayle Marcus (F)	6 3	13 12	Hammersmith	28	9 70	Rangers
Glass Stephen (M)	5 9	10 11	Dundee	23	5 76	Newcastle U
Godfrey Elliott (M)			Toronto	22	2 83	Scholar
Hand Jamie (M)	6 0	11 08	Uxbridge	7	2 84	Scholar
Helguson Heidar (F)	5 10	12 04	Akureyri	22	8 77	Lillestrom
Hughes Stephen (M)	6 0	12 12	Wokingham	18	9 76	Everton
Hyde Micah (M)	5 10	11 07	Newham	10 11 74		Cambridge U
Ifil Jerel (D)	6 1	12 11	London	27	6 82	Academy
Issa Pierre (D)	6 4	14 00	Johannesburg	11	9 75	Chelsea
Johnson Richard (M)	5 10	11 13	Kurri Kurri	27	4 74	Trainee
Langston Matthew (D)	6 2	12 04	Brighton	2	4 81	Trainee
Lee Richard (G)	6 0	12 07	Oxford	5 10 82		Scholar
Mahon Gavin (M)	6 0	13 02	Birmingham	2	1 77	Brentford
Matthews Barrie (M)			Forest of Dean	1	2 83	Scholar
McNamee Anthony (F)	5 5	9 06	Lambeth	13	7 83	Scholar
Mead Daniel (M)			Luton	19	9 84	Scholar
Nielsen Allan (M)	5 8	11 02	Esbjerg	13	3 71	Tottenham H
Noel-Williams Gifton (F)	6 4	14 00	Islington	21	1 80	Trainee
Norville Jason (F)	5 11	10 07	Trinidad & Tobago	9	9 83	Scholar
Patterson Simon (M)			Northwick	4	9 82	
Robinson Paul (D)	5 9	11 11	Watford	14 12 78		Trainee
Saunders Neil (M)			Barking	7	5 83	Scholar
Smith Jack (D)			Hemel Hempstead	14 10 83		Scholar
Smith Tommy (F)	5 9	10 00	Hemel Hempstead	22	5 80	Trainee
Swonnell Sam (M)	5 10	11 10	Brentwood	13	9 82	Scholar
Vega Ramon (D)	6 3	14 00	Olten	14	6 71	Celtic
Vernazza Paulo (M)	5 10	10 13	Islington	1 11 79		Arsenal
Williams Nick (D)	6 1	12 10	Cheltenham	16	2 83	
Wright Nick (F)	5 10	11 08	Derby	15 10 75		Carlisle U

League Appearances: Baardsen, E. 14; Blondeau, P. 24(1); Brown, W. 10(1); Chamberlain, A. 32; Cook, L. 6(4); Cox, N. 39(1); Doyley, L. 11(9); Fisken, G. 12(5); Foley, D. 1; Galli, F. 27(1); Gayle, M. 28(8); Gibbs, N. (1); Glass, S. 29(2); Hand, J. 4(6); Helguson, H. 11(23); Hughes, S. 11(4); Hyde, M. 37(2); Issa, P. 12(3); Mahon, G. 6; McNamee, A. 2(5); Nielsen, A. 19(3); Noble, D. 5(10); Noel-Williams, G. 15(14); Norville, J. 2(2); Okon, P. 14(1); Panayi, J. 2(2); Pennant, J. 9; Robinson, P. 38; Smith, T. 35(5); Vega, R. 23(4); Vernazza, P. 21; Ward, D. (1); Webber, D. 4(1); Wooter, N. 7(10).

Goals – League (62): Smith 11 (1 pen), Helguson 6, Nielsen 6, Noel-Williams 6, Gayle 4, Hyde 4, Brown 3, Glass 3 (1 pen), Robinson 3, Cox 2, Pennant 2, Webber 2, Fisken 1, Galli 1, Issa 1, McNamee 1, Noble 1, Vega 1, Wooter 1, own goals 3.
Worthington Cup (11): Gayle 2 (1 pen), Hyde 2, Noel-Williams 2, Vega 2, Helguson 1, Robinson 1, Vernazza 1.
FA Cup (2): Gayle 1, Noel-Williams 1.
Ground: Vicarage Road Stadium, Watford WD18 0ER. Telephone (01923) 496000.
Record attendance: 34,099 v Manchester U, FA Cup 4th rd (replay), 3 February 1969. **Capacity:** 20,800.
Manager: To be appointed.
Secretary: Catherine Alexander.
Most League Goals: 92, Division 4, 1959–60.
Highest League Scorer in Season: Cliff Holton, 42, Division 4, 1959–60.
Most League Goals in Total Aggregate: Luther Blissett, 148, 1976–83, 1984–88, 1991–92.
Most Capped Player: John Barnes, 31 (79), England and Kenny Jackett, 31, Wales.
Most League Appearances: Luther Blissett, 415, 1976–83, 1984–88, 1991–92.
Honours – Football League: Division 3 Champions – 1968–69. Division 2 Champions – 1997–98. Division 4 Champions – 1977–78.
Colours: Yellow shirts, red shorts, red stockings with black and yellow turnover.

WEST BROMWICH ALBION   FA PREMIERSHIP

Name	Ht	Wt	Birthplace	Birthdate	Club/Status
Adamson Chris (G)	6 3	12 00	Ashington	4 11 78	Trainee
Appleton Michael (M)	5 8	11 00	Salford	4 12 75	Preston NE
Balis Igor (D)	5 11	11 00	Czech Republic	5 1 70	Spartak Trnava
Briggs Mark (M)	6 1	11 01	Wolverhampton	16 2 82	Scholar
Chambers Adam (D)	5 10	11 08	Sandwell	20 11 80	Trainee
Chambers James (D)	5 10	11 08	Sandwell	20 11 80	Trainee
Clement Neil (D)	6 0	14 07	Reading	3 10 78	Chelsea
Dichio Danny (F)	6 4	13 10	Hammersmith	19 10 74	Sunderland
Dobie Scott (F)	6 2	12 09	Workington	10 10 78	Carlisle U
Dyer Lloyd (M)			Birmingham	13 9 82	
Gilchrist Phil (D)	6 0	13 03	Stockton	25 8 73	Leicester C
Hoult Russell (G)	6 4	14 01	Ashby	22 11 72	Portsmouth
Jensen Brian (G)	6 1	12 04	Copenhagen	8 6 75	AZ
Johnson Andy (M)	6 0	13 03	Bristol	2 5 74	Nottingham F
Jordao (M)	6 0	12 07	Malanje	30 8 71	Braga
McInnes Derek (M)	5 7	11 04	Paisley	5 7 71	Toulouse
Moore Darren (D)	6 3	15 08	Birmingham	22 4 74	Portsmouth
Oliver Adam (M)	5 9	11 02	Sandwell	25 10 80	Trainee
Roberts Jason (F)	6 1	13 06	Park Royal	25 1 78	Bristol R
Scott Mark (F)	6 1	12 02	Sandwell	16 7 82	Scholar
Taylor Bob (F)	5 11	13 05	Easington	3 2 67	Bolton W
Turner Matt (M)	5 9	10 00	Nottingham	29 12 81	Nottingham F

League Appearances: Appleton, M. 18; Balis, I. 32(2); Benjamin, T. (3); Butler, T. 14(5); Chambers, A. 24(8); Chambers, J. 1(4); Clement, N. 45; Cummings, W. 6(8); Dichio, D. 26(1); Dobie, S. 32(11); Fox, R. 2(18); Gilchrist, P. 43; Hoult, R. 45; Jensen, B. 1; Johnson, A. 28(4); Jordao 19(6); Lyttle, D. 13(10); McInnes, D. 45; Moore, D. 31(1); Quinn, J. 1(6); Roberts, J. 12(2); Rosler, U. 5; Sigurdsson, L. 42(1); Taylor, B. 18(16); Varga, S. 3(1).
Goals – League (61): Dobie 10, Dichio 9, Roberts 7, Taylor 7, Clement 6 (1 pen), Jordao 5, Johnson 4, McInnes 3, Balis 2 (1 pen), Moore 2, Benjamin 1, Fox 1, Rosler 1, Sigurdsson 1, own goals 2.
Worthington Cup (3): Dobie 2, Jordao 1.
FA Cup (4): Clement 2 (2 pens), Dichio 1, Johnson 1.
Ground: The Hawthorns, West Bromwich B71 4LF. Telephone (0121) 525 8888.
Record attendance: 64,815 v Arsenal, FA Cup 6th rd, 6 March 1937. **Capacity:** 28,000.
Manager: Gary Megson.
Secretary: Dr. John J. Evans BA, PHD. (Wales).
Most League Goals: 105, Division 2, 1929–30.
Highest League Scorer in Season: William 'Ginger' Richardson, 39, Division 1, 1935–36.
Most League Goals in Total Aggregate: Tony Brown, 218, 1963–79.
Most Capped Player: Stuart Williams, 33 (43), Wales.
Most League Appearances: Tony Brown, 574, 1963–80.
Honours – Football League: Division 1 Champions – 1919–20. Division 2 Champions – 1901–02, 1910–11. **FA Cup:** Winners 1888, 1892, 1931, 1954, 1968. **Football League Cup:** Winners 1965–66.
Colours: Navy blue and white striped shirts, white shorts, blue and white stockings.

WEST HAM UNITED   FA PREMIERSHIP

Name	Ht	Wt	Birthplace	Birthdate	Club/Status
Britton Leon (M)			South London	16 9 82	Trainee
Byrne Shaun (D)	5 9	11 08	Taplow	21 1 81	Trainee

Bywater Steve (G)	6 2	12 00	Manchester	7 6 81	Trainee
Camara Titi (F)	6 0	13 00	Conakry	17 11 72	Liverpool
Carrick Michael (M)	6 1	11 10	Wallsend	28 7 81	Trainee
Charles Gary (D)	5 9	11 08	East London	13 4 70	Benfica
Cole Joe (M)	5 7	9 08	Islington	8.11 81	Trainee
Courtois Laurent (M)	5 7	10 11	Lyon	11 9 78	Toulouse
Dailly Christian (D)	6 0	12 10	Dundee	23 10 73	Blackburn R
Defoe Jermain (F)	5 7	10 04	Beckton	7 10 82	Charlton Ath
Di Canio Paolo (F)	5 9	11 09	Rome	9 7 68	Sheffield W
Forde David (G)	6 2	13 06	Galway	20 12 79	Barry T
Foxe Hayden (D)	6 3	13 05	Sydney	23 6 77	Mechelen
Garcia Richard (F)	5 11	12 00	Perth	9 4 81	Trainee
Hutchison Don (M)	6 1	11 08	Gateshead	9 5 71	Sunderland
Iriekpen Ezomo (D)	6 1	12 02	East London	14 5 82	Trainee
James David (G)	6 5	14 02	Welwyn	1 8 70	Aston Villa
Johnson Glen (D)			London	23 8 84	Scholar
Kanoute Frederic (F)	6 3	13 08	Ste. Foy-Les-Lyon	2 9 77	Lyon
Labant Vladimir (D)	6 0	13 00	Zilina	8 6 74	Sparta Prague
Lomas Steve (M)	6 0	12 08	Hanover	14 3 72	Manchester C
McCann Grant (M)	5 10	11 00	Belfast	14 4 80	Trainee
McMahon Daryl (M)			Dublin	10 10 83	
Minto Scott (D)	5 10	10 00	Wirral	6 8 71	Benfica
Moncur John (M)	5 8	9 10	Mile End	22 9 66	Swindon T
Pearce Ian (D)	6 3	14 04	Bury St Edmunds	7 5 74	Blackburn R
Repka Tomas (D)	6 0	12 04	Slavicin Zlin	2 1 74	Fiorentina
Schemmel Sebastian (D)	5 8	11 13	Nancy	2 6 75	Metz
Sinclair Trevor (M)	5 10	12 05	Dulwich	2 3 73	QPR
Soma Ragnvald (D)	6 2	12 02	Bryne	10 11 79	Bryne
Song Rigobert (D)	6 0	13 00	Nkanglicock	1 7 76	Liverpool
Ward Elliott (D)			Harrow	19 1 85	Scholar
Winterburn Nigel (D)	5 8	11 04	Coventry	11 12 63	Arsenal

League Appearances: Byrne, S. (1); Camara, T. (1); Carrick, M. 30; Cole, J. 29(1); Courtois, L. 5(2); Dailly, C. 38; Defoe, J. 14(21); Di Canio, P. 26; Foxe, H. 4(2); Garcia, R. 2(6); Hislop, S. 12; Hutchison, D. 24; James, D. 26; Kanoute, F. 27; Kit son, P. 3(4); Labant, V. 7(5); Lomas, S. 14(1); McCann, G. (3); Minto, S. 5; Moncur, J. 7(12); Pearce, I. 8(1); Repka, T. 31; Schemmel, S. 35; Sinclair, T. 34; Soma, R. 1(2); Song, R. 5; Todorov, S. 2(4); Winterburn, N. 29(2).

Goals – League (48): Kanoute 11, Defoe 10, Di Canio 9 (4 pens), Sinclair 5, Lomas 4, Kitson 3, Carrick 2, Pearce 2, Hutchison 1, Schemmel 1.

Worthington Cup (0).

FA Cup (6): Defoe 4, Cole 1, Kanoute 1.

Ground: Boleyn Ground, Green Street, Upton Park, London E13 9AZ. Telephone (020) 8548 2748.

Record attendance: 42,322 v Tottenham H, Division 1, 17 October 1970. **Capacity:** 35,595.

Manager: Glenn Roeder.

Secretary: Peter Barnes.

Most League Goals: 101, Division 2, 1957–58.

Highest League Scorer in Season: Vic Watson, 42, Division 1, 1929–30.

Most League Goals in Total Aggregate: Vic Watson, 298, 1920–35.

Most Capped Player: Bobby Moore, 108, England.

Most League Appearances: Billy Bonds, 663, 1967–88.

Honours – Football League: Division 2 Champions – 1957–58, 1980–81. **FA Cup:** Winners 1964, 1975, 1980. **European Competitions: European Cup-Winners' Cup winners:** 1964–65. **Intertoto Cup winners** 1999.

Colours: Claret shirts with sky blue sleeves, white shorts, white stockings.

WIGAN ATHLETIC   DIV. 2

Ashcroft Lee (F)	5 9	13 04	Preston	7	9 72	Grimsby T
Brannan Ged (M)	6 0	13 09	Liverpool	15	1 72	Motherwell
De Vos Jason (D)	6 4	13 10	Ontario	2	1 74	Dundee U
Dinning Tony (M)	5 11	12 00	Wallsend	12	4 75	Wolverhampton W
Ellington Nathan (F)	5 10	13 06	Bradford	2	7 81	Bristol R
Filan John (G)	6 2	14 11	Sydney	8	2 70	Blackburn R
Green Scott (D)	5 10	13 02	Walsall	15	1 70	Bolton W
Jackson Matt (D)	6 0	14 00	Leeds	19	10 71	Norwich C
Jarrett Jason (M)	6 0	13 03	Bury	14	9 79	Bury
Kennedy Peter (M)	5 10	11 12	Lisburn	10	9 73	Watford
Kerr Stewart (G)	6 2	14 08	Bellshill	13	11 74	Celtic
Liddell Andy (F)	5 8	11 13	Leeds	28	6 73	Barnsley
McCulloch Lee (F)	6 1	13 10	Bellshill	14	5 78	Motherwell
McMillan Steve (D)	5 8	12 00	Edinburgh	19	1 76	Motherwell
Mitchell Paul (D)	5 9	12 03	Manchester	26	8 81	Scholar
Pendlebury Ian (D)			Bolton	3	9 83	Trainee
Roberts Neil (F)	5 10	13 08	Wrexham	7	4 78	Wrexham
Teale Gary (F)	5 9	12 04	Glasgow	21	7 78	Ayr U

League Appearances: Adamczuk, D. 3; Ashcroft, L. 14(2); Brannan, G. 31(2); Bukran, G. 1; Cook, P. 6; Croft, G. 7; Dalglish, P. 17(12); De Vos, J. 19(1); De Zeeuw, A. 42; Dinning, T. 32(1); Ellington, N. 3; Filan, J. 25; Green, S. 35(4); Haworth, S. 19(8); Jackson, M. 26; Jarrett, J. 5; Kenna, J. 6; Kennedy, P. 29(2); Kerr, S. 8; Kilford, I. 7(13); Liddell, A. 33(1); McCulloch, L. 24(10); McGibbon, P. 18; McLoughlin, A. 1(2); McMillan, S. 29; Mitchell, P. 16(7); Nolan, I. 5(3); Pendlebury, I. 4; Roberts, N. 5(12); Santus, P. (1); Sharp, K. 1(1); Stillie, D. 13; Teale, G. 22(1); Traynor, G. (1).
Goals – League (66): Liddell 18 (3 pens), Haworth 10, McCulloch 6, De Vos 5, Dinning 5 (1 pen), Roberts 4, Ashcroft 3 (2 pens), Green 3, Dalglish 2, De Zeeuw 2, Ellington 2, Kenna 1, McGibbon 1, Teale 1, own goals 3.
Worthington Cup (2): Brannan 1, Haworth 1.
FA Cup (0).
Ground: J. J. B. Stadium, Robin Park, Newtown, Wigan WN6 7BA. Telephone (01942) 774 000.
Record attendance: 27,500 v Hereford U, FA Cup 2nd rd, 12 December 1953.
Capacity: 25,000
Manager: Paul Jewell.
Secretary: Mrs Brenda Spencer.
Most League Goals: 84, Division 3, 1996–97.
Highest League Scorer in Season: Graeme Jones, 31, Division 3, 1996–97.
Most League Goals in Total Aggregate: David Lowe, 66, 1982–87 and 1995–99.
Most Capped Player: Roy Carroll, 9 (11), Northern Ireland.
Most League Appearances: Kevin Langley, 317, 1981–86, 1990–94.
Honours – Football League: Division 3 Champions – 1996–97. **Freight Rover Trophy:** Winners 1984–85. **Auto Windscreens Shield:** Winners 1998–99.
Colours: All blue.

WIMBLEDON   DIV. 1

Agyemang Patrick (F)	6 1	12 00	Walthamstow	29	9 80	Trainee
Andersen Trond (M)	6 0	11 06	Kristiansund	6	1 75	Molde
Berni Tommaso (G)	6 0	11 04	Florence	6	3 83	Internazionale
Burwood John (D)	5 10	11 00	Newcastle	18	9 84	Scholar
Byrne Des (D)	6 1	12 07	Dublin	10	4 81	Sr Patrick's Ath
Connolly David (F)	5 9	10 09	Willesden	6	6 77	Feyenoord

Cunningham Kenny (D)	5 11	11 04	Dublin	28 6 71	Millwall
Darlington Jermaine (D)	5 9	12 09	Hackney	11 4 74	QPR
Davis Kelvin (G)	6 1	11 04	Bedford	29 9 76	Luton T
Francis Damien (M)	6 0	10 10	Wandsworth	27 2 79	Trainee
Gier Robert (D)	5 10	11 07	Ascot	6 1 80	Trainee
Gore Shane (G)	5 10	11 02	Ashford	28 10 81	Scholar
Gray Wayne (F)	5 10	11 07	South London	7 11 80	Trainee
Haara Heikki (D)	6 1	11 04	Lahti	20 11 82	
Harding Ben (M)	5 10	11 02	Carshalton	6 9 84	Scholar
Hawkins Peter (D)	6 0	11 04	Maidstone	19 9 78	Trainee
Herzig Nico (M)	5 10	11 00	Pobneck	10 12 83	Carl Zeiss Jena
Holloway Darren (D)	6 0	12 00	Crook	3 10 77	Sunderland
Hughes Michael (M)	5 6	10 08	Larne	2 8 71	West Ham U
Jupp Duncan (D)	6 0	12 04	Guildford	25 1 75	Fulham
Karlsson Par (M)	5 8	10 11	Gothenburg	29 5 78	IFK Gothenburg
Leigertwood Mikele (D)	6 1	11 04	Enfield	12 11 82	
Lund Andreas (F)	6 1	11 07	Kristiansund	7 5 75	Molde
McAnuff Joel (F)	5 11	11 04	Edmonton	9 11 81	Scholar
Mild Hakan (M)	5 11	11 02	Trollhattan	14 6 71	IFK Gothenburg
Morgan Lionel (F)	5 11	11 00	Tottenham	17 2 83	Scholar
Nowland Adam (F)	5 11	11 06	Preston	6 7 81	Blackpool
Reo-Coker Nigel (M)			Southwark	14 5 84	Scholar
Robinson Paul (F)	5 11	12 00	Sunderland	20 11 78	Newcastle U
Selley Ian (M)	5 10	10 11	Chertsey	14 6 74	Fulham
Shipperley Neil (F)	6 0	13 11	Chatham	30 10 74	Barnsley
Tapp Alex (M)	5 8	11 09	Redhill	7 6 82	Trainee
Waehler Kjetil (M)	5 10	11 04	Oslo	16 3 76	Lyn
Williams Mark (D)	6 0	12 04	Stalybridge	28 9 70	Watford
Willmott Chris (D)	5 11	10 12	Bedford	30 9 77	Luton T

League Appearances: Agyemang, P. 17(16); Ainsworth, G. (2); Andersen, T. 27(3); Ardley, N. 27(2); Brown, W. 17; Byrne, D. (1); Connolly, D. 35; Cooper, K. 39(1); Cunningham, K. 34; Darlington, J. 25(4); Davis, K. 40; Feuer, I. 2(2); Francis, D. 21(2); Gier, R. 3; Gore, S. (1); Hawkins, P. 25(4); Heald, P. 4; Holloway, D. 32; Hughes, M. 24(2); Jupp, D. 1(1); Karlsson, P. 1(6); Kimble, A. 7(2); Leigertwood, M. 1; McAnuff, J. 22(16); Mild, H. 8(1); Morgan, L. 4(7); Nielsen, D. 6(6); Nowland, A. 1(6); Reo-Coker, N. (1); Roberts, A. 18; Robinson, P. (1); Shipperley, N. 36(5); Williams, M. 4(1); Willmott, C. 25(2).

Goals – League (63): Connolly 18 (3 pens), Shipperley 12, Cooper 10, Agyemang 4, Hughes 4, McAnuff 4, Ardley 3, Nielsen 2, Brown 1, Francis 1, Morgan 1, Roberts 1, Willmott 1, own goal 1.

Worthington Cup (1): Williams 1.

FA Cup (0).

Ground: Selhurst Park, South Norwood, London SE25 6PY. Telephone (020) 8771 2233.

Record attendance: 30,115 v Manchester U, FA Premier League, 9 May 1993.

Capacity: 26,297.

Manager: Stuart Murdoch.

Secretary: Steve Rooke.

Most League Goals: 97, Division 3, 1983–84.

Highest League Scorer in Season: Alan Cork, 29, 1983–84.

Most League Goals in Total Aggregate: Alan Cork, 145, 1977–92.

Most Capped Player: Kenny Cunningham, 40, Republic of Ireland.

Most League Appearances: Alan Cork, 430, 1977–92.

Honours – Football League: Division 4 Champions – 1982–83. **FA Cup:** Winners 1987–88.

Colours: All navy blue with yellow trim.

WOLVERHAMPTON WANDERERS   DIV. 1

Andrews Keith (M)	6 0	13 05	Dublin	13 9 80	Trainee
Bazeley Darren (D)	5 11	11 09	Northampton	5 10 72	Watford
Blake Nathan (F)	5 11	13 12	Cardiff	27 1 72	Blackburn R
Branch Michael (F)	5 10	11 07	Liverpool	18 10 78	Everton
Butler Paul (D)	6 0	14 09	Manchester	2 11 72	Sunderland
Camara Mohammed (D)	5 11	11 09	Conakry	25 6 75	Le Havre
Cameron Colin (M)	5 8	11 00	Kirkcaldy	23 10 72	Hearts
Clingan Sammy (M)	5 11	11 06	Belfast	13 1 84	Scholar
Clyde Mark (D)	6 1	12 00	Limavady	27 12 82	Scholar
Coleman Ken (D)	6 0	12 00	Cork	20 9 82	Scholar
Connelly Sean (D)	5 10	11 10	Sheffield	26 6 70	Stockport Co
Cooper Kevin (M)	5 8	10 04	Derby	8 2 75	Wimbledon
Kennedy Mark (M)	5 11	11 09	Dublin	15 5 76	Manchester C
Larkin Colin (F)	5 9	10 02	Dundalk	27 4 82	Trainee
Lescott Jolean (D)	6 2	14 00	Birmingham	16 8 82	Trainee
McChrystal Mark (D)	6 1	13 07	Derry	25 6 84	Scholar
McGrane Ian (M)	5 10	12 00	Dublin	4 8 84	Scholar
Melligan John (M)	5 9	11 02	Dublin	11 2 82	Trainee
Miller Kenny (F)	5 10	11 04	Edinburgh	23 12 79	Rangers
Murray Matt (G)	6 4	13 10	Solihull	2 5 81	Trainee
Naylor Lee (D)	5 10	12 00	Bloxwich	19 3 80	Trainee
Ndah George (F)	6 1	12 06	Dulwich	23 12 74	Swindon T
Newton Shaun (M)	5 8	11 00	Camberwell	20 8 75	Charlton Ath
Oakes Michael (G)	6 2	14 00	Northwich	30 10 73	Aston Villa
Pollet Ludovic (D)	5 11	11 07	Vieux-conde	18 6 70	Le Havre
Proudlock Adam (F)	6 0	13 07	Wellington	9 5 81	Trainee
Rae Alex (M)	5 10	11 09	Glasgow	30 9 69	Sunderland
Roussel Cedric (F)	6 3	13 12	Mons	6 1 78	Coventry C
Sturridge Dean (F)	5 8	12 02	Birmingham	27 7 73	Leicester C
Ward Graham (M)	5 8	11 09	Dublin	25 2 83	Scholar

League Appearances: Andrews, K. 4(7); Blake, N. 38(1); Branch, M. 5(2); Butler, P. 43; Camara, M. 23(4); Cameron, C. 38(3); Connelly, S. 5(3); Cooper, K. 4(1); Dinning, T. 4; Halle, G. 4(1); Kennedy, M. 35; Ketsbaia, T. (2); Lescott, J. 44; Miller, K. 5(15); Muscat, K. 37; Naylor, L. 26(1); Ndah, G. 1(14); Newton, S. 45; Oakes, M. 46; Pollet, L. 5(3); Proudlock, A. 12(7); Rae, A. 31(5); Robinson, C. 15(8); Roussel, C. 6(11); Sinton, A. 3(4); Sturridge, D. 27.
Goals – League (76): Sturridge 20 (2 pens), Blake 11, Newton 8, Rae 7, Kennedy 5, Lescott 5, Cameron 4, Proudlock 3, Miller 2, Robinson 2, Roussel 2, Butler 1, Ndah 1, Sinton 1, own goals 4.
Worthington Cup (1): Dinning 1.
FA Cup (0).
Ground: Molineux Grounds, Wolverhampton WV1 4QR. Telephone (01902) 655000.
Record attendance: 61,315 v Liverpool, FA Cup 5th rd, 11 February 1939.
Capacity: 28,525.
Manager: Dave Jones.
Secretary: Richard Skirrow.
Most League Goals: 115, Division 2, 1931–32.
Highest League Scorer in Season: Dennis Westcott, 38, Division 1, 1946–47.
Most League Goals in Total Aggregate: Steve Bull, 250, 1986–99.
Most Capped Player: Billy Wright, 105, England (70 consecutive).
Most League Appearances: Derek Parkin, 501, 1967–82.
Honours – Football League: Division 1 Champions – 1953–54, 1957–58, 1958–59. Division 2 Champions – 1931–32, 1976–77. Division 3 (N) Champions – 1923–24. Division 3 Champions – 1988–89. Division 4 Champions – 1987–88. **FA Cup:** Winners 1893, 1908, 1949, 1960. **Football League Cup:** Winners 1973–74, 1979–80.

Sherpa Van Trophy winners 1988.
Colours: Gold shirts, black shorts, black stockings.

WREXHAM   DIV. 3

Carey Brian (D)	6 3	13 02	Cork	31	5 68	Leicester C
Edwards Carlos (F)	5 11	11 01	Trinidad	24	10 78	
Ferguson Darren (M)	5 10	11 10	Glasgow	9	2 72	Wolverhampton W
Holmes Shaun (D)	5 9	10 07	Derry	27	12 80	Manchester C
Lawrence Dennis (D)	6 7	11 13	Trinidad	1	8 74	Defence Force
Roberts Steve (D)	6 2	11 06	Wrexham	24	2 80	Trainee
Rogers Kristian (G)	6 0	11 12	Chester	2	10 80	
Sam Hector (F)	5 9	11 05	Trinidad	25	2 78	San Juan Jabloteh
Thomas Steve (M)	5 10	11 07	Hartlepool	23	6 79	Trainee
Trundle Lee (F)	6 0	11 11	Liverpool	10	10 76	Rhyl
Whitfield Paul (G)			St Asaph	6	5 82	Scholar

League Appearances: Barrett, P. 10(5); Bennett, D. 5(1); Blackwood, M. 21(10); Carey, B. 16(2); Chalk, M. 17(7); Edwards, C. 10(16); Evans, M. (4); Faulconbridge, C. 36(1); Ferguson, D. 37(1); Gibson, R. 11(7); Hill, K. 12; Holmes, S. 39(1); Jones, L. 3(1); Lawrence, D. 29(3); Miller, W. 5; Moody, A. (1); Morgan, C. (2); Morrell, A. 13(12); Pejic, S. 11(1); Phillips, W. 27; Roberts, S. 24; Rogers, K. 27; Rovde, M. 12; Russell, K. 8(2); Sam, H. 15(14); Sharp, K. 12(3); Thomas, S. 30(8); Trundle, L. 30(6); Walsh, D. 7(2); Warren, D. 5; Whitley, J. 34.
Goals – League (56): Faulconbridge 13, Trundle 8 (1 pen), Edwards 5, Jones 5, Sam 5 (2 pens), Chalk 3 (1 pen), Ferguson 3 (1 pen), Thomas 3, Blackwood 2, Carey 2, Lawrence 2, Morrell 2, Hill 1, Phillips 1, Roberts 1.
Worthington Cup (2): Faulconbridge 1, Russell 1.
FA Cup (0).
Ground: Racecourse Ground, Mold Road, Wrexham LL11 2AH. Telephone (01978) 262129.
Record attendance: 34,445 v Manchester U, FA Cup 4th rd, 26 January 1957.
Capacity: 15,500.
Manager: Denis Smith.
Secretary: D. L. Rhodes.
Most League Goals: 106, Division 3 (N), 1932–33.
Highest League Scorer in Season: Tom Bamford, 44, Division 3 (N), 1933–34.
Most League Goals in Total Aggregate: Tom Bamford, 175, 1928–34.
Most Capped Player: Joey Jones, 29 (72), Wales.
Most League Appearances: Arfon Griffiths, 592, 1959–61, 1962–79.
Honours – Football League: Division 3 Champions – 1977–78. **Welsh Cup:** Winners 22 times.
Colours: Red shirts, white shorts, red stockings.

WYCOMBE WANDERERS   DIV. 2

Brown Steve (M)	5 10	11 12	Northampton	6	7 66	Northampton T
Bulman Dannie (M)	5 9	11 12	Ashford	24	1 79	Ashford T
Currie Darren (M)	5 10	12 07	Hampstead	29	11 74	Barnet
Devine Sean (F)	5 11	13 00	Lewisham	6	9 72	Barnet
Harris Richard (F)	5 11	10 09	Croydon	23	10 80	Crystal Palace
Holligan Gavin (F)	5 10	13 00	Lambeth	30	6 80	West Ham U
Johnson Roger (D)	6 3	11 00	Ashford	28	4 83	Trainee
Leach Marc (D)			Hemel Hempstead	12	7 83	
Lee Martyn (M)	5 6	9 00	Guildford	10	8 80	Trainee
McCarthy Paul (D)	5 10	13 10	Cork	4	8 71	Brighton & HA

McSporran Jermaine (F)	5 10	10 12	Manchester	1 1 77	Oxford C
Osborn Mark (G)	6 0	14 01	Bletchley	19 6 81	Trainee
Rammell Andy (F)	6 1	13 12	Nuneaton	10 2 67	Walsall
Roberts Stuart (M)	5 6	9 08	Carmarthen	22 7 80	Swansea C
Rogers Mark (D)	5 11	12 12	Geulph	3 11 75	
Ryan Keith (M)	5 10	12 06	Northampton	25 6 70	Berkhamsted T
Senda Danny (F)	5 10	10 02	Harrow	17 4 81	Southampton
Simpemba Ian (M)			Dublin	28 3 83	Scholar
Simpson Michael (M)	5 8	11 07	Nottingham	28 2 74	Notts Co
Taylor Martin (G)	6 0	13 11	Tamworth	9 12 66	Derby Co
Thomson Andy (D)	6 3	14 03	Swindon	28 3 74	Bristol R
Townsend Ben (D)	5 10	11 03	Reading	8 10 81	Scholar
Vinnicombe Chris (D)	5 9	10 12	Exeter	20 10 70	Burnley
Williams Steven (G)			Oxford	21 4 83	Scholar

League Appearances: Baird, A. 1(5); Brown, S. 31(8); Bulman, D. 37(9); Carroll, D. 1(11); Cousins, J. 13(6); Currie, D. 44(2); Devine, S. 19(1); Emblen, P. 5(7); Harris, R. 2(1); Holligan, G. 11(9); Johnson, R. 7; Leach, M. 1; Lee, M. 2(5); Lopez, C. 1; Marsh, C. (1); McCarthy, P. 28; McSporran, J. 19(13); Phelan, L. (1); Rammell, A. 27; Roberts, S. 18(8); Rogers, M. 39(2); Ryan, K. 12(23); Senda, D. 38(5); Simpson, M. 43; Taylor, M. 46; Thomson, A. 3; Townsend, B. 2; Tuttle, D. 4; Vinnicombe, C. 42; Walker, R. 10(2).
Goals – League (58): Rammell 11 (1 pen), Brown 8 (4 pens), McSporran 7, Bulman 5, Devine 5, Holligan 4, Currie 3, McCarthy 3, Walker 3, Rogers 2, Emblen 1, Johnson 1, Ryan 1, Simpson 1, Vinnicombe 1, own goals 2.
Worthington Cup (0).
FA Cup (9): Currie 3, Rammell 2, Brown 1 (pen), Bulman 1, McSporran 1, Walker 1.
Ground: Adams Park, Hillbottom Road, Sands, High Wycombe HP12 4HJ. Telephone (01494) 472100.
Record attendance: 9002 v West Ham U, FA Cup 3rd rd, 7 January 1995. **Capacity:** 10,000 (7350 seats).
Manager: Lawrie Sanchez.
Secretary: Keith J. Allen.
Most League Goals: 67, Division 3, 1993–94.
Highest League Goalscorer in Season: Sean Devine, 23, 1999–2000.
Most League Goals in Total Aggregate: Dave Carroll, 41, 1993–2002.
Most Capped Player: Mark Rogers, 5, Canada.
Most League Appearances: Steve Brown, 309, 1994–2002.
Honours – GM Vauxhall Conference winners: 1993. **FA Trophy winners:** 1991, 1993.
Colours: Light and dark blue quartered shirts, navy shorts, light blue stockings.

YORK CITY   DIV. 3

Basham Mike (D)	6 0	13 09	Barking	27 9 73	Barnet
Brackstone Stephen (M)	5 11	10 08	Hartlepool	19 9 82	Middlesbrough
Brass Chris (M)	5 10	11 11	Easington	24 7 75	Burnley
Bullock Lee (M)	6 0	12 12	Stockton	22 5 81	Trainee
Cooper Richard (M)	5 8	11 01	Nottingham	27 9 79	Nottingham F
Fettis Alan (G)	6 0	13 09	Newtownards	1 2 71	Blackburn R
Fox Christian (M)	5 10	11 12	Auchenbrae	11 4 81	Trainee
Grant Lee (D)	6 0	11 00	York	31 12 85	
Hobson Gary (D)	6 1	13 04	North Ferriby	12 11 72	Chester C
Howarth Russell (G)	6 2	14 07	York	27 3 82	Scholar
Mathie Alex (F)	5 10	12 00	Bathgate	20 12 68	Preston NE
Nogan Lee (F)	5 10	11 09	Cardiff	21 5 69	Darlington
O'Kane Aiden (M)	5 9	11 03	Belfast	24 11 79	

Parkin Jonathan (D)	6 1	15 00	Barnsley	30 12 81	Barnsley
Potter Graham (D)	5 11	11 13	Solihull	20 5 75	WBA
Smith Christopher (D)	5 11	13 01	Derby	30 6 81	Reading
Wood Leigh (M)	5 11	11 10	Selby	21 5 83	Scholar

League Appearances: Basham, M. 26(3); Brackstone, S. 6(3); Brass, C. 41; Bullock, L. 39(1); Cooper, R. 23(2); Darlow, K. 1(1); Duffield, P. 7(4); Edmondson, D. 34(2); Emmerson, S. (6); Evans, M. 1(1); Fettis, A. 45; Fielding, J. 9; Fox, C. 5(7); Grant, L. (1); Hobson, G. 14(2); Hocking, M. 29(4); Howarth, R. 1(1); Jones, S. 7(1); Maley, M. 11(2); Mathie, A. 11(12); Nogan, L. 40(2); O'Kane, A. 11(1); Parkin, J. 18; Potter, G. 37;·Proctor, M. 40(1); Rhodes, B. (1); Richardson, N. 17(5); Salvati, M. 1(7); Smith, C. 12(3); Stamp, N. 5(2); Wise, S. 3(3); Wood, L. 12(2).

Goals – League (54): Proctor 14, Nogan 13, Bullock 8, Duffield 3, Basham 2, Brass 2, Mathie 2, Parkin 2, Potter 2, Cooper 1, Fielding 1, Jones S 1, Salvati 1, own goals 2.

Worthington Cup (2): Brass 1, Bullock 1.
FA Cup (5): Potter 2, Brass 1, Richardson 1, own goal 1.
Ground: Bootham Crescent, York YO3 7AQ. Telephone (01904) 624447.
Record attendance: 28,123 v Huddersfield T, FA Cup 6th rd, 5 March 1938.
Capacity: 9496.
Manager: Terry Dolan.
Secretary: Keith Usher.
Most League Goals: 96, Division 4, 1983–84.
Highest League Scorer in Season: Bill Fenton, 31, Division 3 (N), 1951–52; Arthur Bottom, 31, Division 3 (N), 1954–55 and 1955–56.
Most League Goals in Total Aggregate: Norman Wilkinson, 125, 1954–66.
Most Capped Player: Peter Scott, 7 (10), Northern Ireland.
Most League Appearances: Barry Jackson, 481, 1958–70.
Honours – Football League: Division 4 Champions – 1983–84.
Colours: Red shirts, red shorts, red stockings.

LEAGUE POSITIONS: FA PREMIER from 1992–93 and DIVISION 1 1976–77 to 1991–92

	2000–01	1999–2000	1998–99	1997–98	1996–97	1995–96	1994–95	1993–94	1992–93	1991–92	1990–91	1989–90	1988–89
Arsenal	2	2	2	1	3	5	12	4	10	4	1	4	1
Aston Villa	8	6	6	7	5	4	18	10	2	7	17	2	17
Barnsley	–	–	–	19	–	–	–	–	–	–	–	–	–
Birmingham C	–	–	–	–	–	–	–	–	–	–	–	–	–
Blackburn R	–	–	19	6	13	7	1	2	4	–	–	–	–
Bolton W	–	–	–	18	–	20	–	–	–	–	–	–	–
Bradford C	20	17	–	–	–	–	–	–	–	–	–	–	–
Brighton & HA	–	–	–	–	–	–	–	–	–	–	–	–	–
Bristol C	–	–	–	–	–	–	–	–	–	–	–	–	–
Charlton Ath	9	–	18	–	–	–	–	–	–	–	–	19	14
Chelsea	6	5	3	4	6	11	11	14	11	14	11	5	–
Coventry C	19	14	15	11	17	16	16	11	15	19	16	12	7
Crystal Palace	–	–	–	20	–	–	19	–	20	10	3	15	–
Derby Co	17	16	8	9	12	–	–	–	–	–	20	16	5
Everton	16	13	14	17	15	6	15	17	13	12	9	6	8
Ipswich T	5	–	–	–	–	–	22	19	16	–	–	–	–
Leeds U	4	3	4	5	11	13	5	5	17	1	4	–	–
Leicester C	13	8	10	10	9	–	21	–	–	–	–	–	–
Liverpool	3	4	7	3	4	3	4	8	6	6	2	1	2
Luton T	–	–	–	–	–	–	–	–	–	20	18	17	16
Manchester C	18	–	–	–	–	18	17	16	9	5	5	14	–
Manchester U	1	1	1	2	1	1	2	1	1	2	6	13	11
Middlesbrough	14	12	9	–	19	12	–	–	21	–	–	–	18
Millwall	–	–	–	–	–	–	–	–	–	–	–	20	10
Newcastle U	11	11	13	13	2	2	6	3	–	–	–	–	20
Norwich C	–	–	–	–	–	–	20	12	3	18	15	10	4
Nottingham F	–	–	20	–	20	9	3	–	22	8	8	9	3
Notts Co	–	–	–	–	–	–	–	–	–	21	–	–	–
Oldham Ath	–	–	–	–	–	–	21	19	17	–	–	–	–
Oxford U	–	–	–	–	–	–	–	–	–	–	–	–	–
Portsmouth	–	–	–	–	–	–	–	–	–	–	–	–	–
QPR	–	–	–	–	19	8	9	5	11	12	11	9	–
Sheffield U	–	–	–	–	–	–	20	14	9	13	–	–	–
Sheffield W	–	19	12	16	7	15	13	7	7	3	–	18	15
Southampton	10	15	17	12	16	17	10	18	18	16	14	7	13
Stoke C	–	–	–	–	–	–	–	–	–	–	–	–	–
Sunderland	7	7	–	–	18	–	–	–	–	–	19	–	–
Swansea C	–	–	–	–	–	–	–	–	–	–	–	–	–
Swindon T	–	–	–	–	–	–	–	22	–	–	–	–	–
Tottenham H	12	10	11	14	10	8	7	15	8	15	10	3	6
Watford	–	20	–	–	–	–	–	–	–	–	–	–	–
WBA	–	–	–	–	–	–	–	–	–	–	–	–	–
West Ham U	15	9	5	8	14	10	14	13	–	22	–	–	19
Wimbledon	–	18	16	15	8	14	9	6	12	13	7	8	12
Wolv'hampton W	–	–	–	–	–	–	–	–	–	–	–	–	–

1987–88	1986–87	1985–86	1984–85	1983–84	1982–83	1981–82	1980–81	1979–80	1978–79	1977–78	1976–77	
6	4	7	7	6	10	5	3	4	7	5	8	Arsenal
–	22	16	10	10	6	11	1	7	8	8	4	Aston Villa
–	–	–	–	–	–	–	–	–	–	–	–	Barnsley
–	–	21	–	20	17	16	13	–	21	11	13	Birmingham C
–	–	–	–	–	–	–	–	–	–	–	–	Blackburn R
–	–	–	–	–	–	22	17	–	–	–	–	Bolton W
–	–	–	–	–	–	–	–	–	–	–	–	Bradford C
–	–	–	–	22	13	19	16	–	–	–	–	Brighton & HA
–	–	–	–	–	–	–	–	20	13	17	18	Bristol C
17	19	–	–	–	–	–	–	–	–	–	–	Charlton Ath
18	14	6	6	–	–	–	–	–	22	16	–	Chelsea
10	10	17	18	19	19	14	16	15	10	7	19	Coventry C
–	–	–	–	–	–	22	13	–	–	–	–	Crystal Palace
15	–	–	–	–	–	–	–	21	19	12	15	Derby Co
4	1	2	1	7	7	8	15	19	4	3	9	Everton
–	–	20	17	12	9	2	2	3	6	18	3	Ipswich T
–	–	–	–	–	20	9	11	5	9	10	–	Leeds U
–	20	19	15	15	–	–	21	–	–	22	11	Leicester C
1	2	1	2	1	1	1	5	1	1	2	1	Liverpool
9	7	9	13	16	18	–	–	–	–	–	–	Luton T
–	21	15	–	–	20	10	12	17	15	4	2	Manchester C
2	11	4	4	4	3	3	8	2	9	10	6	Manchester U
–	–	–	–	–	–	22	14	9	12	14	12	Middlesbrough
–	–	–	–	–	–	–	–	–	–	–	–	Millwall
8	17	11	14	–	–	–	–	–	–	21	5	Newcastle U
14	5	–	20	14	14	–	20	12	16	13	16	Norwich C
3	8	8	9	3	5	12	7	5	2	1	–	Nottingham F
–	–	–	21	15	15	–	–	–	–	–	–	Notts Co
–	–	–	–	–	–	–	–	–	–	–	–	Oldham Ath
21	18	18	–	–	–	–	–	–	–	–	–	Oxford U
19	–	–	–	–	–	–	–	–	–	–	–	Portsmouth
5	16	13	19	5	–	–	–	–	20	19	14	QPR
–	–	–	–	–	–	–	–	–	–	–	–	Sheffield U
11	13	5	8	–	–	–	–	–	–	–	–	Sheffield W
12	12	14	5	2	12	7	6	8	14	–	–	Southampton
–	–	–	22	18	13	18	11	18	–	–	21	Stoke C
–	–	–	21	13	16	19	17	–	–	–	20	Sunderland
–	–	–	–	–	21	6	–	–	–	–	–	Swansea C
–	–	–	–	–	–	–	–	–	–	–	–	Swindon T
13	3	10	3	8	4	4	10	14	11	–	22	Tottenham H
20	9	12	11	11	2	–	–	–	–	–	–	Watford
–	–	22	12	17	11	17	4	10	3	6	7	WBA
16	15	3	16	9	8	9	–	–	–	20	17	West Ham U
7	6	–	–	–	–	–	–	–	–	–	–	Wimbledon
–	–	–	–	22	–	21	18	6	18	15	–	Wolv'hampton W

LEAGUE POSITIONS: DIVISION 1 from 1992–93 and DIVISION 2 1976–77 to 1991–92

	2000–01	1999–2000	1998–99	1997–98	1996–97	1995–96	1994–95	1993–94	1992–93	1991–92	1990–91	1989–90	1988–89
Aston Villa	–	–	–	–	–	–	–	–	–	–	–	–	–
Barnsley	16	4	13	–	2	10	6	18	13	16	8	19	7
Birmingham C	5	5	4	7	10	15	–	22	19	–	–	–	23
Blackburn R	2	11	–	–	–	–	–	–	–	6	19	5	5
Blackpool	–	–	–	–	–	–	–	–	–	–	–	–	–
Bolton W	3	6	6	–	1	–	3	14	–	–	–	–	–
Bournemouth	–	–	–	–	–	–	–	–	–	–	–	22	12
Bradford C	–	–	2	13	21	–	–	–	–	–	–	23	14
Brentford	–	–	–	–	–	–	–	–	22	–	–	–	–
Brighton & HA	–	–	–	–	–	–	–	–	–	23	6	18	19
Bristol C	–	–	24	–	–	–	23	13	15	17	9	–	–
Bristol R	–	–	–	–	–	–	–	–	24	13	13	–	–
Burnley	7	–	–	–	–	–	22	–	–	–	–	–	–
Bury	–	–	22	17	–	–	–	–	–	–	–	–	–
Cambridge U	–	–	–	–	–	–	–	–	23	5	–	–	–
Cardiff C	–	–	–	–	–	–	–	–	–	–	–	–	–
Carlisle U	–	–	–	–	–	–	–	–	–	–	–	–	–
Charlton Ath	–	1	–	4	15	6	15	11	12	7	16	–	–
Chelsea	–	–	–	–	–	–	–	–	–	–	–	–	1
Crewe Alex	14	19	18	11	–	–	–	–	–	–	–	–	–
Crystal Palace	21	15	14	–	6	3	–	1	–	–	–	–	3
Derby Co	–	–	–	–	2	9	6	8	3	–	–	–	–
Fulham	1	9	–	–	–	–	–	–	–	–	–	–	–
Gillingham	13	–	–	–	–	–	–	–	–	–	–	–	–
Grimsby T	18	20	11	–	22	17	10	16	9	19	–	–	–
Hereford U	–	–	–	–	–	–	–	–	–	–	–	–	–
Huddersfield T	22	8	10	16	20	8	–	–	–	–	–	–	–
Hull C	–	–	–	–	–	–	–	–	–	–	24	14	21
Ipswich T	–	3	3	5	4	7	–	–	–	1	14	9	8
Leeds U	–	–	–	–	–	–	–	–	–	–	–	1	10
Leicester C	–	–	–	–	–	5	–	4	6	4	22	13	15
Leyton Orient	–	–	–	–	–	–	–	–	–	–	–	–	–
Luton T	–	–	–	–	24	16	20	20	–	–	–	–	–
Manchester C	–	2	–	22	14	–	–	–	–	–	–	–	2
Mansfield T	–	–	–	–	–	–	–	–	–	–	–	–	–
Middlesbrough	–	–	–	2	–	1	9	–	2	7	21	–	–
Millwall	–	–	–	–	22	12	3	7	15	5	–	–	–
Newcastle U	–	–	–	–	–	–	–	1	20	11	3	–	–
Norwich C	15	12	9	15	13	16	–	–	–	–	–	–	–
Nottingham F	11	14	–	1	–	–	–	2	–	–	–	–	–
Notts Co	–	–	–	–	–	24	7	17	–	4	–	–	–
Oldham Ath	–	–	–	–	23	18	14	–	–	–	1	8	16
Oxford U	–	–	23	12	17	–	–	23	14	21	10	17	17
Peterborough U	–	–	–	–	–	–	–	24	10	–	–	–	–
Plymouth Arg	–	–	–	–	–	–	–	–	–	22	18	16	18
Port Vale	–	23	21	19	8	12	17	–	–	24	15	11	–
Portsmouth	20	18	19	20	7	21	18	17	3	9	17	12	20
Preston NE	4	–	–	–	–	–	–	–	–	–	–	–	–
QPR	23	10	20	21	9	–	–	–	–	–	–	–	–

Club	1987-88	1986-87	1985-86	1984-85	1983-84	1982-83	1981-82	1980-81	1979-80	1978-79	1977-78	1976-77
Aston Villa	2	–	–	–	–	–	–	–	–	–	–	–
Barnsley	14	11	12	11	14	10	6	–	–	–	–	–
Birmingham C	19	19	–	2	–	–	–	3	–	–	–	–
Blackburn R	5	12	19	5	6	11	10	4	–	22	5	12
Blackpool	–	–	–	–	–	–	–	–	–	–	20	5
Bolton W	–	–	–	–	22	19	18	–	–	–	1	4
Bournemouth	17	–	–	–	–	–	–	–	–	–	–	–
Bradford C	4	10	13	–	–	–	–	–	–	–	–	–
Brentford	–	–	–	–	–	–	–	–	–	–	–	–
Brighton & HA	–	22	11	6	9	–	–	–	–	2	4	–
Bristol C	–	–	–	–	–	–	21	–	–	–	–	–
Bristol R	–	–	–	–	–	–	22	19	16	18	15	–
Burnley	–	–	–	–	21	–	–	21	13	11	16	–
Bury	–	–	–	–	–	–	–	–	–	–	–	22
Cambridge U	–	–	–	22	12	14	13	8	12	–	–	–
Cardiff C	–	–	21	15	–	20	19	15	9	19	18	–
Carlisle U	–	20	16	7	14	–	–	–	–	–	–	20
Charlton Ath	–	–	2	17	13	17	13	–	22	19	17	7
Chelsea	–	–	–	–	1	18	12	12	4	–	–	2
Crewe Alex	–	–	–	–	–	–	–	–	–	–	–	–
Crystal Palace	6	6	5	15	18	15	15	–	–	1	9	–
Derby Co	–	1	–	–	20	13	16	6	–	–	–	–
Fulham	–	–	22	9	11	4	–	–	20	10	10	17
Gillingham	–	–	–	–	–	–	–	–	–	–	–	–
Grimsby T	–	21	15	10	5	19	17	7	–	–	–	–
Hereford U	–	–	–	–	–	–	–	–	–	–	–	22
Huddersfield T	23	17	16	13	12	–	–	–	–	–	–	–
Hull C	15	14	6	–	–	–	–	–	–	–	22	14
Ipswich T	8	5	–	–	–	–	–	–	–	–	–	–
Leeds U	7	4	14	7	10	8	–	–	–	–	–	–
Leicester C	13	–	–	–	–	3	8	–	1	17	–	–
Leyton Orient	–	–	–	–	–	22	17	14	11	14	19	–
Luton T	–	–	–	–	–	–	1	5	6	18	13	6
Manchester C	9	–	–	3	4	–	–	–	–	–	–	–
Mansfield T	–	–	–	–	–	–	–	–	–	21	–	–
Middlesbrough	3	–	21	19	17	16	–	–	–	–	–	–
Millwall	1	16	9	–	–	–	–	–	21	16	10	–
Newcastle U	–	–	–	–	3	5	9	11	9	8	–	–
Norwich C	–	–	1	–	–	–	3	–	–	–	–	–
Nottingham F	–	–	–	–	–	–	–	–	–	–	–	3
Notts Co	–	–	–	20	–	–	2	17	6	15	8	–
Oldham Ath	10	3	8	14	19	7	11	15	11	14	8	13
Oxford U	–	–	–	1	–	–	–	–	–	–	–	–
Peterborough U	–	–	–	–	–	–	–	–	–	–	–	–
Plymouth Arg	16	7	–	–	–	–	–	–	–	–	–	21
Port Vale	–	–	–	–	–	–	–	–	–	–	–	–
Portsmouth	–	2	4	4	16	–	–	–	–	–	–	–
Preston NE	–	–	–	–	–	–	20	10	7	–	–	–
QPR	–	–	–	–	1	5	8	5	–	–	–	–

LEAGUE POSITIONS: DIVISION 1 from 1992–93 and DIVISION 2 1976–77 to 1991–92 (cont.)

	2000-01	1999-2000	1998-99	1997-98	1996-97	1995-96	1994-95	1993-94	1992-93	1991-92	1990-91	1989-90	1988-89
Reading	–	–	–	24	18	19	2	–	–	–	–	–	–
Rotherham U	–	–	–	–	–	–	–	–	–	–	–	–	–
Sheffield U	10	16	8	6	5	9	8	–	–	–	–	2	–
Sheffield W	17	–	–	–	–	–	–	–	–	–	3	–	–
Shrewsbury T	–	–	–	–	–	–	–	–	–	–	–	–	22
Southampton	–	–	–	–	–	–	–	–	–	–	–	–	–
Southend U	–	–	–	–	24	14	13	15	18	12	–	–	–
Stockport Co	19	17	16	8	–	–	–	–	–	–	–	–	–
Stoke C	–	–	–	23	12	4	11	10	–	–	–	24	13
Sunderland	–	–	1	3	–	1	20	12	21	18	–	6	11
Swansea C	–	–	–	–	–	–	–	–	–	–	–	–	–
Swindon T	–	24	17	18	19	–	21	–	5	8	21	4	6
Tottenham H	–	–	–	–	–	–	–	–	–	–	–	–	–
Tranmere R	24	13	15	14	11	13	5	5	4	14	–	–	–
Walsall	–	22	–	–	–	–	–	–	–	–	–	–	24
Watford	9	–	5	–	–	23	7	19	16	10	20	15	4
WBA	6	21	12	10	16	11	19	21	–	–	23	20	9
West Ham U	–	–	–	–	–	–	–	–	–	2	–	2	7
Wimbledon	8	–	–	–	–	–	–	–	–	–	–	–	–
Wolv'hampton W	12	7	7	9	3	20	4	8	11	11	12	10	–
Wrexham	–	–	–	–	–	–	–	–	–	–	–	–	–

LEAGUE POSITIONS: DIVISION 2 from 1992–93 and DIVISION 3 1976–77 to 1991–92

	2000-01	1999-2000	1998-99	1997-98	1996-97	1995-96	1994-95	1993-94	1992-93	1991-92	1990-91	1989-90	1988-89
Aldershot	–	–	–	–	–	–	–	–	–	–	–	–	24
Barnet	–	–	–	–	–	–	24	–	–	–	–	–	–
Barnsley	–	–	–	–	–	–	–	–	–	–	–	–	–
Birmingham C	–	–	–	–	–	–	1	–	–	2	12	7	–
Blackburn R	–	–	–	–	–	–	–	–	–	–	–	–	–
Blackpool	–	22	14	12	7	3	12	20	18	–	–	23	19
Bolton W	–	–	–	–	–	–	–	–	2	13	4	6	10
Bournemouth	7	16	7	9	16	14	19	17	17	8	9	–	–
Bradford C	–	–	–	–	–	6	14	7	10	16	8	–	–
Brentford	14	17	–	21	4	15	2	16	–	1	6	13	7
Brighton & HA	–	–	–	–	–	23	16	14	9	–	–	–	–
Bristol C	9	9	–	2	5	13	–	–	–	–	–	2	11
Bristol R	21	7	13	5	17	10	4	8	–	–	–	1	5
Burnley	–	2	15	20	9	17	–	6	13	–	–	–	–
Bury	16	15	–	–	1	–	–	–	–	21	7	5	13
Cambridge U	19	19	–	–	–	–	20	10	–	–	1	–	–

	1987–88	1986–87	1985–86	1984–85	1983–84	1982–83	1981–82	1980–81	1979–80	1978–79	1977–78	1976–77
Reading	22	13	–	–	–	20	7	–	–	–	–	–
Rotherham U	–	–	–	–	–	20	7	–	–	–	–	–
Sheffield U	21	9	7	18	–	–	–	–	–	20	12	11
Sheffield W	–	–	–	–	2	6	4	10	–	–	–	–
Shrewsbury T	18	18	17	8	8	9	18	14	13	–	–	–
Southampton	–	–	–	–	–	–	–	–	–	–	2	9
Southend U	–	–	–	–	–	–	–	–	–	–	–	–
Stockport Co	–	–	–	–	–	–	–	–	–	–	–	–
Stoke C	11	8	10	–	–	–	–	–	–	3	7	–
Sunderland	–	20	18	–	–	–	–	2	4	6	–	
Swansea C	–	–	–	–	21	–	–	3	12	–	–	–
Swindon T	12	–	–	–	–	–	–	–	–	–	–	–
Tottenham H	–	–	–	–	–	–	–	–	–	–	3	–
Tranmere R	–	–	–	–	–	–	–	–	–	–	–	–
Walsall	–	–	–	–	–	–	–	–	–	–	–	–
Watford	–	–	–	–	–	2	9	18	–	–	–	–
WBA	20	15	–	–	–	–	–	–	–	–	–	–
West Ham U	–	–	–	–	–	–	1	7	5	–	–	–
Wimbledon	–	–	3	12	–	–	–	–	–	–	–	–
Wolv'hampton W	–	–	–	22	–	2	–	–	–	–	–	1
Wrexham	–	–	–	–	–	–	21	16	16	15	–	–

	1987–88	1986–87	1985–86	1984–85	1983–84	1982–83	1981–82	1980–81	1979–80	1978–79	1977–78	1976–77
Aldershot	20	–	–	–	–	–	–	–	–	–	–	–
Barnet	–	–	–	–	–	–	–	–	–	–	–	–
Barnsley	–	–	–	–	–	–	2	11	–	–	–	–
Birmingham C	–	–	–	–	–	–	–	–	–	–	–	–
Blackburn R	–	–	–	–	–	–	–	2	–	–	–	–
Blackpool	10	9	12	–	–	–	23	18	12	–	–	–
Bolton W	–	21	18	17	10	–	–	–	–	–	–	–
Bournemouth	–	1	15	10	17	14	–	–	–	–	–	–
Bradford C	–	–	–	1	7	12	–	–	–	–	22	–
Brentford	12	11	10	13	20	9	8	9	19	10	–	–
Brighton & HA	2	–	–	–	–	–	–	–	–	–	–	2
Bristol C	5	6	9	5	–	–	23	–	–	–	–	–
Bristol R	8	19	16	6	5	7	15	–	–	–	–	–
Burnley	–	–	–	21	12	–	1	8	–	–	–	–
Bury	14	16	20	–	–	–	–	–	21	19	15	7
Cambridge U	–	–	–	24	–	–	–	–	–	–	2	–

LEAGUE POSITIONS: DIVISION 2 from 1992–93 and DIVISION 3 1976–77 to 1991–92 (cont.)

	2000-01	1999-2000	1998-99	1997-98	1996-97	1995-96	1994-95	1993-94	1992-93	1991-92	1990-91	1989-90	1988-89
Cardiff C	–	21	–	–	–	–	22	19	–	–	–	21	16
Carlisle U	–	–	–	23	–	21	–	–	–	–	–	–	–
Charlton Ath	–	–	–	–	–	–	–	–	–	–	–	–	–
Chester C	–	–	–	–	–	–	23	–	24	18	19	16	8
Chesterfield	–	24	9	10	10	7	–	–	–	–	–	–	22
Colchester U	17	18	18	–	–	–	–	–	–	–	–	–	–
Crewe Alex	–	–	–	–	6	5	3	–	–	–	22	12	–
Crystal Palace	–	–	–	–	–	–	–	–	–	–	–	–	–
Darlington	–	–	–	–	–	–	–	–	–	24	–	–	–
Derby Co	–	–	–	–	–	–	–	–	–	–	–	–	–
Doncaster R	–	–	–	–	–	–	–	–	–	–	–	–	–
Exeter C	–	–	–	–	–	–	–	22	19	20	16	–	–
Fulham	–	–	1	6	–	–	–	21	12	9	21	20	4
Gillingham	–	3	4	8	11	–	–	–	–	–	–	–	23
Grimsby T	–	–	–	3	–	–	–	–	–	3	–	–	22
Halifax T	–	–	–	–	–	–	–	–	–	–	–	–	–
Hartlepool U	–	–	–	–	–	–	–	23	16	11	–	–	–
Hereford U	–	–	–	–	–	–	–	–	–	–	–	–	–
Huddersfield T	–	–	–	–	–	–	5	11	15	3	11	8	14
Hull C	–	–	–	–	24	8	9	20	14	–	–	–	–
Leyton Orient	–	–	23	–	–	–	24	18	7	10	13	14	–
Lincoln C	–	–	23	–	–	–	–	–	–	–	–	–	–
Luton T	22	13	12	17	3	–	–	–	–	–	–	–	–
Macclesfield T	–	–	24	–	–	–	–	–	–	–	–	–	–
Manchester C	–	–	3	–	–	–	–	–	–	–	–	–	–
Mansfield T	–	–	–	–	–	–	–	–	22	–	24	15	15
Middlesbrough	–	–	–	–	–	–	–	–	–	–	–	–	–
Millwall	1	5	10	18	14	–	–	–	–	–	–	–	–
Newport Co	–	–	–	–	–	–	–	–	–	–	–	–	–
Northampton T	18	–	22	4	–	–	–	–	–	–	–	22	20
Notts Co	8	8	16	–	24	4	–	–	–	–	–	3	9
Oldham Ath	15	14	20	13	–	–	–	–	–	–	–	–	–
Oxford U	24	20	–	–	–	2	7	–	–	–	–	–	–
Peterborough U	12	–	–	–	21	19	15	–	–	6	–	–	–
Plymouth Arg	–	–	–	22	19	–	21	3	14	–	–	–	–
Portsmouth	–	–	–	–	–	–	–	–	–	–	–	–	–
Port Vale	11	–	–	–	–	–	–	2	3	–	–	–	3
Preston NE	–	1	5	15	15	–	–	–	21	17	17	19	6
Reading	3	10	11	–	–	–	–	1	8	12	15	10	18
Rochdale	–	–	–	–	–	–	–	–	–	–	–	–	–
Rotherham U	2	–	–	–	23	16	17	15	11	–	23	9	–
Scunthorpe U	–	23	–	–	–	–	–	–	–	–	–	–	–
Sheffield U	–	–	–	–	–	–	–	–	–	–	–	–	–
Sheffield W	–	–	–	–	–	–	–	–	–	–	–	–	2
Shrewsbury T	–	–	–	–	22	18	18	–	–	22	18	11	–
Southend U	–	–	–	24	–	–	–	–	–	–	2	–	21

1987–88	1986–87	1985–86	1984–85	1983–84	1982–83	1981–82	1980–81	1979–80	1978–79	1977–78	1976–77	
–	–	22	–	–	2	–	–	–	–	–	–	Cardiff C
–	22	–	–	–	–	2	19	6	6	13	–	Carlisle U
–	–	–	–	–	–	–	3	–	–	–	–	Charlton Ath
15	15	–	–	–	24	18	9	16	5	13	–	Chester C
18	17	17	–	–	24	11	5	4	20	9	18	Chesterfield
–	–	–	–	–	–	22	5	7	8	–	–	Colchester U
–	–	–	–	–	–	–	–	–	–	–	–	Crewe Alex
–	–	–	–	–	–	–	–	–	–	–	3	Crystal Palace
–	22	13	–	–	–	–	–	–	–	–	–	Darlington
–	–	3	7	–	–	–	–	–	–	–	–	Derby Co
24	13	11	14	–	23	19	–	–	–	–	–	Doncaster R
–	–	–	24	19	18	11	8	9	17	–	–	Exeter C
9	18	–	–	–	–	3	13	–	–	–	–	Fulham
13	5	5	4	8	13	6	15	16	4	7	12	Gillingham
–	–	–	–	–	–	–	–	1	–	–	23	Grimsby T
–	–	–	–	–	–	–	–	–	–	–	–	Halifax T
–	–	–	–	–	–	–	–	–	–	–	–	Hartlepool U
–	–	–	–	–	–	–	–	–	23	–	–	Hereford U
–	–	–	–	3	17	4	–	–	–	–	–	Huddersfield T
–	–	–	3	4	–	–	24	20	8	–	–	Hull C
–	–	–	22	11	20	–	–	–	–	–	–	Leyton Orient
–	21	19	14	6	4	–	–	24	16	9	–	Lincoln C
–	–	–	–	–	–	–	–	–	–	–	–	Luton T
–	–	–	–	–	–	–	–	–	–	–	–	Macclesfield T
–	–	–	–	–	–	–	–	–	–	–	–	Manchester C
19	10	–	–	–	–	–	23	18	–	–	1	Mansfield T
–	2	–	–	–	–	–	–	–	–	–	–	Middlesbrough
–	–	–	2	9	17	9	16	14	–	–	–	Millwall
–	23	19	18	13	4	16	12	–	–	–	–	Newport Co
6	–	–	–	–	–	–	–	–	–	–	22	Northampton T
4	7	8	–	–	–	–	–	–	–	–	–	Notts Co
–	–	–	–	–	–	–	–	–	–	–	–	Oldham Ath
–	–	–	–	1	5	5	14	17	11	18	17	Oxford U
–	–	–	–	–	–	–	–	–	21	4	16	Peterborough U
–	–	2	15	19	8	10	7	15	15	19	–	Plymouth Arg
–	–	–	–	1	13	6	–	–	24	20	–	Portsmouth
11	12	–	–	23	–	–	–	–	–	21	19	Port Vale
16	–	–	23	16	16	14	–	–	–	3	6	Preston NE
–	1	9	–	21	12	10	7	–	–	–	21	Reading
–	–	–	–	–	–	–	–	–	–	–	–	Rochdale
21	14	14	12	18	–	–	1	13	17	20	4	Rotherham U
–	–	–	–	21	–	–	–	–	–	–	–	Scunthorpe U
–	–	–	3	11	–	21	12	–	–	–	–	Sheffield U
–	–	–	–	–	–	–	3	14	14	8	–	Sheffield W
–	–	–	–	–	–	–	–	–	1	11	10	Shrewsbury T
17	–	–	–	22	15	7	–	22	13	–	–	Southend U

LEAGUE POSITIONS: DIVISION 2 from 1992–93 and DIVISION 3 1976–77 to 1991–92 (cont.)

	2000–01	1999–2000	1998–99	1997–98	1996–97	1995–96	1994–95	1993–94	1992–93	1991–92	1990–91	1989–90	1988–89
Stockport Co	–	–	–	–	2	9	11	4	6	5	–	–	–
Stoke C	5	6	8	–	–	–	–	–	1	4	14	–	–
Sunderland	–	–	–	–	–	–	–	–	–	–	–	–	–
Swansea C	23	–	–	–	–	22	10	13	5	19	20	17	12
Swindon T	20	–	–	–	–	1	–	–	–	–	–	–	–
Torquay U	–	–	–	–	–	–	–	–	–	23	–	–	–
Tranmere R	–	–	–	–	–	–	–	–	–	–	5	4	–
Walsall	4	–	2	19	12	11	–	–	5	–	–	24	–
Watford	–	–	–	1	13	–	–	–	–	–	–	–	–
WBA	–	–	–	–	–	–	–	–	4	7	–	–	–
Wigan Ath	6	4	6	11	–	–	–	–	23	15	10	18	17
Wimbledon	–	–	–	–	–	–	–	–	–	–	–	–	–
Wolv'hampton W	–	–	–	–	–	–	–	–	–	–	–	–	1
Wrexham	10	11	17	7	8	8	13	12	–	–	–	–	–
Wycombe W	13	12	19	14	18	12	6	–	–	–	–	–	–
York C	–	–	21	16	20	20	9	5	–	–	–	–	–

LEAGUE POSITIONS: DIVISION 3 from 1992–93 and DIVISION 4 1976–77 to 1991–92

	2000–01	1999–2000	1998–99	1997–98	1996–97	1995–96	1994–95	1993–94	1992–93	1991–92	1990–91	1989–90	1988–89
Aldershot	–	–	–	–	–	–	–	–	–	*	23	22	–
Barnet	24	6	16	7	15	9	11	–	3	7	–	–	–
Barnsley	–	–	–	–	–	–	–	–	–	–	–	–	–
Blackpool	7	–	–	–	–	–	–	–	–	4	5	–	–
Bolton W	–	–	–	–	–	–	–	–	–	–	–	–	–
Bournemouth	–	–	–	–	–	–	–	–	–	–	–	–	–
Bradford C	–	–	–	–	–	–	–	–	–	–	–	–	–
Brentford	–	–	–	–	–	–	–	–	–	–	–	–	–
Brighton & HA	1	11	17	23	23	–	–	–	–	–	–	–	–
Bristol C	–	–	–	–	–	–	–	–	–	–	–	–	–
Burnley	–	–	15	–	–	–	–	–	–	1	6	16	16
Bury	–	–	–	–	–	3	4	13	7	–	–	–	–
Cambridge U	–	–	2	16	10	16	–	–	–	–	–	6	8
Cardiff C	2	–	3	21	7	22	–	–	1	9	13	–	–
Carlisle U	22	23	23	–	3	–	1	7	18	22	20	8	12
Cheltenham T	9	8	–	–	–	–	–	–	–	–	–	–	–
Chester C	–	24	14	14	6	8	–	2	–	–	–	–	–
Chesterfield	3	–	–	–	–	–	3	8	12	13	18	7	–

*Record expunged

1987–88	1986–87	1985–86	1984–85	1983–84	1982–83	1981–82	1980–81	1979–80	1978–79	1977–78	1976–77	
–	–	–	–	–	–	–	–	–	–	–	–	Stockport Co
–	–	–	–	–	–	–	–	–	–	–	–	Stoke C
1	–	–	–	–	–	–	–	–	–	–	–	Sunderland
–	–	24	20	–	–	–	–	–	3	–	–	Swansea C
–	3	–	–	–	–	22	17	10	5	10	11	Swindon T
–	–	–	–	–	–	–	–	–	–	–	–	Torquay U
–	–	–	–	–	–	–	–	–	23	12	14	Tranmere R
3	8	6	11	6	10	20	20	–	22	6	15	Walsall
–	–	–	–	–	–	–	–	–	2	–	–	Watford
–	–	–	–	–	–	–	–	–	–	–	–	WBA
7	4	4	16	15	18	–	–	–	–	–	–	Wigan Ath
–	–	–	–	2	–	21	–	24	–	–	–	Wimbledon
–	–	23										Wolv'hampton W
–	–	–	–	–	22	–	–	–	–	1	5	Wrexham
–	–	–	–	–	–	–	–	–	–	–	–	Wycombe W
23	20	7	8	–	–	–	–	–	–	–	24	York C

1987–88	1986–87	1985–86	1984–85	1983–84	1982–83	1981–82	1980–81	1979–80	1978–79	1977–78	1976–77	
–	6	16	13	5	18	16	6	10	5	5	17	Aldershot
–	–	–	–	–	–	–	–	–	–	–	–	Barnet
–	–	–	–	–	–	–	–	–	4	7	6	Barnsley
–	–	–	2	6	21	12	–	–	–	–	–	Blackpool
3	–	–	–	–	–	–	–	–	–	–	–	Bolton W
–	–	–	–	–	4	13	11	18	17	13		Bournemouth
–	–	–	–	–	2	14	5	15	–	4		Bradford C
–	–	–	–	–	–	–	–	–	4	15		Brentford
–	–	–	–	–	–	–	–	–	–	–	–	Brighton & HA
–	–	–	–	4	14	–	–	–	–	–	–	Bristol C
10	22	14	–	–	–	–	–	–	–	–	–	Burnley
–	–	–	4	15	5	9	12	–	–	–	–	Bury
15	11	22	–	–	–	–	–	–	–	–	1	Cambridge U
2	13	–	–	–	–	–	–	–	–	–	–	Cardiff C
23	–	–	–	–	–	–	–	–	–	–	–	Carlisle U
–	–	–	–	–	–	–	–	–	–	–	–	Cheltenham T
–	–	2	16	24	13	9	–	–	–	–	–	Chester C
–	–	–	1	13	–	–	–	–	–	–	–	Chesterfield

	2000–01	1999–2000	1998–99	1997–98	1996–97	1995–96	1994–95	1993–94	1992–93	1991–92	1990–91	1989–90	1988–89
Colchester U	–	–	–	4	8	7	10	17	10	–	–	24	22
Crewe Alex	–	–	–	–	–	–	–	3	6	6	–	–	3
Darlington	20	4	11	19	18	5	20	21	15	–	1	–	24
Doncaster R	–	–	–	24	19	13	9	15	16	21	11	20	23
Exeter C	19	21	12	15	22	14	22	–	–	–	–	1	13
Fulham	–	–	–	–	2	17	8	–	–	–	–	–	–
Gillingham	–	–	–	–	–	2	19	16	21	11	15	14	–
Grimsby T	–	–	–	–	–	–	–	–	–	–	–	2	9
Halifax T	23	18	10	–	–	–	–	–	22	20	22	23	21
Hartlepool U	4	7	22	17	20	20	18	–	–	–	3	19	19
Hereford U	–	–	–	–	24	6	16	20	17	17	17	17	15
Huddersfield T	–	–	–	–	–	–	–	–	–	–	–	–	–
Hull C	6	14	21	22	17	–	–	–	–	–	–	–	–
Kidderminster H	16	–	–	–	–	–	–	–	–	–	–	–	–
Leyton Orient	5	19	6	11	16	21	–	–	–	–	–	–	6
Lincoln C	18	15	–	3	9	18	12	18	8	10	14	10	10
Macclesfield T	14	13	–	2	–	–	–	–	–	–	–	–	–
Maidstone U	–	–	–	–	–	–	–	–	–	18	19	5	–
Mansfield T	13	17	8	12	11	19	6	12	–	3	–	–	–
Newport Co	–	–	–	–	–	–	–	–	–	–	–	–	–
Northampton T	–	3	–	–	4	11	17	22	20	16	10	–	–
Notts Co	–	–	–	1	–	–	–	–	–	–	–	–	–
Peterborough U	–	5	9	10	–	–	–	–	–	–	4	9	17
Plymouth Arg	12	12	13	–	–	4	–	–	–	–	–	–	–
Portsmouth	–	–	–	–	–	–	–	–	–	–	–	–	–
Port Vale	–	–	–	–	–	–	–	–	–	–	–	–	–
Preston NE	–	–	–	–	–	1	5	5	–	–	–	–	–
Reading	–	–	–	–	–	–	–	–	–	–	–	–	–
Rochdale	8	10	19	18	14	15	15	9	11	8	12	12	18
Rotherham U	–	2	5	9	–	–	–	–	–	–	2	–	1
Scarborough	–	–	24	6	12	23	21	14	13	12	9	18	5
Scunthorpe U	10	–	4	8	13	12	7	11	14	5	8	11	4
Sheffield U	–	–	–	–	–	–	–	–	–	–	–	–	–
Shrewsbury T	15	22	15	13	–	–	–	1	9	–	–	–	–
Southend U	11	16	18	–	–	–	–	–	–	–	–	3	–
Southport	–	–	–	–	–	–	–	–	–	–	–	–	–
Stockport Co	–	–	–	–	–	–	–	–	–	–	2	4	20
Swansea C	–	1	7	20	5	–	–	–	–	–	–	–	–
Swindon T	–	–	–	–	–	–	–	–	–	–	–	–	–
Torquay U	21	9	20	5	21	24	13	6	19	–	7	15	14
Tranmere R	–	–	–	–	–	–	–	–	–	–	–	–	2
Walsall	–	–	–	–	–	2	10	5	15	16	–	–	–
Watford	–	–	–	–	–	–	–	–	–	–	–	–	–
Wigan Ath	–	–	–	–	1	10	14	19	–	–	–	–	–
Wimbledon	–	–	–	–	–	–	–	–	–	–	–	–	–
Wolv'hampton W	–	–	–	–	–	–	–	–	–	–	–	–	–
Workington	–	–	–	–	–	–	–	–	–	–	–	–	–
Wrexham	–	–	–	–	–	–	–	2	14	24	21	7	–
Wycombe W	–	–	–	–	–	–	4	–	–	–	–	–	–
York C	17	20	–	–	–	–	–	–	4	19	21	13	11

	1987-88	1986-87	1985-86	1984-85	1983-84	1982-83	1981-82	1980-81	1979-80	1978-79	1977-78	1976-77
Colchester U	9	5	6	7	8	6	6	–	–	–	–	3
Crewe Alex	17	17	12	10	16	23	24	18	23	24	15	12
Darlington	13	–	–	3	14	17	3	8	22	21	19	11
Doncaster R	–	–	–	2	–	–	3	12	22	12	8	
Exeter C	22	14	21	18	–	–	–	–	–	–	–	2
Fulham	–	–	–	–	–	–	–	–	–	–	–	–
Gillingham	–	–	–	–	–	–	–	–	–	–	–	–
Grimsby T	–	–	–	–	–	–	–	–	2	6	–	–
Halifax T	18	15	20	21	21	11	19	23	18	23	20	21
Hartlepool U	16	18	7	19	23	22	14	9	19	13	21	22
Hereford U	19	16	10	5	11	24	10	-22	21	14	–	–
Huddersfield T	–	–	–	–	–	–	–	1	9	11	9	
Hull C	–	–	–	–	2	8	–	–	–	–	–	–
Kidderminster H	–	–	–	–	–	–	–	–	–	–	–	–
Leyton Orient	8	7	5	–	–	–	–	–	–	–	–	–
Lincoln C	–	24	–	–	–	–	2	7	–	–	–	–
Macclesfield T	–	–	–	–	–	–	–	–	–	–	–	–
Maidstone U	–	–	–	–	–	–	–	–	–	–	–	–
Mansfield T	–	–	3	14	19	10	20	7	–	–	–	–
Newport C	24	–	–	–	–	–	–	–	3	8	16	19
Northampton T	–	1	8	23	18	15	22	10	13	19	10	–
Notts Co	–	–	–	–	–	–	–	–	–	–	–	–
Peterborough U	7	10	17	11	7	9	5	5	8	–	–	–
Plymouth Arg	–	–	–	–	–	–	–	–	–	–	–	–
Portsmouth	–	–	–	–	–	–	–	4	7	–	–	
Port Vale	–	–	4	12	–	3	7	19	20	16	–	–
Preston NE	–	2	·23	–	–	–	–	–	–	1	8	–
Reading	–	–	–	3	–	–	–	–	–	–	–	–
Rochdale	21	21	18	17	22	20	21	15	24	20	24	18
Rotherham U	–	–	–	–	–	–	–	–	–	–	–	
Scarborough	12	–	–	–	–	–	–	–	–	–	–	
Scunthorpe U	4	8	15	9	–	4	23	16	14	12	14	20
Sheffield U	–	–	–	–	–	–	1	–	–	–	–	
Shrewsbury T	–	–	–	–	–	–	–	–	–	–	–	
Southend U	–	3	9	20	–	–	–	1	–	–	2	10
Southport	–	–	–	–	–	–	–	–	–	–	23	23
Stockport Co	20	19	11	22	12	16	18	20	16	17	18	14
Swansea C	6	12	–	–	–	–	–	–	–	–	3	5
Swindon T	–	–	1	8	17	8	–	–	–	–	–	–
Torquay U	5	23	24	24	9	12	15	17	9	11	9	16
Tranmere R	14	20	19	6	10	19	11	21	15	–	–	–
Walsall	–	–	–	–	–	–	–	–	2	–	–	–
Watford	–	–	–	–	–	–	–	–	–	–	1	7
Wigan Ath	–	–	–	–	3	11	6	6	–	–	–	–
Wimbledon	–	–	–	–	1	–	4	–	3	13	–	–
Wolv'hampton W	1	4	–	–	–	–	–	–	–	–	–	–
Workington	–	–	–	–	–	–	–	–	–	–	–	24
Wrexham	11	9	13	15	20	–	–	–	–	–	–	–
Wycombe W	–	–	–	–	–	–	–	–	–	–	–	–
York C	–	–	–	–	1	7	17	24	17	10	22	–

LEAGUE CHAMPIONSHIP HONOURS
FA PREMIER LEAGUE
Maximum points: 126

	First	Pts	Second	Pts	Third	Pts
1992–93	Manchester U	84	Aston Villa	74	Norwich C	72
1993–94	Manchester U	92	Blackburn R	84	Newcastle U	77
1994–95	Blackburn R	89	Manchester U	88	Nottingham F	77

Maximum points: 114

	First	Pts	Second	Pts	Third	Pts
1995–96	Manchester U	82	Newcastle U	78	Liverpool	71
1996–97	Manchester U	75	Newcastle U*	68	Arsenal*	68
1997–98	Arsenal	78	Manchester U	77	Liverpool	65
1998–99	Manchester U	79	Arsenal	78	Chelsea	75
1999–00	Manchester U	91	Arsenal	73	Leeds U	69
2000–01	Manchester U	80	Arsenal	70	Liverpool	69
2001–02	Arsenal	87	Liverpool	80	Manchester U	77

DIVISION 1
Maximum points: 138

	First	Pts	Second	Pts	Third	Pts
1992–93	Newcastle U	96	West Ham U*	88	Portsmouth††	88
1993–94	Crystal Palace	90	Nottingham F	83	Millwall††	74
1994–95	Middlesbrough	82	Reading††	79	Bolton W	77
1995–96	Sunderland	83	Derby Co	79	Crystal Palace††	75
1996–97	Bolton W	98	Barnsley	80	Wolverhampton W††	76
1997–98	Nottingham F	94	Middlesbrough	91	Sunderland††	90
1998–99	Sunderland	105	Bradford C	87	Ipswich T††	86
1999–00	Charlton Ath	91	Manchester C	89	Ipswich T	87
2000–01	Fulham	101	Blackburn R	91	Bolton W	87
2001–02	Manchester C	99	WBA	89	Wolverhampton W††	86

DIVISION 2
Maximum points: 138

	First	Pts	Second	Pts	Third	Pts
1992–93	Stoke C	93	Bolton W	90	Port Vale††	89
1993–94	Reading	89	Port Vale	88	Plymouth Arg††	85
1994–95	Birmingham C	89	Brentford††	85	Crewe Alex††	83
1995–96	Swindon T	92	Oxford U	83	Blackpool††	82
1996–97	Bury	84	Stockport Co	82	Luton T††	78
1997–98	Watford	88	Bristol C	85	Grimsby T	72
1998–99	Fulham	101	Walsall	87	Manchester C	82
1999–00	Preston NE	95	Burnley	88	Gillingham	85
2000–01	Millwall	93	Rotherham U	91	Reading††	86
2001–02	Brighton & HA	90	Reading	84	Brentford*††	83

DIVISION 3
Maximum points: 126

	First	Pts	Second	Pts	Third	Pts
1992–93	Cardiff C	83	Wrexham	80	Barnet	79
1993–94	Shrewsbury T	79	Chester C	74	Crewe Alex	73
1994–95	Carlisle U	91	Walsall	83	Chesterfield	81

Maximum points: 138

	First	Pts	Second	Pts	Third	Pts
1995–96	Preston NE	86	Gillingham	83	Bury	79
1996–97	Wigan Ath*	87	Fulham	87	Carlisle U	84
1997–98	Notts Co	99	Macclesfield T	82	Lincoln C	75
1998–99	Brentford	85	Cambridge U	81	Cardiff C	80
1999–00	Swansea C	85	Rotherham U	84	Northampton T	82
2000–01	Brighton & HA	92	Cardiff C	82	Chesterfield¶	80
2001–02	Plymouth Arg	102	Luton T	97	Mansfield T	79

Won or placed on goal average (ratio)/goal difference.
†† Not promoted after play-offs. ¶ 9 pts deducted for irregularities.

FOOTBALL LEAGUE
Maximum points: a 44; b 60

	First	Pts	Second	Pts	Third	Pts
1888–89a	Preston NE	40	Aston Villa	29	Wolverhampton W	28
1889–90a	Preston NE	33	Everton	31	Blackburn R	27
1890–91a	Everton	29	Preston NE	27	Notts Co	26
1891–92b	Sunderland	42	Preston NE	37	Bolton W	36

Maximum points: a 44; b 52; c 60; d 68; e 76; f 84; g 126; h 120; k 114.

	First	Pts	Second	Pts	Third	Pts
1892–93c	Sunderland	48	Preston NE	37	Everton	36
1893–94c	Aston Villa	44	Sunderland	38	Derby Co	36
1894–95c	Sunderland	47	Everton	42	Aston Villa	39
1895–96c	Aston Villa	45	Derby Co	41	Everton	39
1896–97c	Aston Villa	47	Sheffield U*	36	Derby Co	36
1897–98c	Sheffield U	42	Sunderland	37	Wolverhampton W*	35
1898–99d	Aston Villa	45	Liverpool	43	Burnley	39
1899–1900d	Aston Villa	50	Sheffield U	48	Sunderland	41
1900–01d	Liverpool	45	Sunderland	43	Notts Co	40
1901–02d	Sunderland	44	Everton	41	Newcastle U	37
1902–03d	The Wednesday	42	Aston Villa*	41	Sunderland	41
1903–04d	The Wednesday	47	Manchester C	44	Everton	43
1904–05d	Newcastle U	48	Everton	47	Manchester C	46
1905–06e	Liverpool	51	Preston NE	47	The Wednesday	44
1906–07e	Newcastle U	51	Bristol C	48	Everton*	45
1907–08e	Manchester U	52	Aston Villa*	43	Manchester C	43
1908–09e	Newcastle U	53	Everton	46	Sunderland	44
1909–10e	Aston Villa	53	Liverpool	48	Blackburn R*	45
1910–11e	Manchester U	52	Aston Villa	51	Sunderland*	45
1911–12e	Blackburn R	49	Everton	46	Newcastle U	44
1912–13e	Sunderland	54	Aston Villa	50	Sheffield W	49
1913–14e	Blackburn R	51	Aston Villa	44	Middlesbrough*	43
1914–15e	Everton	46	Oldham Ath	45	Blackburn R*	43
1919–20f	WBA	60	Burnley	51	Chelsea	49
1920–21f	Burnley	59	Manchester C	54	Bolton W	52
1921–22f	Liverpool	57	Tottenham H	51	Burnley	49
1922–23f	Liverpool	60	Sunderland	54	Huddersfield T	53
1923–24f	Huddersfield T*	57	Cardiff C	57	Sunderland	53
1924–25f	Huddersfield T	58	WBA	56	Bolton W	55
1925–26f	Huddersfield T	57	Arsenal	52	Sunderland	48
1926–27f	Newcastle U	56	Huddersfield T	51	Sunderland	49
1927–28f	Everton	53	Huddersfield T	51	Leicester C	48
1928–29f	Sheffield W	52	Leicester C	51	Aston Villa	50
1929–30f	Sheffield W	60	Derby Co	50	Manchester C*	47
1930–31f	Arsenal	66	Aston Villa	59	Sheffield W	52
1931–32f	Everton	56	Arsenal	54	Sheffield W	50
1932–33f	Arsenal	58	Aston Villa	54	Sheffield W	51
1933–34f	Arsenal	59	Huddersfield T	56	Tottenham H	49
1934–35f	Arsenal	58	Sunderland	54	Sheffield W	49
1935–36f	Sunderland	56	Derby Co*	48	Huddersfield T	48
1936–37f	Manchester C	57	Charlton Ath	54	Arsenal	52
1937–38f	Arsenal	52	Wolverhampton W	51	Preston NE	49
1938–39f	Everton	59	Wolverhampton W	55	Charlton Ath	50
1946–47f	Liverpool	57	Manchester U*	56	Wolverhampton W	56
1947–48f	Arsenal	59	Manchester U*	52	Burnley	52
1948–49f	Portsmouth	58	Manchester U*	53	Derby Co	53
1949–50f	Portsmouth*	53	Wolverhampton W	53	Sunderland	52
1950–51f	Tottenham H	60	Manchester U	56	Blackpool	50
1951–52f	Manchester U	57	Tottenham H*	53	Arsenal	53
1952–53f	Arsenal*	54	Preston NE	54	Wolverhampton W	51
1953–54f	Wolverhampton W	57	WBA	53	Huddersfield T	51
1954–55f	Chelsea	52	Wolverhampton W*	48	Portsmouth*	48
1955–56f	Manchester U	60	Blackpool*	49	Wolverhampton W	49
1956–57f	Manchester U	64	Tottenham H*	56	Preston NE	56
1957–58f	Wolverhampton W	64	Preston NE	59	Tottenham H	51
1958–59f	Wolverhampton W	61	Manchester U	55	Arsenal*	50

	First	Pts	Second	Pts	Third	Pts
1959–60f	Burnley	55	Wolverhampton W	54	Tottenham H	53
1960–61f	Tottenham H	66	Sheffield W	58	Wolverhampton W	57
1961–62f	Ipswich T	56	Burnley	53	Tottenham H	52
1962–63f	Everton	61	Tottenham H	55	Burnley	54
1963–64f	Liverpool	57	Manchester U	53	Everton	52
1964–65f	Manchester U*	61	Leeds U	61	Chelsea	56
1965–66f	Liverpool	61	Leeds U*	55	Burnley	55
1966–67f	Manchester U	60	Nottingham F*	56	Tottenham H	56
1967–68f	Manchester C	58	Manchester U	56	Liverpool	55
1968–69f	Leeds U	67	Liverpool	61	Everton	57
1969–70f	Everton	66	Leeds U	57	Chelsea	55
1970–71f	Arsenal	65	Leeds U	64	Tottenham H*	52
1971–72f	Derby Co	58	Leeds U*	57	Liverpool*	57
1972–73f	Liverpool	60	Arsenal	57	Leeds U	53
1973–74f	Leeds U	62	Liverpool	57	Derby Co	48
1974–75f	Derby Co	53	Liverpool*	51	Ipswich T	51
1975–76f	Liverpool	60	QPR	59	Manchester U	56
1976–77f	Liverpool	57	Manchester C	56	Ipswich T	52
1977–78f	Nottingham F	64	Liverpool	57	Everton	55
1978–79f	Liverpool	68	Nottingham F	60	WBA	59
1979–80f	Liverpool	60	Manchester U	58	Ipswich T	53
1980–81f	Aston Villa	60	Ipswich T	56	Arsenal	53
1981–82g	Liverpool	87	Ipswich T	83	Manchester U	78
1982–83g	Liverpool	82	Watford	71	Manchester U	70
1983–84g	Liverpool	80	Southampton	77	Nottingham F*	74
1984–85g	Everton	90	Liverpool*	77	Tottenham H	77
1985–86g	Liverpool	88	Everton	86	West Ham U	84
1986–87g	Everton	86	Liverpool	77	Tottenham H	71
1987–88h	Liverpool	90	Manchester U	81	Nottingham F	73
1988–89k	Arsenal*	76	Liverpool	76	Nottingham F	64
1989–90k	Liverpool	79	Aston Villa	70	Tottenham H	63
1990–91k	Arsenal†	83	Liverpool	76	Crystal Palace	69
1991–92g	Leeds U	82	Manchester U	78	Sheffield W	75

No official competition during 1915–19 and 1939–46; Regional Leagues operating.
* Won or placed on goal average (ratio)/goal difference.
† 2 pts deducted

DIVISION 2 to 1991–92

Maximum points: a 44; b 56; c 60; d 68; e 76; f 84; g 126; h 132; k 138.

1892–93a	Small Heath	36	Sheffield U	35	Darwen	30
1893–94b	Liverpool	50	Small Heath	42	Notts Co	39
1894–95c	Bury	48	Notts Co	39	Newton Heath*	38
1895–96c	Liverpool*	46	Manchester C	46	Grimsby T*	42
1896–97c	Notts Co	42	Newton Heath	39	Grimsby T	38
1897–98c	Burnley	48	Newcastle U	45	Manchester C	39
1898–99d	Manchester C	52	Glossop NE	46	Leicester Fosse	45
1899–1900d	The Wednesday	54	Bolton W	52	Small Heath	46
1900–01d	Grimsby T	49	Small Heath	48	Burnley	44
1901–02d	WBA	55	Middlesbrough	51	Preston NE*	42
1902–03d	Manchester C	54	Small Heath	51	Woolwich A	48
1903–04d	Preston NE	50	Woolwich A	49	Manchester U	48
1904–05d	Liverpool	58	Bolton W	56	Manchester U	53
1905–06e	Bristol C	66	Manchester U	62	Chelsea	53
1906–07e	Nottingham F	60	Chelsea	57	Leicester Fosse	48
1907–08e	Bradford C	54	Leicester Fosse	52	Oldham Ath	50
1908–09e	Bolton W	52	Tottenham H*	51	WBA	51
1909–10e	Manchester C	54	Oldham Ath*	53	Hull C*	53
1910–11e	WBA	53	Bolton W	51	Chelsea	49

126

	First	Pts	Second	Pts	Third	Pts
1911–12e	Derby Co*	54	Chelsea	54	Burnley	52
1912–13e	Preston NE	53	Burnley	50	Birmingham	46
1913–14e	Notts Co	53	Bradford PA*	49	Woolwich A	49
1914–15e	Derby Co	53	Preston NE	50	Barnsley	47
1919–20f	Tottenham H	70	Huddersfield T	64	Birmingham	56
1920–21f	Birmingham*	58	Cardiff C	58	Bristol C	51
1921–22f	Nottingham F	56	Stoke C*	52	Barnsley	52
1922–23f	Notts Co	53	West Ham U	51	Leicester C	51
1923–24f	Leeds U	54	Bury*	51	Derby Co	51
1924–25f	Leicester C	59	Manchester U	57	Derby Co	55
1925–26f	Sheffield W	60	Derby Co	57	Chelsea	52
1926–27f	Middlesbrough	62	Portsmouth*	54	Manchester C	54
1927–28f	Manchester C	59	Leeds U	57	Chelsea	54
1928–29f	Middlesbrough	55	Grimsby T	53	Bradford PA*	48
1929–30f	Blackpool	58	Chelsea	55	Oldham Ath	53
1930–31f	Everton	61	WBA	54	Tottenham H	51
1931–32f	Wolverhampton W	56	Leeds U	54	Stoke C	52
1932–33f	Stoke C	56	Tottenham H	55	Fulham	50
1933–34f	Grimsby T	59	Preston NE	52	Bolton W*	51
1934–35f	Brentford	61	Bolton W*	56	West Ham U	56
1935–36f	Manchester U	56	Charlton Ath	55	Sheffield U*	52
1936–37f	Leicester C	56	Blackpool	55	Bury	52
1937–38f	Aston Villa	57	Manchester U*	53	Sheffield U	53
1938–39f	Blackburn R	55	Sheffield U	54	Sheffield W	53
1946–47f	Manchester C	62	Burnley	58	Birmingham C	55
1947–48f	Birmingham C	59	Newcastle U	56	Southampton	52
1948–49f	Fulham	57	WBA	56	Southampton	55
1949–50f	Tottenham H	61	Sheffield W*	52	Sheffield U*	52
1950–51f	Preston NE	57	Manchester C	52	Cardiff C	50
1951–52f	Sheffield W	53	Cardiff C*	51	Birmingham C	51
1952–53f	Sheffield U	60	Huddersfield T	58	Luton T	52
1953–54f	Leicester C*	56	Everton	56	Blackburn R	55
1954–55f	Birmingham C*	54	Luton T*	54	Rotherham U	54
1955–56f	Sheffield W	55	Leeds U	52	Liverpool*	48
1956–57f	Leicester C	61	Nottingham F	54	Liverpool	53
1957–58f	West Ham U	57	Blackburn R	56	Charlton Ath	55
1958–59f	Sheffield W	62	Fulham	60	Sheffield U*	53
1959–60f	Aston Villa	59	Cardiff C	58	Liverpool*	50
1960–61f	Ipswich T	59	Sheffield U	58	Liverpool	52
1961–62f	Liverpool	62	Leyton Orient	54	Sunderland	53
1962–63f	Stoke C	53	Chelsea*	52	Sunderland	52
1963–64f	Leeds U	63	Sunderland	61	Preston NE	56
1964–65f	Newcastle U	57	Northampton T	56	Bolton W	50
1965–66f	Manchester C	59	Southampton	54	Coventry C	53
1966–67f	Coventry C	59	Wolverhampton W	58	Carlisle U	52
1967–68f	Ipswich T	59	QPR*	58	Blackpool	58
1968–69f	Derby Co	63	Crystal Palace	56	Charlton Ath	50
1969–70f	Huddersfield T	60	Blackpool	53	Leicester C	51
1970–71f	Leicester C	59	Sheffield U	56	Cardiff C*	53
1971–72f	Norwich C	57	Birmingham C	56	Millwall	55
1972–73f	Burnley	62	QPR	61	Aston Villa	50
1973–74f	Middlesbrough	65	Luton T	50	Carlisle U	49
1974–75f	Manchester U	61	Aston Villa	58	Norwich C	53
1975–76f	Sunderland	56	Bristol C*	53	WBA	53
1976–77f	Wolverhampton W	57	Chelsea	55	Nottingham F	52
1977–78f	Bolton W	58	Southampton	57	Tottenham H*	56
1978–79f	Crystal Palace	57	Brighton & HA*	56	Stoke C	56
1979–80f	Leicester C	55	Sunderland	54	Birmingham C*	53
1980–81f	West Ham U	66	Notts Co	53	Swansea C*	50

127

	First	Pts		Second	Pts		Third	Pts
1981–82g	Luton T	88		Watford	80		Norwich C	71
1982–83g	QPR	85		Wolverhampton W	75		Leicester C	70
1983–84g	Chelsea*	88		Sheffield W	88		Newcastle U	80
1984–85g	Oxford U	84		Birmingham C	82		Manchester C	74
1985–86g	Norwich C	84		Charlton Ath	77		Wimbledon	76
1986–87g	Derby Co	84		Portsmouth	78		Oldham Ath††	75
1987–88h	Millwall	82		Aston Villa*	78		Middlesbrough	78
1988–89k	Chelsea	99		Manchester C	82		Crystal Palace	81
1989–90k	Leeds U*	85		Sheffield U	85		Newcastle U††	80
1990–91k	Oldham Ath	88		West Ham U	87		Sheffield W	82
1991–92k	Ipswich T	84		Middlesbrough	80		Derby Co	78

No official competition during 1915–19 and 1939–46; Regional Leagues operating.
* Won or placed on goal average (ratio)/goal difference.
†† Not promoted after play-offs.

DIVISION 3 to 1991–92
Maximum points: 92; 138 from 1981–82.

	First	Pts		Second	Pts		Third	Pts
1958–59	Plymouth Arg	62		Hull C	61		Brentford*	57
1959–60	Southampton	61		Norwich C	59		Shrewsbury T*	52
1960–61	Bury	68		Walsall	62		QPR	60
1961–62	Portsmouth	65		Grimsby T	62		Bournemouth*	59
1962–63	Northampton T	62		Swindon T	58		Port Vale	54
1963–64	Coventry C*	60		Crystal Palace	60		Watford	58
1964–65	Carlisle U	60		Bristol C*	59		Mansfield T	59
1965–66	Hull C	69		Millwall	65		QPR	57
1966–67	QPR	67		Middlesbrough	55		Watford	54
1967–68	Oxford U	57		Bury	56		Shrewsbury T	55
1968–69	Watford*	64		Swindon T	64		Luton T	61
1969–70	Orient	62		Luton T	60		Bristol R	56
1970–71	Preston NE	61		Fulham	60		Halifax T	56
1971–72	Aston Villa	70		Brighton & HA	65		Bournemouth*	62
1972–73	Bolton W	61		Notts Co	57		Blackburn R	55
1973–74	Oldham Ath	62		Bristol R*	61		York C	61
1974–75	Blackburn R	60		Plymouth Arg	59		Charlton Ath	55
1975–76	Hereford U	63		Cardiff C	57		Millwall	56
1976–77	Mansfield T	64		Brighton & HA	61		Crystal Palace*	59
1977–78	Wrexham	61		Cambridge U	58		Preston NE*	56
1978–79	Shrewsbury T	61		Watford*	60		Swansea C	60
1979–80	Grimsby T	62		Blackburn R	59		Sheffield W	58
1980–81	Rotherham U	61		Barnsley*	59		Charlton Ath	59
1981–82	Burnley*	80		Carlisle U	80		Fulham	78
1982–83	Portsmouth	91		Cardiff C	86		Huddersfield T	82
1983–84	Oxford U	95		Wimbledon	87		Sheffield U*	83
1984–85	Bradford C	94		Millwall	90		Hull C	87
1985–86	Reading	94		Plymouth Arg	87		Derby Co	84
1986–87	Bournemouth	97		Middlesbrough	94		Swindon T	87
1987–88	Sunderland	93		Brighton & HA	84		Walsall	82
1988–89	Wolverhampton W	92		Sheffield U*	84		Port Vale	84
1989–90	Bristol R	93		Bristol C	91		Notts Co	87
1990–91	Cambridge U	86		Southend U	85		Grimsby T*	83
1991–92	Brentford	82		Birmingham C	81		Huddersfield T	78

* Won or placed on goal average (ratio)/goal difference.

DIVISION 4 (1958–1992)

Maximum points: 92; 138 from 1981–82.

	First	Pts	Second	Pts	Third	Pts
1958–59	Port Vale	64	Coventry C*	60	York C	60
1959–60	Walsall	65	Notts Co*	60	Torquay U	60
1960–61	Peterborough U	66	Crystal Palace	64	Northampton T*	60
1961–62†	Millwall	56	Colchester U	55	Wrexham	53
1962–63	Brentford	62	Oldham Ath*	59	Crewe Alex	59
1963–64	Gillingham*	60	Carlisle U	60	Workington	59
1964–65	Brighton & HA	63	Millwall*	62	York C	62
1965–66	Doncaster R*	59	Darlington	59	Torquay U	58
1966–67	Stockport Co	64	Southport*	59	Barrow	59
1967–68	Luton T	66	Barnsley	61	Hartlepools U	60
1968–69	Doncaster R	59	Halifax T	57	Rochdale*	56
1969–70	Chesterfield	64	Wrexham	61	Swansea C	60
1970–71	Notts Co	69	Bournemouth	60	Oldham Ath	59
1971–72	Grimsby T	63	Southend U	60	Brentford	59
1972–73	Southport	62	Hereford U	58	Cambridge U	57
1973–74	Peterborough U	65	Gillingham	62	Colchester U	60
1974–75	Mansfield T	68	Shrewsbury T	62	Rotherham U	59
1975–76	Lincoln C	74	Northampton T	68	Reading	60
1976–77	Cambridge U	65	Exeter C	62	Colchester U*	59
1977–78	Watford	71	Southend U	60	Swansea C*	56
1978–79	Reading	65	Grimsby T*	61	Wimbledon*	61
1979–80	Huddersfield T	66	Walsall	64	Newport Co	61
1980–81	Southend U	67	Lincoln C	65	Doncaster R	56
1981–82	Sheffield U	96	Bradford C*	91	Wigan Ath	91
1982–83	Wimbledon	98	Hull C	90	Port Vale	88
1983–84	York C	101	Doncaster R	85	Reading*	82
1984–85	Chesterfield	91	Blackpool	86	Darlington	85
1985–86	Swindon T	102	Chester C	84	Mansfield T	81
1986–87	Northampton T	99	Preston NE	90	Southend U	80
1987–88	Wolverhampton W	90	Cardiff C	85	Bolton W	78
1988–89	Rotherham U	82	Tranmere R	80	Crewe Alex	78
1989–90	Exeter C	89	Grimsby T	79	Southend U	75
1990–91	Darlington	83	Stockport Co*	82	Hartlepool U	82
1991–92§	Burnley	83	Rotherham U*	77	Mansfield T	77

* *Won or placed on goal average (ratio)/goal difference.*
†*Maximum points: 88 owing to Accrington Stanley's resignation.* ††*Not promoted after play-offs.*
§*Maximum points: 126 owing to Aldershot being expelled.*

DIVISION 3—SOUTH (1920–1958)

1920–21 Season as Division 3.
Maximum points: a 84; b 92.

	First		Second		Third	
1920–21a	Crystal Palace	59	Southampton	54	QPR	53
1921–22a	Southampton*	61	Plymouth Arg	61	Portsmouth	53
1922–23a	Bristol C	59	Plymouth Arg*	53	Swansea T	53
1923–24a	Portsmouth	59	Plymouth Arg	55	Millwall	54
1924–25a	Swansea T	57	Plymouth Arg	56	Bristol C	53
1925–26a	Reading	57	Plymouth Arg	56	Millwall	53
1926–27a	Bristol C	62	Plymouth Arg	60	Millwall	56
1927–28a	Millwall	65	Northampton T	55	Plymouth Arg	53
1928–29a	Charlton Ath*	54	Crystal Palace	54	Northampton T*	52
1929–30a	Plymouth Arg	68	Brentford	61	QPR	51
1930–31a	Notts Co	59	Crystal Palace	51	Brentford	50
1931–32a	Fulham	57	Reading	55	Southend U	53
1932–33a	Brentford	62	Exeter C	58	Norwich C	57
1933–34a	Norwich C	61	Coventry C*	54	Reading*	54

	First	Pts	Second	Pts	Third	Pts
1934–35a	Charlton Ath	61	Reading	53	Coventry C	51
1935–36a	Coventry C	57	Luton T	56	Reading	54
1936–37a	Luton T	58	Notts Co	56	Brighton & HA	53
1937–38a	Millwall	56	Bristol C	55	QPR*	53
1938–39a	Newport Co	55	Crystal Palace	52	Brighton & HA	49
1939–46	Competition cancelled owing to war.					
1946–47a	Cardiff C	66	QPR	57	Bristol C	51
1947–48a	QPR	61	Bournemouth	57	Walsall	51
1948–49a	Swansea T	62	Reading	55	Bournemouth	52
1949–50a	Notts Co	58	Northampton T*	51	Southend U	51
1950–51b	Nottingham F	70	Norwich C	64	Reading*	57
1951–52b	Plymouth Arg	66	Reading*	61	Norwich C	61
1952–53b	Bristol R	64	Millwall*	62	Northampton T	62
1953–54b	Ipswich T	64	Brighton & HA	61	Bristol C	56
1954–55b	Bristol C	70	Leyton Orient	61	Southampton	59
1955–56b	Leyton Orient	66	Brighton & HA	65	Ipswich T	64
1956–57b	Ipswich T*	59	Torquay U	59	Colchester U	58
1957–58b	Brighton & HA	60	Brentford*	58	Plymouth Arg	58

* Won or placed on goal average (ratio).

DIVISION 3—NORTH (1921–1958)

Maximum points: a 76; b 84; c 80; d 92.

	First	Pts	Second	Pts	Third	Pts
1921–22a	Stockport Co	56	Darlington*	50	Grimsby T	50
1922–23a	Nelson	51	Bradford PA	47	Walsall	46
1923–24b	Wolverhampton W	63	Rochdale	62	Chesterfield	54
1924–25b	Darlington	58	Nelson*	53	New Brighton	53
1925–26b	Grimsby T	61	Bradford PA	60	Rochdale	59
1926–27b	Stoke C	63	Rochdale	58	Bradford PA	55
1927–28b	Bradford PA	63	Lincoln C	55	Stockport Co	54
1928–29g	Bradford C	63	Stockport Co	62	Wrexham	52
1929–30b	Port Vale	67	Stockport Co	63	Darlington*	50
1930–31b	Chesterfield	58	Lincoln C	57	Wrexham*	54
1931–32c	Lincoln C*	57	Gateshead	57	Chester	50
1932–33b	Hull C	59	Wrexham	57	Stockport Co	54
1933–34b	Barnsley	62	Chesterfield	61	Stockport Co	59
1934–35b	Doncaster R	57	Halifax T	55	Chester	54
1935–36b	Chesterfield	60	Chester*	55	Tranmere R	55
1936–37b	Stockport Co	60	Lincoln C	57	Chester	53
1937–38b	Tranmere R	56	Doncaster R	54	Hull C	53
1938–39b	Barnsley	67	Doncaster R	56	Bradford C	52
1939–46	Competition cancelled owing to war.					
1946–47b	Doncaster R	72	Rotherham U	60	Chester	56
1947–48b	Lincoln C	60	Rotherham U	59	Wrexham	50
1948–49b	Hull C	65	Rotherham U	62	Doncaster R	50
1949–50b	Doncaster R	55	Gateshead	53	Rochdale*	51
1950–51d	Rotherham U	71	Mansfield T	64	Carlisle U	62
1951–52d	Lincoln C	69	Grimsby T	66	Stockport Co	59
1952–53d	Oldham Ath	59	Port Vale	58	Wrexham	56
1953–54d	Port Vale	69	Barnsley	58	Scunthorpe U	57
1954–55d	Barnsley	65	Accrington S	61	Scunthorpe U*	58
1955–56d	Grimsby T	68	Derby Co	63	Accrington S	59
1956–57d	Derby Co	63	Hartlepools U	59	Accrington S*	58
1957–58d	Scunthorpe U	66	Accrington S	59	Bradford C	57

* Won or placed on goal average (ratio).

PROMOTED AFTER PLAY-OFFS
(Not accounted for in previous section)
1986–87 Aldershot to Division 3.
1987–88 Swansea C to Division 3.
1988–89 Leyton Orient to Division 3.
1989–90 Cambridge U to Division 3; Notts Co to Division 2; Sunderland to Division 1.
1990–91 Notts Co to Division 1; Tranmere R to Division 2; Torquay U to Division 3.
1991–92 Blackburn R to Premier League; Peterborough U to Division 1.
1992–93 Swindon T to Premier League; WBA to Division 1; York C to Division 2.
1993–94 Leicester C to Premier League; Burnley to Division 1; Wycombe W to
         Division 2.
1994–95 Huddersfield T to Division 1.
1995–96 Leicester C to Premier League; Bradford C to Division 1; Plymouth Arg to
         Division 2.
1996–97 Crystal Palace to Premier League; Crewe Alex to Division 1; Northampton T
         to Division 2.
1997–98 Charlton Ath to Premier League; Colchester U to Division 2.
1998–99 Watford to Premier League; Scunthorpe to Division 2.
1999–00 Peterborough U to Division 2.
2000–01 Walsall to Division 1; Blackpool to Division 2.
2001–02 Birmingham C to Premier League; Stoke C to Division 1; Cheltenham T to
         Division 2.

RELEGATED CLUBS

FA PREMIER LEAGUE TO DIVISION 1

1992–93 Crystal Palace, Middlesbrough, Nottingham F
1993–94 Sheffield U, Oldham Ath, Swindon T
1994–95 Crystal Palace, Norwich C, Leicester C, Ipswich T
1995–96 Manchester C, QPR, Bolton W
1996–97 Sunderland, Middlesbrough, Nottingham F
1997–98 Bolton W, Barnsley, Crystal Palace
1998–99 Charlton Ath, Blackburn R, Nottingham F
1999–00 Wimbledon, Sheffield W, Watford
2000–01 Manchester C, Coventry C, Bradford C.
2001–02 Ipswich T, Derby Co, Leicester C.

DIVISION 1 TO DIVISION 2

1898–99 Bolton W and Sheffield W	1925–26 Manchester C and Notts Co
1899–1900 Burnley and Glossop	1926–27 Leeds U and WBA
1900–01 Preston NE and WBA	1927–28 Tottenham H and Middlesbrough
1901–02 Small Heath and Manchester C	1928–29 Bury and Cardiff C
1902–03 Grimsby T and Bolton W	1929–30 Burnley and Everton
1903–04 Liverpool and WBA	1930–31 Leeds U and Manchester U
1904–05 League extended. Bury and	1931–32 Grimsby T and West Ham U
Notts Co, two bottom clubs in	1932–33 Bolton W and Blackpool
First Division, re-elected.	1933–34 Newcastle U and Sheffield U
1905–06 Nottingham F and	1934–35 Leicester C and Tottenham H
Wolverhampton W	1935–36 Aston Villa and Blackburn R
1906–07 Derby Co and Stoke C	1936–37 Manchester U and Sheffield W
1907–08 Bolton W and Birmingham C	1937–38 Manchester C and WBA
1908–09 Manchester C and Leicester Fosse	1938–39 Birmingham C and Leicester C
1909–10 Bolton W and Chelsea	1946–47 Brentford and Leeds U
1910–11 Bristol C and Nottingham F	1947–48 Blackburn R and Grimsby T
1911–12 Preston NE and Bury	1948–49 Preston NE and Sheffield U
1912–13 Notts Co and Woolwich Arsenal	1949–50 Manchester C and
1913–14 Preston NE and Derby Co	Birmingham C
1914–15 Tottenham H and Chelsea*	1950–51 Sheffield W and Everton
1919–20 Notts Co and Sheffield W	1951–52 Huddersfield T and Fulham
1920–21 Derby Co and Bradford PA	1952–53 Stoke C and Derby Co
1921–22 Bradford C and Manchester U	1953–54 Middlesbrough and Liverpool
1922–23 Stoke C and Oldham Ath	1954–55 Leicester C and Sheffield W
1923–24 Chelsea and Middlesbrough	1955–56 Huddersfield T and Sheffield U
1924–25 Preston NE and Nottingham F	1956–57 Charlton Ath and Cardiff C

1957–58 Sheffield W and Sunderland
1958–59 Portsmouth and Aston Villa
1959–60 Luton T and Leeds U
1960–61 Preston NE and Newcastle U
1961–62 Chelsea and Cardiff C
1962–63 Manchester C and Leyton Orient
1963–64 Bolton W and Ipswich T
1964–65 Wolverhampton W and Birmingham C
1965–66 Northampton T and Blackburn R
1966–67 Aston Villa and Blackpool
1967–68 Fulham and Sheffield U
1968–69 Leicester C and QPR
1969–70 Sunderland and Sheffield W
1970–71 Burnley and Blackpool
1971–72 Huddersfield T and Nottingham F
1972–73 Crystal Palace and WBA
1973–74 Southampton, Manchester U, Norwich C
1974–75 Luton T, Chelsea, Carlisle U
1975–76 Wolverhampton W, Burnley, Sheffield U
1976–77 Sunderland, Stoke C, Tottenham H
1977–78 West Ham U, Newcastle U, Leicester C
1978–79 QPR, Birmingham C, Chelsea
1979–80 Bristol C, Derby Co, Bolton W
1980–81 Norwich C, Leicester C, Crystal Palace
1981–82 Leeds U, Wolverhampton W, Middlesbrough
1982–83 Manchester C, Swansea C, Brighton & HA
1983–84 Birmingham C, Notts Co, Wolverhampton W
1984–85 Norwich C, Sunderland, Stoke C
1985–86 Ipswich T, Birmingham C, WBA
1986–87 Leicester C, Manchester C, Aston Villa
1987–88 Chelsea**, Portsmouth, Watford, Oxford U
1988–89 Middlesbrough, West Ham U, Newcastle U
1989–90 Sheffield W, Charlton Ath, Millwall
1990–91 Sunderland and Derby Co
1991–92 Luton T, Notts Co, West Ham U
1992–93 Brentford, Cambridge U, Bristol R
1993–94 Birmingham C, Oxford U, Peterborough U
1994–95 Swindon T, Burnley, Bristol C, Notts Co
1995–96 Millwall, Watford, Luton T
1996–97 Grimsby T, Oldham Ath, Southend U
1997–98 Manchester C, Stoke C, Reading
1998–99 Bury, Oxford U, Bristol C
1999 00 Walsall, Port Vale, Swindon T
2000–01 Huddersfield T, QPR, Tranmere R
2001–02 Crewe Alex, Barnsley, Stockport Co

**Relegated after play-offs.
*Subsequently re-elected to Division 1 when League was extended after the War.

DIVISION 2 TO DIVISION 3

1920–21 Stockport Co
1921–22 Bradford PA and Bristol C
1922–23 Rotherham Co and Wolverhampton W
1923–24 Nelson and Bristol C
1924–25 Crystal Palace and Coventry C
1925–26 Stoke C and Stockport Co
1926–27 Darlington and Bradford C
1927–28 Fulham and South Shields
1928–29 Port Vale and Clapton Orient
1929–30 Hull C and Notts Co
1930–31 Reading and Cardiff C
1931–32 Barnsley and Bristol C
1932–33 Chesterfield and Charlton Ath
1933–34 Millwall and Lincoln C
1934–35 Oldham Ath and Notts Co
1935–36 Port Vale and Hull C
1936–37 Doncaster R and Bradford C
1937–38 Barnsley and Stockport Co
1938–39 Norwich C and Tranmere R
1946–47 Swansea T and Newport Co
1947–48 Doncaster R and Millwall
1948–49 Nottingham F and Lincoln C
1949–50 Plymouth Arg and Bradford PA
1950–51 Grimsby T and Chesterfield
1951–52 Coventry C and QPR
1952–53 Southampton and Barnsley
1953–54 Brentford and Oldham Ath
1954–55 Ipswich T and Derby Co
1955–56 Plymouth Arg and Hull C
1956–57 Port Vale and Bury
1957–58 Doncaster R and Notts Co
1958–59 Barnsley and Grimsby T
1959–60 Bristol C and Hull C
1960–61 Lincoln C and Portsmouth
1961–62 Brighton & HA and Bristol R
1962–63 Walsall and Luton T
1963–64 Grimsby T and Scunthorpe U
1964–65 Swindon T and Swansea T
1965–66 Middlesbrough and Leyton Orient
1966–67 Northampton T and Bury
1967–68 Plymouth Arg and Rotherham U
1968–69 Fulham and Bury
1969–70 Preston NE and Aston Villa
1970–71 Blackburn R and Bolton W
1971–72 Charlton Ath and Watford
1972–73 Huddersfield T and Brighton & HA
1973–74 Crystal Palace, Preston NE, Swindon T
1974–75 Millwall, Cardiff C, Sheffield W

1975–76	Oxford U, York C, Portsmouth
1976–77	Carlisle U, Plymouth Arg, Hereford U
1977–78	Blackpool, Mansfield T, Hull C
1978–79	Sheffield U, Millwall, Blackburn R
1979–80	Fulham, Burnley, Charlton Ath
1980–81	Preston NE, Bristol C, Bristol R
1981–82	Cardiff C, Wrexham, Orient
1982–83	Rotherham U, Burnley, Bolton W
1983–84	Derby Co, Swansea C, Cambridge U
1984–85	Notts Co, Cardiff C, Wolverhampton W
1985–86	Carlisle U, Middlesbrough, Fulham
1986–87	Sunderland**, Grimsby T, Brighton & HA
1987–88	Huddersfield T, Reading, Sheffield U**
1988–89	Shrewsbury T, Birmingham C, Walsall
1989–90	Bournemouth, Bradford C, Stoke C
1990–91	WBA and Hull C
1991–92	Plymouth Arg, Brighton & HA, Port Vale
1992–93	Preston NE, Mansfield T, Wigan Ath, Chester C
1993–94	Fulham, Exeter C, Hartlepool U, Barnet
1994–95	Cambridge U, Plymouth Arg, Cardiff C, Chester C, Leyton Orient
1995–96	Carlisle U, Swansea C, Brighton & HA, Hull C
1996–97	Peterborough U, Shrewsbury T, Rotherham U, Notts Co
1997–98	Brentford, Plymouth Arg, Carlisle U, Southend U
1998–99	York C, Northampton T, Lincoln C, Macclesfield T
1999–00	Cardiff C, Blackpool, Scunthorpe U, Chesterfield
2000–01	Bristol R, Luton T, Swansea C, Oxford U
2001–02	Bournemouth, Bury, Wrexham, Cambridge U

DIVISION 3 TO DIVISION 4

1958–59	Rochdale, Notts Co, Doncaster R, Stockport Co
1959–60	Accrington S, Wrexham, Mansfield T, York C
1960–61	Chesterfield, Colchester U, Bradford C, Tranmere R
1961–62	Newport Co, Brentford, Lincoln C, Torquay U
1962–63	Bradford PA, Brighton & HA, Carlisle U, Halifax T
1963–64	Millwall, Crewe Alex, Wrexham, Notts Co
1964–65	Luton T, Port Vale, Colchester U, Barnsley
1965–66	Southend U, Exeter C, Brentford, York C
1966–67	Doncaster R, Workington, Darlington, Swansea T
1967–68	Scunthorpe U, Colchester U, Grimsby T, Peterborough U (demoted)
1968–69	Oldham Ath, Crewe Alex, Hartlepool, Northampton T
1969–70	Bournemouth, Southport, Barrow, Stockport Co
1970–71	Reading, Bury, Doncaster R, Gillingham
1971–72	Mansfield T, Barnsley, Torquay U, Bradford C
1972–73	Rotherham U, Brentford, Swansea C, Scunthorpe U
1973–74	Cambridge U, Shrewsbury T, Southport, Rochdale
1974–75	Bournemouth, Tranmere R, Watford, Huddersfield T
1975–76	Aldershot, Colchester U, Southend U, Halifax T
1976–77	Reading, Northampton T, Grimsby T, York C
1977–78	Port Vale, Bradford C, Hereford U, Portsmouth
1978–79	Peterborough U, Walsall, Tranmere R, Lincoln C
1979–80	Bury, Southend U, Mansfield T, Wimbledon
1980–81	Sheffield U, Colchester U, Blackpool, Hull C
1981–82	Wimbledon, Swindon T, Bristol C, Chester
1982–83	Reading, Wrexham, Doncaster R, Chesterfield
1983–84	Scunthorpe U, Southend U, Port Vale, Exeter C
1984–85	Burnley, Orient, Preston NE, Cambridge U
1985–86	Lincoln C, Cardiff C, Wolverhampton W, Swansea C
1986–87	Bolton W**, Carlisle U, Darlington, Newport Co
1987–88	Doncaster R, York C, Grimsby T, Rotherham U**
1988–89	Southend U, Chesterfield, Gillingham, Aldershot
1989–90	Cardiff C, Northampton T, Blackpool, Walsall
1990–91	Crewe Alex, Rotherham U, Mansfield T
1991–92	Bury, Shrewsbury T, Torquay U, Darlington

**Relegated after play-offs.*

LEAGUE TITLE WINS

FA PREMIER LEAGUE – Manchester U 7, Arsenal 2, Blackburn R 1.

LEAGUE DIVISION 1 – Liverpool 18, Arsenal 10, Everton 9, Sunderland 8, Manchester U 7, Aston Villa 7, Newcastle U 5, Sheffield W 4, Huddersfield T 3, Leeds U 3, Manchester C 3, Wolverhampton W 3, Blackburn R 2, Nottingham F 2, Portsmouth 2, Preston NE 2, Burnley 2, Tottenham H 2, Derby Co 2, Bolton W 1, Chelsea 1, Sheffield U 1, WBA 1, Ipswich T 1, Crystal Palace 1, Middlesbrough 1, Charlton Ath 1, Fulham 1.

LEAGUE DIVISION 2 – Leicester C 6, Manchester C 6, Sheffield W 5, Birmingham C (one as Small Heath) 5, Derby Co 4, Liverpool 4, Preston NE 4, Ipswich T 3, Leeds U 3, Notts Co 3, Middlesbrough 3, Stoke C 3, Bury 2, Grimsby T 2, Norwich C 2, Nottingham F 2, Tottenham H 2, WBA 2, Aston Villa 2, Burnley 2, Chelsea 2, Manchester U 2, Millwall 2, West Ham U 2, Wolverhampton W 2, Bolton W 2, Fulham 2, Swindon T, Huddersfield T, Bristol C, Brentford, Bradford C, Everton, Sheffield U, Newcastle U, Coventry C, Blackpool, Blackburn R, Brighton & HA, Sunderland, Crystal Palace, Luton T, QPR, Oxford U, Oldham Ath, Reading, Watford 1 each.

LEAGUE DIVISION 3 – Portsmouth 2, Oxford U 2, Carlisle U 2, Preston NE 2, Shrewsbury T 2, Brentford 2, Plymouth Arg 2, Southampton, Bury, Northampton T, Coventry C, Hull C, QPR, Watford, Leyton Orient, Aston Villa, Bolton W, Oldham Ath, Blackburn R, Hereford U, Mansfield T, Wrexham, Grimsby T, Rotherham U, Burnley, Bradford C, Bournemouth, Reading, Sunderland, Wolverhampton W, Bristol R, Cambridge U, Cardiff C, Wigan Ath, Notts Co, Swansea C, Brighton & HA 1 each.

LEAGUE DIVISION 4 – Chesterfield 2, Doncaster R 2, Peterborough U 2, Port Vale, Walsall, Millwall, Brentford, Gillingham, Brighton, Stockport Co, Luton T, Notts Co, Grimsby T, Southport, Mansfield T, Lincoln C, Cambridge U, Watford, Reading, Huddersfield T, Southend U, Sheffield U, Wimbledon, York C, Swindon T, Northampton T, Wolverhampton W, Rotherham U, Exeter C, Darlington, Burnley 1 each.

To 1957–58

DIVISION 3 (South) – Bristol C 3; Charlton Ath, Ipswich T, Millwall, Notts Co, Plymouth Arg, Swansea T 2 each; Brentford, Bristol R, Cardiff C, Crystal Palace, Coventry C, Fulham, Leyton Orient, Luton T, Newport Co, Nottingham F, Norwich C, Portsmouth, QPR, Reading, Southampton, Brighton & HA 1 each.

DIVISION 3 (North) – Barnsley, Doncaster R, Lincoln C 3 each; Chesterfield, Grimsby T, Hull C, Port Vale, Stockport Co 2 each; Bradford PA, Bradford C, Darlington, Derby Co, Nelson, Oldham Ath, Rotherham U, Stoke C, Tranmere R, Wolverhampton W, Scunthorpe U 1 each.

LEAGUE ATTENDANCES 2001–2002

FA BARCLAYCARD PREMIERSHIP ATTENDANCES

	Average Gate			Season 2001/02	
	2000/01	2001/02	+/–%	Highest	Lowest
Arsenal	37,975	38,054	+0.21	38,240	37,898
Aston Villa	31,597	35,012	+10.81	42,632	27,701
Blackburn Rovers	20,740	25,984	+25.28	30,487	21,873
Bolton Wanderers	16,062	25,098	+56.26	27,351	20,747
Charlton Athletic	20,020	24,135	+20.56	26,551	20,451
Chelsea	34,698	39,033	+12.49	41,725	33,504
Derby County	28,551	29,818	+4.44	33,297	25,712
Everton	34,130	34,004	–0.37	39,948	29,503
Fulham	14,985	19,545	+30.43	21,159	15,885
Ipswich Town	22,524	24,396	+8.31	28,286	21,133
Leeds United	39,016	39,789	+1.98	40,287	38,337
Leicester City	20,453	19,835	–3.02	21,886	15,412
Liverpool	43,699	43,389	–0.71	44,371	37,163
Manchester United	67,543	67,586	+0.06	67,683	67,534
Middlesbrough	30,730	28,450	–7.42	34,358	24,041
Newcastle United	51,290	51,373	+0.16	52,130	49,185
Southampton	15,115	30,633	+102.66	31,973	26,794
Sunderland	45,069	44,108	–2.13	47,989	39,730
Tottenham Hotspur	35,216	34,878	–0.96	36,075	29,596
West Ham United	25,697	31,359	+22.04	35,546	24,517

NATIONWIDE FOOTBALL LEAGUE: DIVISION ONE ATTENDANCES

	Average Gate			Season 2001/02	
	2000/01	2001/02	+/–%	Highest	Lowest
Barnsley	14,465	13,292	–8.1	18,303	10,976
Birmingham City	21,283	21,854	+2.7	29,178	17,310
Bradford City	18,511	15,489	–16.3	20,209	12,846
Burnley	16,234	15,252	–6.0	21,823	13,162
Coventry City	20,535	15,436	–24.8	22,902	12,448
Crewe Alexandra	6,698	7,113	+6.2	10,092	5,419
Crystal Palace	17,061	17,177	+0.7	22,080	13,970
Gillingham	9,293	8,569	–7.8	10,477	6,575
Grimsby Town	5,646	6,430	+13.9	9,275	4,859
Manchester City	34,058	33,059	–2.9	34,657	30,238
Millwall	11,442	13,253	+15.8	17,058	10,021
Norwich City	16,525	18,738	+13.4	21,251	15,710
Nottingham Forest	20,615	21,701	+5.3	28,546	15,632
Portsmouth	13,533	15,117	+11.7	19,103	12,336
Preston North End	14,617	14,883	+1.8	21,014	11,371
Rotherham United	5,652	7,488	+32.5	11,426	5,586
Sheffield United	17,211	18,020	+4.7	29,364	14,180
Sheffield Wednesday	19,268	20,864	+8.3	29,772	15,592
Stockport County	7,031	6,244	–11.2	9,537	4,086
Walsall	5,632	6,816	+21.0	9,181	5,080
Watford	13,941	14,896	+6.9	18,911	12,160
West Bromwich Albion	17,657	20,691	+17.2	26,712	17,335
Wimbledon	7,901	6,958	–11.9	13,564	4,249
Wolverhampton Wanderers	19,258	23,796	+23.6	28,015	19,231

Nationwide attendance averages and highest crowd figures for 2001–02 supplied by Football League. Other attendances unofficial.

NATIONWIDE FOOTBALL LEAGUE: DIVISION TWO ATTENDANCES

	Average Gate			Season 2001/02	
	2000/01	2001/02	+/–%	Highest	Lowest
Blackpool	4,457	5,682	+27.5	9,333	4,118
AFC Bournemouth	4,403	5,062	+15.0	8,147	2,908
Brentford	4,645	6,729	+44.9	11,303	4,561
Brighton & Hove Albion	6,603	6,559	–0.7	6,870	6,117
Bristol City	10,369	11,241	+8.4	15,609	8,299
Bury	3,444	3,914	+13.6	7,953	2,459
Cambridge United	4,403	3,505	–20.4	5,665	2,379
Cardiff City	7,962	12,523	+57.3	17,403	8,013
Chesterfield	4,846	4,305	–11.2	5,442	3,538
Colchester United	3,555	3,822	+7.5	5,186	2,835
Huddersfield Town	12,808	10,880	–15.1	16,041	7,179
Northampton Town	5,654	5,246	–7.2	6,723	3,909
Notts County	5,201	5,956	+14.5	15,618	3,140
Oldham Athletic	4,972	5,812	+16.9	8,859	3,970
Peterborough United	6,252	5,420	–13.3	8,656	3,445
Port Vale	4,458	5,214	+17.0	10,344	3,514
Queens Park Rangers	12,013	11,750	–2.2	18,346	8,519
Reading	12,647	14,115	+11.6	22,151	8,081
Stoke City	13,767	13,966	+1.4	23,019	9,515
Swindon Town	6,187	5,840	–5.6	9,264	3,821
Tranmere Rovers	9,045	8,656	–4.3	12,201	7,342
Wigan Athletic	6,774	5,651	–16.6	7,783	3,535
Wrexham	3,600	3,782	+5.1	5,832	2,470
Wycombe Wanderers	5,513	6,681	+21.2	9,250	5,400

NATIONWIDE FOOTBALL LEAGUE: DIVISION THREE ATTENDANCES

	Average Gate			Season 2001/02	
	2000/01	2001/02	+/–%	Highest	Lowest
Bristol Rovers	7,275	6,565	–9.8	10,127	4,457
Carlisle United	3,670	3,214	–14.5	5,226	1,849
Cheltenham Town	3,695	4,052	+9.7	7,013	2,402
Darlington	3,844	3,842	–0.1	6,339	2,729
Exeter City	3,692	3,313	–10.3	5,756	2,038
Halifax Town	2,214	1,717	–22.4	3,400	1,227
Hartlepool United	3,423	3,566	+4.2	4,842	2,599
Hull City	6,684	9,506	+42.2	12,529	8,419
Kidderminster Harriers	3,422	2,984	–12.8	4,147	2,002
Leyton Orient	4,528	4,550	+0.6	6,540	3,284
Lincoln City	3,273	2,673	–18.3	5,849	1,935
Luton Town	5,754	7,413	+28.8	9,585	5,066
Macclesfield Town	2,064	2,128	+3.1	3,002	1,356
Mansfield Town	2,706	4,896	+80.9	8,638	2,681
Oxford United	5,148	6,258	+21.6	11,121	4,964
Plymouth Argyle	4,945	8,788	+77.7	18,517	3,850
Rochdale	3,249	3,412	+5.0	5,292	2,819
Rushden & Diamonds	3,876	4,404	+13.6	5,876	2,771
Scunthorpe United	3,446	3,800	+10.3	6,479	2,574
Shrewsbury Town	2,898	3,849	+32.8	7,858	2,576
Southend United	4,322	3,986	–7.8	5,973	2,477
Swansea City	4,913	3,693	–24.8	5,501	2,677
Torquay United	2,556	2,534	–0.9	4,217	1,702
York City	3,026	3,143	+3.9	6,495	1,840

TRANSFERS 2001–2002

June 2001 *From* *To*

	From	To
8 Alcide, Colin J.	York City	Cambridge United
21 Alexander, Gary G.	Swindon Town	Hull City
4 Campbell, Stuart P.	Leicester City	Grimsby Town
25 Crichton, Paul A.	Burnley	Norwich City
19 Easton, Clint J.	Watford	Norwich City
14 Freeman, Mark W.	Cheltenham Town	Boston United
20 Glennon, Mathew W.	Bolton Wanderers	Hull City
27 Jeffers, Francis	Everton	Arsenal
27 Kerr, Scott A.	Bradford City	Hull City
11 McLaren, Paul A.	Luton Town	Sheffield Wednesday
20 Pitcher, Geoffrey	Kingstonian	Brighton & Hove Albion
5 Pollitt, Michael F.	Chesterfield	Rotherham United
28 Rivers, Mark A.	Crewe Alexandra	Norwich City
1 Simpkins, Michael	Chesterfield	Cardiff City
20 Vaesen, Nico	Huddersfield Town	Birmingham City
4 Warner, Philip	Southampton	Cambridge United
23 Wise, Dennis F.	Chelsea	Leicester City

July 2001

	From	To
11 Bellamy, Craig D.	Coventry City	Newcastle United
27 Carroll, Roy E.	Wigan Athletic	Manchester United
20 Clarke, Darrell J.	Mansfield Town	Hartlepool United
6 Conlon, Barry J.	York City	Darlington
18 Cresswell, Richard P.W.	Leicester City	Preston North End
11 Crouch, Peter J.	Queens Park Rangers	Portsmouth
14 Currie, Darren	Barnet	Wycombe Wanderers
16 Darlington, Jermaine C.	Queens Park Rangers	Wimbledon
21 Delap, Rory J.	Derby County	Southampton
11 Dobie, Scott R.	Carlisle United	West Bromwich Albion
7 Dudfield, Lawrie G.	Leicester City	Hull City
12 Emblen, Neil R.	Wolverhampton Wanderers	Norwich City
6 Euell, Jason J.	Wimbledon	Charlton Athletic
21 Fletcher, Gary	Northwich Victoria	Leyton Orient
24 Forbes, Adrian E.	Norwich City	Luton Town
24 Gorre, Dean	Huddersfield Town	Barnsley
10 Griffiths, Carl B.	Leyton Orient	Luton Town
16 Hackworth, Anthony	Leeds United	Notts County
9 Hadji, Moustapha	Coventry City	Aston Villa
16 Hughes, Andrew J.	Notts County	Reading
19 Ireland, Craig	Dundee	Notts County
17 James, David B.	Aston Villa	West Ham United
26 Jevons, Philip	Everton	Grimsby Town
11 Joachim, Julian K.	Aston Villa	Coventry City
4 Jones, Stephen G.	Leigh RMI	Crewe Alexandra
6 Kavanagh, Graham A.	Stoke City	Cardiff City
7 Kennedy, Mark J.	Manchester City	Wolverhampton Wanderers
18 Kennedy, Peter H.J.	Watford	Wigan Athletic
3 Lampard, Frank J.	West Ham United	Chelsea
16 Mildenhall, Stephen J.	Swindon Town	Notts County
17 Miller, Thomas W.	Hartlepool United	Ipswich Town
17 Palmer, Stephen L.	Watford	Queens Park Rangers
12 Peschisolido, Paul P.	Fulham	Sheffield United
10 Poyet, Gustavo D.A.	Chelsea	Tottenham Hotspur
3 Prior, Spencer J.	Manchester City	Cardiff City
16 Reddington, Stuart	Chelsea	Mansfield Town
24 Richards, Tony S.	Barnet	Southend United
31 Scowcroft, James B.	Ipswich Town	Leicester City
25 Shipperley, Neil J.	Barnsley	Wimbledon
14 Southgate, Gareth	Aston Villa	Middlesbrough
13 Stockley, Sam J.	Barnet	Oxford United
26 Walker, Ian M.	Tottenham Hotspur	Leicester City

9 Williams, Ryan N.	Chesterfield	Hull City
13 Williams, Thomas A.	West Ham United	Peterborough United
13 Wright, Richard I.	Ipswich Town	Arsenal
27 Young, Luke P.	Tottenham Hotspur	Charlton Athletic

Temporary transfers

17 Bywater, Stephen M.	West Ham United	Wolverhampton Wanderers
9 Clarke, Matthew J.	Bradford City	Fulham
25 Cummings, Warren	Chelsea	West Bromwich Albion
10 Noble, David J.	Arsenal	Watford
4 Parkin, Sam	Chelsea	Northampton Town
4 Wolleaston, Robert A.	Chelsea	Northampton Town

August 2001

6 Alexander, Neil	Livingston	Cardiff City
2 Berkovic, Eyal	Celtic	Manchester City
10 Brammer, David	Port Vale	Crewe Alexandra
24 Burchill, Mark J.	Celtic	Portsmouth
24 Cameron, Colin	Heart of Midlothian	Wolverhampton Wanderers
9 Clements, Matthew	Mildenhall Town	Cambridge United
8 De Vos, Jason R.	Dundee United	Wigan Athletic
9 Evans, Gareth J.	Leeds United	Huddersfield Town
9 Forbes, Adrian E.	Norwich City	Luton Town
8 Gayle, Marcus A.	Rangers	Watford
9 Greening, Jonathan	Manchester United	Middlesbrough
8 Harley, Jon	Chelsea	Fulham
2 Hartson, John	Coventry City	Celtic
9 Holmes, Shaun P.	Manchester City	Wrexham
8 Hughes, Lee	West Bromwich Albion	Coventry City
31 Hutchison, Donald	Sunderland	West Ham United
15 Kelly, Leon M.	Atherstone United	Cambridge United
24 Kerr, James S.R.	Celtic	Wigan Athletic
31 Kirkland, Christopher	Coventry City	Liverpool
23 Lucketti, Christopher J.	Huddersfield Town	Preston North End
20 McNeil, Martin J.	Cambridge United	Torquay United
10 Newton, Shaun O.	Charlton Athletic	Wolverhampton Wanderers
3 Nicholls, Kevin J.	Wigan Athletic	Luton Town
2 Nowland, Adam C.	Blackpool	Wimbledon
9 O'Neill, Keith P.	Middlesbrough	Coventry City
9 Perpetuini, David P.	Watford	Gillingham
10 Perrett, Russell	Cardiff City	Luton Town
23 Wainwright, Neil	Sunderland	Darlington
9 Wilson, Mark A.	Manchester United	Middlesbrough
1 Ziege, Christian	Liverpool	Tottenham Hotspur

Temporary transfers

10 Adamczuk, Dariuz	Rangers	Wigan Athletic
18 Beharall, David	Newcastle United	Grimsby Town
18 Beresford, Marlon	Middlesbrough	Wolverhampton Wanderers
25 Berkley, Austin J.	Barnet	Carlisle United
10 Birch, Gary S.	Walsall	Exeter City
18 Burgess, Benjamin K.	Blackburn Rovers	Brentford
9 Byrne, Desmond	Wimbledon	Cambridge United
31 Capleton, Melvin D.R.	Southend United	Grays Athletic
17 Chillingworth, Daniel T.	Cambridge United	Cambridge City
2 Constantine, Leon	Millwall	Leyton Orient
16 Croudson, Steven D.	Grimsby Town	Scunthorpe United
11 Crowe, Dean A.	Stoke City	Plymouth Argyle
23 Dichio, Daniele S.E.	Sunderland	West Bromwich Albion
18 Dorrian, Christopher S.	Leyton Orient	Dover Athletic
10 Evatt, Ian R.	Derby County	Northampton Town
15 Futcher, Benjamin P.	Oldham Athletic	Stalybridge Celtic
31 Hammond, Elvis Z.	Fulham	Bristol Rovers
18 Hillier, Ian M.	Tottenham Hotspur	Luton Town
17 Hodgson, Steven G.	Macclesfield Town	Nuneaton Borough
18 Hyde, Graham	Birmingham City	Chesterfield

24 Kelly, Alan T.	Blackburn Rovers	Birmingham City
17 McIntosh, Martin	Hibernian	Rotherham United
9 McNeil, Martin J.	Cambridge United	Torquay United
24 Myers, Peter W.	Halifax Town	Guiseley
9 Navarro, Alan E.	Liverpool	Crewe Alexandra
17 O'Flynn, John	Peterborough United	Cambridge City
17 Okikiolu, Samuel K.	Wimbledon	Clyde
18 Opara, Kelechi C.	Leyton Orient	Billericay Town
24 Osei-Kuffour, Jonathan	Arsenal	Swindon Town
8 Page, Robert J.	Watford	Sheffield United
25 Parsons, David	Leyton Orient	Dover Athletic
6 Peacock, Gavin K.	Queens Park Rangers	Charlton Athletic
9 Proctor, Michael A.	Sunderland	York City
10 Pullen, James	Ipswich Town	Blackpool
7 Ramsay, Scott A.	Brighton & Hove Albion	Yeovil Town
10 Richards, Marc J.	Blackburn Rovers	Crewe Alexandra
24 Robinson, Paul M.J.	Millwall	Fisher Athletic
25 Salt, Philip T.	Oldham Athletic	Leigh RMI
7 Savic, Sinisa	Barnsley	Frickley Athletic
14 Smart, Allan A.C.	Watford	Hibernian
30 Taylor, Robert A.	Wolverhampton Wanderers	Queens Park Rangers
21 Tod, Andrew	Dunfermline Athletic	Bradford City
30 Tyson, Nathan	Reading	Swansea City
17 Wainwright, Neil	Sunderland	Darlington
24 Webb, Paul A.	Kidderminster Harriers	Hereford United
16 Whitfield, Paul M.	Wrexham	Connah's Quay Nomads
10 Wilkie, Lee	Dundee	Notts County
23 Woozley, David J.	Crystal Palace	Torquay United

September 2001

13 Belgrave, Barrington	Yeovil Town	Southend United
13 Blake, Nathan A.	Blackburn Rovers	Wolverhampton Wanderers
7 Clarke, Matthew J.	Bradford City	Crystal Palace
8 Coyne, Christopher J.	Dundee	Luton Town
10 Dinning, Tony	Wolverhampton Wanderers	Wigan Athletic
21 Goodhind, Warren	Barnet	Cambridge United
13 Hanlon, Ritchie K.	Peterborough United	Rushden & Diamonds
5 Jackson, Justin J.	Rushden & Diamonds	Doncaster Rovers
19 Johnson, Andrew J.	Nottingham Forest	West Bromwich Albion
6 Marsh, Christopher J.	Wycombe Wanderers	Northampton Town
24 Moody, Paul	Millwall	Oxford United
14 Moore, Darren M.	Portsmouth	West Bromwich Albion
7 Neill, Lucas E.	Millwall	Blackburn Rovers
14 Page, Robert J.	Watford	Sheffield United
13 Partridge, Scott M.	Brentford	Rushden & Diamonds
13 Patmore, Warren J.	Rushden & Diamonds	Woking
21 Rae, Alexander S.	Sunderland	Wolverhampton Wanderers
24 Richards, Dean I.	Southampton	Tottenham Hotspur
28 Richardson, Marcus G.	Cambridge United	Torquay United
13 Thorne, Peter L.	Stoke City	Cardiff City

Temporary transfers

7 Andrews, John H.	Mansfield Town	Hucknall Town
24 Antony, Paul M.	Carlisle United	Newry Town
29 Arphexad, Pegguy M.	Liverpool	Stockport County
11 Barrett, Graham	Arsenal	Crewe Alexandra
14 Beharall, David	Newcastle United	Grimsby Town
21 Bennion, Christopher	Middlesbrough	Scunthorpe United
7 Bettney, Scott	Sheffield Wednesday	Worksop Town
7 Bragstad, Bjorn O.	Derby County	Birmingham City
5 Broomes, Marlon C.	Blackburn Rovers	Grimsby Town
14 Brown, Wayne L.	Ipswich Town	Wimbledon
19 Burgess, Benjamin K.	Blackburn Rovers	Brentford
7 Caceres, Adrian C.	Southampton	Brentford
21 Capaldi, Anthony C.	Birmingham City	Hereford United
17 Casey, Ryan P.	Swansea City	Merthyr Tydfil

28 Castle, Stephen C.	Leyton Orient	Stevenage Borough
25 Chettle, Stephen	Barnsley	Walsall
16 Chillingworth, Daniel T.	Cambridge United	Cambridge City
25 Cockrill, Dale	Cambridge United	Aylesbury United
28 Constantine, Leon	Millwall	Leyton Orient
29 Crowe, Dean	Stoke City	Luton Town
20 Curtis, Thomas D.	Portsmouth	Walsall
7 Dinning, Tony	Wolverhampton Wanderers	Wigan Athletic
10 Evatt, Ian R.	Derby County	Northampton Town
15 Futcher, Benjamin P.	Oldham Athletic	Stalybridge Celtic
5 Gould, Ronny D.	Leyton Orient	Heybridge Swifts
6 Grayson, Simon N.	Blackburn Rovers	Notts County
14 Gregg, Matthew S.	Crystal Palace	Exeter City
10 Hanlon, Ritchie K.	Peterborough United	Rushden & Diamonds
28 Harris, Richard L.S.	Crystal Palace	Mansfield Town
20 Hillier, Ian M.	Tottenham Hotspur	Luton Town
14 Holmes, Derek	Ross County	AFC Bournemouth
20 Hoolickin, Lee	Carlisle United	Gretna
14 Hunter, Barry V.	Reading	Rushden & Diamonds
8 Hyde, Graham	Birmingham City	Chesterfield
7 Ilic, Sasa	Charlton Athletic	Portsmouth
4 Kelly, Leon M.	Cambridge United	Stalybridge Celtic
24 Killen, Christopher J.	Manchester City	Port Vale
14 Larkin, Colin	Wolverhampton Wanderers	Kidderminster Harriers
21 Lewis, Craig	Carlisle United	Workington
12 Liddle, Graham	Darlington	Whitby Town
18 Lockwood, Adam B.	Reading	Yeovil Town
27 Maley, Mark	Sunderland	York City
21 May, Kyle	Carlisle United	Gretna
3 McCready, Christopher J.	Crewe Alexandra	Hyde United
3 McElholm, Brendan A.	Leyton Orient	Chelmsford City
7 McGill, Brendan	Sunderland	Carlisle United
7 Miller, Kenneth	Rangers	Wolverhampton Wanderers
18 Miller, William	Dundee	Wrexham
2 Moody, Paul	Millwall	Oxford United
18 Murphy, Danny	Queens Park Rangers	Hampton & Richmond Borough
8 Murray, Jade A.	Leyton Orient	Sutton United
17 Mustoe, Neil J.	Cambridge United	Cambridge City
9 Navarro, Alan E.	Liverpool	Crewe Alexandra
21 Nelson, Craig M.	Middlesbrough	Gateshead
21 Ormerod, Anthony	Middlesbrough	Hartlepool United
7 Palmer, Carlton L.	Coventry City	Sheffield Wednesday
9 Proctor, Michael A.	Sunderland	York City
10 Pullen, James	Ipswich Town	Blackpool
21 Reddy, Michael	Sunderland	Hull City
18 Richardson, Marcus G.	Cambridge United	Torquay United
23 Robinson, Paul M.J.	Millwall	Fisher Athletic
28 Rustem, Adam R.	Queens Park Rangers	Chertsey Town
26 Salt, Philip T.	Oldham Athletic	Leigh RMI
11 Singh, Harpal	Leeds United	Bury
7 Smith, Grant G.	Sheffield United	Halifax Town
5 Stamp, Philip L.	Middlesbrough	Millwall
28 Summerbell, Mark	Middlesbrough	Bristol City
8 Tate, Christopher D.	Leyton Orient	Stevenage Borough
25 Uka, Niam	Leyton Orient	Wingate & Finchley
20 Vickers, Stephen	Middlesbrough	Crystal Palace
13 Walker, Richard M.	Aston Villa	Wycombe Wanderers
28 Ward, Christopher	Birmingham City	Forest Green Rovers
28 Webb, Paul A.	Kidderminster Harriers	Hereford United
27 Wheatcroft, Paul M.	Bolton Wanderers	Rochdale
22 White, Jason G.	Cheltenham Town	Mansfield Town
7 Wilford, Aron L.	Middlesbrough	Scarborough
21 Williams, Lee	Mansfield Town	Cheltenham Town

| 23 Woozley, David J. | Crystal Palace | Torquay United |
| 28 Wright, Daniel J. | Queens Park Rangers | Chertsey Town |

October 2001

22 Armstrong, Christopher	Bury	Oldham Athletic
27 Crowe, Dean A.	Stoke City	Luton Town
12 Gill, Wayne J.	Tranmere Rovers	Oldham Athletic
11 Grant, Anthony J.	Manchester City	Burnley
19 Green, Ryan M.	Wolverhampton Wanderers	Millwall
19 Johnson, Seth A.M.	Derby County	Leeds United
19 McAteer, Jason W.	Blackburn Rovers	Sunderland
8 Mullin, John	Burnley	Rotherham United
19 Neilson, Alan B.	Fulham	Grimsby Town
19 Roberts, Stuart I.	Swansea City	Wycombe Wanderers
1 Sharpling, Christopher	Crystal Palace	Woking
3 Ward, Darren P.	Watford	Millwall
31 Williams, Paul D.	Coventry City	Southampton

Temporary transfers

19 Beharall, David	Newcastle United	Grimsby Town
21 Bennion, Christopher	Middlesbrough	Scunthorpe United
11 Betts, Robert	Coventry City	Lincoln City
19 Boardman, Jonathan G.	Crystal Palace	Margate
8 Broomes, Marlon C.	Blackburn Rovers	Grimsby Town
16 Browne, Ricky D.	Queens Park Rangers	Enfield
14 Brown, Wayne L.	Ipswich Town	Wimbledon
22 Bullock, Matthew	Stoke City	Macclesfield Town
2 Butterworth, Adam L.	Cambridge United	Heybridge Swifts
12 Caldwell, Stephen	Newcastle United	Blackpool
18 Carbone, Benito	Bradford City	Derby County
21 Carlisle, Wayne T.	Crystal Palace	Swindon Town
28 Castle, Stephen C.	Leyton Orient	Stevenage Borough
9 Charles, Anthony D.	Crewe Alexandra	Hayes
29 Charles, Julian	Brentford	Farnborough Town
19 Clements, Matthew	Cambridge United	Stalybridge Celtic
26 De-Vulgt, Leigh S.	Swansea City	Merthyr Tydfil
23 Douglas, Stuart A.	Luton Town	Oxford United
23 Etherington, Matthew	Tottenham Hotspur	Bradford City
12 Feuer, Anthony I.	Wimbledon	Derby County
19 Flowers, Timothy D.	Leicester City	Stockport County
5 Folan, Caleb C.	Leeds United	Rushden & Diamonds
25 Foley, Dominic J.	Watford	Queens Park Rangers
8 Ford, Ryan	Notts County	Gresley Rovers
15 Futcher, Benjamin P.	Oldham Athletic	Stalybridge Celtic
9 Gray, Philip	Oxford United	Boston United
11 Grayson, Simon N.	Blackburn Rovers	Notts County
27 Grimsdell, Daniel B.	Leyton Orient	Aveley
12 Hahnemann, Marcus S.	Fulham	Rochdale
4 Hammond, Elvis Z.	Fulham	Bristol Rovers
19 Hankin, Sean A.	Crystal Palace	Torquay United
11 Hill, Keith J.	Cheltenham Town	Wrexham
16 Hillier, Ian M.	Tottenham Hotspur	Luton Town
27 Hitzlsperger, Thomas	Aston Villa	Chesterfield
12 Holden, Dean T.J.	Bolton Wanderers	Oldham Athletic
18 Hoolickin, Lee	Carlisle United	Gretna
19 Jackson, Matthew A.	Norwich City	Wigan Athletic
24 Killen, Christopher J.	Manchester City	Port Vale
23 Knight, Leon L.	Chelsea	Huddersfield Town
5 Larkin, Colin	Wolverhampton Wanderers	Kidderminster Harriers
24 Liddle, Gareth J.C.	Crewe Alexandra	Hyde United
1 Lovett, Jay	Brentford	Crawley Town
8 Lumsdon, Christopher	Sunderland	Barnsley
26 Maley, Mark	Sunderland	York City
19 May, Kyle	Carlisle United	Gretna
20 McClare, Sean P.	Barnsley	Port Vale
10 McGill, Brendan	Sunderland	Carlisle United

27 Moore, Stefan	Aston Villa	Chesterfield
5 Mullin, John	Burnley	Rotherham United
9 Murray, Jade	Leyton Orient	Sutton United
19 Nacca, Francesco	Cambridge United	Cambridge City
22 Nelson, Craig M.	Middlesbrough	Gateshead
5 O'Brien, Christopher T.	Liverpool	Chester City
19 Odejayi, Olukayode	Bristol City	Forest Green Rovers
4 O'Flynn, John	Peterborough United	Cambridge City
27 Opara, Kelechi C.	Leyton Orient	Purfleet
22 Ormerod, Anthony	Middlesbrough	Hartlepool United
19 Oster, John	Sunderland	Barnsley
26 O'Sullivan, Christopher	Swansea City	Aberystwyth Town
9 Peacock, Gavin K.	Queens Park Rangers	Charlton Athletic
26 Pearce, Alexander G.	Chesterfield	Ilkeston Town
8 Proctor, Michael A.	Sunderland	York City
10 Pullen, James	Ipswich Town	Blackpool
12 Richards, Marc J.	Blackburn Rovers	Oldham Athletic
5 Risbridger, Gareth	Southend United	Dover Athletic
30 Rosler, Uwe	Southampton	West Bromwich Albion
23 Ross, Neil J.	Stockport County	Bristol Rovers
26 Rustem, Adam R.	Queens Park Rangers	Chertsey Town
26 Samuel, J. Lloyd	Aston Villa	Gillingham
11 Sandford, Lee R.	Sheffield United	Stockport County
23 Shittu, Daniel O.	Charlton Athletic	Queens Park Rangers
23 Sidwell, Steven J.	Arsenal	Brentford
14 Singh, Harpal	Leeds United	Bury
8 Skinner, Stephen K.	Gretna	Carlisle United
9 Smith, Grant G.	Sheffield United	Halifax Town
8 Taylor, Robert A.	Wolverhampton Wanderers	Gillingham
26 Thogersen, Thomas	Portsmouth	Walsall
22 Tudor, Shane A.	Wolverhampton Wanderers	Cambridge United
5 Varty, John W.	Carlisle United	Workington
14 Walker, Richard M.	Aston Villa	Wycombe Wanderers
29 Wheatcroft, Paul M.	Bolton Wanderers	Rochdale
16 White, Thomas J.C.	Portsmouth	Havant & Waterlooville
7 Wilford, Aron L.	Middlesbrough	Scarborough
22 Williams, Paul D.	Coventry City	Southampton
26 Wright, Daniel J.	Queens Park Rangers	Chertsey Town

November 2001

23 Bent, Marcus N.	Blackburn Rovers	Ipswich Town
14 Clark, Ian D.	Hartlepool United	Darlington
30 Deane, Brian C.	Middlesbrough	Leicester City
30 Ellison, Kevin	Leicester City	Stockport County
7 Folan, Anthony S.	Brentford	Bohemians
30 Fowler, Robert B.	Liverpool	Leeds United
20 Gallen, Kevin A.	Barnsley	Queens Park Rangers
9 Hamilton, Ian R.	Notts County	Lincoln City
6 Hillier, Ian M.	Tottenham Hotspur	Luton Town
28 Holmes, Derek	Ross County	AFC Bournemouth
20 Jackson, Matthew A.	Norwich City	Wigan Athletic
30 Jones, Gary R.	Rochdale	Barnsley
16 Jones, Mark A.	Chesterfield	Raith Rovers
14 Lescott, Aaron A.	Sheffield Wednesday	Stockport County
29 McClare, Sean P.	Barnsley	Port Vale
15 McIntosh, Martin	Hibernian	Rotherham United
16 Rogers, Alan	Nottingham Forest	Leicester City
30 Smart, Allan A.C.	Watford	Oldham Athletic
19 Tod, Andrew	Dunfermline Athletic	Bradford City
23 Tudor, Shane A.	Wolverhampton Wanderers	Cambridge United
2 Zhiyi, Fan	Crystal Palace	Dundee

Temporary transfers

9 Appleby, Richard D.	Swansea City	Kidderminster Harriers
15 Armstrong, Joel	Chesterfield	Hucknall Town
19 Beharall, David	Newcastle United	Oldham Athletic

Name		
21 Bennion, Christopher	Middlesbrough	Scunthorpe United
13 Bloomfield, Daniel R.	Norwich City	King's Lynn
23 Broad, Joseph R.	Plymouth Argyle	Yeovil Town
14 Broomes, Marlon C.	Blackburn Rovers	Grimsby Town
12 Brown, Wayne L.	Ipswich Town	Wimbledon
2 Burgess, Benjamin K.	Blackburn Rovers	Brentford
28 Burns, John C.	Bristol City	Shelbourne
20 Caldwell, Gary	Newcastle United	Darlington
3 Capaldi, Anthony C.	Birmingham City	Hereford United
21 Charles, Anthony D.	Crewe Alexandra	Hayes
30 Charles, Julian	Brentford	Farnborough Town
19 Chillingworth, Daniel T.	Cambridge United	Darlington
1 Chilvers, Liam C.	Arsenal	Notts County
19 Clark, Steven T.	West Ham United	Southend United
30 Cook, Paul A.	Burnley	Wigan Athletic
15 Delaney, Damien	Leicester City	Stockport County
31 Dichio, Daniele S.E.	Sunderland	West Bromwich Albion
27 Dryden, Richard A.	Luton Town	Scarborough
24 Dunning, Darren	Blackburn Rovers	Rochdale
16 Edwards, Christian N.H.	Nottingham Forest	Crystal Palace
27 Etherington, Matthew	Tottenham Hotspur	Bradford City
15 Evans, Rhys K.	Chelsea	Queens Park Rangers
9 Evans, Stephen J.	Crystal Palace	Swansea City
16 Fleming, Curtis	Middlesbrough	Birmingham City
30 Folan, Caleb C.	Leeds United	Hull City
9 Ford, Ryan	Notts County	Gresley Rovers
23 Gordon, Dean D.	Middlesbrough	Cardiff City
2 Grant, John A.C.	Crewe Alexandra	Rushden & Diamonds
30 Gray, Wayne W.	Wimbledon	Leyton Orient
20 Hadland, Philip J.	Leyton Orient	Carlisle United
15 Hankin, Sean A.	Crystal Palace	Torquay United
23 Hanson, Christian	Middlesbrough	Torquay United
2 Hillier, Ian M.	Tottenham Hotspur	Luton Town
27 Hitzlsperger, Thomas	Aston Villa	Chesterfield
13 Holden, Dean T.J.	Bolton Wanderers	Oldham Athletic
8 Kelly, Leon M.	Cambridge United	Nuneaton Borough
2 Kenna, Jeffrey J.	Blackburn Rovers	Wigan Athletic
16 Knight, Leon L.	Chelsea	Huddersfield Town
14 Larkin, Colin	Wolverhampton Wanderers	Kidderminster Harriers
19 Leigertwood, Mikele B.	Wimbledon	Leyton Orient
16 Lovett, Jay	Brentford	Crawley Town
9 Lumsdon, Christopher	Sunderland	Barnsley
26 Maley, Mark	Sunderland	York City
23 Marsh, Adam	Darlington	Whitby Town
6 Marshall, Ian P.	Bolton Wanderers	Blackpool
22 May, Kyle	Carlisle United	Gretna
30 McSheffrey, Gary	Coventry City	Stockport County
30 Melligan, John J.	Wolverhampton Wanderers	AFC Bournemouth
28 Mills, Rowan L.	Portsmouth	Coventry City
22 Nacca, Francesco	Cambridge United	Cambridge City
9 Navarro, Alan E.	Liverpool	Tranmere Rovers
18 Odejayi, Olukayode	Bristol City	Forest Green Rovers
23 Oleksewycz, Stephen M.	Halifax Town	Frickley Athletic
26 Pearce, Alexander G.	Chesterfield	Ilkeston Town
23 Phelan, Leeyon	Wycombe Wanderers	Ashford Town (Middlesex)
20 Piper, Matthew J.	Leicester City	Mansfield Town
5 Proctor, Michael A.	Sunderland	York City
6 Pullen, James	Ipswich Town	Blackpool
30 Quinn, Stephen J.	West Bromwich Albion	Notts County
12 Rachubka, Paul S.	Manchester United	Oldham Athletic
12 Richards, Marc J.	Blackburn Rovers	Oldham Athletic
9 Richardson, Leam N.	Bolton Wanderers	Notts County
2 Salako, John A.	Charlton Athletic	Reading
28 Samuel, J. Lloyd	Aston Villa	Gillingham
2 Scott, Dion E.	Walsall	Boston United

143

23 Shields, Dene	Sunderland	Scarborough
26 Shittu, Daniel O.	Charlton Athletic	Queens Park Rangers
22 Sidwell, Steven J.	Arsenal	Brentford
19 Singh, Harpal	Leeds United	Bury
6 Smart, Allan A.C.	Watford	Stoke City
8 Smith, Andrew W.	Sheffield United	Glenavon
23 Smith, Jeffrey	Bolton Wanderers	Macclesfield Town
20 Street, Kevin	Crewe Alexandra	Luton Town
23 Sturridge, Dean C.	Leicester City	Wolverhampton Wanderers
5 Tait, Paul	Crewe Alexandra	Hull City
5 Thomson, Peter D.	Luton Town	Rushden & Diamonds
9 Trainer, Philip A.	Crewe Alexandra	Hednesford Town
16 Vickers, Stephen	Middlesbrough	Birmingham City
15 Walker, Richard M.	Aston Villa	Wycombe Wanderers
23 Ward, Scott	Luton Town	Boreham Wood
2 Watson, Kevin E.	Rotherham United	Reading
23 Webber, Daniel V.	Manchester United	Port Vale
7 Williams, Lee	Mansfield Town	Cheltenham Town
24 Wright, Daniel J.	Queens Park Rangers	Chertsey Town
23 Wright, Mark A.	Walsall	Nuneaton Borough

December 2001

14 Appleby, Richard D.	Swansea City	Kidderminster Harriers
14 Beckett, Luke J.	Chesterfield	Stockport County
13 Broomes, Marlon C.	Blackburn Rovers	Sheffield Wednesday
29 Cole, Andrew A.	Manchester United	Blackburn Rovers
21 Coote, Adrian	Norwich City	Colchester United
13 Crosby, Andrew K.	Brighton & Hove Albion	Oxford United
5 Dichio, Daniele S.E.	Sunderland	West Bromwich Albion
14 Filan, John R.	Blackburn Rovers	Wigan Athletic
31 Fleming, Curtis	Middlesbrough	Crystal Palace
28 Granville, Daniel P.	Manchester City	Crystal Palace
9 Hamilton, Ian R.	Notts County	Lincoln City
7 Hankin, Sean A.	Crystal Palace	Torquay United
14 Hurst, Glynn	Stockport County	Chesterfield
12 Lumsdon, Christopher	Sunderland	Barnsley
24 McEvilly, Lee	Burscough	Rochdale
14 Miller, Kenneth	Rangers	Wolverhampton Wanderers
12 Murray, Paul	Southampton	Oldham Athletic
24 O'Brien, Christopher T.	Liverpool	Chester City
7 Ormerod, Brett R.	Blackpool	Southampton
24 Sturridge, Dean C.	Leicester City	Wolverhampton Wanderers
7 Symons, Christopher J.	Fulham	Crystal Palace
14 Teale, Gary	Ayr United	Wigan Athletic
18 Vickers, Stephen	Middlesbrough	Birmingham City
21 Walker, Richard M.	Aston Villa	Blackpool

Temporary transfers

7 Aldridge, Paul J.	Tranmere Rovers	Vauxhall Motors
19 Allott, Mark S.	Oldham Athletic	Chesterfield
24 Artell, David J.	Rotherham United	Chesterfield
14 Banks, Steven	Bolton Wanderers	Rochdale
14 Barrett, Graham	Arsenal	Colchester United
3 Bart-Williams, Christopher G.	Nottingham Forest	Charlton Athletic
20 Benjamin, Trevor J.	Leicester City	Crystal Palace
22 Birch, Gary S.	Walsall	Nuneaton Borough
11 Bloomfield, Daniel	Norwich City	Kings Lynn
21 Bound, Matthew T.	Swansea City	Oxford United
15 Brown, Craig V.	Leyton Orient	Sutton United
7 Caldwell, Stephen	Newcastle United	Bradford City
24 Carey, Shaun P.	Rushden & Diamonds	Stevenage Borough
24 Clark, Steven T.	West Ham United	Southend United
10 Cleary, Sean J.	Derby County	Gresley Rovers
14 Clements, Matthew C.	Cambridge United	Kings Lynn
14 Cockrill, Dale	Cambridge United	Wisbech Town
28 Day, Rhys	Manchester City	Blackpool

20 Delaney, Damien	Leicester City	Stockport County
7 Djordjic, Bojan	Manchester United	Sheffield Wednesday
5 Dryden, Richard A.	Luton Town	Scarborough
18 Edwards, Christian	Nottingham Forest	Crystal Palace
14 Fallon, Rory M.	Barnsley	Shrewsbury Town
21 Fletcher, Gary	Leyton Orient	Grays Athletic
14 Ford, Ryan	Notts County	Gresley Rovers
29 Gough, Neil	Leyton Orient	Chelmsford City
14 Green, Stuart	Newcastle United	Carlisle United
7 Hadley, Stewart A.	Kidderminster Harriers	Worcester City
14 Hahnemann, Marcus S.	Fulham	Reading
21 Hanson, Christian	Middlesbrough	Torquay United
19 Ingham, Michael G.	Sunderland	Stoke City
19 Innes, Mark	Oldham Athletic	Chesterfield
24 Kenna, Jeffrey J.	Blackburn Rovers	Birmingham City
21 Larkin, Colin	Wolverhampton Wanderers	Kidderminster Harriers
18 Leigertwood, Mikele B.	Wimbledon	Leyton Orient
6 Liddle, Gareth J.C.	Crewe Alexandra	Hyde United
13 Logan, Richard J.	Ipswich Town	Torquay United
23 Lovell, Mark	Gillingham	St Leonards
15 Lovett, Jay	Brentford	Crawley Town
12 Macauley, Steven R.	Crewe Alexandra	Macclesfield Town
20 Maley, Mark	Sunderland	York City
5 Marshall, Ian P.	Bolton Wanderers	Blackpool
3 McGill, Brendan	Sunderland	Carlisle United
14 McSwegan, Gary J.	Heart of Midlothian	Barnsley
31 Melligan, John J.	Wolverhampton Wanderers	AFC Bournemouth
28 Mills, Rowan L.	Portsmouth	Coventry City
21 Milosevic, Dejan	Leeds United	Wolverhampton Wanderers
14 Morley, David T.	Carlisle United	Oxford United
28 Muggleton, Carl D.	Cheltenham Town	Bradford City
14 Murray, Frederick A.	Blackburn Rovers	Cambridge United
14 Nielsen, David	Wimbledon	Norwich City
24 Oleksewycz, Steven	Halifax Town	Worksop Town
28 Panopoulos, Michael	Portsmouth	Dunfermline Athletic
7 Parkin, Jonathan	Barnsley	Hartlepool United
6 Payton, Andrew P.	Burnley	Blackpool
22 Piper, Matthew J.	Leicester City	Mansfield Town
2 Rachubka, Paul S.	Manchester United	Oldham Athletic
21 Ramsay, Scott A.	Brighton & Hove Albion	Bognor Regis Town
19 Reeves, David	Chesterfield	Oldham Athletic
31 Rodrigues, Daniel F.	Southampton	Bristol City
4 Royce, Simon E.	Leicester City	Brighton & Hove Albion
14 Samuels, Anthony	Chelmsford City	Welling United
28 Scott, Dion E.	Walsall	Boston United
21 Shields, Dene	Sunderland	Scarborough
24 Smith, Jeff	Bolton Wanderers	Macclesfield Town
6 Thomson, Peter	Luton Town	Rushden & Diamonds
21 Toner, Ciaran	Tottenham Hotspur	Peterborough United
10 Trainer, Philip A.	Crewe Alexandra	Hednesford Town
21 Traore, Demba	Cambridge United	Aylesbury United
12 Webb, Daniel J.	Southend United	Brighton & Hove Albion
6 White, Ben	Gillingham	Dover Athletic
21 Wilkinson, Shaun F.	Brighton & Hove Albion	Havant & Waterlooville
6 Windass, Dean	Middlesbrough	Sheffield Wednesday
20 Wright, Mark A.	Walsall	Nuneaton Borough
19 Wright, Mark S.	Preston North End	Glentoran

January 2002

31 Bart-Williams, Christopher G.	Nottingham Forest	Charlton Athletic
25 Blake, Robert J.	Bradford City	Burnley
12 Challinor, David P.	Tranmere Rovers	Stockport County
25 Clark, Steven T.	West Ham United	Southend United
24 Etuhu, Dickson	Manchester City	Preston North End

145

29 Hadley, Stewart	Kidderminster Harriers	Worcester City
28 Hardiker, John	Morecambe	Stockport County
29 Innes, Mark	Oldham Athletic	Chesterfield
11 Kuqi, Shefki	Stockport County	Sheffield Wednesday
11 Lee, David J.F.	Hull City	Brighton & Hove Albion
7 Marshall, Ian P.	Bolton Wanderers	Blackpool
16 Mills, Rowan L.	Portsmouth	Coventry City
18 Morley, David T.	Carlisle United	Oxford United
23 Navarro, Alan E.	Liverpool	Tranmere Rovers
9 Nielsen, David	Wimbledon	Norwich City
9 Reeves, David	Chesterfield	Oldham Athletic
31 Salako, John A.	Charlton Athletic	Reading
8 Shittu, Daniel O.	Charlton Athletic	Queens Park Rangers
11 Wicks, Matthew J.	Brighton & Hove Albion	Hull City
30 Xavier, Abel	Everton	Liverpool

Temporary transfers

10 Adamson, Christopher	West Bromwich Albion	Plymouth Argyle
19 Allott, Mark S.	Oldham Athletic	Chesterfield
15 Appleby, Matthew W.	Barnsley	Oldham Athletic
18 Banks, Steven	Bolton Wanderers	Rochdale
11 Barrett, Daniel T.	Chesterfield	Matlock Town
2 Bart-Williams, Christopher G.	Nottingham Forest	Charlton Athletic
31 Beresford, Marlon	Middlesbrough	Burnley
8 Birch, Gary S.	Walsall	Nuneaton Borough
26 Bolland, Philip C.	Oxford United	Chester City
22 Bound, Matthew T.	Swansea City	Oxford United
30 Brown, Wayne L.	Ipswich Town	Watford
18 Bruce, Joseph M.	Luton Town	Wingate & Finchley
18 Burley, Adam G.	Sheffield United	Scarborough
11 Caldwell, Stephen	Newcastle United	Bradford City
7 Chilvers, Liam C.	Arsenal	Notts County
10 Cleary, Sean J.	Derby County	Gresley Rovers
13 Cockrill, Dale	Cambridge United	Wisbech Town
10 Constantine, Leon	Millwall	Partick Thistle
25 Coppinger, James	Newcastle United	Hartlepool United
19 Cowan, Thomas	Cambridge United	Peterborough United
17 Croft, Gary	Ipswich Town	Wigan Athletic
22 Delaney, Damien	Leicester City	Stockport County
21 De-Vulgt, Leigh S.	Swansea City	Llanelli
26 Douglas, Stuart A.	Luton Town	Rushden & Diamonds
31 Draper, Craig J.	Swansea City	Llanelli
3 Dunning, Darren	Blackburn Rovers	Rochdale
4 Fallon, Rory	Barnsley	Shrewsbury Town
12 Flynn, Michael A.	Stockport County	Stoke City
11 Foley, Dominic J.	Watford	Swindon Town
22 Ghent, Matthew I.	Barnsley	Doncaster Rovers
29 Gough, Neil	Leyton Orient	Chelmsford City
2 Gray, Wayne W.	Wimbledon	Leyton Orient
15 Green, Stuart	Newcastle United	Carlisle United
7 Hadley, Stewart	Kidderminster Harriers	Worcester City
18 Halls, John	Arsenal	Colchester United
25 Hay, Alexander N.	Tranmere Rovers	Morecambe
10 Hazell, Reuben	Tranmere Rovers	Torquay United
22 Heald, Paul A.	Wimbledon	Sheffield Wednesday
29 Healy, Colin	Celtic	Coventry City
18 Holdsworth, David G.	Birmingham City	Walsall
4 Jackson, Kirk S.S.	Darlington	Stevenage Borough
11 Jackson, Michael D.	Cheltenham Town	Weston-Super-Mare
29 Kelly, Leon M.	Cambridge United	Dover Athletic
14 Logan, Richard J.	Ipswich Town	Torquay United
14 Mann, Neil	Hull City	Scarborough
25 Marsh, Adam	Darlington	Hampton & Richmond Borough
10 Melligan, John J.	Wolverhampton Wanderers	AFC Bournemouth

18	Montgomery, Gary S.	Coventry City	Crewe Alexandra
15	Morley, David T.	Carlisle United	Oxford United
13	Murray, Frederick A.	Blackburn Rovers	Cambridge United
18	Mvondo Antangana, Simon P.	Dundee United	Port Vale
21	Myhill, Glyn O.	Aston Villa	Stoke City
29	Naylor, Richard A.	Ipswich Town	Millwall
25	O'Hare, Alan P.J.	Bolton Wanderers	Chesterfield
10	O'Neill, Paul D.	Macclesfield Town	Bangor
9	Parkin, Jonathan	Barnsley	Hartlepool United
18	Partridge, David W.	Dundee United	Leyton Orient
10	Pennant, Jermaine	Arsenal	Watford
24	Piper, Matthew J.	Leicester City	Mansfield Town
18	Pitcher, Geoffrey	Brighton & Hove Albion	Woking
24	Rachubka, Paul S.	Manchester United	Oldham Athletic
29	Reid, Paul M.	Rangers	Preston North End
24	Richards, Justin	Bristol Rovers	Newport County
28	Roberts, Andrew J.	Wimbledon	Norwich City
17	Roberts, Ben J.	Charlton Athletic	Reading
25	Roberts, Neil W.	Wigan Athletic	Hull City
18	Rodwell, James R.	Rushden & Diamonds	Dagenham & Redbridge
22	Rose, Richard A.	Gillingham	Longford Town
3	Salako, John A.	Charlton Athletic	Reading
28	Shandran, Anthony M.	Burnley	St Patrick's Athletic
24	Shields, Anthony G.	Peterborough United	Stevenage Borough
22	Spiller, Daniel	Gillingham	Longford Town
18	Taylor, Robert A.	Wolverhampton Wanderers	Grimsby Town
18	Thompson, Andrew R.	Cardiff City	Shrewsbury Town
11	Trainer, Philip A.	Crewe Alexandra	Hednesford Town
25	Wardley, Stuart J.	Queens Park Rangers	Rushden & Diamonds
9	White, Ben	Gillingham	Dover Athletic
4	Whitehead, Damien S.	Macclesfield Town	Drogheda
20	Wilkinson, Shaun F.	Brighton & Hove Albion	Havant & Waterlooville
18	Woodman, Andrew J.	Colchester United	Oxford United
25	Wright, Daniel J.	Queens Park Rangers	Wealdstone

February 2002

6	Akinbiyi, Adeola P.	Leicester City	Crystal Palace
20	Allott, Mark S.	Oldham Athletic	Chesterfield
18	Appleby, Matthew W.	Barnsley	Oldham Athletic
15	Armstrong, Steven C.	Huddersfield Town	Sheffield Wednesday
1	Barton, Warren D.	Newcastle United	Derby County
27	Brackstone, Stephen	Middlesbrough	York City
20	Clarke, Christopher E.	Halifax Town	Blackpool
19	Clegg, Michael J.	Manchester United	Oldham Athletic
22	Dickov, Paul	Manchester City	Leicester City
28	Haworth, Simon O.	Wigan Athletic	Tranmere Rovers
10	Hazell, Reuben	Tranmere Rovers	Torquay United
15	Howson, Stuart L.	Blackburn Rovers	Chesterfield
8	Jenas, Jermaine A.	Nottingham Forest	Newcastle United
8	John, Stern	Nottingham Forest	Birmingham City
1	Kenna, Jeffrey J.	Blackburn Rovers	Birmingham City
7	Lee, Robert M.	Newcastle United	Derby County
8	Marcelo, Cipriano	Birmingham City	Walsall
15	Mike, Leon J.	Manchester City	Aberdeen
1	N'Diaye, Seyni	Tranmere Rovers	Dunfermline Athletic
8	O'Connor, Martin J.	Birmingham City	Walsall
18	Peters, Mark W.	Southampton	Brentford
12	Reeves, David	Chesterfield	Oldham Athletic
14	Savage, Basir M.	Walton & Hersham	Reading
13	Thomas, Danny J.	Leicester City	AFC Bournemouth
13	Tipton, Matthew J.	Oldham Athletic	Macclesfield Town
28	Uddin, Anwar	West Ham United	Sheffield Wednesday

Temporary transfers

23	Armstrong, Joel	Chesterfield	Ilkeston Town
13	Austin, Neil J.	Barnsley	Gateshead

18 Banks, Steven	Bolton Wanderers	Rochdale
13 Barrett, Daniel	Chesterfield	Matlock Town
11 Barry-Murphy, Brian	Preston North End	Southend United
1 Bedeau, Anthony C.O.	Torquay United	Barnsley
8 Benjamin, Trevor J.	Leicester City	Norwich City
28 Betsy, Kevin E.L.	Fulham	Barnsley
1 Bevan, Scott	Southampton	Stoke City
14 Boardman, Jonathan G.	Crystal Palace	Woking
28 Brown, Wayne L.	Ipswich Town	Watford
22 Bruce, Joseph M.	Luton Town	Wingate & Finchley
22 Burton, Deon J.	Derby County	Stoke City
27 Cameron, Martin G.W.	Bristol Rovers	Partick Thistle
25 Campbell, Andrew P.	Middlesbrough	Cardiff City
8 Carbone, Benito	Bradford City	Middlesbrough
8 Carsley, Lee K.	Coventry City	Everton
11 Charles, Anthony D.	Crewe Alexandra	Hayes
6 Clements, Matthew C.	Cambridge United	Kings Lynn
1 Combe, Alan	Dundee United	Bradford City
17 Cowan, Thomas	Cambridge United	Peterborough United
15 Cudworth, Thomas J.S.	Coventry City	Evesham United
5 Deeney, Saul	Notts County	Gresley Rovers
8 Devlin, Paul J.	Sheffield United	Birmingham City
1 Dudley, Craig B.	Oldham Athletic	Scunthorpe United
7 Evans, Kevin	Cardiff City	Boston United
19 Flowers, Timothy D.	Leicester City	Coventry City
2 Fox, Christian	York City	Larne
8 Furlong, Paul A.	Birmingham City	Sheffield United
15 Grant, John A.C.	Crewe Alexandra	Northwich Victoria
3 Gray, Wayne W.	Wimbledon	Leyton Orient
15 Grayson, Simon N.	Blackburn Rovers	Bradford City
26 Heald, Paul A.	Wimbledon	Sheffield Wednesday
28 Hendry, Edward C.J.	Bolton Wanderers	Preston North End
19 Holdsworth, David G.	Birmingham City	Walsall
4 Hooper, Dean R.	Peterborough United	Dagenham & Redbridge
14 Jackman, Daniel J.	Aston Villa	Cambridge United
5 Johnson, David A.	Nottingham Forest	Sheffield Wednesday
5 Jones, Stephen G.	Crewe Alexandra	Rochdale
8 Lee, Andrew J.	Bradford City	Emley
8 Lewis, Karl J.	Leicester City	Brighton & Hove Albion
22 Liddle, Gareth J.C.	Crewe Alexandra	Leek Town
15 Logan, Richard J.	Ipswich Town	Torquay United
15 Lormor, Anthony	Hartlepool United	Shrewsbury Town
15 Macauley, Steven R.	Crewe Alexandra	Macclesfield Town
15 Macdonald, Charles L.	Charlton Athletic	Torquay United
5 Maddison, Lee R.	Carlisle United	Oxford United
25 Marsh, Adam	Darlington	Hampton & Richmond Borough
15 McAnespie, Kieran	Fulham	AFC Bournemouth
18 McElhatton, Michael T.	Rushden & Diamonds	Chester City
18 McGibbon, Patrick C.G.	Wigan Athletic	Scunthorpe United
15 McSweegan, Gary J.	Heart of Midlothian	Luton Town
1 Murphy, Shaun P.	Sheffield United	Crystal Palace
26 Murray, Adam D.	Derby County	Mansfield Town
15 Murray, Frederick A.	Blackburn Rovers	Cambridge United
15 Nicholls, Ashley	Ipswich Town	Canvey Island
15 Oleksewycz, Stephen M.	Halifax Town	Worksop Town
7 Parkin, Jonathan	Hartlepool United	York City
1 Pennock, Anthony	Rushden & Diamonds	Farnborough Town
21 Pringle, Ulf M.	Charlton Athletic	Grimsby Town
12 Richards, Marc J.	Blackburn Rovers	Halifax Town
14 Roget, Leo T.E.	Stockport County	Reading
3 Selley, Ian	Wimbledon	Southend United
19 Sheppard, Kyle D.	Bristol City	Merthyr Tydfil
19 Shields, Greg	Charlton Athletic	Walsall
1 Smith, David C.	Stockport County	Macclesfield Town

15 Stirling, Jude B.	Luton Town	Stevenage Borough
4 Strachan, Gavin D.	Coventry City	Motherwell
8 Thomas, Danny J.	Leicester City	AFC Bournemouth
21 Todd, Andrew J.J.	Charlton Athletic	Grimsby Town
26 Tuttle, David P.	Millwall	Wycombe Wanderers
7 Varty, John W.	Carlisle United	Workington
27 Wardley, Stuart	Queens Park Rangers	Rushden & Diamonds
8 Ward, Mark	Sheffield United	Aldershot Town
26 Wheatcroft, Paul M.	Bolton Wanderers	Mansfield Town
19 Woodman, Andrew J.	Colchester United	Oxford United

March 2002

6 Beharall, David	Newcastle United	Oldham Athletic
28 Betsy, Kevin E.L.	Fulham	Barnsley
4 Bolland, Philip	Oxford United	Chester City
26 Campbell, Andrew P.	Middlesbrough	Cardiff City
15 Carsley, Lee K.	Coventry City	Everton
26 Cooper, Kevin L.	Wimbledon	Wolverhampton Wanderers
24 Crouch, Peter J.	Portsmouth	Aston Villa
28 Ellington, Nathan L.F.	Bristol Rovers	Wigan Athletic
7 Finnigan, John F.	Lincoln City	Cheltenham Town
18 Gascoigne, Paul J.	Everton	Burnley
15 Hall, Fitz	Chesham United	Oldham Athletic
28 Howe, Edward J.F.	AFC Bournemouth	Portsmouth
27 Jarrett, Jason L.M.	Bury	Wigan Athletic
8 Johnson, Damien M.	Blackburn Rovers	Birmingham City
21 Kearney, Thomas J.	Everton	Bradford City
6 Macken, Jonathan P.	Preston North End	Manchester City
4 Mahon, Gavin A.	Brentford	Watford
8 Murray, Frederick A.	Blackburn Rovers	Cambridge United
6 Parkin, Jonathan	Barnsley	York City
26 Petterson, Andrew K.	Portsmouth	West Bromwich Albion
26 Roberts, Christian J.	Exeter City	Bristol City
22 Simpson, Paul D.	Blackpool	Rochdale
22 Tebily, Olivier	Celtic	Birmingham City
28 Thomson, Andrew J.	Bristol Rovers	Wycombe Wanderers
20 Todorov, Svetoslav	West Ham United	Portsmouth
14 Watson, Kevin E.	Rotherham United	Reading
6 Williams, Eifion W.	Torquay United	Hartlepool United
13 Williams, Thomas A.	Peterborough United	Birmingham City
28 Woodman, Andrew J.	Colchester United	Oxford United

Temporary transfers

20 Adebola, Bamberdele O.	Birmingham City	Oldham Athletic
28 ✦Ainsworth, Gareth	Wimbledon	Preston North End
22 Armstrong, Joel	Chesterfield	Ilkeston Town
29 Armstrong, Joel	Chesterfield	Bradford Park Avenue
28 Ashdown, Jamie L.	Reading	Arsenal
9 Attwell, Jamie W.	Bristol City	Tiverton Town
15 Barrett, Daniel T.	Chesterfield	Matlock Town
27 Benjamin, Trevor J.	Leicester City	West Bromwich Albion
4 Beresford, Marlon	Middlesbrough	Burnley
15 Bevan, Scott	Southampton	Woking
22 Bloomer, Matthew B.	Hull City	Lincoln City
21 Branch, Paul M.	Wolverhampton Wanderers	Reading
19 Bruce, Joseph M.	Luton Town	Wingate & Finchley
22 Buchanan, Wayne B.	Bolton Wanderers	Chesterfield
25 Bull, Nikki	Queens Park Rangers	Hayes
1 Burrows, Mark	Exeter City	Merthyr Tydfil
25 Burton, Deon J.	Derby County	Stoke City
25 Bywater, Stephen M.	West Ham United	Cardiff City
22 Carbonari, Horacio A.	Derby County	Coventry City
2 Cole, Timothy	Dagenham & Redbridge	Billericay Town
8 Cooke, Stephen L.	Aston Villa	AFC Bournemouth
26 Coppinger, James	Newcastle United	Hartlepool United
28 Croft, Gary	Ipswich Town	Cardiff City

22 Davies, Gareth	Chesterfield	Matlock Town
29 Deeney, Saul	Notts County	Ilkeston Town
28 Delaney, Damien	Leicester City	Huddersfield Town
11 Devlin, Paul J.	Sheffield United	Birmingham City
27 Dinning, Tony	Wigan Athletic	Stoke City
28 Dublin, Dion	Aston Villa	Millwall
11 Duff, Shane	Cheltenham Town	Evesham United
28 Dunning, Darren	Blackburn Rovers	Blackpool
27 Esson, Ryan	Aberdeen	Rotherham United
28 Evers, Sean A.	Plymouth Argyle	Stevenage Borough
11 Flynn, Michael A.	Stockport County	Stoke City
28 Foley, Dominic J.	Watford	Queens Park Rangers
28 Galloway, Michael A.	Carlisle United	Gretna
18 Grant, John	Crewe Alexandra	Northwich Victoria
27 Gray, Wayne W.	Wimbledon	Brighton & Hove Albion
28 Halle, Gunnar	Bradford City	Wolverhampton Wanderers
1 Healey, Stephen J.	Swansea City	Llanelli
28 Hicks, Mark	Millwall	Farnborough Town
21 Holmes, Richard	Notts County	Hereford United
1 Hoolickin, Lee	Carlisle United	Gretna
5 Hooper, Dean R.	Peterborough United	Dagenham & Redbridge
14 Hopkins, Gareth	Cheltenham Town	Forest Green Rovers
28 Hore, John S.	Carlisle United	Workington
28 Hughes, Michael E.	Wimbledon	Birmingham City
28 Ifil, Jerel C.	Watford	Huddersfield Town
28 Jackman, Daniel J.	Aston Villa	Cambridge United
14 Jeffrey, Michael R.	Grimsby Town	Scunthorpe United
12 Johnson, David A.	Nottingham Forest	Burnley
28 Jones, Philip L.	Oswestry Town	Wrexham
26 Jones, Scott	Bristol Rovers	York City
7 Jones, Stephen G.	Crewe Alexandra	Rochdale
28 Joyce, Damien D.	Manchester City	Hyde United
28 Kabba, Steven	Crystal Palace	Luton Town
1 Kendall, Lee M.	Cardiff City	Haverfordwest
15 Kimble, Alan F.	Wimbledon	Peterborough United
28 Knight, Richard	Oxford United	Colchester United
27 Laursen, Jacob	Leicester City	Wolverhampton Wanderers
28 Lee, Martyn J.	Wycombe Wanderers	Cheltenham Town
4 Lewis, Craig	Carlisle United	Workington
20 Lightbourne, Kyle L.	Macclesfield Town	Hull City
19 Lovell, Stephen W.H.	Portsmouth	Sheffield United
28 Lowndes, Nathan	St Johnstone	Rotherham United
27 Macdonald, Charles L.	Charlton Athletic	Colchester United
5 Macken, Jonathan P.	Preston North End	Manchester City
8 Maddison, Lee R.	Carlisle United	Oxford United
1 Mann, Neil	Hull City	Scarborough
1 Marchant, Ross	Sunderland	Whitby Town
25 Marsh, Adam	Darlington	Worksop Town
28 McAnespie, Kieran	Fulham	AFC Bournemouth
28 McCarthy, Jonathan D.	Birmingham City	Sheffield Wednesday
25 McElhatton, Michael T.	Rushden & Diamonds	Chester City
15 McPhail, Stephen J.P.	Leeds United	Millwall
28 Montgomery, Gary S.	Coventry City	Kidderminster Harriers
8 Murphy, Daryl	Luton Town	Harrow Borough
5 Murphy, Shaun P.	Sheffield United	Crystal Palace
26 Murray, Adam D.	Derby County	Mansfield Town
4 Naylor, Richard A.	Ipswich Town	Barnsley
8 Newton, Adam L.	West Ham United	Leyton Orient
4 Norris, David M.	Bolton Wanderers	Hull City
5 O'Hare, Alan	Bolton Wanderers	Chesterfield
18 Pennock, Anthony	Rushden & Diamonds	Farnborough Town
28 Pettinger, Paul A.	Lincoln City	Kettering Town
22 Price, Michael D.	Hull City	North Ferriby United
26 Proudlock, Adam D.	Wolverhampton Wanderers	Nottingham Forest
22 Quinn, Stephen J.	West Bromwich Albion	Bristol Rovers

28 Reddy, Michael	Sunderland	Barnsley
28 Robinson, Paul D.	Wimbledon	Grimsby Town
18 Robinson, Stephen	Preston North End	Bristol City
8 Roget, Leo T.E.	Stockport County	Reading
7 Ross, Brian S.	Hartlepool United	Harrogate Town
15 Royce, Simon E.	Leicester City	Manchester City
18 Russell, Samuel I.	Middlesbrough	Gateshead
15 Selley, Ian	Wimbledon	Southend United
28 Shandran, Anthony M.	Burnley	Stalybridge Celtic
19 Shields, Greg	Charlton Athletic	Walsall
8 Singh, Harpal	Leeds United	Bristol City
4 Steel, Luke D.	Peterborough United	Manchester United
28 Summerbell, Mark	Middlesbrough	Portsmouth
4 Tate, Christopher D.	Leyton Orient	Chester City
22 Thomas, James A.	Blackburn Rovers	Bristol Rovers
27 Thomas, Jerome W.	Arsenal	Queens Park Rangers
1 Thurston, Mark R.	Carlisle United	Gretna
28 Tod, Andrew	Bradford City	Heart of Midlothian
21 Todd, Andrew J.J.	Charlton Athletic	Grimsby Town
28 Trainer, Philip A.	Crewe Alexandra	Stalybridge Celtic
22 Tunnicliffe, Andrew J.	Manchester City	Altrincham
22 Tyson, Nathan	Reading	Cheltenham Town
28 Uhlenbeek, Gustav R.	Sheffield United	Walsall
25 Varga, Stanislav	Sunderland	West Bromwich Albion
8 Varty, John W.	Carlisle United	Workington
26 Vaughan, Anthony J.	Nottingham Forest	Scunthorpe United
28 Ward, Christopher	Birmingham City	Southport
28 Wardley, Stuart	Queens Park Rangers	Rushden & Diamonds
28 Waterman, David G.	Portsmouth	Oxford United
28 Webber, Daniel V.	Manchester United	Watford
28 Whalley, Gareth	Bradford City	Crewe Alexandra
15 Whiteman, Marc C.	Bury	Altrincham
21 Whitley, Jeffrey	Manchester City	Notts County
12 Williams, Thomas A.	Peterborough United	Birmingham City
28 Wilson, Scott P.	Rangers	Portsmouth
29 Wright, Daniel J.	Queens Park Rangers	Molesey

April 2002

4 Byfield, Darren	Walsall	Rotherham United
30 Lambert, Rickie L.	Macclesfield Town	Stockport County
18 Redknapp, Jamie F.	Liverpool	Tottenham Hotspur
30 Walters, Jonathan R.	Blackburn Rovers	Bolton Wanderers
17 Waterman, David	Portsmouth	Oxford United

Temporary transfers

28 Bull, Nikki	Queens Park Rangers	Hayes
3 Deeney, Saul	Notts County	Ilkeston Town
12 Devlin, Paul J.	Sheffield United	Birmingham City
23 Dublin, Dion	Aston Villa	Millwall
16 Duff, Shane	Cheltenham Town	Evesham United
29 Galloway, Michael A.	Carlisle United	Gretna
17 Grant, John	Crewe Alexandra	Northwich Victoria
28 Hooper, Dean R.	Peterborough United	Dagenham & Redbridge
15 Hopkins, Gareth	Cheltenham Town	Forest Green Rovers
18 Jeffrey, Michael R.	Grimsby Town	Scunthorpe United
9 Johnson, David A.	Nottingham Forest	Burnley
28 Lee, Martyn J.	Wycombe Wanderers	Cheltenham Town
5 Newton, Adam L.	West Ham United	Leyton Orient
4 O'Hare, Alan	Bolton Wanderers	Chesterfield
24 Osborn, Mark	Wycombe Wanderers	Farnborough Town
17 Russell, Samuel I.	Middlesbrough	Gateshead
2 Thurston, Mark R.	Carlisle United	Gretna
22 Tyson, Nathan	Reading	Cheltenham Town

FA CUP REVIEW 2001–2002

You had a sense that it was not to be Chelsea's day when on the morning of the match John Terry reported sick at their headquarters, just hours away from the 2002 FA Cup final.

The portents were already not good, Jimmy Floyd Hasselbaink was known to be struggling to shake off an injury and facing an Arsenal team which confidently chasing the double, they needed to be at a peak to overcome the odds.

Worse, too, it was the injured Celestine Babayaro who had to retreat from the fray at half-time surprisingly to be replaced by Terry. Hasselbaink had to go off at last for Gianfranco Zola in the 68th minute and well though Chelsea had contained their opponents, they had desperately needed a piece of luck to score.

It was not to be and two minutes after Chelsea's second substitution, Ray Parlour saved his first goal of the season for a well-taken effort from 25 yards which swerved into the top right-hand corner of the net. One sensed this was it for Chelsea and ten minutes later the Swede Frederik Ljungberg added a second for Arsenal with a fine individual goal.

It was Arsenal's eighth FA Cup trophy in their 15th final, the latter figure equalling Manchester United's record. But as we know the competition is all about the minnows and the magic and if you look hard enough you can still find them.

The first round as usual brought a few names once associated with the Football League, now hoping to be the surprises themselves. Newport County drew at Blackpool 2-2, Barrow 1-1 at Oldham Athletic and Aldershot Town 0-0 at home to Bristol Rovers, while recently deposed Barnet had a similar result with visiting Carlisle United. But mostly it was no joy, with one notable exception. Hereford United, heroes of 1971–72 in ousting Newcastle United when they were in the League themselves, beat Wrexham 1-0.

Yet there were other non-league axe-wielders. Canvey Island chopped down Wigan Athletic 1-0, while Tamworth drew 1-1 with Rochdale as did Whitby Town with Plymouth Argyle. Forest Green Rovers earned a replay after 2-2 at Macclesfield Town as did Bedford Town goalless with Peterborough United. Top scorers of the round were fairly recent newcomers to the League, Cheltenham Town 6-1 at Kettering Town. The replays accounted for the pretenders, though Forest Green only failed after a marathon penalty shoot-out 11-10.

Round Two's initial top heroes were again Canvey of the Ryman League, conquerors of Northampton Town 1-0 on the island. Hereford bowed out 3-2 at Swindon Town, but Dagenham had a goalless draw at Exeter City to raise further hopes in Essex. Sensationally these were confirmed in a 3-0 replay success for the Daggers.

Alas, both retreated in a third round fragmented by adverse weather conditions, losing 4-1; Canvey at Burnley, Dagenham at home to Ipswich. Still the mighty toppled. Leeds lost 2-1 at Second Division Cardiff City where crowd disturbances marred the occasion and even more surprisingly Derby County 3-1 at home to Third Division strugglers Bristol Rovers. Sunderland were beaten 2-1 at home by West Bromwich Albion, Southampton 2-1 at Rotherham United. Wycombe Wanderers held Fulham to a 2-2 draw before losing the replay 1-0.

Meanwhile Arsenal had won 4-2 at Watford, Chelsea 4-0 after a goalless draw with Norwich City. Yet surprises continued in Round Four. Walsall won 2-1 at Charlton Athletic, Leicester City lost 1-0 at West Bromwich and Ipswich Town 4-1 at home to Manchester City. Arsenal won a stormy affair with Liverpool 1-0 but Chelsea required a replay before beating West Ham United 3-2. Cardiff went out 3-1 at Tranmere.

Cheltenham who had done well throughout lost in the fifth round 1-0 at West Bromwich, Arsenal beat plucky Gillingham 5-2 and Chelsea overcame Preston North End 3-1. Crewe Alexandra did well to draw 0-0 at Everton but lost the replay by the odd goal in three.

In the quarter-finals, Chelsea revenged themselves on Spurs for their FA Cup defeat winning 4-0 at White Hart Lane, Arsenal had to replay with Newcastle United after a 1-1 draw, but won it 3-0. Fulham succeeded 1-0 at West Bromwich and Middlesbrough took three goals off Everton without reply.

The semi-finals were uninspiring; a goal settled each, Chelsea over Fulham, Arsenal via an opponent against Middlesbrough. But then the cup has all kinds of everything.

AXA FA CUP 2001–2002

FIRST ROUND

Hayes	(2) 3	Wycombe W	(2) 4
Aldershot T	(0) 0	Bristol R	(0) 0
Altrincham	(1) 1	Lancaster C	(1) 1
Barnet	(0) 0	Carlisle U	(0) 0
Bedford T	(0) 0	Peterborough U	(0) 0
Blackpool	(1) 2	Newport Co	(2) 2
Bournemouth	(2) 3	Worksop T	(0) 0
Brentford	(0) 1	Morecambe	(0) 0
Brighton & HA	(1) 1	Shrewsbury T	(0) 0
Bristol C	(0) 0	Leyton Orient	(1) 1
Cambridge U	(0) 1	Notts Co	(1) 1
Colchester U	(0) 0	York C	(0) 0
Dagenham & R	(1) 1	Southport	(0) 0
Doncaster R	(1) 2	Scunthorpe U	(2) 3
Exeter C	(1) 3	Cambridge C	(0) 0
Grays Ath	(0) 1	Hinckley U	(0) 2
Halifax T	(1) 2	Farnborough T	(0) 1
Huddersfield T	(0) 2	Gravesend & N	(1) 1
Kettering T	(1) 1	Cheltenham T	(2) 6
Kidderminster H	(0) 0	Darlington	(0) 1
Lincoln C	(0) 1	Bury	(0) 1
Macclesfield T	(1) 2	Forest Green R	(1) 2
Mansfield T	(1) 1	Oxford U	(0) 0
Northwich Vic	(0) 2	Hull C	(3) 5
Oldham Ath	(1) 1	Barrow	(1) 1
Port Vale	(0) 3	Aylesbury U	(0) 0
Reading	(0) 1	Welling U	(0) 0
Southend U	(1) 3	Luton T	(1) 2
Stalybridge C	(0) 0	Chesterfield	(2) 3
Swindon T	(2) 3	Hartlepool U	(1) 1
Tamworth	(1) 1	Rochdale	(1) 1
Tiverton T	(0) 1	Cardiff C	(1) 3
(at Cardiff.)			
Torquay U	(0) 1	Northampton T	(2) 2
Tranmere R	(1) 4	Brigg T	(0) 1
Whitby T	(1) 1	Plymouth Arg	(0) 1
Wigan Ath	(0) 0	Canvey Island	(0) 1
Worcester C	(0) 0	Rushden & D	(0) 1
Hereford U	(1) 1	Wrexham	(0) 0
Lewes	(0) 0	Stoke C	(1) 2
(at Stoke.)			
Swansea C	(2) 4	QPR	(0) 0

FIRST ROUND REPLAYS

Barrow	(0) 0	Oldham Ath	(1) 1
Bristol R	(0) 1	Aldershot T	(0) 0
Bury	(0) 1	Lincoln C	(1) 1
(aet; Lincoln C won 3-2 on penalties.)			
Carlisle U	(0) 1	Barnet	(0) 0
Lancaster C	(1) 1	Altrincham	(1) 4
(aet.)			
Notts Co	(1) 2	Cambridge U	(0) 0
Peterborough U	(1) 2	Bedford T	(0) 1

Plymouth Arg	(3) 3	Whitby T	(0) 2
Rochdale	(0) 1	Tamworth	(0) 0
York C	(1) 2	Colchester U	(0) 2

(aet; York C won 3-2 on penalties.)

| Forest Green R | (1) 1 | Macclesfield T | (1) 1 |

(aet; Macclesfield T won 11-10 on penalties.)

| Newport Co | (1) 1 | Blackpool | (0) 4 |

(aet.)

SECOND ROUND

Altrincham	(0) 1	Darlington	(1) 2
Blackpool	(2) 2	Rochdale	(0) 0
Brighton & HA	(1) 2	Rushden & D	(0) 1
Cardiff C	(1) 3	Port Vale	(0) 0
Chesterfield	(0) 1	Southend U	(0) 1
Exeter C	(0) 0	Dagenham & R	(0) 0
Halifax T	(0) 1	Stoke C	(1) 1
Hinckley U	(0) 0	Cheltenham T	(1) 2
Hull C	(1) 2	Oldham Ath	(1) 3
Leyton Orient	(0) 2	Lincoln C	(1) 1
Macclesfield T	(0) 4	Swansea C	(0) 1
Mansfield T	(2) 4	Huddersfield T	(0) 0
Peterborough U	(1) 1	Bournemouth	(0) 0
Plymouth Arg	(1) 1	Bristol R	(0) 1
Scunthorpe U	(2) 3	Brentford	(1) 2
Swindon T	(1) 3	Hereford U	(2) 2
Tranmere R	(4) 6	Carlisle U	(0) 1
Wycombe W	(0) 3	Notts Co	(0) 0
York C	(2) 2	Reading	(0) 0
Canvey Island	(0) 1	Northampton T	(0) 0

SECOND ROUND REPLAYS

Stoke C	(2) 3	Halifax T	(0) 0
Bristol R	(0) 3	Plymouth Arg	(0) 2
Southend U	(1) 2	Chesterfield	(0) 0
Dagenham & R	(3) 3	Exeter C	(0) 0

THIRD ROUND

Barnsley	(0) 1	Blackburn R	(0) 1
Burnley	(2) 4	Canvey Island	(0) 1
Charlton Ath	(0) 2	Blackpool	(1) 1
Dagenham & R	(1) 1	Ipswich T	(2) 4
Grimsby T	(0) 0	York C	(0) 0
Leicester C	(1) 2	Mansfield T	(1) 1
Liverpool	(2) 3	Birmingham C	(0) 0
Manchester C	(1) 2	Swindon T	(0) 0
Millwall	(1) 2	Scunthorpe U	(1) 1
Newcastle U	(1) 2	Crystal Palace	(0) 0
Norwich C	(0) 0	Chelsea	(0) 0
Portsmouth	(1) 1	Leyton Orient	(0) 4
Sheffield U	(0) 1	Nottingham F	(0) 0
Stoke C	(0) 0	Everton	(0) 1
Sunderland	(1) 1	WBA	(1) 2
Watford	(1) 2	Arsenal	(2) 4
Wolverhampton W	(0) 0	Gillingham	(0) 1
Aston Villa	(0) 2	Manchester U	(0) 3

Cardiff C	(1) 2	Leeds U	(1) 1
Cheltenham T	(1) 2	Oldham Ath	(1) 1
Derby Co	(0) 1	Bristol R	(2) 3
Macclesfield T	(0) 0	West Ham U	(1) 3
Southend U	(0) 1	Tranmere R	(0) 3
Walsall	(0) 2	Bradford C	(0) 0
Wimbledon	(0) 0	Middlesbrough	(0) 0
Wycombe W	(0) 2	Fulham	(0) 2
Brighton & HA	(0) 0	Preston NE	(1) 2
Crewe Alex	(1) 2	Sheffield W	(1) 1
Darlington	(1) 2	Peterborough U	(0) 2
Coventry C	(0) 0	Tottenham H	(1) 2
Rotherham U	(1) 2	Southampton	(0) 1
Stockport Co	(0) 1	Bolton W	(2) 4

THIRD ROUND REPLAYS

Fulham	(0) 1	Wycombe W	(0) 0
Middlesbrough	(1) 2	Wimbledon	(0) 0
York C	(1) 1	Grimsby T	(0) 0
Blackburn R	(2) 3	Barnsley	(0) 1
Chelsea	(1) 4	Norwich C	(0) 0
Peterborough U	(0) 2	Darlington	(0) 0

FOURTH ROUND

Charlton Ath	(0) 1	Walsall	(1) 2
Chelsea	(1) 1	West Ham U	(0) 1
Everton	(3) 4	Leyton Orient	(1) 1
Middlesbrough	(0) 2	Manchester U	(0) 0
Millwall	(0) 0	Blackburn R	(0) 1
Preston NE	(0) 2	Sheffield U	(1) 1
Rotherham U	(2) 2	Crewe Alex	(1) 4
WBA	(0) 1	Leicester C	(0) 0
York C	(0) 0	Fulham	(1) 2
Arsenal	(1) 1	Liverpool	(0) 0
Cheltenham T	(2) 2	Burnley	(1) 1
Ipswich T	(0) 1	Manchester C	(1) 4
Peterborough U	(0) 2	Newcastle U	(2) 4
Tranmere R	(1) 3	Cardiff C	(1) 1
Gillingham	(1) 1	Bristol R	(0) 0
Tottenham H	(2) 4	Bolton W	(0) 0

FOURTH ROUND REPLAY

West Ham U	(1) 2	Chelsea	(1) 3

FIFTH ROUND

Arsenal	(1) 5	Gillingham	(0) 2
Middlesbrough	(0) 1	Blackburn R	(0) 0
WBA	(0) 1	Cheltenham T	(0) 0
Walsall	(0) 1	Fulham	(1) 2
Chelsea	(2) 3	Preston NE	(1) 1
Everton	(0) 0	Crewe Alex	(0) 0
Newcastle U	(0) 1	Manchester C	(0) 0
Tottenham H	(2) 4	Tranmere R	(0) 0

FIFTH ROUND REPLAY

Crewe Alex	(1) 1	Everton	(1) 2

SIXTH ROUND

Newcastle U	(0) 1	Arsenal	(1) 1
Middlesbrough	(3) 3	Everton	(0) 0
Tottenham H	(0) 0	Chelsea	(1) 4
WBA	(0) 0	Fulham	(0) 1

SIXTH ROUND REPLAY

Arsenal	(2) 3	Newcastle U	(0) 0

SEMI-FINALS

Fulham	(0) 0	Chelsea	(1) 1
Middlesbrough	(0) 0	Arsenal	(1) 1

FINAL (at Millennium Stadium)

4 MAY

Arsenal (0) 2 *(Parlour 70, Ljungberg 80)*
Chelsea (0) 0   73,963

Arsenal: Seaman; Lauren, Cole, Vieira, Campbell, Adams, Wiltord (Keown), Parlour, Henry (Kanu), Bergkamp (Edu), Ljungberg.
Chelsea: Cudicini; Melchiot (Zenden), Babayaro (Terry), Petit, Gallas, Desailly, Gronkjaer, Lampard, Hasselbaink (Zola), Gudjohnsen, Le Saux.
Referee: M. Riley (Leeds).

PAST FA CUP FINALS

Details of one goalscorer is not available in 1878.

1872	The Wanderers 1	Royal Engineers 0
	Betts	
1873	The Wanderers 2	Oxford University 0
	Kinnaird, Wollaston	
1874	Oxford University................2	Royal Engineers 0
	Mackarness, Patton	
1875	Royal Engineers 1	Old Etonians.....................................1*
	Renny-Tailyour	*Bonsor*
Replay	Royal Engineers 2	Old Etonians 0
	Renny-Tailyour, Stafford	
1876	The Wanderers 1	Old Etonians.....................................1*
	Edwards	*Bonsor*
Replay	The Wanderers 3	Old Etonians 0
	Wollaston, Hughes 2	
1877	The Wanderers 2	Oxford University 1*
	Lindsay, Kenrick	*Kinnaird (og)*
1878	The Wanderers 3	Royal Engineers 1
	Kenrick 2, Kinnaird	*Unknown*
1879	Old Etonians 1	Clapham Rovers 0
	Clerke	
1880	Clapham Rovers 1	Oxford University 0
	Lloyd-Jones	
1881	Old Carthusians 3	Old Etonians 0
	Wyngard, Parry, Todd	
1882	Old Etonians 1	Blackburn Rovers...............................0
	Anderson	
1883	Blackburn Olympic 2	Old Etonians.....................................1*
	Costley, Matthews	*Goodhart*
1884	Blackburn Rovers...............2	Queen's Park, Glasgow 1
	Sowerbutts, Forrest	*Christie*
1885	Blackburn Rovers...............2	Queen's Park, Glasgow 0
	Forrest, Brown	
1886	Blackburn Rovers...............0	West Bromwich Albion 0
Replay	Blackburn Rovers...............2	West Bromwich Albion 0
	Brown, Sowerbutts	
1887	Aston Villa 2	West Bromwich Albion 0
	Hunter, Hodgetts	
1888	West Bromwich Albion 2	Preston NE 1
	Woodhall, Bayliss	*Dewhurst*
1889	Preston NE 3	Wolverhampton W 0
	Dewhurst, J. Ross, Thompson	
1890	Blackburn Rovers...............6	Sheffield W 1
	Walton, John Southworth, Lofthouse, Townley 3	*Bennett*
1891	Blackburn Rovers...............3	Notts Co...1
	Dewar, John Southworth, Townley	*Oswald*

Year	Winner	Score	Runner-up	Score
1892	West Bromwich Albion	3	Aston Villa	0
	Geddes, Nicholls, Reynolds			
1893	Wolverhampton W	1	Everton	0
	Allen			
1894	Notts Co	4	Bolton W	1
	Watson, Logan 3		*Cassidy*	
1895	Aston Villa	1	West Bromwich Albion	0
	J. Devey			
1896	Sheffield W	2	Wolverhampton W	1
	Spiksley 2		*Black*	
1897	Aston Villa	3	Everton	2
	Campbell, Wheldon, Crabtree		*Boyle, Bell*	
1898	Nottingham F	3	Derby Co	1
	Cape 2, McPherson		*Bloomer*	
1899	Sheffield U	4	Derby Co	1
	Bennett, Beers, Almond, Priest		*Boag*	
1900	Bury	4	Southampton	0
	McLuckie 2, Wood, Plant			
1901	Tottenham H	2	Sheffield U	2
	Brown 2		*Bennett, Priest*	
Replay	Tottenham H	3	Sheffield U	1
	Cameron, Smith, Brown		*Priest*	
1902	Sheffield U	1	Southampton	1
	Common		*Wood*	
Replay	Sheffield U	2	Southampton	1
	Hedley, Barnes		*Brown*	
1903	Bury	6	Derby Co	0
	Ross, Sagar, Leeming 2, Wood, Plant			
1904	Manchester C	1	Bolton W	0
	Meredith			
1905	Aston Villa	2	Newcastle U	0
	Hampton 2			
1906	Everton	1	Newcastle U	0
	Young			
1907	Sheffield W	2	Everton	1
	Stewart, Simpson		*Sharp*	
1908	Wolverhampton W	3	Newcastle U	1
	Hunt, Hedley, Harrison		*Howey*	
1909	Manchester U	1	Bristol C	0
	A. Turnbull			
1910	Newcastle U	1	Barnsley	1
	Rutherford		*Tufnell*	
Replay	Newcastle U	2	Barnsley	0
	Shepherd 2 (1 pen)			
1911	Bradford C	0	Newcastle U	0
Replay	Bradford C	1	Newcastle U	0
	Speirs			
1912	Barnsley	0	West Bromwich Albion	0
Replay	Barnsley	1	West Bromwich Albion	0*
	Tufnell			

Year	Winner	Score	Runner-up	Score
1913	Aston Villa	1	Sunderland	0
	Barber			
1914	Burnley	1	Liverpool	0
	Freeman			
1915	Sheffield U	3	Chelsea	0
	Simmons, Masterman, Kitchen			
1920	Aston Villa	1	Huddersfield T	0*
	Kirton			
1921	Tottenham H	1	Wolverhampton W	0
	Dimmock			
1922	Huddersfield T	1	Preston NE	0
	Smith (pen)			
1923	Bolton W	2	West Ham U	0
	Jack, J.R. Smith			
1924	Newcastle U	2	Aston Villa	0
	Harris, Seymour			
1925	Sheffield U	1	Cardiff C	0
	Tunstall			
1926	Bolton W	1	Manchester C	0
	Jack			
1927	Cardiff C	1	Arsenal	0
	Ferguson			
1928	Blackburn Rovers	3	Huddersfield T	1
	Roscamp 2, McLean		*A. Jackson*	
1929	Bolton W	2	Portsmouth	0
	Butler, Blackmore			
1930	Arsenal	2	Huddersfield T	0
	James, Lambert			
1931	West Bromwich Albion	2	Birmingham	1
	W.G. Richardson 2		*Bradford*	
1932	Newcastle U	2	Arsenal	1
	Allen 2		*John*	
1933	Everton	3	Manchester C	0
	Stein, Dean, Dunn			
1934	Manchester C	2	Portsmouth	1
	Tilson 2		*Rutherford*	
1935	Sheffield W	4	West Bromwich Albion	2
	Rimmer 2, Palethorpe, Hooper		*Boyes, Sandford*	
1936	Arsenal	1	Sheffield U	0
	Drake			
1937	Sunderland	3	Preston NE	1
	Gurney, Carter, Burbanks		*F. O'Donnell*	
1938	Preston NE	1	Huddersfield T	0*
	Mutch (pen)			
1939	Portsmouth	4	Wolverhampton W	1
	Parker 2, Barlow, Anderson		*Dorsett*	
1946	Derby Co	4	Charlton Ath	1*
	H. Turner (og), Doherty, Stamps 2		*H. Turner*	

Year	Winner	Score	Runner-up	Score
1947	Charlton Ath	1	Burnley	0*
	Duffy			
1948	Manchester U	4	Blackpool	2
	Rowley 2, Pearson, Anderson		*Shimwell (pen), Mortensen*	
1949	Wolverhampton W	3	Leicester C	1
	Pye 2, Smyth,		*Griffiths*	
1950	Arsenal	2	Liverpool	0
	Lewis 2			
1951	Newcastle U	2	Blackpool	0
	Milburn 2			
1952	Newcastle U	1	Arsenal	0
	G. Robledo			
1953	Blackpool	4	Bolton W	3
	Mortensen 3, Perry		*Lofthouse, Moir, Bell*	
1954	West Bromwich Albion	3	Preston NE	2
	Allen 2 (1 pen), Griffin		*Morrison, Wayman*	
1955	Newcastle U	3	Manchester C	1
	Milburn, Mitchell, Hannah		*Johnstone*	
1956	Manchester C	3	Birmingham C	1
	Hayes, Dyson, Johnstone		*Kinsey*	
1957	Aston Villa	2	Manchester U	1
	McParland 2		*T. Taylor*	
1958	Bolton W	2	Manchester U	0
	Lofthouse 2			
1959	Nottingham F	2	Luton T	1
	Dwight, Wilson		*Pacey*	
1960	Wolverhampton W	3	Blackburn Rovers	0
	McGrath (og), Deeley 2			
1961	Tottenham H	2	Leicester C	0
	Smith, Dyson			
1962	Tottenham H	3	Burnley	1
	Greaves, Smith, Blanchflower (pen)		*Robson*	
1963	Manchester U	3	Leicester C	1
	Herd 2, Law		*Keyworth*	
1964	West Ham U	3	Preston NE	2
	Sissons, Hurst, Boyce		*Holden, Dawson*	
1965	Liverpool	2	Leeds U	1*
	Hunt, St John		*Bremner*	
1966	Everton	3	Sheffield W	2
	Trebilcock 2, Temple		*McCalliog, Ford*	
1967	Tottenham H	2	Chelsea	1
	Robertson, Saul		*Tambling*	
1968	West Browmwich Albion	1	Everton	0*
	Astle			
1969	Manchester C	1	Leicester C	0
	Young			
1970	Chelsea	2	Leeds U	2*
	Houseman, Hutchinson		*Charlton, Jones*	

Replay	Chelsea.................................2	Leeds U 1*	
	Osgood, Webb	*Jones*	
1971	Arsenal.................................2	Liverpool 1*	
	Kelly, George	*Heighway*	
1972	Leeds U................................1	Arsenal 0	
	Clarke		
1973	Sunderland 1	Leeds U 0	
	Porterfield		
1974	Liverpool 3	Newcastle 0	
	Keegan 2, Heighway		
1975	West Ham U...........................2	Fulham 0	
	A. Taylor 2		
1976	Southampton..........................1	Manchester U 0	
	Stokes		
1977	Manchester U.........................2	Liverpool 1	
	Pearson, J. Greenhoff	*Case*	
1978	Ipswich T 1	Arsenal 0	
	Osborne		
1979	Arsenal.................................3	Manchester U 2	
	Talbot, Stapleton,	*McQueen, McIlroy*	
	Sunderland		
1980	West Ham U...........................1	Arsenal 0	
	Brooking		
1981	Tottenham H...........................1	Manchester C.........................1*	
	Hutchison (og)	*Hutchison*	
Replay	Tottenham H...........................3	Manchester C.........................2	
	Villa 2, Crooks	*MacKenzie, Reeves (pen)*	
1982	Tottenham H...........................1	QPR 1*	
	Hoddle	*Fenwick*	
Replay	Tottenham H...........................1	QPR 0	
	Hoddle (pen)		
1983	Manchester U.........................2	Brighton & HA........................2*	
	Stapleton, Wilkins	*Smith, Stevens*	
Replay	Manchester U.........................4	Brighton & HA........................0	
	Robson 2, Whiteside, Muhren (pen)		
1984	Everton 2	Watford.................................0	
	Sharp, Gray		
1985	Manchester U.........................1	Everton 0*	
	Whiteside		
1986	Liverpool 3	Everton 1	
	Rush 2, Johnston	*Lineker*	
1987	Coventry C 3	Tottenham H..........................2*	
	Bennett, Houchen,	*C. Allen, Kilcline (og)*	
	Mabbutt (og)		
1988	Wimbledon.............................1	Liverpool 0	
	Sanchez		
1989	Liverpool 3	Everton 2*	
	Aldridge, Rush 2	*McCall 2*	
1990	Manchester U.........................3	Crystal Palace 3*	
	Robson, Hughes 2	*O'Reilly, Wright 2*	
Replay	Manchester U.........................1	Crystal Palace 0	
	Martin		

1991	Tottenham H	2	Nottingham F	1*
	Stewart, Walker (og)		*Pearce*	
1992	Liverpool	2	Sunderland	0
	Thomas, Rush			
1993	Arsenal	1	Sheffield W	1*
	Wright		*Hirst*	
Replay	Arsenal	2	Sheffield W	1*
	Wright, Linighan		*Waddle*	
1994	Manchester U	4	Chelsea	0
	Cantona 2 (2 pens),			
	Hughes, McClair			
1995	Everton	1	Manchester U	0
	Rideout			
1996	Manchester U	1	Liverpool	0
	Cantona			
1997	Chelsea	2	Middlesbrough	0
	Di Matteo, Newton			
1998	Arsenal	2	Newcastle U	0
	Overmars, Anelka			
1999	Manchester U	2	Newcastle U	0
	Sheringham, Scholes			
2000	Chelsea	1	Aston Villa	0
	Di Matteo			
2001	Liverpool	2	Arsenal	1
	Owen 2		*Ljungberg*	
2002	Arsenal	2	Chelsea	0
	Parlour, Ljungberg			

*After extra time

SUMMARY OF FA CUP WINNERS SINCE 1871

Manchester United	10
Arsenal	8
Tottenham Hotspur	8
Aston Villa	7
Blackburn Rovers	6
Liverpool	6
Newcastle United	6
Everton	5
The Wanderers	5
West Bromwich Albion	5
Bolton Wanderers	4
Manchester City	4
Sheffield United	4
Wolverhampton Wanderers	4
Chelsea	3
Sheffield Wednesday	3
West Ham United	3
Bury	2
Nottingham Forest	2
Old Etonians	2
Preston North End	2
Sunderland	2
Barnsley	1
Blackburn Olympic	1
Blackpool	1
Bradford City	1
Burnley	1
Cardiff City	1
Charlton Athletic	1
Clapham Rovers	1
Coventry City	1
Derby County	1
Huddersfield Town	1
Ipswich Town	1
Leeds United	1
Notts County	1
Old Carthusians	1
Oxford University	1
Portsmouth	1
Royal Engineers	1
Southampton	1
Wimbledon	1

APPEARANCES IN FA CUP FINAL

Arsenal	15
Manchester United	15
Newcastle United	13
Everton	12
Liverpool	12
Aston Villa	10
West Bromwich Albion	10
Tottenham Hotspur	9
Blackburn Rovers	8
Manchester City	8
Wolverhampton Wanderers	8
Bolton Wanderers	7
Chelsea	7
Preston North End	7
Old Etonians	6
Sheffield United	6
Sheffield Wednesday	6
Huddersfield Town	5
The Wanderers	5
Derby County	4
Leeds United	4
Leicester City	4
Oxford University	4
Royal Engineers	4
Sunderland	4
West Ham United	4
Blackpool	3
Burnley	3
Nottingham Forest	3
Portsmouth	3
Southampton	3
Barnsley	2
Birmingham City	2
Bury	2
Cardiff City	2
Charlton Athletic	2
Clapham Rovers	2
Notts County	2
Queen's Park (Glasgow)	2
Blackburn Olympic	1
Bradford City	1
Brighton & Hove Albion	1
Bristol City	1
Coventry City	1
Crystal Palace	1
Fulham	1
Ipswich Town	1
Luton Town	1
Middlesbrough	1
Old Carthusians	1
Queen's Park Rangers	1
Watford	1
Wimbledon	1

WORTHINGTON CUP REVIEW 2001–2002

Blackburn Rovers may not have flirted too seriously with the League Cup in the past – two semi-final places as far apart as 1962 and 1993 being the top of their achievements – but they proved tenacious underdogs in the 2002 Worthington Cup final to upset the favourites Tottenham Hotspur.

At the time of the final on 24 February, Blackburn were looking in a fairly sorry state in the FA Premier League, third from bottom and really should have been concentrating on the bread and butter rather than the cream of the cup. Moreover they had the week previously lost in the FA Cup fifth round 1-0 to Middlesbrough.

But these were fringe worries on the day at the Millennium Stadium in Cardiff with 72,500 packed in. Then when Matt Jansen put Rovers ahead in the 25th minute, perhaps there was to be a turn-up after all. Indeed the circumstances of the opening goal were slightly fortuitous for them.

Keith Gillespie's shot took a deflection and fell invitingly for Jansen, who had time to size up the situation before putting the ball past Neil Sullivan in the Spurs goal. However, the elation of the moment had started to subside when Christian Ziege levelled the scores eight minutes later. Les Ferdinand made ground on the right flank and pulled the ball back for the wing-back to make it 1-1 with ease.

This certainly made the prospects for the second half interesting for both teams, yet it was Blackburn who finally broke the deadlock in the 69th minute through Andy Cole as he was the quickest to react in the area when neither defenders nor other attackers were able to respond in a positive manner.

For Cole, recently signed from Manchester United, it was a further indication of his value to the club and undoubtedly helped in their major aim of staying in the Premier League.

And while there had been much discussion over which team shared the dressing-room with the hoodoo on it, a more relevant fact was that in the previous seven finals at the ground, the supporters in the North Stand had seen their team emerge as winners. It was no different for Blackburn.

Of course when they entered the 2001–02 competition it was a League Cup with a difference: no two-legged matches in the initial stages. Rovers started with a 2-0 win over Oldham Athletic, while Tottenham were similarly disposing of Torquay United.

Middlesbrough were Blackburn's next victims 2-1 at Ewood Park, but Spurs won comfortably by four clear goals at Tranmere Rovers. Round Four had Rovers drawn at home yet again this time to Manchester City and once more they came through 2-0. Spurs won 2-1 at Fulham.

For the fourth time in a row Blackburn did not need to travel and comprehensively beat a reserve-looking Arsenal side 4-0, a feat topped by Spurs who took six goals off Bolton Wanderers without reply.

Blackburn again had the easier draw in the semi-finals, playing Sheffield Wednesday while Tottenham had London rivals Chelsea with which to contend. Rovers won 2-1 at Hillsbrough and 4-2 at home in the two-legged affair, but Tottenham lost 2-1 at Stamford Bridge to make their tie more open. At least that was the theory before the event, as Spurs gave one of their best performances of the season in overturning Chelsea's first game lead to win 5-1 on the night.

Giant-killing acts were scarce early on, though Crystal Palace did win 5-4 on penalties after a 1-1 draw at Everton in the second round. There were more shocks in the third round, notably Liverpool losing 2-1 at home to Grimsby Town. Leeds United whacked six goals past Leicester City at Filbert Street, Fulham beat Derby County 5-2 and Manchester City were other six-shooters at the expense of Birmingham City, Darren Huckerby scoring four times.

Premier League casualties in the fourth round were Charlton Athletic losing 3-2 at Watford and Aston Villa losing out at Villa Park to Sheffield Wednesday by the only goal. In the clash of the victors in the quarter-finals, Wednesday beat Watford 4-0 while Chelsea eased out Newcastle United by a single goal, in the ties not involving the eventual finalists.

Matt Jansen of Blackburn was the top scorer in the competition with six goals and his team hit 18, three fewer than Tottenham's 21 shared by 11 different scorers.

There was also some speculation that the League Cup would one day become a British Cup to allow Celtic and Rangers to join in.

WORTHINGTON CUP 2001–2002

FIRST ROUND

Darlington	(0) 0	Sheffield U	(0) 1
Hartlepool U	(0) 0	Nottingham F	(1) 2
Scunthorpe U	(0) 0	Rotherham U	(2) 2
Barnsley	(1) 2	Halifax T	(0) 0
Blackpool	(0) 3	Wigan Ath	(0) 2
Bournemouth	(0) 0	Torquay U	(1) 2
Brentford	(0) 1	Norwich C	(0) 0
Brighton & HA	(0) 2	Wimbledon	(0) 1
Bristol C	(1) 2	Cheltenham T	(0) 1
Burnley	(0) 2	Rushden & D	(1) 3
Bury	(0) 1	Sheffield W	(1) 3
Exeter C	(0) 0	Walsall	(0) 1
Grimsby T	(0) 2	Lincoln C	(1) 1
Huddersfield T	(0) 0	Rochdale	(1) 1
Kidderminster H	(2) 2	Preston NE	(0) 3
(aet.)			
Leyton Orient	(2) 2	Crystal Palace	(1) 4
Macclesfield T	(0) 1	Bradford C	(0) 2
(aet.)			
Mansfield T	(2) 3	Notts Co	(4) 4
Millwall	(1) 2	Cardiff C	(1) 1
Northampton T	(0) 2	QPR	(1) 1
(aet.)			
Oxford U	(1) 1	Gillingham	(0) 2
(aet.)			
Port Vale	(2) 2	Chesterfield	(1) 1
Portsmouth	(0) 1	Colchester U	(0) 2
Reading	(2) 4	Luton T	(0) 0
Stockport Co	(1) 3	Carlisle U	(0) 0
Swansea C	(0) 0	Peterborough U	(1) 2
Tranmere R	(1) 3	Shrewsbury T	(0) 1
Watford	(0) 1	Plymouth Arg	(0) 0
Wrexham	(0) 2	Hull C	(1) 3
Wycombe W	(0) 0	Bristol R	(0) 1
York C	(1) 2	Crewe Alex	(1) 2
(aet; Crewe Alex won 6-5 on penalties.)			
Birmingham C	(2) 3	Southend U	(0) 0
Cambridge U	(0) 1	WBA	(1) 1
(aet; WBA won 4-3 on penalties.)			
Stoke C	(0) 0	Oldham Ath	(0) 0
(aet; Oldham Ath won 6-5 on penalties.)			
Wolverhampton W	(0) 1	Swindon T	(0) 2

SECOND ROUND

Blackpool	(0) 0	Leicester C	(1) 1
Bolton W	(0) 4	Walsall	(0) 3
(aet.)			
Brighton & HA	(0) 0	Southampton	(1) 3
Bristol R	(0) 0	Birmingham C	(1) 3
Colchester U	(0) 1	Barnsley	(1) 3
Crewe Alex	(0) 2	Rushden & D	(0) 0
(aet.)			
Gillingham	(1) 2	Millwall	(0) 1
Grimsby T	(1) 3	Sheffield U	(0) 3
(aet; Grimsby T won 4-2 on penalties.)			

Middlesbrough	(0) 3	Northampton T	(0) 1
Notts Co	(0) 2	Manchester C	(0) 4
(aet.)			
Peterborough U	(0) 2	Coventry C	(0) 2
(aet; Coventry C won 4-2 on penalties.)			
Reading	(0) 0	West Ham U	(0) 0
(aet; Reading won 6-5 on penalties.)			
Rochdale	(0) 2	Fulham	(1) 2
(aet; Fulham won 6-5 on penalties.)			
Rotherham U	(0) 0	Bradford C	(3) 4
Tranmere R	(2) 4	Preston NE	(1) 1
WBA	(0) 2	Swindon T	(0) 0
(aet.)			
Blackburn R	(1) 2	Oldham Ath	(0) 0
Bristol C	(0) 2	Watford	(0) 3
Charlton Ath	(1) 2	Port Vale	(0) 0
Derby Co	(1) 3	Hull C	(0) 0
Everton	(1) 1	Crystal Palace	(1) 1
(aet; Crystal Palace won 5-4 on penalties.)			
Newcastle U	(0) 4	Brentford	(1) 1
(aet.)			
Nottingham F	(1) 1	Stockport Co	(1) 1
(aet; Nottingham F won 8-7 on penalties.)			
Sheffield W	(2) 4	Sunderland	(1) 2
(aet.)			
Tottenham H	(0) 2	Torquay U	(0) 0

THIRD ROUND

Bolton W	(1) 1	Nottingham F	(0) 0
Barnsley	(0) 0	Newcastle U	(0) 1
Coventry C	(0) 0	Chelsea	(0) 2
Crewe Alex	(1) 2	Ipswich T	(2) 3
Gillingham	(0) 0	Southampton	(1) 2
Leicester C	(0) 0	Leeds U	(3) 6
Liverpool	(0) 1	Grimsby T	(0) 2
(aet.)			
Tranmere R	(0) 0	Tottenham H	(2) 4
WBA	(0) 0	Charlton Ath	(1) 1
Watford	(2) 4	Bradford C	(0) 1
Aston Villa	(1) 1	Reading	(0) 0
Blackburn R	(1) 2	Middlesbrough	(1) 1
(aet.)			
Fulham	(1) 5	Derby Co	(1) 2
Manchester C	(3) 6	Birmingham C	(0) 0
Sheffield W	(0) 2	Crystal Palace	(1) 2
(aet; Sheffield W won 3-1 on penalties.)			
Arsenal	(3) 4	Manchester U	(0) 0

FOURTH ROUND

Arsenal	(1) 2	Grimsby T	(0) 0
Bolton W	(0) 2	Southampton	(0) 2
(aet; Bolton W won 6-5 on penalties.)			
Newcastle U	(4) 4	Ipswich T	(0) 1
Watford	(1) 3	Charlton Ath	(1) 2
(aet.)			
Aston Villa	(0) 0	Sheffield W	(1) 1
Blackburn R	(1) 2	Manchester C	(0) 0
Leeds U	(0) 0	Chelsea	(0) 2
Fulham	(1) 1	Tottenham H	(1) 2

FIFTH ROUND

Blackburn R	(3) 4	Arsenal	(0) 0
Tottenham H	(4) 6	Bolton W	(0) 0
Chelsea	(0) 1	Newcastle U	(0) 0
Sheffield W	(1) 4	Watford	(0) 0

SEMI-FINAL, FIRST LEG

Sheffield W	(0) 1	Blackburn R	(2) 2
Chelsea	(1) 2	Tottenham H	(0) 1

SEMI-FINAL, SECOND LEG

Blackburn R	(2) 4	Sheffield W	(0) 2
(Blackburn R won 6-3 on aggregate.)			
Tottenham H	(2) 5	Chelsea	(0) 1
(Tottenham H won 6-3 on aggregate.)			

FINAL (at Millennium Stadium)

24 FEB

Blackburn R (1) 2 *(Jansen 25, Cole 69)*
Tottenham H (1) 1 *(Ziege 33)*   72,500

Blackburn R: Friedel; Taylor, Bjornebye, Dunn, Berg, Johansson, Gillespie (Hignett), Jansen (Yordi), Cole, Hughes, Duff.
Tottenham H: Sullivan; Taricco (Davies), Ziege, Thatcher, Perry, King, Anderton, Sherwood, Ferdinand, Sheringham, Poyet (Iversen).
Referee: G. Poll.

PAST LEAGUE CUP FINALS

Played as two legs up to 1966

1961	Rotherham U 2	Aston Villa 0
	Webster, Kirkman	
	Aston Villa 3	Rotherham U 0*
	O'Neill, Burrows, McParland	
1962	Rochdale 0	Norwich C 3
	Lythgoe 2, Punton	
	Norwich C...............................1	Rochdale 0
	Hill	
1963	Birmingham C 3	Aston Villa 1
	Leek 2, Bloomfield	*Thomson*
	Aston Villa 0	Birmingham C 0
1964	Stoke C....................................1	Leicester C...............................1
	Bebbington	*Gibson*
	Leicester C...............................3	Stoke C....................................2
	Stringfellow, Gibson, Riley	*Viollet, Kinnell*
1965	Chelsea....................................3	Leicester C...............................2
	Tambling, Venables (pen),	*Appleton, Goodfellow*
	McCreadie	
	Leicester C...............................0	Chelsea....................................0
1966	West Ham U.............................2	WBA 1
	Moore, Byrne	*Astle*
	WBA 4	West Ham U.............................1
	Kaye, Brown, Clark, Williams	*Peters*
1967	QPR 3	WBA 2
	Morgan R, Marsh, Lazarus	*Clark C 2*
1968	Leeds U....................................1	Arsenal 0
	Cooper	
1969	Swindon T................................3	Arsenal....................................1*
	Smart, Rogers 2	*Gould*
1970	Manchester C 2	WBA 1*
	Doyle, Pardoe	*Astle*
1971	Tottenham H 2	Aston Villa 0
	Chivers 2	
1972	Chelsea....................................1	Stoke C....................................2
	Osgood	*Conroy, Eastham*
1973	Tottenham H 1	Norwich C 0
	Coates	
1974	Wolverhampton W 2	Manchester C 1
	Hibbitt, Richards	*Bell*
1975	Aston Villa 1	Norwich C...............................0
	Graydon	
1976	Manchester C 2	Newcastle U 1
	Barnes, Tueart	*Gowling*
1977	Aston Villa 0	Everton 0
Replay	Aston Villa 1	Everton 1*
	Kenyon (og)	*Latchford*
Replay	Aston Villa 3	Everton 2*
	Little 2, Nicholl	*Latchford, Lyons*
1978	Nottingham F 0	Liverpool 0*
Replay	Nottingham F 1	Liverpool 0
	Robertson (pen)	

Year	Winner	Score	Runner-up	Score
1979	Nottingham F	3	Southampton	2
	Birtles 2, Woodcock		*Peach, Holmes*	
1980	Wolverhampton W	1	Nottingham F	0
	Gray			
1981	Liverpool	1	West Ham U	1*
	Kennedy A		*Stewart (pen)*	
Replay	Liverpool	2	West Ham U	1
	Dalglish, Hansen		*Goddard*	
1982	Liverpool	3	Tottenham H	1*
	Whelan 2, Rush		*Archibald*	
1983	Liverpool	2	Manchester U	1*
	Kennedy A, Whelan		*Whiteside*	
1984	Liverpool	0	Everton	0*
Replay	Liverpool	1	Everton	0
	Souness			
1985	Norwich C	1	Sunderland	0
	Chisholm (og)			
1986	Oxford U	3	QPR	0
	Hebberd, Houghton, Charles			
1987	Arsenal	2	Liverpool	1
	Nicholas 2		*Rush*	
1988	Luton T	3	Arsenal	2
	Stein B 2, Wilson		*Hayes, Smith*	
1989	Nottingham F	3	Luton T	1
	Clough 2, Webb		*Harford*	
1990	Nottingham F	1	Oldham Ath	0
	Jemson			
1991	Sheffield W	1	Manchester U	0
	Sheridan			
1992	Manchester U	1	Nottingham F	0
	McClair			
1993	Arsenal	2	Sheffield W	1
	Merson, Morrow		*Harkes*	
1994	Aston Villa	3	Manchester U	1
	Atkinson, Saunders 2 (1 pen)		*Hughes*	
1995	Liverpool	2	Bolton W	1
	McManaman 2		*Thompson*	
1996	Aston Villa	3	Leeds U	0
	Milosevic, Taylor, Yorke			
1997	Leicester C	1	Middlesbrough	1*
	Heskey		*Ravanelli*	
Replay	Leicester C	1	Middlesbrough	0*
	Claridge			
1998	Chelsea	2	Middlesbrough	0*
	Sinclair, Di Matteo			
1999	Tottenham H	1	Leicester C	0
	Nielsen			
2000	Leicester C	2	Tranmere R	1
	Elliott 2		*Kelly*	
2001	Liverpool	1	Birmingham C	1
	Fowler		*Purse (pen)*	
Liverpool won 5-4 on penalties.				
2002	Blackburn	2	Tottenham H	1
	Jansen, Cole		*Ziege*	

*After extra time

LDV VANS TROPHY 2001–2002

FIRST ROUND

Stevenage Bor	(0) 1	Southend U	(3) 4
Barnet	(0) 2	Bournemouth	(1) 1
(aet; Barnet won on sudden death.)			
Blackpool	(1) 3	Stoke C	(0) 2
Bristol C	(0) 1	Torquay U	(0) 0
(aet; Bristol C won on sudden death.)			
Cardiff C	(4) 7	Rushden & D	(0) 1
Cheltenham T	(0) 2	Plymouth Arg	(1) 1
Colchester U	(0) 1	Swindon T	(0) 0
Dagenham & R	(0) 3	Leyton Orient	(1) 2
(aet; Dagenham & R won on sudden death.)			
Darlington	(0) 2	Macclesfield T	(1) 1
Doncaster R	(0) 0	Kidderminster H	(0) 1
Exeter C	(1) 1	Cambridge U	(1) 2
(aet; Cambridge U won on sudden death.)			
Hartlepool U	(0) 0	Bury	(0) 1
(aet; Bury won on sudden death.)			
Huddersfield T	(0) 0	Halifax T	(0) 0
(aet; Huddersfield T won 4-3 on penalties.)			
Leigh RMI	(0) 2	Scarborough	(0) 1
(aet; Leigh RMI won on sudden death.)			
Northampton T	(2) 2	Oxford U	(0) 0
Notts Co	(0) 2	York C	(0) 0
Port Vale	(0) 2	Carlisle U	(1) 1
Rochdale	(1) 2	Southport	(0) 0
Scunthorpe U	(1) 3	Lincoln C	(0) 1
Shrewsbury T	(0) 0	Chesterfield	(0) 1
Swansea C	(1) 1	Brighton & HA	(1) 2
Wrexham	(1) 5	Wigan Ath	(1) 1
Yeovil T	(1) 3	QPR	(0) 0
Wycombe W	(0) 1	Brentford	(0) 0

SECOND ROUND

Brighton & HA	(1) 2	Wycombe W	(0) 1
(aet; Brighton & HA won on sudden death.)			
Bury	(1) 2	Notts Co	(1) 3
(aet; Notts Co won on sudden death.)			
Cambridge U	(1) 1	Cheltenham T	(0) 1
(aet; Cambridge U won 5-4 on penalties.)			
Cardiff C	(0) 1	Peterborough U	(1) 3
Chesterfield	(0) 1	Kidderminster H	(0) 0
(aet; Chesterfield won on sudden death.)			
Dagenham & R	(0) 3	Luton T	(0) 2
(aet; Dagenham & R won on sudden death.)			
Hull C	(1) 3	Leigh RMI	(0) 0
Mansfield T	(0) 0	Blackpool	(1) 4
Northampton T	(0) 0	Barnet	(0) 1
Oldham Ath	(1) 2	Tranmere R	(0) 0
Reading	(1) 2	Colchester U	(0) 1
Rochdale	(0) 1	Port Vale	(0) 2
Scunthorpe U	(0) 3	Darlington	(0) 0
Southend U	(0) 0	Bristol C	(0) 2
Wrexham	(0) 0	Huddersfield T	(1) 1
Bristol R	(0) 1	Yeovil T	(1) 1
(aet; Bristol R won 5-4 on penalties.)			

QUARTER-FINALS

Barnet	(2) 4	Reading	(1) 1
Bristol C	(1) 2	Peterborough U	(1) 1

(aet; Bristol C won on sudden death.)

Cambridge U	(1) 2	Brighton & HA	(1) 1

(aet; Cambridge U won on sudden death.)

Chesterfield	(0) 0	Blackpool	(1) 3
Huddersfield T	(1) 4	Scunthorpe U	(0) 1
Hull C	(1) 2	Port Vale	(1) 1
Notts Co	(0) 0	Oldham Ath	(1) 1
Bristol R	(2) 4	Dagenham & R	(0) 1

NORTHERN SEMI-FINALS

Hull C	(0) 0	Huddersfield T	(1) 1
Oldham Ath	(1) 2	Blackpool	(2) 5

SOUTHERN SEMI-FINALS

Cambridge U	(1) 2	Barnet	(0) 0
Bristol C	(2) 3	Bristol R	(0) 0

NORTHERN FINAL, FIRST LEG

Blackpool	(2) 3	Huddersfield T	(0) 1

NORTHERN FINAL, SECOND LEG

Huddersfield T	(2) 2	Blackpool	(0) 1

(3-3 on aggregate aet; Blackpool won on sudden death.)

SOUTHERN FINAL, FIRST LEG

Cambridge U	(0) 0	Bristol C	(0) 0

SOUTHERN FINAL, SECOND LEG

Bristol C	(0) 0	Cambridge U	(1) 2

(Cambridge U won 2-0 on aggregate.)

FINAL (at Millennium Stadium)

24 MAR

Blackpool (1) 4 *(Murphy J 6, Clarke 54, Hills 77, Taylor 82)*
Cambridge U (1) 1 *(Wanless 28 (pen))*   20,287

Blackpool: Barnes; O'Kane, Jaszczun, Collins, Clarke, Marshall (Hughes), Wellens (Simpson), Bullock, Murphy J, Taylor (Walker), Hills.
Cambridge U: Perez; Angus (Goodhind), Murray, Duncan, Tann, Ashbee, Wanless, Tudor (Jackman), Kitson (One), Youngs, Guttridge.
Referee: R. Furnandiz.

FA CHARITY SHIELD WINNERS 1908–2001

1908 Manchester U v QPR	
4-0 after 1-1 draw	
1909 Newcastle U v Northampton T 2-0	
1910 Brighton v Aston Villa	1-0
1911 Manchester U v Swindon T	8-4
1912 Blackburn R v QPR	2-1
1913 Professionals v Amateurs	7-2
1920 Tottenham H v Burnley	2-0
1921 Huddersfield T v Liverpool	1-0
1922 Not played	
1923 Professionals v Amateurs	2-0
1924 Professionals v Amateurs	3-1
1925 Amateurs v Professionals	6-1
1926 Amateurs v Professionals	6-3
1927 Cardiff C v Corinthians	2-1
1928 Everton v Blackburn R	2-1
1929 Professionals v Amateurs	3-0
1930 Arsenal v Sheffield W	2-1
1931 Arsenal v WBA	1-0
1932 Everton v Newcastle U	5-3
1933 Arsenal v Everton	3-0
1934 Arsenal v Manchester C	4-0
1935 Sheffield W v Arsenal	1-0
1936 Sunderland v Arsenal	2-1
1937 Manchester C v Sunderland	2-0
1938 Arsenal v Preston NE	2-1
1948 Arsenal v Manchester U	4-3
1949 Portsmouth v Wolverhampton W	1-1*
1950 World Cup Team v	4-2
Canadian Touring Team	
1951 Tottenham H v Newcastle U	2-1
1952 Manchester U v Newcastle U	4-2
1953 Arsenal v Blackpool	3-1
1954 Wolverhampton W v WBA	4-4*
1955 Chelsea v Newcastle U	3-0
1956 Manchester U v Manchester C	1-0
1957 Manchester U v Aston Villa	4-0
1958 Bolton W v Wolverhampton W	4-1
1959 Wolverhampton W v	3-1
Nottingham F	
1960 Burnley v Wolverhampton W	2-2*

1961 Tottenham H v FA XI	3-2
1962 Tottenham H v Ipswich T	5-1
1963 Everton v Manchester U	4-0
1964 Liverpool v West Ham U	2-2*
1965 Manchester U v Liverpool	2-2*
1966 Liverpool v Everton	1-0
1967 Manchester U v Tottenham H	3-3*
1968 Manchester C v WBA	6-1
1969 Leeds U v Manchester C	2-1
1970 Everton v Chelsea	2-1
1971 Leicester C v Liverpool	1-0
1972 Manchester C v Aston Villa	1-0
1973 Burnley v Manchester C	1-0
1974 Liverpool† v Leeds U	1-1
1975 Derby Co v West Ham U	2-0
1976 Liverpool v Southampton	1-0
1977 Liverpool v Manchester U	0-0*
1978 Nottingham F v Ipswich T	5-0
1979 Liverpool v Arsenal	3-1
1980 Liverpool v West Ham U	1-0
1981 Aston Villa v Tottenham H	2-2*
1982 Liverpool v Tottenham H	1-0
1983 Manchester U v Liverpool	2-0
1984 Everton v Liverpool	1-0
1985 Everton v Manchester U	2-0
1986 Everton v Liverpool	1-1*
1987 Everton v Coventry C	1-0
1988 Liverpool v Wimbledon	2-1
1989 Liverpool v Arsenal	1-0
1990 Liverpool v Manchester U	1-1*
1991 Arsenal v Tottenham H	0-0*
1992 Leeds U v Liverpool	4-3
1993 Manchester U† v Arsenal	1-1
1994 Manchester U v Blackburn R	2-0
1995 Everton v Blackburn R	1-0
1996 Manchester U v Newcastle U	4-0
1997 Manchester U† v Chelsea	1-1
1998 Arsenal v Manchester U	3-0
1999 Arsenal v Manchester U	2-1
2000 Chelsea v Manchester U	2-0

*Each club retained shield for six months. †Won on penalties.

ONE2ONE CHARITY SHIELD 2001

Manchester U (0) 1, Liverpool (2) 2

At Millennium Stadium, 12 August 2001, attendance 70,227

Manchester U: Barthez; Irwin, Silvestre, Neville G, Keane, Stam, Beckham, Butt (Yorke), Van Nistelrooy, Scholes, Giggs.

Scorer: Van Nistelrooy 51.

Liverpool: Westerveld; Babbel, Riise (Carragher), Hamann, Henchoz, Hyypia, Murphy (Berger), McAllister, Heskey, Owen, Barmby (Biscan).

Scorers: McAllister 2 (pen), Owen 16.

Referee: A. D'Urso (Billericay).

SCOTTISH LEAGUE REVIEW 2001–2002

To say that Scottish football is in some bother is clearly the understatement of all time. With the prospect of both Celtic and Rangers wanting to play in England rather than their own native land, the other Premier League clubs already giving notice that they intend resigning from the competition, the domestic scene is one serious problem. The national team now under the leadership of the German Bertie Vogts is very much in the second category and under reconstruction.

The second season of the new formula in the Premier League with top and bottom halves splitting after 33 matches was again less than satisfactory. At the time Celtic needed only one more win to take the title and in the cellar, St Johnstone required a miracle to save them from relegation.

Celtic then confirmed their title by beating Livingston 5-1 to claim their 38th overall title and the second in a row, the first occasion in 20 years they had taken successive championships. The remaining interest was in the chase for places in Europe.

It was not such a poor season for Rangers as in the 2000–01 campaign because they did manage to beat Celtic 3-2 in the Tennent's Scottish Cup final, and beat Ayr United 4-0 in the CIS Insurance Cup final after eliminating Celtic 2-1 in the semi-finals. However their finishing position in the league was 18 points adrift of Celtic, three worse than the previous season.

Rangers' first defeat of the season was 2-0 at Ibrox against Celtic on 30 September. For some wiseacres the writing was already on the wall in green and white. It was harder still to erase the colours by 25 November when Celtic completed a double at Parkhead by winning 2-1 to extend the gap to ten points with around a third of the season played.

But before Christmas, Celtic suffered what was to prove their sole reverse in the league when they were beaten 2-0 at Aberdeen, though the margin at the top was still ten points and Rangers had played one more match than Celtic.

When the brief winter pause arrived, there seemed little to predict outside of the obvious. Rangers did draw with Celtic on 10 March and appropriately in view of their overall performance, Livingston inflicted Rangers' third defeat on 13 April by a 2-1 scoreline.

Thus third place went to Livingston, a tremendous effort by the newcomers to the top flight. But to put that into context, they did finish 27 points behind Rangers. Aberdeen were fourth in what was a better season for them and Hearts fifth as in 2000–01. Dunfermline made the cut this time, but Hibernian, Kilmarnock and Dundee disappointed in failing so to do.

The Scottish League season ended in bizarre fashion. At Ayr a pitch invasion by unhappy Airdrie supporters ended the match after only 21 minutes with United leading 1-0. Airdrie on the brink of financial extinction had been runners-up to Partick Thistle in the Division One race and were the reigning Bell's Scottish League Challenge Cup holders having beaten Alloa 2-1 in October.

Airdrie's demise clearly upset the likelihood of normal promotion and relegation elsewhere in the league, but certainly Falkirk and Raith Rovers were due to go down from the First Division until Falkirk were given a reprieve. The replacements were Queen of the South and Alloa.

Stenhousemuir and Morton were on the way down from the Second Division before Stenhousemuir escaped, while Brechin City and Dumbarton went up. Not that financial problems were confined to Airdrie, because Motherwell in the Scottish Premier League were in dire straits and put into administration during the season. Clydebank were also in some bother on the fiscal front while Hamilton Academical players were threatening to go on strike over non-payment of wages. However, a vacancy to be filled was the close season priority for the Scottish League.

Seven candidates put themselves forward: Gretna, Gala Fairydean, Huntly, Cove Rangers, Edinburgh City, Preston Athletic and the newly formed Airdrie United. The winner proved to be Gretna, Scottish based but having been playing in England since 1947 and members of the Unibond League.

Then came the next bombshell. Clydebank folded. A consortium of their fans put forward a rescue proposal and they and Airdrie United went cap-in-hand to the administrator, each hoping to fill the new vacancy. But peace may have broken out on the Premier front.

SCOTTISH LEAGUE TABLES 2001–2002

Premier League	P	W	D	L	F	A	W	D	L	F	A	Pts	GD
			Home		*Goals*			*Away*		*Goals*			
Celtic	38	18	1	0	51	9	15	3	1	43	9	103	76
Rangers	38	14	4	1	42	11	11	6	2	40	16	85	55
Livingston	38	9	5	4	23	17	7	5	8	27	30	58	3
Aberdeen	38	12	2	5	31	19	4	5	10	20	30	55	2
Hearts	38	8	3	8	30	27	6	3	10	22	30	48	−5
Dunfermline Ath	38	9	4	6	25	24	3	5	11	16	40	45	−23
Kilmarnock	38	7	6	6	24	26	6	4	9	20	28	49	−10
Dundee U	38	6	5	8	18	30	6	5	8	20	29	46	−21
Dundee	38	8	5	6	23	24	4	3	12	18	31	44	−14
Hibernian	38	6	6	7	35	30	4	5	10	16	26	41	−5
Motherwell	38	8	5	6	30	25	3	2	14	19	44	40	−20
St Johnstone	38	2	3	15	11	32	3	3	12	13	30	21	−38

First Division	P	W	D	L	F	A	W	D	L	F	A	Pts	GD
			Home		*Goals*			*Away*		*Goals*			
Partick T	36	12	6	0	38	15	7	3	8	23	23	66	23
Airdrieonians	36	8	6	4	31	19	7	5	6	28	21	56	19
Ayr U	36	8	6	4	25	16	5	7	6	28	28	52	9
Ross Co	36	10	2	6	33	21	4	8	6	18	22	52	8
Clyde	36	8	6	4	27	21	5	4	9	24	35	49	−5
Inverness CT	36	11	3	4	47	22	2	6	10	13	29	48	9
Arbroath	36	9	3	6	22	28	5	3	10	20	31	48	−17
St Mirren	36	6	8	4	19	19	5	4	9	24	34	45	−10
Falkirk	36	5	5	8	24	36	5	4	9	25	37	39	−24
Raith R	36	7	5	6	31	25	1	6	11	19	37	35	−12

Second Division	P	W	D	L	F	A	W	D	L	F	A	Pts	GD
			Home		*Goals*			*Away*		*Goals*			
Queen of the S	36	12	4	2	33	19	8	5	5	31	23	67	22
Alloa Ath	36	8	8	2	35	17	7	6	5	20	16	59	22
Forfar Ath	36	8	3	7	25	25	7	5	6	26	22	53	4
Clydebank	36	8	4	6	25	23	6	5	7	19	22	51	−1
Hamilton A	36	9	5	4	26	15	4	4	10	23	29	48	5
Berwick R	36	6	4	8	19	28	6	7	5	25	24	47	−8
Stranraer	36	7	5	6	27	25	3	10	5	21	26	45	−3
Cowdenbeath	36	5	8	5	27	28	6	3	9	22	23	44	−2
Stenhousemuir	36	3	8	7	15	25	5	4	9	18	32	36	−24
Morton	36	3	8	7	20	28	4	6	8	28	35	35	−15

Third Division	P	W	D	L	F	A	W	D	L	F	A	Pts	GD
			Home		*Goals*			*Away*		*Goals*			
Brechin C	36	12	4	2	38	14	10	3	5	29	24	73	29
Dumbarton	36	10	4	4	30	22	8	3	7	29	26	61	11
Albion R	36	8	5	5	28	23	8	6	4	23	19	59	9
Peterhead	36	9	4	5	36	26	8	1	9	27	26	56	11
Montrose	36	9	2	7	25	20	7	5	6	18	19	55	4
Elgin C	36	9	3	6	26	20	4	5	9	19	27	47	−2
East Stirlingshire	36	8	1	9	27	27	4	3	11	24	31	40	−7
East Fife	36	6	4	8	23	26	5	3	10	16	30	40	−17
Stirling Albion	36	6	4	8	23	29	3	6	9	22	39	37	−23
Queen's Park	36	4	6	8	17	21	5	2	11	21	32	35	−15

BANK OF SCOTLAND SCOTTISH LEAGUE—PREMIER LEAGUE

RESULTS 2001–2002

	Aberdeen	Celtic	Dundee	Dundee U	Dunfermline Ath	Hearts	Hibernian	Kilmarnock	Livingston	Motherwell	Rangers	St Johnstone
Aberdeen	—	2-0	0-0	2-1	3-2	3-2	2-0	2-0	0-3	4-2	0-3	1-0
Celtic	0-1	—	3-1	4-0	1-0	2-3	3-0	1-1	3-0	1-0	0-1	3-0
Dundee	2-0	0-4	—	5-1	5-0	2-0	2-1	1-0	3-2	2-0	2-1	2-1
Dundee U	1-4	0-3	2-2	—	2-2	1-1	1-0	1-2	1-0	3-1	1-1	1-1
Dunfermline Ath	1-0	0-4	2-0	0-1	—	0-2	1-2	0-2	1-2	5-2	1-4	0-0
Hearts	1-0	0-1	3-1	1-2	2-0	—	1-0	2-0	2-3	3-1	1-4	2-1
Hibernian	1-0	3-1	2-0	6-1	5-1	2-1	—	2-2	1-3	1-0	2-4	3-0
Kilmarnock	3-4	1-1	0-1	2-0	1-1	1-2	0-0	—	2-3	4-0	2-2	4-0
Livingston	3-1	0-1	3-2	2-2	0-0	3-3	1-0	0-1	—	2-0	0-2	3-0
Motherwell	0-0	0-2	4-2	2-1	4-1	2-0	0-3	2-2	0-0	—	2-1	1-0
Rangers	3-2	1-2	2-1	3-2	4-0	2-0	1-1	5-0	3-0	3-0	—	1-1

175

BELL'S SCOTTISH LEAGUE—DIVISION ONE RESULTS 2001–2002

	Airdrie	Arbroath	Ayr U	Clyde	Falkirk	Inverness CT	Partick Th	Raith R	Ross Co	St Mirren
Airdrie	—	3-1	2-1	1-2	2-1	6-0	1-0	2-2	1-1	0-0
Arbroath	0-6	—	1-2	2-2	1-0	3-0	1-1	1-1	0-2	2-3
Ayr U	2-1	3-2	—	2-1	1-0	3-2	1-3	2-2	2-1	0-2
Clyde	1-3	0-1	2-0	—	0-1	1-0	1-0	1-1	1-1	0-3
Falkirk	1-0	0-0	2-2	2-1	—	3-0	0-2	3-1	2-0	4-2
Inverness CT	0-3	1-0	2-2	0-1	0-0	—	1-1	1-0	0-0	4-1
Partick Th	0-1	1-1	1-2	1-1	1-2	1-1	—	1-2	3-0	1-1
Raith R	1-2	5-1	2-1	1-6	3-2	1-0	2-1	—	0-0	3-1
Ross Co	2-2	0-2	1-1	4-0	4-2	2-1	3-2	4-2	—	3-2
St Mirren	1-2	2-0	3-2	2-1	5-1	0-0	1-0	1-0	1-1	—

BELL'S SCOTTISH LEAGUE—DIVISION TWO RESULTS 2001–2002

	Alloa	Berwick R	Clydebank	Cowdenbeath	Forfar	Hamilton	Morton	Queen of the South	Stenhousemuir	Stranraer
Alloa	—	2-2	1-0	5-1	1-2	2-1	1-1	2-0	0-1	2-2
Berwick R	0-4	—	2-2	0-0	1-1	2-2	4-0	4-1	4-0	0-0
Clydebank	0-1	1-2	—	2-5	0-2	1-1	2-0	0-4	1-1	2-2
Cowdenbeath	1-0	0-2	1-0	—	3-2	3-2	0-0	3-0	2-1	4-1
Forfar	1-2	2-4	1-1	1-0	—	3-0	1-2	0-1	3-2	1-3
Hamilton	0-1	1-1	1-2	2-1	1-4	—	1-4	1-1	2-4	1-2
Morton	4-1	3-1	3-0	0-2	2-0	2-1	—	3-1	2-3	2-2
Queen of the South	0-1	2-2	1-0	1-3	1-2	3-1	6-5	—	4-1	1-1
Stenhousemuir	1-0	3-0	2-2	0-3	0-0	2-0	4-0	1-1	—	1-1
Stranraer	1-1	2-2	1-1	2-1	2-0	3-2	0-0	1-2	1-0	—

BELL'S SCOTTISH LEAGUE—DIVISION THREE RESULTS 2001–2002

	Albion R	Brechin C	Dumbarton	East Fife	East Stirling	Elgin C	Montrose	Peterhead	Queens Park	Stirling A
Albion R	—	1-2	0-2	3-0	0-4	4-4	0-0	1-0	2-1	1-3
Brechin C	0-1	—	1-1	2-1	5-1	2-2	0-0	2-1	2-0	2-0
Dumbarton	4-1	3-2	—	6-0	1-0	1-0	0-0	4-3	2-1	3-1
East Fife	2-0	2-1	1-0	—	2-0	3-0	0-5	0-1	5-0	2-1
East Stirling	0-0	0-0	2-4	0-4	—	3-1	1-2	0-3	1-1	4-1
Elgin C	2-3	3-4	1-0	2-2	2-1	—	2-0	2-3	1-4	2-0
Montrose	1-2	2-0	0-3	2-0	2-2	0-2	—	4-1	0-3	1-1
Peterhead	2-0	0-1	1-3	2-1	2-0	1-0	4-0	—	0-1	1-1
Queens Park	0-0	3-1	4-0	1-2	2-3	3-0	2-2	2-0	—	3-0
Stirling A	0-3	1-3	2-1	0-1	1-0	3-1	1-1	2-0	3-2	—

ABERDEEN   PREMIER LEAGUE

Ground: Pittodrie Stadium, Aberdeen AB24 5QH (01224) 650400
Ground capacity: 22,199. **Colours:** All red with white trim.
Manager: Ebbe Skovdahl.
League Appearances: Anderson R 17(7); Belabed R (1); Bett C 1(2); Bisconti R 31; Clark C 1(7); Dadi E 20(8); Esson R 7(2); Guntweit C 16(2); Kjaer P 23; Mackie D 28(7); McAllister J 26(3); McGuire P 38; McNaughton K 33(1); Mike L 7(2); O'Donoghue R (1); Peat M 1; Precec D 7(1); Rutkiewicz K 1(3); Solberg T 10(5); Thornley B 15(9); Tiernan F 11(12); Whyte D 30(1); Winters R 34; Young Dk 23(9); Young Dn 32; Zerouali H 6(12).
Goals – League (51): Winters 13 (5 pens), Mackie 8, Zerouali 8, Dadi 4, McGuire 3, Mike 3, Thornley 3, Derek Young 3, Anderson 1, Bisconti 1, Guntweit 1, Rutkiewicz 1, Solberg 1, Darren Young 1.
Scottish Cup (4): McAllister 1, Thornley 1, Winters 1, Darren Young 1.
CIS Cup (3): Dadi 1, Mackie 1, Thornley 1.
Honours – Division 1: Champions – 1954-55, **Premier Division:** Champions – 1979-80, 1983-84, 1984-85. **Scottish Cup winners** 1947, 1970, 1982, 1983, 1984, 1986, 1990. **League Cup winners** 1956, 1977, 1986, 1990, 1996. **European Cup-Winners' Cup winners** 1983.

AIRDRIEONIANS   WITHDRAWN FROM LEAGUE

Ground: Shyberry Excelsior Stadium, Airdrie ML6 8QZ (01236) 622000
Ground capacity: 10,000 (all seated). **Colours:** White shirts with red diamond, white shorts.
League Appearances: Armstrong P 30(2); Beasley D 4(6); Bennett N 10(1); Coyle O 36; Docherty S 11(8); Dunn R (14); Ferguson A 26; Gardner L 8(14); Henry J 21(1); James K 34; Lawrence A (1); Macdonald S 4(6); Macfarlane N 28; McAlpine J (1); McCulloch S 3; McDonald C (4); McManus A 28; McPherson C 29(3); Reilly M 6; Roberts M 34(2); Ronald P (6); Smith A 26(6); Stewart A 25(3); Taylor S 24(8); Vareille J 9(3).
Goals – League (59): Coyle 23 (3 pens), Roberts 12, Taylor 8, McPherson 4, Macfarlane 3, Smith 2, Vareille 2, Armstrong 1, Gardner 1, James 1, McDonald C 1, own goal 1.
Scottish Cup (0):
CIS Cup (5): Coyle 1, James 1, Macfarlane 1, Roberts 1, own goal 1.
Challenge Cup (11): Coyle 3, Roberts 3, McPherson 2, Taylor 2, James 1.
Honours – Division II: Champions – 1902-03, 1954-55, 1973-74. **Scottish Cup winners** 1924. **B&Q Cup winners** 1995. **Bell's League Challenge winners** 2000-01, 2001-02.

ALBION ROVERS   DIV. 3

Ground: Cliftonhill Stadium, Main Street, Coatbridge ML5 3RB (01236) 606334
Ground capacity: 2496. **Colours:** Scarlet and yellow shirts, scarlet shorts.
Manager: Peter Hetherston.
League Appearances: Bonar P 19(2); Booth M 31; Carr D 5(9); Coulter J 1; Coulter R 10(2); Diack I 19(7); Donnelly K 2(2); Easton S 25(2); Fahey C 27; Hamilton S 32(1); Harty M 23(4); Ingram S (2); Lumsden T 22; McCormick S 11(6); McKenna G 25(9); McKenzie J 18(5); McLean C 19(8); McLees J (2); McMullan R 8(20); Murdoch S (3); Rankin I (3); Rodden P (2); Shearer S 9(1); Silvestro C 15(3); Smith J 20; Stirling J 4; Struthers W 1; Tait T 15; Waldie C 35(1).
Goals – League (51): McLean 11 (1 pen), Booth 8 (2 pens), Diack 7 (1 pen), Harty 5, McKenzie 3, Bonar 2, Carr 2, McMullan 2, Silvestro 2, Smith 2, Donnelly 1, Hamilton 1, McCormick 1, McKenna 1, Stirling 1 (pen), Waldie 1, own goal 1.

Scottish Cup (3): McLean 2, Harty 1.
CIS Cup (0):
Challenge Cup (3): Bonar 1, Hamilton 1, McMullan 1.
Honours – Division II: Champions – 1933-34. **Second Division:** Champions 1988-89.

ALLOA ATHLETIC   DIV. 1

Ground: Recreation Park, Alloa FK10 1RY (01259) 722695
Ground capacity: 3100. **Colours:** Gold shirts with black trim, black shorts with gold stripe.
Manager: Terry Christie.
League Appearances: Anderson D 7(3); Brown T 7(3); Christie M 16(6); Cowan M 8(2); Curran H 19(12); Donnachie S 2(11); Evans G 7(4); Evans J 5(1); Fisher J 26(4); Hamilton R 24(10); Hutchison G 32(3); Irvine W 2(5); Kerr C 1; Knox K 28; Little I 29(5); Raeside R 22(1); Seaton A 21(6); Soutar D 31; Thomson S 31(1); Valentine C 33; Walker R 23(9); Watson G 17; Whalen S 5.
Goals – League (55): Hutchison 14, Hamilton 7 (1 pen), Seaton 6 (1 pen), Knox 5, Little 5, Curran 4, Raeside 3 (1 pen), Walker 3, Donnachie 2, Fisher 2, Brown 1, Christie 1, Thomson 1, Watson 1.
Scottish Cup (4): Evans 2, Hutchison 1, Little 1.
CIS Cup (4): Curran 1, Little 1, Thomson 1, Walker 1.
Challenge Cup (10): Evans 2, Hamilton 2, Little 2, Curran 1, Fisher 1, Hutchison 1, Irvine 1.
Honours – Division II: Champions – 1921-22. **Third Division:** Champions – 1997-98. **Bell's League Challenge winners** 2000.

ARBROATH   DIV. 1

Ground: Gayfield Park, Arbroath DD11 1QB (01241) 872157
Ground capacity: 4020. **Colours:** Maroon shirts with white trim, white shorts.
Manager: John Brownlie.
League Appearances: Arbuckle D (3); Bayne G 33(1); Brownlie P 26(5); Cargill A 29(3); Cusick J 23(6); Durno P (1); Fallon S 3; Florence S 25(2); Gardner J 3(6); Graham E 1; Heenan K 9(12); Henslee G 2(11); Hinchcliffe C 35; Mackay D 5; Mallan S 14(9); McAulay J 7(13); McGlashan J 32; McInally D 17(2); McKinnon C 20(9); Mercer J 6(12); Moffat S 6(2); Ritchie I 31; Roddie A 3(1); Rowe G 31; Swankie S 3(6); Tait J 31; Wight C 1.
Goals – League (42): Bayne 6, McGlashan 6, Mallan 6 (2 pens), McKinnon 5, Ritchie 5, Cargill 4, Cusick 4, Rowe 3, Brownlie 1, Heenan 1, McAulay 1.
Scottish Cup (0):
CIS Cup (0):
Challenge Cup (1): Brownlie 1.
Honours – Nil.

AYR UNITED   DIV. 1

Ground: Somerset Park, Ayr KA8 9NB (01292) 263435
Ground capacity: 10,243 (1549 seated). **Colours:** White shirts with black trim, black shorts.
Manager: Gordon Dalziel.
League Appearances: Annand E 21(7); Bradford J (10); Bruce R (1); Chaplain S 4(4); Crabbe S 20; Craig D 27(1); Dodds J 1; Duffy C 21(1); Dunlop M 1; Grady J 24(7); Hughes J 30; Kean S 4(4); Latta J (1); Lovering P 27(5); McEwan C 15(7); McGinley P 27; McLaughlin B 8(11); Molloy T (1); Moss D 5; Nelson C 35; Robertson J 36; Scally N 5(2); Sharp L 9(12); Sheerin P 33(1); Smyth M 4; Stevenson C (1); Teale G 18; Twaddle K 1; Wilson M 20(6).

Goals – League (53): Annand 14 (6 pens), Grady 8 (1 pen), Sheerin 6, McGinlay 5, Teale 4, Crabbe 3, Kean 3, Robertson 2, Wilson 2, Hughes 1, Lovering 1, McEwan 1, McLaughlin 1, Moss 1, Scally 1
Scottish Cup (13): Crabbe 3, Annand 2, Grady 2, McGinlay 2, Sheerin 2, Robertson 1, own goal 1.
CIS Cup (10): Annand 4, Grady 2, McGinlay 1, Robertson 1, Sharp 1, Teale 1.
Challenge Cup (5): Annand 1, Bradford 1, McGinlay 1, Sheerin 1, Teale 1.
Honours – Division II: Champions – 1911-12, 1912-13, 1927-28, 1936-37, 1958-59, 1965-66. **Second Division:** Champions – 1987-88, 1996-97.

BERWICK RANGERS   DIV. 2

Ground: Shielfield Park, Berwick-on-Tweed TD15 2EF (01289) 307424
Ground capacity: 4131. **Colours:** Black with four inch gold stripe, black shorts with white trim.
Manager: Paul Smith.
League Appearances: Anthony M 23(4); Bennett N 25(2); Bradley M 17(11); Brannigan K 5; Crawford D 1(2); Duthie M 1; Farrell G 21(1); Feroz C 20(2); Forrest G 25(6); Glancy M 6(3); Gray D 1(3); Harvey J 1(3); Huxford R 11(3); Mathers P 6; May E 3(3); McCulloch W 24; McDonald C 7(4); McDowell M 10(6); McNicoll G 13(4); Murie D 35; Neil M 19(4); Neill A 36; O'Connor G 6; Rae D 1(2); Ritchie I 4; Robertson A 8; Ronald P 7(3); Smith A 5; Smith D 19(8); Thomas K 3(2); Whelan J 6(4); Wood G 28.
Goals – League (44): Wood 9, McDowell 7, Anthony 5, Bennett 5 (1 pen), Feroz 4, Smith D 3, Forrest 2, Neil M 2, Brannigan 1, Duthie 1, Glancy 1, Neill A 1, Robertson 1, Smith A 1, Thomas 1.
Scottish Cup (1): Feroz 1.
CIS Cup (0):
Challenge Cup (3): Glancy 1, Ritchie 1, Wood 1.
Honours – Second Division: Champions – 1978-79.

BRECHIN CITY   DIV. 2

Ground: Glebe Park, Brechin DD9 6BJ (01356) 622856
Ground capacity: 3980. **Colours:** Red with white trim.
Manager: Dick Campbell.
League Appearances: Bain K 29(2); Black R 29(5); Cairney H 32; Cairns M 26; Campbell P 11(11); Clark D 24(3); Craig D 2(3); Dewar G (3); Donachie B 3(4); Ewart J 4(2); Fotheringham K 32; Grant R 23(2); Henderson R (6); Honeyman B 6(13); Kernaghan A 3; King C 36; Leask M 1(7); McAllister S 1(1); McKeown K 10; Miller G 26; O'Boyle G 4(1); Riley P 13(9); Smith D 17(15); Smith J 30; Templeman C 34(1).
Goals – League (67): Templeman 15, Grant 10, Bain 7 (2 pens), King 7, Fotheringham 6, Smith J 6, Clark 4, Honeyman 3, Campbell 2, Miller 2, O'Boyle 2, Black 1, Leask 1, Smith D 1.
Scottish Cup (4): O'Boyle 2, Fotheringham 1, Grant 1.
CIS Cup (0):
Challenge Cup (11): Fotheringham 3 (1 pen), Smith 3, Grant 2, Bain 1, Kernaghan 1, Templeman 1.
Honours – Second Division: Champions – 1982-83, 1989-90. **C Division:** Champions – 1953-54.

CELTIC   PREMIER LEAGUE

Ground: Celtic Park, Glasgow G40 3RE (0141) 556 2611
Ground capacity: 60,832 (all seated). **Colours:** Green and white hooped shirts, white shorts.
Manager: Martin O'Neill.

League Appearances: Agathe D 21; Balde B 22; Boyd T 9; Crainey S 10(5); Douglas R 35; Gould J 1; Guppy S 10(6); Hartson J 26(5); Healy C 2(2); Kennedy J 1; Kharine D 2(1); Lambert P 33(1); Larsson H 33; Lennon N 32(1); Lynch S 1; Maloney S 3(13); McNamara J 9(11); Mjällby J 35; Moravcik L 17(7); Petrov S 25(2); Petta B 12(6); Smith J 3(9); Sutton C 18; Sylla M 7(1); Tebily O 8(3); Thompson A 22(3); Valgaeren J 19; Wieghorst M 2(1).
Goals – League (94): Larsson 29 (2 pens), Hartson 19 (1 pen), Moravcik 6, Petrov 6, Thompson 6 (1 pen), Lambert 5, Maloney 5, Sutton 4, Mjällby 3, Balde 2, Lynch 2, Valgaeren 2, Agathe 1, Lennon 1, Smith 1, Sylla 1, own goal 1.
Scottish Cup (14): Balde 2, Hartson 2, Larsson 2, Thompson 2, Maloney 1, Petrov 1, Petta 1, Sylla 1, Wieghorst 1, own goal 1.
CIS Cup (11): Maloney 4, Hartson 3, Balde 2, Healy 1, Tebily 1.
Honours – Division I: Champions – 1892-93, 1893-94, 1895-96, 1897-98, 1904-05, 1905-06, 1906-07, 1907-08, 1908-09, 1909-10, 1913-14, 1914-15, 1915-16, 1916-17, 1918-19, 1921-22, 1925-26, 1935-36, 1937-38, 1953-54, 1965-66, 1966-67, 1967-68, 1968-69, 1969-70, 1970-71, 1971-72, 1972-73, 1973-74. **Premier Division: Champions** – 1976-77, 1978-79, 1980-81, 1981-82, 1985-86, 1987-88, 1997-98, 2000-01, 2001-02. **Scottish Cup winners** 1892, 1899, 1900, 1904, 1907, 1908, 1911, 1912, 1914, 1923, 1925, 1927, 1931, 1933, 1937, 1951, 1954, 1965, 1967, 1969, 1971, 1972, 1974, 1975, 1977, 1980, 1985, 1988, 1989, 1995, 2001. **League Cup winners** 1957, 1958, 1966, 1967, 1968, 1969, 1970, 1975, 1983, 1998, 2000, 2001. **European Cup winners** 1967.

CLYDE   DIV. 1

Ground: Broadwood Stadium, Cumbernauld G68 9NE (01236) 451511
Ground capacity: 8200. **Colours:** White shirts with red and black trim, black shorts.
Manager: Alan Kernaghan.
League Appearances: Aitken C 2(3); Bingham C 10(6); Budinauckas K 10(2); Carrigan B 9; Convery S 13(15); Cranmer C 8(5); Crawford B 8(9); De Gregorio R 4(5); Dunn D 22(5); Fraser J 22; Graham M 2; Grant A (1); Hagen D 16(12); Halliwell B 24(1); Hinds L 24(8); Kane A 1(9); Kane P 4(1); Keogh P 28(3); Kernaghan A 15; McClay A 3(1); McCusker R (1); McDowell M 1(3); McLaughlin M 12(2); McPhee B 4; Mensing S 23; Millen A 31; Mitchell J 31; Murray D 9; Okikiolu S 2(1); Potter J 6; Ross J 27; Smith B 25(1).
Goals – League (51): Hinds 11, Keogh 10 (2 pens), Mitchell 5 (1 pen), Carrigan 4 (1 pen), Fraser 3, Millen 3, Ross 3, Convery 2, Crawford 2, Hagen 2, Kernaghan 1, McCusker 1 (pen), McLaughlin 1, Mensing 1, Potter 1, own goal 1.
Scottish Cup (2): Fraser 1, Mensing 1.
CIS Cup (3): Crawford 2, Kane A 1.
Challenge Cup (9): Kane A 2, Keogh 2, Ross 2, Convery 1, McCusker 1, Mitchell 1.
Honours – Division II: Champions – 1904-05, 1951-52, 1956-57, 1961-62, 1972-73.
Second Division: Champions – 1977-78, 1981-82, 1992-93, 1999-2000. **Scottish Cup winners** 1939, 1955, 1958.

CLYDEBANK   WITHDRAWN FROM LEAGUE

Ground: Sharing with Morton – Cappielow Park, Greenock (01475) 723571
Ground capacity: 14,891. **Colours:** Red and white stripes, black shorts.
League Appearances: Bossy F 27(3); Brannigan K (1); Burke A 17(10); Carrigan B 7(3); Dick J 4(5); Falconer W 1; Ferguson D 28; George L 2; Gow A 3(2); Graham A 9(12); Hamilton B 27; Jackson D 7(7); Kinnaird P (4); Klein D 1; Lavety B 7(1); McColligan B 25(4); McGowan N 31(1); McGrillen P 19(16); McKinlay W 8; McKinnon R 20; McNally M 18(1); McPeak A 3; McVey W 5(2); Miller J 1(2); Mooney G 2(1); Nicholls M 5(4); O'Neill M 19; Paton E 31(5); Robertson S 9(2); Shaw G 1; Shields P 13(2); Smith H 26; Stirling J 1; Vella S 9; Whiteford A 10(4).

Goals – League (44): Burke 9 (2 pens), Paton 8 (2 pens), McGrillen 7, O'Neill 4, Lavety 3, Shields 3, Graham 2, Jackson 2, Ferguson 1, McColligan 1, McKinnon 1, own goals 3.
Scottish Cup (1): Paton 1
CIS Cup (0):
Challenge Cup (1): Burke 1
Honours – Second Division: Champions – 1975-76.

COWDENBEATH   DIV. 2

Ground: Central Park, Cowdenbeath KY4 9EY (01383) 610166
Ground capacity: 5268. **Colours:** Royal blue with white cuffs and collar, white shorts.
Manager: Keith Wright.
League Appearances: Boyle J 34(1); Brown G 35; Burns J 1(1); Byle K 1(2); Campbell A 12(2); Crabbe G 1(1); Dixon J 5(5); Elliot J 6(6); French H 33(1); Gibb S 1; Gordon C 13; Huggon R 2(3); King T 9; Kwik Ajet W 1; Lawrence A 21(2); Martin J 4; Mauchlen I 13(9); McMillan C (5); Miller C (1); Milne K 9; Moffat A 3; Neeson C 11(3); O'Connor G 19; Raynes S 12(3); Renwick M 7; Robertson A 1; Sullivan V 2(2); Swift S 31(2); Welsh B 1(1); White D 30; Wilson K 32; Wilson P 1; Winter C 25; Wright K 13(12); Young C 7(8).
Goals – League (49): Brown 17, Wright 9, French 4, Mauchlen 4, White 3 (1 pen), Lawrence 2, Swift 2, Crabbe 1, Dixon 1, Elliot 1, King 1, Wilson K 1, Young 1, own goals 2
Scottish Cup (0):
CIS Cup (2): Wilson K 1, Wright 1
Challenge Cup (0):
Honours – Division II: Champions – 1913-14, 1914-15, 1938-39.

DUMBARTON   DIV. 2

Ground: Strathclyde Homes Stadium, Dumbarton G82 1JJ.
Ground capacity: 2050. **Colours:** Yellow shirts with black facing, shorts yellow with black stripe.
Manager: David Winnie.
League Appearances: Bonar S 19(13); Brittain C 27(5); Brown A 35; Bruce J 10; Connolly J 2, Crilly M 29(1); Dickie M 23; Dillon J 15(18); Dunn R 11(2); Flannery P 32(1); Hillcoat J 12; Jack S 25(3); Lauchlan M 9(2); Lynes C 5(15); McCann K 19; McKelvie D 2(20); McKeown J 23; Murdoch S 5; O'Neill M 26(3); Robertson J 28(6); Stewart D 17; Wight J 22.
Goals – League (59): Flannery 18 (2 pens), Crilly 10, Robertson 8, Brown 7, Dunn 4, Brittain 2, McCann 2, O'Neill 2, Bonar 1, Dillon 1, Lauchlan 1, Lynes 1, McKeown 1, Stewart 1
Scottish Cup (1): McKeown 1.
CIS Cup (2): Brown 1, Flannery 1.
Challenge Cup (0):
Honours – Division I: Champions – 1890-91 (Shared), 1891-92. **Division II:** Champions – 1910-11, 1971-72. **Second Division:** Champions – 1991-92. **Scottish Cup winners** 1883.

DUNDEE   PREMIER LEAGUE

Ground: Dens Park, Dundee DD3 7JY (01382) 889966
Ground capacity: 11,760 (all seated). **Colours:** Navy shirts with red, blue and white stripes on front, white shorts with navy and red piping.
Manager: Jim Duffy.

League Appearances: Artero J 12(9); Beghetto M 21; Beith G 1(2); Boylan C (1); Caballero F 28(4); Carranza A 23(3); Coyne C (2); Del Rio W 31(2); Forbes B 2(2); Garrido B 8(10); Gatti L (4); Kemas K 2(10); Ketsbaia T 22; Khizanishvili Z 18; Langfield J 21; Mackay D 13(4); Marrocco M 12; Milne S 15(15); Naveda B (2); Nemsadze G 10(1); Rae G 36; Robb S (1); Robertson M 7(9); Romano A 17(4); Sara J 25(3); Smith B 36(2); Speroni J 17; Torres E 19; Traverso G (2); Wilkie L 8; Zhiyi F 14.
Goals – League (41): Sara 11 (1 pen), Caballero 6 (1 pen), Ketsbaia 6, Rae 6, Milne 5, Zhiyi 2, Carranza 1, Kemas 1, Mackay 1, Nemsadze 1, Torres 1.
Scottish Cup (4): Milne 1, Sara 1, Torres 1, Zhiyi 1.
CIS Cup (3): Boylan 1, Caballero 1, Milne 1.
Honours – Division I: Champions – 1961-62. **First Division:** Champions – 1978-79, 1991-92, 1997-98. **Division II:** Champions – 1946-47. **Scottish Cup winners** 1910. **League Cup winners** 1952, 1953, 1974. **B&Q (Centenary) Cup winners** 1991.

DUNDEE UNITED　　　　　　PREMIER LEAGUE

Ground: Tannadice Park, Dundee DD3 7JW (01382) 833166
Ground capacity: 14,223. **Colours:** Tangerine shirts, black shorts.
Manager: Alex Smith.
League Appearances: Aljofree H 27; Buchan J 6(1); Carson S 6(7); Cocozza M 1(1); Duff S 9; Easton C 33(3); Fullarton J 11; Gallacher P 38; Griffin D 29; Hamilton J 20(4); Hannah D 16(4); Jarvie P (1); Lauchlan J 33; Lilley D 19(7); McConalogue S 5(7); McCracken D 16(3); McCunnie J 27(1); McIntyre J 16(3); Miller C 31(3); O'Brien R 2(6); O'Donnell S 1(5); Ogunmade D (2); Partridge D 13; Paterson J 12(15); Thompson S 20(12); Venetis A 14(10); Wilson M 1; Winters D 4(9); Wright S 8(1).
Goals – League (38): Lilley 6, McIntyre 6, Thompson 6, Hamilton 5 (1 pen), Miller 4, Easton 3, Aljofree 2 (1 pen), Griffin 2, Paterson 2, McConalogue 1, Venetis 1.
Scottish Cup (9): Aljofree 3, Thompson 2, Winters 2, Easton 1, Miller 1.
CIS Cup (6): Thompson 2, Easton 1, Griffin 1, Hamilton 1, Paterson 1.
Honours – Premier Division: Champions – 1982-83. **Division II:** Champions – 1924-25, 1928-29. **Scottish Cup winners** 1994. **League Cup winners** 1980, 1981.

DUNFERMLINE ATHLETIC　　　PREMIER LEAGUE

Ground: East End Park, Dunfermline KY12 7RB (01383) 724295
Ground capacity: 12,500. **Colours:** Black and white striped shirts, white shorts with black piping.
Manager: Jim Calderwood.
League Appearances: Blair B (1); Bullen L 25(6); Crawford S 36; Dair J 17(11); de Gier J 12; Doesburg M 4(5); Ferguson I 20; Hampshire S 13(10); Karnebeek A 3(2); Kilgannon S 3(7); MacPherson A 22(2); Mason G 33(2); McGarty M (2); McGroarty C 17(5); McLeish K 1(1); N'Diaye S 6(3); Nicholls D 12(11); Nicholson B 36(1); Nish C 2(12); Panopoulos M 7(2); Petrie S 14(9); Potter J 2(2); Rossi Y 9(1); Ruitenbeek M 29; Skerla A 36; Skinner J 18(8); Thomson SM 32; Thomson SY 9.
Goals – League (41): Nicholson 7, Crawford 6, Thomson SM 6 (1 pen), de Gier 5, Bullen 4, Hampshire 3, Mason 3, Petrie 2, Dair 1, N'Diaye 1, Nicholls 1, Skerla 1, own goal 1.
Scottish Cup (3): Crawford 2, Thomson SM 1.
CIS Cup (4): Mason 2, Hampshire 1, Nicholson 1.
Honours – First Division: Champions – 1988-89, 1995-96. **Division II:** Champions – 1925-26. **Second Division:** Champions – 1985-86. **Scottish Cup winners** 1961, 1968.

EAST FIFE   DIV. 3

Ground: Bayview Park, Methil, Fife KY8 3RW (01333) 426323
Ground capacity: 2000 (all seated). **Colours:** Gold and black shirts, white shorts.
Manager: James Moffat.
League Appearances: Allan J 18(15); Bailey L 27(3); Brown S (1); Clyde R 1;
Coulston D 4; Courts C (1); Cunningham G 28(4); Gallagher J 35; Geisler M (1);
Gibson K 24; Gilbert G 3(2); Godfrey R 36; Graham R 12(4); Herkes J 19(11);
Lofting A 2(8); Macdonald A (1); McManus P 32(2); Mortimer P 35; Munro K 33;
Nairn J 13(8); Oliver N 15; Ovenstone J 6(2); Rae J 3(1); Spink D 1(2); Tejero A 1;
Thomson J 12; Wilson W 36.
Goals – League (39): McManus 11, Bailey 5, Cunningham 3, Gibson 3, Mortimer 3,
Allan 2, Gallagher 2, Graham 2, Herkes 2, Gilbert 1, Munro 1, Nairn 1. Oliver 1,
Wilson 1, own goal 1.
Scottish Cup (4): McManus 3, Bailey 1.
CIS Cup (1): McManus 1.
Challenge Cup (2): Graham 1, McManus 1.
Honours – Division II: Champions – 1947-48. **Scottish Cup winners** 1938. **League
Cup winners** 1948, 1950, 1954.

EAST STIRLINGSHIRE   DIV. 3

Ground: Firs Park, Falkirk FK2 7AY (01324) 623583
Ground capacity: 1880. **Colours:** Black shirts with white hoops, black shorts with
white and red stripes.
Head Coach: Danny Diver.
League Appearances: Aitken A (2); Ferguson B 22(2); Gilbert G (1); Gordon K
23(9); Hall M 21(2); Hay D 27; Hunter M 1(8); Kristjansson T 1; Lorimer D 23(5);
Lyle D 16(1); Maughan R 29(3); McAuley S 31(2); McCheyne G 28; McDonald I
25(2); McGhee G 24(2); McKechnie G 16(4); McLaren G 1(4); McLaughlin P 2;
Menelaws D 7; Robertson S 1; Russell G 30; Scott A 19(4); Todd C 8(1); Todd D
24(6); Tolland M 4(2); Ure D 13(5); Wood D (2).
Goals – League (51): Gordon 11 (1 pen), Lyle 10, McKechnie 6, Menelaws 5 (1
pen), Lorimer 3, Ure 3, McAuley 2, McCheyne 2, Maughan 2, Ferguson 1, Hall 1,
McDonald 1, McGhee 1, Scott 1, Todd D 1, own goal 1.
Scottish Cup (2): Lyle 1, McDonald 1.
CIS Cup (0):
Challenge Cup (0):
Honours – Division II: Champions – 1931-32. **C Division:** Champions – 1947-48.

ELGIN CITY   DIV. 3

Ground: Borough Briggs, Elgin IV30 1AP (01343) 551114
Ground capacity: 5000 (478 seated). **Colours:** Black and white vertical stripes, black
shorts.
Manager: Alex Caldwell.
League Appearances: Bremner F 1(1); Campbell C 22(6); Craig D 11(17); Craig R
4(7); Dlugonski B 22; Furphy W 12(1); Gilzean I 33(1); Hamilton G 2; Hind D
23(4); James R 9; Kelly J 12(7); MacDonald J 14(8); MacDonald S 22(1); Mackay
D 8; Mackay S 12; Mailer C 17(2); McBride R 25(1); McGlashan C 11(3); Morrison
M 6; Pirie M 33; Rae D 5(1); Rae M 1; Ross D 28(1); Rutherford R 4(5); Sander-
son M 15(1); Teasdale M 10; Tully C 34.
Goals – League (45): Gilzean 12, Kelly 6 (1 pen), James 4, Tully 4 (1 pen), Camp-
bell 3, Hind 2, Mackay S 2, Ross 2, Craig D 1, Dlugonski 1, McBride 1, MacDonald
S 1, Mailer 1, Rae D 1, Rutherford 1, Sanderson 1, Teasdale 1, own goal 1.
Scottish Cup (0):

CIS Cup (2): Gilzean 1, McGlashan 1.
Challenge Cup (0):

FALKIRK   DIV. 1

Ground: Brockville Park, Falkirk FK1 5AX (01324) 624121
Ground capacity: 9706. **Colours:** Navy blue shirts with white, white shorts.
Manager: Ian McCall.
League Appearances: Brown K 5; Christie K 29; Convery D 3; Craig S 19(10);
Denham G 9; Deuchar K 3(10); Henry J 9; Hill D 5; Hogarth M 31; Kerr M 28(2);
Lawrie A 14; Mair L 19(1); McAllister K 21(7); McQuilken J 35; McStay G 8(9);
Miller L 27; Morris I 18(16); Moss D 3; Murray N 8; Oponga C 3; Pearson C 1(1);
Rennie S 28(2); Rodgers A 4(10); Tano P 4(2); Waddell R 17(12); Watson S 4(2);
Wilkie L 9; Wright P 12(2).
Goals – League (49): Miller 11, Morris 5, Christie 4, Craig 4 (1 pen), Kerr 3, Ren-
nie 3, Waddell 3, Henry 2, Lawrie 2, McQuilken 2, Wilkie 2, Wright 2 (pens),
Brown 1, Deuchar 1, McAllister 1, Rodgers 1, Watson 1, own goal 1.
Scottish Cup (1): Rodgers 1.
CIS Cup (2): Craig 1, Lawrie 1.
Challenge Cup (4): Watson 2 (1 pen), Craig 1, Kerr 1.
Honours – Division II: Champions – 1935-36, 1969-70, 1974-75. **First Division:**
Champions – 1990-91, 1993-94. **Second Division:** Champions – 1979-80. **Scottish
Cup winners** 1913, 1957. **League Challenge Cup winners** 1998.

FORFAR ATHLETIC   DIV. 2

Ground: Station Park, Forfar, Angus (01307) 463576
Ground capacity: 4640. **Colours:** Sky blue shirts with navy flashes, navy shorts.
Manager: Neil Cooper.
League Appearances: Bett C 8; Bowman D 11(1); Brown M 36; Byers K 34(1);
Christie S 12(19); Donaldson E 10(5); Farnan C 1(8); Good I 26; Henry J 18(4);
Horn R 20(1); Lunan P 16(9); Mallan S 3; McCloy B 25(1); McCulloch S 9; Milne
K 23(1); Moffat B 17(8); Morris R 12(7); Rattray A 29; Sellars B 24; Stewart W
22(10); Taylor S 1(3); Tosh P 30; Walker D (3); Williams D 5(7); Yardley M 4.
Goals – League (51): Tosh 19 (2 pens), Byers 9, Christie 5, Sellars 5, Moffat 3,
Stewart 3, Yardley 3, Horn 1, McCulloch 1, own goals 3.
Scottish Cup (9): Sellars 3, Tosh 3, Byers 2, Yardley 1.
CIS Cup (1): Tosh 1.
Challenge Cup (2): Moffat 1, own goal 1
Honours – Second Division: Champions – 1983-84. **Third Division:** Champions –
1994-95.

HAMILTON ACADEMICAL   DIV. 2

Ground: New Douglas Park, Cadzow Avenue, Hamilton ML3 0FT (01698) 286103
Ground capacity: 5330. **Colours:** Red and white hooped shirts, white shorts.
Manager: Ally Dawson
League Appearances: Armstrong G 5(2); Bonnar M 26(1); Callaghan S 32; Cun-
nington E 19; Davidson S (1); Elfallah M 1(3); Gaughan P 17(1); Goram A 1; Gra-
ham A 25(7); Herbet M 5; Kwik Ajet W 2(3); Lurinsky A 1(2); MacLaren R 11(4);
Macfarlane I 14; Martin M 18(5); McCreadie I 6(1); McDonald P 15(4); McFarlane
D 12(4); McLaughlin S (2); McNiven D 25(1); McPhee B 15(2); Miller D (1);
Moore M 25(5); Nelson M 27(4); Nicholls M 2; O'Neil K 3(13); Potter G 14(3);
Renicks S 29(1); Russell A 7(5); Sherry J 13(3); Stewart C 2; Sweeney S 24(2);
Walker J (3).

Goals – League (49): Moore 12, Callaghan 7 (1 pen), McFarlane D 7, McNiven 6, Bonnar 3, McPhee 3, Martin 2, Nicholls 2, Armstrong 1, Gaughan 1, Graham 1, Russell 1, Sherry 1, Sweeney 1, own goal 1.
Scottish Cup (5): McPhee 2, Callaghan 1, McFarlane D 1, McNiven 1.
CIS Cup (1): Moore 1
Challenge Cup (0):
Honours – First Division: Champions – 1985-86, 1987-88. **Divison II:** Champions – 1903-04. **Division III:** Champions – 2000-01. **B&Q Cup winners** 1992, 1993.

HEART OF MIDLOTHIAN   PREMIER LEAGUE

Ground: Tynecastle Park, Gorgie Road, Edinburgh EH11 2NL (0131) 200 7200
Ground capacity: 18,000. **Colours:** Maroon shirts, white shorts.
Manager: Craig Levein.
League Appearances: Adam S 12(7); Boyack S 6(13); Cameron C 4; Davidson R (2); Flögel T 29(3); Fuller S 27; Fulton S 27(8); Grönlund T 22(1); Hamill J 1(2); Juanjo 5(4); Kirk A 4(16); Mahe S 35; Maybury A 27; McCann A 4(2); McKenna K 31(2); McKenzie R 6; McMullan P 1(); McSwegan G 1(4); Milne K 3(1); Neilson R 2; Niemi A 32; Pressley S 30; Severin S 24(3); Simmons S 24(9); Sloan R 4(2); Tod A 3; Tomaschek R 6(1); Wales G 21(11); Webster A 25(2); Weir G 3(6).
Goals – League (52): McKenna 9, Fuller 8, Wales 6, Simmons 5 (2 pens), Adam 3, Cameron 3, Fulton 3 (1 pen), Severin 3, Grönlund 2, Juanjo 2, Mahe 2, Pressley 2 (pens), Kirk 1, Sloan 1, Tod 1, Webster 1.
Scottish Cup (3): Fuller 2, Wales 1.
CIS Cup (0):
Honours – Division I: Champions – 1894-95, 1896-97, 1957-58, 1959-60. **First Division:** Champions – 1979-80. **Scottish Cup winners** 1891, 1896, 1901, 1906, 1956, 1998. **League Cup winners** 1955, 1959, 1960, 1963.

HIBERNIAN   PREMIER LEAGUE

Ground: Easter Road Stadium, Edinburgh EH7 5QG (0131) 661 2159
Ground capacity: 17,500. **Colours:** Green shirts with white sleeves and collar, white shorts with green stripe.
Manager: Bobby Williamson.
League Appearances: Andrews L (?); Arpinon F 16(4); Brebner G 23(5); Brewster C 23(2); Caig A 8; Caldwell G 10(1); Colgan N 30; Daquin F 1(1); de la Cruz U 25(7); Dempsie A 2(1); Fenwick P 22; Hilland P 3; Hurtado E 4(8); Jack M 28(3); Laursen U 23(1); Luna F 16(9); Martin L 1; McManus T 14(7); Murray I 30(2); Nicol K 2(); O'Connor G 14(5); O'Neill J 32; Orman A 30; Reid A (2); Riordan D 1(5); Sauzee F 10; Smart A 2(3); Smith G 30; Townsley D 7(11); Whittaker S (1); Wiss J 6(5); Zitelli D 7(14).
Goals – League (51): O'Connor 10, Luna 7, Townsley 5, Sauzee 4 (3 pens), Brewster 3, Fenwick 3, McManus 3, O'Neil 3, Arpinon 2, Brebner 2, de la Cruz 2, Murray 2, Hurtado 1, Laursen 1, Orman 1, Smart 1, own goal 1.
Scottish Cup (5): Brebner 1, Hurtado 1, Luna 1, Smith 1, Zitelli 1.
CIS Cup (4): Brewster 2, Luna 1, McManus 1.
Honours – Division I: Champions – 1902-03, 1947-48, 1950-51, 1951-52. **First Division:** Champions – 1980-81, 1998-99. **Division II:** Champions – 1893-94, 1894-95, 1932-33. **Scottish Cup winners** 1887, 1902. **League Cup winners** 1973, 1992.

INVERNESS CALEDONIAN THISTLE   DIV. 1

Ground: Caledonian Stadium, East Longman, Inverness IV1 1FF (01463) 222880
Ground capacity: 6500. **Colours:** Royal blue shirts with red stripes, royal blue shorts.
Manager: Steven W. Paterson.

League Appearances: Bagan D 10(7); Bavidge M 23(11); Bradshaw P 2; Calder J 9(1); Christie C 30(3); Duncan R 25(6); Golabek S 5(10); Macdonald N (11); Mann R 34; McBain R 33; McCaffrey S 32; Munro G 18; Ritchie P 29(5); Robson B 33(1); Stewart G 3(17); Teasdale M 14(3); Tokely R 34; Walker J 27; Wyness D 35(1).
Goals – League (60): Wyness 18, Ritchie 15, Mann 7 (3 pens), Bavidge 4, Tokely 3, Bagan 2, Christie 2, McBain 2, Robson 2, Duncan 1, Macdonald 1, Munro 1, Stewart 1, own goal 1.
Scottish Cup (7): Wyness 3, Bagan 1, Ritchie 1, Robson 1, Tokely 1.
CIS Cup (7): Ritchie 2, Robson 2, Bavidge 1, Teasdale 1, Tokely 1.
Challenge Cup (5): Ritchie 2, Bavidge 1, Christie 1, Wyness 1.
Honours – Third Division: Champions – 1996-97.

KILMARNOCK   PREMIER LEAGUE

Ground: Rugby Park, Kilmarnock KA1 2DP (01563) 525184
Ground capacity: 18,128. **Colours:** Blue and white striped shirts, white shorts.
Manager: Jim Jefferies.
League Appearances: Baker M 6; Boyd K 11(17); Calderon A 9(8); Canero P 31(1); Canning M (1); Cocard C 4(6); Dargo C 25(4); Di Giacomo P 15(8); Dillon S 1(1); Dindeleux F 27; Durrant I (1); Fowler J 22(7); Hay G 26; Hessey S 13(2); Innes C 20; Jaconelli E (3); Johnson T 7(3); Mahood A 33; Marshall G 36; McCutcheon G 2(1); McDonald G 1(5); McGowne K 22; McLaren A 13(15); Meldrum C 2(1); Mitchell A 33(1); Murray S 16(3); Ngonge M 7(2); Pizzo M 10(3); Reilly M (1); Sanjuan J 18(2); Shields G 5; Vareille J 3.
Goals – League (44): Johnson 7 (1 pen), Dargo 6, Boyd 4, McLaren 4, Di Giacomo 3, Mitchell 3, Ngonge 3, McGowne 2, Mahood 2, Murray 2, Calderon 1, Canero 1, Cocard 1, Dindeleux 1, Innes 1, Pizzo 1, own goals 2.
Scottish Cup (3): Canero 1, Mitchell 1, Sanjuan 1.
CIS Cup (0):
Honours – Division I: Champions – 1964-65. **Division II:** Champions – 1897-98, 1898-99. **Scottish Cup winners** 1920, 1929, 1997.

LIVINGSTON   PREMIER LEAGUE

Ground: Almondvale Stadium, Livingston EH54 7DN (01506) 417 000
Ground capacity: 10,024. **Colours:** Gold shirts with black and white trim, black shorts with gold and white trim.
Manager: Jim Leishman.
League Appearances: Anderson J 10(1); Andrews M 35; Aurellio D 5(9); Bingham D 31(6); Bollan G 20(1); Brinquin P 23; Brittain R (2); Broto J 17; Caputo M 4(17); Culkin N 21; Deas P 1; Del Nero S (1); Fernandez D 30(3); Hart M 14(7); Jokovic N (3); Keith M (1); Lovell S 26(1); Lowndes N 7(14); Makel L 9(4); McCulloch M (2); McEwan D (1); Petersen M 2(1); Quino F 34(2); Rubio O 33; Santini D 21; Tosh S 21(10); Toure-Mamman C 3(6); Wilson B 32(5); Xausa D 19(9).
Goals – League (50): Wilson 9 (1 pen), Quino 8, Xausa 7, Bingham 6, Fernandez 6, Andrews 3, Lovell 3, Lowndes 3, Tosh 2, Aurellio 1 (pen), Brinquin 1, Rubio 1.
Scottish Cup (4): Bingham 2, Fernandez 1, Wilson 1.
CIS Cup (9): Caputo 4, Wilson 2, Bingham 1, Lovell 1, Tosh 1.
Honours – First Division: Champions – 2000-01. **Second Division:** Champions – 1986-87, 1998-99. **Third Division:** Champions – 1995-96.

MONTROSE   DIV. 3

Ground: Links Park, Montrose DD10 8QD (01674) 673200
Ground capacity: 3292. **Colours:** Royal blue shirts and shorts.
Manager: Kevin Drinkell.

League Appearances: Allison J 26(5); Brand R 22(4); Butter J 4; Christie G 33; Conway F 20(1); Craib M 10(1); Craig D 26(3); Ferguson S 34(2); Hutcheon A 3(23); Johnson G 31; Kerrigan S 23(2); Laidlaw S 18(14); Leask M 6(1); Lowe B 1(6); Magee K 5(4); McGlynn G 32(2); McKellar J 12(11); McKinnon R 21; McQuillan J 27; Mitchell J 6(13); Muirhead D 1(1); Sharp G (1); Sharp R 25; Stewart S 4; Thomas K 3; Webster K 1; Yates M 2(2).
Goals – League (43): Laidlaw 13 (1 pen), Kerrigan 7, Conway 3, Ferguson 3, Brand 2, Christie 2, Johnson 2, McKellar 2, McKinnon 2, Sharp R 2, Allison 1, Leask 1, Magee 1, Mitchell 1, Stewart 1.
Scottish Cup (4): Laidlaw 3 (1 pen), Lowe 1
CIS Cup (0):
Challenge Cup (0):
Honours – Second Division: Champions – 1984-85.

MORTON   DIV. 3

Ground: Cappielow Park, Greenock (01475) 723571
Ground capacity: 14,891. **Colours:** Royal blue and white hooped shirts, white shorts with royal blue panel down side.
Manager: Dave McPherson.
League Appearances: Aitken C 7(12); Bannerman S 31; Bottiglieri E 15(11); Cannie P 8; Carmichael D 1(3); Collins D 32; Compston M (2); Correia A 1(1); Coyle C 33; Curran S 9(1); Frail S 24; Gibson J 14(8); Greacen S 15; Hawke W 19; Kearney D 2(4); Kerr D 21(1); MacGregor D 32; Maisano M 11; Mapes C 1(1); McAneny P 5; McMillan A (2); McPherson D 16; Miller S 16(4); Moffat C 2(1); Moore A 11(4); O'Connor S 20(1); Redmond G 2(16); Reid A 9; Renwick M 2; Riddle S 1(3); Ross K 3(1); Tweedie G 19(12); Votinen J 1; Wright P 13.
Goals – League (48): Bannerman 8 (2 pens), O'Connor 8, Tweedie 5, McPherson 4, Miller 4 (1 pen), Wright 4 (1 pen), Bottiglieri 2, Cannie 2, Hawke 2, Kerr 2, Reid 2, Aitken 1, Gibson 1, Moore 1, Redmond 1, Votinen 1.
Scottish Cup (1): Aitken 1.
CIS Cup (0):
Challenge Cup (1): O'Connor 1.
Honours – First Division: Champions – 1977-78, 1983-84, 1986-87. **Division II:** Champions – 1949-50, 1963-64, 1966-67. **Second Division:** Champions – 1994-95.
Scottish Cup winners 1922.

MOTHERWELL   PREMIER LEAGUE

Ground: Fir Park, Motherwell ML1 2QN (01698) 333333
Ground capacity: 13,742. **Colours:** Amber shirts with claret hoop and trim, white shorts.
Manager: Terry Butcher.
League Appearances: Adams D 19(9); Bernhard F 2(1); Brown M 19; Clarke D (1); Clarkson D (1); Corrigan M 26(4); Cosgrove S (2); Deloumeaux E 22(1); Dow A 7(2); Dubourdeau F 4; Elliott S 30(7); Fagan S (2); Ferrere D 7(2); Forrest E 9(5); Hammell S 37(1); Harvey P (2); Kelly D 19; Kinniburgh W 1; Lasley K 25(3); Lehmann D 10(1); Leitch S 26; MacDonald K (1); Martinez R 8(9); McFadden J 20(4); Nicholas S 5(11); Pearson S 19(8); Ramsay D 2; Ready K 35(1); Soloy Y 11(1); Strong G 31(1); Tarrant N 2(3); Twaddle K 7(5); Woods S 15(1).
Goals – League (49): Elliott 10, McFadden 10 (1 pen), Kelly 6 (3 pens), Lehmann 4, Ferrere 3, Ready 3, Adams 2, Lasley 2, Nicholas 2, Pearson 2, Strong 2, Dow 1, Hammell 1, Soloy 1.
Scottish Cup (1): Elliott 1.
CIS Cup (1): Kelly 1.
Honours – Division I: Champions – 1931-32. **First Division:** Champions – 1981-82, 1984-85. **Division II:** Champions – 1953-54, 1968-69. **Scottish Cup winners** 1952, 1991. **League Cup winners** 1951.

PARTICK THISTLE   PREMIER LEAGUE

Ground: Firhill Park, Glasgow G20 7AL (0141) 579 1971
Ground capacity: 14,538. **Colours:** Red and yellow striped shirts, red shorts.
Manager: John Lambie.
League Appearances: Archibald A 31(2); Arthur K 22(1); Britton G 24(9); Budin-auckas K 4; Burns A 13; Cameron M 6(2); Connaghan D 8; Constantine L 2; Craigan S 31(1); Deas P 25; Dolan J 19(7); Elliot B 2(6); Fleming D 24(5); Gibson A 1(3); Gow G 5; Hardie M 22(9); Howie W (2); Huxford R 2(4); Javary J (1); Kelly P 9(1), Klein D 5; Lennon D 32(3); Lyle D (2); McAnespie S (1); McCulloch M 14(2); McDowell M (4); McKinstry J 21(2); McLean S 23(6); Nicholls M 1; Paterson S 36; Roddie A 1(2); Smith J (1); Walker P 12(16); Watson S 1.
Goals – League (61): Britton 12 (2 pens), Hardie 11, McLean 9 (1 pen), Fleming 7, Burns 4, Lennon 4, Walker 4, Archibald 2, Dolan 2, McKinstry 2, Cameron 1, Elliot 1, McCulloch 1, own goal 1.
Scottish Cup (10): Hardie 2, McLean 2, Paterson 2, Walker 2, Britton 1, Gibson 1.
CIS Cup (6): Lennon 2, McLean 2, Hardie 1, McDowell 1
Challenge Cup (10): Britton 2, Fleming 2, Hardie 2, Lennon 2, McCallum 1, McDowell 1.
Honours – First Division: Champions – 1975-76, 2001-02. **Division II:** Champions – 1896-97, 1899-1900, 1970-71. **Second Division:** Champions 2000-01. **Scottish Cup winners** 1921. **League Cup winners** 1972.

PETERHEAD   DIV. 3

Ground: Balmoor Stadium, Peterhead AB42 1EU (01779) 478256
Ground capacity: 3250 (1000 seated). **Colours:** Royal blue with white shirts, royal blue shorts.
Manager: Ian Wilson.
League Appearances: Bisset K 11(16); Brown S 1; Buchanan R 1; Canning M 21; Clark G (3); Clark S 19(6); Cooper C 21(4); Duffy J 2(3); Findlay C 5(9); Johnston M 29(6); King S 24(4); Livingstone B 24(5); Mackay S 32(3); Marrs V (1); Mathers P 10; McQuade J 4; McSkimming S 4(5); Murray I (1); Pirie I 25; Rennie K (1); Robertson K 7(3); Simpson M 33; Slater M 6(1); Smith G 28(1); Stewart I 32(1); Tindal K 33; Wood M 7(1); Yeats C 17(14).
Goals – League (63): Stewart 19 (2 pens), Johnston 18, Yeats 5, Tindal 4, Cooper 3 (2 pens), Mackay 3, Robertson 3, Bisset 2, Wood 2, Clark S 1, Findlay 1, Livingstone 1, McSkimming 1.
Scottish Cup (0):
CIS Cup (0):
Challenge Cup (2): Stewart 2.

QUEEN OF THE SOUTH   DIV. 1

Ground: Palmerston Park, Dumfries DG2 9BA (01387) 254853
Ground capacity: 8352. **Colours:** Royal blue shirts with white sleeves, white shorts with blue piping.
Manager: John Connolly.
League Appearances: Aitken A 25(1); Allan D 11(2); Anderson D 15(1); Armstrong G (2), Atkinson P 23(4); Bowey S 5(3); Burns G (1); Campbell J 3(1); Connell G 26(6); Connelly G 27(4); Connolly S (2); Crawford J 16(3); Davidson S 7(9); Dawson S (1); Donald B 6(5); Feroz C 8; Glancy M 2(1); Gray A 34(1); Hawke W 6; Hogg A (3); Hollier P (3); Lyle D 13; McAlpine J 27(3); McDowell M 2; McGhie G (1); McKeown D 2(1); McMahon D (1); Moore A 2(10); O'Boyle G 7; O'Connor S 4(4); O'Neil J 27(5); Patterson M 1(1); Poston T 1; Scott C 33; Sunderland J 2(6); Thomson J 32(1); Walker L (2); Weatherson P 26(7).

Goals – League (64): O'Neil 19 (7 pens), Weatherson 15, Lyle 6, McAlpine 6, Atkinson 3, O'Boyle 3, O'Connor 3, Davidson 2, Bowey 1, Connelly 1, Feroz 1, Gray 1, Moore 1, own goals 2.
Scottish Cup (2): O'Neil 2.
CIS Cup (4): Feroz 4.
Challenge Cup (0):
Honours – Division II: Champions – 1950-51. **Second Division:** Champions – 2001-02

QUEEN'S PARK   DIV. 3

Ground: Hampden Park, Glasgow G42 9BA (0141) 632 1275
Ground capacity: 52,000. **Colours:** Black and white hooped shirts, white shorts.
Coach/Player: John McCormack.
League Appearances: Borland P 21; Brown J 7(11); Bruce J 11(1); Canning S 27(9); Carberry A 2(1); Caven R 16; Clark R (2); Collins N 28; Cunningham J 7(1); Dunning A 7(4); Ewing C 5(2); Ferry D 26(1); Fisher C 6(10); Gallagher M 10(2); Gallagher P 4(3); Gemmell J 7(5); Jackson R 18(11); Marshall S 22(2); Martin W 9(16); McPhee G 2(2); McVey W 6(1); Miller B 2(4); Miller G 7(1); Miller K 3; Mitchell A 12; Orr S 1(3); Patterson P 9(5); Proudfoot K 2(1); Quinn A 33(2); Rae D 5(1); Sinclair R 11(1); Smith G 24; Stevenson C 18; Whelan J 21; White J 7.
Goals – League (38): Canning 5, Jackson 5, Whelan 4 (1 pen), Fisher 3, Gemmell 3, Quinn 3, Martin 3, Caven 2 (pens), Dunning 2, Gallagher M 2, Marshall 2, Ferry 1, Miller G 1, Proudfoot 1, own goal 1.
Scottish Cup (2): Jackson 2.
CIS Cup (0):
Challenge Cup (0):
Honours – Division II: Champions – 1922-23. **B Division:** Champions – 1955-56. **Second Division:** Champions – 1980-81. **Third Division:** Champions – 1999-2000. **Scottish Cup winners** 1874, 1875, 1876, 1880, 1881, 1882, 1884, 1886, 1890, 1893.

RAITH ROVERS   DIV. 2

Ground: Stark's Park, Pratt Street, Kirkcaldy KY1 1SA (01592) 263514
Ground capacity: 10,104 (all seated). **Colours:** Navy blue shirts with white trim, white shorts with navy blue edges.
Manager: Antonio Calderon.
League Appearances: Browne P 34(1); Clark A 1(11); Clark J 1(2); Crabbe S 11; Davidson H 10(1); Dennis S 26; Ellis L 19(2); Hampshire P 4(3); Henderson D 28(1); Henderson R 8; Javary P 8; Jones M 8(7); Matheson R 13(2); McCulloch G 25(1); McGarty M 3(5); Millar M 8; Miller J 2(3); Miller W 3; Miotto S 9; Monin S 27; Nanou W 13(9); Novo I 33; O'Boyle G 2(3); Quesada A 14(3); Rivas F 14(1); Smith A 32; Stein J 22(6); Zoco J 18(1).
Goals – League (50): Novo 19 (3 pens), Smith A 11, Crabbe 6, Henderson D 3, Dennis 2, Jones 2, Stein 2 (1 pen), Clark A 1, Davidson H 1, Miller J 1, Quesada 1, Rivas 1.
Scottish Cup (0):
CIS Cup (3): Henderson D 1, Novo 1, Smith A 1.
Challenge Cup (6): Novo 3, Dennis 1, Matheson 1, Zoco 1.
Honours – First Division: Champions – 1992-93, 1994-95. **Division II:** Champions – 1907-08, 1909-10 (Shared), 1937-38, 1948-49. **League Cup winners** 1995.

RANGERS   PREMIER LEAGUE

Ground: Ibrox Stadium, Glasgow G51 2XD (0870) 600 1972
Ground capacity: 50,444. **Colours:** Royal blue shirts with red and white trim and red piping at front, white shorts with royal blue trim.
Manager: Alex McLeish.

League Appearances: Amoruso L 28; Arveladze S 21(1); Ball M 5(2); Brighton T 1; Burke C 1(1); Caniggia C 16(7); Christiansen J (1); de Boer R 19(5); Dodds W 5(6); Dowie A (1); Ferguson B 21(1); Flo T 25(5); Gibson J (1); Hughes S 12(5); Johnston A 1; Kanchelskis A 6(4); Klos S 36; Konterman B 26; Latapy R 14(2); Lovenkrands P 10(8); Malcolm R 6(1); McCann N 13(12); McGregor A 2; Miller K (3); Mols M 8(7); Moore C 18; Nerlinger C 7(1); Numan A 28(2); Penttila T (1); Reyna C 10; Ricksen F 31; Ross M 19(2); Vidmar T 23(2); Wilson S 6.
Goals – League (82): Flo 17, Arveladze 11, de Boer 7, McCann 7, Caniggia 5, Latapy 5, Amoruso 4, Ricksen 4, Konterman 3, Mols 3, Moore 3, Dodds 2, Lovenkrands 2, Reyna 2, Burke 1, Ferguson 1, Kanchelskis 1, Nerlinger 1, Numan 1, Vidmar 1, own goal 1.
Scottish Cup (19): Dodds 4, Arveladze 3, Lovenkrands 3, Ferguson 2, Flo 2, Nerlinger 2, Amoruso 1, Kanchelskis 1, Konterman 1.
CIS Cup (11): Arveladze 3, Caniggia 2, Ferguson 1 (pen), Flo 1, Konterman 1, Lovenkrands 1, Numan 1, Reyna 1.
Honours – Division I: Champions – 1890-91 (Shared), 1898-99, 1899-1900, 1900-01, 1901-02, 1910-11, 1911-12, 1912-13, 1917-18, 1919-20, 1920-21, 1922-23, 1923-24, 1924-25, 1926-27, 1927-28, 1928-29, 1929-30, 1930-31, 1932-33, 1933-34, 1934-35, 1936-37, 1938-39, 1946-47, 1948-49, 1949-50, 1952-53, 1955-56, 1956-57, 1958-59, 1960-61, 1962-63, 1963-64, 1974-75. **Premier Division:** Champions – 1975-76, 1977-78, 1986-87, 1988-89, 1989-90, 1990-91, 1991-92, 1992-93, 1993-94, 1994-95, 1995-96, 1996-97. **Premier League:** Champions – 1998-99, 1999-2000. **Scottish Cup winners** 1894, 1897, 1898, 1903, 1928, 1930, 1932, 1934, 1935, 1936, 1948, 1949, 1950, 1953, 1960, 1962, 1963, 1964, 1966, 1973, 1976, 1978, 1979, 1981, 1992, 1993, 1996, 1999, 2000, 2002. **League Cup winners** 1947, 1949, 1961, 1962, 1964, 1965, 1971, 1976, 1978, 1979, 1982, 1984, 1985, 1987, 1988, 1989, 1991, 1993, 1994, 1997, 1999, 2002. **European Cup-Winners' Cup winners** 1972.

ROSS COUNTY   DIV. 1

Ground: Victoria Park, Dingwall IV15 9QW (01349) 860860
Ground capacity: 6700. **Colours:** Navy blue, white and red.
Manager: Neale Cooper.
League Appearances: Anselin C 7(4); Blackley D (1); Bone A 27(4); Boukraa K 10(6); Bullock A 33; Campbell C (2); Canning M 7; Cowie D 14(4); Dlugonski B 3; Ferguson S 26(2); Fraser J 4; Fridge L 1; Gethins C 11(13); Gilbert K 15; Gonzales R 2(1); Hastings R 26(2); Hislop S 29(4); Holmes D 2(1); Irvine B 29(1); Jack D (1); Kuyper N (1); Lilley D 5(1); MacDonald K (1); Mackay S 3(10); Maxwell I 35; McCormick M 11(9); McQuade J 5(2); Perry M 36; Prest M 2(6); Robertson H 36; Tarrant N 2(5); Webb S 15(4).
Goals – League (51): Hislop 14, Bone 9 (2 pens), Gethins 6, Robertson 6, Ferguson 4, McCormick 3, Boukraa 2, Irvine 2, Campbell 1, Gilbert 1, Prest 1, own goals 2.
Scottish Cup (1): Perry 1.
CIS Cup (6): Bone 2, Boukraa 2, Irvine 1, Mackay 1.
Challenge Cup (4): Hislop 3, McQuade 1.
Honours – Third Division: Champions – 1998-99.

ST JOHNSTONE   DIV. 1

Ground: McDiarmid Park, Crieff Road, Perth PH1 2SJ (01738) 459090
Ground capacity: 10,673. **Colours:** Royal blue shirts with white trim, white shorts.
Manager: Billy Stark.
League Appearances: Connolly P 21(8); Cuthbert K 11(1); Dasovic N 22(2); Djebaili R 4(9); Dods D 32; Falconer W 16(9); Ferry M (2); Forsyth R 15(1); Fotheringham M 2(4); Hartley P 32; Jackson D 6(3); Jones G 7(6); Kane P 15; Kemble B 14; Lovenkrands T 28(1); Lynch M 20; MacDonald P 12(16); Maher M 4(6); Main A 7; McBride J 15(6); McClune D 5(2); McCluskey S 19(4); McCulloch M 4(2);

Miller A 18; Murray G 38; Panther E 5(2); Parker K 14(7); Roy L 2; Russell C 7(6); Sylla M 1; Weir J 17; Youssouf S 5.
Goals – League (24): Hartley 5, Falconer 3, MacDonald 3, Dods 2, Lovenkrands 2, Connolly 1, Jackson 1 (pen), Jones 1, McBride 1 (pen), Murray 1, Parker 1, Russell 1, Weir 1, Youssouf 1.
Scottish Cup (0):
CIS Cup (4): MacDonald 2, Dods 1, Hartley 1.
Honours – First Division: Champions – 1982-83, 1989-90, 1996-97. **Division II:** Champions – 1923-24, 1959-60, 1962-63.

ST MIRREN   DIV. 1

Ground: St Mirren Park, Paisley PA3 2EJ (0141) 889 2558, 840 1337
Ground capacity: 10,866 (all seated). **Colours:** Black and white striped shirts, shorts white with black trim.
Manager: Tom Hendrie.
League Appearances: Baltacha S 9(4); Bowman G 17(2); Burns A 16(6); Dempster J (1); Gillies R 27(4); Guy G (1); Hillcoat J 9; Keogh L (1); Kerr C 11(5); Lapping S (1); Lowing D 2; Mackenzie S 26(2); McCann R (1); McGarry S 11(10); McGinty B 20(1); McGowan J 24; McKnight P 6(8); McLaughlin B 31; Murray H 27(5); Nicolson I 17(6); Quitongo J 33(1); Robertson K 1(2); Robinson R (1); Ross I 23(2); Roy L 25; Rudden P 2(5); Strang S 1; Turner T 8(1); Walker S 34; Wreh C (5); Yardley M 16(7).
Goals – League (43): Gillies 6 (3 pens), McGinty 6 (2 pens), McLaughlin 5, Quitongo 5, Ross 5, Yardley 4, Walker 3, Nicolson 2, McGarry 2, Baltacha 1, Burns 1, Kerr 1, McGowan 1, own goal 1.
Scottish Cup (0):
CIS Cup (1): Quitongo 1.
Challenge Cup (1): Yardley 1.
Honours – First Division: Champions – 1976-77, 1999-2000.
Division II: Champions – 1967-68. **Scottish Cup winners** 1926, 1959, 1987.

STENHOUSEMUIR   DIV. 2

Ground: Ochilview Park, Stenhousemuir FK5 5QL (01324) 562992
Ground capacity: 2374. **Colours:** Maroon shirts, white shorts.
Manager: John McVeigh.
League Appearances: Abbott G 8(1); Black G (1); Carlin A 17; Clyde R 1(1); Connaghan D 4; Cormack P 13(3); Davidson G 10; Dick J 1; Donald B 4(7); Donald G 20(3); Donaldson E 13(2); English I 25(6); Ferguson I 24; Forrest F 2(1); Graham D 16(9); Graham M 10; Grant M 4(2); Harvey P 2(1); Irvine W 11(11); Jackson C 32; Jarvie P 5; McGurk R 4; McKeown D 25; Miller P (3); Milne D 20(1); Mooney M 11(6); Murphy S 3(2); Sandison J 8(1); Shanks P 1(1); Shearer G (4); Stone M 35; Storrar A 27(6); Taggart C (2); Vella S 10(2); Wilson M 15; Wood C 15(6).
Goals – League (33): Irvine 7 (5 pens), English 6, Ferguson 6 (1 pen), Donald G 5, Graham D 2, Mooney 2, Jackson 1, Milne 1, Stone 1, Storrar 1, Wood 1.
Scottish Cup (0):
CIS Cup (2): Abbott 1, Ferguson 1.
Challenge Cup (1): Mooney 1.
Honours – League Challenge Cup: Winners – 1996.

STIRLING ALBION   DIV. 3

Ground: Forthbank Stadium, Springkerse Industrial Estate, Stirling FK7 7UJ (01786) 450399
Ground capacity: 3808. **Colours:** Red and white halved shirts, shorts red with white piping.
Player Coach: Allan Moore.

League Appearances: Bailey L (1); Beveridge R 1(1); Brannigan K 19; Butler D 3(1); Cosgrove S 9(1); Cremin B 2(3); Crozier B 13; Davies D 1; De Gregorio R 1; Devine S 24(1); Edwards C 4(2); Geraghty M 24(2); Goldie D 12; Hay P 29(3); Heighton H 3; Henderson N 14; Higgins G 9(4); Hutchison S 3(2); Kearney D 9(1); Kelly G 2(2); McCallion K 13(9); McLellan K 21(5); Middleton G 2; Moriarty T 13; Morrison G 16(3); Munro G 11(12); Nugent P 22; O'Brien D 9(3); Raeside R 6; Reid C 33; Reilly S 27; Ross D 4(19); Stuart W 6(11); Williams A 29(3); Wilson D (1); Zujovic G 2(1).
Goals – League (45): Williams 17 (1 pen), Geraghty 6. Devine 5, Henderson 4 (2 pens), Higgins 3, Ross 3, Brannigan 1, Cremin 1, Crozier 1, Goldie 1, Hay 1, Nugent 1, own goal 1.
Scottish Cup (2): Munro 1, Williams 1.
CIS Cup (5): Williams 4, Munro 1.
Challenge Cup (1): Henderson 1.
Honours – Division II: Champions – 1952-53, 1957-58, 1960-61, 1964-65. **Second Division:** Champions – 1976-77, 1990-91, 1995-96.

STRANRAER   DIV. 2

Ground: Stair Park, Stranraer DG9 8BS (01776) 703271
Ground capacity: 5600. **Colours:** Blue shirts with white side panels, blue shorts with white side panels.
Manager: Billy McLaren.
League Appearances: Aitken S 36; Blair P 11(10); Bradford J 3; Dempster J 3(2); Duthie M 2; Farrell D 21(2); Finlayson K 24(6); Gallagher M 2(6); Gallagher P 0(2); Gaughan K 15(4); George D 3(3); Glancy M 5(1); Grace A 16(5); Harty I 28(2); Hodge A 21(3); Jenkins A 13(11); Johnstone D 8; Kerr P 2; Macdonald W 32; McGeown M 35; O'Neill S (1); Paterson A 10(3); Rodosthenous M (1); Shaw G 27(2); Sherry M 1(1); Stewart C 1; Stirling J 11(2); Weir M 1(7); Wingate D 34; Wright F 31(2).
Goals – League (48): Harty 16 (3 pens), Finlayson 7, Shaw 4, Wright 4, Aitken 3, Grace 2, Kerr 2, Wingate 2, Blair 1, Bradford 1, Farrell 1, Gaughan 1, Hodge 1, Jenkins 1, Macdonald 1, own goal 1.
Scottish Cup (1): Harty 1.
CIS Cup (3): Finlayson 1, Harty 1, Shaw 1.
Challenge Cup (10): Gallagher M 3, Wright 2, Finlayson 1, Gaughan 1, Harty 1, Jenkins 1, Johnstone 1.
Honours – Second Division: Champions – 1993-94, 1997-98. **League Challenge Cup winners** 1997.

GRETNA   DIV. 3

Ground: Raydale Park, Gretna DG16 5AP (01461) 337602
Ground capacity: 2200.
Manager: Rowan Alexander.

SCOTTISH LEAGUE HONOURS

*On goal average (ratio)/difference. †Held jointly after indecisive play-off.
‡Won on deciding match. ††Held jointly. ¶Two points deducted for fielding
ineligible player. Competition suspended 1940–45 during war; Regional Leagues
operating. ‡‡Two points deducted for registration irregularities.

PREMIER LEAGUE
Maximum points: 108

	First	Pts	Second	Pts	Third	Pts
1998–99	Rangers	77	Celtic	71	St Johnstone	57
1999–00	Rangers	90	Celtic	69	Hearts	54

Maximum points: 114

2000–01	Celtic	97	Rangers	82	Hibernian	66
2001–02	Celtic	103	Rangers	85	Livingston	58

PREMIER DIVISION
Maximum points: 72

1975–76	Rangers	54	Celtic	48	Hibernian	43
1976–77	Celtic	55	Rangers	46	Aberdeen	43
1977–78	Rangers	55	Aberdeen	53	Dundee U	40
1978–79	Celtic	48	Rangers	45	Dundee U	44
1979–80	Aberdeen	48	Celtic	47	St Mirren	42
1980–81	Celtic	56	Aberdeen	49	Rangers*	44
1981–82	Celtic	55	Aberdeen	53	Rangers	43
1982–83	Dundee U	56	Celtic*	55	Aberdeen	55
1983–84	Aberdeen	57	Celtic	50	Dundee U	47
1984–85	Aberdeen	59	Celtic	52	Dundee U	47
1985–86	Celtic*	50	Hearts	50	Dundee U	47

Maximum points: 88

1986–87	Rangers	69	Celtic	63	Dundee U	60
1987–88	Celtic	72	Hearts	62	Rangers	60

Maximum points: 72

1988–89	Rangers	56	Aberdeen	50	Celtic	46
1989–90	Rangers	51	Aberdeen*	44	Hearts	44
1990–91	Rangers	55	Aberdeen	53	Celtic*	41

Maximum points: 88

1991–92	Rangers	72	Hearts	63	Celtic	62
1992–93	Rangers	73	Aberdeen	64	Celtic	60
1993–94	Rangers	58	Aberdeen	55	Motherwell	54

Maximum points: 108

1994–95	Rangers	69	Motherwell	54	Hibernian	53
1995–96	Rangers	87	Celtic	83	Aberdeen*	55
1996–97	Rangers	80	Celtic	75	Dundee U	60
1997–98	Celtic	74	Rangers	72	Hearts	67

DIVISION 1
Maximum points: 52

1975–76	Partick T	41	Kilmarnock	35	Montrose	30

Maximum points: 78

1976–77	St Mirren	62	Clydebank	58	Dundee	51
1977–78	Morton*	58	Hearts	58	Dundee	57
1978–79	Dundee	55	Kilmarnock*	54	Clydebank	54
1979–80	Hearts	53	Airdrieonians	51	Ayr U*	44
1980–81	Hibernian	57	Dundee	52	St Johnstone	51
1981–82	Motherwell	61	Kilmarnock	51	Hearts	50
1982–83	St Johnstone	55	Hearts	54	Clydebank	50
1983–84	Morton	54	Dumbarton	51	Partick T	46
1984–85	Motherwell	50	Clydebank	48	Falkirk	45
1985–86	Hamilton A	56	Falkirk	45	Kilmarnock	44

		Maximum points: 88			
1986–87	Morton	57	Dunfermline Ath	56	Dumbarton	53
1987–88	Hamilton A	56	Meadowbank T	52	Clydebank	49

		Maximum points: 78			
1988–89	Dunfermline Ath	54	Falkirk	52	Clydebank	48
1989–90	St Johnstone	58	Airdrieonians	54	Clydebank	44
1990–91	Falkirk	54	Airdrieonians	53	Dundee	52

		Maximum points: 88			
1991–92	Dundee	58	Partick T*	57	Hamilton A	57
1992–93	Raith R	65	Kilmarnock	54	Dunfermline Ath	52
1993–94	Falkirk	66	Dunfermline Ath	65	Airdrieonians	54

		Maximum points: 108			
1994–95	Raith R	69	Dunfermline Ath*	68	Dundee	68
1995–96	Dunfermline Ath	71	Dundee U*	67	Morton	67
1996–97	St Johnstone	80	Airdrieonians	60	Dundee*	58
1997–98	Dundee	70	Falkirk	65	Raith R*	60
1998–99	Hibernian	89	Falkirk	66	Ayr U	62
1999–00	St Mirren	76	Dunfermline Ath	71	Falkirk	68
2000–01	Livingston	76	Ayr U	69	Falkirk	56
2001–02	Partick T	66	Airdrieonians	56	Ayr U	52

DIVISION 2

		Maximum points: 52			
1975–76	Clydebank*	40	Raith R	40	Alloa	35

		Maximum points: 78			
1976–77	Stirling A	55	Alloa	51	Dunfermline Ath	50
1977–78	Clyde*	53	Raith R	53	Dunfermline Ath	48
1978–79	Berwick R	54	Dunfermline Ath	52	Falkirk	50
1979–80	Falkirk	50	East Stirling	49	Forfar Ath	46
1980–81	Queen's Park	50	Queen of the S	46	Cowdenbeath	45
1981–82	Clyde	59	Alloa*	50	Arbroath	50
1982–83	Brechin C	55	Meadowbank T	54	Arbroath	49
1983–84	Forfar Ath	63	East Fife	47	Berwick R	43
1984–85	Montrose	53	Alloa	50	Dunfermline Ath	49
1985–86	Dunfermline Ath	57	Queen of the S	55	Meadowbank T	49
1986–87	Meadowbank T	55	Raith R*	52	Stirling A*	52
1987–88	Ayr U	61	St Johnstone	59	Queen's Park	51
1988–89	Albion R	50	Alloa	45	Brechin C	43
1989–90	Brechin C	49	Kilmarnock	48	Stirling A	47
1990–91	Stirling A	54	Montrose	46	Cowdenbeath	45
1991–92	Dumbarton	52	Cowdenbeath	51	Alloa	50
1992–93	Clyde	54	Brechin C*	53	Stranraer	53
1993–94	Stranraer	56	Berwick R	48	Stenhousemuir*	47

		Maximum points: 108			
1994–95	Morton	64	Dumbarton	60	Stirling A	58
1995–96	Stirling A	81	East Fife	67	Berwick R	60
1996–97	Ayr U	77	Hamilton A	74	Livingston	64
1997–98	Stranraer	61	Clydebank	60	Livingston	59
1998–99	Livingston	77	Inverness CT	72	Clyde	53
1999–00	Clyde	65	Alloa	64	Ross County	62
2000–01	Partick T	75	Arbroath	58	Berwick R*	54
2001–02	Queen of the S	67	Alloa	59	Forfar Ath	53

DIVISION 3

		Maximum points: 108			
1994–95	Forfar Ath	80	Montrose	67	Ross Co	60
1995–96	Livingston	72	Brechin C	63	Caledonian T	57
1996–97	Inverness CT	76	Forfar Ath*	67	Ross Co	67
1997–98	Alloa	76	Arbroath	68	Ross Co*	67
1998–99	Ross Co	77	Stenhousemuir	64	Brechin C	59
1999–00	Queen's Park	69	Berwick R	66	Forfar Ath	61
2000–01	Hamilton A*	76	Cowdenbeath	76	Brechin C	72
2001–02	Brechin C	73	Dumbarton	61	Albion R	59

Maximum points: a 36; *b* 44; *c* 40; *d* 52; *e* 60; *f* 68; *g* 76; *h* 84.

	First	Pts	Second	Pts	Third	Pts
1890–91a	Dumbarton††	29	Rangers††	29	Celtic	21
1891–92b	Dumbarton	37	Celtic	35	Hearts	34
1892–93a	Celtic	29	Rangers	28	St Mirren	20
1893–94a	Celtic	29	Hearts	26	St Bernard's	23
1894–95a	Hearts	31	Celtic	26	Rangers	22
1895–96a	Celtic	30	Rangers	26	Hibernian	24
1896–97a	Hearts	28	Hibernian	26	Rangers	25
1897–98a	Celtic	33	Rangers	29	Hibernian	22
1898–99a	Rangers	36	Hearts	26	Celtic	24
1899–						
1900a	Rangers	32	Celtic	25	Hibernian	24
1900–01c	Rangers	35	Celtic	29	Hibernian	25
1901–02a	Rangers	28	Celtic	26	Hearts	22
1902–03b	Hibernian	37	Dundee	31	Rangers	29
1903–04d	Third Lanark	43	Hearts	39	Celtic*	38
1904–05d	Celtic‡	41	Rangers	41	Third Lanark	35
1905–06e	Celtic	49	Hearts	43	Airdrieonians	38
1906–07f	Celtic	55	Dundee	48	Rangers	45
1907–08f	Celtic	55	Falkirk	51	Rangers	50
1908–09f	Celtic	51	Dundee	50	Clyde	48
1909–10f	Celtic	54	Falkirk	52	Rangers	46
1910–11f	Rangers	52	Aberdeen	48	Falkirk	44
1911–12f	Rangers	51	Celtic	45	Clyde	42
1912–13f	Rangers	53	Celtic	49	Hearts*	41
1913–14g	Celtic	65	Rangers	59	Hearts*	54
1914–15g	Celtic	65	Hearts	61	Rangers	50
1915–16g	Celtic	67	Rangers	56	Morton	51
1916–17g	Celtic	64	Morton	54	Rangers	53
1917–18f	Rangers	56	Celtic	55	Kilmarnock*	43
1918–19f	Celtic	58	Rangers	57	Morton	47
1919–20h	Rangers	71	Celtic	68	Motherwell	57
1920–21h	Rangers	76	Celtic	66	Hearts	50
1921–22h	Celtic	67	Rangers	66	Raith R	51
1922–23g	Rangers	55	Airdrieonians	50	Celtic	46
1923–24g	Rangers	59	Airdrieonians	50	Celtic	46
1924–25g	Rangers	60	Airdrieonians	57	Hibernian	52
1925–26g	Celtic	58	Airdrieonians*	50	Hearts	50
1926–27g	Rangers	56	Motherwell	51	Celtic	49
1927–28g	Rangers	60	Celtic*	55	Motherwell	55
1928–29g	Rangers	67	Celtic	51	Motherwell	50
1929–30g	Rangers	60	Motherwell	55	Aberdeen	53
1930–31g	Rangers	60	Celtic	58	Motherwell	56
1931–32g	Motherwell	66	Rangers	61	Celtic	48
1932–33g	Rangers	62	Motherwell	59	Hearts	50
1933–34g	Rangers	66	Motherwell	62	Celtic	47
1934–35g	Rangers	55	Celtic	52	Hearts	50
1935–36g	Celtic	66	Rangers*	61	Aberdeen	61
1936–37g	Rangers	61	Aberdeen	54	Celtic	52
1937–38g	Celtic	61	Hearts	58	Rangers	49
1938–39g	Rangers	59	Celtic	48	Aberdeen	46
1946–47e	Rangers	46	Hibernian	44	Aberdeen	39
1947–48e	Hibernian	48	Rangers	46	Partick T	36
1948–49e	Rangers	46	Dundee	45	Hibernian	39
1949–50e	Rangers	50	Hibernian	49	Hearts	43

1950–51e	Hibernian	48	Rangers*	38	Dundee	38
1951–52e	Hibernian	45	Rangers	41	East Fife	37
1952–53e	Rangers*	43	Hibernian	43	East Fife	39
1953–54e	Celtic	43	Hearts	38	Partick T	35
1954–55e	Aberdeen	49	Celtic	46	Rangers	41
1955–56f	Rangers	52	Aberdeen	46	Hearts*	45
1956–57f	Rangers	55	Hearts	53	Kilmarnock	42
1957–58f	Hearts	62	Rangers	49	Celtic	46
1958–59f	Rangers	50	Hearts	48	Motherwell	44
1959–60f	Hearts	54	Kilmarnock	50	Rangers*	42
1960–61f	Rangers	51	Kilmarnock	50	Third Lanark	42
1961–62f	Dundee	54	Rangers	51	Celtic	46
1962–63f	Rangers	57	Kilmarnock	48	Partick T	46
1963–64f	Rangers	55	Kilmarnock	49	Celtic*	47
1964–65f	Kilmarnock*	50	Hearts	50	Dunfermline Ath	49
1965–66f	Celtic	57	Rangers	55	Kilmarnock	45
1966–67f	Celtic	58	Rangers	55	Clyde	46
1967–68f	Celtic	63	Rangers	61	Hibernian	45
1968–69f	Celtic	54	Rangers	49	Dunfermline Ath	45
1969–70f	Celtic	57	Rangers	45	Hibernian	44
1970–71f	Celtic	56	Aberdeen	54	St Johnstone	44
1971–72f	Celtic	60	Aberdeen	50	Rangers	44
1972–73f	Celtic	57	Rangers	56	Hibernian	45
1973–74f	Celtic	53	Hibernian	49	Rangers	48
1974–75f	Rangers	56	Hibernian	49	Celtic	45

DIVISION 2 to 1974–75

Maximum points: a 76; b 72; c 68; d 52; e 60; f 36; g 44.

1893–94f	Hibernian	29	Cowlairs	27	Clyde	24
1894–95f	Hibernian	30	Motherwell	22	Port Glasgow	20
1895–96f	Abercorn	27	Leith Ath	23	Renton	21
1896–97f	Partick T	31	Leith Ath	27	Kilmarnock*	21
1897–98f	Kilmarnock	29	Port Glasgow	25	Morton	22
1898–99f	Kilmarnock	32	Leith Ath	27	Port Glasgow	25
1899–						
1900f	Partick T	29	Morton	28	Port Glasgow	20
1900–01f	St Bernard's	25	Airdrieonians	23	Abercorn	21
1901–02g	Port Glasgow	32	Partick T	31	Motherwell	26
1902–03g	Airdrieonians	35	Motherwell	28	Ayr U*	27
1903–04g	Hamilton A	37	Clyde	29	Ayr U	28
1904–05g	Clyde	32	Falkirk	28	Hamilton A	27
1905–06g	Leith Ath	34	Clyde	31	Albion R	27
1906–07g	St Bernard's	32	Vale of Leven*	27	Arthurlie	27
1907–08g	Raith R	30	Dumbarton	‡‡27	Ayr U	27
1908–09g	Abercorn	31	Raith R*	28	Vale of Leven	28
1909–10g	Leith Ath‡	33	Raith R	33	St Bernard's	27
1910–11g	Dumbarton	31	Ayr U	27	Albion R	25
1911–12g	Ayr U	35	Abercorn	30	Dumbarton	27
1912–13d	Ayr U	34	Dunfermline Ath	33	East Stirling	32
1913–14g	Cowdenbeath	31	Albion R	27	Dunfermline Ath*	26
1914–15d	Cowdenbeath*	37	St Bernard's*	37	Leith Ath	37
1921–22a	Alloa	60	Cowdenbeath	47	Armadale	45
1922–23a	Queen's Park	57	Clydebank ¶	50	St Johnstone ¶	45
1923–24a	St Johnstone	56	Cowdenbeath	55	Bathgate	44
1924–25a	Dundee U	50	Clydebank	48	Clyde	47
1925–26a	Dunfermline Ath	59	Clyde	53	Ayr U	52

1926–27a	Bo'ness	56	Raith R	49	Clydebank	45
1927–28a	Ayr U	54	Third Lanark	45	King's Park	44
1928–29b	Dundee U	51	Morton	50	Arbroath	47
1929–30a	Leith Ath*	57	East Fife	57	Albion R	54
1930–31a	Third Lanark	61	Dundee U	50	Dunfermline Ath	47
1931–32a	East Stirling*	55	St Johnstone	55	Raith R*	46
1932–33c	Hibernian	54	Queen of the S	49	Dunfermline Ath	47
1933–34c	Albion R	45	Dunfermline Ath*	44	Arbroath	44
1934–35c	Third Lanark	52	Arbroath	50	St Bernard's	47
1935–36c	Falkirk	59	St Mirren	52	Morton	48
1936–37c	Ayr U	54	Morton	51	St Bernard's	48
1937–38c	Raith R	59	Albion R	48	Airdrieonians	47
1938–39c	Cowdenbeath	60	Alloa*	48	East Fife	48
1946–47d	Dundee	45	Airdrieonians	42	East Fife	31
1947–48e	East Fife	53	Albion R	42	Hamilton A	40
1948–49e	Raith R*	42	Stirling A	42	Airdrieonians*	41
1949–50e	Morton	47	Airdrieonians	44	Dunfermline Ath*	36
1950–51e	Queen of the S*	45	Stirling A	45	Ayr U*	36
1951–52e	Clyde	44	Falkirk	43	Ayr U	39
1952–53e	Stirling A	44	Hamilton A	43	Queen's Park	37
1953–54e	Motherwell	45	Kilmarnock	42	Third Lanark*	36
1954–55e	Airdrieonians	46	Dunfermline Ath	42	Hamilton A	39
1955–56b	Queen's Park	54	Ayr U	51	St Johnstone	49
1956–57b	Clyde	64	Third Lanark	51	Cowdenbeath	45
1957–58b	Stirling A	55	Dunfermline Ath	53	Arbroath	47
1958–59b	Ayr U	60	Arbroath	51	Stenhousemuir	46
1959–60b	St Johnstone	53	Dundee U	50	Queen of the S	49
1960–61b	Stirling A	55	Falkirk	54	Stenhousemuir	50
1961–62b	Clyde	54	Queen of the S	53	Morton	44
1962 63b	St Johnstone	55	East Stirling	49	Morton	48
1963–64b	Morton	67	Clyde	53	Arbroath	46
1964–65b	Stirling A	59	Hamilton A	50	Queen of the S	45
1965–66b	Ayr U	53	Airdrieonians	50	Queen of the S	47
1966–67a	Morton	69	Raith R	58	Arbroath	57
1967–68b	St Mirren	62	Arbroath	53	East Fife	49
1968 69b	Motherwell	64	Ayr U	53	East Fife*	48
1969–70b	Falkirk	56	Cowdenbeath	55	Queen of the S	50
1970–71b	Partick T	56	East Fife	51	Arbroath	46
1971–72b	Dumbarton*	52	Arbroath	52	Stirling A	50
1972–73b	Clyde	56	Dunfermline Ath	52	Raith R*	47
1973–74b	Airdrieonians	60	Kilmarnock	58	Hamilton A	55
1974–75a	Falkirk	54	Queen of the S*	53	Montrose	53

Elected to Division 1: 1894 Clyde; 1895 Hibernian; 1896 Abercorn; 1897 Partick T;
1899 Kilmarnock; 1900 Morton and Partick T; 1902 Port Glasgow and Partick T;
1903 Airdrieonians and Motherwell; 1905 Falkirk and Aberdeen; 1906 Clyde and
Hamilton A; 1910 Raith R; 1913 Ayr U and Dumbarton.

RELEGATED CLUBS

From Premier League
1998–99 Dunfermline Ath *(No relegation 1999–2000)*
2000–01 St Mirren
2001–02 St Johnstone

From Premier Division
1974–75 *No relegation due to League reorganisation*
1975–76 Dundee, St Johnstone
1976–77 Hearts, Kilmarnock
1977–78 Ayr U, Clydebank
1978–79 Hearts, Motherwell
1979–80 Dundee, Hibernian
1980–81 Kilmarnock, Hearts
1981–82 Partick T, Airdrieonians
1982–83 Morton, Kilmarnock
1983–84 St Johnstone, Motherwell
1984–85 Dumbarton, Morton
1985–86 *No relegation due to League reorganization*
1986–87 Clydebank, Hamilton A
1987–88 Falkirk, Dunfermline Ath, Morton
1988–89 Hamilton A
1989–90 Dundee
1990–91 None
1991–92 St Mirren, Dunfermline Ath
1992–93 Falkirk, Airdrieonians
1993–94 *See footnote*
1994–95 Dundee U
1995–96 Partick T, Falkirk
1996–97 Raith R
1997–98 Hibernian

From Division 1
1974–75 *No relegation due to League reorganisation*
1975–76 Dunfermline Ath, Clyde
1976–77 Raith R, Falkirk
1977–78 Alloa Ath, East Fife
1978–79 Montrose, Queen of the S
1979–80 Arbroath, Clyde
1980–81 Stirling A, Berwick R
1981–82 East Stirling, Queen of the S
1982–83 Dunfermline Ath, Queen's Park
1983–84 Raith R, Alloa
1984–85 Meadowbank T, St Johnstone
1985–86 Ayr U, Alloa
1986–87 Brechin C, Montrose
1987–88 East Fife, Dumbarton
1988–89 Kilmarnock, Queen of the S
1989–90 Albion R, Alloa
1990–91 Clyde, Brechin C
1991–92 Montrose, Forfar Ath
1992–93 Meadowbank T, Cowdenbeath
1993–94 *See footnote*
1994–95 Ayr U, Stranraer
1995–96 Hamilton A, Dumbarton
1996–97 Clydebank, East Fife
1997–98 Partick T, Stirling A
1998–99 Hamilton A, Stranraer
1999–00 Clydebank
2000–01 Morton, Alloa
2001–02 Raith R

Relegated from Division 2
1994–95 Meadowbank T, Brechin C
1995–96 Forfar Ath, Montrose
1996–97 Dumbarton, Berwick R
1997–98 Stenhousemuir, Brechin C
1998–99 East Fife, Forfar Ath
1999–00 Hamilton A**
2000–01 Queen's Park, Stirling A
2001–02 Morton

Relegated from Division 1 1973–74
1921–22 *Queen's Park, Dumbarton, Clydebank
1922–23 Albion R, Alloa Ath
1923–24 Clyde, Clydebank
1924–25 Third Lanark, Ayr U

1925–26 Raith R, Clydebank
1926–27 Morton, Dundee U
1927–28 Dunfermline Ath, Bo'ness
1928–29 Third Lanark, Raith R
1929–30 St Johnstone, Dundee U
1930–31 Hibernian, East Fife

1931–32 Dundee U, Leith Ath
1932–33 Morton, East Stirling
1933–34 Third Lanark, Cowdenbeath
1934–35 St Mirren, Falkirk
1935–36 Airdrieonians, Ayr U
1936–37 Dunfermline Ath, Albion R
1937–38 Dundee, Morton
1938–39 Queen's Park, Raith R
1946–47 Kilmarnock, Hamilton A
1947–48 Airdrieonians, Queen's Park
1948–49 Morton, Albion R
1949–50 Queen of the S, Stirling A
1950–51 Clyde, Falkirk
1951–52 Morton, Stirling A
1952–53 Motherwell, Third Lanark
1953–54 Airdrieonians, Hamilton A
1954–55 *No clubs relegated*
1955–56 Stirling A, Clyde

1956–57 Dunfermline Ath, Ayr U
1957–58 East Fife, Queen's Park
1958–59 Queen of the S, Falkirk
1959–60 Arbroath, Stirling A
1960–61 Ayr U, Clyde
1961–62 St Johnstone, Stirling A
1962–63 Clyde, Raith R
1963–64 Queen of the S, East Stirling
1964–65 Airdrieonians, Third Lanark
1965–66 Morton, Hamilton A
1966–67 St Mirren, Ayr U
1967–68 Motherwell, Stirling A
1968–69 Falkirk, Arbroath
1969–70 Raith R, Partick T
1970–71 St Mirren, Cowdenbeath
1971–72 Clyde, Dunfermline Ath
1972–73 Kilmarnock, Airdrieonians
1973–74 East Fife, Falkirk

*Season 1921–22 – only 1 club promoted, 3 clubs relegated.
**15 pts deducted for failing to field a team.*

Scottish League championship wins: Rangers 49, Celtic 38, Aberdeen 4, Hearts 4, Hibernian 4, Dumbarton 2, Dundee 1, Dundee U 1, Kilmarnock 1, Motherwell 1, Third Lanark 1.

The Scottish Football League was reconstructed into three divisions at the end of the 1974–75 season, so the usual relegation statistics do not apply. Further reorganization took place at the end of the 1985–86 season. From 1986–87, the Premier and First Division had 12 teams each. The Second Division remained at 14. From 1988–89, the Premier Division reverted to 10 teams, and the First Division to 14 teams but in 1991–92 the Premier and First Division reverted to 12. At the end of the 1997–98 season, the top nine clubs in Premier Division broke away from the Scottish League to form a new competition, the Scottish Premier League, with the club promoted from Division One. At the end of the 1999–2000 season two teams were added to the Scottish League. There was no relegation from the Premier League but two promoted from the First Division and three from each of the Second and Third Divisions. One team was relegated from the First Division and one from the Second Division, leaving 12 teams in each division.

PAST SCOTTISH LEAGUE CUP FINALS

1946–47	Rangers	4	Aberdeen	0
1947–48	East Fife	0 4	Falkirk	0* 1
1948–49	Rangers	2	Raith Rovers	0
1949–50	East Fife	3	Dunfermline	0
1950–51	Motherwell	3	Hibernian	0
1951–52	Dundee	3	Rangers	2
1952–53	Dundee	2	Kilmarnock	0
1953–54	East Fife	3	Partick Thistle	2
1954–55	Hearts	4	Motherwell	2
1955–56	Aberdeen	2	St Mirren	1
1956–57	Celtic	0 3	Partick Thistle	0 0
1957–58	Celtic	7	Rangers	1
1958–59	Hearts	5	Partick Thistle	1
1959–60	Hearts	2	Third Lanark	1
1960–61	Rangers	2	Kilmarnock	0
1961–62	Rangers	1 3	Hearts	1 1
1962–63	Hearts	1	Kilmarnock	0
1963–64	Rangers	5	Morton	0
1964–65	Rangers	2	Celtic	1
1965–66	Celtic	2	Rangers	1
1966–67	Celtic	1	Rangers	0
1967–68	Celtic	5	Dundee	3
1968–69	Celtic	6	Hibernian	2
1969–70	Celtic	1	St Johnstone	0
1970–71	Rangers	1	Celtic	0
1971–72	Partick Thistle	4	Celtic	1
1972–73	Hibernian	2	Celtic	1
1973–74	Dundee	1	Celtic	0
1974–75	Celtic	6	Hibernian	3
1975–76	Rangers	1	Celtic	0
1976–77	Aberdeen	2	Celtic	1
1977–78	Rangers	2	Celtic	1*
1978–79	Rangers	2	Aberdeen	1
1979–80	Aberdeen	0 0	Dundee U	0* 3
1980–81	Dundee	0	Dundee U	3
1981–82	Rangers	2	Dundee U	1
1982–83	Celtic	2	Rangers	1
1983–84	Rangers	3	Celtic	2
1984–85	Rangers	1	Dundee U	0
1985–86	Aberdeen	3	Hibernian	0
1986–87	Rangers	2	Celtic	1
1987–88	Rangers†	3	Aberdeen	3*
1988–89	Aberdeen	2	Rangers	3*
1989–90	Aberdeen	2	Rangers	1
1990–91	Rangers	2	Celtic	1
1991–92	Hibernian	2	Dunfermline Ath	0
1992–93	Rangers	2	Aberdeen	1*
1993–94	Rangers	2	Hibernian	1
1994–95	Raith R†	2	Celtic	2*
1995–96	Aberdeen	2	Dundee	0
1996–97	Rangers	4	Hearts	3
1997–98	Celtic	3	Dundee U	0
1998–99	Rangers	2	St Johnstone	1
1999–2000	Celtic	2	Aberdeen	0
2000–01	Celtic	3	Kilmarnock	0
2001–02	Rangers	4	Ayr U	0

†*Won on penalties *After extra time*

CIS SCOTTISH LEAGUE CUP 2001–2002

FIRST ROUND

Elgin C	(1) 2	Stranraer	(1) 3
Airdrieonians	(1) 3	Morton	(0) 0
Albion R	(0) 0	Inverness CT	(0) 2
Alloa Ath	(2) 4	Peterhead	(0) 0
Berwick R	(0) 0	Partick T	(2) 3
Clyde	(0) 2	Stenhousemuir	(1) 2
(aet; Clyde won 4-2 on penalties.)			
Dumbarton	(1) 2	Clydebank	(0) 0
East Fife	(0) 1	Arbroath	(0) 0
East Stirling	(0) 0	Queen of the S	(1) 3
Forfar Ath	(0) 1	Falkirk	(1) 2
Raith R	(1) 1	Montrose	(0) 0
Ross Co	(0) 3	Brechin C	(0) 0
Queen's Park	(0) 0	Hamilton A	(1) 1
Stirling Albion	(2) 3	Cowdenbeath	(1) 2

SECOND ROUND

Airdrieonians	(1) 2	Motherwell	(0) 1
Ayr U	(1) 4	Stranraer	(0) 0
Dundee U	(2) 3	Dumbarton	(0) 0
Falkirk	(0) 0	Raith R	(1) 2
Queen of the S	(0) 1	Aberdeen	(2) 2
Ross Co	(0) 0	Hearts	(0) 0
(aet; Ross Co won 5-4 on penalties.)			
Clyde	(0) 1	St Johnstone	(1) 2
Dunfermline Ath	(1) 3	Alloa Ath	(0) 0
Hamilton A	(0) 0	Dundee	(0) 2
Inverness CT	(1) 3	Partick T	(1) 3
(aet; Inverness CT won 4-2 on penalties.)			
Livingston	(2) 3	East Fife	(0) 0
Stirling Albion	(1) 2	St Mirren	(1) 1

THIRD ROUND

Aberdeen	(0) 1	Livingston	(4) 6
Ayr U	(0) 0	Kilmarnock	(0) 0
(aet; Ayr U won 5-4 on penalties.)			
Celtic	(3) 8	Stirling Albion	(0) 0
Dundee U	(1) 3	St Johnstone	(2) 2
(aet)			
Dunfermline Ath	(0) 1	Inverness CT	(1) 1
(aet; Inverness CT won 4-1 on penalties.)			
Raith R	(0) 0	Hibernian	(0) 2
Rangers	(2) 3	Airdrieonians	(0) 0
Ross Co	(1) 2	Dundee	(0) 1

QUARTER FINALS

Hibernian	(1) 2	Dundee U	(0) 0
Ayr U	(2) 5	Inverness CT	(1) 1
Ross Co	(0) 1	Rangers	(2) 2
Livingston	(0) 0	Celtic	(1) 2

SEMI-FINALS

Rangers	(1) 2	Celtic	(0) 1
(aet)			
Hibernian	(0) 0	Ayr U	(0) 1
(aet)			

FINAL

Rangers	(1) 4	Ayr U	(0) 0

BELL'S LEAGUE CHALLENGE 2001–2002

FIRST ROUND

Airdrieonians	(0) 2	Queen of the South	(0) 0
Albion R	(0) 2	Montrose	(0) 0
(aet)			
Berwick R	(1) 3	Elgin C	(0) 0
Brechin C	(3) 4	Stirling Albion	(0) 1
Cowdenbeath	(0) 0	Ross Co	(0) 2
(aet)			
East Fife	(0) 2	Raith R	(0) 3
East Stirling	(0) 0	Alloa Ath	(0) 1
Falkirk	(2) 4	Arbroath	(1) 1
Inverness CT	(2) 3	Forfar Ath	(1) 2
(aet)			
Morton	(1) 1	Clyde	(2) 3
Partick T	(3) 5	Queen's Park	(0) 0
Peterhead	(1) 2	Hamilton A	(0) 0
St Mirren	(0) 1	Ayr U	(1) 3
Stenhousemuir	(1) 1	Stranraer	(1) 4

SECOND ROUND

Albion R	(0) 1	Airdrieonians	(2) 4
Alloa Ath	(1) 3	Inverness CT	(1) 2
(aet)			
Brechin C	(1) 4	Peterhead	(0) 0
Clyde	(3) 5	Berwick R	(0) 0
Dumbarton	(0) 0	Ross Co	(0) 2
Falkirk	(0) 0	Clydebank	(0) 0
(aet; Clydebank won 5-4 on penalties.)			
Raith R	(2) 3	Partick T	(1) 5
(aet)			
Stranraer	(1) 3	Ayr U	(1) 2

QUARTER-FINALS

Alloa Ath	(3) 4	Stranraer	(1) 3
(aet)			
Clyde	(0) 1	Partick T	(0) 0
Clydebank	(1) 1	Airdrieonians	(2) 2
Ross Co	(0) 0	Brechin C	(1) 2

SEMI-FINALS

Airdrieonians	(1) 1	Brechin C	(0) 1
(aet; Airdrieonians won 4-3 on penalties.)			
Clyde	(0) 0	Alloa Ath	(0) 1

FINAL

Airdrieonians	(0) 2	Alloa Ath	(0) 1

TENNENT'S SCOTTISH CUP 2001–2002

FIRST ROUND

Albion R	(0) 0	Elgin C	(0) 0
Alloa A	(2) 3	Dumbarton	(0) 1
Brechin C	(0) 4	Stenhousemuir	(0) 0
Morton	(1) 1	Queen of the S	(2) 2
Stirling Albion	(0) 2	Buckie Thistle	(1) 1
Tarff Rovers	(0) 1	Montrose	(2) 4
Wick Academy	(0) 2	Threave Rovers	(2) 3
Clydebank	(0) 1	Peterhead	(0) 0

FIRST ROUND REPLAY

Elgin C	(0) 0	Albion R	(1) 1

SECOND ROUND

Alloa Ath	(1) 1	Queen of the S	(0) 0
Berwick R	(1) 1	Cowdenbeath	(0) 0
Brechin C	(0) 0	Albion R	(1) 1
Clydebank	(0) 0	Stranraer	(0) 1
Deveronvale	(0) 0	Spartans	(0) 0
East Stirlingshire	(0) 1	Forres Mechanics	(1) 1
Forfar Ath	(2) 2	Threave Rovers	(0) 0
Gala Fairydean	(1) 1	Stirling Albion	(0) 0
Hamilton A	(3) 4	Montrose	(0) 0
Queen's Park	(0) 0	East Fife	(0) 0

SECOND ROUND REPLAYS

Forres Mechanics	(1) 3	East Stirling	(1) 1
Spartans	(0) 1	Deveronvale	(0) 2
East Fife	(1) 2	Queen's Park	(1) 2

(aet; East Fife won 4-2 on penalties.)

THIRD ROUND

Deveronvale	(0) 0	Ayr U	(4) 6
Dundee U	(0) 3	Forres Mechanics	(0) 0
Dunfermline Ath	(2) 3	Motherwell	(0) 1
Hearts	(0) 2	Ross Co	(0) 1
Kilmarnock	(3) 3	Airdrieonians	(0) 0
Stranraer	(0) 0	Hibernian	(0) 0
Dundee	(0) 1	Falkirk	(0) 1
Albion R	(0) 0	Livingston	(0) 0

(match abandoned at half-time; floodlighting failure)

Alloa Ath	(0) 0	Celtic	(2) 5
Arbroath	(0) 0	Inverness CT	(1) 2
Berwick R	(0) 0	Rangers	(0) 0
Clyde	(0) 1	St Mirren	(0) 0
East Fife	(1) 2	Partick T	(3) 4
Hamilton A	(0) 1	Raith R	(0) 0
St Johnstone	(0) 0	Aberdeen	(0) 2
Gala Fairydean	(0) 0	Forfar Ath	(3) 5

THIRD ROUND REPLAYS

Albion R	(1) 1	Livingston	(2) 4
Hibernian	(2) 4	Stranraer	(0) 0
Falkirk	(0) 0	Dundee	(1) 1
Rangers	(0) 3	Berwick R	(0) 0

FOURTH ROUND

Aberdeen	(2) 2	Livingston	(0) 0
Ayr U	(2) 3	Dunfermline Ath	(0) 0
Clyde	(1) 1	Forfar Ath	(1) 2
Hearts	(1) 1	Inverness CT	(1) 3
Kilmarnock	(0) 0	Celtic	(0) 2
Partick T	(0) 1	Dundee	(0) 1
Rangers	(2) 4	Hibernian	(1) 1
Dundee U	(0) 4	Hamilton A	(0) 0

FOURTH ROUND REPLAY

Dundee	(0) 1	Partick T	(1) 2

QUARTER-FINALS

Dundee U	(2) 2	Ayr U	(1) 2
Partick T	(0) 2	Inverness CT	(1) 2
Aberdeen	(0) 0	Celtic	(1) 2
Forfar Ath	(0) 0	Rangers	(4) 6

QUARTER-FINAL REPLAYS

Inverness CT	(0) 0	Partick T	(0) 1
Ayr U	(1) 2	Dundee U	(0) 0

SEMI-FINALS

Ayr U	(0) 0	Celtic	(0) 3
Rangers	(1) 3	Partick T	(0) 0

FINAL

Celtic	(1) 2	Rangers	(1) 3

PAST SCOTTISH CUP FINALS

Year	Winner	Score	Opponent	Score
1874	Queen's Park	2	Clydesdale	0
1875	Queen's Park	3	Renton	0
1876	Queen's Park	1 2	Third Lanark	1 0
1877	Vale of Leven	0 1 3	Rangers	0 1 2
1878	Vale of Leven	1	Third Lanark	0
1879	Vale of Leven	1	Rangers	1

Vale of Leven awarded cup, Rangers did not appear for replay

Year	Winner	Score	Opponent	Score
1880	Queen's Park	3	Thornlibank	0
1881	Queen's Park	2 3	Dumbarton	1 1

Replayed because of protest

Year	Winner	Score	Opponent	Score
1882	Queen's Park	2 4	Dumbarton	2 1
1883	Dumbarton	2 2	Vale of Leven	2 1
1884	*Queen's Park awarded cup when Vale of Leven did not appear for the final*			
1885	Renton	0 3	Vale of Leven	0 1
1886	Queen's Park	3	Renton	1
1887	Hibernian	2	Dumbarton	1
1888	Renton	6	Cambuslang	1
1889	Third Lanark	3 2	Celtic	0 1

Replayed because of protest

Year	Winner	Score	Opponent	Score
1890	Queen's Park	1 2	Vale of Leven	1 1
1891	Hearts	1	Dumbarton	0
1892	Celtic	1 5	Queen's Park	0 1

Replayed because of protest

Year	Winner	Score	Opponent	Score
1893	Queen's Park	2	Celtic	1
1894	Rangers	3	Celtic	1
1895	St Bernards	3	Renton	1
1896	Hearts	3	Hibernian	1
1897	Rangers	5	Dumbarton	1
1898	Rangers	2	Kilmarnock	0
1899	Celtic	2	Rangers	0
1900	Celtic	4	Queen's Park	3
1901	Hearts	4	Celtic	3
1902	Hibernian	1	Celtic	0
1903	Rangers	1 0 2	Hearts	1 0 0
1904	Celtic	3	Rangers	2
1905	Third Lanark	0 3	Rangers	0 1
1906	Hearts	1	Third Lanark	0
1907	Celtic	3	Hearts	0
1908	Celtic	5	St Mirren	1
1909	*After two drawn games between Celtic and Rangers, 2.2, 1.1, there was a riot and the cup was withheld*			
1910	Dundee	2 0 2	Clyde	2 0 1
1911	Celtic	0 2	Hamilton Acad	0 0
1912	Celtic	2	Clyde	0
1913	Falkirk	2	Raith R	0
1914	Celtic	0 4	Hibernian	0 1
1920	Kilmarnock	3	Albion R	2
1921	Partick Th	1	Rangers	0
1922	Morton	1	Rangers	0
1923	Celtic	1	Hibernian	0
1924	Airdrieonians	2	Hibernian	0
1925	Celtic	2	Dundee	1
1926	St Mirren	2	Celtic	0
1927	Celtic	3	East Fife	1
1928	Rangers	4	Celtic	0
1929	Kilmarnock	2	Rangers	0
1930	Rangers	0 2	Partick Th	0 1
1931	Celtic	2 4	Motherwell	2 2
1932	Rangers	1 3	Kilmarnock	1 0
1933	Celtic	1	Motherwell	0

Year	Winner	Score	Runner-up	Score
1934	Rangers	5	St Mirren	0
1935	Rangers	2	Hamilton Acad	1
1936	Rangers	1	Third Lanark	0
1937	Celtic	2	Aberdeen	1
1938	East Fife	1 4	Kilmarnock	1 2
1939	Clyde	4	Motherwell	0
1947	Aberdeen	2	Hibernian	1
1948	Rangers	1 1	Morton	1 0
1949	Rangers	4	Clyde	1
1950	Rangers	3	East Fife	0
1951	Celtic	1	Motherwell	0
1952	Motherwell	4	Dundee	0
1953	Rangers	1 1	Aberdeen	1 0
1954	Celtic	2	Aberdeen	1
1955	Clyde	1 1	Celtic	1 0
1956	Hearts	3	Celtic	1
1957	Falkirk	1 2	Kilmarnock	1 1
1958	Clyde	1	Hibernian	0
1959	St Mirren	3	Aberdeen	1
1960	Rangers	2	Kilmarnock	0
1961	Dunfermline Ath	0 2	Celtic	0 0
1962	Rangers	2	St Mirren	0
1963	Rangers	1 3	Celtic	1 0
1964	Rangers	3	Dundee	1
1965	Celtic	3	Dunfermline Ath	2
1966	Rangers	0 1	Celtic	0 0
1967	Celtic	2	Aberdeen	0
1968	Dunfermline Ath	3	Hearts	1
1969	Celtic	4	Rangers	0
1970	Aberdeen	3	Celtic	1
1971	Celtic	1 2	Rangers	1 1
1972	Celtic	6	Hibernian	1
1973	Rangers	3	Celtic	2
1974	Celtic	3	Dundee U	0
1975	Celtic	3	Airdrieonians	1
1976	Rangers	3	Hearts	1
1977	Celtic	1	Rangers	0
1978	Rangers	2	Aberdeen	1
1979	Rangers	0 0 3	Hibernian	0 0 2
1980	Celtic	1	Rangers	0
1981	Rangers	0 4	Dundee U	0 1
1982	Aberdeen	4	Rangers	1 (aet)
1983	Aberdeen	1	Rangers	0 (aet)
1984	Aberdeen	2	Celtic	1 (aet)
1985	Celtic	2	Dundee U	1
1986	Aberdeen	3	Hearts	0
1987	St Mirren	1	Dundee U	0 (aet)
1988	Celtic	2	Dundee U	1
1989	Celtic	1	Rangers	0
1990	Aberdeen†	0	Celtic	0
1991	Motherwell	4	Dundee U	3 (aet)
1992	Rangers	2	Airdrieonians	1
1993	Rangers	2	Aberdeen	1
1994	Dundee U	1	Rangers	0
1995	Celtic	1	Airdrieonians	0
1996	Rangers	5	Hearts	1
1997	Kilmarnock	1	Falkirk	0
1998	Hearts	2	Rangers	1
1999	Rangers	1	Celtic	0
2000	Rangers	4	Aberdeen	0
2001	Celtic	3	Hibernian	0
2002	Rangers	3	Celtic	2

†won on penalties

WELSH LEAGUE 2001–2002

LEAGUE OF WALES

	P	Home W	D	L	Goals F	A	Away W	D	L	Goals F	A	GD	Pts
Barry Town	34	13	2	2	47	11	10	6	1	35	18	53	77
Total Network Solutions.	34	12	3	2	35	13	9	4	4	30	20	32	70
Bangor City	34	13	3	1	40	13	8	3	6	43	25	45	69
Caersws	34	11	2	4	33	17	7	2	8	32	27	21	58
Afan Lido	34	12	2	3	27	11	6	2	9	15	25	6	58
Rhyl	34	11	2	4	28	19	6	3	8	25	26	8	56
Cwmbran Town	34	8	3	6	40	31	9	1	7	36	22	13	55
Connah's Quay Nomads	34	7	6	4	32	25	7	3	7	24	21	10	51
Aberystwyth Town	34	8	7	2	29	16	6	2	9	24	32	5	51
Carmarthen Town	34	9	3	5	33	17	4	6	7	18	20	14	48
Caernarfon Town	34	8	2	7	38	31	4	6	7	26	33	0	44
Port Talbot Town	34	7	3	7	28	27	5	4	8	16	28	–11	43
Newtown	34	7	6	4	21	19	2	5	10	14	25	–9	38
Flexsys Cefn Druids	34	4	2	11	23	38	4	6	7	26	41	–30	32
Llanelli	34	4	6	7	21	31	4	1	12	20	33	–23	31
Oswestry Town	34	4	4	9	17	33	4	2	11	22	51	–45	30
Haverfordwest County	34	4	5	8	27	33	2	5	10	20	43	–29	28
Rhayader Town	34	2	3	12	17	43	1	3	13	12	46	–60	15

NORTHERN IRELAND LEAGUE 2001–2002

SMIRNOFF IFL

Premiership	P	W	D	L	F	A	GD	Pts
Portadown	36	22	9	5	75	34	+41	75
Glentoran	36	21	11	4	63	23	+40	74
Linfield	36	17	11	8	64	35	+29	62
Coleraine	36	19	2	15	64	58	+6	59
Omagh Town	36	15	9	12	55	55	0	54
Cliftonville	36	9	11	16	37	46	–9	38
Glenavon	36	9	9	18	37	57	–20	36
Newry Town	36	8	12	16	40	62	–22	36
Crusaders	36	9	7	20	41	65	–24	34
Ards	36	6	9	21	30	71	–41	27

LEAGUE OF WALES – RESULTS 2001–2002

	Aberystwyth Town	Afan Lido	Bangor City	Barry Town	Caernarfon	Caersws	Carmarthen Town	Connah's Quay Nomads	Cwmbran Town	Flexsys Cefn Druids	Haverfordwest County	Llanelli	Newtown	Oswestry Town	Port Talbot Town	Rhayader Town	Rhyl	Total Network Solutions
Aberystwyth Town	—	2-0	1-0	1-1	2-2	1-3	1-1	2-0	3-0	3-0	1-1	3-1	2-2	3-0	4-1	1-0	1-1	1-3
Afan Lido	0-1	—	1-0	2-2	1-0	1-1	3-0	0-1	2-1	2-0	0-0	0-0	1-3	0-3	2-1	1-0	1-1	0-2
Bangor City	2-0	3-0	—	1-1	3-3	1-1	3-0	2-1	1-3	6-0	5-0	2-0	3-1	1-0	1-0	1-0	3-0	3-0
Barry Town	4-1	3-2	2-2	—	2-0	0-3	3-0	2-1	1-3	4-2	5-0	3-0	2-0	4-1	3-1	1-0	3-0	3-1
Caernarfon	2-1	6-0	1-1	1-5	—	3-3	1-2	2-0	0-2	4-2	6-0	0-0	0-0	4-1	2-0	5-0	3-2	0-1
Caersws	2-1	3-0	1-1	0-3	2-0	—	2-0	2-1	1-2	2-1	4-5	2-1	3-1	4-1	1-2	1-0	1-0	1-2
Carmarthen Town	2-1	3-0	0-0	0-1	2-1	1-1	—	2-2	1-2	0-2	0-0	0-6	3-1	3-2	0-1	5-0	1-0	3-1
Connah's Quay Nomads	1-2	4-2	2-2	0-1	5-1	3-0	1-0	—	4-2	0-2	1-2	6-1	2-2	5-1	0-0	4-0	2-1	0-0
Cwmbran Town	2-0	0-1	3-7	3-6	1-2	1-2	1-0	0-1	—	2-4	2-2	0-1	1-0	1-2	0-2	4-2	0-3	0-4
Flexsys Cefn Druids	1-2	0-1	3-7	0-2	2-1	2-1	0-4	0-3	2-4	—	5-1	0-1	4-0	4-2	0-2	3-3	2-0	2-2
Haverfordwest County	2-3	1-2	2-4	2-4	1-2	1-0	2-1	0-3	0-3	2-4	—	3-4	1-1	0-5	0-2	2-0	0-1	3-3
Llanelli	3-2	1-2	3-7	0-2	1-2	2-1	2-1	2-1	0-3	2-4	2-2	—	2-1	0-1	2-1	6-1	0-3	1-3
Newtown	1-1	1-3	0-0	0-1	3-3	1-0	1-1	0-0	1-0	0-2	1-1	1-0	—	2-2	4-0	2-2	0-3	0-1
Oswestry Town	2-5	0-3	0-1	1-4	0-1	1-3	1-1	2-3	0-2	0-5	2-2	3-2	2-3	—	5-1	3-3	2-2	1-5
Port Talbot Town	1-1	0-1	2-4	0-1	0-1	2-4	2-6	1-2	1-2	6-2	3-2	2-1	3-0	2-3	—	3-0	2-3	1-0
Rhayader Town	0-2	0-0	0-1	0-3	0-1	2-6	0-1	0-4	1-0	3-4	0-3	0-3	1-0	1-2	1-2	—	1-1	4-0
Rhyl	3-0	1-0	0-3	1-1	3-1	1-3	3-1	2-0	4-0	3-1	2-0	2-0	1-0	2-3	3-1	1-1	—	1-2
Total Network Solutions	2-1	2-0	1-1	1-1	2-2	1-0	3-0	0-1	1-2	3-1	0-0	0-4	3-1	1-0	1-0	1-0	1-3	—

EUROPEAN REVIEW 2001–2002

Hampden Park was the venue for the European Cup Final 2002 style, the first time the Scottish ground had been used for the event since 1976, but as an echo from their first such staging in 1960 it was Real Madrid who again won the trophy.

Back in 1960 the Spaniards had made it five in a row with a splendid victory in what was arguably their finest final in beating Eintracht Frankfurt 7-3. This time there were fresh Germanic opponents in Bayer Leverkusen.

Having just failed to win the Bundesliga when it seemed easier to win it and thrown their own cup chances away, Leverkusen were not perhaps in the best frame of mind for the encounter. When Raul put the Spaniards ahead in the eighth minute, their worst fears seemed to have been realised. But they drew level when Lucio headed in for the Germans.

That was how it stayed until a minute from the interval when Zinedine Zidane made his not insignificant contribution to the proceedings. A centre from Roberto Carlos found the French international just outside the penalty area where he unleashed a left-foot volley of such precision and power that it gave goalkeeper Hans-Jorg Butt no hope of stopping it.

With injuries affecting both teams seven minutes of extra time was added to the second half. During this time Real's replacement goalkeeper Iker Casillas made three heart-stopping saves to keep Real ahead and this after Leverkusen goalkeeper Butt had even had a header of his own at the Spanish end! It was Real Madrid's ninth European Cup success in their centenary year.

As far as the UEFA Cup was concerned, the final worked out brilliantly for Feyenoord as it was played on their own ground in Rotterdam. Again there was German opposition for the Dutch team in the form of Borussia Dortmund. Pierre Van Hooijdonk opened the scoring for Feyenoord from the penalty spot in the 33rd minute and added a second goal seven minutes later. Two goals ahead by the break seemed enough, but Marcio Amoroso reduced the arrears from a penalty two minutes after the restart.

The margin lasted only three minutes before Jon Dahl Tomasson restored Feyenoord's two-goal advantage only for Jan Koller to make it 3-2 in the 50th minute. Thus five goals had been scored in a 17 minute spell either side of the half-time break. For Feyenoord it was their first European trophy for 28 years.

As far as British involvement in the two main European competitions is concerned Manchester United reached the semi-final but lost the tie with Leverkusen at Old Trafford where they had to settle for a 2-2 draw. They did manage another draw in Germany but at 1-1 it was insufficient and gave Leverkusen the tie on away goals.

For Leverkusen it was a second triumph over an English team as they had beaten Liverpool in the quarter-finals. Despite taking a 1-0 lead in the first leg at Anfield, the Merseysiders lost away 4-2.

Arsenal gave one of their poorest performances of the season in the last group game losing 1-0 to the kind of reserve-looking Juventus team, the composition of which is usually expected by English teams not interested in the League Cup.

In the UEFA Cup, Leeds United reached the fourth round before losing to PSV Eindhoven and Rangers went out at the same stage to Feyenoord the eventual winners.

Alas the future of the UEFA Cup seems doubtful. Already it is becoming the poor relation as was the Cup-Winners' Cup which was axed in 1999. The Champions League takes all the plaudits and most of the money and seems likely to be expanded eventually at the expense of the UEFA Cup.

There was a shock for France in the Under-21 championship final, held scoreless by the Czech Republic and then beaten on a penalty shoot-out 3-1 in Switzerland.

Actually the Swiss themselves produced their first trophy winning the UEFA Under-17 title in Denmark. Once again it was the French who lost out. In the final which also regrettably went to penalties before a winner was declared, the Swiss won 4-2 after both teams had failed to score in the match. The Swiss had comprehensively beaten England 3-0 in the semi-finals.

England again disappointed in the Under-21 final stages when it had been expected they would be strong enough to actually win the competition. The Under-20s had fared little better in a tournament in Toulon.

EUROPEAN CUP 2001–2002

FIRST QUALIFYING ROUND, FIRST LEG

Araks	(0) 0	Serif	(0) 1
Barry Town	(0) 2	Shamkir	(0) 0
Bohemians	(2) 3	Levadia	(0) 0
F91 Dudelange	(1) 1	Skonto Riga	(1) 6
KR Reykjavik	(0) 2	Vllaznia	(1) 1
Levski	(3) 4	Zeljeznicar	(0) 0
Linfield	(0) 0	Torpedo Kutaisi	(0) 0
Sloga	(0) 0	Kaunas	(0) 0
Valletta	(0) 0	Haka	(0) 0
VB Vagur	(0) 0	Slavia Mozyr	(0) 0

FIRST QUALIFYING ROUND, SECOND LEG

Haka	(4) 5	Valletta	(0) 0
Kaunas	(0) 1	Sloga	(0) 1
Levadia	(0) 0	Bohemians	(0) 0
Serif	(1) 2	Araks	(0) 0
Shamkir	(0) 0	Barry Town	(0) 1
Skonto Riga	(0) 0	F91 Dudelange	(0) 1
Slavia Mozyr	(5) 5	VB Vagur	(0) 0
Torpedo Kutaisi	(0) 1	Linfield	(0) 0
Vllaznia	(0) 1	KR Reykjavik	(0) 0
Zeljeznicar	(0) 0	Levski	(0) 0

SECOND QUALIFYING ROUND, FIRST LEG

Anderlecht	(2) 4	Serif	(0) 0
Bohemians	(1) 1	Halmstad	(1) 2
Ferencvaros	(0) 0	Hajduk Split	(1) 2
Galatasaray	(1) 2	Vllaznia	(0) 0
Haka	(0) 0	Maccabi Haifa	(1) 1
Levski	(0) 0	Brann	(0) 0
Maribor	(0) 0	Rangers	(1) 3
Omonia	(0) 1	Red Star Belgrade	(1) 1
Porto	(5) 8	Barry Town	(0) 0
Shakhtjor Donetsk	(1) 3	Lugano	(0) 0
Skonto Riga	(0) 1	Wisla	(0) 2
Slavia Mozyr	(0) 0	Inter Bratislava	(1) 1
Steaua	(2) 3	Sloga	(0) 0
Torpedo Kutaisi	(0) 0	FC Copenhagen	(1) 1

SECOND QUALIFYING ROUND, SECOND LEG

Barry Town	(2) 3	Porto	(1) 1
Brann	(1) 1	Levski	(1) 1
FC Copenhagen	(1) 3	Torpedo Kutaisi	(0) 1
Hajduk Split	(0) 0	Ferencvaros	(0) 0
Halmstad	(0) 2	Bohemians	(0) 0
Inter Bratislava	(0) 1	Slavia Mozyr	(0) 0
Lugano	(0) 2	Shakhtjor Donetsk	(1) 1
Maccabi Haifa	(1) 4	Haka	(0) 0

(Match awarded 3-0 to Haka; Maccabi Haifa fielded an ineligible player.)

Rangers	(0) 3	Maribor	(1) 1
Red Star Belgrade	(0) 2	Omonia	(0) 1
Serif	(1) 1	Anderlecht	(1) 2
Sloga	(0) 1	Steaua	(2) 2
Vllaznia	(1) 1	Galatasaray	(1) 4
Wisla	(0) 1	Skonto Riga	(0) 0

THIRD QUALIFYING ROUND, FIRST LEG

Ajax	(1) 1	Celtic	(2) 3
FC Copenhagen	(0) 2	Lazio	(1) 1

Galatasaray	(1) 2	Levski	(0) 1
Hajduk Split	(1) 1	Mallorca	(0) 0
Haka	(0) 0	Liverpool	(1) 5
Halmstad	(1) 2	Anderlecht	(0) 3
Inter Bratislava	(0) 3	Rosenborg	(1) 3
Lokomotiv Moscow	(2) 3	Tirol Innsbruck	(1) 1
Parma	(0) 0	Lille	(0) 2
Porto	(1) 2	Grasshoppers	(0) 2
Rangers	(0) 0	Fenerbahce	(0) 0
Red Star Belgrade	(0) 0	Leverkusen	(0) 0
Shakhtjor Donetsk	(0) 0	Borussia Dortmund	(1) 2
Slavia Prague	(0) 1	Panathinaikos	(1) 2
Steaua	(1) 2	Dynamo Kiev	(3) 4
Wisla	(3) 3	Barcelona	(2) 4

THIRD QUALIFYING ROUND, SECOND LEG

Anderlecht	(0) 1	Halmstad	(1) 1
Barcelona	(0) 1	Wisla	(0) 0
Borussia Dortmund	(0) 3	Shakhtjor Donetsk	(1) 1
Celtic	(0) 0	Ajax	(1) 1
Dynamo Kiev	(0) 1	Steaua	(1) 1
Fenerbahce	(1) 2	Rangers	(0) 1
Grasshoppers	(0) 2	Porto	(2) 3
Lazio	(0) 4	FC Copenhagen	(0) 1
Leverkusen	(2) 3	Red Star Belgrade	(0) 0
Levski	(0) 1	Galatasaray	(0) 1
Lille	(0) 0	Parma	(1) 1
Liverpool	(1) 4	Haka	(1) 1
Mallorca	(1) 2	Hajduk Split	(0) 0
Panathinaikos	(1) 1	Slavia Prague	(0) 0
Rosenborg	(3) 4	Inter Bratislava	(0) 0
Tirol Innsbruck	(0) 0	Lokomotiv Moscow	(0) 1

(result annulled; referee Van der Ende wrongly booked Maminov instead of Pimenov already on a yellow card)

Tirol Innsbruck	(1) 1	Lokomotiv Moscow	(0) 0

CHAMPIONS LEAGUE

GROUP A

Lokomotiv Moscow	(1) 1	Anderlecht	(1) 1
Roma	(0) 1	Real Madrid	(0) 2
Anderlecht	(0) 0	Roma	(0) 0
Real Madrid	(1) 4	Lokomotiv Moscow	(0) 0
Real Madrid	(0) 4	Anderlecht	(1) 1
Roma	(0) 2	Lokomotiv Moscow	(0) 1
Anderlecht	(0) 0	Real Madrid	(2) 2
Lokomotiv Moscow	(0) 0	Roma	(0) 1
Anderlecht	(1) 1	Lokomotiv Moscow	(2) 5
Real Madrid	(0) 1	Roma	(1) 1
Lokomotiv Moscow	(1) 2	Real Madrid	(0) 0
Roma	(0) 1	Anderlecht	(1) 1

Final Table	P	W	D	L	F	A	Pts
Real Madrid	6	4	1	1	13	5	13
Roma	6	2	3	1	6	5	9
Lokomotiv Moscow	6	2	1	3	9	9	7
Anderlecht	6	0	3	3	4	13	3

GROUP B

Dynamo Kiev	(2) 2	Borussia Dortmund	(0) 2
Liverpool	(1) 1	Boavista	(1) 1

Boavista	(3) 3	Dynamo Kiev	(1) 1
Borussia Dortmund	(0) 0	Liverpool	(0) 0
Boavista	(2) 2	Borussia Dortmund	(0) 1
Liverpool	(1) 1	Dynamo Kiev	(0) 0
Borussia Dortmund	(0) 2	Boavista	(1) 1
Dynamo Kiev	(0) 1	Liverpool	(1) 2
Boavista	(0) 1	Liverpool	(1) 1
Borussia Dortmund	(1) 1	Dynamo Kiev	(0) 0
Dynamo Kiev	(0) 1	Boavista	(0) 0
Liverpool	(1) 2	Borussia Dortmund	(0) 0

Final Table	P	W	D	L	F	A	Pts
Liverpool	6	3	3	0	7	3	12
Boavista	6	2	2	2	8	7	8
Borussia Dortmund	6	2	2	2	6	7	8
Dynamo Kiev	6	1	1	4	5	9	4

Boavista qualified on better head-to-head record.

GROUP C

Mallorca	(1) 1	Arsenal	(0) 0
Schalke	(0) 0	Panathinaikos	(0) 2
Arsenal	(2) 3	Schalke	(1) 2
Panathinaikos	(2) 2	Mallorca	(0) 0
Panathinaikos	(1) 1	Arsenal	(0) 0
Schalke	(0) 0	Mallorca	(0) 1
Arsenal	(1) 2	Panathinaikos	(0) 1
Mallorca	(0) 0	Schalke	(2) 4
Arsenal	(0) 3	Mallorca	(0) 1
Panathinaikos	(1) 2	Schalke	(0) 0
Mallorca	(0) 1	Panathinaikos	(0) 0
Schalke	(1) 3	Arsenal	(0) 1

Final Table	P	W	D	L	F	A	Pts
Panathinaikos	6	4	0	2	8	3	12
Arsenal	6	3	0	3	9	9	9
Mallorca	6	3	0	3	4	9	9
Schalke	6	2	0	4	9	9	6

Arsenal qualified on better head-to-head record.

GROUP D

Galatasaray	(0) 1	Lazio	(0) 0
Nantes	(3) 4	PSV Eindhoven	(0) 1
Lazio	(1) 1	Nantes	(1) 3
PSV Eindhoven	(1) 3	Galatasaray	(0) 1
Nantes	(0) 0	Galatasaray	(0) 1
PSV Eindhoven	(1) 1	Lazio	(0) 0
Galatasaray	(0) 0	Nantes	(0) 0
Lazio	(1) 2	PSV Eindhoven	(0) 1
Lazio	(0) 1	Galatasaray	(0) 0
PSV Eindhoven	(0) 0	Nantes	(0) 0
Galatasaray	(1) 2	PSV Eindhoven	(0) 0
Nantes	(0) 1	Lazio	(0) 0

Final Table	P	W	D	L	F	A	Pts
Nantes	6	3	2	1	8	3	11
Galatasaray	6	3	1	2	5	4	10
PSV Eindhoven	6	2	1	3	6	9	7
Lazio	6	2	0	4	4	7	6

GROUP E

Juventus	(1) 3	Celtic	(0) 2
Rosenborg	(0) 1	Porto	(1) 2
Celtic	(1) 1	Porto	(0) 0

Rosenborg	(0) 1	Juventus	(0) 1
Celtic	(1) 1	Rosenborg	(0) 0
Porto	(0) 0	Juventus	(0) 0
Porto	(2) 3	Celtic	(0) 0
Juventus	(1) 1	Rosenborg	(0) 0
Juventus	(1) 3	Porto	(1) 1
Rosenborg	(2) 2	Celtic	(0) 0
Celtic	(2) 4	Juventus	(1) 3
Porto	(1) 1	Rosenborg	(0) 0

Final Table	P	W	D	L	F	A	Pts
Juventus	6	3	2	1	11	8	11
Porto	6	3	1	2	7	5	10
Celtic	6	3	0	3	8	11	9
Rosenborg	6	1	1	4	4	6	4

GROUP F

Fenerbahce	(0) 0	Barcelona	(2) 3
Lyon	(0) 0	Leverkusen	(0) 1
Fenerbahce	(0) 0	Lyon	(0) 1
Leverkusen	(0) 2	Barcelona	(1) 1
Barcelona	(0) 2	Lyon	(0) 0
Leverkusen	(1) 2	Fenerbahce	(1) 1
Barcelona	(2) 2	Leverkusen	(1) 1
Lyon	(1) 3	Fenerbahce	(1) 1
Fenerbahce	(1) 1	Leverkusen	(2) 2
Lyon	(0) 2	Barcelona	(2) 3
Barcelona	(0) 1	Fenerbahce	(0) 0
Leverkusen	(1) 2	Lyon	(2) 4

Final Table	P	W	D	L	F	A	Pts
Barcelona	6	5	0	1	12	5	15
Leverkusen	6	4	0	2	10	9	12
Lyon	6	3	0	3	10	9	9
Fenerbahce	6	0	0	6	3	12	0

GROUP G

La Coruna	(1) 2	Olympiakos	(0) 2
Manchester United	(0) 1	Lille	(0) 0
La Coruna	(0) 2	Manchester United	(1) 1
Lille	(2) 3	Olympiakos	(0) 1
Lille	(0) 1	La Coruna	(0) 1
Olympiakos	(0) 0	Manchester United	(0) 2
Manchester United	(2) 2	La Coruna	(2) 3
Olympiakos	(0) 2	Lille	(1) 1
La Coruna	(1) 1	Lille	(1) 1
Manchester United	(0) 3	Olympiakos	(0) 0
Lille	(0) 1	Manchester United	(1) 1
Olympiakos	(0) 1	La Coruna	(0) 1

Final Table	P	W	D	L	F	A	Pts
La Coruna	6	2	4	0	10	8	10
Manchester United	6	3	1	2	10	6	10
Lille	6	1	3	2	7	7	6
Olympiakos	6	1	2	3	6	12	5

La Coruna finished top on better head-to-head record.

GROUP H

Bayern Munich	(0) 0	Sparta Prague	(0) 0
Spartak Moscow	(0) 2	Feyenoord	(1) 2
Sparta Prague	(2) 4	Feyenoord	(0) 0
Spartak Moscow	(0) 1	Bayern Munich	(2) 3
Feyenoord	(2) 2	Bayern Munich	(1) 2

Sparta Prague	(0) 2	Spartak Moscow	(0) 0
Bayern Munich	(3) 5	Spartak Moscow	(0) 1
Feyenoord	(0) 0	Sparta Prague	(1) 2
Bayern Munich	(2) 3	Feyenoord	(1) 1
Spartak Moscow	(2) 2	Sparta Prague	(1) 2
Feyenoord	(2) 2	Spartak Moscow	(1) 1
Sparta Prague	(0) 0	Bayern Munich	(1) 1

Final Table	P	W	D	L	F	A	Pts
Bayern Munich	6	4	2	0	14	5	14
Sparta Prague	6	3	2	1	10	3	11
Feyenoord	6	1	2	3	7	14	5
Spartak Moscow	6	0	2	4	7	16	2

SECOND STAGE

GROUP A

Bayern Munich	(0) 1	Manchester United	(0) 1
Boavista	(1) 1	Nantes	(0) 0
Manchester United	(1) 3	Boavista	(0) 0
Nantes	(0) 0	Bayern Munich	(0) 1
Boavista	(0) 0	Bayern Munich	(0) 1
Nantes	(1) 1	Manchester United	(0) 1
Bayern Munich	(0) 1	Boavista	(0) 0
Manchester United	(3) 5	Nantes	(1) 1
Manchester United	(0) 0	Bayern Munich	(0) 0
Nantes	(1) 1	Boavista	(0) 1
Bayern Munich	(0) 2	Nantes	(0) 1
Boavista	(0) 0	Manchester United	(2) 3

Final Table	P	W	D	L	F	A	Pts
Manchester United	6	3	3	0	13	3	12
Bayern Munich	6	3	3	0	5	2	12
Boavista	6	1	2	3	2	8	5
Nantes	6	0	2	4	4	11	2

Manchester United finished top on better head-to-head record.

GROUP B

Galatasaray	(1) 1	Roma	(0) 1
Liverpool	(1) 1	Barcelona	(1) 3
Barcelona	(0) 2	Galatasaray	(2) 2
Roma	(0) 0	Liverpool	(0) 0
Barcelona	(0) 1	Roma	(0) 1
Liverpool	(0) 0	Galatasaray	(0) 0
Galatasaray	(0) 1	Liverpool	(0) 1
Roma	(0) 3	Barcelona	(0) 0
Barcelona	(0) 0	Liverpool	(0) 0
Roma	(0) 1	Galatasaray	(1) 1
Galatasaray	(0) 0	Barcelona	(0) 1
Liverpool	(1) 2	Roma	(0) 0

Final Table	P	W	D	L	F	A	Pts
Barcelona	6	2	3	1	7	7	9
Liverpool	6	1	4	1	4	4	7
Roma	6	1	4	1	6	5	7
Galatasaray	6	0	5	1	5	6	5

Liverpool qualified on better head-to-head record.

GROUP C

Panathinaikos	(0) 0	Porto	(0) 0
Sparta Prague	(1) 2	Real Madrid	(2) 3
Porto	(0) 0	Sparta Prague	(0) 1
Real Madrid	(1) 3	Panathinaikos	(0) 0
Real Madrid	(0) 1	Porto	(0) 0
Sparta Prague	(0) 0	Panathinaikos	(1) 2

Panathinaikos	(1) 2	Sparta Prague	(0) 1
Porto	(1) 1	Real Madrid	(2) 2
Porto	(1) 2	Panathinaikos	(0) 1
Real Madrid	(0) 3	Sparta Prague	(0) 0
Panathinaikos	(1) 2	Real Madrid	(1) 2
Sparta Prague	(0) 2	Porto	(0) 0

Final Table	P	W	D	L	F	A	Pts
Real Madrid	6	5	1	0	14	5	16
Panathinaikos	6	2	2	2	7	8	8
Sparta Prague	6	2	0	4	6	10	6
Porto	6	1	1	4	3	7	4

GROUP D

Juventus	(3) 4	Leverkusen	(0) 0
La Coruna	(2) 2	Arsenal	(0) 0
Arsenal	(2) 3	Juventus	(0) 1
Leverkusen	(0) 3	La Coruna	(0) 0
Juventus	(0) 0	La Coruna	(0) 0
Leverkusen	(0) 1	Arsenal	(0) 1
Arsenal	(2) 4	Leverkusen	(0) 1
La Coruna	(1) 2	Juventus	(0) 0
Arsenal	(0) 0	La Coruna	(2) 2
Leverkusen	(1) 3	Juventus	(0) 1
La Coruna	(0) 1	Leverkusen	(1) 3
Juventus	(0) 1	Arsenal	(0) 0

Final Table	P	W	D	L	F	A	Pts
Leverkusen	6	3	1	2	11	11	10
La Coruna	6	3	1	2	7	6	10
Arsenal	6	2	1	3	8	8	7
Juventus	6	2	1	3	7	8	7

Leverkusen finished top on better head-to-head record.

QUARTER-FINALS, FIRST LEG

Bayern Munich	(0) 2	Real Madrid	(1) 1
La Coruna	(0) 0	Manchester United	(2) 2
Liverpool	(1) 1	Leverkusen	(0) 0
Panathinaikos	(0) 1	Barcelona	(0) 0

QUARTER-FINALS, SECOND LEG

Barcelona	(1) 3	Panathinaikos	(1) 1
Leverkusen	(1) 4	Liverpool	(1) 2
Manchester United	(1) 3	La Coruna	(1) 2
Real Madrid	(0) 2	Bayern Munich	(0) 0

SEMI-FINALS, FIRST LEG

| Barcelona | (0) 0 | Real Madrid | (0) 2 |
| Manchester United | (1) 2 | Leverkusen | (0) 2 |

SEMI-FINALS, SECOND LEG

| Leverkusen | (1) 1 | Manchester United | (1) 1 |
| Real Madrid | (1) 1 | Barcelona | (0) 1 |

FINAL
Leverkusen (1) 1, Real Madrid (2) 2
(at Hampden Park, 15 May 2002, 52,000)

Leverkusen: Butt; Sebescen (Kirsten 65), Placente, Ramelow, Zivkovic, Lucio (Babic 90), Schneider, Ballack, Neuville, Basturk, Brdaric (Berbatov 39).
Scorer: Lucio 14.
Real Madrid: Cesar (Casillas 68); Michel Salgado, Roberto Carlos, Makelele (Conceicao 73), Hierro, Helguera, Figo (McManaman 61), Morientes, Raul, Zidane, Solari.
Scorers: Raul 8, Zidane 45.
Referee: Meier (Switzerland).

INTER-TOTO CUP 2001

FIRST ROUND
Carmarthen Town v AIK Stockholm 0-0, 0-3
Dundee v Sartid 0-0, 2-5
Cork City v Metalurgs 0-1, 1-2
Anorthosis v Slaven Belupo 0-2, 0-7
WIT v Ried 1-0, 1-2
Aarhus v Publikum 1-0, 1-7
St Julia v Lausanne 1-3, 0-6
Tatabanya v Shirak 2-3, 3-1
B68 v Lokeren 2-4, 0-0
Uni Craiova v Bylis 3-3, 1-0
Dynamo Minsk v Hobscheid 6-0, 1-1
Groclin v Spartak Varna 1-0, 0-4
Jazz v Gloria 1-0, 1-2
Grindavik v Vilash 1-0, 2-1
Tiligul v Cliftonville 1-0, 3-1
Celik v Denizli 1-0, 5-3
Ekranas v Artmedia 1-1, 1-1
Artmedia won on penalties.
NK Zagreb v Pobeda 1-2, 1-1
Hapoel Haifa v VMK 2-0, 3-0
Zaglebie v Hibernians 4-0, 0-1

SECOND ROUND
Sturm Graz v Lausanne 0-1, 3-3
Celik v Gent 1-0, 0-2
Slaven Belupo v Bastia 1-0, 1-0
Dynamo Minsk v Hapoel Haifa 2-0, 1-0
Pobeda v Rize 2-1, 2-0
Basle v Grindavik 3-0, 2-0
Troyes v WIT 6-0, 1-1
Spartak Varna v Tavriya 0-3, 2-2
Tiligul v Tatabanya 1-1, 0-4
Odense v AIK Stockholm 2-2, 0-2

Zaglebie v Lokeren 2-2, 1-2
Paris St Germain v Jazz 3-0, 4-1
1860 Munich v Sartid 3-1, 3-2
Metalurgs v Heerenveen 3-2, 1-6
Synot v Uni Craiova 3-2, 2-2
Publikum v Artmedia 5-0, 1-1

THIRD ROUND
Chmel v Pobeda 0-0, 1-0
Lokeren v Newcastle United 0-4, 0-1
Publikum v Lausanne 1-1, 0-0
Slaven Belupo v Aston Villa 2-1, 0-2
Basle v Heerenveen 2-1, 3-2
Werder Bremen v Gent 2-3, 1-0
Wolfsburg v Dynamo Minsk 4-3, 0-0
Brescia v Tatabanya 2-1, 1-1
Tavriya v Paris St Germain 0-1, 0-4
RKC v 1860 Munich 1-2, 1-3
Troyes v AIK Stockholm 2-1, 2-1
Rennes v Synot 5-0, 2-4

SEMI-FINALS
Gent v Paris St Germain 0-0, 1-7
Troyes v Wolfsburg 1-0, 2-2
Rennes v Aston Villa 2-1, 0-1
1860 Munich v Newcastle United 2-3, 1-3
Chmel v Brescia 1-2, 2-2

FINALS
Troyes v Newcastle United 0-0, 4-4
Troyes won on away goals.
Basle v Aston Villa 1-1, 1-4
Paris St Germain v Brescia 0-0, 1-1

UEFA CUP 2001–2002

QUALIFYING ROUND, FIRST LEG

AEK Athens	(2) 6	Grevenmacher	(0) 0
Ararat Erevan	(0) 0	Hapoel Tel Aviv	(2) 2
Atlantas	(0) 0	Rapid Bucharest	(1) 4
Birkirkara	(0) 0	Lokomotiv Tbilisi	(0) 0
Brasov	(3) 5	Mika	(0) 1
Brondby	(1) 2	Shelbourne	(0) 0
FC Brugge	(0) 4	IA Akranes	(0) 0
Cosmos	(0) 0	Rapid Vienna	(1) 1
CSKA Kiev	(1) 2	Jokerit	(0) 0
Cwmbran Town	(0) 0	Slovan Bratislava	(2) 4
Debrecen	(2) 3	Otaci	(0) 0
Dinaburg	(0) 2	Osijek	(0) 1
Dinamo Bucharest	(1) 1	Dinamo Tirana	(0) 0
Dynamo Tbilisi	(1) 2	BATE Borisov	(0) 1
Dynamo Zagreb	(0) 1	Flora	(0) 0
Etzella	(0) 0	Legia	(3) 4
Fylkir	(2) 2	Pogon	(0) 1
Glenavon	(0) 0	Kilmarnock	(0) 1
HB Torshavn	(0) 2	Graz	(0) 2
HJK Helsinki	(1) 2	Ventspils	(0) 1
Longford Town	(1) 1	Liteks	(0) 1
Maccabi Tel Aviv	(3) 6	Zalgiris	(0) 0
Maritimo	(1) 1	Sarajevo	(0) 0
Matador	(1) 3	Sliema Wanderers	(0) 0
Midtjylland	(1) 1	Glentoran	(0) 1
MyPa	(0) 1	Helsingborg	(1) 3
Neftchi	(0) 0	Gorica	(0) 0
Obilic	(2) 4	GI Gotu	(0) 0
Olimpija	(1) 4	Shafa	(0) 0
Omonia	(0) 2	Dunaferr	(1) 2
Pelister	(0) 0	St Gallen	(1) 2
Polonia	(0) 4	TNS	(0) 0
Ruzomberok	(2) 3	Belshina	(0) 1
Shakhter	(0) 1	CSKA Sofia	(0) 2
SK Tirana	(0) 3	Apollon	(1) 2
Santa Coloma	(0) 0	Partizan Belgrade	(1) 1
Trans	(0) 1	Elfsborg	(2) 3
Vaduz	(1) 3	Varteks	(0) 3
Vardar	(0) 0	Standard Liege	(1) 3
Viking	(0) 1	Brotnjo	(0) 0
Zimbru Chisinau	(0) 0	Gaziantep	(0) 0

QUALIFYING ROUND, SECOND LEG

Apollon	(0) 3	SK Tirana	(1) 1
BATE Borisov	(2) 4	Dynamo Tbilisi	(0) 0
Belshina	(0) 0	Ruzomberok	(0) 0
Brotnjo	(1) 1	Viking	(1) 1
CSKA Sofia	(1) 3	Shakhter	(0) 1
Dinamo Tirana	(0) 1	Dinamo Bucharest	(2) 3
Dunaferr	(0) 2	Olympiakos	(2) 4
Elfsborg	(1) 5	Trans	(0) 0
Flora	(0) 0	Dynamo Zagreb	(1) 1
Gaziantep	(2) 4	Zimbru Chisinau	(1) 1
GI Gotu	(1) 1	Obilic	(1) 1

219

Glentoran	(0) 0	Midtjylland	(1) 4
Gorica	(0) 1	Neftchi	(0) 0
Graz	(2) 4	HB Torshavn	(0) 0
Grevenmacher	(0) 0	AEK Athens	(1) 2
Hapoel Tel Aviv	(2) 3	Ararat	(0) 0
Helsingborg	(1) 2	MyPa	(1) 1
IA Akranes	(1) 1	FC Brugge	(1) 6
Jokerit	(0) 0	CSKA Kiev	(0) 2
Kilmarnock	(0) 1	Glenavon	(0) 0
Legia	(1) 2	Etzella	(0) 1
Liteks	(0) 2	Longford Town	(0) 0
Lokomotiv Tbilisi	(0) 1	Birkirkara	(1) 1
Mika	(0) 0	Brasov	(1) 2
Osijek	(1) 1	Dinaburg	(0) 0
Otaci	(0) 1	Debrecen	(0) 0
Partizan Belgrade	(2) 7	Santa Coloma	(1) 1
Pogon	(1) 1	Fylkir	(0) 1
Rapid Bucharest	(2) 8	Atlantas	(0) 0
Rapid Vienna	(1) 2	Cosmos	(0) 0
Sarajevo	(0) 0	Maritimo	(0) 1
Shafa	(0) 0	Olimpija	(1) 3
Shelbourne	(0) 0	Brondby	(1) 3
Sliema Wanderers	(1) 2	Matador	(0) 1
Slovan Bratislava	(0) 1	Cwmbran Town	(0) 0
St Gallen	(0) 2	Pelister	(0) 3
Standard Liege	(0) 3	Vardar	(0) 1
TNS	(0) 0	Polonia	(1) 2
Varteks	(3) 6	Vaduz	(0) 1
Ventspils	(0) 0	HJK Helsinki	(1) 1
Zalgiris	(0) 0	Maccabi Tel Aviv	(0) 1

FIRST ROUND, FIRST LEG

AEK Athens	(0) 2	Hibernian	(0) 0
Ajax	(1) 2	Apollon	(0) 0
Aston Villa	(0) 2	Varteks	(1) 3
BATE Borisov	(0) 0	AC Milan	(0) 2
Bordeaux	(2) 5	Debrecen	(1) 1
Celta Vigo	(1) 4	Olomouc	(0) 0
Chelsea	(1) 3	Levski	(0) 0
Chernomorets	(0) 0	Valencia	(0) 1
FC Copenhagen	(1) 2	Obilic	(0) 0
CSKA Kiev	(1) 3	Red Star Belgrade	(1) 2
CSKA Sofia	(2) 3	Shakhtjor Donetsk	(0) 0
Dinamo Bucharest	(0) 1	Grasshoppers	(1) 3
Dnepr	(0) 0	Fiorentina	(0) 0
Dynamo Moscow	(1) 1	Birkirkara	(0) 0
Dynamo Zagreb	(0) 2	Maccabi Tel Aviv	(2) 2
Genclerbirligi	(0) 1	Halmstad	(1) 1
Gorica	(0) 1	Osijek	(0) 2
Hajduk Split	(1) 2	Wisla	(0) 2
Haka	(1) 1	Union Berlin	(0) 1
Hapoel Tel Aviv	(0) 1	Gaziantep	(0) 0
Inter Bratislava	(0) 1	Liteks	(0) 0
Internazionale	(3) 3	Brasov	(0) 0
(in Trieste).			
Ipswich Town	(0) 1	Torpedo Moscow	(1) 1
Karnten	(0) 0	PAOK Salonika	(0) 0
Kilmarnock	(0) 1	Viking	(1) 1
Legia	(1) 4	Elfsborg	(1) 1

Liberec	(1) 2	Slovan Bratislava	(0) 0
Maritimo	(1) 1	Leeds United	(0) 0
Matador	(0) 0	Freiburg	(0) 0
Midtjylland	(0) 0	Sporting Lisbon	(0) 3
Odd Grenland	(2) 2	Helsingborg	(1) 2
Olimpija	(1) 2	Brondby	(1) 4
Olympiakos	(1) 2	FC Brugge	(1) 2
Paris St Germain	(0) 0	Rapid Bucharest	(0) 0
Parma	(1) 1	HJK Helsinki	(0) 0
Partizan Belgrade	(0) 1	Rapid Vienna	(0) 0
Polonia	(0) 1	Twente	(0) 2
Pribram	(1) 4	Sedan	(0) 0
Roda	(1) 3	Fylkir	(0) 0
Servette	(0) 1	Slavia Prague	(0) 0
St Gallen	(1) 2	Steaua	(1) 1
Standard Liege	(1) 2	Strasbourg	(0) 0
Troyes	(3) 6	Ruzomberok	(0) 1
Utrecht	(2) 3	Graz	(0) 0
Viktoria Zizkov	(0) 0	Tirol Innsbruck	(0) 0
Westerlo	(0) 0	Hertha Berlin	(1) 2
Zaragoza	(0) 3	Silkeborg	(0) 0

FIRST ROUND, SECOND LEG

Apollon	(0) 0	Ajax	(1) 3
Birkirkara	(0) 0	Dynamo Moscow	(0) 0
Brasov	(0) 0	Internazionale	(2) 3
Brondby	(0) 0	Olimpija	(0) 0
FC Brugge	(2) 7	Olympiakos	(0) 1
Debrecen	(1) 3	Bordeaux	(0) 1
Elfsborg	(0) 1	Legia	(1) 6
Fiorentina	(0) 2	Dnepr	(0) 1
Freiburg	(1) 2	Matador	(0) 1
Fylkir	(0) 1	Roda	(0) 3
Gaziantep	(0) 1	Hapoel Tel Aviv	(1) 1
Grasshoppers	(2) 3	Dinamo Bucharest	(0) 1
Graz	(3) 3	Utrecht	(0) 3
Halmstad	(1) 1	Genclerbirligi	(0) 0
Helsingborg	(1) 1	Odd Grenland	(1) 1
Hertha Berlin	(0) 1	Westerlo	(0) 0
Hibernian	(0) 3	AEK Athens	(0) 2
HJK Helsinki	(0) 0	Parma	(0) 2
Leeds United	(2) 3	Maritimo	(0) 0
Levski	(0) 0	Chelsea	(2) 2
Liteks	(2) 3	Inter Bratislava	(0) 0
Maccabi Tel Aviv	(1) 1	Dynamo Zagreb	(1) 1
AC Milan	(2) 4	BATE Borisov	(0) 0
Obilic	(1) 2	FC Copenhagen	(0) 2
Olomouc	(0) 4	Celta Vigo	(2) 3
Osijek	(0) 1	Gorica	(0) 0
PAOK Salonika	(1) 4	Karnten	(0) 0
Rapid Bucharest	(0) 0	Paris St Germain	(0) 1

*(abandoned after 113 minutes; floodlight failure. Game awarded 3-0 to PSG as
Rapid failed to have necessary back-up generator).*

Rapid Vienna	(2) 5	Partizan Belgrade	(0) 1
Red Star Belgrade	(0) 0	CSKA Kiev	(0) 0
Ruzomberok	(0) 1	Troyes	(0) 0
Sedan	(1) 3	Pribram	(0) 1
Shakhtjor Donetsk	(1) 2	CSKA Sofia	(0) 1
Silkeborg	(1) 1	Zaragoza	(1) 2

Slavia Prague	(0) 1	Servette	(1) 1
Slovan Bratislava	(1) 1	Liberec	(0) 0
Sporting Lisbon	(2) 3	Midtjylland	(0) 2
Steaua	(1) 1	St Gallen	(0) 1
Strasbourg	(2) 2	Standard Liege	(0) 2
Tirol Innsbruck	(0) 1	Viktoria Zizkov	(0) 0
Torpedo Moscow	(0) 1	Ipswich Town	(0) 2
Twente	(0) 2	Polonia	(0) 0
Union Berlin	(2) 3	Haka	(0) 0
Valencia	(3) 5	Chernomorets	(0) 0
Varteks	(0) 0	Aston Villa	(0) 1
Viking	(2) 2	Kilmarnock	(0) 0
Wisla	(1) 1	Hajduk Split	(0) 0
Anzhi	(0) 0	Rangers	(0) 1

(Tie decided over one match played in Warsaw).

SECOND ROUND, FIRST LEG

Bordeaux	(2) 2	Standard Liege	(0) 0
Celta Vigo	(1) 3	Liberec	(0) 1
FC Copenhagen	(0) 0	Ajax	(0) 0
CSKA Kiev	(0) 0	FC Brugge	(1) 2
Fiorentina	(0) 2	Tirol Innsbruck	(0) 0
Freiburg	(0) 0	St Gallen	(0) 1
Grasshoppers	(2) 4	Twente	(0) 1
Halmstad	(0) 0	Sporting Lisbon	(0) 1
Hapoel Tel Aviv	(0) 2	Chelsea	(0) 0
Internazionale	(0) 2	Wisla	(0) 0
Ipswich Town	(0) 0	Helsingborg	(0) 0
Leeds United	(3) 4	Troyes	(1) 2
Legia	(1) 1	Valencia	(0) 0
AC Milan	(1) 2	CSKA Sofia	(0) 0
Osijek	(0) 1	AEK Athens	(1) 2
PAOK Salonika	(3) 6	Pribram	(0) 1
Paris St Germain	(2) 4	Rapid Vienna	(0) 0
Rangers	(1) 3	Dynamo Moscow	(0) 1
Roda	(2) 4	Maccabi Tel Aviv	(0) 1
Union Berlin	(0) 0	Liteks	(0) 2
Utrecht	(0) 1	Parma	(1) 3
Varteks	(0) 3	Brondby	(0) 1
Viking	(0) 0	Hertha Berlin	(1) 1
Zaragoza	(0) 0	Servette	(0) 0

SECOND ROUND, SECOND LEG

AEK Athens	(2) 3	Osijek	(2) 2
Ajax	(0) 0	FC Copenhagen	(0) 1
Brondby	(2) 5	Varteks	(0) 0
FC Brugge	(3) 5	CSKA Kiev	(0) 0
Chelsea	(0) 1	Hapoel Tel Aviv	(1) 1
CSKA Sofia	(0) 0	AC Milan	(0) 1
Dynamo Moscow	(1) 1	Rangers	(3) 4
Helsingborg	(1) 1	Ipswich Town	(0) 3
Hertha Berlin	(2) 2	Viking	(0) 0
Liberec	(1) 3	Celta Vigo	(0) 0
Liteks	(0) 0	Union Berlin	(0) 0
Maccabi Tel Aviv	(1) 2	Roda	(1) 1
Parma	(0) 0	Utrecht	(0) 0
Pribram	(1) 2	PAOK Salonika	(1) 2
Rapid Vienna	(2) 2	Paris St Germain	(0) 2
St Gallen	(1) 1	Freiburg	(2) 4

Servette	(0) 1	Zaragoza	(0) 0
Sporting Lisbon	(2) 6	Halmstad	(1) 1
Standard Liege	(0) 0	Bordeaux	(0) 2
Tirol Innsbruck	(1) 2	Fiorentina	(2) 2
Troyes	(2) 3	Leeds United	(1) 2
Twente	(2) 4	Grasshoppers	(0) 2
Valencia	(4) 6	Legia	(0) 1
Wisla	(1) 1	Internazionale	(0) 0

THIRD ROUND, FIRST LEG

AEK Athens	(3) 3	Liteks	(1) 2
Bordeaux	(0) 1	Roda	(0) 0
FC Brugge	(1) 4	Lyon	(0) 1
FC Copenhagen	(0) 0	Borussia Dortmund	(0) 1
Feyenoord	(0) 1	Freiburg	(0) 0
Fiorentina	(0) 0	Lille	(1) 1
Grasshoppers	(1) 1	Leeds United	(0) 2
Hapoel Tel Aviv	(1) 2	Lokomotiv Moscow	(0) 1
Ipswich Town	(0) 1	Internazionale	(0) 0
Liberec	(2) 3	Mallorca	(0) 1
AC Milan	(1) 2	Sporting Lisbon	(0) 0
PAOK Salonika	(2) 3	PSV Eindhoven	(1) 2
Parma	(1) 1	Brondby	(0) 1
Rangers	(0) 0	Paris St Germain	(0) 0
Servette	(0) 0	Hertha Berlin	(0) 0
Valencia	(0) 1	Celtic	(0) 0

THIRD ROUND, SECOND LEG

Borussia Dortmund	(0) 1	FC Copenhagen	(0) 0
Brondby	(0) 0	Parma	(1) 3
Celtic	(1) 1	Valencia	(0) 0
aet; Valencia won 5-4 on penalties.			
Freiburg	(1) 2	Feyenoord	(0) 2
Hertha Berlin	(0) 0	Servette	(1) 3
Internazionale	(2) 4	Ipswich Town	(0) 1
Leeds United	(2) 2	Grasshoppers	(1) 2
Lille	(1) 2	Fiorentina	(0) 0
Liteks	(0) 1	AEK Athens	(1) 1
Lokomotiv Moscow	(0) 0	Hapoel Tel Aviv	(0) 1
Lyon	(2) 3	FC Brugge	(0) 0
Mallorca	(0) 1	Liberec	(0) 2
Paris St Germain	(0) 0	Rangers	(0) 0
aet; Rangers won 4-3 on penalties.			
PSV Eindhoven	(2) 4	PAOK Salonika	(0) 1
Roda	(0) 2	Bordeaux	(0) 0
Sporting Lisbon	(0) 1	AC Milan	(0) 1

FOURTH ROUND, FIRST LEG

Hapoel Tel Aviv	(0) 0	Parma	(0) 0
Internazionale	(2) 3	AEK Athens	(1) 1
Lille	(0) 1	Borussia Dortmund	(0) 1
Lyon	(1) 1	Liberec	(1) 1
PSV Eindhoven	(0) 0	Leeds United	(0) 1
Rangers	(0) 1	Feyenoord	(0) 1
Roda	(0) 0	AC Milan	(1) 1
Valencia	(1) 3	Servette	(0) 0

FOURTH ROUND, SECOND LEG

AC Milan	(0) 0	Roda	(0) 1

(aet; AC Milan won 3-2 on penalties).

AEK Athens	(1) 2	Internazionale	(1) 2
Borussia Dortmund	(0) 0	Lille	(0) 0
Feyenoord	(2) 3	Rangers	(1) 2
Leeds United	(0) 0	PSV Eindhoven	(0) 1
Liberec	(1) 4	Lyon	(1) 1
Parma	(0) 1	Hapoel Tel Aviv	(1) 2
Servette	(1) 2	Valencia	(2) 2

QUARTER-FINALS, FIRST LEG

Hapoel Tel Aviv	(1) 1	AC Milan	(0) 0

(in Nicosia).

Internazionale	(0) 1	Valencia	(0) 1
Liberec	(0) 0	Borussia Dortmund	(0) 0

(in Prague).

PSV Eindhoven	(0) 1	Feyenoord	(1) 1

QUARTER-FINALS, SECOND LEG

Borussia Dortmund	(0) 4	Liberec	(0) 0
Feyenoord	(0) 1	PSV Eindhoven	(1) 1

(aet; Feyenoord won 5-4 on penalties).

AC Milan	(2) 2	Hapoel Tel Aviv	(0) 0
Valencia	(0) 0	Internazionale	(1) 1

SEMI-FINALS, FIRST LEG

Borussia Dortmund	(3) 4	AC Milan	(0) 0
Internazionale	(0) 0	Feyenoord	(0) 1

SEMI-FINALS, SECOND LEG

Feyenoord	(2) 2	Internazionale	(0) 2
AC Milan	(2) 3	Borussia Dortmund	(0) 1

FINAL

Feyenoord (2) 3, Borussia Dortmund (0) 2

(in Rotterdam, 8 May 2002, 45,000)

Feyenoord: Zoetebier; Gyan, Rzasa, Ono (De Haan 75), Van Wonderen, Paauwe, Bosvelt, Kalou (Elmander 75), Van Hooijdonk, Van Persie (Leonardo 62), Tomasson.
Scorers: Van Hooijdonk 33 (pen), 40, Tomasson 50.
Borussia Dortmund: Lehmann; Evanilson, Dede, Ricken (Heinrich 69), Worns, Kohler, Reuter, Ewerthon (Addo 61), Koller, Amoroso, Rosicky.
Scorers: Amoroso 47 (pen), Koller 58.
Referee: Pereira (Portugal).

PAST EUROPEAN CUP FINALS

Year	Team	Score	Opponent	Score
1956	Real Madrid	4	Stade de Rheims	3
1957	Real Madrid	2	Fiorentina	0
1958	Real Madrid	3	AC Milan	2*
1959	Real Madrid	2	Stade de Rheims	0
1960	Real Madrid	7	Eintracht Frankfurt	3
1961	Benfica	3	Barcelona	2
1962	Benfica	5	Real Madrid	3
1963	AC Milan	2	Benfica	1
1964	Internazionale	3	Real Madrid	1
1965	Internazionale	1	SL Benfica	0
1966	Real Madrid	2	Partizan Belgrade	1
1967	Celtic	2	Internazionale	1
1968	Manchester U	4	Benfica	1*
1969	AC Milan	4	Ajax	1
1970	Feyenoord	2	Celtic	1*
1971	Ajax	2	Panathinaikos	0
1972	Ajax	2	Internazionale	0
1973	Ajax	1	Juventus	0
1974	Bayern Munich	1 4	Atletico Madrid	1 0
1975	Bayern Munich	2	Leeds U	0
1976	Bayern Munich	1	St Etienne	0
1977	Liverpool	3	Borussia Moenchengladbach	1
1978	Liverpool	1	FC Brugge	0
1979	Nottingham F	1	Malmö	0
1980	Nottingham F	1	Hamburg	0
1981	Liverpool	1	Real Madrid	0
1982	Aston Villa	1	Bayern Munich	0
1983	Hamburg	1	Juventus	0
1984	Liverpool†	1	Roma	1
1985	Juventus	1	Liverpool	0
1986	Steaua Bucharest†	0	Barcelona	0
1987	Porto	2	Bayern Munich	1
1988	PSV Eindhoven†	0	Benfica	0
1989	AC Milan	4	Steaua Bucharest	0
1990	AC Milan	1	Benfica	0
1991	Red Star Belgrade†	0	Marseille	0
1992	Barcelona	1	Sampdoria	0
1993	Marseille	1	AC Milan	0

(Marseille subsequently stripped of title)

Year	Team	Score	Opponent	Score
1994	AC Milan	4	Barcelona	0
1995	Ajax	1	AC Milan	0
1996	Juventus†	1	Ajax	1
1997	Borussia Dortmund	3	Juventus	1
1998	Real Madrid	1	Juventus	0
1999	Manchester U	2	Bayern Munich	1
2000	Real Madrid	3	Valencia	0
2001	Bayern Munich†	1	Valencia	1
2002	Real Madrid	2	Leverkusen	1

† aet; won on penalties.
* aet.

PAST EUROPEAN CUP-WINNERS FINALS

Year	Team	Score	Opponent	Score
1961	Fiorentina	4	Rangers	1‡
1962	Atletico Madrid	1 3	Fiorentina	1 0
1963	Tottenham H	5	Atletico Madrid	1
1964	Sporting Lisbon	3 1	MTK Budapest	3* 0

1965	West Ham U	2	Munich 1860	0
1966	Borussia Dortmund	2	Liverpool	1*
1967	Bayern Munich	1	Rangers	0*
1968	AC Milan	2	Hamburg	0
1969	Slovan Bratislava	3	Barcelona	2
1970	Manchester C	2	Gornik Zabrze	1
1971	Chelsea	1 2	Real Madrid	1* 1*
1972	Rangers	3	Dynamo Moscow	2
1973	AC Milan	1	Leeds U	0
1974	Magdeburg	2	AC Milan	0
1975	Dynamo Kiev	3	Ferencvaros	0
1976	Anderlecht	4	West Ham U	2
1977	Hamburg	2	Anderlecht	0
1978	Anderlecht	4	Austria Vienna	0
1979	Barcelona	4	Fortuna Dusseldorf	3*
1980	Valencia†	0	Arsenal	0
1981	Dynamo Tbilisi	2	Carl Zeiss Jena	1
1982	Barcelona	2	Standard Liege	1
1983	Aberdeen	2	Real Madrid	1*
1984	Juventus	2	Porto	1
1985	Everton	3	Rapid Vienna	1
1986	Dynamo Kiev	3	Atletico Madrid	0
1987	Ajax	1	Lokomotiv Leipzig	0
1988	Mechelen	1	Ajax	0
1989	Barcelona	2	Sampdoria	0
1990	Sampdoria	2	Anderlecht	0
1991	Manchester U	2	Barcelona	1
1992	Werder Bremen	2	Monaco	0
1993	Parma	3	Antwerp	1
1994	Arsenal	1	Parma	0
1995	Real Zaragoza	2	Arsenal	1*
1996	Paris St Germain	1	Rapid Vienna	0
1997	Barcelona	1	Paris St Germain	0
1998	Chelsea	1	Stuttgart	0
1999	Lazio	2	Mallorca	1

PAST FAIRS CUP FINALS

1958	Barcelona	8	London	2‡
1960	Barcelona	4	Birmingham C	1‡
1961	Roma	4	Birmingham C	2‡
1962	Valencia	7	Barcelona	3‡
1963	Valencia	4	Dynamo Zagreb	1‡
1964	Real Zaragoza	2	Valencia	1
1965	Ferencvaros	1	Juventus	0
1966	Barcelona	4	Real Zaragoza	3‡
1967	Dynamo Zagreb	2	Leeds U	0‡
1968	Leeds U	1	Ferencvaros	0‡
1969	Newcastle U	6	Ujpest Dozsa	2‡
1970	Arsenal	4	Anderlecht	3‡
1971	Leeds U**	3	Juventus	3‡

PAST UEFA CUP FINALS

1972	Tottenham H	2 1	Wolverhampton W	1 1
1973	Liverpool	3 0	Borussia Moenchengladbach	0 2
1974	Feyenoord	2 2	Tottenham H	2 0
1975	Borussia Moenchengladbach	0 5	Twente Enschede	0 1
1976	Liverpool†	3 1	FC Brugge	2 1
1977	Juventus**	1 1	Athletic Bilbao	0 2

Year	Winner			Runner-up		
1978	PSV Eindhoven	0	3	SEC Bastia	0	0
1979	Borussia Moenchengladbach	1	1	Red Star Belgrade	1	0
1980	Borussia Moenchengladbach	3	0	Eintracht Frankfurt**	2	1
1981	Ipswich T	3	2	AZ 67 Alkmaar	0	4
1982	IFK Gothenburg	1	3	SV Hamburg	0	1
1983	Anderlecht	1	1	Benfica	0	1
1984	Tottenham H†	1	1	RSC Anderlecht	1	1
1985	Real Madrid	3	0	Videoton	0	1
1986	Real Madrid	5	0	Cologne	1	2
1987	IFK Gothenburg	1	1	Dundee U	0	1
1988	Bayer Leverkusen†	0	3	Espanol	0	3
1989	Napoli	2	3	Stuttgart	1	3
1990	Juventus	3	0	Fiorentina	1	0
1991	Internazionale	2	0	AS Roma	0	1
1992	Ajax**	0	2	Torino	0	2
1993	Juventus	3	3	Borussia Dortmund	1	0
1994	Internazionale	1	1	Salzburg	0	0
1995	Parma	1	1	Juventus	0	1
1996	Bayern Munich	2	3	Bordeaux	0	1
1997	Schalke*†	1	0	Internazionale	0	1
1998	Internazionale	3		Lazio	0	
1999	Parma	3		Marseille	0	
2000	Galatasaray†	0		Arsenal	4	
2001	Liverpool§	5		Alaves	4	
2002	Feyenoord	3		Borussia Dortmund	2	

*After extra time   **Won on away goals   †Won on penalties   ‡Aggregate score
§Won on sudden death.

EUROPEAN CHAMPIONS LEAGUE 2002–2003

DRAW 2002–2003

FIRST QUALIFYING ROUND
To be played July 17 and 24
Tampere United v FC Pyunik
Skonto v Barry Town
Portadown v Belshina Bobruisk
F91 Dudelange v Vardar
FBK Kaunas v Dinamo Tirana
Flora v Apoel Nicosia
FK Zeljeznikar v IA Akranes
Hibernians v Shelbourne
Torpedo Kutaisi v B36 Torshavn
Sheriff Tiraspol v Zhenis Aspana.

SECOND QUALIFYING ROUND
To be played July 31 and August 7
Zalaegerszegi TE v NK Zagreb
Club Brugge v Dinamo Bucharest
MSK Zilina v FC Basel
Skonto or Barry v PFC Levski Sofia.
Dynamo Kiev v Tampere United or FC
  Pyunik
Brondby IF v FBK Kaunas or Dinamo
  Tirana
NK Maribor v Flora or Apoel Nicosia
F91 Dudelange or Vardar v Legia Warsaw
Boavista v Hibernians or Shelbourne

Maccabi Haifa v Portadown or Belshina
  Bobruisk
Lillestrom v FK Zeljeznikar v IA Akranes
Hammarby v FK Partizan
Sparta Prague v Torpedo Kutaisi v B36
  Torshavn
Sheriff Tiraspol v Zhenis Aspana v Grazer
  AK

SEEDINGS:
Pot 1: Real Madrid, Bayern
Munich*, Manchester United*, Barcelona*,
Valencia, Juventus, Arsenal,
Internazionale*
Pot 2: Deportivo La Coruna, Bayer
Leverkusen, Liverpool, Galatasaray, Roma,
Lyon, Borussia Dortmund, Feyenoord*.
Pot 3: Milan*, PSV Eindhoven, Dinamo
Kiev*, Spartak Moscow, Lokomotiv
Moscow*, Olympiakos, AEK Athens*,
Sparta Prague*.
Pot 4: Ajax, Rosenborg*, Lens, Newcastle*,
Brugge*, Sturm Graz*, Boavista*, Celtic*.
* denotes team has to pre-qualify.
Teams from the same pot cannot be drawn
to face each other.

Draw for the first round proper will take
place on August 29, with the eight groups
consisting of one team from each pot.

PAST EUROPEAN CHAMPIONSHIP FINALS

Year	Winners		Runners-up		Venue	Attendance
1960	USSR	2	Yugoslavia	1	Paris	17,966
1964	Spain	2	USSR	1	Madrid	120,000
1968	Italy	2	Yugoslavia	0	Rome	60,000
	After 1-1 draw					75,000
1972	West Germany	3	USSR	0	Brussels	43,437
1976	Czechoslovakia	2	West Germany	2	Belgrade	45,000
	(Czechoslovakia won on penalties)					
1980	West Germany	2	Belgium	1	Rome	47,864
1984	France	2	Spain	0	Paris	48,000
1988	Holland	2	USSR	0	Munich	72,308
1992	Denmark	2	Germany	0	Gothenburg	37,800
1996	Germany	2	Czech Republic	1	Wembley	73,611
	(Germany won on sudden death)					
2000	France	2	Italy	1	Rotterdam	50,000
	(France won on sudden death)					

EURO 2004 – FIXTURES

Group 1
Cyprus, France, Israel, Malta, Slovenia.
07.09.02 Slovenia v Malta
07.09.02 Cyprus v France
12.10.02 France v Slovenia
12.10.02 Malta v Israel
16.10.02 Israel v Cyprus
16.10.02 Malta v France
20.11.02 Cyprus v Malta
29.03.03 Cyprus v Israel
29.03.03 France v Malta
02.04.03 Slovenia v Cyprus
02.04.03 Israel v France
30.04.03 Malta v Slovenia
07.06.03 Israel v Slovenia
07.06.03 Malta v Cyprus
06.09.03 France v Cyprus
06.09.03 Slovenia v Israel
10.09.03 Israel v Malta
10.09.03 Slovenia v France
11.10.03 Cyprus v Slovenia
11.10.03 France v Israel

Group 2
Denmark, Luxembourg, Norway, Romania, Bosnia.
07.09.02 Norway v Denmark
07.09.02 Bosnia v Romania
12.10.02 Denmark v Luxembourg
12.10.02 Romania v Norway
16.10.02 Norway v Bosnia
16.10.02 Luxembourg v Romania
29.03.03 Bosnia v Luxembourg
29.03.03 Romania v Denmark
02.04.03 Luxembourg v Norway
02.04.03 Denmark v Bosnia
07.06.03 Denmark v Norway
07.06.03 Romania v Bosnia
11.06.03 Luxembourg v Denmark
11.06.03 Norway v Romania
06.09.03 Bosnia v Norway
06.09.03 Romania v Luxembourg
10.09.03 Luxembourg v Bosnia
10.09.03 Denmark v Romania
11.10.03 Norway v Luxembourg
11.10.03 Bosnia v Denmark

Group 3
Austria, Holland, Belarus, Moldova, Czech Republic.
07.09.02 Austria v Moldova
07.09.02 Holland v Belarus
12.10.02 Belarus v Austria
13.10.02 Moldova v Czech Republic
16.10.02 Austria v Holland
16.10.02 Czech Republic v Belarus
29.03.03 Belarus v Moldova
29.03.03 Holland v Czech Republic
02.04.03 Czech Republic v Austria
02.04.03 Moldova v Holland
07.06.03 Moldova v Austria
07.06.03 Belarus v Holland
11.06.03 Czech Republic v Moldova
11.06.03 Austria v Belarus
06.09.03 Holland v Austria
06.09.03 Belarus v Czech Republic
10.09.03 Czech Republic v Holland
10.09.03 Moldova v Belarus
11.10.03 Austria v Czech Republic
11.10.03 Holland v Moldova

Group 4
Hungary, Poland, Sweden, San Marino, Latvia.
07.09.02 San Marino v Poland
07.09.02 Latvia v Sweden
12.10.02 Sweden v Hungary
12.10.02 Poland v Latvia
16.10.02 Hungary v San Marino
20.11.02 San Marino v Latvia
29.03.03 Poland v Hungary
02.04.03 Poland v San Marino
02.04.03 Hungary v Sweden
30.04.03 Latvia v San Marino
07.06.03 Hungary v Latvia
07.06.03 San Marino v Sweden
11.06.03 Sweden v Poland
11.06.03 San Marino v Hungary
06.09.03 Latvia v Poland
06.09.03 Sweden v San Marino
10.09.03 Poland v Sweden
10.09.03 Latvia v Hungary
11.10.03 Sweden v Latvia
11.10.03 Hungary v Poland

Group 5
Germany, Iceland, Scotland,
Faeroes, Lithuania.
07.09.02 Lithuania v
Germany
07.09.02 Faeroes v Scotland
12.10.02 Lithuania v Faeroes
12.10.02 Iceland v Scotland
16.10.02 Germany v Faeroes
16.10.02 Iceland v Lithuania
29.03.03 Germany v
Lithuania
29.03.03 Scotland v Iceland
02.04.03 Lithuania v Scotland
07.06.03 Scotland v Germany
07.06.03 Iceland v Faeroes
11.06.03 Faeroes v Germany
11.06.03 Lithuania v Iceland
20.08.03 Faeroes v Iceland
06.09.03 Scotland v Faeroes
06.09.03 Iceland v Germany
10.09.03 Germany v Scotland
10.09.03 Faeroes v Lithuania
11.10.03 Scotland v Lithuania
11.10.03 Germany v Iceland

Group 6
Greece, Northern Ireland,
Spain, Ukraine, Armenia.
07.09.02 Greece v Spain
07.09.02 Armenia v Ukraine
12.10.02 Spain v Northern
Ireland
12.10.02 Ukraine v Greece
16.10.02 Greece v Armenia
16.10.02 Northern Ireland v
Ukraine
29.03.03 Armenia v Northern
Ireland
29.03.03 Ukraine v Spain
02.04.03 Northern Ireland v
Greece
02.04.03 Spain v Armenia
07.06.03 Spain v Greece
07.06.03 Ukraine v Armenia
11.06.03 Northern Ireland v
Spain
11.06.03 Greece v Ukraine
06.09.03 Armenia v Greece
06.09.03 Ukraine v Northern
Ireland
10.09.03 Northern Ireland v
Armenia
10.09.03 Spain v Ukraine
11.10.03 Greece v Northern
Ireland
11.10.03 Armenia v Spain

Group 7
England, Liechtenstein,
Turkey, Slovakia, Macedonia.
07.09.02 Turkey v Slovakia
07.09.02 Liechtenstein v
Macedonia
12.10.02 Slovakia v England

12.10.02 Macedonia v Turkey
16.10.02 Turkey v
Liechtenstein
16.10.02 Liechtenstein v
Macedonia
29.03.03 Liechtenstein v
England
29.03.03 Macedonia v
Slovakia
02.04.03 England v Turkey
02.04.03 Slovakia v
Liechtenstein
07.06.03 Slovakia v Turkey
07.06.03 Macedonia v
Liechtenstein
11.06.03 England v Slovakia
11.06.03 Turkey v Macedonia
06.09.03 Liechtenstein v
Turkey
06.09.03 Macedonia v
England
10.09.03 England v
Liechtenstein
10.09.03 Slovakia v
Macedonia
11.10.03 Turkey v England
11.10.03 Liechtenstein v
Slovakia

Group 8
Belgium, Bulgaria, Croatia,
Estonia, Andorra.
07.09.02 Belgium v Bulgaria
07.09.02 Croatia v Estonia
12.10.02 Andorra v Belgium
12.10.02 Bulgaria v Croatia
16.10.02 Estonia v Belgium
16.10.02 Bulgaria v Andorra
29.03.03 Croatia v Belgium
02.04.03 Estonia v Bulgaria
02.04.03 Croatia v Andorra
30.04.03 Andorra v Estonia
07.06.03 Bulgaria v Belgium
07.06.03 Estonia v Andorra
11.06.03 Estonia v Croatia
11.06.03 Belgium v Andorra
06.09.03 Bulgaria v Estonia
06.09.03 Andorra v Croatia
10.09.03 Belgium v Croatia
10.09.03 Andorra v Bulgaria
11.10.03 Croatia v Bulgaria
11.10.03 Belgium v Estonia

Group 9
Finland, Italy, Wales,
Yugoslavia, Azerbaijan.
07.09.02 Azerbaijan v Italy
07.09.02 Finland v Wales
12.10.02 Italy v Yugoslavia
12.10.02 Finland v Azerbaijan
16.10.02 Wales v Italy
16.10.02 Yugoslavia v Finland
20.11.02 Azerbaijan v Wales
29.03.03 Italy v Finland
29.03.03 Wales v Azerbaijan

02.04.03 Yugoslavia v Wales
30.04.03 Azerbaijan v
Yugoslavia
07.06.03 Finland v Yugoslavia
11.06.03 Finland v Italy
11.06.03 Yugoslavia v
Azerbaijan
06.09.03 Italy v Wales
06.09.03 Azerbaijan v Finland
10.09.03 Wales v Finland
10.09.03 Yugoslavia v Italy
11.10.03 Italy v Azerbaijan
11.10.03 Wales v Yugoslavia

Group 10
Albania, Republic of Ireland,
Switzerland, Georgia, Russia.
07.09.02 Russia v Republic of
Ireland
07.09.02 Switzerland v
Georgia
12.10.02 Albania v
Switzerland
12.10.02 Georgia v Russia
16.10.02 Republic of Ireland
v Switzerland
16.10.02 Russia v Albania
29.03.03 Georgia v Republic
of Ireland
29.03.03 Albania v Russia
02.04.03 Albania v Republic
of Ireland
02.04.03 Georgia v
Switzerland
07.06.03 Switzerland v Russia
07.06.03 Republic of Ireland
v Albania
11.06.03 Republic of Ireland
v Georgia
11.06.03 Switzerland v
Albania
06.09.03 Republic of Ireland
v Russia
06.09.03 Georgia v Albania
10.09.03 Russia v Switzerland
10.09.03 Albania v Georgia
11.10.03 Russia v Georgia
11.10.03 Switzerland v
Republic of Ireland

Play-offs
15/19.11.03

Group Matches
12/19.06.04; 04/19.07.04

Quarter-finals
30.06.04

Semi-finals
01.07.04

Final
04.07.04

PAST WORLD CUP FINALS

Year	Winners		Runners-up		Venue	Att.	Referee
1930	Uruguay	4	Argentina	2	Montevideo	90,000	Langenus (B)
1934	Italy	2	Czechoslovakia	1	Rome	50,000	Eklind (Se)
	(after extra time)						
1938	Italy	4	Hungary	2	Paris	45,000	Capdeville (F)
1950	Uruguay	2	Brazil	1	Rio de Janeiro	199,854	Reader (E)
1954	West Germany	3	Hungary	2	Berne	60,000	Ling (E)
1958	Brazil	5	Sweden	2	Stockholm	49,737	Guigue (F)
1962	Brazil	3	Czechoslovakia	1	Santiago	68,679	Latychev (USSR)
1966	England	4	West Germany	2	Wembley	93,802	Dienst (Sw)
	(after extra time)						
1970	Brazil	4	Italy	1	Mexico City	107,412	Glockner (EG)
1974	West Germany	2	Holland	1	Munich	77,833	Taylor (E)
1978	Argentina	3	Holland	1	Buenos Aires	77,000	Gonella (I)
	(after extra time)						
1982	Italy	3	West Germany	1	Madrid	90,080	Coelho (Br)
1986	Argentina	3	West Germany	2	Mexico City	114,580	Filho (Br)
1990	West Germany	1	Argentina	0	Rome	73,603	Codesal (Mex)
1994	Brazil	0	Italy	0	Los Angeles	94,194	Puhl (H)
	(Brazil won 3-2 on penalties aet)						
1998	France	3	Brazil	0	St-Denis	75,000	Belqola (Mor)
2002	Brazil	2	Germany	0	Yokohama	69,029	Collina (I)

FIFA WORLD CUP 2002 QUALIFYING COMPETITION RESULTS

EUROPE
(Members 51, Entries 51)

GROUP 1

Zurich, 2 September 2000, 14,500

Switzerland (0) 0   Russia (0) 1 *(Bestchastnykh 74)*

Switzerland: Pascolo; Lubamba, Henchoz, Muller P, Mazzarelli (Buhlmann 72), Cantaluppi (Wicky 64), Vogel, Sforza, Comisetti, Rey, Yakin H (N'Kufo 64).
Russia: Nigmatullin; Khlestov, Chugainov, Smertin, Gusev (Alenichev 52), Drozdov, Onopko, Karpin, Titov (Panov 46) (Semak 88), Mostovoi, Bestchastnykh.
Referee: Nielsen (Denmark).

Toftir, 3 September 2000, 3200

Faeroes (0) 2 *(Arge 87, Hansen O 90)*   **Slovenia (1) 2** *(Udovic 25, Osterc 86)*

Faeroes: Mikkelsen; Hansen HF, Johannesen O, Hansen JK, Morkore A, Joensen S, Petersen (Joensen J 78), Johnsson, Hansen O, Arge, Jonsson T (Morkore K 57).
Slovenia: Simeunovic; Bulajic, Vugdalic, Milinovic, Novak, Karic, Ceh A, Pavlin, Zahovic, Rudonja (Zlogar 89), Udovic (Osterc 71).
Referee: Vuorela (Finland).

Luxembourg, 3 September 2000, 3305

Luxembourg (0) 0   Yugoslavia (2) 2 *(Milosevic 4, Jokanovic 26)*

Luxembourg: Besic; Vanek, Schauls, Funck, Strasser, Deville L, Saibene, Alverdi (Theis 84), Holtz (Ferron 89), Schneider, Zaritski (Huss 62).
Yugoslavia: Cicovic; Mirkovic, Dudic (Sakic 62), Jokanovic, Bunjevcevic, Djordjevic, Lazetic, Stankovic D (Ilic I 73), Drulovic, Mijatovic (Kovacevic 70), Milosevic.
Referee: Smolik (Belarus).

Luxembourg, 7 October 2000, 1788

Luxembourg (0) 1 *(Strasser 46)*   **Slovenia (2) 2** *(Zahovic 39, Milinovic 41)*

Luxembourg: Besic; Vanek, Schauls, Funck, Strasser (Posing 88), Saibene, Peters, Holtz, Schneider, Cardoni (Zaritski 80), Huss (Braun 73).
Slovenia: Dabanovic; Milinovic, Vugdalic, Karic, Knavs, Novak, Ceh A, Siljak (Udovic 80), Zahovic, Pavlin (Pavlovic 67), Acimovic.
Referee: Benes (Czech Republic).

Zurich, 7 October 2000, 9500

Switzerland (4) 5 *(Zwyssig 26, Fournier 35, Turkyilmaz 43 (pen), 45 (pen), 53 (pen))*
Faeroes (1) 1 *(Petersen 4)*

Switzerland: Zuberbuhler; Lubamba (Wicky 66), Henchoz, Zwyssig, Fournier, Sesa, Vogel (Celestini 66), Sforza, Comisetti, Chapuisat, Turkyilmaz (Cantaluppi 76).
Faeroes: Mikkelsen; Morkore A, Johannesen O, Hansen JK, Hansen HF, Petersen (Jacobsen R 63), Joensen S (Joensen J 63), Johnsson, Hansen O, Hansen JB, Arge.
Referee: Kapitanis (Cyprus).

Moscow, 11 October 2000, 12,000

Russia (1) 3 *(Buznikin 19, Khokhlov 57, Titov 90)*   **Luxembourg (0) 0**

Russia: Nigmatullin; Khlestov, Khokhlov, Smertin, Tetradze, Buznikin, Onopko, Karpin, Titov, Mostovoi, Bestchastnykh.
Luxembourg: Gillet; Funck (Ferron 86), Schauls, Vanek, Strasser, Saibene, Peters, Holtz, Schneider (Posing 77), Cardoni, Huss (Zaritski 61).
Referee: Ferry (Northern Ireland).

Ljubljana, 11 October 2000, 7000

Slovenia (1) 2 *(Siljak 44, Acimovic 78)*   **Switzerland (1) 2** *(Turkyilmaz 20, 66)*

Slovenia: Dabanovic; Milinovic, Vugdalic, Knavs, Novak, Ceh A, Pavlin (Acimovic 69), Karic, Udovic (Tavcar 46), Zahovic, Siljak (Osterc 59).
Switzerland: Zuberbuhler; Zellweger, Mazzarelli, Zwyssig, Fournier (Magnin 64) (Muller P 72), Wicky (Cantaluppi 46), Comisetti, Vogel, Chapuisat, Sforza, Turkyilmaz.
Referee: Durkin (England).

Luxembourg, 24 March 2001, 2380

Luxembourg (0) 0   Faeroes (0) 2 *(Jacobsen C 75, Morkore K 82)*

Luxembourg: Besic; Deville L, Schauls, Posing, Strasser, Saibene, Peters (Huss 46), Holtz, Zaritski, Cardoni, Schneider (Braun 77).
Faeroes: Mikkelsen; Johannesen O, Hansen JB, Borg (Olsen 84), Hansen HF, Hansen O, Benjaminsen (Jacobsen R 73), Johnsson, Morkore K, Jonsson T (Jacobsen C 20), Petersen J.
Referee: Hanacsek (Hungary).

Moscow, 24 March 2001, 35,000

Russia (1) 1 *(Khlestov 8)*   **Slovenia (1) 1** *(Knavs 22)*

Russia: Nigmatulin; Khlestov, Nikiforov, Kovtun, Tetradze, Karpin, Smertin (Bestchastnykh 46), Onopko, Alenichev (Semak 66), Titov, Buznikin.
Slovenia: Simeunovic; Gajser, Milinovic, Knavs, Bulajic, Novak, Ceh A, Pavlin, Rudonja (Pavlovic 88), Zahovic, Osterc (Cimerotic 66).
Referee: Dallas (Scotland).

Belgrade, 24 March 2001, 36,000

Yugoslavia (0) 1 *(Mihajlovic 68)*   **Switzerland (0) 1** *(Chapuisat 84)*

Yugoslavia: Kocic; Duljaj, Djukic, Mihajlovic, Obradovic, Lazetic (Stefanovic 78), Jugovic, Stankovic D (Ivic 56), Djordjevic (Kovacevic 64), Kezman, Milosevic.
Switzerland: Pascolo; Zellweger, Henchoz, Muller P, Quentin, Lombardo (Buhlmann 72), Vogel, Fournier, Lonfat, Yakin H (Frei 58), Chapuisat (Vega 86).
Referee: Nilsson (Sweden).

Moscow, 28 March 2001, 10,500

Russia (1) 1 *(Mostovoi 19)*   **Faeroes (0) 0**

Russia: Nigmatulin; Tetradze (Alenichev 46), Nikiforov, Kovtun, Karpin, Gusev (Drozdov 46), Onopko, Khokhlov, Mostovoi, Titov, Buznikin (Bestchastnykh 67).
Faeroes: Mikkelsen; Johannesen O, Thorsteinsson, Borg, Hansen O, Hansen HF, Benjaminsen, Johnsson, Morkore K (Joensen S 75), Jacobsen C, Petersen J.
Referee: Irvine (Republic of Ireland).

Ljubljana, 28 March 2001, 10,000

Slovenia (0) 1 *(Zahovic 90)*   **Yugoslavia (1) 1** *(Milosevic 32)*

Slovenia: Simeunovic; Gajser (Acimovic 37), Vugdalic, Bulajic, Knavs, Novak, Ceh A, Osterc (Cimerotic 46), Pavlin (Pavlovic 62), Zahovic, Rudonja.
Yugoslavia: Kocic; Obradovic, Djukic, Mihajlovic, Krstajic, Stefanovic, Jokanovic (Duljaj 68), Lazetic, Djordjevic, Milosevic (Ivic 79), Kezman (Drulic 57).
Referee: Jol (Holland).

Zurich, 28 March 2001, 8600

Switzerland (2) 5 *(Frei 9, 31, 90, Lonfat 64, Chapuisat 72)*   **Luxembourg (0) 0**

Switzerland: Pascolo; Zellweger, Henchoz, Muller P, Quentin, Lonfat (Buhlmann 74), Vogel, Fournier, Lombardo (Muller S 86), Frei, Chapuisat (Yakin H 79).
Luxembourg: Besic; Schauls, Saibene, Deville L, Peters (Reiter 77), Cardoni, Strasser, Posing, Holtz, Schneider (Schaack 53), Huss (Zaritski 68).
Referee: Larsen (Denmark).

Belgrade, 25 April 2001, 48,000

Yugoslavia (0) 0   Russia (0) 1 *(Bestchastnykh 72)*

Yugoslavia: Ilic II; Dudic, Djukic, Bunjevcevic, Krstajic (Stefanovic 84), Jokanovic, Mihajlovic, Lazetic, Tomic, Drulic (Stankovic D 73), Kezman (Djordjevic 63).
Russia: Nigmatullin; Tugaynov, Onopko, Drozdov (Tetradze 47), Kovtun, Alenichev, Mostovoi, Khokhlov, Gusev (Semak 87), Titov, Fedkov (Bestchastnykh 46).
Referee: Plautz (Austria).

Toftir, 2 June 2001, 4000

Faeroes (0) 0   Switzerland (0) 1 *(Frei 81)*

Faeroes: Mikkelsen; Hansen HF, Johannesen O, Hansen JB, Borg, Benjaminsen, Petersen J (Petersen H 87), Johnsson, Hansen O, Arge (Jacobsen J 78), Jacobsen C.
Switzerland: Pascolo; Zellweger, Henchoz, Muller P, Quentin, Wicky, Vogel, Sforza (Lonfat 69), Lombardo, Sesa (N'Kufo 58), Frei (Magnin 87).
Referee: McDonald (Scotland).

Moscow, 2 June 2001, 70,000

Russia (1) 1 *(Kovtun 25)*   **Yugoslavia (1) 1** *(Mijatovic 38)*

Russia: Nigmatullin; Smertin, Chugainov, Onopko, Kovtun, Karpin, Titov, Mostovoi, Khokhlov, Alenichev, Bestchastnykh (Buznikin 71).
Yugoslavia: Radakovic; Obradovic, Djukic, Mihajlovic, Djorovic, Mirkovic (Bunjevcevic 85), Lazetic (Drulovic 71), Dmitrovic, Tomic, Mijatovic (Kezman 65), Milosevic.
Referee: Fandel (Germany).

Ljubljana, 2 June 2001, 5000

Slovenia (1) 2 *(Zahovic 35, 65 (pen))*   **Luxembourg (0) 0**

Slovenia: Simeunovic; Galic, Milinovic, Knavs, Novak, Ceh A, Pavlin, Cimerotic (Osterc 80), Karic (Rudonja 46), Zahovic, Acimovic (Pavlovic 62).
Luxembourg: Gillet; Deville L, Schauls, Theis, Strasser, Saibene, Peters, Holtz, Huss (Mischo 46), Cardoni (Braun 82), Schneider.
Referee: Brugger (Austria).

Toftir, 6 June 2001, 4371

Faeroes (0) 0   Yugoslavia (2) 6 *(Stankovic D 20, 55, Kezman 29, 87, 90, Milosevic 68)*

Faeroes: Mikkelsen; Hansen HF, Benjaminsen, Hansen JB, Borg, Hansen O, Joensen S (Jacobsen R 88), Johnsson (Morkore A 75), Jacobsen C (Petersen H 75), Arge, Petersen J.
Yugoslavia: Radakovic; Mirkovic (Bunjevcevic 46), Mihajlovic, Djorovic, Dmitrovic, Lazetic (Obradovic 46), Stankovic D, Drulovic (Ilic I 74), Mijatovic, Milosevic, Kezman.
Referee: Jara (Czech Republic).

Luxembourg, 6 June 2001, 2200

Luxembourg (0) 1 *(Schneider 48)*   **Russia (1) 2** *(Alenichev 16, Semak 76)*

Luxembourg: Gillet; Schauls, Deville L, Theis, Strasser, Peters (Reiter 89), Saibene, Holtz, Cardoni, Schneider (Braun 83), Huss (Christophe 64).
Russia: Nigmatullin; Smertin (Popov 52), Nikiforov, Onopko, Kovtun, Karpin, Titov, Mostovoi, Khokhlov, Alenichev (Semak 61), Bestchastnykh (Fedkov 66).
Referee: Skjervold (Norway).

Basle, 6 June 2001, 26,000

Switzerland (0) 0   Slovenia (0) 1 *(Cimerotic 83)*

Switzerland: Pascolo; Zellweger, Henchoz, Muller P, Quentin, Wicky (Lonfat 66), Vogel, Fournier, Lombardo (Sforza 56), N'Kufo, Frei (Sesa 79).
Slovenia: Simeunovic; Galic, Milinovic, Knavs, Novak, Ceh A, Pavlin, Rudonja, Karic (Cimerotic 32), Zahovic, Osterc (Acimovic 46).
Referee: Granat (Poland).

Belgrade, 15 August 2001, 20,000

Yugoslavia (1) 2 *(Mihajlovic 23, Djukic 85)*   **Faeroes (0) 0**

Yugoslavia: Kralj; Mirkovic, Djukic, Mihajlovic, Djorovic, Tomic, Dmitrovic (Djordjevic 68), Drulovic (Lazetic 62), Mijatovic, Kezman, Milosevic (Kovacevic 46).
Faeroes: Mikkelsen; Hansen JB, Hansen HF, Johannesen O, Hansen JK, Borg, Benjaminsen (Jacobsen R 90), Johnsson, Hansen O, Petersen J (Olsen 84), Jacobsen C.
Referee: Pratas (Portugal).

Toftir, 1 September 2001, 1470

Faeroes (0) 1 *(Hansen JK 85 (pen))*   **Luxembourg (0) 0**

Faeroes: Mikkelsen; Hansen HF, Johannesen O, Hansen JK, Hansen JB, Olsen (Lakjuni 59), Borg, Benjaminsen, Petersen J, Johnsson J, Jacobsen C.
Luxembourg: Gillet; Schauls, Schaack, Reiter, Saibene (Schneider 46), Strasser, Peters, Holtz, Braun (Huss 67), Cardoni, Posing.
Referee: Siric (Croatia).

Ljubljana, 1 September 2001, 8000

Slovenia (0) 2 *(Osterc 62, Acimovic 90 (pen))*   **Russia (0) 1** *(Titov 73)*

Slovenia: Simeunovic; Karic, Milinovic, Galic, Knavs, Novak, Ceh A, Pavlin, Rudonja (Pavlovic 78), Cimerotic (Osterc 46), Acimovic.
Russia: Nigmatullin; Khokhlov (Izmailov 46), Dayev, Tugaynov, Gusev (Semak 65), Kovtun, Onopko, Karpin, Titov, Mostovoi, Bestchastnykh (Shirko 79).
Referee: Poll (England).

Basle, 1 September 2001, 28,190

Switzerland (1) 1 *(Yakin H 24)*   **Yugoslavia (1) 2** *(Milosevic 39, Krstajic 74)*

Switzerland: Pascolo; Zellweger (Frei 75), Yakin M, Muller P, Berner, Sesa (Chapuisat 75), Vogel, Fournier, Comisetti (Sforza 69), Yakin H, Turkyilmaz.
Yugoslavia: Kralj; Mirkovic, Djukic, Krstajic, Lazetic (Drulovic 67), Jokanovic, Djordjevic, Dmitrovic, Mijatovic (Stankovic D 80), Kezman, Milosevic (Kovacevic 69).
Referee: Colombo (France).

Torshavn, 5 September 2001, 2927

Faeroes (0) 0   Russia (2) 3 *(Bestchastnykh 20, 31, Shirko 88)*

Faeroes: Mikkelsen; Johannesen O, Hansen JK, Hansen JB, Hansen HF, Hansen O, Benjaminsen, Johnsson, Borg (Olsen 81), Petersen J, Jacobsen C (Morkore K 46).
Russia: Nigmatullin; Drozdov, Nikiforov, Semak (Khokhlov 53), Alenichev (Koriaka 83), Kovtun, Onopko, Karpin, Titov, Izmailov, Bestchastnykh (Shirko 46).
Referee: Byrne (Republic of Ireland).

Luxembourg, 5 September 2001, 2312

Luxembourg (0) 0   Switzerland (1) 3 *(Frei 12, Turkyilmaz 57, 84)*

Luxembourg: Gillet; Schauls, Schaack, Posing, Strasser, Saibene, Peters (Rohmann 89), Holtz (Mischo 46), Braun (Huss 66), Cardoni, Christophe.
Switzerland: Stiel; Haas, Yakin M, Muller P, Quentin, Sesa (Lonfat 46), Vogel (Mazzarelli 67), Sforza, Comisetti (Fournier 46), Frei, Turkyilmaz.
Referee: Corpodean (Romania).

Belgrade, 5 September 2001, 22,000

Yugoslavia (0) 1 *(Djordjevic 52)*   **Slovenia (1) 1** *(Milinovic 11)*

Yugoslavia: Kralj; Djorovic, Djukic, Krstajic (Gvozdenovic 65), Lazetic (Stankovic D 73), Jokanovic, Djordjevic, Dmitrovic, Mijatovic, Kezman (Kovacevic 76), Milosevic.
Slovenia: Simeunovic (Dabanovic 81); Milinovic, Galic, Knavs, Gajser, Ceh A, Pavlin, Zahovic (Acimovic 56), Karic, Rudonja (Cimerotic 37), Osterc.
Referee: Nieto (Spain).

Moscow, 6 October 2001, 20,000

Russia (3) 4 *(Bestchastnykh 14 (pen), 18, 38, Titov 83)*   **Switzerland (0) 0**

Russia: Nigmatullin; Smertin (Khokhlov 88), Drozdov (Dayev 25), Tugaynov, Alenichev, Kovtun, Onopko, Gusev (Semak 74), Titov, Izmailov, Bestchastnykh.
Switzerland: Stiel; Zellweger, Quentin, Yakin M (Zwyssig 46), Muller P, Mazzarelli, Sesa, Comisetti (Lonfat 79), Yakin H, Sforza, Di Jorio (Lombardo 46).
Referee: Fisker (Denmark).

Ljubljana, 6 October 2001, 10,000

Slovenia (2) 3 *(Ceh N 13, 31, Tiganj 82)*   **Faeroes (0) 0**

Slovenia: Simeunovic; Milinovic, Galic, Knavs, Novak, Osterc (Tiganj 67), Ceh N (Bulajic 90), Rakovic (Tavcar 53), Rudonja, Gajser, Pavlovic.
Faeroes: Mikkelsen; Johannesen O, Hansen JK, Hansen JB (Danielsen 80), Hansen HF, Hansen O (Olsen 73), Jacobsen R, Morkore K, Borg, Petersen J, Jacobsen C (Jacobsen JR 74).
Referee: Kasnaferis (Greece).

Belgrade, 6 October 2001, 1758

Yugoslavia (1) 6 *(Jokanovic 19, Mijatovic 58, Kezman 61, 71, Milosevic 62, 68)*
Luxembourg (1) 2 *(Peters 38, Christophe 52)*

Yugoslavia: Stevanovic; Mirkovic, Djorovic (Ilic I 56), Jokanovic, Krstajic, Djordjevic, Mijatovic, Milosevic, Kezman (Tomic 73), Stankovic D, Lazetic (Drulovic 44).
Luxembourg: Gillet; Ferron, Schauls, Deville F, Strasser, Saibene, Peters (Reiter 85), Posing, Christophe, Cardoni (Deville L 15), Schneider (Theis 75).
Referee: Irvine (Northern Ireland).

234

Group 1 Table

	P	W	D	L	F	A	Pts
Russia	10	7	2	1	18	5	23
Slovenia	10	5	5	0	17	9	20
Yugoslavia	10	5	4	1	22	8	19
Switzerland	10	4	2	4	18	12	14
Faeroes	10	2	1	7	6	23	7
Luxembourg	10	0	0	10	4	28	0

GROUP 2

Tallinn, 16 August 2000, 1695

Estonia (0) 1 *(Reim 64 (pen))*   **Andorra (0) 0**

Estonia: Tohver; Allas, Lemsalu, Stepanovs, Rooba U, Piiroja (Jurisson 73), Reim, Alonen (Anniste 67), Terehhov, Oper, Zelinski (Ustritski 87).
Andorra: Koldo; Felix Alvarez (Soria 71), Jonas, Txema, Lima I, Escura, Sonejee, Emiliano (Pujol 74), Jimenez, Ruiz, Sanchez J.
Referee: Arsic (Yugoslavia).

La Vella, 2 September 2000, 1000

Andorra (1) 2 *(Emiliano 45, Lima I 51)*
Cyprus (1) 3 *(Constantinou M 25 (pen), 90, Agathocleous 77)*

Andorra: Koldo; Ramirez, Txema, Jonas, Sonejee, Lima I, Emiliano (Lucendo 89), Escura, Ruiz, Jimenez, Sanchez J.
Cyprus: Panayiotou N; Theodotou, Charalambous C (Agathocleous 54), Ioannou D, Charalambous M, Ioakim, Engomitis, Aristocleous (Yiasoumi 71), Christodolou M, Okkas (Kotsonis 85), Constantinou M.
Referee: Yarmenchuk (Ukraine).

Amsterdam, 2 September 2000, 50,000

Holland (0) 2 *(Talan 71, Van Bronckhorst 84)*
Republic of Ireland (1) 2 *(Robbie Keane 21, McAteer 65)*

Holland: Van der Sar; Reiziger (Seedorf 46), Konterman (Talan 66), Frank de Boer, Van Bronckhorst, Witschge (Bruggink 59), Ronald de Boer, Bosvelt, Cocu, Bouma, Kluivert.
Republic of Ireland: Kelly A; Carr, Harte, Dunne, Breen, Roy Keane, McAteer (Kelly G 75), Kinsella, Quinn (Connolly 71), Robbie Keane, Kilbane (Staunton 79).
Referee: Michel (Slovakia).

Tallinn, 3 September 2000, 4700

Estonia (0) 1 *(Oper 81)*   **Portugal (1) 3** *(Rui Costa 15, Figo 49, Sa Pinto 57)*

Estonia: Poom; Allas, Stepanovs, Lemsalu, Rooba U, Jurisson (Haavistu 71), Alonen (Anniste 36), Reim, Terehhov, Zelinski (Viikmae 67), Oper.
Portugal: Quim; Nelson (Costinha 64), Fernando Couto, Jorge Costa, Rui Jorge, Figo, Rui Costa, Paulo Sousa, Simao (Vidigal 71), Sa Pinto, Joao Pinto (Pauleta 74).
Referee: Agins (Malta).

La Vella, 7 October 2000, 800

Andorra (0) 1 *(Ruiz 90 (pen))*   **Estonia (0) 2** *(Reim 54, Oper 65)*

Andorra: Koldo; Ramirez, Txema, Jonas, Lima A, Lima I, Emiliano, Sonejee (Lucendo 60), Sanchez J, Jimenez (Soria 83), Ruiz.
Estonia: Poom; Allas, Rooba U, Lemsalu, Stepanovs, Viikmae (Haavistu 80), Terehhov, Oper, Kristal (Anniste 58), Reim, Zelinski (Ustritski 46).
Referee: Koren (Israel).

Nicosia, 7 October 2000, 12,000

Cyprus (0) 0   Holland (0) 4 *(Seedorf 69, 78, Overmars 81, Kluivert 90)*

Cyprus: Panayiotou N; Theodotou, Charalambous C, Ioannou D, Charalambous M (Poyiatzis 62), Pounnas (Gjurev 80), Melanarkitis, Spoljaric, Ioakim, Malekkos (Okkas 77), Agathocleous.
Holland: Van der Sar; Bosvelt (Van Bommel 75), Reiziger, Frank de Boer, Van Bronckhorst, Cocu, Talan (Seedorf 58), Davids, Kluivert, Ronald de Boer (Bouma 80), Overmars.
Referee: Cesari (Italy).

Lisbon, 7 October 2000, 65,000

Portugal (0) 1 *(Conceicao 57)*   **Republic of Ireland (0) 1** *(Holland 72)*

Portugal: Quim; Beto, Fernando Couto, Jorge Costa, Dimas (Capucho 88), Conceicao, Rui Costa, Vidigal, Figo, Sa Pinto (Pauleta 76), Joao Pinto (Simao 76).
Republic of Ireland: Kelly A; Carr, Harte, Dunne, Breen, Roy Keane, McAteer (Duff 69), Kinsella, Quinn (Holland 46), Robbie Keane (Finnan 83), Kilbane.
Referee: Ouzounov (Bulgaria).

Rotterdam, 11 October 2000, 48,000

Holland (0) 0   Portugal (2) 2 *(Conceicao 11, Pauleta 44)*

Holland: Van der Sar; Melchiot, Frank de Boer, Cocu, Reiziger, Van Bommel (Bosvelt 72), Overmars (Talan 46), Davids, Kluivert (Vennegoor of Hesselink 65), Seedorf, Bouma.
Portugal: Quim; Jorge Costa, Dimas, Secretario, Fernando Couto, Vidigal (Fernando Meira 90), Figo, Bino, Pauleta (Simeo 90), Rui Costa (Sa Pinto 87), Conceicao.
Referee: Poll (England).

Dublin, 11 October 2000, 34,562

Republic of Ireland (1) 2 *(Kinsella 25, Dunne 50)*   **Estonia (0) 0**

Republic of Ireland: Kelly A; Carr, Harte, Dunne, Breen, Roy Keane, McAteer (Duff 46), Kinsella, Quinn, Robbie Keane (Foley 87), Kilbane (Finnan 87).
Estonia: Poom; Allas, Stepanovs, Lemsalu, Saviauk, Viikmae (Haavistu 68), Reim, Anniste, Terehhov, Oper, Zelinski (Ustritski 68).
Referee: Hauge (Norway).

Nicosia, 15 November 2000, 8000

Cyprus (3) 5 *(Okkas 10, 18, Agathocleous 42, Christodoulou M 74, Spoljaric 90 (pen))*
Andorra (0) 0

Cyprus: Panayiotou N; Konnafis, Charalambous C, Ioannou D (Nicolaou N 82), Charalambous M, Pounnas, Ioakim, Spoljaric, Okkas, Agathocleous (Neophytou 74), Constantinou M (Christodoulou M 46).
Andorra: Koldo; Txema, Marc, Jonas, Sonejee, Lima I (Soria 88), Emiliano (Ramirez 59), Sanchez J, Lucendo, Jimenez, Ruiz (Escura 78).
Referee: Johansson (Sweden).

Madeira, 28 February 2001, 12,000

Portugal (2) 3 *(Figo 1, 48, Pauleta 36)*   **Andorra (0) 0**

Portugal: Quim; Xavier, Rui Jorge, Fernando Couto (Capucho 46), Beto, Paulo Bento (Joao Pinto 63), Rui Costa, Conceicao, Figo, Nuno Gomes (Tomas 75), Pauleta.
Andorra: Koldo; Pol, Ramirez, Jonas, Lucendo (Soria 89), Txema, Emiliano (Escura 61), Sonejee, Ruiz, Marc, Sanchez J (Garcia 89).
Referee: Allaerts (Belgium).

Barcelona, 24 March 2001, 1000

Andorra (0) 0
Holland (2) 5 *(Kluivert 9, Hasselbaink 36, Van Hooijdonk 60, 71, Van Bommel 85)*

Andorra: Sanchez A; Pol, Jonas, Sonejee, Lima I, Ramirez, Emiliano (Escura 85), Txema, Lucendo (Jimenez 64), Ruiz (Fernandez 90), Sanchez J.
Holland: Van der Sar; Bosvelt, Stam (Bouma 72), Frank de Boer, Cocu, Van Bommel, Davids (Paauwe 46), Zenden, Hasselbaink, Kluivert (Van Hooijdonk 58), Overmars.
Referee: Trivkovic (Croatia).

Nicosia, 24 March 2001, 13,000

Cyprus (0) 0   Republic of Ireland (2) 4 *(Roy Keane 32, 89, Harte 42 (pen), Kelly 81)*

Cyprus: Panayiotou N; Melanarkitis (Filippou 56), Konnafis, Charalambous M, Christodoulou M, Theodotou, Pounnas (Malekkos 43), Ioakim, Spoljaric, Constandinou M, Okkas (Agathocleous 75).

Republic of Ireland: Given; Kelly G, Harte, Roy Keane, Breen, Cunningham, McAteer (Holland 78), Kinsella, Connolly, Robbie Keane (Doherty 89), Kilbane (Duff 82).
Referee: De Bleeckere (Belgium).

Barcelona, 28 March 2001, 5000

Andorra (0) 0   Republic of Ireland (1) 3 *(Harte 33 (pen), Kilbane 76, Holland 80)*

Andorra: Sanchez A; Pol, Jonas (Soria 90), Lima A, Lucendo, Lima I, Sonejee, Txema, Sanchez J (Jimenez 87), Emiliano (Escura 80), Ruiz.
Republic of Ireland: Given; Kelly G, Harte, Roy Keane, Breen, Cunningham, Holland, Kilbane (Finnan 84), Connolly (Doherty 25), Robbie Keane, Duff.
Referee: Ishchenko (Ukraine).

Limassol, 28 March 2001, 5000

Cyprus (0) 2 *(Constantinou M 48, Okkas 66)*   **Estonia (0) 2** *(Kristal 77, Piiroja 79)*

Cyprus: Panayiotou; Ioakim, Germanou, Charalambous M, Theodotou, Konnafis, Agathocleous (Christodolou M 63), Engomitis (Melanarkitis 69), Malekkos (Spoljaric 46), Okkas, Constantinou M.
Estonia: Kaalma; Rooba M, Stepanovs, Piiroja, Rooba U, Novikov (Alonen 81), Reim, Kristal, Haavistu (Terehhov 54), Zelinski (Viikmae 59), Oper.
Referee: Mikulski (Poland).

Oporto, 28 March 2001, 45,000

Portugal (0) 2 *(Pauleta 83, Figo 90 (pen))*
Holland (1) 2 *(Hasselbaink 17 (pen), Kluivert 47)*

Portugal: Quim; Secretario, Litos, Fernando Couto, Rui Jorge, Costinha, Paulo Bento (Capucho 32), Conceicao (Nuno Gomes 57), Figo, Rui Costa, Pauleta.
Holland: Van der Sar; Reiziger, Frank de Boer, Stam, Cocu, Zenden (Makaay 72), Davids, Van Bommel (Bosvelt 68), Overmars, Kluivert, Hasselbaink (Van Hooijdonk 80).
Referee: Meier (Switzerland).

Eindhoven, 25 April 2001, 30,000

Holland (3) 4 *(Hasselbaink 29, Overmars 35, Kluivert 44, Van Nistelrooy 82)*
Cyprus (0) 0

Holland: Van der Sar; Melchiot, Hofland, Frank de Boer, Cocu, Zenden, Seedorf (Van Nistelrooy 71), Van Bommel, Overmars (Sikora 83), Kluivert, Hasselbaink (Van Hooijdonk 71).
Cyprus: Morphis; Konnafis, Filippou, Charalambous M, Germanou, Melanarkitis, Engomitis (Kaiafas 89), Christodolou M (Yiasoumi 76), Satsias, Okkas (Agathocleous 84), Constandinou M.
Referee: Baskakov (Russia).

Dublin, 25 April 2001, 34,000

Republic of Ireland (2) 3 *(Kilbane 34, Kinsella 36, Breen 76)*   **Andorra (1) 1** *(Lima I 32)*

Republic of Ireland: Given; Kelly G, Harte, Breen (Staunton 84), Dunne, Holland, Kennedy (Carr 66), Kinsella (Finnan 79), Connolly, Doherty, Kilbane.
Andorra: Sanchez A; Escura, Lima I, Lima A, Jonas, Txema, Emiliano (Soria 86), Ruiz, Sonejee, Jimenez (Pujol 81), Sanchez J (Fernandez 90).
Referee: Jakobsson (Iceland).

Tallinn, 2 June 2001, 9500

Estonia (0) 2 *(Oper 65, Zelinski 78)*
Holland (0) 4 *(Frank de Boer 68, Van Nistelrooy 82, 90, Kluivert 89)*

Estonia: Kaalma; Saviauk, Stepanovs, Piiroja, Rooba U, Viikmae (Zelinski 29), Reim, Haavistu (Rahn 70), Novikov, Kristal, Oper.
Holland: Van der Sar; Reiziger, Melchiot, Frank de Boer, Cocu, Paauwe (Landzaat 60), Zenden, Makaay (Van Hooijdonk 69), Hasselbaink (Van Nistelrooy 60), Kluivert, Overmars.
Referee: Richards (Wales).

Dublin, 2 June 2001, 34,000

Republic of Ireland (0) 1 *(Roy Keane 65)*   **Portugal (0) 1** *(Figo 79)*

Republic of Ireland: Given; Carr, Harte, Kelly G, Dunne, Staunton, Kinsella (Doherty 79), Roy Keane, Quinn (Holland 75), Robbie Keane (Duff 60), Kilbane.
Portugal: Ricardo; Frechaut, Litos (Boa Morte 87), Jorge Costa, Rui Jorge (Joao Pinto 74), Beto, Petit, Barbosa (Capucho 71), Figo, Rui Costa, Pauleta.
Referee: Fisker (Denmark).

Tallinn, 6 June 2001, 9000

Estonia (0) 0   Republic of Ireland (2) 2 *(Dunne 9, Holland 39)*

Estonia: Kaalma; Saviauk, Stepanovs, Piiroja, Rooba U (Allas 69), Reim, Novikov (Ustritski 72), Haavistu (Terehhov 49), Kristal, Oper, Zelinski.
Republic of Ireland: Given; Carr, Harte, Kelly G, Dunne, Staunton, Kinsella, Holland, Quinn (Doherty 37), Kilbane, Duff (O'Brien 89).
Referee: Mircea (Romania).

Lisbon, 6 June 2001, 35,000

Portugal (1) 6 *(Pauleta 36, 71, Barbosa 55, 59, Joao Pinto 76, 81)*   **Cyprus (0) 0**

Portugal: Ricardo; Frechaut, Jorge Costa (Nuno Gomes 82), Beto, Rui Jorge, Petit (Paulo Bento 87), Rui Costa, Barbosa (Sa Pinto 72), Capucho, Pauleta, Joao Pinto.
Cyprus: Morphis; Theodotou, Filippou, Charalambous M, Ioakim, Satsias, Engomitis (Yiasoumi 69), Christodoulou M (Melanarkitis 61), Germanou, Okkas (Stavrou 83), Constantinou M.
Referee: Farina (Italy).

Tallinn, 15 August 2001, 5000

Estonia (0) 2 *(Zelinski 51, Novikov 86)*   **Cyprus (1) 2** *(Constantinou M 39 (pen), 69)*

Estonia: Kaalma; Allas, Lemsalu (Rooba U 79), Piiroja, Saviauk, Reim, Viikmae (Svets 75), Novikov, Zelinski, Kristal, Oper.
Cyprus: Petrides; Konnafis, Georgiou, Melanarkitis, Charalambous M, Nicolaou C, Theodotou, Kaiafas (Agathocleous 75), Okkas, Christodoulou M (Yiasemakis 90), Constantinou M.
Referee: Chikun (Belarus).

Lleida, 1 September 2001, 4876

Andorra (1) 1 *(Jonas 41)*
Portugal (5) 7 *(Nuno Gomes 36, 40, 44, 90, Pauleta 39, Rui Jorge 45, Conceicao 58)*

Andorra: Koldo; Ramirez, Lucendo (Txema 60), Jonas, Lima A, Sonejee, Emiliano (Jimenez 76), Sanchez J, Escura, Pol, Ruiz (Garcia 90).
Portugal: Ricardo; Frechaut, Beto, Jorge Costa, Rui Jorge (Nuno Gomes 32), Petit (Fernando Meira 61), Figo, Capucho (Simao 46), Conceicao, Joao Pinto, Pauleta.
Referee: Hauge (Norway).

Dublin, 1 September 2001, 49,000

Republic of Ireland (0) 1 *(McAteer 67)*   **Holland (0) 0**

Republic of Ireland: Given; Kelly G, Harte, Dunne, Staunton, Holland, McAteer (O'Brien 90), Roy Keane, Robbie Keane (Finnan 58), Kilbane, Duff (Quinn 88).
Holland: Van der Sar; Melchiot, Numan (Van Hooijdonk 63), Cocu, Stam, Hofland, Zenden (Hasselbaink 55), Van Bommel, Kluivert, Van Nistelrooy, Overmars (Van Bronckhorst 71).
Referee: Krug (Germany).

Larnaca, 5 September 2001, 6000

Cyprus (1) 1 *(Constantinou M 24)*
Portugal (0) 3 *(Nuno Gomes 48, Pauleta 63, Conceicao 71)*

Cyprus: Petrides; Theodotou, Konnafis, Charalambous M, Ioakim, Georgiou, Satsias (Themistocleous 88), Engomitis (Nicolaou N 58), Christodoulou M, Okkas (Agathocleous 58), Constantinou M.

Portugal: Ricardo; Frechaut, Beto, Jorge Costa (Capucho 34), Rui Jorge, Petit, Fernando Meira, Figo, Conceicao, Joao Pinto (Nuno Gomes 34), Pauleta (Simao 80).
Referee: Nilsson (Sweden).

Eindhoven, 5 September 2001, 28,500

Holland (5) 5 *(Zenden 15, Van Bommel 26, 39, Cocu 30, Van Nistelrooy 43)*
Estonia (0) 0

Holland: Van der Sar; Melchiot, Numan, Cocu, Stam, Hofland, Zenden, Van Bommel, Kluivert, Van Nistelrooy (Hasselbaink 46), Overmars (Makaay 46) (Van Hooijdonk 63).
Estonia: Kaalma; Rooba U, Piiroja, Stepanovs, Saviauk, Novikov, Kristal, Reim, Oper, Zelinski, Viikmae (Anniste 46).
Referee: Vassaras (Greece).

Arnhem, 6 October 2001, 20,000

Holland (2) 4 *(Van Hooijdonk 4 (pen), Seedorf 45, Van Nistelrooy 54, 90)*
Andorra (0) 0

Holland: Van der Sar; Melchiot (Numan 72), Landzaat, Seedorf, Hofland, Van Bronckhorst, Sikora (Van der Vaart 67), Davids, Van Hooijdonk, Van Nistelrooy, Zenden.
Andorra: Koldo; Escura, Txema, Jonas, Lima A, Fernandez, Emiliano (Gil 90), Sonejee, Jimenez, Ferron (Benet 90), Ruiz.
Referee: Erdemir (Turkey).

Lisbon, 6 October 2001, 80,000

Portugal (1) 5 *(Joao Pinto 29, Nuno Gomes 49, 64, Pauleta 58, Figo 78)*   **Estonia (0) 0**

Portugal: Ricardo; Frechaut (Nuno Gomes 39), Fernando Couto, Jorge Costa, Rui Jorge, Figo, Petit, Rui Costa, Capucho (Paulo Sousa 66), Joao Pinto (Simao 46), Pauleta.
Estonia: Kaalma; Saviauk (Allas 55), Stepanovs, Piiroja, Rooba U, Kristal, Reim, Novikov (Anniste 68), Haavistu (Alonen 68), Oper, Zelinski.
Referee: Strampe (Germany).

Dublin, 6 October 2001, 35,000

Republic of Ireland (2) 4 *(Harte 3, Quinn 11, Connolly 63, Roy Keane 68)*   **Cyprus (0) 0**

Republic of Ireland: Given; Finnan, Harte, Breen, Staunton, Holland, Kennedy (Carsley 65), Roy Keane, Quinn (Morrison 70), Connolly, Kilbane (McPhail 85).
Cyprus: Panayiotou N; Konnafis (Louka 70), Koutsonis, Theodotou, Melanarkitis, Daskalakis, Nicolaou N, Okkas (Themistocleous 85), Satsias, Christodolou M, Yiasoumi (Kontoletterou 90).
Referee: Roca (Spain).

Group 2 Table	P	W	D	L	F	A	Pts
Portugal	10	7	3	0	33	7	24
Republic of Ireland	10	7	3	0	23	5	24
Holland	10	6	2	2	30	9	20
Estonia	10	2	2	6	10	26	8
Cyprus	10	2	2	6	13	31	8
Andorra	10	0	0	10	5	36	0

GROUP 3

Sofia, 2 September 2000, 15,000

Bulgaria (0) 0   Czech Republic (0) 1 *(Poborsky 73 (pen))*

Bulgaria: Zdravkov; Peev, Markov, Ivanov B, Kirilov (Topuzakov 76), Petrov S, Todorov (Ivanov G 63), Stoyanov, Yovov (Petrov M 33), Balakov, Iliev.
Czech Republic: Srnicek; Repka, Rada, Nedved, Fukal, Horvath (Rosicky 77), Tyce, Poborsky, Koller (Lokvenc 63), Smicer (Vicek 90), Bejbl.
Referee: Marin (Spain).

239

Reykjavik, 2 September 2000, 7072

Iceland (1) 1 *(Sverrisson E 12)*   **Denmark (1) 2** *(Tomasson 26, Bisgaard 49)*

Iceland: Arason; Helgason A (Gunnarsson B 29), Hreidarsson, Marteinsson, Kolvidsson, Kristinsson R, Gudmundsson (Helguson 70), Sverrisson E, Gudjohnsen E, Gudjonsson T (Sigurdsson H 70), Dadason.
Denmark: Schmeichel; Goldbaek (Nielsen A 76), Henriksen, Gravesen, Heintze, Helveg, Steen-Nielsen, Rommedahl (Michaelsen 81), Tomasson, Bisgaard (Jensen C 70), Sand.
Referee: Bre (France).

Belfast, 2 September 2000, 8227

Northern Ireland (0) 1 *(Gray 70)*   **Malta (0) 0**

Northern Ireland: Carroll; Nolan, Hughes, Murdock, Taggart, Horlock, Johnson, Magilton, Healy, Elliott (Gray 61), Lomas.
Malta: Barry; Dimech, Debono, Said, Carabott, Sylla (Brincat 46), Thuma, Camilleri (Veselji 78), Chetcuti, Busuttil, Mallia (Turner 58).
Referee: Bezubiak (Russia).

Sofia, 7 October 2000, 4000

Bulgaria (1) 3 *(Ivanov G 39, 65, Todorov 90)*   **Malta (0) 0**

Bulgaria: Zdravkov; Markov, Pazin, Petrov S, Hristov, Stoyanov (Petkov M 59), Ivanov G (Todorov 88), Balakov, Iliev (Petkov I 70), Peev, Petrov M.
Malta: Barry; Carabott, Chetcuti, Said, Debono, Dimech (Holland 67), Busuttil (Mallia 60), Giglio, Nwoko, Brincat (Agius 75), Zahra.
Referee: Caljia (Bosnia).

Teplice, 7 October 2000, 9843

Czech Republic (3) 4 *(Koller 17, 41, Nedved 44, 90)*   **Iceland (0) 0**

Czech Republic: Srnicek; Repka, Rada, Nedved, Fukal, Horvath (Rosicky 79), Tyce, Poborsky (Latal 68), Koller (Lokvenc 75), Sionko, Bejbl.
Iceland: Kristinsson B; Helgason A, Hreidarsson, Marteinsson (Gudmundsson 46), Kolvidsson, Kristinsson R (Gretarsson 85), Jonsson S, Sverrisson E, Gudjohnsen E, Helguson, Dadason (Gudjonsson T 46).
Referee: Vassaros (Greece).

Belfast, 7 October 2000, 11,823

Northern Ireland (1) 1 *(Healy 38)*   **Denmark (0) 1** *(Rommedahl 60)*

Northern Ireland: Carroll; Lomas, Hughes, Murdock, Taggart, Horlock, Magilton, Jeff Whitley (Mulryne 72), Healy, Elliott (Gray 84), Lennon.
Denmark: Schmeichel; Helveg, Henriksen, Gravesen, Heintze, Steen-Nielsen, Tofting, Rommedahl, Tomasson, Sand (Jensen C 82), Gronkjaer (Bisgaard 63).
Referee: Pereira (Portugal).

Copenhagen, 11 October 2000, 39,847

Denmark (0) 1 *(Sand 73)*   **Bulgaria (0) 1** *(Berbatov 82)*

Denmark: Schmeichel; Helveg, Henriksen, Gravesen, Heintze, Rommedahl, Tofting, Steen-Nielsen (Jensen C 46), Gronkjaer (Mikaelsen 55), Tomasson (Nielsen A 79), Sand.
Bulgaria: Zdravkov; Kishishev, Petkov M (Todorov 77), Kirilov, Pazin, Petrov S, Hristov (Peev 68), Ivanov B, Balakov, Ivanov G (Berbatov 64), Petrov M.
Referee: Sarvan (Turkey).

Reykjavik, 11 October 2000, 5415

Iceland (0) 1 *(Gudjonsson T 89)*   **Northern Ireland (0) 0**

Iceland: Kristinsson B; Helgason A, Hreidarsson, Sverrisson E, Vidarsson, Helguson, Gunnarsson B, Kristinsson R (Gretarsson 46), Gudjonsson T, Gudjohnsen E, Dadason (Sigurdsson H 64).
Northern Ireland: Carroll; Lomas, Hughes, Murdock, Taggart (Williams 46), Horlock, Lennon, Johnson, Healy, Magilton, Elliott (Gray 82).
Referee: Merk (Germany).

Valletta, 11 October 2000, 4000

Malta (0) 0   Czech Republic (0) 0

Malta: Muscat; Said, Chetcuti (Camilleri 61), Spiteri, Debono, Agius, Busuttil, Giglio (Turner 75), Brincat (Theuma 63), Nwoko, Zahra.
Czech Republic: Srnicek; Fukal (Latal 46), Rada, Repka, Tyce, Poborsky, Nedved, Bejbl, Horvath (Vicek 65), Koller, Sionko (Lokvenc 82).
Referee: Siric (Croatia).

Sofia, 24 March 2001, 20,000

Bulgaria (1) 2 *(Chamokov 36, Berbatov 78)*   **Iceland (1) 1** *(Hreidarsson 24)*

Bulgaria: Zdravkov; Kishishev (Peev 63), Pazin, Chomakov, Markov, Kirilov (Todorov 77), Petkov M, Balakov, Hristov, Ivanov G (Berbatov 63), Petrov.
Iceland: Arason; Sigurdsson L, Hreidarsson, Vidarsson, Gunnarsson B, Kristinsson R, Helguson (Gudmundsson 76), Sverrisson E, Gudjonsson T (Gretarsson 59), Gudjohnsen E (Sigthorsson 61), Dadason.
Referee: Riley (England).

Valletta, 24 March 2001, 2500

Malta (0) 0   Denmark (1) 5 *(Sand 8, 65, 80, Heintze 50, Jensen C 76)*

Malta: Muscat; Turner (Okoh 46), Carabott, Dimech (Holland 65), Zahra, Debono, Giglio (Camilleri 65), Busuttil, Saliba, Nwoko, Brincat.
Denmark: Sorensen; Tofting, Henriksen, Laursen, Heintze, Helveg (Goldbaek 68), Gravesen (Steen-Nielsen 63), Gronkjaer, Rommedahl, Sand, Martin Jorgensen (Jensen C 75).
Referee: McCurry (Scotland).

Belfast, 24 March 2001, 10,368

Northern Ireland (0) 0   Czech Republic (0) 1 *(Nedved 11)*

Northern Ireland: Carroll; Griffin, Hughes A, Elliott (Gray 78), Williams, Murdock, Gillespie, Lennon, Healy (Ferguson 78), Magilton, Hughes M.
Czech Republic: Srnicek; Fukal, Votava, Ujfalusi, Tyce, Poborsky, Bejbl, Rosicky (Jarosik 81), Nedved, Smicer (Nemec 90), Koller (Lokvenc 73).
Referee: Gonzalez (Spain).

Sofia, 28 March 2001, 20,000

Bulgaria (2) 4 *(Balakov 10, Petrov M 17, 78, Chomakov 72)*
Northern Ireland (1) 3 *(Williams 14, Elliott 83, Healy 90 (pen))*

Bulgaria: Zdravkov; Kishishev, Petkov M (Stoilov 58), Markov, Chomakov, Pazin, Ivanov R, Hristov (Petrov Sv 87), Berbatov (Ivanov G 81), Dalakov, Petrov M.
Northern Ireland: Carroll; Griffin, Nolan (McCarthy 90), Elliott, Willams, Murdock, Gillespie (Johnson 85), Lennon (Kennedy 85), Healy, Magilton, Hughes M.
Referee: Hrinak (Slovakia).

Prague, 28 March 2001, 16,354

Czech Republic (0) 0   Denmark (0) 0

Czech Republic: Srnicek; Fukal, Votava, Ujfalusi, Poborsky, Rosicky (Jarosik 86), Bejbl, Nedved, Nemec, Smicer (Kuka 67), Koller (Lokvenc 89).
Denmark: Sorensen; Helveg, Henriksen, Laursen, Heintze (Nygaard 88), Rommedahl (Jensen C 78), Tofting, Gravesen, Gronkjaer (Martin Jorgensen 46), Tomasson, Sand.
Referee: Barber (England).

Valletta, 25 April 2001, 1500

Malta (1) 1 *(Mifsud 14)*
Iceland (2) 4 *(Gudmundsson 42, Sigurdsson H 45, Gudjohnsen E 83, Gudjonsson T 90)*

Malta: Muscat; Debono, Said, Carabott, Spiteri, Giglio (Theuma 63), Busuttil, Mifsud, Zahra (Mallia 70), Nwoko, Brincat (Turner 56).
Iceland: Arason; Vidarsson, Sverrisson E (Marteinsson 67), Hreidarsson, Kristinsson R, Gudmundsson, Gretarsson, Gunnarsson B, Sigurdsson H (Gudjonsson T 84), Gudjohnsen E, Sigthorsson (Dadason 84).
Referee: Zotta (Romania).

241

Copenhagen, 2 June 2001, 41,669

Denmark (1) 2 *(Sand 6, Tomasson 82)*   **Czech Republic (1) 1** *(Tyce 40)*

Denmark: Sorensen; Helveg, Henriksen, Laursen, Heintze, Tofting, Tomasson, Steen-Nielsen (Jensen C 58), Rommedahl (Gronkjaer 74), Sand, Martin Jorgensen (Nielsen A 87).
Czech Republic: Srnicek; Johana, Ujfalusi, Votava, Tyce (Rada 60), Poborsky (Kuka 85), Nedved, Galasek, Berger, Lokvenc (Koller 68), Smicer.
Referee: Merk (Germany).

Reykjavik, 2 June 2001, 3554

Iceland (2) 3 *(Gudmundsson 7, Dadason 38, Gudjohnsen E 68)*   **Malta (0) 0**

Iceland: Arason; Helgason, Vidarsson, Gretarsson, Gunnarsson B, Kristinsson R (Kolvidsson 74), Gudmundsson, Sverrisson E (Marteinsson 74), Gudjohnsen E, Sigurdsson H, Dadason (Helguson 74).
Malta: Muscat; Said, Turner, Spiteri, Theuma, Dimech, Agius, Giglio (Suda 74), Mifsud, Brincat (Camilleri 46), Mallia (Nwoko 69).
Referee: Lajuks (Latvia).

Belfast, 2 June 2001, 7663

Northern Ireland (0) 0   Bulgaria (0) 1 *(Ivanov G 52)*

Northern Ireland: Taylor; Nolan (Quinn 86), Griffin, Murdock, Hughes A, Lennon (Mulryne 79), Gillespie, Johnson, Healy, Elliott (Ferguson 79), Hughes M.
Bulgaria: Zdravkov; Ivanov B, Markov, Pazin, Kishishev (Peev 23), Hristov (Stoilov 87), Petrov M (Kirilov 77), Balakov, Chomakov, Petkov M, Ivanov G.
Referee: Busacca (Switzerland).

Teplice, 6 June 2001, 14,850

Czech Republic (1) 3 *(Kuka 40, 88, Baros 90)*   **Northern Ireland (1) 1** *(Mulryne 45)*

Czech Republic: Srnicek; Repka, Votava (Bejbl 46), Tyce, Poborsky (Lokvenc 83), Nedved, Galasek, Rosicky, Berger, Koller (Baros 65), Kuka.
Northern Ireland: Taylor; Nolan, Hughes A, Murdock, Williams, Griffin, Johnson (Ferguson 76), Mulryne (Kennedy 81), Healy, Elliott (Quinn 65), Hughes M.
Referee: Sundell (Sweden).

Copenhagen, 6 June 2001, 38,499

Denmark (1) 2 *(Sand 43, 83)*   **Malta (1) 1** *(Mallia 8)*

Denmark: Sorensen; Helveg, Henriksen, Heintze, Tofting (Nielsen A 75), Tomasson (Nygaard 68), Gravesen, Jensen C, Rommedahl (Gronkjaer 55), Sand, Martin Jorgensen.
Malta: Barry; Debono, Said, Theuma, Camilleri, Turner, Brincat (Holland 73), Mallia (Nwoko 65), Dimech, Agius (Okoh 78), Mifsud.
Referee: Shmolik (Belarus).

Reykjavik, 6 June 2001, 4316

Iceland (1) 1 *(Dadason 43)*   **Bulgaria (0) 1** *(Berbatov 81)*

Iceland: Arason; Helgason, Vidarsson, Gretarsson, Gunnarsson B, Kristinsson R, Hreidarsson, Sverrisson E, Gudjohnsen E, Sigurdsson H, Dadason (Helguson 46).
Bulgaria: Zdravkov; Pazin (Petrov Sv 54), Markov, Ivanov B, Stoilov, Chomakov (Petrov M 65), Balakov (Todorov 73), Kirilov, Peev, Ivanov G, Berbatov.
Referee: Gallagher (England).

Copenhagen, 1 September 2001, 41,500

Denmark (1) 1 *(Rommedahl 3)*   **Northern Ireland (0) 1** *(Mulryne 73)*

Denmark: Sorensen (Kjaer 11); Helveg, Heintze, Tofting, Laursen, Henriksen, Rommedahl, Nielsen P (Frandsen 68), Tomasson (Nygaard 78), Sand, Gronkjaer.
Northern Ireland: Taylor; Griffin, Kennedy, Murdock, Hughes A, Horlock, Gillespie, Magilton, Healy, Mulryne, Hughes M (Elliott 70).
Referee: Wojcik (Poland).

Reykjavik, 1 September 2001, 6011

Iceland (1) 3 *(Sverrisson E 45, 77, Sigthorsson 65)*   **Czech Republic (0) 1** *(Jankulovski 88)*

Iceland: Arason; Helgason, Sverrisson E, Hreidarsson, Vidarsson, Gretarsson, Marteinsson (Sigurdsson L 83), Gudjonsson J, Sigurdsson H (Helguson 73), Sigthorsson, Gudjohnsen E (Baldvinsson 73).

Czech Republic: Srnicek; Grygera (Horvath 66), Novotny, Johana, Tyce, Poborsky (Lokvenc 66), Jarosik (Jankulovski 46), Rosicky, Nedved, Koller, Baros.

Referee: Messina (Italy).

Valletta, 1 September 2001, 409

Malta (0) 0   Bulgaria (0) 2 *(Berbatov 75, 80)*

Malta: Muscat; Said, Turner, Spiteri, Theuma, Carabott, Agius (Zahra 36), Giglio (Ciantar 67), Mifsud, Debono, Nwoko (Licari 87).

Bulgaria: Zdravkov; Pazin, Markov, Ivanov B, Petrov S, Peev, Chomakov (Balakov 54) (Stoilov 82), Alexandrov (Yanchev 70), Petkov M, Ivanov G, Berbatov.

Referee: Strampe (Germany).

Sofia, 5 September 2001, 21,500

Bulgaria (0) 0   Denmark (0) 2 *(Tomasson 47, 90)*

Bulgaria: Zdravkov; Markov, Pazin, Ivanov B, Petkov M (Todorov 76), Petrov S (Yanchev 62), Balakov, Peev, Petkov I, Ivanov G (Petrov M 62), Berbatov.

Denmark: Kjaer; Tofting, Henriksen, Laursen, Heintze, Helveg, Nielsen P (Nielsen A 46) (Steen-Nielsen 78), Gronkjaer (Michaelsen 73), Tomasson, Rommedahl, Sand.

Referee: Wegereef (Holland).

Teplice, 5 September 2001, 9218

Czech Republic (2) 3 *(Jankulovski 20, Lokvenc 37, Baros 68)*
Malta (1) 2 *(Carabott 22 (pen), Agius 55)*

Czech Republic: Srnicek; Grygera, Jankulovski, Novotny, Johana, Jarosik (Horvath 66), Baranek, Rosicky, Poborsky, Kuka (Baros 54), Lokvenc (Velkoborsky 90).

Malta: Muscat; Said (Dimech 79), Carabott, Spiteri, Debono, Agius, Giglio, Mifsud (Licari 74), Turner, Zahra (Ciantar 88), Nwoko.

Referee: Mammedov (Azerbaijan).

Belfast, 5 September 2001, 6625

Northern Ireland (0) 3 *(Healy 48, Hughes M 58, McCartney 60)*   **Iceland (0) 0**

Northern Ireland: Taylor; Griffin, Kennedy, Horlock, Hughes A, McCartney, Gillespie (McVeigh 88), Magilton, Healy, Mulryne, Hughes M.

Iceland: Arason; Helgason (Helguson 62), Vidarsson, Sverrisson E, Hreidarsson, Marteinsson, Gudjonsson J, Gretarsson, Gudjohnsen E, Sigurdsson H (Baldvinsson 86), Sigthorsson.

Referee: Hanacsek (Hungary).

Prague, 6 October 2001, 15,020

Czech Republic (3) 6 *(Rosicky 5, 70, Nedved 16, 76, Baros 28, Lokvenc 66)*   **Bulgaria (0) 0**

Czech Republic: Srnicek; Grygera, Novotny, Repka, Tyce (Hasek 26), Jankulovski, Poborsky (Baranek 78), Rosicky, Nedved, Lokvenc (Smicer 68), Baros.

Bulgaria: Zdravkov; Pazin, Markov, Ivanov B, Petrov S, Petkov M (Peev 72), Balakov, Zhelev, Yanchev (Berbatov 20), Ivanov G (Manchev 65), Petrov M.

Referee: Colombo (France).

Copenhagen, 6 October 2001, 42,000

Denmark (4) 6 *(Rommedahl 12, Sand 14, 67, Gravesen 30, 35, Michaelsen 90)*   **Iceland (0) 0**

Denmark: Sorensen; Helveg, Laursen, Henriksen, Heintze, Tofting, Gravesen, Tomasson (Mads Jorgensen 80), Rommedahl (Michaelsen 55), Martin Jorgensen, Sand (Madsen 68).

Iceland: Arason; Sigurdsson L (Vidarsson 69), Marteinsson, Sverrisson E, Hreidarsson, Gudjonsson J, Gretarsson, Gunnarsson B, Kristinsson R, Baldvinsson (Sigthorsson 74), Gudjohnsen E.

Referee: Ibanez (Spain).

Valletta, 6 October 2001, 3223

Malta (0) 0   Northern Ireland (0) 1 *(Healy 57 (pen))*

Malta: Muscat; Said, Spiteri, Debono, Carabott, Agius, Theuma (Mallia 65), Zahra (Suda 80), Chetcuti, Mifsud, Nwoko.
Northern Ireland: Taylor; Griffin, Kennedy, Horlock, Murdock, McCartney, Johnson, Magilton, Healy (McCann 80), Elliott (Quinn J 80), Hughes M.
Referee: Schuttengruber (Austria).

Group 3 Table	P	W	D	L	F	A	Pts
Denmark	10	6	4	0	22	6	22
Czech Republic	10	6	2	2	20	8	20
Bulgaria	10	5	2	3	14	15	17
Iceland	10	4	1	5	14	20	13
Northern Ireland	10	3	2	5	11	12	11
Malta	10	0	1	9	4	24	1

GROUP 4

Baku, 2 September 2000, 20,000

Azerbaijan (0) 0   Sweden (1) 1 *(Svensson A 10)*

Azerbaijan: Kramarenko; Kuliyev E, Agayev, Akhmedov, Yadullayev, Kuliyev K, Mamedov R (Imamaliev 86), Tagizade, Musayev B (Kurbanov M 65), Vasilyev, Kvaratskhelia.
Sweden: Hedman; Nilsson R, Andersson P, Bjorklund, Mellberg, Mjallby, Alexandersson, Svensson A (Mild 75), Ljungberg, Andersson K, Larsson.
Referee: Luinge (Holland).

Istanbul, 2 September 2000, 22,000

Turkey (1) 2 *(Okan 45, Emre 70)*   **Moldova (0) 0**

Turkey: Rustu; Umit D, Ogun, Fatih, Emre, Bulent K, Okan (Tayfur 60), Suat (Tayfun 65), Hakan Sukur, Cenk (Umit K 84), Unsal.
Moldova: Dinov; Covalenco, Sosnovschi, Testimitanu, Rebeja, Stroenco, Curtianu (Sischin 46), Oprea (Tanurkov 77), Catinsus, Epureanu (Stratulat 34), Rogaciov.
Referee: Benko (Austria).

Bratislava, 3 September 2000, 4011

Slovakia (1) 2 *(Lazarevski 3 (og), Demo 74)*   **Macedonia (0) 0**

Slovakia: Konig; Dzurik, Karhan, Timko, Leitner, Balis, Kratochvil, Moravcik (Nemeth P 46), Ujlaky (Demo 46), Jancula (Meszaros 76), Nemeth S.
Macedonia: Filevski; Veselinovski, Stojanovski (Lazarevski 64), Sedloski, Nikolovski, Stavrevski, Serafimovski, Micevski (Gerasimovski 69), Hristov, Ciric (Beciri 77), Savevski.
Referee: Hamer (Luxembourg).

Skopje, 6 October 2000, 4000

Macedonia (2) 3 *(Hristov 35, 42, Beciri 75)*   **Azerbaijan (0) 0**

Macedonia: Filevski; Lazarevski (Veselinovski 70), Stavrevski, Sedloski, Nikolovski (Gerasimovski 20), Serafimovski, Sainovski, Micevski, Hristov, Sakiri, Beciri (Miserdovski 80).
Azerbaijan: Kramarenko; Asadov, Yadullayev, Akhmedov, Agayev, Kuliyev K (Kvaratskhelia 55), Kurbanov M (Musayev R 65), Tagizade, Musayev B, Vasilyev (Lychkin 75), Kuliyev E.
Referee: Fisker (Denmark).

Chisinau, 7 October 2000, 5000

Moldova (0) 0   Slovakia (0) 1 *(Nemeth S 79)*

Moldova: Dinov; Covalenco, Catinsus, Testimitanu, Rebeja, Stroenco, Curtianu, Sischin (Rogaciov 60), Sosnovschi (Epureanu 82), Gaidamasciuc (Stratulat 72), Clescenco.

Slovakia: Konig; Dzurik, Sobona, Suchancok, Karhan, Demo (Nemeth P 74), Valachovic, Leitner, Pinte, Nemeth S (Prohaszka 88), Moravcik (Meszaros 53).
Referee: Stuchlik (Austria).

Gothenburg, 7 October 2000, 42,152

Sweden (0) 1 *(Larsson 68)*   **Turkey (0) 1** *(Tayfur 90 (pen))*

Sweden: Hedman; Nilsson R, Andersson P, Bjorklund, Alexandersson (Corneliusson 55), Jonsson (Svensson A 63), Mjallby, Ljungberg, Mild, Andersson K, Larsson (Osmanovski 90).
Turkey: Rustu; Ogun, Fatih, Bulent K, Arif, Ergun (Abdullah 80), Suat (Tayfur 64), Hakan Sukur, Nihat, Izzet (Hasan Sas 75), Unsal.
Referee: Krug (Germany).

Baku, 11 October 2000, 40,000

Azerbaijan (0) 0   Turkey (0) 1 *(Hakan Sukur 72)*

Azerbaijan: Kramarenko; Agayev, Yadullayev, Akhmedov, Lychkin (Mamedov R 85), Kuliyev K, Kurbanov M, Tagizade (Gambarov 72), Musayev B (Kerimov 58), Vasilyev, Kuliyev E.
Turkey: Rustu; Nihat (Fatih 46), Ogun, Bulent K, Alpay, Arif (Tayfur 90), Ergun, Suat, Hakan Sukur, Izzet (Hasan Sas 62), Unsal.
Referee: Snoddy (Northern Ireland).

Chisinau, 11 October 2000, 4000

Moldova (0) 0   Macedonia (0) 0

Moldova: Hmaruc; Stratulat, Catinsus, Testimitanu, Rebeja (Epureanu 46), Stroenco, Curtianu (Boret 65), Sischin (Rogaciov 56), Sosnovschi, Gaidamasciuc, Clescenco.
Macedonia: Filevski; Stavrevski, Lazarevski, Sedloski, Gerasimovski, Serafimovski (Veselinovski 70), Sainovski (Karanfilovski 76), Micevski, Hristov, Ciric (Miserdovski 85), Sakiri.
Referee: Ibanez (Spain).

Bratislava, 11 October 2000, 11,227

Slovakia (0) 0   Sweden (0) 0

Slovakia: Konig; Dzurik, Sobona, Timko, Karhan, Suchancok, Balis, Leitner, Meszaros (Prohaszka 86), Nemeth S, Moravcik (Gresko 58).
Sweden: Hedman; Nilsson R, Andersson P, Bjorklund, Mellberg, Mjallby, Svensson A (Osmanovski 70), Jonsson (Mild 47), Ljungberg, Andersson K (Andersson D 82), Larsson.
Referee: Dallas (Scotland).

Baku, 24 March 2001, 20,000

Azerbaijan (0) 0   Moldova (0) 0

Azerbaijan: Kramarenko; Agayev, Akhmedov, Kuliyev E (Getman 68), Yadullayev, Niftaliyev (Ismailov 46), Kuliyev K, Tagizade, Rzayev, Lychkin (Kuliyev R 80), Vasiliev.
Moldova: Hmaruc; Covalenco, Rebeja, Testimitanu (Romanenco 13), Sosnovschi, Catinsus, Epureanu, Gaidamasciuc, Sischin, Rogaciov (Oprea 46), Clescenco (Pogreban 61).
Referee: Stark (Germany).

Gothenburg, 24 March 2001, 22,106

Sweden (1) 1 *(Svensson A 43)*   **Macedonia (0) 0**

Sweden: Hedman; Mellberg, Andersson P, Matovac, Corneliusson, Linderoth (Andersson D 64), Schwarz (Selakovic 80), Svensson A (Mild 66), Ljungberg, Osmanovski, Larsson.
Macedonia: Milosevski; Mitrevski, Stavrevski, Sedloski, Zdravevski (Krstev S 68), Veselinovski, Serafimovski, Micevski, Lazarevski, Sakiri, Beciri (Sainovski 82).
Referee: Wegereef (Holland).

Istanbul, 24 March 2001, 23,000

Turkey (0) 1 *(Hakan Sukur 53 (pen))*   **Slovakia (0) 1** *(Tomaschek 68)*

Turkey: Rustu; Bulent K, Ogun, Fatih, Alpay, Okan (Arif 77) (Tayfun 83), Umit, Ergun (Tayfun 83), Abdullah, Hakan Sukur, Hasan Sas.
Slovakia: Konig; Karhan, Valachovic, Varga, Dzurik, Demo (Nemeth P 89), Labant, Tomaschek, Gresko, Nemeth S, Pinte.
Referee: Wojcik (Poland).

Chisinau, 28 March 2001, 8000

Macedonia (1) 1 *(Micevski 20)*   **Turkey (0) 2** *(Mitrevski 68 (og), Umit D 69)*

Macedonia: Milosevski; Stavrevski, Zdravevski (Krstev S 82), Sedloski, Mitrevski, Serafimovski (Georgieski 75), Micevski (Krsevski 75), Hristov, Beciri, Sakiri, Lazarevski.
Turkey: Rustu; Fatih, Alpay, Tayfur, Okan (Tayfun 82), Umit D, Ogun (Umit O 37), Ergun (Ozer 59), Abdullah, Hakan Sukur, Hasan Sas.
Referee: Colombo (France).

Skopje, 28 March 2001, 7000

Moldova (0) 0   Sweden (0) 2 *(Allback 89, 90)*

Moldova: Romanenco; Covalenco, Rebeja, Catinsus, Sosnovschi, Gaidamasciuc, Rogaciov (Pogreban 67), Oprea (Berco 72), Cebotari (Lungu 55), Sischin, Clescenco.
Sweden: Hedman; Mellberg, Andersson P, Matovac, Corneliusson, Selakovic (Andersson D 55), Schwarz, Mild (Jonsson 44), Ljungberg, Larsson, Svensson A (Allback 78).
Referee: Duhamel (France).

Trnava, 28 March 2001, 10,000

Slovakia (2) 3 *(Nemeth S 1, 10, Meszaros 57)*   **Azerbaijan (1) 1** *(Vasilyev 3 (pen))*

Slovakia: Konig; Varga, Karhan, Meszaros, Tomaschek, Labant, Pinte, Dzurik (Ujlaky 64), Demo (Jancula 78), Gresko, Nemeth S (Valachovic 68).
Azerbaijan: Kramarenko; Agayev, Yadullayev, Akhmedov, Kuliyev E, Kuliyev K, Kurbanov M, Imamaliev, Niftaliyev, Vasilyev (Musayev S 82), Lychkin (Aliev 46).
Referee: Kapitanis (Cyprus).

Skopje, 2 June 2001, 3000

Macedonia (1) 2 *(Sakiri 20 (pen), Krstev M 65)*
Moldova (1) 2 *(Pogreban 10, Barburos 72)*

Macedonia: Zekir; Stavrevski, Stojanov, Guzelov, Nikolovski (Trajanov 46), Jovanovski Z, Serafimovski (Jovanovski G 70), Krstev M, Krstev S, Sakiri, Beciri (Nacevski 46).
Moldova: Romanenco; Covalenco, Rebeja, Testimitanu (Osipenco 65), Sosnovschi, Stroenco, Sischin (Barburos 70), Catinsus, Pogreban (Epureanu 46), Gaidamasciuc, Clescenco.
Referee: Van Hulten (Holland).

Stockholm, 2 June 2001, 34,327

Sweden (1) 2 *(Allback 45, 51)*   **Slovakia (0) 0**

Sweden: Hedman; Mellberg, Andersson P, Saarenpaa, Lucic, Alexandersson (Jonsson 73), Linderoth (Svensson A 90), Magnus Svensson, Allback (Andersson D 88), Larsson, Ljungberg.
Slovakia: Konig; Karhan, Timko, Varga, Dzurik, Tomaschek, Demo (Janocko 58), Nemeth S (Vittek 58), Gresko (Babnic 82), Labant, Pinte.
Referee: Aranda (Spain).

Istanbul, 2 June 2001, 25,000

Turkey (3) 3 *(Tayfun 2, Oktay 29, Hakan Sukur 33)*   **Azerbaijan (0) 0**

Turkey: Rustu; Umit D, Alpay, Bulent K, Abdullah, Tayfun, Okan (Basturk 61), Tugay, Emre (Ergun 80), Hakan Sukur, Oktay (Ozer 37).

Azerbaijan: Gasanadze; Yunusov, Mamedov A (Niftaliyev 68), Akhmedov, Mamedov R, Kurbanov K, Kuliyev K, Tagizade (Kuliyev R 80), Rzayev (Orudzev 50), Kurbanov M, Mardanov.
Referee: Roca (Spain).

Baku, 6 June 2001, 20,000

Azerbaijan (1) 2 *(Vasilyev 26, Tagizade 55)*   **Slovakia (0) 0**

Azerbaijan: Gasanadze; Yunusov, Akhmedov, Mamedov R, Niftaliyev, Kurbanov M, Yadullayev, Tagizade (Kuliyev R 82), Kurbanov K (Ismailov 89), Getman, Vasilyev (Rzayev 75).
Slovakia: Konig; Dzurik, Vittek (Bencik 69), Varga, Karhan, Tomaschek, Janocko, Nemeth S, Labant, Gresko, Pinte (Babnic 62).
Referee: Vollquartz (Denmark).

Gothenburg, 6 June 2001, 30,233

Sweden (1) 6 *(Larsson 38 (pen), 58, 68 (pen), 79 (pen), Alexandersson 74, Allback 77)*
Moldova (0) 0

Sweden: Hedman; Mellberg, Andersson P, Saarenpaa (Andersson C 34), Lucic, Alexandersson, Linderoth, Magnus Svensson (Mathias Svensson 83), Svensson A (Andersson D 71), Allback, Larsson.
Moldova: Romanenco; Covalenco, Stroenco, Rebeja (Osipenco 63), Catinsus, Gaidamasciuc, Epureanu, Testimitanu, Oprea, Pogreban (Barburos 46), Clescenco (Sischin 78).
Referee: Dunn (England).

Bursa, 6 June 2001, 20,000

Turkey (1) 3 *(Alpay 43, 58, 70)*   **Macedonia (2) 3** *(Sakiri 7, Serafimovski 20, Nikolovski 62)*

Turkey: Rustu; Umit D, Bulent K, Alpay, Abdullah, Tayfun (Fatih 84), Okan (Basturk 69), Tugay, Emre, Hakan Sukur, Oktay (Ozer 46).
Macedonia: Filevski; Stavrevski, Nikolovski, Mitreveski, Stojanov, Serafimovski (Trajanov 72), Krstev M, Guzelov, Sakiri, Nacevski (Lazarevski 48), Beciri (Pandev 66).
Referee: Rodomonti (Italy).

Skopje, 1 September 2001, 8000

Macedonia (0) 1 *(Nacevski 63)*   **Sweden (2) 2** *(Larsson 27, Andersson P 32)*

Macedonia: Gruevski; Nikolovski, Guzelov, Mitrevski, Jovanovski Z, Stavrevski, Trajanov (Stojanov 61), Serafimovski (Ignjatov 83), Sakiri, Beciri (Nacevski 46), Maznov.
Sweden: Hedman; Mellberg, Andersson P, Mjallby (Andersson C 66), Kaamark (Saarenpaa 83), Linderoth, Alexandersson, Svensson A (Andersson D 64), Ljungberg, Allback, Larsson.
Referee: Levnikov (Russia).

Chisinau, 1 September 2001, 4000

Moldova (1) 2 *(Clescenco 15, Covalciuc 85)*   **Azerbaijan (0) 0**

Moldova: Romanenco; Olexic, Rebeja, Berco, Sosnovschi, Catinsus, Curtianu (Boret 68), Comleonoc, Sischin (Andronic 54), Rogaciov (Covalciuc 83), Clescenco.
Azerbaijan: Gasanadze; Getman (Kuliyev R 66), Yunusov, Niftaliyev (Mamedov A 72), Mamedov R, Kuliyev K, Kurbanov M, Tagizade, Ismailov (Vasilyev 69), Aliyev, Kuliyev E.
Referee: Melnychuk (Ukraine).

Bratislava, 1 September 2001, 8783

Slovakia (0) 0   Turkey (1) 1 *(Hakan Sukur 34)*

Slovakia: Bucek; Kozak, Varga, Timko (Labant 78), Balis (Pinte 46), Karhan, Janocko, Demo, Gresko, Nemeth S (Vittek 46), Oravec.
Turkey: Rustu; Fatih, Alpay, Umit O, Umit D, Basturk (Nihat 61), Tayfur, Ogun (Tayfun 87), Hasan Sas (Arif 78), Abdullah, Hakan Sukur.
Referee: Pereira (Portugal).

Baku, 5 September 2001, 7000

Azerbaijan (0) 1 *(Ismailov 90)*   **Macedonia (1) 1** *(Trajanov 12)*

Azerbaijan: Gasanzade; Yadullayev, Yunusov, Mamedov A, Kuliyev E, Kuliyev K, Kurbanov, Tagizade, Vasilyev (Ismailov 71), Kuliyev R (Aliyev 58), Musayev R.
Macedonia: Gruevski; Stojanov, Guzelov (Pikolavski 25), Nikolovski, Stavrevski, Serafimovski, Ivanovski, Trajanov (Ignjatov 81), Sakiri, Maznov, Baciri (Nacevski 71).
Referee: Ross (Northern Ireland).

Trencin, 5 September 2001, 2789

Slovakia (0) 4 *(Nemeth P 54, Nemeth S 59, 73, Demo 65)*
Moldova (1) 2 *(Clescenco 11, Rebeja 76)*

Slovakia: Hyll; Karhan, Kozak (Demo 22), Varga, Labant, Janocko, Nemeth P, Dzurik, Gresko (Balis 80), Oravec (Nemeth S 46), Vittek.
Moldova: Romanenco; Sosnovschi, Catinsus, Rebeja, Olexic, Berco, Sischin (Covalciuc 46), Curtianu (Boret 46), Comleonoc (Andronic 88), Rogaciov, Clescenco.
Referee: Vuorela (Finland).

Istanbul, 5 September 2001, 22,000

Turkey (0) 1 *(Hakan Sukur 51)*   **Sweden (0) 2** *(Larsson 87, Andersson A 90)*

Turkey: Rustu; Fatih, Alpay, Umit O, Umit D, Emre (Arif 46), Tayfur, Basturk (Tayfun 63), Abdullah, Hasan Sas (Ergun 88), Hakan Sukur.
Sweden: Hedman; Mellberg, Saarenpaa, Andersson P, Kaamark (Andersson A 64), Linderoth, Alexandersson (Jonsson 80), Ljungberg, Andersson D (Svensson A 64), Allback, Larsson.
Referee: Braschi (Italy).

Skopje, 7 October 2001, 5000

Macedonia (0) 0   Slovakia (1) 5 *(Reiter 27, Dzurik 57, Nemeth P 72, Pinte 81, Oravec 90)*

Macedonia: Gruevski; Stavrevski, Stojanov (Kapinkovski 66), Sedloski, Mitreveski, Jovanovski G (Beciri 64), Lazarevski, Trajanov, Maznov, Sakiri (Ignjatov 64), Nacevski.
Slovakia: Bucek; Karhan, Kozak, Hornyak, Varga, Nemeth P, Dzurik (Soitis 84), Reiter (Janocko 75), Gresko, Nemeth S (Oravec 66), Pinte.
Referee: Riley (England).

Chisinau, 7 October 2001, 3000

Moldova (0) 0   Turkey (1) 3 *(Emre 5, Nihat 75, Ilhan 83)*

Moldova: Romanenco; Andronic, Olexic, Ivanov, Cebotari, Catinsus, Epureanu, Sischin (Covalciuc 72), Miterev (Pogreban 76), Gaidamasciuc, Berco.
Turkey: Rustu; Mehmet, Emre, Umit O, Unsal, Okan, Tugay, Nihat, Hasan Sas (Ergun 84), Arif (Ilhan 75), Umit K (Basturk 68).
Referee: De Bleeckere (Belgium).

Stockholm, 7 October 2001, 32,786

Sweden (0) 3 *(Svensson A 53, Larsson 61 (pen), Ibrahimovic 69)*   **Azerbaijan (0) 0**

Sweden: Hedman; Saarenpaa, Andersson P (Michael Svensson 36), Mjallby, Andersson C, Linderoth, Alexandersson, Andersson D (Svensson A 46), Ljungberg, Allback (Ibrahimovic 66), Larsson.
Azerbaijan: Gasanzade; Yadullayev, Sadykhov, Mamedov A, Asadov, Kuliyev E (Getman 77), Akhmedov, Tagizade, Kurbanov M, Kurbanov K (Vasilyev 83), Guseynov (Aliev 75).
Referee: Wojcik (Poland).

Group 4 Table	P	W	D	L	F	A	Pts
Sweden	10	8	2	0	20	3	26
Turkey	10	6	3	1	18	8	21
Slovakia	10	5	2	3	16	9	17
Macedonia	10	1	4	5	11	18	7
Moldova	10	1	3	6	6	20	6
Azerbaijan	10	1	2	7	4	17	5

GROUP 5

Minsk, 2 September 2000, 35,000

Belarus (1) 2 *(Khatskevich 40, Belkevich 56)*   **Wales (0) 1** *(Speed 89)*

Belarus: Tumilovich; Lukhvich, Yakhimovich, Shtanyuk, Gurenko, Khatskevich, Yaskovich (Shuneiko 71), Orlovski (Skripchenko 85), Vasilyuk, Romashchenko M (Ryndyuk 28), Belkevich.
Wales: Jones P; Page, Roberts G, Savage, Coleman, Melville, Robinson, Speed, Bellamy, Roberts I (Blake 73), Giggs.
Referee: Trentalange (Italy).

Oslo, 2 September 2000, 19,201

Norway (0) 0   Armenia (0) 0

Norway: Olsen F; Bergdolmo, Hoftun, Berg, Riseth (Basma 49), Mykland, Leonhardsen, Iversen, Flo T (Helstad 85), Solskjaer, Skammelsrud (Strand R 70).
Armenia: Berezovski; Soukiassian, Hovsepian, Khodgoyan, Vardanian, Khachatrian, Art Petrossian (Minasian 90), Voskanian, Dokhoyan K, Shahgeldian (Demirchian 65), Movsissian (Arm Karamian 85).
Referee: Young (Scotland).

Kiev, 2 September 2000, 50,000

Ukraine (1) 1 *(Shevchenko 13)*   **Poland (2) 3** *(Olisadebe 3, 33, Kaluzny 57)*

Ukraine: Kernozenko; Luzhny, Tymoschuk (Zubov 46), Golovko, Vashchuk, Dmitrulin, Gusin, Popov (Kossovski V 75), Vorobei (Yashkin 61), Shevchenko, Rebrov.
Poland: Dudek; Klos (Hajto 85), Zielinski, Michal Zewlakow, Waldoch, Kozminski (Krzynowek 89), Swierczewski, Iwan, Juskowiak (Gilewicz 70), Kaluzny, Olisadebe.
Referee: Aranda (Spain).

Erevan, 7 October 2000, 14,000

Armenia (2) 2 *(Art Petrossian 17, 44)*   **Ukraine (1) 3** *(Shevchenko 45, 59, Gusin 55)*

Armenia: Berezovski; Soukiassian, Khodgoyan (Arm Karamian 63), Hovsepian, Vardanian, Khachatrian, Art Petrossian, Voskanian, Dokhoyan K, Shahgeldian (Aram Hakopian 77), Movsissian (Art Karamian 63).
Ukraine: Shovkovskyi; Luzhny, Nesmachni, Golovko, Vashchuk, Dmitrulin, Shevchenko, Gusin, Vorobei (Mikhailenko 67), Tymoschuk (Yashkin 46), Rebrov.
Referee: Larsen (Denmark)

Lodz, 7 October 2000, 7000

Poland (1) 3 *(Kaluzny 24, 62, 73)*   **Belarus (1) 1** *(Ryndyuk 37)*

Poland: Dudek; Klos, Zielinksi, Michal Zewlakow, Waldoch, Krzynowek, Swierczewski, Karwan (Iwan 81), Juskowiak (Kryszalowicz 46), Kaluzny, Olisadebe.
Belarus: Varivonchik; Yakhimovich, Ostrovski, Lukhvich, Shtanyuk, Gurenko, Baranov (Lavrik 74), Belkevich, Romashchenko M, Vasilyuk (Ryndyuk 30), Skripchenko (Orlovski 68).
Referee: Frisk (Sweden).

Cardiff, 7 October 2000, 51,000

Wales (0) 1 *(Blake 60)*   **Norway (0) 1** *(Helstad 80)*

Wales: Jones P; Delaney, Savage, Page, Coleman, Melville, Robinson, Speed, Hartson (Roberts I 86), Blake, Giggs.
Norway: Olsen F; Basma, Bjornebye, Leonhardsen, Berg, Johnsen R, Bakke (Helstad 78), Mykland, Iversen (Flo T 59), Solskjaer, Strand R.
Referee: Strampe (Germany).

Minsk, 11 October 2000, 20,000

Belarus (2) 2 *(Khatskevich 23, Ryndyuk 34)*   **Armenia (0) 1** *(Khodgoyan 50)*

Belarus: Tumilovich; Yakhimovich, Ostrovski, Lukhvich, Lavrik, Gurenko, Khatskevich, Belkevich, Romashchenko M (Skripchenko 89), Vasilyuk (Shuneiko 60), Ryndyuk.
Armenia: Abramian; Soukiassian, Khodgoyan (Art Karamian 61), Hovsepian, Vardanian, Khachatrian, Art Petrossian (Arm Karamian 85), Voskanian, Dokhoyan K, Shahgeldian, Movsissian.
Referee: Corpodean (Romania).

Oslo, 11 October 2000, 23,612

Norway (0) 0   Ukraine (0) 1 *(Shevchenko 49)*

Norway: Olsen F; Basma, Johnsen R, Berg, Bergdolmo, Bakke (Helstad 75), Mykland, Iversen, Solskjaer, Leonhardsen (Flo T 54), Strand R.
Ukraine: Shovkovskyi; Luzhny (Fedorov 80), Nesmachni, Golovko, Vashchuk, Dmitrulin, Shevchenko, Gusin, Vorobei, Popov (Yashkin 50), Rebrov.
Referee: Meier (Switzerland).

Warsaw, 11 October 2000, 14,000

Poland (0) 0   Wales (0) 0

Poland: Dudek; Klos, Zielinski, Waldoch, Michal Zewlakow, Karwan, Kaluzny, Swierczewski, Krzynowek (Rzasa 70), Gilewicz (Kryszalowicz 56), Juskowiak (Olisabede 75).
Wales: Jones P; Delaney, Savage, Page, Coleman, Melville, Robinson, Speed, Hartson (Jones N 75), Blake, Giggs.
Referee: Cortez (Portugal).

Erevan, 24 March 2001, 12,000

Armenia (1) 2 *(Minasian 32, Movsissian 71)*   **Wales (1) 2** *(Hartson 41, 48)*

Armenia: Abramian; Vardanian, Hovsepian, Khodgoyan (Art Karamian 58), Sargsyan, Art Petrossian, Voskanian (Aram Hakopian 70), Dokhoyan K, Minasian (Demirchian 39), Shahgeldian, Movsissian.
Wales: Jones P; Delaney, Legg, Melville, Page, Pembridge (Jones M 46), Saunders (Robinson C 70), Speed, Bellamy, Hartson (Roberts I 79), Robinson J.
Referee: Kasnaferis (Greece).

Oslo, 24 March 2001, 15,077

Norway (0) 2 *(Carew 58, Solskjaer 66)*   **Poland (2) 3** *(Olisadebe 23, 29, Karwan 80)*

Norway: Myhre; Bergdolmo, Berg, Lundekvam, Stensaas (Flo T 84), Winsnes, Larsen T, Tessem, Solskjaer, Carew, Helstad (Iversen 60).
Poland: Matysek (Dudek 64); Klos, Hajto, Zielinski, Michal Zewlakow, Iwan (Karwan 64), Kaluzny, Swierczewski (Zdebel 88), Kozminski, Kryszalowicz, Olisadebe.
Referee: Dougal (Scotland).

Kiev, 24 March 2001, 75,000

Ukraine (0) 0   Belarus (0) 0

Ukraine: Shovkovskyi; Luzhny, Golovko, Vashchuk, Nesmachni, Popov (Vorobei 61), Dmitrulin (Tymoshchuk 78), Kardash, Yashkin, Shevchenko, Rebrov.
Belarus: Tumilovich; Shuneiko, Ostrovski, Shtanyuk, Yaskovich, Gurenko, Khatskevich, Belkevich, Vasilyuk, Milevski, Romashchenko M (Lavrik 73).
Referee: Marin (Spain).

Minsk, 28 March 2001, 39,000

Belarus (1) 2 *(Khatskevich 19, Vasilyuk 90)*   **Norway (0) 1** *(Solskjaer 68)*

Belarus: Tumilovich; Shuneiko, Yakhimovich, Shtanyuk, Lukhvich, Gurenko, Khatskevich, Belkevich, Vasilyuk, Milevski (Lavrik 46), Romashchenko M.
Norway: Myhre; Riseth, Berg, Eggen, Bergdolmo, Tessem (Helstad 87), Larsen T, Winsnes, Solskjaer, Carew, Iversen (Flo T 46).
Referee: Vassaras (Greece).

Warsaw, 28 March 2001, 11,000

Poland (2) 4 *(Michal Zewlakow 15 (pen), Olisadebe 41, Marcin Zewlakow 81, Karwan 88)*
Armenia (0) 0

Poland: Dudek; Klos, Zielinski, Hajto, Michal Zewlakow (Krzynowek 76), Swierczewski, Iwan (Karwan 67), Kaluzny, Kozminski, Kryszalowicz (Marcin Zewlakow 79), Olisadebe.
Armenia: Abramian; Mkrchian, Demirchian, Hovsepian, Vardanian, Khachatrian, Art Petrossian, Voskanian (Art Karamian 66), Dokhoyan K, Shahgeldian (Arm Karamian 73), Movsissian.
Referee: Poulat (France).

Cardiff, 28 March 2001, 46,750

Wales (1) 1 *(Hartson 12)*   **Ukraine (0) 1** *(Shevchenko 52)*

Wales: Jones P; Delaney, Barnard, Melville, Page, Jones M (Davies 55), Robinson C, Speed, Bellamy, Hartson (Saunders 70), Giggs.
Ukraine: Shovkovskyi; Luzhny, Golovko, Vashchuk, Nesmachni, Tymoshchuk, Popov (Melashchenko 70), Yashkin, Rebrov (Kardash 46), Vorobei, Shevchenko.
Referee: Romain (Belgium).

Erevan, 2 June 2001, 10,000

Armenia (0) 0   Belarus (0) 0

Armenia: Abramian; Soukiassian, Khodgoyan, Demirchian (Dokhoyan A 65), Vardanian A, Khachatrian, Art Petrossian, Minasian (Art Karamian 36), Sargsyan, Arm Karamian (Gevorgian 69), Dokhoyan K.
Belarus: Tumilovic; Yakhimovich, Ostrovski, Lukhvich, Shtanyuk (Kulchi 84), Gurenko, Khatskevich, Belkevich, Shuneiko, Vasilyuk (Tarlovski 79), Milevski (Yaskovich 72).
Referee: Guenov (Bulgaria).

Kiev, 2 June 2001, 42,000

Ukraine (0) 0   Norway (0) 0

Ukraine: Shovkovskyi; Starostyak, Golovko, Vashchuk, Dmitrulin, Parfenov, Tymoshchuk, Zubov, Vorobei (Spivak 68), Shevchenko, Yashkin (Rebrov 46).
Norway: Myhre; Basma, Hoftun, Berg, Riseth, Rudi, Leonhardsen, Andersen T, Bakke, Strand R (Helstad 78), Carew.
Referee: Maric (Croatia).

Cardiff, 2 June 2001, 48,500

Wales (1) 1 *(Blake 13)*   **Poland (1) 2** *(Olisadebe 32, Kryszalowicz 72)*

Wales: Jones P; Page (Jenkins 84), Barnard (Jones M 79), Melville, Symons, Pembridge, Savage, Speed, Hartson, Blake, Giggs.
Poland: Dudek; Klos, Bak J, Hajto, Michal Zewlakow, Iwan, Zdebel (Krynowek 62), Bak A, Kozminski, Juskowiak (Kryszalowicz 54), Olisadebe (Marcin Zewlakow 90).
Referee: Ersoy (Turkey).

Erevan, 6 June 2001, 10,000

Armenia (1) 1 *(Art Petrossian 11)*   **Poland (1) 1** *(Kaluzny 4)*

Armenia: Abramian; Soukiassian, Khodgoyan, Hovsepian, Vardanian (Demirchian 41), Khachatrian, Art Petrossian, Dokhoyan A (Ara Hakopian 33) (Gevorgian 66), Dokhoyan K, Sargsyan, Art Karamian.
Poland: Dudek; Kukielka, Hajto, Bak J, Michal Zewlakow, Swierczewski, Bak A, Kaluzny (Krzynowek 36), Kozminski (Zdebel 84), Juskowiak (Marcin Zewlakow 64), Kryszalowicz.
Referee: Romain (Belgium).

Oslo, 6 June 2001, 17,164

Norway (0) 1 *(Carew 80)*   **Belarus (1) 1** *(Belkevich 23)*

Norway: Myhre; Basma (Aas 90), Hoftun, Berg, Riseth, Johnsen F, Leonhardsen, Andersen T, Bakke (Rudi 69), Strand R (Nevland 69), Carew.
Belarus: Tumilovich; Yakhimovich, Ostrovski (Tarlovski 85), Lukhvich, Shtanyuk, Gurenko, Khatskevich, Belkevich, Shuneiko, Vasilyuk (Khomutovsky 81), Milevski (Yaskovich 50).
Referee: Radoman (Yugoslavia).

Kiev, 6 June 2001, 33,000

Ukraine (1) 1 *(Zubov 44)*   **Wales (0) 1** *(Pembridge 74)*

Ukraine: Shovkovskyi (Levytsky 90); Starostiak (Luzhny 46), Golovko, Vashchuk, Dmitrulin (Nesmachni 46), Parfenov, Tymoshchuk, Zubov, Vorobei, Shevchenko, Rebrov.
Wales: Jones P; Delaney (Jenkins 38), Barnard, Page, Melville, Pembridge, Davies, Speed, Hartson, Blake (Koumas 73), Giggs.
Referee: Gomes (Portugal).

Minsk, 1 September 2001, 44,000

Belarus (0) 0   Ukraine (1) 2 *(Shevchenko 45, 56)*

Belarus: Khomutovsky; Yakhimovich, Ostrovski (Yaskovich 53), Lukhvich, Shtanyuk, Gurenko, Khatskevich (Tarlovski 46), Belkevich (Romashchenko M 60), Shuneiko, Volodenkov, Katchuro.
Ukraine: Virt; Luzhny, Golovko, Vashchuk, Nesmachni, Tymoshchuk, Parfenov, Zubov, Shevchenko, Vorobei (Melaschenko 71), Rebrov.
Referee: Sars (France).

Chorzow, 1 September 2001, 42,500

Poland (1) 3 *(Kryszalowicz 45, Olisadebe 77, Marcin Zewlakow 88)*   **Norway (0) 0**

Poland: Dudek; Klos, Hajto, Waldoch, Michal Zewlakow, Karwan, Kaluzny, Swierczewski (Bak A 90), Kozminski (Krzynowek 81), Kryszalowicz (Marcin Zewlakow 74), Olisadebe.
Norway: Myhre; Basma, Johnsen R, Berg, Bergdolmo, Strand R (Riise 62), Rudi, Sorensen, Leonhardsen (Rushfeldt 80), Iversen (Strand P 89), Solskjaer.
Referee: Liba (Czech Republic).

Cardiff, 1 September 2001, 18,000

Wales (0) 0   Armenia (0) 0

Wales: Jones P; Delaney, Jenkins (Barnard 80), Robinson C (Jones M 80), Symons, Melville, Savage, Davies, Roberts I, Bellamy, Giggs.
Armenia: Berezovski; Soukiassian, Hovsepian, Vardanian, Dokhoyan A, Art Petrossian (Demirchian 80), Khachatrian, Voskanian (Harutyunian 67), Dokhoyan K, Shahgeldian (Simonian 75), Movsissian.
Referee: Attard (Malta).

Minsk, 5 September 2001, 24,302

Belarus (1) 4 *(Vasilyuk 8, 46, 51, 62)*   **Poland (0) 1** *(Marcin Zewlakow 77)*

Belarus: Tumilovich; Yakhimovich, Milevski (Yaskovich 61), Lukhvich, Shtanyuk, Gurenko, Romashchenko M, Kulchi, Shuneiko, Kachuro, Vasilyuk (Ryndyuk 70) (Ostrovski 83).
Poland: Dudek; Klos, Karwan, Michal Zewlakow, Waldoch, Kukielka, Swierczewski, Kozminski (Krzynowek 46), Kryszalowicz (Marcin Zewlakow 46), Bak A, Olisadebe (Gilewicz 61).
Referee: Plautz (Austria).

Oslo, 5 September 2001, 18,211

Norway (1) 3 *(Johnsen R 17, Carew 65, Johnsen F 83)*
Wales (2) 2 *(Savage 10, Bellamy 27)*

Norway: Myhre; Basma, Johnsen R, Berg, Riise, Sorensen (Johnsen F 46), Strand R, Rudi, Leonhardsen (Strand P 90), Iversen (Carew 5), Solskjaer.
Wales: Jones P; Delaney, Jenkins, Robinson C (Jones M 84), Symons, Page, Savage, Davies (Robinson J 77), Hartson (Blake 83), Bellamy, Giggs.
Referee: Stuchlik (Austria).

Lviv, 5 September 2001, 27,000

Ukraine (1) 3 *(Shevchenko 13, Vorobei 84, 90)*   **Armenia (0) 0**

Ukraine: Virt; Luzhny, Nesmachni, Golovko, Vashchuk, Serebrennikov (Shyshchenko 65), Shevchenko, Parfenov, Zubov (Popov 46), Melaschenko (Vorobei 74), Rebrov.
Armenia: Berezovski; Soukiassian, Dokhoyan K, Hovsepian, Vardanian, Khachatrian, Art Petrossian, Dokhoyan A (Harutyunian 82), Sarkissian, Shahgeldian (Hakopian H 70), Movsissian.
Referee: Loizou (Cyprus).

Erevan, 6 October 2001, 10,000

Armenia (0) 1 *(Hakopian H 71)*   **Norway (0) 4** *(Borgersen 50, 80, Carew 70, 89)*

Armenia: Berezovski; Khodgoyan (Art Karamian 63), Dokhoyan A (Minasian 74), Hovsepian, Vardanian, Khachatrian, Art Petrossian, Dokhoyan K, Sarkissian, Voskanian (Hakopian H 59), Arm Karamian.
Norway: Myhre; Bergdolmo, Johnsen R (Borgersen 46), Basma, Riise, Sorensen (Riseth 83), Bakke, Strand R, Rudi, Johnsen F (Flo T 90), Carew.
Referee: Schluchter (Switzerland).

Chorzow, 6 October 2001, 20,900

Poland (1) 1 *(Olisadebe 40)*   **Ukraine (0) 1** *(Shevchenko 81)*

Poland: Dudek; Klos, Hajto, Waldoch, Michal Zewlakow, Świerczewski (Bak J 77), Karwan, Bak A, Kozminski (Krzynowek 65), Marcin Zewlakow (Kryszalowicz 46), Olisadebe.
Ukraine: Reva; Luzhny, Golovko, Vashchuk (Fedorov 79), Nesmachni (Zadorozhni 84), Zubov, Popov, Melaschenko (Shyshchenko 46), Tymoshchuk, Shevchenko, Vorobei.
Referee: Dallas (Scotland).

Cardiff, 6 October 2001, 12,000

Wales (0) 1 *(Hartson 47)*   **Belarus (0) 0**

Wales: Jones P; Delaney, Speed, Jones M (Robinson C 65), Symons (Page 17), Melville, Robinson J, Davies, Hartson (Roberts I 90), Bellamy, Pembridge.
Belarus: Tumilovich; Lukhvich, Yakhimovich, Shtanyuk, Gurenko, Shuneiko, Kulchi, Yaskovich, Baranov (Gleb 67), Vasilyuk (Ryndyuk 44), Katchuro.
Referee: Rodomonti (Italy).

Group 5 Table	P	W	D	L	F	A	Pts
Poland	10	6	3	1	21	11	21
Ukraine	10	4	5	1	13	8	17
Belarus	10	4	3	3	12	11	15
Norway	10	2	4	4	12	14	10
Wales	10	1	6	3	10	12	9
Armenia	10	0	5	5	7	19	5

GROUP 6

Brussels, 2 September 2000, 40,000

Belgium (0) 0   Croatia (0) 0

Belgium: De Vlieger; Deflandre, Valgaeren, Van Meir, Van Kerckhoven, Vander-haeghe, Wilmots, Goor (Hendrikx 88), Mpenza E (Mpenza M 74), Strupar (Peeters 60), Verheyen.
Croatia: Pletikosa; Kovac R, Jarni, Soldo, Stimac, Simic, Vugrinec (Biscan 46), Jurcic, Suker, Kovac N, Balaban (Tudor 90).
Referee: Levnikov (Russia).

Riga, 2 September 2000, 9500

Latvia (0) 0   Scotland (0) 1 *(McCann 89)*

Latvia: Kolinko; Laizans, Lobanyov, Stepanovs, Blagonadezhdin, Bleidelis, Ivanov, Astafjevs, Rubins, Pahars, Stolcers.
Scotland: Sullivan; Boyd, Davidson (Naysmith 46), Weir (Cameron 46), Hendry, Dailly, Ferguson B, Elliott, Dodds (Holt 90), Hutchison, McCann.
Referee: Schluchter (Switzerland).

Riga, 7 October 2000, 9000

Latvia (0) 0   Belgium (2) 4 *(Wilmots 5, Peeters 13, Cavens 82, Verheyen 90)*

Latvia: Kolinko; Stepanovs, Laizans, Lobanyov (Zemlinsky 75), Blagonadezhdin (Polyakov 63), Astafjevs, Bleidelis, Ivanov, Pahars, Rubins, Stolcers (Peltsis 68).
Belgium: De Vlieger; Deflandre, Valgaeren, Van Meir, Van Kerckhoven, Vander-haeghe, Wilmots (Goossens 88), Goor, Peeters (Cavens 80), Walem (Boffin 85), Ver-heyen.
Referee: Irvine (Northern Ireland).

Serravalle, 7 October 2000, 4377

San Marino (0) 0   Scotland (0) 2 *(Elliott 71, Hutchison 73)*

San Marino: Gasperoni F; Gennari, Gobbi, Matteoni (Valentini V 74), Bacciocchi, Marani, Gasperoni B, Zonzini (Della Valle 80), Manzaroli, Muccioli, Montagna (De Luigi 60).
Scotland: Sullivan; McNamara, Naysmith, Elliott, Hendry, Dailly (Weir 36), Cameron, Gallacher (Dickov 65), Dodds, Hutchison, McCann (Johnston 46).
Referee: Orrason (Iceland).

Zagreb, 11 October 2000, 30,000

Croatia (1) 1 *(Boksic 16)*   **Scotland (1) 1** *(Gallacher 24)*

Croatia: Pavlovic; Kovac R, Stimac, Simic, Saric, Kovac N, Soldo (Biscan 46), Jarni (Zivkovic 46), Prosinecki, Balaban, Boksic (Vugrinec 75).
Scotland: Sullivan; Boyd, Naysmith, Elliott, Hendry, Weir, Cameron, Burley, Gal-lacher, Hutchison, Johnston (Dickov 46) (Holt 90).
Referee: Veissiere (France).

Serravalle, 15 November 2000, 537

San Marino (0) 0   Latvia (1) 1 *(Yeliseyev 9)*

San Marino: Gasperoni F; Gennari, Marani, Valentini V, Matteoni, Bacciocchi, Mucci-oli, Zonzoni (Selva R 84), Montagna (De Luigi 78), Manzaroli (Bugli 74), Selva A.
Latvia: Kolinko; Stepanovs, Laizans, Zemlinsky, Blagonadezhdin, Bleidelis, Troitsky, Astafjevs, Pahars, Rubins (Verpakovsky 66), Yeliseyev (Ivanov 84).
Referee: Cheferin (Slovakia).

Brussels, 28 February 2001, 40,104

Belgium (3) 10 *(Vanderhaeghe 10, 50, Mpenza E 13, Goor 26, 60, Baseggio 64, Wilmots 72, Peeters 76, 84, 88)* **San Marino (0) 1** *(Selva A 90)*

Belgium: De Vlieger; Deflandre (Crasson 67), Van Meir, Van Buyten, Dheedene, Englebert (Peeters 59), Vanderhaeghe, Baseggio (Vermant 75), Goor, Mpenza E, Wilmots.
San Marino: Gasperoni F; Gennari, Gobbi, Della Balda (Manzaroli 69), Marani, Matteoni, Muccioli, Selva A, Valentini, Zonzini (Vannucci 78), De Luigi (Bugli 87).
Referee: Kaldma (Estonia).

Osijek, 24 March 2001, 18,000

Croatia (3) 4 *(Balaban 8, 43, 45, Vugrinec 89)* **Latvia (0) 1** *(Stolcers 60)*

Croatia: Pletikosa; Simic, Tudor, Kovac R (Vranjes 77), Jarni, Zivkovic, Stanic (Cvitanovic 46), Prosinecki (Bjelica 63), Balaban, Suker, Vugrinec.
Latvia: Kolinko; Troitsky, Stepanovs, Zemlinsky, Blagonadezhdin, Bleidelis (Verpakovsky 39), Astafjevs, Laizans, Rubins (Rimkus 73), Pahars, Yeliseyev (Stolcers 54).
Referee: Ingvarsson (Sweden).

Glasgow, 24 March 2001, 37,480

Scotland (2) 2 *(Dodds 1, 28 (pen))* **Belgium (0) 2** *(Wilmots 58, Van Buyten 90)*

Scotland: Sullivan; Weir, Boyd, Elliott, Hendry, Ferguson B, Burley, Lambert, Dodds (Gallacher 88), Hutchison, Matteo.
Belgium: De Vlieger; Mpenza E, Wilmots, Goor, Vanderhaege, Baseggio (Vermant 79), Hendrikx (Peeters 46), Dheedene, De Boeck, Valgaeren (Van Buyten 57), Deflandre.
Referee: Nielsen (Denmark).

Glasgow, 28 March 2001, 27,313

Scotland (3) 4 *(Hendry 22, 33, Dodds 34, Cameron 65)* **San Marino (0) 0**

Scotland: Sullivan; Johnston, Matteo (Gallacher 64), Elliott (Boyd 46), Hendry, Weir, Burley, Lambert, Dodds, Hutchison, Cameron (Gemmill 82).
San Marino: Gasperoni F; Della Balda (Albani 90), Marani, Gobbi, Matteoni, Bacciocchi, Manzaroli (Selva R 80), Zonzini, Muccioli, Vannucci (Bugli 69), Selva A.
Referee: Kari (Finland).

Riga, 25 April 2001, 4000

Latvia (1) 1 *(Pahars 1)* **San Marino (0) 1** *(Albani 59)*

Latvia: Kolinko; Astafjevs, Stepanovs, Zemlinsky, Kolesnichenko (Mikholap 46), Ivanov (Zakreshevski 77), Blagonadezhdin, Rubins, Rimkus (Yeliseyev 66), Pahars, Stolcers.
San Marino: Gasperoni F; Albani, Vannucci, Della Balda, Matteoni, Bugli (Selva R 80), Bacciocchi, Muccioli, Zonzini, Manzaroli (Nanni 90), Selva A (Montagna 83).
Referee: Nalbandian (Albania).

Brussels, 2 June 2001, 30,000

Belgium (2) 3 *(Wilmots 2, Mpenza E 12, Zemlinsky 49 (og))* **Latvia (0) 1** *(Pahars 51)*

Belgium: De Vlieger; Crasson, Valgaeren, Van Meir, Van der Heyden, Simons, Wilmots (Vermant 83), Goor (Boffin 68), Mpenza E (Sonck 78), Walem, Verheyen.
Latvia: Kolinko; Stepanovs, Astafjevs (Stolcers 67), Zemlinsky, Laizans, Blagonadezhdin (Zakreshevsky 68), Ivanov, Bleidelis, Pahars (Mikholap 71), Rubins, Isakov.
Referee: Dobrinov (Bulgaria).

Varazdin, 2 June 2001, 15,000

Croatia (2) 4 *(Vlaovic 3, Balaban 29, Suker 54 (pen), Vugrinec 61)*   **San Marino (0) 0**

Croatia: Pletikosa; Saric, Tudor, Simic, Jarni, Kovac R, Kovac N (Agic 64), Prosinecki, Vugrinec (Vucko 76), Vlaovic, Balaban (Suker 46).
San Marino: Gasperoni F; Albani, Della Balda, Matteoni (Manzaroli 26), Bacciocchi, Marani, Gennari, Vannucci, Gasperoni B (Ugolini 86), Zonzini (Selva R 76), Selva A.
Referee: Timofejev (Estonia).

Riga, 6 June 2001, 5000

Latvia (0) 0   Croatia (1) 1 *(Balaban 40)*

Latvia: Kolinko; Stepanovs, Astafjevs (Mikholap 71), Zemlinsky, Laizans, Blagonadezhdin, Zakreshevsky, Bleidelis (Dobretsov 88), Isakov, Rubins (Verpakovsky 61), Stolcers.
Croatia: Pletikosa; Saric, Jarni, Tomas, Tudor, Simic, Rapaic (Vugrinec 75), Prosinecki, Suker, Kovac N (Agic 90), Balaban (Vlaovic 65).
Referee: McDermott (Republic of Ireland).

Serraville, 6 June 2001, 1000

San Marino (1) 1 *(Selva A 11)*
Belgium (1) 4 *(Wilmots 10, 89 (pen), Verheyen 60, Sonck 68)*

San Marino: Gasperoni F; Albani (Selva R 69), Della Balda, Bacciocchi, Marani, Gennari, Muccioli, Vannucci, Zonzini (Ugolini 82), Selva A, Gasperoni B (Bugli 74).
Belgium: De Vlieger; Deflandre, Van Meir, Valgaeren, Van Kerckhoven (Boffin 79), Verheyen, Vanderhaeghe, Walem, Goor (Vermant 75), Peeters (Sonck 52), Wilmots.
Referee: Yakov (Israel).

Glasgow, 1 September 2001, 47,384

Scotland (0) 0   Croatia (0) 0

Scotland: Sullivan; Weir, Naysmith (Gemmill 84), Elliott, Matteo, Dailly, Burley, Hutchison, Booth (Dodds 72), Lambert, McCann (Cameron 52).
Croatia: Pletikosa; Tudor, Stimac, Kovac R, Zivkovic, Soldo, Tomas (Biscan 84), Jarni, Prosinecki (Vugrinec 78), Stanic (Suker 71), Balaban.
Referee: Michel (Slovakia).

Brussels, 5 September 2001, 48,500

Belgium (1) 2 *(Van Kerckhoven 28, Goor 90)*   **Scotland (0) 0**

Belgium: De Vlieger; Deflandre, De Boeck, Van Meir, Van Kerckhoven, Verheyen, Vanderhaeghe, Walem (Simons 89), Goor, Wilmots, Sonck (Peeters 82).
Scotland: Sullivan; Weir (Cameron 66), Boyd (Booth 57), Elliott, Matteo, Dailly, Burley (McNamara 82), Hutchison, Dodds, Lambert, Naysmith.
Referee: Gonzalez (Spain).

Serravalle, 5 September 2001, 1500

San Marino (0) 0   Croatia (1) 4 *(Kovac N 40, Prosinecki 49 (pen), 90, Soldo 77)*

San Marino: Gasperoni F; Della Balda, Matteoni, Gobbi, Gennari, Marani (Bugli 49), Gasperoni B, Zonzini (Nanni 88), Muccioli, Selva A, Montagna (Ugolini 62).
Croatia: Butina; Zivkovic, Jarni, Stimac, Simic, Soldo, Stanic (Suker 78), Kovac N, Prosinecki, Vlaovic (Balaban 63), Vugrinec (Saric 63).
Referee: Stadsgaard (Denmark).

Zagreb, 6 October 2001, 36,077

Croatia (0) 1 *(Boksic 75)*   **Belgium (0) 0**

Croatia: Pletikosa; Simic, Tudor, Kovac R, Zivkovic, Tomas, Soldo (Rapajic 72), Jarni, Prosinecki (Vranjes 79), Vlaovic (Balaban 63), Boksic.
Belgium: De Vlieger; Deflandre (Peeters 83), Van Meir, De Boeck, Van Kerckhoven, Verheyen, Vanderhaeghe, Baseggio, Goor (Hendrikx 81), Wilmots (Sonck 71), Mpenza E.
Referee: Krug (Germany).

Glasgow, 6 October 2001, 23,228

Scotland (1) 2 *(Freedman 44, Weir 53)* **Latvia (1) 1** *(Rubins 21)*

Scotland: Sullivan; Nicholson B (Booth 63), Davidson, Weir, Dailly (Rae 71), Elliott, Burley, Hutchison (Severin 76), Freedman, Cameron, McCann.
Latvia: Kolinko; Isakov, Zakreshevsky, Stepanovs, Blagonadezhdin, Bleidelis (Kolesnichenko 76), Laizans, Astafjevs, Rubins (Dobretsov 82), Pahars, Verpakovsky.
Referee: Hauge (Norway).

Group 6 Table	P	W	D	L	F	A	Pts
Croatia	8	5	3	0	15	2	18
Belgium	8	5	2	1	25	6	17
Scotland	8	4	3	1	12	6	15
Latvia	8	1	1	6	5	16	4
San Marino	8	0	1	7	3	30	1

GROUP 7

Sarajevo, 2 September 2000, 35,000

Bosnia (1) 1 *(Baljic 41)* **Spain (1) 2** *(Gerard 39, Etxeberria 72)*

Bosnia: Guso; Akrapovic, Hujdurovic, Mujcin (Topic 79), Varesanovic, Hibic, Bolic, Sabic (Muratovic 86), Barbarez, Salihamidzic, Baljic.
Spain: Casillas; Manuel Pablo, Sergi, Paco, Abelardo, Mendieta, Helguera, Gerard (Guerrero 85), Urzaiz (Celades 70), Raul, Munitis (Etxeberria 58).
Referee: Fandel (Germany).

Ramat Gan, 3 September 2000, 14,000

Israel (1) 2 *(Mizrahi A 1, Balili 79)* **Liechtenstein (0) 0**

Israel: Davidovich; Talker (Benayoun 66), Shelach, Gershon, Harazi A, Keissi, Berkovic (Zohar 82), Tal (Balili 77), Nimny, Mizrahi A, Banin.
Liechtenstein: Jehle; Ospelt, Zech, Hasler D, Frick C (Gigon 76), Martin Stocklasa (Hanselmann 85), Michael Stocklasa (Burgmeier 85), Hefti, Telser, Frick M, Beck T.
Referee: O'Hanlon (Republic of Ireland).

Vaduz, 7 October 2000, 3500

Liechtenstein (0) 0 **Austria (1) 1** *(Flogel 20)*

Liechtenstein: Jehle; Ospelt, Hasler D, Telser, Martin Stocklasa, Hanselmann, Hefti, Michael Stocklasa (Nigg 74), Gigon, Beck T, Frick M.
Austria: Wohlfahrt; Martin Hiden, Baur, Stranzl, Schopp (Hortnagl 67), Kuhbauer, Herzog, Flogel, Kirchler, Brunmayr (Kitzbichler 46), Mayrleb.
Referee: Rowbotham (Scotland).

Madrid, 7 October 2000, 80,000

Spain (1) 2 *(Gerard 22, Hierro 53)* **Israel (0) 0**

Spain: Casillas; Hierro, Manuel Pablo, Abelardo, Sergi, Helguera, Gerard (Baraja 31), Mendieta, Munitis, Raul (Guerrero 85), Urzaiz (Catanha 75).
Israel: Davidovich; Halfon, Talker, Shelach, Benado, Keissi, Tal, Nimny (Benayoun 65), Badir (Berkovic 75), Revivo, Mizrahi A.
Referee: Colombo (France).

Vienna, 11 October 2000, 48,000

Austria (1) 1 *(Baur 21)* **Spain (1) 1** *(Baraja 27)*

Austria: Wohlfahrt; Hatz, Baur, Martin Hiden, Stranzl (Hortnagl 46), Flogel, Cerny, Kuhbauer (Schopp 75), Mayrleb, Herzog, Kocijan (Kirchler 54).
Spain: Casillas; Hierro, Abelardo, Sergi, Baraja, Helguera, Mendieta, Urzaiz (Catanha 60), Raul (Guerrero 88), Victor Sanchez (Rufete 46), Manuel Pablo.
Referee: Ivanov (Russia).

Tel Aviv, 11 October 2000, 30,000

Israel (1) 3 *(Berkovic 12, Abuksis 62, Katan 76)* Bosnia (0) 1 *(Akrapovic 48)*

Israel: Davidovich; Benado, Talker, Shelach, Gershon, Keissi (Ben-Dayan 86), Tal, Revivo, Abuksis, Berkovic (Benayoun 60), Mizrahi A (Katan 73).
Bosnia: Guso; Akrapovic, Music, Hujdurovic (Krupinac 79), Varesanovic, Hibic, Bolic, Demirovich (Joldic 73), Barbarez, Salihamidzic, Baljic.
Referee: Jol (Holland).

Sarajevo, 24 March 2001, 25,000

Bosnia (1) 1 *(Barbarez 42)* Austria (0) 1 *(Baur 61)*

Bosnia: Piplica; Varesanovic, Hujdurovic, Hibic, Rizvic (Hota 70), Sabic, Akrapovic, Barbarez, Music, Bolic, Baljic (Topic 83).
Austria: Wohlfahrt; Baur, Martin Hiden, Neukirchner (Prilasnig 54), Cerny (Schopp 46), Kuhbauer, Stranzl, Herzog (Haas 71), Flogel, Vastic, Mayrleb.
Referee: Ovrebo (Norway).

Alicante, 24 March 2001, 29,900

Spain (2) 5 *(Helguera 20, Mendieta 36, 81, Hierro 54 (pen), Raul 68)*
Liechtenstein (0) 0

Spain: Casillas; Manuel Pablo, Hierro, Nadal, Romero, Mendieta, Guardiola (Sergio 82), Helguera (Baraja 67), Raul, Javi Moreno, Munitis (Etxeberria 39).
Liechtenstein: Jehle; Ospelt, Zech, Hefti, Hasler D, Gigon, Beck T (Buchel R 88), Martin Stocklasa (Gerster 90), Telser, Michael Stocklasa, Frick M.
Referee: Ceferin (Slovakia).

Vienna, 28 March 2001, 21,000

Austria (2) 2 *(Baur 9, Herzog 41 (pen))* Israel (1) 1 *(Baur 6 (og))*

Austria: Wohlfahrt; Baur, Martin Hiden, Prilasnig, Schopp, Kuhbauer, Herzog (Kitzbichler 90), Stranzl, Flogel, Vastic (Hortnagl 57), Mayrleb (Haas 63).
Israel: Davidovich; Benado (Mizrahi A 57), Talker, Shelach (Brumer 46), Gershon, Banin (Tal 72), Keissi, Nimny, Berkovic, Zeituni, Benayoun.
Referee: Trentalange (Italy).

Vaduz, 28 March 2001, 3400

Liechtenstein (0) 0 Bosnia (1) 3 *(Barbarez 10, 72, Hota 89)*

Liechtenstein: Jehle; Ospelt, Hefti, Zech, Martin Stocklasa, Hasler D, Beck T (Nigg 73), Telser (Buchel R 46), Michael Stocklasa (Ritter 90), Gigon, Frick M.
Bosnia: Piplica; Varesanovic, Hujdurovic, Hibic, Music, Salihamidzic, Akrapovic, Sabic (Rivzic 90), Barbarez, Bolic (Topic 63), Baljic (Hota 81).
Referee: Sipailo (Latvia).

Innsbruck, 25 April 2001, 13,000

Austria (1) 2 *(Glieder 43, Flogel 75)* Liechtenstein (0) 0

Austria: Manninger; Prilasnig, Baur, Martin Hiden, Kitzbichler (Ibertsberger 75), Kirchler, Flogel, Herzog (Wallner 89), Hortnagl, Vastic (Weissenberger 61), Glieder.
Liechtenstein: Jehle; Ospelt (Buchel R 66), Hefti, Ritter, Zech, Beck T (D'Elia 52), Hasler D, Telser, Martin Stocklasa, Gigon, Frick M (Michael Stocklasa 81).
Referee: Malcolm (Northern Ireland).

Vaduz, 2 June 2001, 1500

Liechtenstein (0) 0 Israel (3) 3 *(Revivo 2, Tal 6, Nimny 17)*

Liechtenstein: Jehle; Ospelt, Ritter, Zech, Martin Stocklasa, Michael Stocklasa, Beck T (Gerster 85), Buchel R (Beck M 71), Telser, Gigon, Hasler H (D'Elia 65).
Israel: Davidovich; Ben-Dayan (Badir 65), Talker, Benado, Gershon, Keissi, Zeituni, Revivo (Mizrahi A 74), Nimny, Berkovic (Benayoun 65), Tal.
Referee: Isaksen (Faeroes).

Oviedo, 2 June 2001, 27,000

Spain (1) 4 *(Hierro 26, Javi Moreno 75, Raul 88, Diego Tristan 90)*
Bosnia (1) 1 *(Beslija 41)*

Spain: Canizares; Manuel Pablo, Hierro, Nadal, Juanfran, Mendieta (Munitis 55), Guardiola, Helguera (Valeron 46), Luis Enrique (Javi Moreno 75), Raul, Diego Tristan.
Bosnia: Piplica; Hujdurovic, Varesanovic, Hibic, Beslija, Akrapovic, Mujcin, Barbarez, Music (Hota 70), Baljic, Bolic (Demirovic 82).
Referee: Olsen (Norway).

Tel Aviv, 6 June 2001, 25,000

Israel (1) 1 *(Revivo 4)*   **Spain (0) 1** *(Raul 63)*

Israel: Davidovich (Auat 46); Brumer, Talker, Benado, Gershon, Keissi, Zeituni, Berkovic (Benayoun 87), Tal, Nimny, Revivo (Banin 70).
Spain: Canizares; Manuel Pablo, Hierro, Nadal, Sergi, Valeron (Helguera 76), Guardiola (Diego Tristan 60), Baraja, Luis Enrique (Puyol 83), Javi Moreno, Raul.
Referee: Frisk (Sweden).

Sarajevo, 1 September 2001, 7700

Bosnia (0) 0   Israel (0) 0

Bosnia: Piplica; Beslija, Music, Konjic, Akrapovic, Hibic, Sabic, Salihamidzic, Topic (Muharemovic 74), Mujcin (Hota 82), Baljic (Saranovic 79).
Israel: Auat; Talker (Harazi 46), Shelach, Gershon, Benado, Keissi, Zeituni, Banin, Tal, Nimny, Revivo (Katan 70).
Referee: Schoch (Switzerland).

Valencia, 1 September 2001, 35,000

Spain (1) 4 *(Diego Tristan 44, Morientes 78, 83, Mendieta 90)*   **Austria (0) 0**

Spain: Canizares; Manuel Pablo, Hierro, Nadal, Aranzabal, Victor Sanchez (Mendieta 79), Valeron, Xavi, Vicente (Luis Enrique 83), Raul, Diego Tristan (Morientes 71).
Austria: Wohlfahrt; Baur, Prilasnig, Martin Hiden, Kogler, Flogel, Herzog, Ibertsberger (Winklhofer 69), Hortnagl, Vastic (Brunmayr 65), Weissenberger (Kitzbichler 57).
Referee: Elizondo (Argentina).

Vienna, 5 September 2001, 23,200

Austria (1) 2 *(Herzog 38, 86)*   **Bosnia (0) 0**

Austria: Wohlfahrt; Baur, Kogler, Martin Hiden, Ibertsberger (Winklhofer 83), Kuhbauer, Prilasnig, Herzog (Kitzbichler 88), Flogel, Vastic, Haas (Weissenberger 81).
Bosnia: Piplica; Beslija, Ikanovic (Hota 68), Konjic, Hibic, Salihamidzic, Sabic, Mujcin, Music, Baljic, Barbarez (Topic 71).
Referee: Barber (England).

Vaduz, 5 September 2001, 4648

Liechtenstein (0) 0   Spain (1) 2 *(Raul 17, Nadal 77)*

Liechtenstein: Jehle; Telser, Ospelt, Zech, Michael Stocklasa, Gigon, Beck T (Nigg 88), Martin Stocklasa, Gerster, Beck M (Burgmeier 67), Buchel R (Buchel M 82).
Spain: Casillas; Puyol, Tellez, Hierro (Nadal 46), Aranzabal, Etxeberria, Mendieta, Albelda, Luis Enrique (Diego Tristan 72), Raul (Jose Ignacio 46), Morientes.
Referee: Dobrinov (Bulgaria).

Zenica, 7 October 2001, 7000

Bosnia (2) 5 *(Konjic 34, Baljic 45 (pen), 82 (pen), Sabic 69, Dodik 86)*   **Liechtenstein (0) 0**

Bosnia: Piplica; Beslija (Hota 72), Music, Konjic, Hibic, Akrapovic (Biscevic 71), Sabic, Salihamidzic (Ikanovic 58), Dodik, Muharemovic, Baljic.
Liechtenstein: Jehle; Ospelt, Martin Stocklasa, Hefti, Michael Stocklasa, Gerster, Telser, Buchel R (D'Elia 76), Beck T (Nigg 46), Burgmeier (Beck M 71), Gigon.
Referee: McDermott (Republic of Ireland).

259

Tel Aviv, 27 October 2001, 41,000

Israel (0) 1 *(Gershon 56 (pen))*   **Austria (0) 1** *(Herzog 90)*

Israel: Auat; Ben Dayan, Benado, Gershon, Talker, Keissi, Banin (Tal 26), Berkovic, Nimny, Revivo (Katan 52), Abuksis.
Austria: Wohlfahrt; Strafner (Wallner 69), Winklhofer, Prilasnig, Vukovic, Schopp (Lexa 60), Kitzbichler (Kocijan 74), Markus Hiden, Herzog, Vastic, Haas.
Referee: Pereira (Portugal).

Group 7 Table	P	W	D	L	F	A	Pts
Spain	8	6	2	0	21	4	20
Austria	8	4	3	1	10	8	15
Israel	8	3	3	2	11	7	12
Bosnia	8	2	2	4	12	12	8
Liechtenstein	8	0	0	8	0	23	0

GROUP 8

Budapest, 3 September 2000, 57,000

Hungary (1) 2 *(Horvath 29, 78)*   **Italy (1) 2** *(Inzaghi F 26, 35)*

Hungary: Kiraly; Korsos G, Sebok V, Matyus (Peto 46), Feher C, Halmai, Hamar (Lendvai 89), Illes, Lisztes, Horvath, Tokoli (Dombi 75).
Italy: Toldo; Cannavaro, Nesta, Iuliano, Zambrotta, Albertini, Maldini, Fiore (Gattuso 80), Totti, Inzaghi F, Del Piero (Delvecchio 73).
Referee: Barber (England).

Bucharest, 3 September 2000, 4500

Romania (0) 1 *(Ganea 89)*   **Lithuania (0) 0**

Romania: Stelea; Ciobotariu (Mutu 49), Filipescu, Belodedici, Contra (Petre 58), Petrescu, Munteanu C, Munteanu D, Chivu, Moldovan (Ganea 67), Vladoiu.
Lithuania: Padimanskas; Kancelskis, Gleveckas, Skerla, Zvirgzdauskas, Zutautas D, Danilevicius, Semberas, Preiksaitis (Buitkus 46), Maciulevicius (Mikalajunas 46), Fomenka (Radzius 80).
Referee: Norman (Sweden).

Milan, 7 October 2000, 54,297

Italy (3) 3 *(Inzaghi F 13, Delvecchio 17, Totti 42)*   **Romania (0) 0**

Italy: Toldo; Cannavaro, Nesta, Maldini, Di Livio, Albertini, Fiore (Pancaro 55), Coco, Totti, Inzaghi F (Del Piero 81), Delvecchio (Gattuso 71).
Romania: Stelea; Petrescu (Contra 46), Belodedici, Filipescu, Chivu, Rosu, Galca, Lupescu, Munteanu D (Munteanu C 62), Moldovan (Mutu 58), Ganea.
Referee: Wegereef (Holland).

Vilnius, 7 October 2000, 5000

Lithuania (0) 0   Georgia (2) 4 *(Ketsbaia 18, 33, Kinkladze 46, Arveladze A 84)*

Lithuania: Padimanskas; Skerla, Gleveckas, Graziunas (Maciulevicius 39), Zutatas D, Buitkus, Semberas, Ivanauskas (Morinas 46), Fomenka (Zvinglas 55), Danilevicius, Jankauskas.
Georgia: Gvaramadze; Silagadze, Kobiashvili, Rekhviashvili, Khizanishvili, Kaladze, Nemsadze, Kavelashvili, Ketsbaia (Menteshashvili 67), Kinkladze (Jamarauli 70), Demetradze (Arveladze A 56).
Referee: Wojcik (Poland).

Ancona, 11 October 2000, 26,000

Italy (0) 2 *(Del Piero 47 (pen), 88 (pen))*   **Georgia (0) 0**

Italy: Toldo; Cannavaro, Nesta, Bertotto, Di Livio, Albertini, Fiore (Pancaro 76), Coco, Totti (Montella 83), Delvecchio (Gattuso 52), Del Piero.
Georgia: Gvaramadze; Silagadze, Kobiashvili, Rekhviashvili, Khizanishvili, Kaladze, Nemsadze, Kavelashvili, Ketsbaia (Menteshashvili 68), Kinkladze (Jamarauli 61), Arveladze A (Demetradze 61).
Referee: Nilsson (Sweden).

Vilnius, 11 October 2000, 2000

Lithuania (0) 1 *(Buitkus 71)*   **Hungary (2) 6** *(Illes 24, Feher M 36, 62, 72, Horvath 66, Lisztes 84 (pen))*
Lithuania: Padimanskas; Skerla, Gleveckas, Radzius, Kancelskis (Graziunas 69), Buitkus, Semberas, Ivanauskas (Maciulevicius 70), Preiksaitis, Morinas (Danielvicius 83), Jankauskas.
Hungary: Kiraly; Korsos G (Bodnar 84), Feher C (Juhar 78), Matyus (Dombi 73), Sebok V, Peto, Feher M, Lisztes, Horvath, Illes, Hamar.
Referee: Erdemir (Turkey).

Budapest, 24 March 2001, 20,000

Hungary (0) 1 *(Sebok V 70 (pen))*   **Lithuania (0) 1** *(Razanauskas 74)*
Hungary: Kiraly; Feher C, Sebok V, Korsos G, Juhar, Miriuta, Dardai, Illes, Hamar (Egressy 46), Horvath, Feher M (Dombi 64).
Lithuania: Stauce; Skarbalius, Dedura (Dziaukstas 35), Gleveckas, Zvirgzdauskas, Razanauskas (Joksas 89), Zutautas R, Poskus, Morinas, Semberas, Mikalajunas.
Referee: Melnischuk (Ukraine).

Bucharest, 24 March 2001, 24,500

Romania (0) 0   Italy (2) 2 *(Inzaghi F 29, 32)*
Romania: Stelea; Radoi (Serban 71), Filipescu, Prodan, Contra, Codrea, Galca (Munteanu C 59), Munteanu D, Moldovan (Ganea 78), Niculae, Ilie A.
Italy: Buffon; Cannavaro, Nesta, Maldini, Zambrotta, Tommasi, Fiore (Tacchinardi 62), Albertini, Pancaro, Inzaghi F (Montella 86), Del Piero.
Referee: Fandel (Germany).

Tbilisi, 28 March 2001, 27,000

Georgia (0) 0   Romania (0) 2 *(Munteanu D 68, Contra 81)*
Georgia: Gvaramadze; Silagadze, Rekhviashvili (Iashvili 73), Kobiashvili, Khizanishvili, Nemsadze, Kaladze, Kavelashvili (Janashia 52), Ketsbaia (Kemoklidze 62), Arveladze S, Kinkladze.
Romania: Stelea; Contra, Filipescu, Prodan, Radoi (Galca 58), Munteanu C, Codrea, Chivu, Munteanu D, Moldovan (Stoica 82), Ilie A (Niculae 21).
Referee: Pedersen (Norway).

Trieste, 28 March 2001, 14,800

Italy (1) 4 *(Inzaghi F 17, 63, Del Piero 49, 79)*   **Lithuania (0) 0**
Italy: Buffon; Cannavaro, Nesta, Maldini, Zambrotta, Tommasi, Tacchinardi, Coco, Totti (Fiore 75), Inzaghi F (Montella 69), Del Piero (Di Livio 83).
Lithuania: Stauce; Zvirgzdauskas, Skarbalius, Joksas, Dziaukstas, Razanauskas (Danilevicius 30), Zutautas R, Semberas, Morinas, Poskus (Zvingilas 77), Mikalajunas (Jankauskas 65).
Referee: Shmolik (Belarus).

Tbilisi, 2 June 2001, 28,000

Georgia (0) 1 *(Gakhokidze 80)*   **Italy (1) 2** *(Delvecchio 45, Totti 66)*
Georgia: Zoidze; Silagadze, Abramidze, Kaladze, Kobiashvili, Khizanishvili (Gakhokidze 79), Nemsadze (Arveladze S 80), Rekhviashvili, Menteshashvili (Arveladze A 60), Ketsbaia, Kavelashvili.
Italy: Buffon; Cannavaro, Nesta (Materazzi 74), Maldini, Zambrotta, Tommasi, Tacchinardi, Pancaro, Totti, Delvecchio (Montella 79), Del Piero (Di Livio 58).
Referee: Iturralde (Spain).

Bucharest, 2 June 2001, 22,000

Romania (1) 2 *(Niculae 4, 54)*   **Hungary (0) 0**
Romania: Stelea; Contra, Radoi (Prodan 64), Ciobotariu, Chivu, Munteanu D, Codrea, Ilie A (Munteanu C 75), Dumitru, Moldovan (Ganea 72), Niculae.
Hungary: Kiraly; Feher C, Korsos G, Sebok V, Matyus, Peto, Lisztes, Sowunmi (Kabat 73), Dardai, Horvath (Korsos A 46), Hamar (Dombi 41).
Referee: Poulat (France).

Budapest, 6 June 2001, 10,000

Hungary (2) 4 *(Matyus 40, Sebok V 45 (pen), Korsos A 55, 62)*
Georgia (0) 1 *(Kobiashvili 77)*

Hungary: Kiraly; Korsos G, Sebok V, Peto, Matyus, Lisztes (Lendvai 80), Halmai (Dardai 70), Illes, Korsos A (Dombi 77), Horvath, Kabat.
Georgia: Zoidze; Abramidze, Kaladze (Todua 67), Arveladze A, Kobiashvili, Nemsadze (Kemoklidze 67), Rekhviashvili, Khizanishvili, Ketsbaia, Arveladze S, Kavelashvili (Kinkladze 53).
Referee: Strampe (Germany).

Kaunas, 6 June 2001, 7000

Lithuania (0) 1 *(Fomenka 87)* **Romania (1) 2** *(Ilie A 31, Moldovan 49)*

Lithuania: Stauce; Zvirgzdauskas, Dedura, Skarbalius, Graziunas, Morinas (Fomenka 46), Zutautas R, Mikalajunas, Semberas, Razanauskas (Buitkus 73), Poskus.
Romania: Stelea; Contra (Ganea 54), Radoi, Filipescu, Chivu, Dumitru, Niculae, Kodrea, Munteanu D, Moldovan (Prodan 57), Ilie A (Mutu 63).
Referee: Stredak (Slovakia).

Tbilisi, 1 September 2001, 8000

Georgia (1) 3 *(Arveladze S 34, Jamarauli 49, Iashvili 64)* **Hungary (1) 1** *(Matyus 44)*

Georgia: Gvaramadze; Kobiashvili, Khizanishvili, Rekhviashvili, Kaladze, Tskitishvili (Sajala 78), Nemsadze, Kavelashvili (Iashvili 46), Jamarauli, Kinkladze, Arveladze S (Demetradze 62).
Hungary: Kiraly; Korsos G, Peto, Matyus, Sebok V, Halmai (Dardai 53), Kabat, Lisztes, Horvath (Tokoli 62), Illes (Lendvai 66), Korsos A.
Referee: Kos (Slovenia).

Kaunas, 1 September 2001, 5500

Lithuania (0) 0 Italy (0) 0

Lithuania: Stauce; Skarbalius, Stankevicius, Gleveckas, Dziaukstas, Razanauskas (Narbekovas 88), Zutautas R, Morinas, Mikalajunas, Jankauskas, Poskus (Semberas 85).
Italy: Buffon; Cannavaro, Nesta, Maldini, Zambrotta (Coco 82), Tommasi, Tacchinardi, Pancaro, Totti (Fiore 88), Vieri, Del Piero (Inzaghi F 61).
Referee: Van der Ende (Holland).

Tbilisi, 5 September 2001, 18,000

Georgia (0) 2 *(Iashvili 85, 87)* **Lithuania (0) 0**

Georgia: Gvaramadze; Kobiashvili, Khizanishvili, Sajala, Kaladze, Tskitishvili, Nemsadze, Kavelashvili (Demetradze 46), Alexidze (Burduli 74), Kinkladze, Iashvili (Arveladze S 90).
Lithuania: Stauce; Stankevicius, Dziaukstas, Gleveckas, Skarbalius, Morinas, Zutautas R, Mikalajunas (Jankauskas 86), Semberas, Razanauskas, Poskus.
Referee: Yakov (Israel).

Budapest, 5 September 2001, 8000

Hungary (0) 0 Romania (2) 2 *(Ilie A 10, Niculae 26)*

Hungary: Kiraly; Korsos G (Kabat 46), Sebok V, Juhar, Matyus, Dardai, Lisztes, Lendvai (Gyori 63), Korsos A (Fuzi 55), Tokoli, Horvath.
Romania: Lobont; Filipescu (Kirita 73), Popescu G, Radoi, Chivu, Contra, Sabau, Munteanu D, Mutu, Ilie A (Rosu 75), Niculae (Ganea 80).
Referee: Dallas (Scotland).

Parma, 6 October 2001, 20,805

Italy (1) 1 *(Del Piero 45)* **Hungary (0) 0**

Italy: Buffon; Cannavaro, Materazzi, Maldini, Zambrotta (Di Livio 80), Tommasi, Albertini (Di Biagio 73), Coco, Totti, Del Piero (Gattuso 57), Inzaghi F.
Hungary: Kiraly; Bodnar, Kuttor, Juhar, Matyus, Peto, Sebok V, Miriuta (Lisztes 55), Dardai, Tokoli (Egressy 77), Kabat (Ferenczi 66).
Referee: Chavez (Paraguay).

Bucharest, 6 October 2001, 16,500

Romania (0) 1 *(Popescu G 88)*   **Georgia (0) 1** *(Iashvili 54)*

Romania: Lobont; Kirita, Lacusta, Miu, Parvu (Mihalcea 61), Popescu G, Dumitru, Munteanu D, Niculae, Mutu (Rosu 46), Ilie A (Pancu 70).
Georgia: Gvaramadze; Kobiashvili, Khizanishvili, Rekhviashvili, Sajala, Tskitishvili, Kaladze, Jamarauli, Iashvili (Alexidze 80), Kinkladze (Ketsbaia 63), Kavelashvili (Burduli 75).
Referee: Michel (Slovakia).

Group 8 Table	P	W	D	L	F	A	Pts
Italy	8	6	2	0	16	3	20
Romania	8	5	1	2	10	7	16
Georgia	8	3	1	4	12	12	10
Hungary	8	2	2	4	14	13	8
Lithuania	8	0	2	6	3	20	2

GROUP 9

Helsinki, 2 September 2000, 10,770

Finland (1) 2 *(Litmanen 45, Riihilahti 67)*   **Albania (0) 1** *(Murati 63)*

Finland: Jaaskelainen; Saarinen, Turpeinen, Hyypia, Tihinen, Nurmela (Johansson 57), Koppinen (Riihilahti 46), Valakari, Forssell (Ylonen 77), Litmanen, Kolkka.
Albania: Strakosha; Lala, Cipi, Xhumba, Vata R, Murati (Bushi 76), Haxhi, Muka (Skela 46), Kola, Rraklli, Tare.
Referee: Timmink (Holland).

Hamburg, 2 September 2000, 48,500

Germany (1) 2 *(Deisler 17, Ouzounidis 75 (og))*   **Greece (0) 0**

Germany: Kahn; Rehmer, Nowotny, Heinrich (Linke 46), Deisler, Ramelow, Ballack, Bode, Scholl, Jancker, Zickler (Rink 71).
Greece: Eleftheropoulos; Ouzounidis, Goumas, Amanatidis, Georgatos, Poursanidis (Choutos 66), Mavrogenidis (Patsatzoglou 23), Tsartas, Zagorakis, Liberopoulos, Georgiadis (Lakis 76).
Referee: Nieto (Spain).

Wembley, 7 October 2000, 76,377

England (0) 0   Germany (1) 1 *(Hamann 14)*

England: Seaman; Neville G (Dyer 46), Le Saux (Barry 77), Southgate, Keown, Adams, Beckham (Parlour 82), Barmby, Cole, Owen, Scholes.
Germany: Kahn; Rehmer, Nowotny, Linke, Deisler, Ramelow, Hamann, Ballack, Bode (Ziege 86), Scholl, Bierhoff.
Referee: Braschi (Italy).

Athens, 7 October 2000, 14,800

Greece (0) 1 *(Liberopoulos 59)*   **Finland (0) 0**

Greece: Nikopolidis; Georgatos (Venetidis 72), Patsatzoglou, Amanatidis, Ouzounidis, Karagounis (Lakis 76), Zagorakis, Basinas, Liberopoulos, Georgiadis, Choutos (Antzas 83).
Finland: Niemi; Reini, Helin, Hyypia, Tihinen, Nurmela, Wiss (Kottila 81), Valakari, Johansson (Kuqi 64), Litmanen, Kolkka (Forssell 46).
Referee: Collina (Italy).

Tirana, 11 October 2000, 11,000

Albania (0) 2 *(Bushi 50, Fakaj 90)*   **Greece (0) 0**

Albania: Strakosha; Muka, Cipi, Xhumba (Fakaj 75), Vata R, Vata F (Basha 78), Skela, Kola, Haxhi, Bushi, Tare (Bogdani 86).
Greece: Nikopolidis; Basinas, Venetidis (Kyparissis 72), Patsatzogolou, Ouzounidis, Zagorakis (Lakis 70), Georgiadis, Karagounis, Choutos, Liberopoulos, Zikos (Poursanidis 70).
Referee: Pedersen (Norway).

Helsinki, 11 October 2000, 36,210

Finland (0) 0   England (0) 0

Finland: Niemi; Helin (Reini 36), Tihinen, Hyypia, Saarinen (Salli 66), Nurmela, Wiss, Valakari, Johansson, Litmanen, Forssell (Kuqi 76).
England: Seaman; Neville P, Barry (Brown 69), Southgate, Keown, Wise, Parlour, Scholes, Cole, Sheringham (McManaman 69), Heskey.
Referee: Sars (France).

Liverpool, 24 March 2001, 44,262

England (1) 2 *(Owen 43, Beckham 50)*   **Finland (1) 1** *(Neville G 26 (og))*

England: Seaman; Neville G, Powell, Ferdinand R, Campbell, Scholes, Beckham, Gerrard, Cole (Fowler 82), Owen (Butt 90), McManaman (Heskey 72).
Finland: Niemi; Pasanen, Hyypia, Tihinen, Ylonen (Helin 89), Wiss, Nurmela (Forssell 63), Riihilahti, Litmanen, Kolkka (Kuqi 63), Johansson.
Referee: Ivanov (Russia).

Leverkusen, 24 March 2001, 22,500

Germany (0) 2 *(Deisler 50, Klose 88)*   **Albania (0) 1** *(Kola 65)*

Germany: Kahn; Nowotny, Worns, Jeremies, Ramelow, Deisler, Hamann (Rehmer 46), Bode, Neuville (Klose 73), Bierhoff (Jancker 46), Scholl.
Albania: Strakosha; Cipi, Vata R, Lala, Xhumba, Vata F (Skela 79), Hasi (Fakaj 86), Kola, Murati, Tare, Bushi (Rraklli 67).
Referee: Cesari (Italy).

Tirana, 28 March 2001, 18,000

Albania (0) 1 *(Rraklli 90)*   **England (0) 3** *(Owen 73, Scholes 85, Andy Cole 90)*

Albania: Strakosha; Cipi, Fakaj, Lala, Xhumba, Hasi, Vata F (Rraklli 88), Kola (Muka 82), Bellai, Tare (Skela 90), Bushi.
England: Seaman; Neville G, Ashley Cole, Ferdinand R, Campbell (Brown 29), Butt, Beckham, Scholes, Andy Cole, Owen (Sheringham 84), McManaman (Heskey 46).
Referee: Hamer (Luxembourg).

Athens, 28 March 2001, 53,000

Greece (2) 2 *(Haristeas 21, Georgiadis 44)*
Germany (2) 4 *(Rehmer 6, Ballack 25 (pen), Klose 82, Bode 90)*

Greece: Eleftheropoulos; Patsatzoglou, Kostoulas (Mavrogenidis 35), Goumas, Basinas, Karagounis (Niniadis 75), Zagorakis, Georgiadis, Haristeas (Alexandris 84), Liberopoulos, Georgatos.
Germany: Kahn; Worns, Nowotny, Heinrich, Rehmer, Jeremies (Ramelow 90), Deisler, Ballack, Ziege, Jancker (Bode 78), Neuville (Klose 67).
Referee: Pereira (Portugal).

Helsinki, 2 June 2001, 35,774

Finland (2) 2 *(Forssell 28, 43)*   **Germany (0) 2** *(Ballack 68 (pen), Jancker 72)*

Finland: Niemi; Pasanen, Nylund, Hyypia, Tihinen, Nurmela (Johansson 71), Riihilahti (Gronlund 80), Litmanen, Rantanen, Forssell, Kolkka (Kuqi 85).
Germany: Kahn; Rehmer, Nowotny, Linke, Asamoah, Ramelow, Ballack, Bode (Ziege 69), Ricken, Neuville (Klose 62), Jancker (Bierhoff 83).
Referee: Jol (Holland).

Iraklion, 2 June 2001, 4000

Greece (1) 1 *(Mahlas 72)*   **Albania (0) 0**

Greece: Nikopolidis; Patsatzogolou, Dabizas, Venetidis, Zagorakis, Goumas, Ouzounidis, Georgiadis (Basinas 85), Karagounis, Alexandris (Haristeas 62), Liberopoulos (Mahlas 46).
Albania: Strakosha; Cipi, Vata R, Lala, Xhumba, Hasi, Haxhi (Skela 76), Bushi, Vata F, Murati, Tare (Bogdani 71).
Referee: Levnikov (Russia).

Tirana, 6 June 2001, 18,000

Albania (0) 0   Germany (1) 2 *(Rehmer 28, Ballack 68)*

Albania: Strakosha; Vata R, Cipi, Xhumba (Bellai 46), Lala, Vata F, Murati, Hasi (Skela 61), Haxhi (Muka 81), Bushi, Tare.
Germany: Kahn; Rehmer, Nowotny, Linke, Asamoah (Ricken 70), Ramelow, Ballack, Ziege, Deisler (Baumann 84), Jancker, Neuville (Zickler 46).
Referee: Veissiere (France).

Athens, 6 June 2001, 46,000

Greece (0) 0   England (0) 2 *(Scholes 64, Beckham 87)*

Greece: Nikopolidis; Goumas, Ouzounidis, Dabizas, Mavrogenidis (Giannakopoulos 70), Basinas, Zagorakis, Fyssas, Karagounis (Liberopoulos 24), Mahlas (Alexandris 64), Vryzas.
England: Seaman; Neville P, Ashley Cole, Gerrard, Keown, Ferdinand, Beckham, Scholes (Butt 88), Fowler (Smith 79), Owen, Heskey (McManaman 74).
Referee: Pedersen (Norway).

Tirana, 1 September 2001, 6400

Albania (0) 0   Finland (0) 2 *(Tainio 57, Kuqi 90)*

Albania: Beqaj; Lala, Cipi, Xhumba, Bellai, Muka (Vata R 62), Haxhi, Vata F, Bushi, Rraklli (Bogdani 64), Tare (Fortuzi 64).
Finland: Niemi; Helin, Saarinen, Hyypia, Kuivasto, Riihilahti, Nurmela (Kuqi 78), Tainio, Forssell (Johansson 66), Litmanen (Ilola 86), Kolkka.
Referee: Ersoy (Turkey).

Munich, 1 September 2001, 63,000

Germany (1) 1 *(Jancker 6)*   **England (2) 5** *(Owen 13, 48, 66, Gerrard 45, Heskey 74)*

Germany: Kahn; Worns (Asamoah 46), Nowotny, Linke, Rehmer, Hamann, Ballack (Klose 67), Bohme, Deisler, Jancker, Neuville (Kehl 78).
England: Seaman; Neville G, Ashley Cole, Gerrard (Hargreaves 78), Ferdinand, Campbell, Beckham, Scholes (Carragher 83), Heskey, Owen, Barmby (McManaman 65).
Referee: Collina (Italy).

Newcastle, 5 September 2001, 51,046

England (1) 2 *(Owen 44, Fowler 88)*   **Albania (0) 0**

England: Seaman; Neville G, Ashley Cole, Gerrard (Carragher 81), Ferdinand, Campbell, Beckham, Scholes, Heskey (Fowler 53), Owen, Barmby (McManaman 62).
Albania: Strakosha; Dede, Fakaj, Cipi, Xhumba, Murati, Vata F, Bellai, Hasi (Bushi 46), Bogdani (Tare 55), Rraklli (Muka 61).
Referee: Marin (Spain).

Helsinki, 5 September 2001, 27,216

Finland (4) 5 *(Forssell 13, 44, Riihilahti 22, Kolkka 40, Litmanen 53 (pen))*
Greece (1) 1 *(Karagounis 32)*

Finland: Niemi; Helin, Saarinen, Hyypia, Tihinen, Riihilahti, Nurmela, Tainio (Wiss 62), Forssell (Johansson 79), Litmanen (Kuqi 72), Kolkka.
Greece: Eleftheropoulos; Basinas (Zikos 46), Dabizas, Georgatos, Amanatidis, Konstantinidis (Georgiadis 25), Haristeas, Zagorakis (Fyssas 82), Vryzas, Mahlas, Karagounis.
Referee: Allaerts (Belgium).

Manchester, 6 October 2001, 66,009

England (0) 2 *(Sheringham 68, Beckham 90)*   **Greece (1) 2** *(Haristeas 36, Nikolaidis 70)*

England: Martyn; Neville G, Ashley Cole (McManaman 78), Gerrard, Ferdinand, Keown, Beckham, Scholes, Heskey, Fowler (Sheringham 67), Barmby (Andy Cole 46).
Greece: Nikopolidis; Patsatzoglou, Dabizas, Konstantinidis, Vokolos, Fyssas, Haristeas (Lakis 73), Zagorakis (Basinas 57), Karagounis, Kassapis, Nikolaidis (Mahlas 86).
Referee: Jol (Holland).

Gelsenkirchen, 6 October 2001, 52,000

Germany (0) 0   Finland (0) 0

Germany: Kahn; Rehmer, Worns, Nowotny, Ziege, Ballack, Ramelow, Deisler, Bohme (Asamoah 46), Bierhoff, Neuville (Klose 76).
Finland: Niemi; Reini (Helin 78), Tihinen, Saarinen, Hyypia, Nurmela, Tainio (Gronlund 83), Riihilahti, Johansson (Kuqi 66), Litmanen, Forssell.
Referee: Frisk (Sweden).

Group 9 Table	P	W	D	L	F	A	Pts
England	8	5	2	1	16	6	17
Germany	8	5	2	1	14	10	17
Finland	8	3	3	2	12	7	12
Greece	8	2	1	5	7	17	7
Albania	8	1	0	7	5	14	3

SOUTH AMERICA

(Members 10, Entries 10)

Five teams qualified: Argentina, Brazil, Ecuador, Paraguay and Uruguay.

Bogota, 28 March 2000, 42,493

Colombia (0) 0   Brazil (0) 0

Colombia: Cordoba O; Bermudez, Cordoba I, Yepes, Martinez, Viveros, Dinas, Rincon, Oviedo (Moreno 74), Angel, Ricard (Maturana 60).
Brazil: Dida; Evanilson, Aldair, Zago, Roberto Carlos, Emerson, Ze Roberto, Vampeta, Alex (Ricardinho 46), Elber (Ronaldinho 68), Jardel (Edilson 46).
Referee: Mendez (Uruguay).

Buenos Aires, 29 March 2000, 50,000

Argentina (2) 4 *(Batistuta 9, Veron 33, 71 (pen), Lopez C 88)*   **Chile (1) 1** *(Tello 29)*

Argentina: Bonano; Pochettino, Ayala, Samuel, Zanetti, Simeone, Kily Gonzalez, Veron, Ortega (Sensini 85), Batistuta (Crespo 89), Lopez C (Lopez G 89).
Chile: Ramirez Ma; Maldonado, Reyes, Margas, Contreras, Ormazabal (Aros 83), Acuna, Tello, Pizarro (Sierra 70), Zamorano, Salas.
Referee: Moreno (Ecuador).

Quito, 29 March 2000, 50,000

Ecuador (1) 2 *(Delgado 17, Aguinaga A 51)*   **Venezuela (0) 0**

Ecuador: Cevallos; De la Cruz, Jacome, Montano, Guagua (Ayovi M 49), Blandon, Tenorio (Chala 73), Aguinaga A, Obregon, Graziani (Poroso 38), Delgado.
Venezuela: Dudamel; Alvarez, Villafraz (Mea Vitali M 62), Becerra, Rey, Urdaneta, Rojas (Arango 55), Bidoglio, Vera J, Casseres, Garcia (Ochoa 55).
Referee: Gamboa (Chile).

Lima, 29 March 2000, 45,000

Peru (0) 2 *(Solano 55 (pen), Palacios 60)*   **Paraguay (0) 0**

Peru: Ibanez; Jorge Soto, Rebosio, Pajuelo, Olivares (Huaman 72), Jayo, Palacios, Del Solar, Solano, Pizarro (Ciurlizza 81), Zuniga (Holsen 59).
Paraguay: Chilavert; Arce, Ayala, Gamarra, Caniza, Enciso (Struway 68), Paredes (Gavilan 74), Acuna, Campos, Santa Cruz, Jose Cardozo (Gonzalez G 68).
Referee: Elizondo (Argentina).

Montevideo, 29 March 2000, 55,000

Uruguay (1) 1 *(Pablo Garcia 26)*   **Bolivia (0) 0**

Uruguay: Carini; Mendez, Lopez, Montero, Rodriguez, Coelho, Pablo Garcia, O'Neill, Cedres (Olivera 58), Alonso (Zalayeta 76), Recoba (Poyet 89).
Bolivia: Fernandez; Ribera, Pena, Oscar Sanchez, Sandy (Rimba 75), Ivan Castillo, Cristaldo, Justiniano, Erwin Sanchez, Gutierrez L (Suarez 59), Moreno (Botero 70).
Referee: Pereira (Argentina).

La Paz, 26 April 2000, 20,000

Bolivia (1) 1 *(Erwin Sanchez 16)*   **Colombia (1) 1** *(Castillo J 32)*

Bolivia: Fernandez; Ribeiro, Pena, Sandy (Rimba 33), Ivan Castillo, Cristaldo, Soria, Gutierrez R (Galindo 63), Erwin Sanchez, Antelo (Suarez 46), Moreno.
Colombia: Cordoba O; Cordoba I, Bermudez, Yepes, Viveros, Martinez (Cardona 79), Dinas, Oviedo (Ortegon 82), Rincon, Ricard (Angel 74), Castillo J.
Referee: Arana (Peru).

Sao Paulo, 26 April 2000, 65,000

Brazil (2) 3 *(Rivaldo 18, 51, Zago 42)*   **Ecuador (1) 2** *(Aguinaga A 12, De la Cruz 76)*

Brazil: Dida; Cafu, Zago, Aldair, Roberto Carlos (Athirson 68), Cesar Sampaio, Vampeta, Rivaldo, Ze Roberto (Alex 68), Amoroso, Edilson.
Ecuador: Cevallos; De la Cruz, Poroso, Capurro, Hurtado I, Tenorio, Obregon, Aguinaga A (Ayovi M 40) (Kaviedes 88), Blandon, Delgado, Graziani (Hurtado E 66).
Referee: Cervantes (Colombia).

Santiago, 26 April 2000, 45,000

Chile (1) 1 *(Margas 42)*   **Peru (1) 1** *(Jayo 38)*

Chile: Tapia N; Vargas, Reyes, Margas, Maldonado (Nunez C 70), Acuna, Rojas F (Nunez R 70), Pizarro (Sierra 58), Tello, Zamorano, Salas.
Peru: Ibanez; Jorge Soto, Rebosio, Pajuelo, Olivares, Jayo, Soria (Zuniga 58), Del Solar, Palacios, Solano, Pizarro.
Referee: Rojas (Paraguay).

Asuncion, 26 April 2000, 15,000

Paraguay (1) 1 *(Ayala 35)*   **Uruguay (0) 0**

Paraguay: Chilavert; Espinola, Gamarra, Ayala, Caniza, Quintana (Gonzalez G 59), Paredes, Struway, Acuna (Enciso 68), Santa Cruz, Baez (Benitez 82).
Uruguay: Carini; Mendez, Ramos, Lembo, Tabare Silva (Guigou 67), Coelho, Pablo Garcia, De los Santos, Poyet (Olivera 63), Recoba, Dario Silva (Alvez 75).
Referee: Sanchez (Argentina).

Maracaibo, 26 April 2000, 27,000

Venezuela (0) 0   Argentina (2) 4 *(Ayala 7, Ortega 23, 76, Crespo 88)*

Venezuela: Dudamel; Rojas, Rey, Villafraz (Luzardo 46), Gonzalez, Mea Vitali M, Bidoglio, Urdaneta, Vera J, Garcia (Martinez 70), Castellin.
Argentina: Bonano; Ayala, Samuel, Sensini, Kily Gonzalez, Zanetti, Simeone, Veron, Ortega (Gallardo 78), Lopez C (Lopez G 68), Crespo.
Referee: Amarilla (Paraguay).

Ascunion, 3 June 2000, 22,000

Paraguay (2) 3 *(Toledo 11, Brizuela 43, 64)*   **Ecuador (0) 1** *(Graziani 87)*

Paraguay: Chilavert; Caniza, Gamarra, Ayala, Toledo, Paredes, Struway (Enciso 82), Quintana, Acuna, Brizuela (Gonzalez G 76), Baez (Benitez 66).
Ecuador: Cevallos; De la Cruz, Poroso (Kaviedes 66), Montano, Capurro, Blandon, Hurtado I, Tenorio (Chala 46), Aguinaga A, Juarez, Delgado (Graziani 61).
Referee: Gallesio (Uruguay).

Montevideo, 3 June 2000, 60,000

Uruguay (2) 2 *(Dario Silva 35, Montero 41)*   **Chile (1) 1** *(Zamorano 39 (pen))*

Uruguay: Carini; Mendez, Montero, Lembo, Rodriguez, Pablo Garcia, Guigou, O'Neill, Olivera, Recoba (Giacomazzi 89), Dario Silva (Alonso 81).
Chile: Tapia N; Rojas R, Vargas, Reyes, Olarra (Rozental 68), Galdames, Estay (Nunez C 87), Villaseca, Tello, Zamorano, Salas.
Referee: Troxler (Paraguay).

Buenos Aires, 4 June 2000, 50,669

Argentina (0) 1 *(Lopez G 83)*   **Bolivia (0) 0**

Argentina: Bonano; Sensini, Ayala, Samuel, Zanetti (Lopez G 71), Simeone, Kily Gonzalez, Veron, Ortega (Aimar 83), Batistuta, Lopez C (Almeyda 88).
Bolivia: Fernandez; Carballo, Pena, Sandy, Ivan Castillo, Ribera, Baldivieso, Cristaldo, Etcheverry (Galindo 78), Suarez (Garcia 65), Botero (Coimbra 83).
Referee: Rezende (Brazil).

Bogota, 4 June 2000, 22,000

Colombia (2) 3 *(Viveros 27, Cordoba I 42 (pen), Valenciano 88)*   **Venezuela (0) 0**

Colombia: Cordoba O; Martinez, Cordoba I,Ortegon, Bedoya, Rincon, Bolano, Oviedo (Candelo 70), Viveros (Dinas 77), Angel, Castillo J (Valenciano 81).
Venezuela: Dudamel; Filosa, Gonzalez, Alvarado, Echenausi, Arango, Vera J (Farias 55), Mea Vitali M, Bidoglio (De Ornelas 67), Castellin (Savarese 52), Moran.
Referee: Godoi (Brazil).

Lima, 4 June 2000, 45,000

Peru (0) 0   Brazil (1) 1 *(Zago 35)*

Peru: Miranda; Jorge Soto, Pajuelo, Olivares, Rebosio, Palacios, Del Solar, Jayo (Serrano 49), Zuniga, Holsen (Ciurlizza 46), Huaman (Maldonado 46).
Brazil: Dida; Cafu, Roberto Carlos, Aldair, Zago, Cesar Sampaio, Alex (Denilson 65), Emerson, Edmundo, Rivaldo (Vampeta 90), Franca (Ze Roberto 77).
Referee: Giminez (Argentina).

Rio, 28 June 2000, 47,715

Brazil (0) 1 *(Rivaldo 85 (pen))*   **Uruguay (1) 1** *(Dario Silva 6)*

Brazil: Dida; Cafu, Zago, Aldair, Roberto Carlos, Emerson, Vampeta (Ze Roberto 70), Rivaldo, Ronaldinho (Guilherme 46), Franca, Savio (Alex 46).
Uruguay: Carini; Tais, Lembo, Montero, Rodriguez, Pablo Garcia, O'Neill (Giacomazzi 82), Recoba (Coelho 59), Olivera, Dario Silva, Guigou.
Referee: Acosta (Colombia).

Santiago, 28 June 2000, 60,000

Chile (2) 3 *(Caniza 18 (og), Salas 35, Zamorano 78 (pen))*
Paraguay (0) 1 *(Jose Cardozo 71)*

Chile: Tapia N; Fuentes, Rojas R, Reyes, Villarroel, Maldonado, Tello, Estay, Nunez C (Pizarro 68), Zamorano, Salas.
Paraguay: Chilavert; Caniza, Zelaya, Ayala, Toledo, Quintana, Struway (Gonzalez G 46), Paredes, Acuna (Gavilan 37), Santa Cruz (Jose Cardozo 76), Brizuela.
Referee: Martin (Argentina).

Bogota, 28 June 2000, 50,000

Colombia (1) 1 *(Oviedo 27)*   **Argentina (2) 3** *(Batistuta 24, 45, Crespo 75)*

Colombia: Cordoba O; Cordoba I, Bermudez, Yepes, Bolano, Oviedo, Rincon, Dinas (Grisales 51) (Candelo 85), Viveros, Angel, Castillo J (Valenciano 58).
Argentina: Bonano; Sensini, Ayala, Samuel, Zanetti, Veron (Lopez G 70), Kily Gonzalez, Ortega (Sorin 86), Simeone, Lopez C, Batistuta (Crespo 70).
Referee: Larrionda (Uruguay).

San Cristobal, 28 June 2000, 7000

Venezuela (2) 4 *(Mea Vitali M 23, Moran 38, Savarese 61, Tortolero 67 (pen))*
Bolivia (0) 2 *(Moreno 49, Baldivieso 59)*

Venezuela: Angelucci; Jimenez, Gonzalez, Alvarado, Martinez, Urdaneta (Echenausi 90), Farias, Tortolero, Mea Vitali M, Moran, Savarese (Galan 72).
Bolivia: Fernandez; Ribera, Etcheverry (Galindo 80), Pena, Sandy, Ivan Castillo, Cristaldo, Erwin Sanchez, Baldivieso, Suarez (Garcia 73), Botero (Moreno 46).
Referee: Zambrano (Ecuador).

Quito, 29 June 2000, 45,000

Ecuador (1) 2 *(Chala 16, Hurtado E 51)*   **Peru (0) 1** *(Pajuelo 76)*

Ecuador: Cevallos; De la Cruz, Hurtado I, Poroso, Ayovi M, Obregon, Blandon, Chala, Aguinaga A (Burbano 70), Delgado (Graziani 70), Hurtado E (Kaviedes 74).
Peru: Ibanez; Jorge Soto, Rebosio, Pajuelo, Olivares (Zuniga 75), Solano, Del Solar, Jayo (Ciurlizza 75), Serrano (Soria 20), Palacios, Pizarro.
Referee: Simon (Brazil).

Asuncion, 18 July 2000, 36,000

Paraguay (1) 2 *(Paredes 6, Campos 84)*   **Brazil (0) 1** *(Rivaldo 75)*

Paraguay: Chilavert; Sarabia, Ayala, Gamarra, Caniza, Gavilan (Quintana 72), Enciso, Acuna, Paredes (Campos 63), Jose Cardozo, Santa Cruz (Avalos 79).
Brazil: Dida; Cafu, Roque Junior, Edmilson, Roberto Carlos, Cesar Sampaio, Flavio Conceicao, Rivaldo, Ze Roberto (Marques 70), Djalminha (Vampeta 60), Franca (Guilherme 46).
Referee: Larrionda (Uruguay).

Montevideo, 18 July 2000, 62,000

Uruguay (1) 3 *(Olivera 29, 89, Rodriguez 52)*   **Venezuela (1) 1** *(Noriega 23)*

Uruguay: Carini; Tais, Lembo, Montero (Ramos 81), Rodriguez, O'Neill, Pablo Garcia, Olivera, Guigou, Recoba, Dario Silva.
Venezuela: Angelucci; Jimenez, Gonzalez, Alvarado, Martinez, Urdaneta, Farias (Vera J 63), Tortolero, Mea Vitali M, Savarese (Perez 73), Noriega (Alvarez 63).
Referee: Ortube (Bolivia).

Buenos Aires, 19 July 2000, 50,000

Argentina (1) 2 *(Crespo 23, Lopez C 50)*   **Ecuador (0) 0**

Argentina: Bonano; Ayala, Sensini, Samuel, Zanetti, Simeone, Kily Gonzalez (Sorin 76), Veron, Ortega, Crespo (Aimar 76), Lopez C.
Ecuador: Cevallos; De la Cruz, Hurtado I, Poroso, Ayovi M, Tenorio, Blandon, Obregon, Aguinaga A (Chala 88), Hurtado E, Delgado (Graziani 73).
Referee: Bello (Uruguay).

La Paz, 19 July 2000, 35,000

Bolivia (0) 1 *(Suarez 84)*   **Chile (0) 0**

Bolivia: Soria M; Ribeiro, Pena, Sandy, Carballo (Rimba 38), Galindo (Colque 65), Garcia, Calustro, Baldivieso, Botero (Gutierrez T 55), Suarez.
Chile: Tapia N; Villarroel, Reyes, Fuentes, Rojas R, Maldonado, Cornejo, Tello, Estay (Tapia H 69), Zamorano (Navia 84), Rozental (Pizarro 69).
Referee: Toro (Colombia).

Lima, 19 July 2000, 45,000

Peru (0) 0   Colombia (0) 1 *(Angel 48)*

Peru: Vegas; Jorge Soto (Carlos Flores 57), Rebosio, Pajuela, Olivares, Jayo, Solano, Del Solar, Palacios, Pizarro, Zuniga (Lobaton 57).
Colombia: Cordoba O; Martinez, Cordoba I, Yepes, Bolano, Candelo (Hernandez 66), Viveros, Luis Garcia (Dinas 77), Bedoya, Angel, Valenciano (Restrepo 46).
Referee: Sanchez (Chile).

Quito, 25 July 2000, 43,000

Ecuador (0) 0   Colombia (0) 0

Ecuador: Cevallos; De la Cruz, Hurtado I, Poroso, Ayovi M, Obregon, Chala (Herrera 68), Aguinaga A, Hurtado Ed, Graziani (Delgado 68), Hurtado E (Juarez 76).
Colombia: Cordoba O; Martinez, Cordoba I, Yepes, Bolano, Candelo (Hurtado 46), Viveros, Luis Garcia, Bedoya, Moreno (Restrepo 46), Preciado (Dinas 78).
Referee: Aquino (Paraguay).

269

San Cristobal, 25 July 2000, 23,000

Venezuela (0) 0   Chile (0) 2 *(Tapia H 69, Zamorano 90)*

Venezuela: Angelucci; Alvarez, Alvarado, Ornella, Martinez, Mea Vitali M (Arango 72), Farias, Tortolero, Urdaneta, Moran, Savarese (Perez 85).
Chile: Tapia N; Fuentes, Rojas R, Margas, Rojas F, Maldonado, Tello, Estay (Cornejo 72), Sierra (Pizarro 65), Zamorano, Rozental (Tapia H 46).
Referee: Baldassi (Argentina).

Sao Paulo, 26 July 2000, 80,000

Brazil (2) 3 *(Alex 4, Vampeta 44, 50)*   **Argentina (1) 1** *(Almeyda 45)*

Brazil: Dida; Evanilson, Zago, Roque Junior, Roberto Carlos, Emerson, Vampeta, Ze Roberto (Marques 60), Alex (Cesar Sampaio 75), Ronaldinho, Rivaldo.
Argentina: Bonano; Sensini, Ayala, Samuel, Zanetti (Almeyda 39), Simeone, Veron, Kily Gonzalez (Sorin 73), Ortega (Lopez G 73), Crespo, Lopez C.
Referee: Mendez (Uruguay).

Montevideo, 26 July 2000, 60,000

Uruguay (0) 0   Peru (0) 0

Uruguay: Carini; Tais, Lembo, Montero, Rodriguez, O'Neill, Pablo Garcia, Olivera, Guigou (Zalayeta 56), Recoba (Coelho 69), Magallanes.
Peru: Vegas; Jorge Soto, Rebosio, Pajuelo, Olivares, Serrano (Torres 81), Jayo, Ciurlizza, Solano, Palacios, Pizarro.
Referee: Godoi (Brazil).

La Paz, 27 July 2000, 40,000

Bolivia (0) 0   Paraguay (0) 0

Bolivia: Soria M; Ribeiro, Pena, Sandy, Rimba (Paz Garcia 38), Calustro (Cardenas 71), Garcia, Colque, Baldivieso, Botero (Gutierrez L 52), Suarez.
Paraguay: Chilavert; Caballero, Ayala, Gamarra, Da Silva, Esteche, Enciso, Acuna (Ortiz 85), Paredes (Struway 55), Gonzalez G (Benitez 58), Jose Cardozo.
Referee: Almeida (Brazil).

Santiago, 15 August 2000, 65,000

Chile (2) 3 *(Estay 26, Zamorano 43, Salas 75)*   **Brazil (0) 0**

Chile: Tapia N; Fuentes, Rojas R, Reyes, Villaseca (Pizarro 13), Rojas F, Galdames, Tello, Estay, Salas (Villarroel 80), Zamorano (Tapia H 87).
Brazil: Dida; Evanilson, Edmilson, Zago, Roberto Carlos, Assuncao (Djalminha 46), Emerson, Alex (Marques 61), Ricardinho, Rivaldo, Amoroso (Luizao 46).
Referee: Gonzalez (Paraguay).

Bogota, 15 August 2000, 32,000

Colombia (0) 1 *(Castillo J 72)*   **Uruguay (0) 0**

Colombia: Cordoba O; Martinez, Cordoba I, Yepes, Bedoya, Luis Garcia (Morantes 64), Bolano, Oviedo, Aristizabal (Dinas 88), Angel, Castillo J (Bezerra 90).
Uruguay: Carini; Mendez, Lembo, Sorondo, Rodriguez, O'Neill, Pablo Garcia, Guigou (Giacomazzi 56), Olivera, Otero (Ruben Da Silva 51), Dario Silva (Magallanes 85).
Referee: Gimenez (Argentina).

Buenos Aires, 16 August 2000, 55,000

Argentina (0) 1 *(Aimar 67)*   **Paraguay (0) 1** *(Acuna 61)*

Argentina: Bonano; Sensini, Ayala, Samuel, Veron, Simeone (Vivas 71), Kily Gonzalez (Sorin 46), Aimar, Ortega, Lopez G (Saviola 75).
Paraguay: Tavarelli; Sarabia, Ayala, Gamarra, Caniza, Esteche, Struway (Quintana 78), Enciso, Acuna, Santa Cruz (Campos 55), Jose Cardozo (Benitez 85).
Referee: Pereira (Brazil).

Quito, 16 August 2000, 25,000

Ecuador (1) 2 *(Delgado 17, 59)*   **Bolivia (0) 0**

Ecuador: Ibarra; De la Cruz, Hurtado I, Poroso, Ayovi M (Reascos 46), Obregon, Chala, Aguinaga A, Ed Hurtado, Graziani (Juarez 62), Delgado.
Bolivia: Soria M; Paz Garcia, Ribera, Sandy, Arana, Garcia, Calustro (Vaca 76), Castillo S, Galindo, Baldivieso (Coimbra 46), Suarez.
Referee: Solorzano (Venezuela).

Lima, 16 August 2000, 40,000

Peru (0) 1 *(Palacios 70)*   **Venezuela (0) 0**

Peru: Ibanez; Jorge Soto, Jose Soto, Pajuelo (Marengo 40), Soria, Solano (Maldonado 67), Jayo, Palacios, Del Solar, Pizarro, Zuniga.
Venezuela: Angelucci; Jimenez, Alvarado, Gonzalez, Martinez, Mea Vitali M (De Ornelas 82), Farias, Tortolero, Urdaneta, Moran, Savarese (Casseres 71).
Referee: Moreno (Ecuador).

Santiago, 2 September 2000, 60,000

Chile (0) 0   Colombia (0) 1 *(Castillo J 66)*

Chile: Tapia N; Fuentes, Rojas R (Contreras 30), Reyes, Rojas F, Galdames, Tello, Estay (Cornejo 63), Sierra (Valencia 63), Zamorano, Salas.
Colombia: Cordoba O; Martinez, Cordoba I, Yepes, Mazziri, Luis Garcia (Viveros 46), Bolano, Grisales, Aristizabal, Castillo J (Dinas 86), Angel.
Referee: Gallesio (Uruguay).

Asuncion, 2 September 2000, 40,000

Paraguay (3) 3 *(Gonzalez G 30, Jose Cardozo 35, Paredes 44)*   **Venezuela (0) 0**

Paraguay: Chilavert; Gamarra (Gonzalez G 21), Sarabia, Arce, Ayala, Caniza, Acuna, Enciso, Paredes, Santa Cruz (Caceres 87), Jose Cardozo (Campos 77).
Venezuela: Angelucci; Jimenez, Alvarado, Gonzalez (Rey 46), Martinez, Mea Vitali M (Garcia 55), Tortolero (Paez 67), Farias, Urdaneta, De Ornelas, Moran.
Referee: Arandia (Bolivia).

Rio de Janeiro, 3 September 2000, 55,000

Brazil (1) 5 *(Romario 11 (pen), 78, 81, Rivaldo 46, Marques 88)*   **Bolivia (0) 0**

Brazil: Rogerio Ceni; Cafu, Zago, Emerson Carvalho, Roque Junior (Athirson 64), Vampeta, Flavio Conceicao, Alex (Juninho Paulista 59), Rivaldo, Ronaldinho (Marques 80), Romario.
Bolivia: Soria M; Ribeiro, Oscar Sanchez, Paz Garcia (Gutierrez I 73), Sandy, Garcia, Baldivieso, Alvarez, Cristaldo, Etcheverry, Moreno (Lider Paz 28).
Referee: Aros (Chile).

Lima, 3 September 2000, 45,000

Peru (0) 1 *(Samuel 69 (og))*   **Argentina (2) 2** *(Crespo 25, Veron 38)*

Peru: Vegas; Solano, Pajuelo, Jose Soto, Olivares (Zuniga 78), Pereda, Jayo, Del Solar (Tempone 46), Palacios, Mendoza, Pizarro.
Argentina: Bonano; Sensini, Ayala, Samuel, Veron, Simeone (Vivas 80), Sorin, Aimar, Ortega (Husain 73), Crespo, Lopez C (Lopez G 84).
Referee: Ruiz (Colombia).

Montevideo, 3 September 2000, 60,000

Uruguay (2) 4 *(Magallanes 14, Dario Silva 37, Olivera 55, Cedres 87)*   **Ecuador (0) 0**

Uruguay: Carini; Tais, Lembo, Rodriguez, Mendez, Pablo Garcia (Fleurquin 68), Cedres, Olivera, Guigou, Dario Silva (Recoba 73), Magallanes (Abreu 63).
Ecuador: Cevallos; De la Cruz, Poroso, Hurtado I, Capurro, Tenorio (Burbano 56), Obregon, Chala (Candelario 46), Aguinaga A, Juarez, Graziani.
Referee: Jimenez (Colombia).

Bogota, 7 October 2000, 46,000

Colombia (0) 0   Paraguay (1) 2 *(Santa Cruz 4, Chilavert 90)*

Colombia: Cordoba O; Cordoba I, Yepes, Mazziri (Grisales 46), Martinez, Dinas, Bolano, Oviedo (Morantes 59), Aristizabal, Bonilla (Castro 67), Angel.
Paraguay: Chilavert; Arce, Sarabia, Ayala, Da Silva, Struway, Quintana (Alvarengo 66), Paredes, Acuna, Santa Cruz (Yegros 66) (Esteche 90), Jose Cardozo.
Referee: Gallesio (Uruguay).

Buenos Aires, 8 October 2000, 60,000

Argentina (2) 2 *(Gallardo 28, Batistuta 42)*   **Uruguay (0) 1** *(Magallanes 48)*

Argentina: Burgos; Vivas, Ayala, Samuel, Sorin, Simeone, Husain, Gallardo (Delgado 80), Kily Gonzalez, Lopez C (Lopez G 73), Batistuta.
Uruguay: Carini; Pablo Garcia, Tais, Lembo, Rodriguez, Sorondo, Cedres (Regueiro 65), Olivera, Guigou, Recoba (Abreu 70), Magallanes (Alonso 87).
Referee: Rezende (Brazil).

La Paz, 8 October 2000, 25,000

Bolivia (1) 1 *(Suarez 4)*   **Peru (0) 0**

Bolivia: Soria M; Ribeiro, Oscar Sanchez, Pena, Paz Garcia, Colque, Calustro, Garcia, Vaca (Gutierrez R 66), Lider Paz (Moreno 46), Suarez (Galindo 80).
Peru: Ibanez; Zeballos, Rebosio, Pajuelo, Soria, Jayo, Solano (Carmona 46), Bernales, Palacios, Pizarro (Lobaton 57), Zuniga (Alba 57).
Referee: Guevara (Ecuador).

Quito, 8 October 2000, 45,000

Ecuador (0) 1 *(Delgado 76)*   **Chile (0) 0**

Ecuador: Cevallos; De la Cruz, Espinoza, Hurtado I, Guerron, Obregon, Tenorio (Fernandez 63), Aguinaga A, Chala (Sanchez 59), Kaviedes (Ordonez 76), Delgado.
Chile: Tapia N; Alvarez, Contreras, Vargas, Olarra, Pizarro (Valencia 85), Maldonado, Tello, Estay (Rozental 78), Navia (Nunez C 46), Zamorano.
Referee: Rendon (Colombia).

San Cristobal, 8 October 2000, 20,000

Venezuela (0) 0

Brazil (5) 6 *(Euller 21, Juninho Paulista 29, Romario 31, 36 (pen), 39, 64)*

Venezuela: Angelucci; Gonzalez, Martinez, Rey, Alvarado, Farias, De Ornelas, Jimenez, Echenausi (Arango 46), Moran (Paez 66), Garcia (Savarese 77).
Brazil: Rogerio Ceni; Cafu, Zago, Cleber, Silvinho, Donizete, Vampeta, Juninho Pernambucano (Ze Roberto 66), Juninho Paulista (Ricardinho 81), Euller (Marques 70), Romario.
Referee: Aquino (Paraguay).

La Paz, 15 November 2000, 29,112

Bolivia (0) 0   Uruguay (0) 0

Bolivia: Soria M; Oscar Sanchez, Sandy, Paz Garcia (Vaca 80), Ribeiro, Calustro, Garcia, Erwin Sanchez, Colque, Menacho, Suarez (Lider Paz 66).
Uruguay: Carini; Varela, Lembo, Sorondo, Rodriguez, Pablo Garcia, Romero, Coelho (Callejas 64), Regueiro, Magallanes (Dario Silva 56), Franco (Cedres 76).
Referee: Elizondo (Argentina).

Sao Paulo, 15 November 2000, 56,213

Brazil (0) 1 *(Roque Junior 90)*   **Colombia (0) 0**

Brazil: Rogerio Ceni; Cafu, Lucio, Roque Junior, Junior, Cesar Sampaio, Vampeta (Juninho Permanbucano 71), Rivaldo, Juninho Paulista, Franca (Adriano 79), Edmundo (Marques 67).
Colombia: Calero; Martinez, Dinas, Yepes, Bedoya, Bolano, Serna, Viveros, Aristizabal, Angel (Bonilla 67), Castillo J.
Referee: Larrionda (Uruguay).

272

Santiago, 15 November 2000, 56,529

Chile (0) 0   Argentina (1) 2 *(Ortega 26, Husain 90)*

Chile: Tapia N; Reyes, Rojas R, Contreras (Navia 79), Galdames, Maldonado (Villarroel 74), Rojas F, Pizarro, Estay (Valencia 64), Salas, Zamorano.
Argentina: Burgos (Bonano 74); Vivas, Ayala, Samuel, Almeyda, Husain, Sorin, Veron (Aimar 52), Kily Gonzalez, Cruz (Berizzo 84), Ortega.
Referee: Amarilla (Paraguay).

Asuncion, 15 November 2000, 30,000

Paraguay (3) 5 *(Santa Cruz 15, Del Solar 25 (og), Jose Cardozo 44, Paredes 65, Chilavert 84 (pen))*   **Peru (0) 1** *(Garcia 78)*

Paraguay: Chilavert; Arce, Sarabia, Ayala, Caniza, Paredes, Enciso, Acuna, Jose Cardozo (Brizuela 76), Alvarenga (Campos 86), Santa Cruz (Ferreira 70).
Peru: Ibanez; Zeballos (Garcia 60), Pajuelo (Velasquez 16), Rebosio, Soria, Bernales, Del Solar, Pereda (Lobaton 46), Palacios, Muchotrigo, Alva.
Referee: Gimenez (Argentina).

Maracaibo, 15 November 2000, 11,000

Venezuela (0) 1 *(Arango 65)*   **Ecuador (2) 2** *(Kaviedes 4, Sanchez 21)*

Venezuela: Angelucci; De Ornelas, Alvarado, Gonzalez, Vallenilla (Paez 86), Mea Vitali M (Luzardo 46), Farias, Urdaneta, Arango, Castellin (Perez 64), Garcia.
Ecuador: Cevallos; De la Cruz, Poroso, Hurtado I, Guerron, Burbano, Chala, Mendez (Zamora 72), Sanchez, Kaviedes (Fernandez 67), Delgado (Espinoza 88).
Referee: Betancourt (Peru).

Bogota, 27 March 2001, 45,000

Colombia (0) 2 *(Angel 53, 73 (pen))*   **Bolivia (0) 0**

Colombia: Cordoba O; Gonzalez, Dinas, Yepes, Bedoya, Serna, Grisales, Aristizabal (Viveros 46), Asprilla, Bonilla (Ferreira 46), Angel (Quintana 84).
Bolivia: Fernandez; Ribeiro, Pena, Sandy, Arana, Colque, Justiniano, Rojas, Vaca, Coimbra (Lider Paz 79), Cardenas (Suarez 57).
Referee: Souza (Brazil).

Lima, 27 March 2001, 45,000

Peru (0) 3 *(Maestri 54, Mendoza 73, Pizarro 81)*   **Chile (0) 1** *(Navia 62)*

Peru: Miranda; Solano, Rebosio, Pajuela, Olivares (Hidalgo 42) Jayo, Palacios, Del Solar (Maestri 46), Muchotrigo (Ciurlizza 75), Mendoza, Pizarro.
Chile: Tapia N; Vargas, Rojas R, Mi Ramirez, Ponce, Parraguez (Mirosevic 25) (Ruiz 65), Maldonado, Osorio, Tello (Tapia H 46), Zamorano, Navia.
Referee: Sanchez (Argentina).

Buenos Aires, 28 March 2001, 32,000

Argentina (2) 5 *(Crespo 13, Sorin 31, Veron 51, Gallardo 60, Samuel 85)*   **Venezuela (0) 0**

Argentina: Burgos; Vivas, Pochettino, Samuel, Sorin (Zanetti 61), Simeone, Veron, Ortega (Lopez G 70), Kily Gonzalez, Gallardo (Lopez C 76), Crespo.
Venezuela: Dudamel; Alvarado, Rey, Vallenilla, De Ornelas (Perez 51), Urdaneta, Vera J (Mea Vitali M 74), Vera L, Rojas (Martinez 65), Noriega, Paez.
Referee: Zamora (Peru).

Quito, 28 March 2001, 40,800

Ecuador (0) 1 *(Delgado 49)*   **Brazil (0) 0**

Ecuador: Cevallos; De la Cruz, Hurtado I, Poroso, Guerron, Tenorio (Sanchez 69), Burbano, Mendez, Aguinaga A, Kaviedes (Obregon 90), Delgado.
Brazil: Rogerio Ceni; Belletti, Lucio, Roque Junior, Silvinho (Cesar Aparecido 59), Emerson, Vampeta, Juninho Paulista, Rivaldo (Luizao 64), Ronaldinho (Euller 46), Romario.
Referee: Rizo (Mexico).

Montevideo, 28 March 2001, 60,000

Uruguay (0) 0   Paraguay (0) 1 *(Alvarenga 64)*

Uruguay: Carini; Varela, Sorondo, Montero, Rodriguez, De los Santos, Fleurquin (O'Neill 69), Olivera, Guigou (Pandiani 49), Dario Silva (Zalayeta 76), Recoba.
Paraguay: Chilavert; Ayala, Gamarra, Sarabia, Quintana (Alvarenga 46), Struway, Paredes, Acuna, Caniza, Caceres (Cuevas 83), Jose Cardozo (Esteche 88).
Referee: Aranda (Spain).

Santiago, 24 April 2001, 51,000

Chile (0) 0   Uruguay (1) 1 *(Diaz 12 (og))*

Chile: Vargas S; Diaz (Valdes 57), Reyes, Contreras, Tello, Maldonado, Galdames, Osorio (Gonzalez 74), Estay, Tapia H (Nunez C 46), Zamorano.
Uruguay: Carini; Mendez, Lembo, Sorondo, Rodriguez, Pablo Garcia, Guigou, Olivera (Regueiro 84), Magallanes, Recoba (Romero 72), Dario Silva (Varela 76).
Referee: Elizóndo (Argentina).

Quito, 24 April 2001, 40,000

Ecuador (1) 2 *(Delgado 45, 54)*   **Paraguay (1) 1** *(Jose Cardozo 26)*

Ecuador: Cevallos; De la Cruz, Hurtado I, Poroso, Guerron, Burbano (Espinoza 46), Chala (Sanchez 68), Aguinaga A (Mendez 46), Tenorio, Kaviedes, Delgado.
Paraguay: Tavarelli; Espinola, Gamarra, Ayala, Da Silva (Quintana 73), Esteche, Struway, Paredes, Alvarenga (Gonzalez G 62), Cuevas (Brizuela 46), Jose Cardozo.
Referee: Sanchez (Argentina).

San Cristobal, 24 April 2001, 35,000

Venezuela (1) 2 *(Rondon 22, Arango 81)*   **Colombia (0) 2** *(Bedoya 83, Bonilla 88)*

Venezuela: Dudamel; Vallenilla, Mea Vitali R, Rey, Rojas, Vera L, Arango, Mea Vitali M (De Ornelas 61), Urdaneta (Paez 70), Savarese (Vera J 55), Rondon.
Colombia: Calero; Martinez, Bermudez, Dinas, Bedoya, Grisales, Viveros (Quintana 70), Bolano (Gonzalez 61), Restrepo (Ferreira 46), Bonilla, Angel.
Referee: Alvaredo (Chile).

La Paz, 25 April 2001, 35,000

Bolivia (1) 3 *(Lider Paz 41, Colque 55, Botero 81)*
Argentina (1) 3 *(Crespo 44, 89, Sorin 90)*

Bolivia: Fernandez; Ribeiro, Pena, Paz Garcia, Sandy, Colque, Justiniano, Baldivieso, Vaca (Rojas 59), Lider Paz (Cardenas 74), Botero.
Argentina: Burgos; Vivas, Ayala, Samuel, Zanetti (Ortega 62), Simeone, Veron, Sorin, Aimar (Gallardo 57), Crespo, Lopez G (Lopez C 46).
Referee: Ruiz (Colombia).

Sao Paolo, 25 April 2001, 40,000

Brazil (0) 1 *(Romario 66)*   **Peru (0) 1** *(Pajuelo 79)*

Brazil: Rogerio Ceni; Alessandro, Edmilson, Lucio, Cesar Aparecido, Leomar, Vampeta (Washington 80), Ricardinho (Mineiro 77), Marcelinho Carioca (Juninho Paulista 46), Ewerthon, Romario.
Peru: Miranda; Rebosio, Pajuelo, Hidalgo, Solano, Jayo, Ciurlizza, Muchotrigo (Mendoza 46), Palacios, Olivares (Tempone 75), Maestri (Pizarro 46).
Referee: Al-Zaid (Saudi Arabia).

Asuncion, 2 June 2001, 45,000

Paraguay (0) 1 *(Paredes 90)*   **Chile (0) 0**

Paraguay: Chilavert; Arce, Sarabia, Ayala, Caniza, Quintana (Amarilla 77), Paredes, Acuna, Alvarenga, Santa Cruz (Cuevas 66), Brizuela (Julio Gonzalez 46).
Chile: Vargas S; Reyes, Vargas, Contreras, Pozo, Osorio, Villaseca, Perez (Valenzuela 78), Tello, Montecinos, Navia (Neira 63).
Referee: Badilla (Costa Rica).

274

Lima, 2 June 2001, 60,000

Peru (1) 1 *(Pizarro 2)*   **Ecuador (1) 2** *(Mendez 12, Delgado 90)*

Peru: Miranda; Pajuelo, Rebosio, Olivares (Hidalgo 62), Solano, Jayo, Palacios, Ciurlizza, Mendoza (Muchotrigo 74), Pizarro, Maestri (Silva 46).
Ecuador: Cevallos; De la Cruz, Hurtado I, Espinoza, Guerron, Obregon (Guagua 71), Tenorio, Chala (Aguinaga J 86), Mendez, Delgado, Kaviedes (Fernandez 81).
Referee: Marrufo (Mexico).

Buenos Aires, 3 June 2001, 40,000

Argentina (3) 3 *(Kily Gonzalez 23, Lopez C 35, Crespo 38)*   **Colombia (0) 0**

Argentina: Cavallero; Vivas, Ayala, Pochettino, Simeone, Zanetti, Veron (Gallardo 84), Sorin, Kily Gonzalez, Lopez C (Aimar 82), Crespo (Delgado 48).
Colombia: Cordoba O; Martinez, Dinas, Yepes, Bedoya, Serna, Rincon, Viveros (Gonzalez 46), Asprilla (Ferreira 46), Castillo J, Angel (Murillo 77).
Referee: Sanchez (Chile).

La Paz, 3 June 2001, 20,000

Bolivia (3) 5 *(Baldivieso 32, 68, Botero 35, 51, Justiniano 38)*   **Venezuela (0) 0**

Bolivia: Arias; Raldes, Pena, Paz Garcia, Ribeiro (Rojas 85), Justiniano, Baldivieso (Pena D 90), Calustro, Colque, Lider Paz (Cardenas 73), Botero.
Venezuela: Sanhouse; Vallenilla, Rey, Mea Vitali R, Martinez, Vera L, Mea Vitali M, Arango (Casseres 67), Gonzalez (Alvarado 54), Paez (Jimenez 42), Rondon.
Referee: Carpio (Ecuador).

Montevideo, 1 July 2001, 62,000

Uruguay (1) 1 *(Magallanes 32 (pen))*   **Brazil (0) 0**

Uruguay: Carini; Mendez, Montero, Sorondo, Guigou, De los Santos, Pablo Garcia, Romero, Recoba (Lembo 76), Dario Silva (Regueiro 62), Magallanes (Giacomazzi 71).
Brazil: Marcos; Cris, Zago (Jardel 76), Roque Junior, Cafu, Emerson, Rivaldo, Juninho Paulista, Roberto Carlos, Elber (Euller 60), Romario.
Referee: Dallas (Scotland).

Santiago, 14 August 2001, 30,000

Chile (1) 2 *(Salas 35 (pen), 77)*   **Bolivia (1) 2** *(Baldivieso 11 (pen), Coimbra 73)*

Chile: Vargas S; Pozo (Solis 33), Reyes, Vargas J, Aros, Chavarria, Valencia (Ahumada 82), Villaseca, Nunez C (Castillo 46), Salas, Montecinos.
Bolivia: Soria M; Raldes, Pena, Oscar Sanchez, Carballo, Justiniano, Rojas, Lider Paz (Colque 84), Baldivieso, Galindo, Coimbra.
Referee: Gimenez (Argentina).

Maracaibo, 14 August 2001, 25,000

Venezuela (0) 2 *(Moran 53, Rondon 90)*   **Uruguay (0) 0**

Venezuela: Dudamel; Vallenilla, Rey, Alvarado, Rojas, Mea Vitali M, Vera L, Arango, Paez (Perez 87), Noriega (Rondon 66), Moran (Jimenez 76).
Uruguay: Carini; Mendez, Sorondo, Montero, Guigou, De los Santos, Giacomazzi (Regueiro 54), Romero (Morales 65), Olivera, Recoba, Dario Silva (Zalayeta 69).
Referee: Mendoza (Mexico).

Porto Alegre, 15 August 2001, 48,000

Brazil (1) 2 *(Marcelinho Carioca 4, Rivaldo 69)*   **Paraguay (0) 0**

Brazil: Marcos; Roque Junior, Cris, Juan, Belletti, Tinga, Eduardo Costa, Rivaldo (Vampeta 85), Roberto Carlos, Marcelinho Carioca (Denilson 63), Edilson (Leonardo 66).
Paraguay: Chilavert; Arce, Sarabia, Cacares, Morel, Struway (Campos 73), Paredes, Acuna, Gavilan, Santa Cruz (Ferreira 58), Jose Cardozo.
Referee: Krug (Germany).

Quito, 15 August 2001, 45,000

Ecuador (0) 0   Argentina (2) 2 *(Veron 19, Crespo 31 (pen))*

Ecuador: Ibarra; De la Cruz, Hurtado I, Espinoza, Guerron, Burbano (Aguinaga J 46), Chala, Guagua (Fernandez 51), Sanchez (Aguinaga A 46), Delgado, Kaviedes.
Argentina: Burgos; Vivas, Ayala, Samuel, Zanetti, Simeone (Almeyda 67), Veron, Sorin, Aimar (Ortega 60), Crespo, Kily Gonzalez (Lopez C 84).
Referee: Braschi (Italy).

Bogota, 16 August 2001, 33,875

Colombia (0) 0   Peru (0) 1 *(Solano 47)*

Colombia: Cordoba O; Cordoba I, Yepes, Serna, Oviedo (Arriaga 54), Hernandez, Aristizabal, Lopez, Murillo (Ramirez 65), Grisales (Castillo J 65), Bedoya.
Peru: Miranda; Rebosio, Hidalgo, Pajuelo, Solano, Jayo (Salazar 73), Pizarro (Jose Soto 82), Palacios, Jorge Soto, Mendoza (Holsen 87), Del Solar.
Referee: Rizo (Mexico).

Santiago, 4 September 2001, 30,000

Chile (0) 0   Venezuela (0) 2 *(Paez 56, Arango 62)*

Chile: Tapia N; Rojas F, Fuentes, Acuna, Navia, Vargas, Tello, Montecinos, Nunez C (Valencia 63), Galdames, Aros (Perez 72).
Venezuela: Dudamel; Vallenilla, Mea Vitali R, Alvarado, Mea Vitali M, Noriega (Jimenez 75), Vera L, Arango, Paez (Martinez 79), Rojas, Moran (Rondon 86).
Referee: Betancourt (Bolivia).

Lima, 4 September 2001, 45,000

Peru (0) 0   Uruguay (2) 2 *(Dario Silva 12, Recoba 45)*

Peru: Miranda; Jorge Soto, Jose Soto, Pajuelo, Hidalgo, Solano, Jayo, Del Solar (Pereda 72), Palacios, Pizarro (Maestri 46), Mendoza.
Uruguay: Carini; Bizera, Lembo, Rodriguez, Tais, Pablo Garcia, De los Santos, Gigou, Recoba (Perez 89), Dario Silva (Regueiro 72), Chevanton (Magallanes 65).
Referee: Frisk (Sweden).

Buenos Aires, 5 September 2001, 51,000

Argentina (0) 2 *(Gellardo 76, Cris 84 (og))*   **Brazil (1) 1** *(Ayala 2 (og))*

Argentina: Burgos; Ayala, Piacente (Ortega 46), Vivas, Samuel, Lopez C (Almeyda 87), Zanetti, Crespo, Simeone, Aimar (Gellardo 64), Kily Gonzalez.
Brazil: Marcos; Cafu, Lucio, Roque Junior, Cris, Roberto Carlos, Eduardo Costa (Denilson 89), Mauro Silva (Vampeta 70), Marcelinho Carioca, Rivaldo, Elber (Euller 65).
Referee: Meier (Switzerland).

Bogota, 5 September 2001, 46,000

Colombia (0) 0   Ecuador (0) 0

Colombia: Cordoba O; Lopez, Cordoba I, Yepes, Bedoya (Cortes 80), Ramirez, Serna, Hernandez, Murillo (Molina 68), Aristizabal (Arriaga 80), Angel.
Ecuador: Cevallos; De la Cruz, Espinoza, Hurtado I, Guerron, Tenorio, Obregon, Gomez (Aguinaga J 68), Mendez, Kaviedes (Fernandez 58), Delgado.
Referee: Al-Aqily (Saudi Arabia).

Asuncion, 5 September 2001, 30,000

Paraguay (2) 5 *(Paredes 33, Jose Cardozo 45, 89, Chilavert 48, Santa Cruz 70)*
Bolivia (1) 1 *(Lider Paz 15)*

Paraguay: Chilavert; Sarabia, Ayala, Gamarra, Paredes (Quintana 56), Arce, Rodriguez, Struway (Morinigo 70), Ferreira (Gavilan 65), Santa Cruz, Jose Cardozo.
Bolivia: Arias; Reyes, Paz Garcia, Raldes, Pena, Rojas, Justiniano, Galindo, Baldivieso, Castillo A (Andaveriz 66), Lider Paz (Calustro 79).
Referee: Solorzano (Venezuela).

La Paz, 6 October 2001, 5000

Bolivia (0) 1 *(Galindo 60)*

Ecuador (2) 5 *(De la Cruz 13, Delgado 23, Kaviedes 58, Fernandez 89, Gomez 90)*

Bolivia: Arias; Raldes, Jiguchi, Carballo, Reyes, Castillo S (Vaca 33), Calustro, Justiniano, Galindo, Lider Paz, Andaveris (Castillo A 46).
Ecuador: Cevallos; De la Cruz, Hurtado I, Espinoza, Guerron, Tenorio (Gomez 90), Obregon (Burbano 90), Mendez, Chala, Kaviedes (Fernandez 77), Delgado.
Referee: Sanchez (Argentina).

San Cristobal, 6 October 2001, 30,000

Venezuela (0) 3 *(Alvarado 49, 67, Moran 78)*   **Peru (0) 0**

Venezuela: Angelucci; Vallenilla, Mea Vitali R, Alvarado, Rojas, Vera L (Jimenez 10), Mea Vitali M, Arango, Paez (Urdaneta 67), Noriega (Martinez 60), Moran.
Peru: Miranda; Huaman (Mi Ramirez 57), Pajuela, Rebosio, Hidalgo, Jorge Soto, Ciurlizza, Jayo, Palacios, Maestri (Garcia 70), Mendoza (Arakaki 46).
Referee: Sanchez (Chile).

Curitiba, 7 October 2001, 52,000

Brazil (0) 2 *(Edilson 53, Rivaldo 67)*   **Chile (0) 0**

Brazil: Marcos; Lucio, Juan, Edmilson, Cafu, Emerson, Vampeta, Rivaldo (Juninho Paulista 89), Roberto Carlos (Belleti 84), Marcelinho Carioca (Denilson 46), Edilson.
Chile: Toro; Vargas, Robles, Munoz, Caniza, Villaseca, Ormazabal, Perez (Melendez 61), Pizarro, Salas, Valenzuela (Navia 55).
Referee: Elizondo (Argentina).

Asuncion, 7 October 2001, 43,000

Paraguay (0) 2 *(Chilavert 52 (pen), Morinigo 70)*

Argentina (0) 2 *(Pochettino 86, Batistuta 73)*

Paraguay: Chilavert; Arce, Ayala (Caceres 80), Caniza, Gamarra, Alvarenga, Morinigo, Quintana (Rodriguez 71), Struway, Jose Cardozo (Caballero 79), Santa Cruz.
Argentina: Cavellero; Ayala, Pochettino, Samuel, Almeyda, Sorin (Lopez C 63), Veron, Zanetti, Batistuta (Cruz 90), Kily Gonzalez, Ortega (Aimar 80).
Referee: Zamora (Peru).

Montevideo, 7 October 2001, 65,000

Uruguay (1) 1 *(Magallanes 35 (pen))*   **Colombia (0) 1** *(Valentierra 68)*

Uruguay: Munua; Lembo, Montero, Rodriguez, Tais, De los Santos, Pablo Garcia, Guigou (Canobbio 83), Recoba, Dario Silva (Morales 75), Magallanes (Chevanton 46).
Colombia: Cordoba O; Lopez, Cordoba I, Yepes, Bedoya (Cortes 46), Grisales, Restrepo, Bolano, Valentierra, Aristizabal (Murillo 71), Asprilla.
Referee: Collina (Italy).

La Paz, 7 November 2001, 32,574

Bolivia (1) 3 *(Lider Paz 41, Baldivieso 69, 89 (pen))*   **Brazil (1) 1** *(Edilson 26)*

Bolivia: Soria M; Pena, Paz Garcia, Colque (Oscar Sanchez 68), Olivares, Ribeiro, Rojas, Botero, Baldivieso, Lider Paz (Castillo A 76), Galindo (Gutierrez L 56).
Brazil: Marcos; Cafu, Lucio, Juan (Juninho Paulista 76), Edmilson, Serginho, Emerson, Vampeta (Gilberto 62), Ze Roberto (Denilson 56), Rivaldo, Edilson.
Referee: Torres (Venezuela).

Bogota, 7 November 2001, 16,050

Colombia (1) 3 *(Grisales 17, Angel 68, Gonzalez 70)*   **Chile (1) 1** *(Riveros 40)*

Colombia: Cordoba O; Cordoba I, Yepes, Cortes, Bolano (Castillo J 46), Valentierra (Mina 74), Angel, Asprilla (Castro 59), Gonzalez, Restrepo, Grisales.
Chile: Vargas S; Munoz, Ormazabal, Riveros (Medina 72), Navia (Martel 73), Vargas, Villarroel, Robles, Villaseca, Cancino, Norambuela (Almendra 77).
Referee: Gimenez (Argentina).

Quito, 7 November 2001, 40,000

Ecuador (0) 1 *(Kaviedes 73)*   **Uruguay (1) 1** *(Olivera 44 (pen))*

Ecuador: Cevallos; Hurtado I, De la Cruz, Obregon, Guerron (Fernandez 68), Kaviedes (Gomez 77), Delgado, Chala (Aguinaga A 58), Espinoza, Mendez, Tenorio.
Uruguay: Carini; Tais, Lembo, Montero, Pablo Garcia, Guigou, Romero, De los Santos, Dario Silva (Morales 74), Olivera (Sanchez 52), Recoba (Perez 84).
Referee: Rizo (Mexico).

Buenos Aires, 8 November 2001, 18,901

Argentina (0) 2 *(Samuel 46, Lopez C 85)*   **Peru (0) 0**

Argentina: Burgos; Pochettino, Ayala, Samuel, Zanetti, Almeyda, Sorin, Veron, Ortega (Aimar 74), Cruz (Lopez C 46), Kily Gonzalez (Romeo 87).
Peru: Miranda; Jorge Soto, Salazar, Pajuelo, Hidalgo (Huaman 62), Ciurlizza, Del Solar (Mendoza 59), Jayo, Palacios, Pizarro, Maestri.
Referee: Larrionda (Uruguay).

San Cristobal, 8 November 2001, 22,500

Venezuela (3) 3 *(Moran 2, Noriega 22, Gonzalez 40)*   **Paraguay (1) 1** *(Arce 27 (pen))*

Venezuela: Angelucci; Gonzalez, Alvarado, Mea Vitali R, Rojas, Vera L, Mea Vitali M, Urdaneta, Paez (Martinez 72), Noriega (Rondon 61), Moran (Perez 79).
Paraguay: Bobadilla; Arce, Gamarra, Caceres, Morel, Acuna, Struway (Alvarenga 46), Paredes, Morinigo (Quintana 46), Brizuela (Masi 72), Jose Cardozo.
Referee: Elizondo (Argentina).

Sao Luis, 14 November 2001, 65,000

Brazil (3) 3 *(Luizao 12, 19, Rivaldo 35)*   **Venezuela (0) 0**

Brazil: Marcos; Lucio, Roque Junior, Edmilson, Belletti, Roberto Carlos, Emerson, Juninho Paulista (Ronaldinho 68), Rivaldo, Luizao (Denilson 58), Edilson (Marcelinho Carioca 75).
Venezuela: Dudamel; Gonzalez, Rey, Mea Vitali R, Rojas, Mea Vitali M, Vera L, Urdaneta (Vallenilla 58), Paez (Martinez 32), Noriega, Moran (Jimenez 51).
Referee: Gimenez (Argentina).

Santiago, 14 November 2001, 19,237

Chile (0) 0   Ecuador (0) 0

Chile: Vargas S; Robles, Torres, Gomez (Almendra 65), Perez, Sanhueza (Ormeno 46), Medina (Ahumada 46), Munoz, Riveros, Martel, Gutierrez.
Ecuador: Cevallos; De la Cruz, Hurtado I, Espinoza, Ayovi M, Obregon, Burbano, Gomez, Mendez, Fernandez, Kaviedes (Tenorio 70).
Referee: Arandia (Bolivia).

Asuncion, 14 November 2001, 25,000

Paraguay (0) 0   Colombia (2) 4 *(Aristizabal 24, 33 (pen), 62, Castillo J 83)*

Paraguay: Bobadilla; Arce (Masi 71), Sanabria, Gamarra, Ayala, Caniza, Quintana (Struway 83), Paredes, Acuna, Gimenez (Brizuela 56), Jose Cardozo.
Colombia: Cordoba O; Vallejo, Cordoba I, Yepes, Bedoya, Serna, Restrepo, Grisales (Castillo J 83), Morantes, Aristizabal (Castro 85), Asprilla.
Referee: Poll (England).

Lima, 14 November 2001, 2374

Peru (1) 1 *(Alva 9)*   **Bolivia (0) 1** *(Castillo A 88)*

Peru: Miranda; Huaman, Hidalgo, Pajuelo, Jayo, Palacios, Mendoza, Jorge Soto (Palomino 46), Salazar, Ciurlizza (Ferrari 69), Alva (Carty 76).
Bolivia: Fernandez; Reyes, Paz Garcia, Oscar Sanchez (Ribeiro 54), Olivares, Rojas, Botero (Castillo A 63), Coimbra, Lider Paz (Justiniano 90), Pena D, Galindo.
Referee: Baldassi (Argentina).

Montevideo, 14 November 2001, 45,000

Uruguay (1) 1 *(Dario Silva 19)*   **Argentina (1) 1** *(Lopez C 45)*

Uruguay: Carini; Tais (Morales R 64), Lembo, Montero, Rodriguez (Regueiro 83), Guigou, Pablo Garcia, De los Santos, Recoba, Magallanes, Dario Silva (Alonso 46).
Argentina: Burgos; Pochettino, Ayala, Samuel, Zanetti, Sorin, Almeyda, Veron, Aimar (Piacente 84), Ortega (Cruz 46), Lopez C.
Referee: Merk (Germany).

SOUTH AMERICA

Table	P	W	D	L	F	A	Pts
Argentina	18	13	4	1	42	15	43
Ecuador	18	9	4	5	23	20	31
Brazil	18	9	3	6	31	17	30
Paraguay	18	9	3	6	29	23	30
Uruguay	18	7	6	5	19	13	27
Colombia	18	7	6	5	20	15	27
Bolivia	18	4	6	8	21	33	18
Peru	18	4	4	10	14	25	16
Venezuela	18	5	1	12	18	44	16
Chile	18	3	3	12	15	27	12

PLAY-OFFS, FIRST LEG

Vienna, 10 November 2001, 48,500

Austria (0) 0   Turkey (0) 1 *(Okan 60)*

Austria: Wohlfahrt; Flogel, Vukovic, Winklhofer, Baur, Schopp (Lexa 54), Strafner, Herzog, Markus Hiden (Kitzbichler 72), Haas, Wallner (Weissenberger 61).
Turkey: Rustu; Umit O, Alpay, Emre, Umit D, Okan (Tayfur 88), Tugay, Ergun (Arif 62), Abdullah, Basturk (Fatih 70), Hakan Sukur.
Referee: Gonzalez (Spain).

Brussels, 10 November 2001, 44,000

Belgium (1) 1 *(Verheyen 29)*   **Czech Republic (0) 0**

Belgium: De Vlieger; Deflandre, Van Meir (De Boeck 46), Clement, Van Kerckhoven, Verheyen, Simons, Vermant, Walem, Goor, Sonck (Van Houdt 79).
Czech Republic: Srnicek; Grygera (Ujfalusi 32), Repka, Novotny, Jankulowski, Poborsky, Hasek, Jarosik, Smicer (Hubschmann 46), Nedved, Baros (Lokvenc 65).
Referee: Meier (Switzerland).

Ljubljana, 10 November 2001, 9000

Slovenia (1) 2 *(Acimovic 41, Osterc 70)*   **Romania (1) 1** *(Niculae 26)*

Slovenia: Simeunovic; Milinovic, Galic, Vugdalic, Karic (Ceh N 40), Pavlin, Ceh A, Novak, Acimovic (Pavlovic 66), Osterc, Rudonja.
Romania: Stelea; Contra, Iencsi, Popescu, Chivu, Sabau (Rosu 84), Miu (Pancu 90), Mutu, Munteanu D, Ilie A (Ghioane 84), Niculae.
Referee: Nielsen (Denmark).

Kiev, 10 November 2001, 85,000

Ukraine (1) 1 *(Zoubov 18)*   **Germany (1) 1** *(Ballack 30)*

Ukraine: Levytsky; Luzhny, Vashchuk, Golovko, Nesmachni, Zoubov, Tymoshchuk (Parfenov 73), Shevchenko, Vorobei (Melaschenko 76), Gusin, Rebrov (Chitchenko 56).
Germany: Kahn; Rehmer, Nowotny, Linke, Schneider (Ricken 80), Ramelow, Ballack, Hamann, Ziege, Asamoah, Zickler (Jancker 68).
Referee: Braschi (Italy).

PLAY-OFFS, SECOND LEG

Prague, 14 November 2001, 18,996

Czech Republic (0) 0   Belgium (0) 1 *(Wilmots 86 (pen))*

Czech Republic: Srnicek; Johana (Jarosik 58), Hubschmann, Novotny, Jankulovski, Poborsky (Sionko 46), Hasek (Smicer 67), Rosicky, Nedved, Baros, Lokvenc.
Belgium: De Vlieger; Deflandre, Clement, De Boeck, Van Kerckhoven, Vermant (Vanderhaeghe 90), Simons, Goor, Walem (Boffin 84), Verheyen, Sonck (Wilmots 63).
Referee: Frisk (Sweden).

Dortmund, 14 November 2001, 52,000

Germany (3) 4 *(Ballack 3, 50, Neuville 10, Rehmer 14)*
Ukraine (0) 1 *(Shevchenko 90)*

Germany: Kahn; Rehmer (Baumann 87), Nowotny, Linke, Schneider, Ramelow, Hamann, Ziege, Ballack, Neuville (Ricken 70), Jancker (Bierhoff 58).
Ukraine: Levytsky; Luzhny, Vashchuk, Golovko, Nesmachni (Chitchenko 55), Skrypnyk, Zubov, Tymoshchuk (Gusin 24), Parfenov, Shevchenko, Vorobei (Rebrov 70).
Referee: Pereira (Portugal).

Bucharest, 14 November 2001, 24,500

Romania (0) 1 *(Contra 65)*   **Slovenia (0) 1** *(Rudonja 57)*

Romania: Lobont; Contra, Popescu, Ghioane (Ganea 58), Chivu, Sabau, Miu (Mihalcea 78), Munteanu D, Mutu (Pancu 58), Niculae, Ilie A.
Slovenia: Simeunovic; Milinovic, Vugdalic, Galic, Novak, Ceh A, Gajser, Pavlin, Acimovic (Sankovic 62), Osterc (Pavlovic 89), Rudonja.
Referee: Krug (Germany).

Istanbul, 14 November 2001, 22,000

Turkey (3) 5 *(Basturk 21, Hakan Sukur 30, Okan 45, Arif 61, 86)*   **Austria (0) 0**

Turkey: Rustu; Umit D, Emre, Alpay, Abudullah, Okan (Sergen 63), Umit O, Tugay, Basturk (Arif 42), Hasan Sas (Ilhan 87), Hakan Sukur.
Austria: Wohlfahrt; Winklhofer, Vukovic, Strafner, Lexa (Schopp 54), Markus Hiden, Prilasnig (Kitzbichler 46), Herzog, Flogel, Vastic (Weissenberger 75), Haas.
Referee: Collina (Italy).

ASIA/EURO PLAY-OFF, FIRST LEG

Dublin, 10 November 2001, 35,000

Republic of Ireland (1) 2 *(Harte 45 (pen), Robbie Keane 50)*   **Iran (0) 0**

Republic of Ireland: Given; Finnan, Harte, Breen, Staunton (Cunningham 75), Holland, McAteer (Kelly G 84), Roy Keane, Robbie Keane, Quinn, Kilbane.
Iran: Mirzapour; Mahdavikia, Vahedinikbakht (Khaziravi 46), Peyrovani, Golmohammadi, Rezaei, Kavianpour, Bagheri, Karimi, Daei, Minavand.
Referee: Da Silva (Brazil).

ASIA/EURO PLAY-OFF, SECOND LEG

Teheran, 15 November 2001, 110,000

Iran (0) 1 *(Golmohammadi 90)*   **Republic of Ireland (0) 0**

Iran: Mirzapour; Mahdavikia, Minavand, Golmohammadi, Rezaei, Kavianpour, Karimi, Bagheri, Daei, Vahedinikbakht, Peyrovani.
Republic of Ireland: Given; Finnan, Harte, Holland, Staunton, Breen, McAteer, Kinsella, Robbie Keane (Morrison 75), Connolly, Kilbane (Kelly G 79).
Referee: Vega (Costa Rica).

STH AMERICA/OCEANIA PLAY-OFFS

Melbourne, 20 November 2001, 84,656

Australia (0) 1 *(Muscat 78 (pen))*   **Uruguay (0) 0**

Australia: Schwarzer; Muscat, Moore, Murphy, Okon, Vidmar, Emerton, Skoko, Viduka, Kewell, Lazaridis (Agostino 46).
Uruguay: Carini; Tais, Montero, Rodriguez, Lembo, Guigou, Pablo Garcia, Recoba, De los Santos, Chevanton (Regueiro 77), Magallanes (Giacomazza 72).
Referee: Cesari (Italy).

Montevideo, 25 November 2001, 62,000

Uruguay (1) 3 *(Dario Silva 14, Morales R 70, 90)*   **Australia (0) 0**

Uruguay: Carini; Tais, Lembo, Montero, Rodriguez, Guigou, Pablo Garcia, Regueiro (De los Santos 64), Recoba, Dario Silva (Sorondo 81), Magallanes (Morales R 65).
Australia: Schwarzer; Muscat (Agostino 62), Moore, Okon, Vidmar, Emerton, Skoko, Viduka, Murphy (Aloisi 81), Kewell, Lazaridis.
Referee: Bujsaim (UAE).

OCEANIA

(Members 11, Entries 10)

Four teams qualified: China, Japan (hosts), Saudi Arabia and South Korea (hosts).

Group 1: Australia, Tonga, Fiji, American Samoa, Samoa.

Samoa 0, Tonga 1; Fiji 13, American Samoa 0; Tonga 0, Australia 22; American Samoa 0, Samoa 8; Samoa 1, Fiji 6; Australia 31, American Samoa 0; Fiji 0, Australia 2; American Samoa 0, Tonga 5; Australia 11, Samoa 0; Tonga 1, Fiji 8.

Group 2: New Zealand, Tahiti, Solomon Islands, Vanuatu, Cook Islands.

Vanuatu 1, Tahiti 6; Solomon Islands 9, Cook Islands 1; Tahiti 0, New Zealand 5; Cook Islands 1, Vanuatu 8; Vanuatu 2, Solomon Islands 7; New Zealand 2, Cook Islands 0; Solomon Islands 1, New Zealand 5; Cook Islands 0, Tahiti 6; New Zealand 7, Vanuatu 0; Tahiti 2, Solomon Islands 0.

Final Round, First Leg: New Zealand 0, Australia 2.

Final Round, Second Leg: Australia 4, New Zealand 1.
Australia lost to Uruguay in play off.

ASIA

(Members 44, Entries 42)

Four teams qualified: China, Japan (hosts), Saudi Arabia and South Korea (hosts).

Group 1: Laos, Oman, Philippines, Syria.
Oman 12, Laos 0; Syria 12, Philippines 0; Philippines 1, Syria 5; Laos 0, Oman 7; Oman 7, Philippines 0; Syria 11, Laos 0; Philippines 0, Oman 2; Laos 0, Syria 9; Syria 3, Oman 3; Laos 2, Philippines 0; Oman 2, Syria 0; Philippines 1, Laos 1.

Group 2: Guam, Iran, Tajikistan.
Iran 19, Guam 0; Tajikistan 16, Guam 0; Iran 2, Tajikistan 0.
(all ties played in Iran)

Group 3: Hong Kong, Malaysia, Palestine, Qatar.
Qatar 5, Malaysia 1; Hong Kong 1, Palestine 1; Palestine 1, Qatar 2; Malaysia 2, Hong Kong 0; Palestine 1, Malaysia 0; Qatar 2, Hong Kong 0; Palestine 1, Hong Kong 0; Malaysia 0, Qatar 0; Qatar 2, Palestine 1; Hong Kong 2, Malaysia 1; Hong Kong 0, Qatar 3; Malaysia 4, Palestine 3.

Group 4: Bahrain, Kuwait, Kyrgyzstan, Singapore.
Bahrain 1, Kuwait 2; Singapore 0, Kyrgyzstan 1; Bahrain 1, Kyrgyzstan 0; Kuwait 1, Singapore 1; Kyrgyzstan 0, Kuwait 3; Singapore 1, Bahrain 2; Kyrgyzstan 1, Bahrain 2; Singapore 0, Kuwait 1; Kuwait 2, Kyrgyzstan 0; Bahrain 2, Singapore 0; Kyrgyzstan 1, Singapore 1; Kuwait 0, Bahrain 1.

Group 5: Lebanon, Pakistan, Sri Lanka, Thailand.
Thailand 4, Sri Lanka 2; Lebanon 6, Pakistan 0; Thailand 3, Pakistan 0; Lebanon 4, Sri Lanka 0; Pakistan 3, Sri Lanka 3; Lebanon 1, Thailand 2; Pakistan 1, Lebanon 8; Sri Lanka 0, Thailand 3; Sri Lanka 0, Lebanon 5; Pakistan 0, Thailand 6; Sri Lanka 3, Pakistan 1; Thailand 2, Lebanon 2.

Group 6: Iraq, Kazakhstan, Macao, Nepal.
Nepal 0, Kazakhstan 6; Iraq 8, Macao 0; Kazakhstan 3, Macao 0; Nepal 1, Iraq 9; Nepal 4, Macao 1; Kazakhstan 1, Iraq 1; Kazakhstan 4, Nepal 0; Macao 0, Iraq 5; Macao 0, Kazakhstan 5; Iraq 4, Nepal 2; Macao 1, Nepal 6; Iraq 1, Kazakhstan 1.

Group 7: Uzbekistan, Jordan, Turkmenistan, Taiwan.
Turkmenistan 2, Jordan 0; Uzbekistan 7, Taiwan 0; Taiwan 0, Jordan 2; Uzbekistan 1, Turkmenistan 0; Taiwan 0, Turkmenistan 5; Uzbekistan 2, Jordan 2; Jordan 6, Taiwan 0; Turkmenistan 2, Uzbekistan 5; Taiwan 0, Uzbekistan 4; Jordan 1, Turkmenistan 2; Turkmenistan 1, Taiwan 0; Jordan 1, Uzbekistan 1.

Group 8: Brunei, India, UAE, Yemen.
Brunei 0, Yemen 5; India 1, UAE 0; Brunei 0, UAE 12; India 1, Yemen 1; UAE 1, India 0; Yemen 1, Brunei 0; Yemen 3, India 3; UAE 4, Brunei 0; Yemen 2, UAE 1; Brunei 0, India 1; UAE 3, Yemen 2; India 5, Brunei 0.

Group 9: Cambodia, China, Indonesia, Maldives.
Maldives 6, Cambodia 0; Indonesia 5, Maldives 0; Cambodia 1, Maldives 1; China 10, Maldives 1; Indonesia 6, Cambodia 0; Maldives 0, China 1; Cambodia 0, Indonesia 2; Cambodia 0, China 4; Maldives 0, Indonesia 2; China 5, Indonesia 1; China 3, Cambodia 1; Indonesia 0, China 2.

Group 10: Bangladesh, Mongolia, Saudi Arabia, Vietnam.
Vietnam 0, Bangladesh 0; Saudi Arabia 6, Mongolia 0; Mongolia 0, Vietnam 1; Bangladesh 0, Saudi Arabia 3; Mongolia 0, Bangladesh 3; Saudi Arabia 5, Vietnam 0; Mongolia 0, Saudi Arabia 6; Bangladesh 0, Vietnam 4; Vietnam 4, Mongolia 0; Saudi Arabia 6, Bangladesh 0; Bangladesh 2, Mongolia 2; Vietnam 0, Saudi Arabia 4.

Second Round
Group A: Iraq 4, Thailand 0; Saudi Arabia 1, Bahrain 1; Bahrain 2, Iraq 0; Iran 2, Saudi Arabia 0; Saudi Arabia 1, Iraq 0; Thailand 0, Iran 0; Bahrain 1, Thailand 1; Iraq 1, Iran 2; Iran 0, Bahrain 0; Thailand 1, Saudi Arabia 3; Bahrain 0, Saudi Arabia 4; Thailand 1, Iraq 1; Iraq 1, Bahrain 0; Saudi Arabia 2, Iran 2; Iran 1, Thailand 0; Iran 1, Saudi Arabia 2; Iran 2, Iraq 1; Thailand 1, Bahrain 1; Bahrain 3, Iran 1; Saudi Arabia 4, Thailand 1.

Group B: Qatar 0, Oman 0; UAE 4, Uzbekistan 1; China 3, UAE 0; Uzbekistan 2, Qatar 1; UAE 0, Qatar 2; Oman 0, China 2; Qatar 1, China 1; Uzbekistan 5, Oman 0; Oman 1, UAE 1; China 2, Uzbekistan 0; Oman 0, Qatar 3; Uzbekistan 0, UAE 1; UAE 0, China 1; Qatar 2, Uzbekistan 2; Qatar 1, UAE 2; China 1, Oman 2; Oman 4, Uzbekistan 2; China 3, Qatar 0; UAE 2, Oman 2; Uzbekistan 1, China 0.

Asian Play-offs: Iran 1, UAE 0; UAE 0, Iran 3.
Saudi Arabia and China qualified for finals.
Iran lost to Republic of Ireland in play-off.

CONCACAF

(Members 35, Entries 35)

Three teams qualified: Costa Rica, Mexico and the USA.

Caribbean Zone
First Round

Group 1: Barbados 2, Grenàda 2; Grenada 2, Barbados 3; Cuba 4, Cayman Islands 0; Cayman Islands 0, Cuba 0; St Lucia 1, Surinam 0; Surinam 1, St Lucia 0 (Surinam won 3-1 on penalties); Aruba 4, Puerto Rico 2; Puerto Rico 2, Aruba 2.

Group 2: St Vincent & Grenadines 9, US Virgin Islands 0; US Virgin Islands 1, St Vincent & Grenadines 5; British Virgin Islands 1, Bermuda 5; Bermuda 9, British Virgin Islands 0; St Kitts & Nevis 8, Turks & Caicos Islands 0; Turks & Caicos Islands 0, St Kitts & Nevis 6; Guyana suspended, Antigua and Barbuda w.o.

Group 3: Trinidad & Tobago 5, Netherlands Antilles 0; Netherlands Antilles 1, Trinidad & Tobago 1; Anguilla 1, Bahamas 3; Bahamas 2, Anguilla 1; Dominican Republic 3, Montserrat 0; Montserrat 1, Dominican Republic 3; Haiti 4, Dominica 0; Dominica 1, Haiti 3.

Caribbean Zone
Second Round

Group 1: Cuba 1, Surinam 0; Surinam 0, Cuba 0; Aruba 1, Barbados 3; Barbados 4, Aruba 0.

Group 2: St Vincent & the Grenadines 1, St Kitts & Nevis 0; St Kitts & Nevis 1, St Vincent & the Grenadines 2; Antigua & Barbuda 0, Bermuda 0; Bermuda 1, Antigua & Barbuda 1.

Group 3: Trinidad & Tobago 3, Dominican Republic 0; Dominican Republic 0, Trinidad & Tobago 1; Haiti 9, Bahamas 0; Bahamas 0, Haiti 4.

Caribbean Zone Finals

Group 1: Cuba 1, Barbados 1, Barbados 1, Cuba 1 (*Barbados won 5-4 on penalties*).

Group 2: Antigua & Barbuda 2, St Vincent & the Grenadines 1; St Vincent & the Grenadines 4, Antigua & Barbuda 0.

Group 3: Trinidad & Tobago 3, Haiti 1; Haiti 1, Trinidad & Tobago 1.

Central American Zone

Group A: El Salvador 5, Belize 0; Belize 1, Guatemala 2; Guatemala 0, El Salvador 1; Belize 1, El Salvador 3; El Salvador 1, Guatemala 1; Guatemala 0, Belize 0.

Group B: Honduras 3, Nicaragua 0; Nicaragua 0, Panama 2; Panama 1, Honduras 0; Nicaragua 0, Honduras 1; Honduras 3, Panama 1; Panama 4, Nicaragua 0

Inter zone round

Group 1: Cuba 0, Canada 1; Canada 0, Cuba 0.

Group 2: Antigua & Barbuda 0, Guatemala 1; Guatemala 8, Antigua & Barbuda 1.

Group 3: Honduras 4, Haiti 0; Haiti 1, Honduras 3.

Semi-final Round
Costa Rica, Jamaica, Mexico and USA qualified.

Group C: Canada, Mexico, Panama, Trinidad & Tobago.
Canada 0, Trinidad & Tobago 2; Panama 0, Mexico 1; Panama 0, Canada 0;
Trinidad & Tobago 1, Mexico 0; Mexico 2, Canada 0; Trinidad & Tobago 6,
Panama 0; Mexico 7, Panama 1; Trinidad & Tobago 4, Canada 0; Mexico 7,
Trinidad & Tobago 0; Canada 1, Panama 0; Canada 0, Mexico 0; Panama 0,
Trinidad & Tobago 1.

Group D: El Salvador, Honduras, Jamaica, St Vincent & the Grenadines.
El Salvador 2, Honduras 5; St Vincent & the Grenadines 0, Jamaica 1; El Salvador
7, St Vincent & the Grenadines 1; Jamaica 3, Honduras 1; Honduras 6, St Vincent
& the Grenadines 0; Jamaica 1, El Salvador 0; Honduras 5, El Salvador 0; Jamaica
2, St Vincent & the Grenadines 0; Honduras 1, Jamaica 0; St Vincent & the
Grenadines 1, El Salvador 2; St Vincent & the Grenadines 0, Honduras 7; El Salvador 2, Jamaica 0.

Group E: Barbados, Costa Rica, Guatemala, USA.
Barbados 2, Costa Rica 1; Guatemala 1, USA 1; Guatemala 2, Barbados 0; Costa
Rica 2, USA 1; Costa Rica 2, Guatemala 1; USA 7, Barbados 0; Costa Rica 3, Bar-
bados 0; USA 1, Guatemala 0; Barbados 1, Guatemala 3; USA 0, Costa Rica 0;
Barbados 0, USA 4; Guatemala 2, Costa Rica 1.

Play-off: Costa Rica 5, Guatemala 0.

Final Round: Costa Rica, Honduras, Jamaica, Mexico, Trinidad & Tobago, USA.
USA 2, Mexico 0; Jamaica 1, Trinidad & Tobago 0; Costa Rica 2, Honduras 2;
Mexico 4, Jamaica 0; Costa Rica 3, Trinidad & Tobago 0; Honduras 1, USA 2;
Jamaica 1, Honduras 1; Trinidad & Tobago 1, Mexico 1; USA 1, Costa Rica 0;
Mexico 1, Costa Rica 2; Trinidad & Tobago 2, Honduras 4; Jamaica 0, USA 0;
USA 2, Trinidad & Tobago 0; Honduras 3, Mexico 1; Costa Rica 2, Jamaica 1;
Trinidad & Tobago 1, Jamaica 2; Mexico 1, USA 0; Honduras 2, Costa Rica 3;
Trinidad & Tobago 0, Costa Rica 2; USA 2, Honduras 3; Jamaica 1, Mexico 2;
Costa Rica 2, USA 0; Honduras 1, Jamaica 0; Mexico 3, Trinidad & Tobago 0;
Costa Rica 0, Mexico 0; Honduras 0, Trinidad & Tobago 1; USA 2, Jamaica 1;
Jamaica 0, Costa Rica 1; Mexico 3, Honduras 0; Trinidad & Tobago 0, USA 0.
Costa Rica, Mexico and USA qualified.

AFRICA

(Members 52, Entries 50)

Five teams qualified: Cameroon, Nigeria, Senegal, South Africa and Tunisia.

First Round

Group A: Mauritania 1, Tunisia 2; Tunisia 3, Mauritania 0; Guinea Bissau 0, Togo
0; Togo 3, Guinea Bissau 0; Benin 1, Senegal 1; Senegal 1, Benin 0; Cape Verde
Islands 0, Algeria 0; Algeria 2, Cape Verde Islands 0; Gambia 0, Morocco 1;
Morocco 2, Gambia 0.

Group B: Botswana 0, Zambia 1; Zambia 1, Botswana 0; Madagascar 2, Gabon 0;
Gabon 1, Madagascar 0; Lesotho 0, South Africa 2; South Africa 1, Lesotho 0;
Sudan 1, Mozambique 0; Mozambique 2, Sudan 1; Swaziland 0, Angola 1; Angola
7, Swaziland 1.

Group C: Sao Tome e Principe 2, Sierra Leone 0; Sierra Leone 4, Sao Tome e
Principe 0; Central African Republic 0, Zimbabwe 1; Zimbabwe 3, Central African
Republic 1; Equatorial Guinea 1, Congo 3; Congo 2, Equatorial Guinea 1; Libya 3,
Mali 0; Mali 3, Libya 1; Rwanda 2, Ivory Coast 2; Ivory Coast 2, Rwanda 0.

284

Group D: Djibouti 1, Congo DR 1; Congo DR 9, Djibouti 1; Seychelles 1, Namibia 1; Namibia 3, Seychelles 0; Eritrea 0, Nigeria 0; Nigeria 4, Eritrea 0; Mauritius 0, Egypt 2; Egypt 4, Mauritius 2; Somalia 0, Cameroon 3; Cameroon 3, Somalia 0.

Group E: Malawi 2, Kenya 0; Kenya v Malawi abandoned 0-0 after 88 minutes; result stands; Tanzania 0, Ghana 1; Ghana 3, Tanzania 2; Uganda 4, Guinea 4; Guinea 3, Uganda 0; Chad 0, Liberia 1; Liberia 0, Chad 0; Ethiopia 2, Burkina Faso 1; Burkina Faso 3, Ethiopia 0.

Second Round

Group A: Angola, Cameroon, Libya, Togo, Zambia.
Angola 2, Zambia 1; Libya 0, Cameroon 3; Zambia 2, Togo 0; Cameroon 3, Angola 0; Angola 3, Libya 1; Togo 0, Cameroon 2; Libya 3, Togo 3; Cameroon 1, Zambia 0; Zambia 2, Libya 0; Togo 1, Angola 1; Zambia 1, Angola 1; Cameroon 1, Libya 0; Togo 3, Zambia 0; Angola 2, Cameroon 0; Libya 1, Angola 1; Cameroon 2, Togo 0; Zambia 2, Cameroon 2; Togo 2, Libya 0; Libya 2, Zambia 4; Angola 1, Togo 1.
Cameroon qualified for finals.

Group B: Ghana, Liberia, Nigeria, Sierra Leone, Sudan.
Nigeria 2, Sierra Leone 0; Sudan 2, Liberia 0; Ghana 5, Sierra Leone 0; Liberia 2, Nigeria 1; Nigeria 3, Sudan 0; Ghana 1, Sudan 1; Ghana 0, Liberia 1; Sierra Leone 0; Sierra Leone 0, Sudan 2; Ghana 0, Nigeria 0; Sierra Leone 1, Nigeria 4; Liberia 2, Sudan 0; Sierra Leone 1, Ghana 1; Nigeria 2, Liberia 0; Sudan 0, Nigeria 1; Liberia 4; Liberia 1, Ghana 2; Sierra Leone 0, Liberia 1; Ghana 1, Sudan 0; Nigeria 3, Ghana 0; Sudan 3, Sierra Leone 0.
Nigeria qualified for finals.

Group C: Algeria, Egypt, Morocco, Namibia, Senegal.
Algeria 1, Senegal 1; Namibia 0, Morocco 0; Morocco 2, Algeria 1; Senegal 0, Egypt 0; Algeria 1, Namibia 0; Egypt 0, Morocco 0; Namibia 1, Egypt 1; Morocco 0, Senegal 0; Senegal 4, Namibia 0; Egypt 5, Algeria 2; Senegal 3, Algeria 0; Morocco 3, Namibia 0; Algeria 1, Morocco 2; Egypt 1, Senegal 0; Morocco 1, Egypt 0; Namibia 0, Algeria 4; Egypt 8, Namibia 2; Senegal 1, Morocco 0; Algeria 1, Egypt 1; Namibia 0, Senegal 5.
Senegal qualified for finals.

Group D: Congo, Congo DR, Ivory Coast, Madagascar, Tunisia.
Ivory Coast 2, Tunisia 2; Madagascar 3, Congo DR 0; Tunisia 1, Madagascar 0; Congo DR 2, Congo 0; Congo 1, Tunisia 2; Madagascar 1, Ivory Coast 3; Tunisia 6, Congo DR 0, Congo DR 1, Ivory Coast 2; Congo DR 1, Madagascar 0; Ivory Coast 2, Congo 0; Congo 2, Madagascar 0; Madagascar 0, Tunisia 2; Congo 1, Congo DR 1, Tunisia 1, Ivory Coast 1; Tunisia 6, Congo 0; Ivory Coast 6, Madagascar 0; Congo 1, Ivory Coast 1; Congo DR 0, Tunisia 3; Ivory Coast 1, Congo DR 2; Madagascar 1, Congo 0.
Tunisia qualified for finals.

Group E: Burkina Faso, Guinea*, Malawi, South Africa, Zimbabwe.
Malawi 1, Burkina Faso 1; Guinea 3, Zimbabwe 0; Burkina Faso 2, Guinea 3; Zimbabwe 0, South Africa 2 (abandoned 82 minutes; result stands); South Africa 1, Burkina Faso 0; Guinea 1, Malawi 1; Burkina Faso 1, Zimbabwe 2; Malawi 1, South Africa 2; Zimbabwe 2, Malawi 0; Burkina Faso 4, Malawi 2; South Africa 2, Zimbabwe 1; Burkina Faso 1, South Africa 1; South Africa 2, Malawi 0; Zimbabwe 1, Burkina Faso 0; Malawi 0, Zimbabwe 1.
*Guinea subsequently suspended; results expunged.
South Africa qualified for finals

FIFA WORLD CUP FINALS REVIEW

It began with a few shocks and ended with traditional finalists who had surprisingly never met each other in the World Cup. Brazil won their fifth title at the expense of Germany, in a fine finale to a disappointing tournament of damaged reputations.

The Germans began with more confidence and dictated play, but it was Brazil who missed five reasonable chances in the first half and hit the bar through Kleberson. Germany also struck the woodwork from an Oliver Neuville free-kick which Marcos got a hand to. But it was finally Ronaldo who clinched it, taking advantage of a fumble by Oliver Kahn and then adding a second when Rivaldo sold the German defence a dummy.

However, it was France, the holders who had been the first to feel the cool breeze of change in losing to Senegal, a team drawn entirely from the ranks of French clubs.

Not overmuch of a problem for Germany, who had only scraped through to the finals via the play-offs, beat the Saudis 8-0. England who had humiliated the Germans in Munich during the qualifying stages by winning 5-1, had a poor second half against Sweden and had to settle for a 1-1 draw.

Brazil were surprised by the fast-running Turks and needed a penalty three minutes from time to win 2-1. There was controversy in the match when Rivaldo collapsed clutching his face after Hakan Unsal who plays for Blackburn Rovers had clearly kicked the ball at his shin! Unsal was sent off to become the second England-based Turk so to do following Alpay of Aston Villa to the dressing-room. Rivaldo was later fined, but not suspended.

South Korea began better than their co-hosts Japan, who were held to a 2-2 draw by Belgium. The Koreans, showing enterprise and fluidity, defeated Poland 2-0. But the next shock was the USA taking a 3-0 lead over fancied Portugal then winning 3-2.

The Republic of Ireland merited a 1-1 draw with Germany, equalising in the last minute through Robbie Keane. His namesake Roy had been banished before the finals by coach Mick McCarthy following a much-publicised bust-up between the two.

France's second effort was as poor as the first. With Thierry Henry sent off against Uruguay, they were held to a goalless draw. Lacking the injured Zinedine Zidane, the French were clearly in trouble. Then came the crunch game for England against Argentina with memories of the meeting in the 1998 World Cup when David Beckham was controversially sent off. But it was sweet revenge for the England captain whose penalty on the stroke of half-time divided the teams.

More surprises followed. Italy were apparently coasting 1-0 against Croatia when they conceded two goals in three minutes and lost 2-1, but they had been poorly served by the officials.

Brazil took four goals off China and Japan's fortunes revived when Junichi Inamoto on a free transfer from Arsenal scored to beat Russia. But in France's group the crucial last matches left everything in the melting pot. Zidane was patched-up and shoved out, but could contribute little enough against Denmark who won 2-0 and eliminated the holders. Senegal led 3-0 at the break until Uruguay revived and should have won after drawing level.

Eliminated France were soon joined by second favourites Argentina held 1-1 by Sweden. Brazil and Costa Rica produced a free-flowing game to delight the purists with the South Americans winning 5-2. And despite losing 3-1 to Poland, the USA emerged from their group along with the Koreans who beat Portugal.

The second round produced more upsets. South Korea's stock soared with a sudden death victory over Italy 2-1, the USA beat Mexico easily 2-0 and England took full advantage of schoolboy errors in the Danish defence to win 3-0. Germany left it late against Paraguay, but the Republic of Ireland lost out to Spain on penalties after missing one in normal time.

Brazil were hard pressed by Belgium until the latter stages before winning 2-0 and Senegal needed sudden death to dispose of Sweden. To the chagrin of locals, Japan lost 1-0 to Turkey.

More question-marks in the quarter-finals. Spain had two apparently perfect goals ruled out in South Korea's win. England led Brazil but fell to ten men when Ronaldinho was harshly sent off. Turkey's speed was too much for Senegal, but still needed sudden death to win and Germany rode their luck again but beat the United States. In the semi-finals just a goal separated Brazil from Turkey and Germany from South Korea. Then the Turks confirmed their improvement by beating the Koreans 3-2 in the match for third place.

FIFA WORLD CUP FINALS RESULTS

GROUP A

Seoul, 31 May 2002, 62,561
France (0) 0   Senegal (1) 1 *(Diop PB 30)*
France: Barthez; Thuram, Lizarazu, Vieira, Leboeuf, Desailly, Wiltord (Cisse 80), Petit, Trezeguet, Henry, Djorkaeff (Dugarry 59).
Senegal: Sylva; Coly, Daf, Diao, Diatta, Diop PM, Ndiaye, Diop PB, Hadji Diouf, Cisse, Fadiga.
Referee: Bujsaim (UAE).

Ulsan, 1 June 2002, 30,157
Uruguay (0) 1 *(Rodriguez 47)*   **Denmark (1) 2** *(Tomasson 45, 83)*
Uruguay: Carini; Mendez, Rodriguez (Magallanes 87), Garcia, Montero, Sorondo, Varela, Guigou, Abreu (Morales 88), Dario Silva, Recoba (Regueiro 80).
Denmark: Sorensen; Helveg, Heintze (Jensen N 58), Gravesen, Laursen, Henriksen, Rommedahl, Tofting, Sand (Poulsen 89), Tomasson, Gronkjaer (Jorgensen 70).
Referee: Mane (Kuwait).

Daegu, 6 June 2002, 43,500
Denmark (1) 1 *(Tomasson 16 (pen))*   **Senegal (0) 1** *(Diao 52)*
Denmark: Sorensen; Helveg, Heintze, Gravesen (Poulsen 82), Laursen, Henriksen, Gronkjaer (Jorgensen 49), Tofting, Tomasson, Sand, Rommedahl (Lovenkrands 86).
Senegal: Sylva; Coly, Sarr (Camara S 46) (Beye 82), Diaye (Camara H 46), Diop PM, Diatta, Diao, Diop PB, Daf, Diouf, Fadiga.
Referee: Batres (Guatemala).

Busan, 6 June 2002, 38,070
France (0) 0   Uruguay (0) 0
France: Barthez; Thuram, Lizarazu, Petit, Leboeuf (Candela 16), Desailly, Wiltord (Dugarry 90), Vieira, Trezeguet (Cisse 81), Henry, Micoud.
Uruguay: Carini; Varela, Rodriguez (Guigou 73), Lembo, Sorondo, Montero, Romero (De Los Santos 71), Garcia, Dario Silva (Magallanes 60), Abreu, Recoba.
Referee: Rizo (Mexico).

Incheon, 11 June 2002, 48,100
Denmark (1) 2 *(Rommedahl 22, Tomasson 67)*   **France (0) 0**
Denmark: Sorensen; Helveg, Jensen N, Gravesen, Laursen, Henriksen, Poulsen (Bogelund 75), Tofting (Steen-Nielsen 80), Tomasson, Jorgensen (Gronkjaer 46), Rommedahl.
France: Barthez; Candela, Lizarazu, Vieira (Micoud 71), Thuram, Desailly, Makelele, Wiltord (Djorkaeff 84), Trezeguet, Zidane, Dugarry (Cisse 54).
Referee: Pereira (Portugal).

Suwon, 11 June 2002, 33,681
Senegal (3) 3 *(Fadiga 20 (pen), Diop PB 26, 38)*   **Uruguay (0) 3** *(Morales 46, Forlan 69, Recoba 88 (pen))*
Senegal: Sylva; Coly (Beye 63), Daf, Ndour (Faye 76), Diatta, Diop PM, Camara (Moussa Ndiaye 66), Cisse, Diouf, Diop PB, Fadiga.
Uruguay: Carini; Varela, Rodriguez, Lembo, Montero, Sorondo (Regueiro 31), Garcia, Romero (Forlan 46), Abreu (Morales 46), Dario Silva, Recoba.
Referee: Wegereef (Holland).

Group A – Table	P	W	D	L	F	A	Pts
Denmark	3	2	1	0	5	2	7
Senegal	3	1	2	0	5	4	5
Uruguay	3	0	2	1	4	5	2
France	3	0	1	2	0	3	1

GROUP B

Busan, 2 June 2002, 25,186

Paraguay (1) 2 *(Santa Cruz 39, Arce 55)* **South Africa (0) 2** *(Struway 63 (og), Fortune 90 (pen))*
Paraguay: Tavarelli; Alvarenga (Gavilan 66), Arce, Ayala, Gamarra, Caniza, Struway (Franco 86), Acuna, Campos (Morinigo 72), Santa Cruz, Caceres.
South Africa: Arendse; Nzama, Carnell, Sibaya, Radebe, Issa (MacDonald 27), Mokoena T, Mokoena A, McCarthy (Koumantarakis 78), Zuma, Fortune.
Referee: Michel (Slovakia).

Gwangju, 2 June 2002, 25,598

Spain (1) 3 *(Raul 44, Valeron 74, Hierro 88 (pen))* **Slovenia (0) 1** *(Cimerotic 81)*
Spain: Casillas; Puyol, Juanfran (Romero 83), Baraja, Hierro, Nadal, Luis Enrique (Helguera 73), Valeron, Diego Tristan (Morientes 66), Raul, De Pedro.
Slovenia: Simeunovic; Novak (Gajser 77), Karic, Milinovic, Galic, Knavs, Ceh A, Pavlin, Osterc (Cimerotic 56), Rudonja, Zahovic (Acimovic 62).
Referee: Guezzaz (Morocco).

Jeonju, 7 June 2002, 24,000

Spain (0) 3 *(Morientes 53, 69, Hierro 83 (pen))* **Paraguay (1) 1** *(Puyol 10 (og))*
Spain: Casillas; Puyol, Juanfran, Baraja, Hierro, Nadal, Luis Enrique (Helguera 46), Valeron (Xavi 85), Diego Tristan (Morientes 46), Raul, De Pedro.
Paraguay: Chilavert; Arce, Caniza (Struway 78), Caceres, Ayala, Gamarra, Acuna, Paredes, Santa Cruz, Gavilan, Cardozo (Campos 63).
Referee: Ghandour (Egypt).

Daegu, 8 June 2002, 47,226

South Africa (1) 1 *(Nomvethe 4)* **Slovenia (0) 0**
South Africa: Arendse; Nzama, Carnell, Sibaya, Mokoena A, Radebe, Zuma, Mokoena T, Nomvethe (Buckley 71), McCarthy (Koumantarakis 80), Fortune (Pule 83).
Slovenia: Simeunovic; Novak, Karic, Milinovic, Vugdalic, Knavs (Bulajic 60), Acimovic (Ceh N 60), Ceh A, Cimerotic (Osterc 41), Rudonja, Pavlin.
Referee: Sanchez (Argentina).

Seogwipo, 12 June 2002, 30,136

Slovenia (1) 1 *(Acimovic 45)* **Paraguay (0) 3** *(Cuevas 66, 84, Campos 73)*
Slovenia: Dabanovic; Bulajic, Tavcar, Ceh A, Milinovic, Karic, Novak, Pavlin (Rudonja 40), Cimirotic, Osterc (Tiganj 78), Acimovic (Ceh N 63).
Paraguay: Chilavert; Arce, Caniza, Caceres, Ayala, Gamarra, Paredes, Acuna, Cardozo (Cuevas 61) (Franco 90), Santa Cruz, Alvarenga (Campos 54).
Referee: Rizo (Mexico).

Daejeon, 12 June 2002, 31,024

Spain (2) 3 *(Raul 4, 56, Mendieta 45)* **South Africa (1) 2** *(McCarthy 31, Radebe 53)*
Spain: Casillas; Torres, Romero, Albelda, Helguera, Nadal, Joaquin, Xavi, Morientes (Luque 75), Raul (Luis Enrique 82), Mendieta.
South Africa: Arendse; Nzama, Carnell, Sibaya, Mokoena A, Radebe (Molefe 79), Zuma, Mokoena T, Nomvethe (Koumantarakis 74), McCarthy, Fortune (Lekgetho 83).
Referee: Mane (Kuwait).

Group B – Table	P	W	D	L	F	A	Pts
Spain	3	3	0	0	9	4	9
Paraguay	3	1	1	1	6	6	4
South Africa	3	1	1	1	5	5	4
Slovenia	3	0	0	3	2	7	0

GROUP C

Ulsan, 3 June 2002, 33,842

Brazil (0) 2 *(Ronaldo 50, Rivaldo 87 (pen))* **Turkey (1) 1** *(Hasan Sas 45)*
Brazil: Marcos; Cafu, Roberto Carlos, Gilberto Silva, Edmilson, Lucio, Roque Junior, Juninho (Vampeta 73), Ronaldo (Luizao 73), Rivaldo, Ronaldinho (Denilson 67).
Turkey: Rustu; Alpay, Hakan Unsal, Tugay (Arif 88), Bulent K (Ilhan 65), Umit O, Fatih, Emre B, Hakan Sukur, Basturk (Umit D 65), Hasan Sas.
Referee: Young-joo (South Korea).

Gwangju, 4 June 2002, 27,217

China (0) 0   Costa Rica (0) 2 *(Gomez 61, Wright 65)*
China: Jin; Yunlong, Chengying, Xiaopeng, Zhiyi (Genwei 75), Weifeng, Jihai (Bo 26), Tie, Chen (Maozhen 65), Haidong, Mingyu.
Costa Rica: Lonnis; Wallace (Bryce 70), Castro, Marin, Wright, Martinez, Solis, Centeno, Wanchope (Lopez 80), Gomez, Fonseca (Medford 57).
Referee: Vassaras (Greece).

Seogwipo, 8 June 2002, 36,750

Brazil (3) 4 *(Roberto Carlos 15, Rivaldo 32, Ronaldinho 45 (pen), Ronaldo 55)*
China (0) 0
Brazil: Marcos; Cafu, Roberto Carlos, Lucio, Roque Junior, Anderson Polga, Gilberto Silva, Juninho (Ricardinho 70), Ronaldo (Edilson 71), Rivaldo, Ronaldinho (Denilson 46).
China: Jin; Yunlong, Chengying, Junzhe, Wei, Weifeng, Xiaopeng, Tie, Haidong (Bo 75), Hong (Jiayi 66), Mingyu (Pu 62).
Referee: Frisk (Sweden).

Incheon, 9 June 2002, 42,299

Costa Rica (0) 1 *(Parks 86)*   **Turkey (0) 1** *(Emre B 56)*
Costa Rica: Lonnis; Wallace (Bryce 77), Castro, Martinez, Wright, Marin, Solis, Centeno (Medford 67), Wanchope, Lopez (Parks 77), Gomes.
Turkey: Rustu; Fatih, Ergun, Tugay (Arif 88), Umit O, Emre A, Umit D, Emre B, Basturk (Nihat 79), Hakan Sukur (Ilhan 75), Hakan Sas.
Referee: Codjia (Benin).

Suwon, 13 June 2002, 38,524

Costa Rica (1) 2 *(Wanchope 39, Gomez 56)*   **Brazil (3) 5** *(Ronaldo 10, 13, Edmilson 38, Rivaldo 62, Junior 64)*
Costa Rica: Lonnis; Wallace (Bryce 46), Castro, Martinez (Parks 74), Wright, Marin, Solis (Fonseca 65), Lopez, Wanchope, Gomez, Centeno.
Brazil: Marcos; Cafu, Gilberto Silva, Lucio, Edmilson, Anderson Polga, Junior, Juninho (Ricardinho 60), Ronaldo, Rivaldo (Kaka 72), Edilson (Kleberson 57).
Referee: Ghandour (Egypt).

Seoul, 13 June 2002, 43,605

Turkey (2) 3 *(Hasan Sas 6, Bulent K 9, Umit D 85)*   **China (0) 0**
Turkey: Rustu (Catkic 35); Fatih, Hakan Unsal, Tugay (Havutgu 84), Bulent K, Emre A, Umit D, Emre B, Hasan Sas, Hakan Sukur, Basturk (Ilhan 70).
China: Jin; Yunlong, Chengying (Jiayi 46), Junzhe, Wei, Weifeng, Xiaopeng, Tie, Chen (Genwei 73), Haidong (Bo 73), Pu.
Referee: Ruiz (Colombia).

Group C – Table	P	W	D	L	F	A	Pts
Brazil	3	3	0	0	11	3	9
Turkey	3	1	1	1	5	3	4
Costa Rica	3	1	1	1	5	6	4
China	3	0	0	3	0	9	0

GROUP D

Busan, 4 June 2002, 55,982

South Korea (1) 2 *(Hwang SH 26, Yoo SC 53)*   **Poland (0) 0**
South Korea: Lee WJ; Song CG, Lee EY, Choi JC, Hong MB, Kim TY, Kim NI, Yoo SC (Lee CS 62), Park JS, Hwang SH (Ahn JH 50), Seol KH (Cha DR 90).
Poland: Dudek; Hajto, Michal Zewlakow, Kaluzny (Marcin Zewlakow 65), Bak J (Klos 51), Waldoch, Kozminski, Swierczewski, Olisadebe, Zurawski (Kryszalowicz 46), Krzynowek.
Referee: Ruiz (Colombia).

Suwon, 5 June 2002, 37,306

USA (3) 3 *(O'Brien 4, Jorge Costa 30 (og), McBride 36)* **Portugal (1) 2** *(Beto 40, Agoos 71 (og))*
USA: Friedel; Agoos, Sanneh, Beasley, Pope (Llamosa 79), Mastroeni, Hejduk, O'Brien, Stewart (Jones 46), McBride, Donovan (Moore 75).
Portugal: Vitor Baia; Jorge Costa (Andrade 73), Conceicao, Beto, Fernando Couto, Rui Jorge (Paulo Bento 68), Rui Costa, Petit, Joao Pinto, Pauleta, Figo.
Referee: Moreno (Ecuador).

Jeonju, 10 June 2002, 31,000

Portugal (1) 4 *(Pauleta 14, 65, 77, Rui Costa 87)* **Poland (0) 0**
Portugal: Vitor Baia; Frechaut (Beto 63), Rui Jorge, Petit, Fernando Couto, Jorge Costa, Conceicao (Capucho 69), Paulo Bento, Pauleta, Joao Pinto (Rui Costa 60), Figo.
Poland: Dudek; Kozminski, Kaluzny (Bak A 16), Krzynowek, Hajto, Waldoch, Zurawski (Marcin Zewlakow 56), Swierczewski, Kryszalowicz, Olisadebe, Michal Zewlakow (Rzasa 71).
Referee: Dallas (Scotland).

Daegu, 10 June 2002, 60,778

South Korea (0) 1 *(Ahn JH 79)* **USA (1) 1** *(Mathis 24)*
South Korea: Lee WJ; Song CG, Park JS (Lee CS 37), Choi JC, Hong MB, Kim TY, Kim NI, Yoo SC (Choi YS 69), Seol KH, Hwang SH (Ahn JH 55), Lee EY.
USA: Friedel; Sanneh, Hejduk, Reyna, Pope, Agoos, Donovan, O'Brien, Mathis (Wolff 82), McBride, Beasley (Lewis 74).
Referee: Meier (Switzerland).

Daejon, 14 June 2002, 26,482

Poland (2) 3 *(Olisadebe 3, Kryszalowicz 5, Marcin Zewlakow 66)* **USA (0) 1** *(Donovan 83)*
Poland: Majdan; Klos (Waldoch 89), Kozminski, Kucharski (Marcin Zewlakow 65), Glowacki, Zielinski, Zurawski, Murawski, Kryszalowicz, Olisadebe (Sibik 86), Krzynowek.
USA: Friedel; Sanneh, Hejduk, Reyna, Pope, Agoos (Beasley 36), Mathis, Stewart (Jones 68), McBride (Moore 58), Donovan, O'Brien.
Referee: Lu (China).

Incheon, 14 June 2002, 50,239

Portugal (0) 0 **South Korea (0) 1** *(Park JS 70)*
Portugal: Vitor Baia; Beto, Rui Jorge (Xavier 73), Petit (Gomes 77), Fernando Couto, Jorge Costa, Conceicao, Paulo Bento, Joao Pinto (Andrade 68), Pauleta, Figo.
South Korea: Lee WJ; Yoo SC, Lee YP, Song CG, Choi JC, Hong MB, Kim TY, Kim NI, Park JS, Seol KH, Ahn JH (Lee CS 90).
Referee: Sanchez (Argentina).

Group D – Table	P	W	D	L	F	A	Pts
South Korea	3	2	1	0	4	1	7
USA	3	1	1	1	5	6	4
Portugal	3	1	0	2	6	4	3
Poland	3	1	0	2	3	7	3

GROUP E

Sapporo, 1 June 2002, 32,218

Germany (4) 8 *(Klose 20, 25, 69, Ballack 40, Jancker 45, Linke 73, Bierhoff 84, Schneider 90)* **Saudi Arabia (0) 0**
Germany: Kahn; Frings, Ziege, Hamann, Metzelder, Ramelow (Jeremies 46), Linke, Schneider, Jancker (Bierhoff 67), Klose (Neuville 77), Ballack.
Saudi Arabia: Al-Deayea; Tukar, Ahmed Al-Dossari, Zubromawi, Noor, Sulimani, Abdullah Al-Shahrani, Khamis Al-Dossari (Ibrahim Al-Shahrani 46), Temyat (Al-Khathran 46), Al-Jaber, Al-Yami (Abdallah Al-Dossari 77).
Referee: Aquino (Paraguay).

Niigata, 1 June 2002, 33,679

Republic of Ireland (0) 1 *(Holland 52)*   **Cameroon (1) 1** *(Mboma 39)*
Republic of Ireland: Given; Kelly G, Harte (Reid 77), Breen, Staunton, Kinsella, McAteer (Finnan 46), Holland, Robbie Keane, Duff, Kilbane.
Cameroon: Alioum; Geremi, Wome, Kalla, Song, Tchato, Lauren, Foe, Mboma (Suffo 69), Eto'o, Olembe.
Referee: Kamikawa (Japan).

Ibaraki, 5 June 2002, 35,854

Germany (1) 1 *(Klose 19)*   **Republic of Ireland (0) 1** *(Robbie Keane 90)*
Germany: Kahn; Frings, Ziege, Linke, Ramelow, Metzelder, Schneider (Jeremies 90), Hamann, Klose (Bode 86), Jancker (Bierhoff 74), Ballack.
Republic of Ireland: Given; Kelly G (Quinn 72), Harte (Reid 72), Breen, Staunton (Cunningham 88), Kinsella, Finnan, Holland, Robbie Keane, Kilbane, Duff.
Referee: Nielsen (Denmark).

Saitama, 6 June 2002, 52,328

Cameroon (0) 1 *(Eto'o 65)*   **Saudi Arabia (0) 0**
Cameroon: Alioum; Wome (Njanka 80), Kalla, Foe, Song, Tchato, Geremi, Lauren, Eto'o, Mboma (Ndiefi 63), Ngom Kome (Olembe 46).
Saudi Arabia: Al-Deayea; Al-Shehri, Temyat, Al-Jahani, Tukar, Zubromawi (Abdullah Al-Dossari 62), Ibrahim Al-Shahrani, Sulimani, Obeid Al-Dossari (Al-Yami 35), Abdullah Al-Shahrani, Al-Khathran (Noor 81).
Referee: Hauge (Norway).

Shizuoka, 11 June 2002, 47,085

Cameroon (0) 0   Germany (0) 2 *(Bode 50, Klose 79)*
Cameroon: Alioum; Wome, Kalla, Foe, Song, Tchato (Suffo 53), Geremi, Lauren, Eto'o, Mboma (Job 80), Olembe (Kome 64).
Germany: Kahn; Ramelow, Frings, Linke, Metzelder, Ziege, Schneider (Jeremies 80), Hamann, Jancker (Bode 46), Klose (Neuville 84), Ballack.
Referee: Nieto (Spain).

Yokohama, 11 June 2002, 65,320

Saudi Arabia (0) 0   Republic of Ireland (1) 3 *(Robbie Keane 7, Breen 61, Duff 87)*
Saudi Arabia: Al-Deayea; Al-Jahani (Ahmed Al-Dossari 78), Sulimani, Tukar, Zubromawi (Abdullah Al-Dossari 67), Al-Shehri, Ibrahim Al-Shahrani, Al-Temyat, Al-Yami, Khamis Al-Dossarı, Al-Khathran (Al-Shalhoub 66).
Republic of Ireland: Given; Finnan, Harte (Quinn 46), Kinsella (Carsley 88), Breen, Staunton, Kelly G (McAteer 79), Holland, Robbie Keane, Kilbane, Duff.
Referee; Ndoye (Senegal).

Group E – Table

	P	W	D	L	F	A	Pts
Germany	3	2	1	0	11	1	7
Republic of Ireland	3	1	2	0	5	2	5
Cameroon	3	1	1	1	2	3	4
Saudi Arabia	3	0	0	3	0	12	0

GROUP F

Ibaraki, 2 June 2002, 34,050

Argentina (0) 1 *(Batistuta 63)*   **Nigeria (0) 0**
Argentina: Cavallero; Zanetti, Sorin, Pochettino, Samuel, Placente, Simeone, Ortega, Veron (Aimar 78), Batistuta (Crespo 81), Lopez C (Kily Gonzalez 46).
Nigeria: Shorunmu; Sodje (Christopher 73), Babayaro, Yobo, West, Okoronkwo, Okocha, Kanu (Ikedia 48), Ogbeche, Aghahowa, Lawal.
Referee: Veissiere (France).

Saitama, 2 June 2002, 52,271

England (1) 1 *(Campbell 24)*   **Sweden (0) 1** *(Alexandersson 59)*
England: Seaman; Mills, Ashley Cole, Scholes, Campbell, Ferdinand, Beckham (Dyer 63), Hargreaves, Vassell (Cole J 73), Owen, Heskey.
Sweden: Hedman; Mellberg, Lucic, Linderoth, Mjallby, Jakobsson, Alexandersson, Ljungberg, Allback (Andersson A 80), Larsson, Magnus Svensson (Svensson A 55).
Referee: Simon (Brazil).

Sapporo, 7 June 2002, 35,927
Argentina (0) 0   England (1) 1 *(Beckham 44 (pen))*
Argentina: Cavallero; Zanetti, Kily Gonzalez (Lopez C 65), Pochettino, Samuel, Placente,
Simeone, Veron (Aimar 46), Batistuta (Crespo 59), Ortega, Sorin.
England: Seaman; Mills, Ashley Cole, Butt, Campbell, Ferdinand, Beckham, Scholes, Hes-
key (Sheringham 55), Owen (Bridge 80), Hargreaves (Sinclair 19).
Referee: Collina (Italy).

Kobe, 7 June 2002, 36,194
Sweden (1) 2 *(Larsson 35, 62 (pen))*   **Nigeria (1) 1** *(Aghahowa 27)*
Sweden: Hedman; Mellberg, Lucic, Linderoth, Mjallby, Jakobsson, Alexandersson, Svens-
son A (Magnus Svensson 84), Allback (Andersson A 64), Larsson, Ljungberg.
Nigeria: Shorunmu; Yobo, Udeze, Okocha, West, Okoronkwo, Christopher, Utaka,
Ogbeche (Ikedia 71), Aghahowa, Babayaro (Kanu 66).
Referee: Ortube (Bolivia).

Miyagi, 12 June 2002, 45,777
Argentina (0) 1 *(Crespo 88)*   **Sweden (0) 1** *(Svensson A 59)*
Argentina: Cavallero; Sorin (Veron 63), Almeyda (Kily Gonzalez 63), Pochettino, Samuel,
Chamot, Aimar, Zanetti, Batistuta (Crespo 58), Lopez C, Ortega.
Sweden: Hedman; Lucic, Jakobsson, Linderoth, Mellberg, Mjallby, Alexandersson, Mag-
nus Svensson, Allback (Andersson A 46), Larsson (Ibrahimovic 88), Svensson A (Jonsson
68).
Referee: Bujsaim (UAE).

Osaka, 12 June 2002, 44,864
Nigeria (0) 0   England (0) 0
Nigeria: Enyeama; Sodje, Udeze, Christopher, Yobo, Okoronkwo, Okocha, Obiorah,
Aghahowa, Akwuegbu, Opabunmi (Ikedia 86).
England: Seaman; Mills, Ashley Cole (Bridge 85), Butt, Campbell, Ferdinand, Beckham,
Scholes, Heskey (Sheringham 69), Owen (Vassell 77), Sinclair.
Referee: Hall (USA).

Group F – Table	P	W	D	L	F	A	Pts
Sweden	3	1	2	0	4	3	5
England	3	1	2	0	2	1	5
Argentina	3	1	1	1	2	2	4
Nigeria	3	0	1	2	1	3	1

GROUP G

Niigata, 3 June 2002, 32,239
Croatia (0) 0   Mexico (0) 1 *(Blanco 60 (pen))*
Croatia: Pletikosa; Zivkovic, Soldo, Kovac R, Simunic, Jarni, Tomas, Prosinecki (Rapaic
46), Suker (Saric 64), Boksic (Stanic 67), Kovac N.
Mexico: Perez; Mercado, Luna, Vidrio, Marquez, Carmona, Caballero, Torrado, Blanco
(Palencia 79), Borgetti (Hernandez 68), Morales.
Referee: Jun Lu (China).

Sapporo, 3 June 2002, 31,081
Italy (2) 2 *(Vieri 7, 27)*   **Ecuador (0) 0**
Italy: Buffon; Panucci, Maldini, Tommasi, Nesta, Cannavaro, Zambrotta, Di Biagio (Gat-
tuso 70), Totti (Del Piero 74), Vieri, Doni (Di Livio 65).
Ecuador: Cevallos; De la Cruz, Guerron, Tenorio E (Ayovi M 60), Hurtado I, Porozo,
Chala, Obregon, Aguinaga (Tenorio C 46), Delgado, Mendez.
Referee: Hall (USA).

Ibaraki, 8 June 2002, 36,472
Italy (0) 1 *(Vieri 55)*   **Croatia (0) 2** *(Olic 73, Rapaic 76)*
Italy: Buffon; Panucci, Maldini, Tommasi, Nesta (Materazzi 24), Cannavaro, Zambrotta,
Zanetti, Vieri, Totti, Doni (Inzaghi 79).
Croatia: Pletikosa; Saric, Jarni, Tomas, Kovac R, Simunic, Kovac N, Soldo (Vranjes 63),
Boksic, Vugrinec (Olic 57), Rapaic (Simic 79).
Referee: Poll (England).

Miyagi, 9 June 2002, 45,610

Mexico (1) 2 *(Borgetti 28, Torrado 57)*   **Ecuador (1) 1** *(Delgado 5)*
Mexico: Perez; Vidrio, Morales, Rodriguez (Cabellero 86), Marquez, Carmona, Arellano, Torrado, Borgetti (Hernandez 76), Blanco (Mercado 90), Luna.
Ecuador: Cevallos; De la Cruz, Guerron, Mendez, Hurtado I, Poroso, Obregon (Aguinaga 58), Tenorio E (Ayovi M 34), Delgado, Kaviedes (Tenorio C 48), Chala.
Referee: Daami (Tunisia).

Yokohama, 13 June 2002, 65,862

Ecuador (0) 1 *(Mendez 48)*   **Croatia (0) 0**
Ecuador: Cevallos; De la Cruz, Guerron, Ayovi M, Hurtado I, Porozo, Mendez, Obregon (Aguinaga 40), Tenorio C (Kaviedes 75), Delgado, Chala.
Croatia: Pletikosa; Saric (Stanic 67), Jarni, Simic (Vugrinec 52), Kovac N (Vranjes 59), Simunic, Tomas, Rapaic, Olic, Boksic, Kovac R.
Referee: Mattus (Costa Rica).

Oita, 13 June 2002, 39,291

Mexico (1) 1 *(Borgetti 34)*   **Italy (0) 1** *(Del Piero 85)*
Mexico: Perez; Arellano, Morales (Garcia 75), Vidrio, Marquez, Carmona, Rodriguez (Caballero 75), Torrado, Borgetti (Palencia 80), Blanco, Luna.
Italy: Buffon; Zambrotta, Panucci (Coco 63), Cannavaro, Nesta, Maldini, Tomassi, Zanetti, Vieri, Totti (Del Piero 78), Inzaghi (Montella 56).
Referee: Simon (Brazil).

Group G – Table	P	W	D	L	F	A	Pts
Mexico	3	2	1	0	4	2	7
Italy	3	1	1	1	4	3	4
Croatia	3	1	0	2	2	3	3
Ecuador	3	1	0	2	2	4	3

GROUP H

Saitama, 4 June 2002, 55,256

Japan (0) 2 *(Suzuki 59, Inamoto 69)*   **Belgium (0) 2** *(Wilmots 57, Van der Heyden 75)*
Japan: Narazaki; Ichikawa, Ono (Alex 64), Matsuda, Morioka (Miyamoto 72), Nakata K, Inamoto, Toda, Suzuki (Morishima 70), Yanagisawa, Nakata H.
Belgium: De Vlieger; Peeters, Goor, Van Buyten, Van Meir, Van der Heyden, Vanderhaeghe, Simons, Wilmots, Verheyen (Strupar 83), Walem (Sonck 70).
Referee: Vega (Costa Rica).

Kobe, 5 June 2002, 30,957

Russia (0) 2 *(Titov 59, Karpin 64 (pen))*   **Tunisia (0) 0**
Russia: Nigmatullin; Solomatin, Izmailov (Alenichev 78), Kovtun, Onopko, Nikiforov, Semshov (Khokhlov 46), Karpin, Bestchastnykh (Sychev 55), Pimenov, Titov.
Tunisia: Boumnijel; Badra (Zitouni 84), Jaidi, Mkacher, Trabelsi, Bouzaiane, Gabsi (Mhadhebi 67), Bouazizi, Jaziri, Sellimi (Baya 67), Achour.
Referee: Prendergast (Jamaica).

Yokohama, 9 June 2002, 66,108

Japan (0) 1 *(Inamoto 51)*   **Russia (0) 0**
Japan: Narazaki; Myojin, Ono (Hattori 75), Matsuda, Miyamoto, Nakata K, Toda, Nakata H, Suzuki (Nakayana 72), Yanagisawa, Inamoto (Fukunishi 85).
Russia: Nigmatullin; Solomatin, Semshov, Kovtun, Nikiforov, Onopko, Karpin, Smertin (Bestchastnykh 57), Izmailov (Khokhlov 52), Pimenov (Sychev 46), Titov.
Referee: Merk (Germany).

Oita, 10 June 2002, 37,900

Tunisia (1) 1 *(Bouzaine 17)*   **Belgium (1) 1** *(Wilmots 13)*
Tunisia: Boumnijel; Trabelsi, Bouzaine, Ghodhbane, Jaidi, Badra, Gabsi (Sellini 67), Bouazizi, Jaziri (Zitouni 78), Ben Achour, Melki (Baya 89).
Belgium: De Vlieger; Deflandre, Van der Heyden, Simons (Mpenza M 74), De Boeck, Van Buyten, Vanderhaeghe, Goor, Wilmots, Strupar (Sonck 46), Verheyen (Vermant 46).
Referee: Shield (Australia).

Shizuoka, 14 June 2002, 46,640

Belgium (1) 3 *(Walem 7, Sonck 78, Wilmots 82)*   **Russia (0) 2** *(Bestchastnykh 52, Sychev 88)*

Belgium: De Vlieger; Peeters, Van Kerckhoven, Walem, De Boeck (Van Meir 90), Van Buyten, Mpenza M (Sonck 71), Vanderhaeghe, Verheyen (Simons 79), Wilmots, Goor.
Russia: Nigmatullin; Karpin (Kerzhakov 83), Alenichev, Nikiforov (Sennikov 44), Onopko, Kovtun, Solomatin, Smertin (Sychev 35), Khokhlov, Bestchastnykh, Titov.
Referee: Nielsen (Denmark).

Osaka, 14 June 2002, 45,213

Tunisia (0) 0   Japan (0) 2 *(Morishima 48, Nakata H 75)*

Tunisia: Boumnijel; Badra, Jaidi, Bouazizi, Trabelsi, Bouzaiane (Zitouni 77), Clayton (Mhadhebi 60), Ben Achour, Jaziri, Jhodhbane, Melki (Baya 46).
Japan: Narazaki; Myojin, Ono, Matsuda, Miyamoto, Nakata K, Inamoto (Ichimata 46), Toda, Suzuki, Yanagisawa (Morishima 46), Nakata H (Ogasawara 84).
Referee: Veissiere (France).

Group H – Table	P	W	D	L	F	A	Pts
Japan	3	2	1	0	5	2	7
Belgium	3	1	2	0	6	5	5
Russia	3	1	0	2	4	4	3
Tunisia	3	0	1	2	1	5	1

SECOND ROUND

Niigata, 15 June 2002, 40,582

Denmark (0) 0   England (3) 3 *(Ferdinand 5, Owen 22, Heskey 44)*

Denmark: Sorensen; Helveg (Bogelund 7), Jensen N, Gravesen, Laursen, Henriksen, Rommedahl, Tofting (Jensen C 58), Sand, Tomasson, Gronkjaer.
England: Seaman; Mills, Ashley Cole, Butt, Campbell, Ferdinand, Beckham, Scholes (Dyer 49), Heskey (Sheringham 69), Owen (Fowler 46), Sinclair.
Referee: Merk (Germany).

Seogwipo, 15 June 2002, 25,176

Germany (0) 1 *(Neuville 88)*   **Paraguay (0) 0**

Germany: Kahn; Frings, Metzelder (Baumann 60), Jeremies, Rehmer (Kehl 46), Linke, Schneider, Ballack, Neuville (Asamoah 90), Klose, Bode.
Paraguay: Chilavert; Arce, Caniza, Gamarra, Ayala, Caceres, Bonet (Gavilan 84), Acuna, Cardozo, Santa Cruz (Campos 29), Struway (Cuevas 90).
Referee: Batres (Guatemala).

Suwon, 16 June 2002, 38,926

Spain (1) 1 *(Morientes 8)*   **Republic of Ireland (0) 1** *(Robbie Keane 90 (pen))*

Spain: Casillas; Puyol, Juanfran, Baraja, Hierro, Helguera, Luis Enrique, Valeron, Morientes (Albelda 71), Raul (Luque 80), De Pedro (Mendieta 65).
Republic of Ireland: Given; Finnan, Harte (Connolly 82), Kinsella, Breen, Staunton (Cunningham 49), Kelly G (Quinn 54), Holland, Robbie Keane, Duff, Kilbane.
aet; Spain won 3-2 on penalties. Keane (scored), Hierro (scored), Holland (missed), Baraja (scored), Connolly (saved), Juanfran (missed), Kilbane (saved), Valeron (missed), Finnan (scored), Mendieta (scored).
Referee: Frisk (Sweden).

Oita, 16 June 2002, 39,747

Sweden (1) 1 *(Larsson 11)*   **Senegal (1) 2** *(Camara 37, 104)*

Sweden: Hedman; Lucic, Jakobsson, Magnus Svensson (Jonsson 99), Mellberg, Mjallby, Alexandersson (Ibrahimovic 76), Linderoth, Allback (Andersson A 65), Larsson, Svensson A.
Senegal: Sylva; Daf, Coly, Cisse, Diop PM (Beye 66), Diatta, Faye, Diouf, Camara, Thiaw, Diop PB.
aet; Senegal won on sudden death.
Referee: Aquino (Paraguay).

Kobe, 17 June 2002, 40,440

Brazil (0) 2 *(Rivaldo 67, Ronaldo 87)* **Belgium (0) 0**
Brazil: Marcos; Cafu, Roberto Carlos, Lucio, Roque Junior, Edmilson, Juninho (Denilson 57), Gilberto Silva, Ronaldo, Rivaldo (Ricardinho 90), Ronaldinho (Kleberson 81).
Belgium: De Vlieger; Verheyen, Goor, Van Kerckhoven, Van Buyten, Peeters (Sonck 73), Simons, Vanderhaeghe, Mpenza M, Wilmots, Walem.
Referee: Prendergast (Jamaica).

Jeonju, 17 June 2002, 36,380

Mexico (0) 0 **USA (1) 2** *(McBride 8, Donovan 65)*
Mexico: Perez; Arellano, Morales, Vidrio (Mercado 46), Mastroeni, Carmona, Rodriguez, Torrado (Garcia Aspe 78), Borgetti, Blanco, Luna.
USA: Friedel; Reyna, Lewis, Sanneh, Pope, Berhalter, Mastroeni (Llamosa 90), Donovan, Wolff (Stewart 59), McBride (Jones 79), O'Brien.
Referee: Pereira (Portugal).

Miyagi, 18 June 2002, 45,666

Japan (0) 0 **Turkey (1) 1** *(Umit D 12)*
Japan: Narazaki; Myojin, Ono, Matsuda, Miyamoto, Nakata K, Toda, Inamoto (Ichikawa 46) (Morishima 86), Alex (Suzuki 46), Nishizawa, Nakata H.
Turkey: Rustu; Fatih, Hakan Unsal, Tugay, Bulent K, Alpay, Ergun, Basturk (Ilhan 90), Umit D (Nihat 74), Hakan Sukur, Hasan Sas (Tayfur 85).
Referee: Collina (Italy).

Daejeon, 18 June 2002, 38,588

South Korea (0) 2 *(Seol KH 88, Ahn JH 116)* **Italy (1) 1** *(Vieri 18)*
South Korea: Lee WJ; Song CG, Lee YP, Choi JC, Hong MB (Cha DR 82), Kim TY (Hwang SH 63), Yoo SC, Kim NI (Lee CS 68), Park JS, Ahn JH, Seol KH.
Italy: Buffon; Panucci, Coco, Tommasi, Iuliano, Maldini, Zambrotta (Di Livio 72), Del Piero (Gattuso 61), Vieri, Totti, Zanetti.
aet; South Korea won on sudden death.
Referee: Moreno (Ecuador).

QUARTER-FINALS

Shizuoka, 21 June 2002, 47,436

England (1) 1 *(Owen 23)* **Brazil (1) 2** *(Rivaldo 45, Ronaldinho 50)*
England: Seaman, Mills, Ashley Cole (Sheringham 80), Butt, Campbell, Ferdinand, Beckham, Scholes, Heskey, Owen (Vassell 79), Sinclair (Dyer 56).
Brazil: Marcos; Cafu, Roberto Carlos, Lucio, Roque Junior, Edmilson, Kleberson, Gilberto Silva, Ronaldo (Edilson 70), Rivaldo, Ronaldinho.
Referee: Rizo (Mexico).

Ulsan, 21 June 2002, 37,337

Germany (1) 1 *(Ballack 39)* **USA (0) 0**
Germany: Kahn; Frings, Ziege, Kehl, Linke, Metzelder, Schneider (Jeremies 61), Hamann, Neuville (Bode 79), Klose (Bierhoff 88), Ballack.
USA: Friedel; Hejduk (Jones 65), Lewis, Sanneh, Pope, Berhalter, Mastroeni (Stewart 79), Reyna, Donovan, McBride (Mathis 58), O'Brien.
Referee: Dallas (Scotland).

Osaka, 22 June 2002, 44,233

Senegal (0) 0 **Turkey (0) 1** *(Ilhan 94)*
Senegal: Sylva; Daf, Coly, Cisse, Diatta, Diop PM, Camara, Fadiga, Diop PB, Diouf, Diao.
Turkey: Rustu; Ergun, Umit D, Alpay, Bulent K, Fatih, Basturk, Tugay, Hakan Sukur (Ilhan 67), Emre B (Arif 90), Hasan Sas.
aet; Turkey won on sudden death.
Referee: Ruiz (Colombia).

Gwangju, 22 June 2002, 42,114

Spain (0) 0   South Korea (0) 0
Spain: Casillas; Puyol, Romero, Helguera (Xavi 93), Hierro, Nadal, Joaquin, Baraja, Morientes, Valeron (Luis Enrique 80), De Pedro (Mendieta 70).
South Korea: Lee WJ; Song CG, Lee YP, Choi JC, Hong MB, Kim TY (Hwang SH 90), Kim NI (Lee EY 32), Park JS, Ahn JH, Seol KH, Yoo SC (Lee CS 60).
aet; South Korea won 5-3 on penalties. Hwang SH (scored), Hierro (scored) Park JS (scored), Baraja (scored), Seol KH (scored), Xavi (scored), Ahn JH (scored, Joaquin (saved), Hong MB (scored).
Referee: Ghandour (Egypt).

SEMI-FINALS

Seoul, 25 June 2002, 65,256

Germany (0) 1 *(Ballack 75)*   **South Korea (0) 0**
Germany: Kahn; Frings, Metzelder, Hamann, Ramelow, Linke, Schneider (Jeremies 85), Ballack, Neuville (Asamoah 88), Klose (Bierhoff 70), Bode.
South Korea: Lee WJ; Song CG, Lee YP, Choi JC (Lee MS 56), Hong MB (Seol KH 80), Kim TY, Yoo SC, Park JS, Cha DR, Hwang SH (Ahn JH 54), Lee CS.
Referee: Meier (Switzerland).

Saitama, 26 June 2002, 61,058

Brazil (0) 1 *(Ronaldo 49)*   **Turkey (0) 0**
Brazil: Marcos; Cafu, Roberto Carlos, Lucio, Edmilson, Roque Junior, Edilson (Denilson 75), Kleberson (Belletti 85), Gilberto Silva, Ronaldo (Luizao 68), Rivaldo.
Turkey: Rustu; Fatih, Ergun, Tugay, Bulent K, Alpay, Umit D (Izzet 74), Basturk (Arif 88), Emre B (Ilhan 62), Hakan Sukur, Hasan Sas.
Referee: Nielsen (Denmark).

MATCH FOR THIRD PLACE

Daegu, 29 June 2002, 63,483

South Korea (1) 2 *(Lee EY 9, Song CG 90)*

Turkey (3) 3 *(Hakan Sukur 1, Ilhan 13, 32)*
South Korea: Lee WJ; Song CG, Lee CS (Cha DR 64), Lee MS, Hong MB (Kim TY 46), Lee EY, Yoo SC, Park JS, Lee YP, Ahn JH, Seol KH (Choi TU 79).
Turkey: Rustu; Fatih, Ergun, Tugay, Alpay, Bulent K, Umit D (Okan 75), Basturk (Tayfur 85), Hakan Sukur, Ilhan, Emre B (Hakan Unsal 41).
Referee: Mane (Kuwait).

FINAL

Yokohama, 30 June 2002, 69,029

Germany (0) 0,

Brazil (0) 2 *(Ronaldo 67, 79)*
Germany: Kahn; Frings, Bode (Ziege 84), Linke, Ramelow, Metzelder, Jeremies (Asamoah 77), Hamann, Neuville, Klose (Bierhoff 74), Schneider.
Brazil: Marcos; Cafu, Roberto Carlos, Lucio, Edmilson, Roque Junior, Kleberson, Gilberto Silva, Ronaldo (Denilson 90), Rivaldo, Ronaldinho (Juninho 85).
Referee: Collina (Italy).

FINAL TOURNAMENT STATISTICS

Average goals per game 2.52; fastest individual goal: Hakan Sukur, Turkey v South Korea 10.8 secs; top scoring team: Brazil 18 goals; top marksman Ronaldo (Brazil) 8 goals; yellow cards 267; red cards 17; Cafu, the Brazilian captain, became the first player to figure in the final match of three World Cup tournaments.

WORLD CLUB CHAMPIONSHIP

Played annually up to 1974 and intermittently since then between the winners of the
European Cup and the winners of the South American Champions Cup — known as
the Copa Libertadores. In 1980 the winners were decided by one match arranged in
Tokyo in February 1981 and the venue has been the same since. AC Milan replaced
Marseille who had been stripped of their European Cup title in 1993.

1960   Real Madrid beat Penarol 0-0, 5-1
1961   Penarol beat Benfica 0-1, 5-0, 2-1
1962   Santos beat Benfica 3-2, 5-2
1963   Santos beat AC Milan 2-4, 4-2, 1-0
1964   Inter-Milan beat Independiente 0-1, 2-0, 1-0
1965   Inter-Milan beat Independiente 3-0, 0-0
1966   Penarol beat Real Madrid 2-0, 2-0
1967   Racing Club beat Celtic 0-1, 2-1, 1-0
1968   Estudiantes beat Manchester United 1-0, 1-1
1969   AC Milan beat Estudiantes 3-0, 1-2
1970   Feyenoord beat Estudiantes 2-2, 1-0
1971   Nacional beat Panathinaikos* 1-1, 2-1
1972   Ajax beat Independiente 1-1, 3-0
1973   Independiente beat Juventus* 1-0
1974   Atlético Madrid* beat Independiente 0-1, 2-0
1975   Independiente and Bayern Munich could not agree dates; no matches.
1976   Bayern Munich beat Cruzeiro 2-0, 0-0
1977   Boca Juniors beat Borussia Moenchengladbach* 2-2, 3-0
1978   Not contested
1979   Olimpia beat Malmö* 1-0, 2-1
1980   Nacional beat Nottingham Forest 1-0
1981   Flamengo beat Liverpool 3-0
1982   Penarol beat Aston Villa 2-0
1983   Gremio Porto Alegre beat SV Hamburg 2-1
1984   Independiente beat Liverpool 1-0
1985   Juventus beat Argentinos Juniors 4-2 on penalties after a 2-2 draw
1986   River Plate beat Steaua Bucharest 1-0
1987   FC Porto beat Penarol 2-1 after extra time
1988   Nacional (Uru) beat PSV Eindhoven 7-6 on penalties after 1-1 draw
1989   AC Milan beat Atletico Nacional (Col) 1-0 after extra time
1990   AC Milan beat Olimpia 3-0
1991   Red Star Belgrade beat Colo Colo 3-0
1992   Sao Paulo beat Barcelona 2-1
1993   Sao Paulo beat AC Milan 3-2
1994   Velez Sarsfield beat AC Milan 2-0
1995   Ajax beat Gremio Porto Alegre 4-3 on penalties after 0-0 draw
1996   Juventus beat River Plate 1-0
1997   Borussia Dortmund beat Cruzeiro 2-0
1998   Real Madrid beat Vasco da Gama 2-1
1999   Manchester U beat Palmeiras 1-0
2000   Boca Juniors beat Real Madrid 2-1

*European Cup runners-up; winners declined to take part.

2001

27 November in Tokyo

Bayern Munich (0) 1

Boca Juniors (0) 0 *aet*   51,360

Bayern Munich: Kahn; Sagnol, Lizarazu, Kovac R, Kuffour, Fink, Hargreaves
(Sforza 76), Kovac N (Jancker 76), Sergio, Elber, Pizarro (Thiam 118).
Scorer: Kuffour 110.
Boca Juniors: Cordoba; Burdisso, Martinez (Calvo 19) (Carreno 112), Schiavi,
Rodriguez, Serna, Villarreal (Pinto 100), Traverso, Riquelme, Delgardo, Schelotto.
Referee: Nielsen (Denmark).

EUROPEAN SUPER CUP

Played annually between the winners of the European Champions' Cup and the European Cup-Winners' Cup (UEFA Cup from 2000). AC Milan replaced Marseille in 1993–94.

Previous Matches
1972   Ajax beat Rangers 3-1, 3-2
1973   Ajax beat AC Milan 0-1, 6-0
1974   Not contested
1975   Dynamo Kiev beat Bayern Munich 1-0, 2-0
1976   Anderlecht beat Bayern Munich 4-1, 1-2
1977   Liverpool beat Hamburg 1-1, 6-0
1978   Anderlecht beat Liverpool 3-1, 1-2
1979   Nottingham F beat Barcelona 1-0, 1-1
1980   Valencia beat Nottingham F 1-0, 1-2
1981   Not contested
1982   Aston Villa beat Barcelona 0-1, 3-0
1983   Aberdeen beat Hamburg 0-0, 2-0
1984   Juventus beat Liverpool 2-0
1985   Juventus v Everton not contested due to UEFA ban on English clubs
1986   Steaua Bucharest beat Dynamo Kiev 1-0
1987   FC Porto beat Ajax 1-0, 1-0
1988   KV Mechelen beat PSV Eindhoven 3-0, 0-1
1989   AC Milan beat Barcelona 1-1, 1-0
1990   AC Milan beat Sampdoria 1-1, 2-0
1991   Manchester U beat Red Star Belgrade 1-0
1992   Barcelona beat Werder Bremen 1-1, 2-1
1993   Parma beat AC Milan 0-1, 2-0
1994   AC Milan beat Arsenal 0-0, 2-0
1995   Ajax beat Zaragoza 1-1, 4-0
1996   Juventus beat Paris St Germain 6-1, 3-1
1997   Barcelona beat Borussia Dortmund 2-0, 1-1
1998   Chelsea beat Real Madrid 1-0
1999   Lazio beat Manchester U 1-0
2000   Galatasaray beat Real Madrid 2-1
(aet; Galatasaray won on sudden death.)

2001

24 August 2001, Monaco

Bayern Munich (0) 2 *(Salihamidzic 57, Jancker 81)*

Liverpool (2) 3 *(Riise 22, Heskey 45, Owen 46)*   15,000
Bayern Munich: Kahn; Sagnol, Lizarazu, Kovac R, Thiam, Linke, Hargreaves, Sforza (Kovac N 65), Elber, Pizarro (Jancker 65), Salihamidzic (Santa Cruz 71).
Liverpool: Westerveld; Babbel, Carragher, Hamann, Henchoz, Hyypia, Gerrard (Biscan 65), McAllister, Heskey, Owen (Fowler 82), Riise (Murphy 68).
Referee: Pereira (Portugal).

OTHER BRITISH AND IRISH INTERNATIONAL MATCHES 2001–2002

Tottenham, 15 August 2001, 35,238

England (0) 0   Holland (2) 2 *(Van Bommel 30, Van Nistelrooy 39)*

England: Martyn (James 46) (Wright 49); Neville G (Mills 46), Ashley Cole (Powell 46), Carragher, Brown (Southgate 46), Keown (Ehiogu 49), Beckham (Lampard 46), Scholes (Carrick 46), Andy Cole (Smith 69), Fowler (Owen 46), Hargreaves (Barmby 46).

Holland: Van der Sar (Walerrius 46); Reiziger, Van Bronckhorst, Cocu (Kamphuis 80), Stam (Melchiot 46), Hofland, Overmars (Davids 46), Van Bommel (Landzaat 72), Kluivert (Van Hooijdonk 89), Van Nistelrooy (Hasselbaink 46), Zenden (Makaay 46).

Referee: Frisk (Sweden).

Old Trafford, 10 November 2001, 64,413

England (1) 1 *(Beckham 28 (pen))*   **Sweden (1) 1** *(Mild 44)*

England: Martyn; Neville G (Mills 57), Carragher (Neville P 86), Butt (Murphy 57), Southgate, Ferdinand, Beckham, Scholes (Lampard 86), Heskey (Sheringham 57), Phillips (Fowler 57), Sinclair (Anderton 57).

Sweden: Hedman (Kihlstedt 46); Andersson C, Mjallby (Jakobsson 62), Edman (Andersson D 46), Linderoth, Magnus Svensson (Svensson A 46), Alexandersson (Soderstrom 85), Mild, Michael Svensson, Allback, Ibrahimovic (Osmanovski 74).

Referee: Colombo (France).

Amsterdam, 13 February 2002, 48,500

Holland (1) 1 *(Kluivert 26)*   **England (0) 1** *(Vassell 61)*

Holland: Van der Sar; Ricksen, Van Bronckhorst, Cocu (Boateng 46), Reiziger, Frank de Boer (Paauwe 67), Ronald de Boer (Sikora 59), Van Bommel (Davids 46), Kluivert, Van Nistelrooy (Hasselbaink 64), Overmars (Makaay 88).

England: Martyn (James 46); Neville G (Neville P 77), Bridge (Powell 46), Gerrard (Lampard 77), Campbell (Southgate 46), Ferdinand, Beckham, Scholes (Butt 77), Vassell (Cole J 77), Ricketts (Phillips 46), Heskey.

Referee: Duhamel (France).

Leeds, 27 March 2002, 36,635

England (0) 1 *(Fowler 63)*   **Italy (0) 2** *(Montella 67, 90 (pen))*

England: Martyn (James 46); Mills (Neville P 46), Bridge (Neville G 87), Lampard (Cole J 46), Southgate (Ehiogu 46), Campbell (King 46), Beckham (Murphy 46), Butt (Hargreaves 46), Heskey (Fowler 46), Owen (Vassell 46), Sinclair (Sheringham 70).

Italy: Buffon; Zambrotta, Panucci (Coco 74), Cannavaro, Nesta (Adani 82), Materazzi (Iuliano 57), Di Biagio (Gattuso 57), Zanetti (Albertini 57), Delvecchio (Maccarone 74), Totti (Montella 46), Doni (Tommasi 74).

Referee: Fandel (Germany).

Anfield, 17 April 2002, 42,713

England (1) 4 *(Owen 4, Murphy 47, Vassell 55, Ayala 81 (og))*   **Paraguay (0) 0**

England: Seaman; Neville G (Lampard 68); Bridge (Neville P 68), Butt (Hargreaves 46), Southgate (Carragher 68), Keown (Mills 46), Gerrard (Sinclair 46), Scholes (Murphy 46), Vassell (Sheringham 68), Owen (Fowler 46), Dyer (Cole J 46).

Paraguay: Tavarelli; Arce, Caniza, Gavilan (Sanabria 55), Ayala, Gamarra (Caceres 80), Struway, Paredes, Cardozo (Baez 46), Santa Cruz, Bonet (Moringo 80).

Referee: Boignino (Italy).

Seoguipo, 21 May 2002, 39,876

South Korea (0) 1 *(Park JS 52)*   **England: (1) 1** *(Owen 26)*

South Korea: Lee WJ; Song CG, Lee YP, Yoo SC, Choi JC, Hong MB, Kim NI (Lee MS 89), Choi TU (Cha DR 76), Seol KH (Ahn JH 56), Lee CS, Park JS.
England: Martyn (James 46); Mills (Brown 68), Ashley Cole (Bridge 46), Murphy (Sinclair 46), Campbell (Keown 46), Ferdinand (Southgate 46), Hargreaves, Scholes (Cole J 46), Vassell, Owen (Sheringham 46), Heskey.
Referee: Supian (Malaysia).

Kobe, 26 May 2002, 42,000

Cameroon (1) 2 *(Eto'o 5, Geremi 58)*   **England (1) 2** *(Vassell 12, Fowler 90)*

Cameroon: Alioum (Songo'o 77); Song (Ndo 68),Tchato,Geremi (Ainoudji 65), Kalla (Mettomo 55), Lauren (Epalle 59), Foe (Djemba-Djemba 53), Wome (Njanka 61), Eto'o (Suffo 59), Mboma (Ndiefi 65), Olembe (Ngom Kome 53).
England: Martyn (James 46); Brown, Bridge, Cole J, Campbell (Keown 46), Ferdinand (Southgate 46), Hargreaves, Scholes (Mills 46), Vassell (Fowler 76), Owen (Sheringham 46), Heskey (Sinclair 46).
Referee: Katayama (Japan).

Paris, 27 March 2002, 80,000

France (4) 5 *(Zidane 12, Trezeguet 23, 42, Henry 32, Marlet 87)*   **Scotland (0) 0**

France: Barthez; Candela (Karembeu 56), Lizarazu, Vieira (Makelele 46), Leboeuf (Christanval 63), Desailly (Silvestre 46), Wiltord (Marlet 56), Petit, Trezeguet (Carriere 74), Zidane (Djorkaeff 81), Henry.
Scotland: Sullivan; Weir, Crainey, Cameron (Holt 46) (McNamara 74), Caldwell G, Dailly, Lambert, Matteo, Freedman (Gemmill 46), Crawford (Thompson 63), McCann.

Aberdeen, 17 April 2002, 20,465

Scotland (1) 1 *(Dailly 7)*   **Nigeria (1) 2** *(Aghahowa 40, 69)*

Scotland: Douglas; Stockdale (Alexander 46), Crainey, Lambert, Weir, Dailly, Williams (Stewart 64), McNaughton, Thompson (O'Connor 74), McCann (Johnston 78), Gemmill (Caldwell G 46).
Nigeria: Ejide (Bankole 46); Sodje (Ifeajigwa 85), Christopher (Adepoju 78), Yobo, Okoronkwo, Ejiofor, Okocha, Utaka, Aghahowa, Kanu, Ogbeche.
Referee: Ovredo (Norway).

Busan, 16 May 2002, 60,000

South Korea (1) 4 *(Lee CS 15, Ahn JH 57, 87, Yoon JH 67)*
Scotland (0) 1 *(Dobie 74)*

South Korea: Kim BJ; Lee CS (Cha DR 72), Hong MB (Yoon JH 65), Choi JC (Lee MS 46), Kim TY, Lee YP, Yoo SC, Hwang SH (Ahn JH 46), Park JS (Choi TU 72), Lee EY, Song CG.
Scotland: Sullivan; Ross, Alexander (Stockdale 62), Caldwell G, Weir, Dailly, Johnston (Kyle 66), O'Connor (Williams 46), Stewart (Severin 46), Dobie, Gemmill.
Referee: Santhan (Singapore).

Hong Kong, 20 May 2002, 3007

South Africa (1) 2 *(Mokoena T 32, Koumantarakis 90)*   **Scotland (0) 0**

South Africa: Vonk; Mokoena A (Nzama 62), Carnell, Sibaya, Radebe, Issa, Zuma (Koumantarakis 82), Pule (Arendse 69), McCarthy, Mokoena T, Fortune (Buckley 84).
Scotland: Douglas; Stockdale (Alexander 69), Ross, Caldwell G (Wilkie 46), Weir, Dailly, Williams (Severin 78), Kyle, Dobie, Gemmill (Stewart 86), Johnston (McFadden 62).
Referee: Chan SK (Hong Kong).

Hong Kong, 23 May 2002, 5000

Hong Kong (0) 0   Scotland (0) 4 *(Kyle, Thompson, Dailly, Gemmill)*
Scotland: Douglas (Gallacher 76); Ross (Cummings 46), Stockdale, Weir, Dailly, Wilkie, Johnston (Williams 62), Severin, Thompson (Dobie 46), Kyle (O'Connor 81), Gemmill (Alexander 88).
(Caps awarded by Scotland; match not considered a full international by FIFA).

Millennium Stadium, 13 February 2002, 65,000

Wales (1) 1 *(Bellamy 34)*   **Argentina (0) 1** *(Cruz 61)*
Wales: Jones P (Crossley 46); Delaney, Speed, Melville, Page, Pembridge (Robinson C 90), Davies, Savage, Hartson, Bellamy, Giggs (Robinson J 61).
Argentina: Saja; Kily Gonzalez, Hussain, Placente, Chamot, Vivas, Sorin, Veron, Caniggia (Galletti 90), Cruz (Saviola 74), Riquelme (Aimar 74).
Referee: McKeown (Ireland).

Ninian Park, 27 March 2002, 22,000

Wales (0) 0   Czech Republic (0) 0
Wales: Ward (Coyne 46); Delaney, Gabbidon, Savage (Evans P 73), Melville, Page, Davies, Robinson J, Hartson (Taylor 73), Blake (Trollope 62), Koumas.
Czech Republic: Cech (Vaniak 46); Fukal, Jankulovski (Holenak 82), Galasek (Koldusek 62), Ujifalusi, Novotny (Johana 46), Poborsky, Rosicky (Sionko 46), Lokvenc (Koller 46), Stajner (Hubschman 46), Smicer.
Referee: Larsen (Denmark).

Millennium Stadium, 14 May 2002, 36,920

Wales (0) 1 *(Earnshaw 46)*   **Germany (0) 0**
Wales: Crossley; Delaney, Speed, Melville, Page, Savage, Davies, Earnshaw (Coleman 90), Hartson, Pembridge, Giggs.
Germany: Kahn; Heinrich, Ziege (Bode 63), Deisler (Asamoah 63), Linke, Metzelder, Jeremies, Hamann (Kehl 73), Bierhoff (Jancker 72), Klose, Frings.
Referee: Olsen (Norway).

Limassol, 13 February 2002, 221

Poland (2) 4 *(Kryszalowicz 6, 67, Kaluzny 11, Marcin Zewlakow 69)*
Northern Ireland (1) 1 *(Lomas 18)*
Poland: Majdan (Bledzewski 90); Krzynowek, Waldoch, Iwan (Smolarek 46), Bak J, Michal Zewlakow (Rzasa 60), Kozminski, Swierczewski (Zdebel 46), Kryszalowicz (Zielinski 82), Kaluzny (Bak A 46), Olisadebe (Marcin Zewlakow 46).
Northern Ireland: Taylor; Griffin (McCartney 46), Kennedy (McCann 82), Mulryne (Lennon 46), Hughes A, Lomas, Gillespie, Magilton (Duff 82), Johnson (McVeigh 66), Healy (Elliott 60), Hughes M.
Referee: Papaioannou (Cyprus).

Vaduz, 27 March 2002, 1080

Liechtenstein (0) 0   Northern Ireland (0) 0
Liechtenstein: Jehle; Hasler, Gigon, Martin Stocklasa, Zech, Michael Stocklasa, Telser, Beck M, Nigg (Burgmeier 73), Buchel, Beck T.
Northern Ireland: Taylor (Carroll 46); Lomas, McCann (Holmes 69), Mulryne, Williams M, McCartney, Gillespie, Magilton, Johnson, Healy (Elliott 84), Feeney (Hughes M 58).
Referee: Rogalla (Switzerland).

Belfast, 17 April 2002, 11,100

Northern Ireland (0) 0
Spain (1) 5 *(Raul 23, 54, Baraja 47, Puyol 69, Morientes 78)*
Northern Ireland: Taylor (Carroll 46); Nolan, McCartney, Horlock, Hughes A, Williams M, Gillespie (McCourt 77), Elliott, Feeney (McEvilly 63), Johnson, Healy.

Spain: Canizares (Casillas 74); Puyol, Juanfran, Albelda (Mendieta 46), Hierro (Sergio 74), Nadal (Torres 46), Joaquin (Helguera 46), Baraja, Morientes, Raul, De Pedro (Valeron 46).
Referee: Clark (Scotland).

Dublin, 15 August 2001, 27,000
Republic of Ireland (1) 2 *(Duff 21, Morrison 77)*   **Croatia (0) 2** *(Vugrinec 80, Suker 90 (pen))*

Republic of Ireland: Given (Kelly A 46); Kelly G (O'Shea 84), Harte (McPhail 46), Carsley, Dunne (O'Brien 46), Staunton, Reid (Finnan 46), Roy Keane (McAteer 46), Robbie Keane (Morrison 52), Duff (Connolly 52), Kennedy (Kilbane 46).
Croatia: Pletikosa; Soldo (Prosinecki 74), Jarni (Saric 62), Kovac R, Tudor, Simic (Tomas 74), Stanic (Biscan 46), Kovac N (Bjelica 82), Balaban (Vugrinec 46), Boksic (Suker 74), Rapaic (Zivkovic 46).
Referee: Schluchter (Switzerland).

Dublin, 13 February 2002, 44,000
Republic of Ireland (2) 2 *(Reid 3, Robbie Keane 20)*   **Russia (0) 0**

Republic of Ireland: Given (Kiely 46); Finnan (McAteer 72) (Quinn 90), Harte (Staunton 72), Roy Keane (Holland 86), O'Brien (Dunne 46), Cunningham (Breen 46), Reid (Kelly G 46), Healy (Carsley 46), Robbie Keane (Sadlier 72), Duff (Morrison 46), Kilbane (Kennedy 46).
Russia: Nigmatullin; Khlestov (Daev 90), Kovtun, Khokhlov (Izmailov 53), Nikiforov (Chugainov 66), Onopko, Karpin, Mostovoi, Alenichev (Semak 72), Bestchastnykh, Titov.
Referee: Gallacher (England).

Dublin, 27 March 2002, 42,000
Republic of Ireland (1) 3 *(Harte 19, Robbie Keane 54, Morrison 90)*
Denmark (0) 0

Republic of Ireland: Kiely (Colgan 65); Kelly G, Harte, Holland, Cunningham, Staunton, McAteer (Reid 65), Kinsella (Healy 63), Robbie Keane (Connolly 75), Morrison, Duff (Dunne 83).
Denmark: Sorensen (Kjaer 46); Rytter, Heintze (Jensen N 80), Steen-Nielsen, Laursen, Henriksen, Poulsen, Nielsen A (Madsen 46), Rommedahl (Lovenkrands 67), Sand, Gronkjaer.
Referee: Lawlor (Wales).

Dublin, 17 April 2002, 39,000
Republic of Ireland (1) 2 *(Kinsella 6, Doherty 83)*   **USA (1) 1** *(Pope 34)*

Republic of Ireland: Given; Finnan (Kelly G 46), Harte (Staunton 46), Kinsella (Holland 46), O'Brien (Cunningham 46), Breen (Doherty 71), Delap, Healy, Robbie Keane (Morrison 83), Duff (Connolly 46), Kilbane (Reid 46).
USA: Friedel (Keller 46); Sanneh, Agoos, Armas, Pope, Berhalter (Vanney 46), Reyna (Hejduk 71), O'Brien (Lewis 46), McBride (Moore 46), Mathis (Wolff 63), Stewart (Donovan 46).
Referee: Leuba (Switzerland).

Dublin, 16 May 2002, 42,652
Republic of Ireland (0) 1 *(Reid 69)*   **Nigeria (1) 2** *(Aghahowa 13, Sodje 47)*

Republic of Ireland: Given; Finnan, Harte, Holland, Cunningham, Staunton, McAteer (Reid 46), Roy Keane (Kinsella 63), Robbie Keane (Morrison 61), Duff (Connolly 61), Kilbane (Kelly G 61).
Nigeria: Shorunmu; Yobo, West, Opabunmi, Udeze, Sodje, Ikedia, Okocha (Oruma 65), Kanu, Aghahowa, Ogbeche.
Referee: Dos Santos (Portugal).

ENGLAND UNDER-21 TEAMS 2001–2002

14 Aug

England (1) 4 *(Vassell 6, Christie 87, Defoe 50, 90)*

Holland (0) 0   19,467

England: Taylor (Bywater 64); Young (Wright 46), Bridge (Johnson S 46), Dunn (Prutton 43), Terry (Riggott 64), Barry (Bramble 46), Greening (Pennant 67), Davis (Parker 46), Vassell (Defoe 48), Jeffers (Christie 46), Chadwick (Wilson 64).

31 Aug

Germany (0) 1 *(Metzelder 90)*   21,400

England (0) 2 *(Cole J 55, Jeffers 90)*

England: Taylor; Wright, Bridge, Davis, King, Barry, Greening, Prutton, Vassell (Jeffers 57), Cole J (Parker 75), Chadwick (Defoe 70).

4 Sept

England (1) 5 *(Jeffers 17, 59, 90, Defoe 71, Greening 89)*

Albania (0) 0   23,118

England: Taylor; Wright, Bridge, Davis (Wilson 75), King, Barry, Greening, Parker (Pennant 70), Jeffers, Defoe, Chadwick (Johnson S 63).

5 Oct

England (1) 2 *(Defoe 10, Christie 85)*

Greece (0) 1 *(Papadopoulos 90 (pen))* 29,164

England: Kirkland; Young, Bridge, Dunn, King, Barry, Pennant, Carrick, Vassell, Defoe (Christie 73), Greening (Prutton 73).

9 Nov

Holland (2) 2 *(Van der Vaart 21, Kuyt 37)*

England (1) 2 *(Davis 45, Dunn 57)* 14,500

England: Kirkland; Young, Bridge, Davis, Terry (Barry 80), King, Pennant, Carrick, Christie (Ameobi 30), Defoe, Dunn.

13 Nov

England (0) 1 *(Carrick 72)*

Holland (0) 0   32,418

England: Kirkland; Wright, Bridge, Davis, Terry, King, Pennant (Greening 68), Carrick, Ameobi, Defoe, Dunn.

12 Feb

Slovenia (0) 0

England (0) 1 *(Ameobi 65)*   350

England: Robinson (Weaver 60); Wright (Knight 60), Konchesky, Dunn (Etherington 46), Riggott, Barry, Pennant, Parker (Prutton 46), Christie, Defoe (Ameobi 61), Jenas.

26 Mar

England (0) 1 *(Barry 59)*

Italy (1) 1 *(Maccarone 15)*   21,642

England: Robinson (Bywater 79); Wright, Samuel, Prutton, Knight (Gardner 79), Barry, Wright-Phillips (Pennant 46), Jenas (Parker 46), Smith, Defoe, Etherington (Crouch 59).

16 Apr

England (0) 0

Portugal (1) 1 *(Tonel 39)*   28,000

England: Robinson (Kirkland 46); Wright (Young 70), Konchesky, Davis (Jenas 55), Riggott, Barry, Dunn (Pennant 46), Carrick, Smith (Zamora 70), Christie (Crouch 46), Johnson S (Defoe 77).

17 May

Switzerland (0) 1 *(Frei 58)*

England (1) 2 *(Defoe 3, Crouch 53)* 16,000

England: Robinson; Young, Konchesky, Davis (Prutton 34), Riggott, Barry, Pennant, Dunn, Crouch (Ameobi 78), Smith, Defoe (Parker 64).

20 May

Italy (0) 2 *(Maccarone 58, 84)*

England (0) 1 *(Barry 64)*   12,980

England: Robinson; Young, Konchesky, Davis, Knight, Riggott, Smith, Dunn, Crouch (Defoe 46), Prutton (Pennant 84), Barry (Zamora 88).

22 May

Portugal (2) 3 *(Teixeira 7, Makukula 20 (pen), Viana 69)*

England (1) 1 *(Smith 43)*   10,000

England: Robinson; Young, Konchesky, Dunn, Knight, Barry, Pennant (Parker 76), Prutton, Smith, Defoe (Zamora 66), Greening (Ameobi 31).

POST-WAR INTERNATIONAL APPEARANCES
As at July 2002 *(Season of first cap given)*

ENGLAND

A'Court, A. (5) 1957/8 Liverpool
Adams, T. A. (66) 1986/7 Arsenal
Allen, C. (5) 1983/4 QPR, Tottenham H
Allen, R. (5) 1951/2 WBA
Allen, T. (3) 1959/60 Stoke C
Anderson, S. (2) 1961/2 Sunderland
Anderson, V. (30) 1978/9 Nottingham F, Arsenal, Manchester U
Anderton, D. R. (30) 1993/4 Tottenham H
Angus, J. (1) 1960/1 Burnley
Armfield, J. (43) 1958/9 Blackpool
Armstrong, D. (3) 1979/80 Middlesbrough, Southampton
Armstrong, K. (1) 1954/5 Chelsea
Astall, G. (2) 1955/6 Birmingham C
Astle, J. (5) 1968/9 WBA
Aston, J. (17) 1948/9 Manchester U
Atyeo, J. (6) 1955/6 Bristol C

Bailey, G. R. (2) 1984/5 Manchester U
Bailey, M. (2) 1963/4 Charlton
Baily, E. (9) 1949/50 Tottenham H
Baker, J. (8) 1959/60 Hibernian, Arsenal
Ball, A. (72) 1964/5 Blackpool, Everton, Arsenal
Ball, M. J. (1) 2000/01 Everton
Banks, G. (73) 1962/3 Leicester C, Stoke C
Banks, T. (6) 1957/8 Bolton W
Bardsley, D. (2) 1992/3 QPR
Barham, M. (2) 1982/3 Norwich C
Barlow, R. (1) 1954/5 WBA
Barmby, N. J. (23) 1994/5 Tottenham H, Middlesbrough, Everton, Liverpool
Barnes, J. (79) 1982/3 Watford, Liverpool
Barnes, P. (22) 1977/8 Manchester C, WBA, Leeds U
Barrass, M. (3) 1951/2 Bolton W
Barrett, E. D. (3) 1990/1 Oldham Ath, Aston Villa
Barry, G. (6) 1999/00 Aston Villa
Barton, W. D. (3) 1994/5 Wimbledon, Blackburn R
Batty, D. (42) 1990/1 Leeds U, Blackburn R, Newcastle U, Leeds U
Baynham, R. (3) 1955/6 Luton T
Beardsley, P. A. (59) 1985/6 Newcastle U, Liverpool, Newcastle U
Beasant, D. J. (2) 1989/90 Chelsea

Beattie, T. K. (9) 1974/5 Ipswich T
Beckham, D. R. J. (54) 1996/7 Manchester U
Bell, C. (48) 1967/8 Manchester C
Bentley, R. (12) 1948/9 Chelsea
Berry, J. (4) 1952/3 Manchester U
Birtles, G. (3) 1979/80 Nottingham F, Manchester U
Blissett, L. (14) 1982/3 Watford, AC Milan
Blockley, J. (1) 1972/3 Arsenal
Blunstone, F. (5) 1954/5 Chelsea
Bonetti, P. (7) 1965/6 Chelsea
Bould, S. A. (2) 1993/4 Arsenal
Bowles, S. (5) 1973/4 QPR
Boyer, P. (1) 1975/6 Norwich C
Brabrook, P. (3) 1957/8 Chelsea
Bracewell, P. W. (3) 1984/5 Everton
Bradford, G. (1) 1955/6 Bristol R
Bradley, W. (3) 1958/9 Manchester U
Bridge, W. M. (7) 2001/02 Southampton
Bridges, B. (4) 1964/5 Chelsea
Broadbent, P. (7) 1957/8 Wolverhampton W
Broadis, I. (14) 1951/2 Manchester C, Newcastle U
Brooking, T. (47) 1973/4 West Ham U
Brooks, J. (3) 1956/7 Tottenham H
Brown, A. (1) 1970/1 WBA
Brown, K. (1) 1959/60 West Ham U
Brown, W. M. (6) 1998/9 Manchester U
Bull, S. G. (13) 1988/9 Wolverhampton W
Butcher, T. (77) 1979/80 Ipswich T, Rangers
Butt, N. (22) 1996/7 Manchester U
Byrne, G. (2) 1962/3 Liverpool
Byrne, J. (11) 1961/2 Crystal P, West Ham U
Byrne, R. (33) 1953/4 Manchester U

Callaghan, I. (4) 1965/6 Liverpool
Campbell, S. (51) 1995/6 Tottenham H, Arsenal
Carragher, J. L. (8) 1998/9 Liverpool
Carrick, M. (2) 2000/01 West Ham U
Carter, H. (7) 1946/7 Derby Co
Chamberlain, M. (8) 1982/3 Stoke C
Channon, M. (46) 1972/3 Southampton, Manchester C
Charles, G. A. (2) 1990/1 Nottingham F
Charlton, J. (35) 1964/5 Leeds U

Charlton, R. (106) 1957/8 Manchester U

Charnley, R. (1) 1961/2 Blackpool

Cherry, T. (27) 1975/6 Leeds U

Chilton, A. (2) 1950/1 Manchester U

Chivers, M. (24) 1970/1 Tottenham H

Clamp, E. (4) 1957/8 Wolverhampton W

Clapton, D. (1) 1958/9 Arsenal

Clarke, A. (19) 1969/70 Leeds U

Clarke, H. (1) 1953/4 Tottenham H

Clayton, R. (35) 1955/6 Blackburn R

Clemence, R (61) 1972/3 Liverpool, Tottenham H

Clement, D. (5) 1975/6 QPR

Clough, B. (2) 1959/60 Middlesbrough

Clough, N. H. (14) 1988/9 Nottingham F

Coates, R. (4) 1969/70 Burnley, Tottenham H

Cockburn, H. (13) 1946/7 Manchester U

Cohen, G. (37) 1963/4 Fulham

Cole, Andy (15) 1994/5 Manchester U

Cole, Ashley (13) 2000/01 Arsenal

Cole, J. J. (7) 2000/01 West Ham U

Collymore, S. V. (3) 1994/5 Nottingham F

Compton, L. (2) 1950/1 Arsenal

Connelly, J. (20) 1959/60 Burnley, Manchester U

Cooper, C. T. (2) 1994/5 Nottingham F

Cooper, T. (20) 1968/9 Leeds U

Coppell, S. (42) 1977/8 Manchester U

Corrigan, J. (9) 1975/6 Manchester C

Cottee, A. R. (7) 1986/7 West Ham U, Everton

Cowans, G. (10) 1982/3 Aston Villa, Bari, Aston Villa

Crawford, R. (2) 1961/2 Ipswich T

Crowe, C. (1) 1962/3 Wolverhampton W

Cunningham, L. (6) 1978/9 WBA, Real Madrid

Curle, K. (3) 1991/2 Manchester C

Currie, A. (17) 1971/2 Sheffield U, Leeds U

Daley, A. M. (7) 1991/2 Aston Villa

Davenport, P. (1) 1984/5 Nottingham F

Deane, B. C. (3) 1990/1 Sheffield U

Deeley, N. (2) 1958/9 Wolverhampton W

Devonshire, A. (8) 1979/80 West Ham U

Dickinson, J. (48) 1948/9 Portsmouth

Ditchburn, E. (6) 1948/9 Tottenham H

Dixon, K. M. (8) 1984/5 Chelsea

Dixon, L. M. (22) 1989/90 Arsenal

Dobson, M. (5) 1973/4 Burnley, Everton

Dorigo, A. R. (15) 1989/90 Chelsea, Leeds U

Douglas, B. (36) 1957/8 Blackburn R

Doyle, M. (5) 1975/6 Manchester C

Dublin, D. (4) 1997/8 Coventry C, Aston Villa

Duxbury, M. (10) 1983/4 Manchester U

Dyer, K. C. (12) 1999/00 Newcastle U

Eastham, G. (19) 1962/3 Arsenal

Eckersley, W. (17) 1949/50 Blackburn R

Edwards, D. (18) 1954/5 Manchester U

Ehiogu, U. (4) 1995/6 Aston Villa, Middlesbrough

Ellerington, W. (2) 1948/9 Southampton

Elliott, W. H. (5) 1951/2 Burnley

Fantham, J. (1) 1961/2 Sheffield W

Fashanu, J. (2) 1988/9 Wimbledon

Fenwick, T. (20) 1983/4 QPR, Tottenham H

Ferdinand, L. (17) 1992/3 QPR, Newcastle U, Tottenham H

Ferdinand, R. G. (27) 1997/8 West Ham U, Leeds U

Finney, T. (76) 1946/7 Preston NE

Flowers, R. (49) 1954/5 Wolverhampton W

Flowers, T. (11) 1992/3 Southampton, Blackburn R

Foster, S. (3) 1981/2 Brighton

Foulkes, W. (1) 1954/5 Manchester U

Fowler, R. B. (26) 1995/6 Liverpool, Leeds U

Francis, G. (12) 1974/5 QPR

Francis, T. (52) 1976/7 Birmingham C, Nottingham F, Manchester C, Sampdoria

Franklin, N. (27) 1946/7 Stoke C

Froggatt, J. (13) 1949/50 Portsmouth

Froggatt, R. (4) 1952/3 Sheffield W

Garrett, T. (3) 1951/2 Blackpool

Gascoigne, P. J. (57) 1988/9 Tottenham H, Lazio, Rangers, Middlesbrough

Gates, E. (2) 1980/1 Ipswich T

George, F. C. (1) 1976/7 Derby Co

Gerrard, S. G. (10) 1999/00 Liverpool

Gidman, J. (1) 1976/7 Aston Villa

Gillard, I. (3) 1974/5 QPR

Goddard, P. (1) 1981/2 West Ham U

Grainger, C. (7) 1955/6 Sheffield U, Sunderland

Gray, A. A. (1) 1991/2 Crystal P
Gray, M. (3) 1998/9 Sunderland
Greaves, J. (57) 1958/9 Chelsea, Tottenham H
Greenhoff, B. (18) 1975/6 Manchester U
Gregory, J. (6) 1982/3 QPR
Guppy, S. (1) 1999/00 Leicester C

Hagan, J. (1) 1948/9 Sheffield U
Haines, J. (1) 1948/9 WBA
Hall, J. (17) 1955/6 Birmingham C
Hancocks, J. (3) 1948/9 Wolverhampton W
Hardwick, G. (13) 1946/7 Middlesbrough
Harford, M. G. (2) 1987/8 Luton T
Hargreaves, O. (8) 2001/02 Bayern Munich
Harris, G. (1) 1965/6 Burnley
Harris, P. (2) 1949/50 Portsmouth
Harvey, C. (1) 1970/1 Everton
Hassall, H. (5) 1950/1 Huddersfield T, Bolton W
Hateley, M. (32) 1983/4 Portsmouth, AC Milan, Monaco, Rangers
Haynes, J. (56) 1954/5 Fulham
Hector, K. (2) 1973/4 Derby Co
Hellawell, M. (2) 1962/3 Birmingham C
Hendrie, L. A. (1) 1998/9 Aston Villa
Henry, R. (1) 1962/3 Tottenham H
Heskey, E. W. (29) 1998/9 Leicester C, Liverpool
Hill, F. (2) 1962/3 Bolton W
Hill, G. (6) 1975/6 Manchester U
Hill, R. (3) 1982/3 Luton T
Hinchcliffe, A. G. (7) 1996/7 Everton, Sheffield W
Hinton, A. (3) 1962/3 Wolverhampton W, Nottingham F
Hirst, D. E. (3) 1990/1 Sheffield W
Hitchens, G. (7) 1960/1 Aston Villa, Internazionale
Hoddle, G. (53) 1979/80 Tottenham H, Monaco
Hodge, S. B. (24) 1985/6 Aston Villa, Tottenham H, Nottingham F
Hodgkinson, A. (5) 1956/7 Sheffield U
Holden, D. (5) 1958/9 Bolton W
Holliday, E. (3) 1959/60 Middlesbrough
Hollins, J. (1) 1966/7 Chelsea
Hopkinson, E. (14) 1957/8 Bolton W
Howe, D. (23) 1957/8 WBA
Howe, J. (3) 1947/8 Derby Co
Howey, S. N. (4) 1994/5 Newcastle U
Hudson, A. (2) 1974/5 Stoke C
Hughes, E. (62) 1969/70 Liverpool, Wolverhampton W

Hughes, L. (3) 1949/50 Liverpool
Hunt, R. (34) 1961/2 Liverpool
Hunt, S. (2) 1983/4 WBA
Hunter, N. (28) 1965/6 Leeds U
Hurst, G. (49) 1965/6 West Ham U

Ince, P. (53) 1992/3 Manchester U, Internazionale, Liverpool, Middlesbrough

James, D. B. (9) 1996/7 Liverpool, Aston Villa, West Ham U
Jezzard, B. (2) 1953/4 Fulham
Johnson, D. (8) 1974/5 Ipswich T, Liverpool
Johnson, S. A. M. (1) 2000/01 Derby Co
Johnston, H. (10) 1946/7 Blackpool
Jones, M. (3) 1964/5 Sheffield U, Leeds U
Jones, R. (8) 1991/2 Liverpool
Jones, W. H. (2) 1949/50 Liverpool

Kay, A. (1) 1962/3 Everton
Keegan, K. (63) 1972/3 Liverpool, SV Hamburg, Southampton
Kennedy, A. (2) 1983/4 Liverpool
Kennedy, R. (17) 1975/6 Liverpool
Keown, M. R. (43) 1991/2 Everton, Arsenal
Kevan, D. (14) 1956/7 WBA
Kidd, B. (2) 1969/70 Manchester U
King, L. B. (1) 2001/02 Tottenham H
Knowles, C. (4) 1967/8 Tottenham H

Labone, B. (26) 1962/3 Everton
Lampard, F. J. (7) 1999/00 West Ham U, Chelsea
Lampard, F. R. G. (2) 1972/3 West Ham U
Langley, J. (3) 1957/8 Fulham
Langton, R. (11) 1946/7 Blackburn R, Preston NE, Bolton W
Latchford, R. (12) 1977/8 Everton
Lawler, C. (4) 1970/1 Liverpool
Lawton, T. (15) 1946/7 Chelsea, Notts Co
Lee, F. (27) 1968/9 Manchester C
Lee, J. (1) 1950/1 Derby C
Lee, R. M. (21) 1994/5 Newcastle U
Lee, S. (14) 1982/3 Liverpool
Le Saux, G. P. (36) 1993/4 Blackburn R, Chelsea
Le Tissier, M. P. (8) 1993/4 Southampton
Lindsay, A. (4) 1973/4 Liverpool
Lineker, G. (80) 1983/4 Leicester C, Everton, Barcelona, Tottenham H
Little, B. (1) 1974/5 Aston Villa
Lloyd, L. (4) 1970/1 Liverpool, Nottingham F

Lofthouse, N. (33) 1950/1 Bolton W
Lowe, E. (3) 1946/7 Aston Villa

Mabbutt, G. (16) 1982/3 Tottenham H
Macdonald, M. (14) 1971/2 Newcastle U, Arsenal
Madeley, P. (24) 1970/1 Leeds U
Mannion, W. (26) 1946/7 Middlesbrough
Mariner, P. (35) 1976/7 Ipswich T, Arsenal
Marsh, R. (9) 1971/2 QPR, Manchester C
Martin, A. (17) 1980/1 West Ham U
Martyn, A. N. (23) 1991/2 Crystal P, Leeds U
Marwood, B. (1) 1988/9 Arsenal
Matthews, R. (5) 1955/6 Coventry C
Matthews, S. (37) 1946/7 Stoke C, Blackpool
McCann, G. P. (1) 2000/01 Sunderland
McDermott, T. (25) 1977/8 Liverpool
McDonald, C. (8) 1957/8 Burnley
McFarland, R. (28) 1970/1 Derby C
McGarry, W. (4) 1953/4 Huddersfield T
McGuinness, W. (2) 1958/9 Manchester U
McMahon, S. (17) 1987/8 Liverpool
McManaman, S. (37) 1994/5 Liverpool, Real Madrid
McNab, R. (4) 1968/9 Arsenal
McNeil, M. (9) 1960/1 Middlesbrough
Meadows, J. (1) 1954/5 Manchester C
Medley, L. 1950/1 Tottenham H
Melia, J. (2) 1962/3 Liverpool
Merrick, G. (23) 1951/2 Birmingham C
Merson, P. C. (21) 1991/2 Arsenal, Middlesbrough, Aston Villa
Metcalfe, V. (2) 1950/1 Huddersfield T
Milburn, J. (13) 1948/9 Newcastle U
Miller, B. (1) 1960/1 Burnley
Mills, D. J. (12) 2000/01 Leeds U
Mills, M. (42) 1972/3 Ipswich T
Milne, G. (14) 1962/3 Liverpool
Milton, C. A. (1) 1951/2 Arsenal
Moore, R. (108) 1961/2 West Ham U
Morley, A. (6) 1981/2 Aston Villa
Morris, J. (3) 1948/9 Derby Co
Mortensen, S. (25) 1946/7 Blackpool
Mozley, B. (3) 1949/50 Derby Co
Mullen, J. (12) 1946/7 Wolverhampton W
Mullery, A. (35) 1964/5 Tottenham H
Murphy, D. B. (4) 2001/02 Liverpool

Neal, P. (50) 1975/6 Liverpool
Neville, G. A. (52) 1994/5 Manchester U
Neville, P. J. (37) 1995/6 Manchester U

Newton, K. (27) 1965/6 Blackburn R, Everton
Nicholls, J. (2) 1953/4 WBA
Nicholson, W. (1) 1950/1 Tottenham H
Nish, D. (5) 1972/3 Derby Co
Norman, M. (23) 1961/2 Tottenham H

O'Grady, M. (2) 1962/3 Huddersfield T, Leeds U
Osgood, P. (4) 1969/70 Chelsea
Osman, R. (11) 1979/80 Ipswich T
Owen, M. J. (41) 1997/8 Liverpool
Owen, S. (3) 1953/4 Luton T

Paine, T. (19) 1962/3 Southampton
Pallister, G. (22) 1987/8 Middlesbrough, Manchester U
Palmer, C. L. (18) 1991/2 Sheffield W
Parker, P. A. (19) 1988/9 QPR, Manchester U
Parkes, P. (1) 1973/4 QPR
Parlour, R. (10) 1998/9 Arsenal
Parry, R. (2) 1959/60 Bolton W
Peacock, A. (6) 1961/2 Middlesbrough, Leeds U
Pearce, S. (78) 1986/7 Nottingham F, West Ham U
Pearson, Stan (8) 1947/8 Manchester U
Pearson, Stuart (15) 1975/6 Manchester U
Pegg, D. (1) 1956/7 Manchester U
Pejic, M. (4) 1973/4 Stoke C
Perry, W. (3) 1955/6 Blackpool
Perryman, S. (1) 1981/2 Tottenham H
Peters, M. (67) 1965/6 West Ham U, Tottenham H
Phelan, M. C. (1) 1989/90 Manchester U
Phillips, K (8) 1998/9 Sunderland
Phillips, L. (3) 1951/2 Portsmouth
Pickering, F. (3) 1963/4 Everton
Pickering, N. (1) 1982/3 Sunderland
Pilkington, B. (1) 1954/5 Burnley
Platt, D. (62) 1989/90 Aston Villa, Bari, Juventus, Sampdoria, Arsenal
Pointer, R. (3) 1961/2 Burnley
Powell, C. G. (5) 2000/01 Charlton Ath
Pye, J. (1) 1949/50 Wolverhampton W

Quixall, A. (5) 1953/4 Sheffield W

Radford, J. (2) 1968/9 Arsenal
Ramsey, A. (32) 1948/9 Southampton, Tottenham H
Reaney, P. (3) 1968/9 Leeds U
Redknapp, J. F. (17) 1995/6 Liverpool
Reeves, K. (2) 1979/80 Norwich C
Regis, C. (5) 1981/2 WBA, Coventry C
Reid, P. (13) 1984/5 Everton
Revie, D. (6) 1954/5 Manchester C

Richards, J. (1) 1972/3 Wolverhampton W
Richardson, K. (1) 1993/4 Aston Villa
Rickaby, S. (1) 1953/4 WBA
Ricketts, M. B. (1) 2001/02 Bolton W
Rimmer, J. (1) 1975/6 Arsenal
Ripley, S. E. (2) 1993/4 Blackburn R
Rix, G. (17) 1980/1 Arsenal
Robb, G. (1) 1953/4 Tottenham H
Roberts, G. (6) 1982/3 Tottenham H
Robson, B. (90) 1979/80 WBA, Manchester U
Robson, R. (20) 1957/8 WBA
Rocastle, D. (14) 1988/9 Arsenal
Rowley, J. (6) 1948/9 Manchester U
Royle, J. (6) 1970/1 Everton, Manchester C
Ruddock, N. (1) 1994/5 Liverpool

Sadler, D. (4) 1967/8 Manchester U
Salako, J. A. (5) 1990/1 Crystal P
Sansom, K. (86) 1978/9 Crystal P, Arsenal
Scales, J. R. (3) 1994/5 Liverpool
Scholes, P. (49) 1996/7 Manchester U
Scott, L. (17) 1946/7 Arsenal
Seaman, D. A. (73) 1988/9 QPR, Arsenal
Sewell, J. (6) 1951/2 Sheffield W
Shackleton, L. (5) 1948/9 Sunderland
Sharpe, L. S. (8) 1990/1 Manchester U
Shaw, G. (5) 1958/9 Sheffield U
Shearer, A. (63) 1991/2 Southampton, Blackburn R, Newcastle U
Shellito, K. (1) 1962/3 Chelsea
Sheringham, E. (51) 1992/3 Tottenham H, Manchester U, Tottenham H
Sherwood, T. A. (3) 1998/9 Tottenham H
Shilton, P. (125) 1970/1 Leicester C, Stoke C, Nottingham F, Southampton, Derby Co
Shimwell, E. (1) 1948/9 Blackpool
Sillett, P. (3) 1954/5 Chelsea
Sinclair, T. (9) 2001/02 West Ham U
Sinton, A. (12) 1991/2 QPR, Sheffield W
Slater, W. (12) 1954/5 Wolverhampton W
Smith, A. (3) 2000/01 Leeds U
Smith, A. M. (13) 1988/9 Arsenal
Smith, L. (5) 1950/1 Arsenal
Smith, R. (15) 1960/1 Tottenham H
Smith, Tom (1) 1970/1 Liverpool
Smith, Trevor (2) 1959/60 Birmingham C
Southgate, G. (49) 1995/6 Aston Villa, Middlesbrough
Spink, N. (1) 1982/3 Aston Villa
Springett, R. (33) 1959/60 Sheffield W

Staniforth, R. (8) 1953/4 Huddersfield T
Statham, D. (3) 1982/3 WBA
Stein, B. (1) 1983/4 Luton T
Stepney, A. (1) 1967/8 Manchester U
Sterland, M. (1) 1988/9 Sheffield W
Steven, T. M. (36) 1984/5 Everton, Rangers, Marseille
Stevens, G. A. (7) 1984/5 Tottenham H
Stevens, M. G. (46) 1984/5 Everton, Rangers
Stewart, P. A. (3) 1991/2 Tottenham H
Stiles, N. (28) 1964/5 Manchester U
Stone, S. B. (9) 1995/6 Nottingham F
Storey-Moore, I. (1) 1969/70 Nottingham F
Storey, P. (19) 1970/1 Arsenal
Streten, B. (1) 1949/50 Luton T
Summerbee, M. (8) 1967/8 Manchester C
Sunderland, A. (1) 1979/80 Arsenal
Sutton, C. R. (1) 1997/8 Blackburn R
Swan, P. (19) 1959/60 Sheffield W
Swift, F. (19) 1946/7 Manchester C

Talbot, B. (6) 1976/7 Ipswich T
Tambling, R. (3) 1962/3 Chelsea
Taylor, E. (1) 1953/4 Blackpool
Taylor, J. (2) 1950/1 Fulham
Taylor, P. H. (3) 1947/8 Liverpool
Taylor, P. J. (4) 1975/6 Crystal P
Taylor, T. (19) 1952/3 Manchester U
Temple, D. (1) 1964/5 Everton
Thomas, Danny (2) 1982/3 Coventry C
Thomas, Dave (8) 1974/5 QPR
Thomas, G. R. (9) 1990/1 Crystal P
Thomas, M. L. (2) 1988/9 Arsenal
Thompson, P. (16) 1963/4 Liverpool
Thompson, P. B. (42) 1975/6 Liverpool
Thompson, T. (2) 1951/2 Aston Villa, Preston NE
Thomson, R. (8) 1963/4 Wolverhampton W
Todd, C. (27) 1971/2 Derby Co
Towers, T. (3) 1975/6 Sunderland
Tueart, D. (6) 1974/5 Manchester C

Ufton, D. (1) 1953/4 Charlton Ath
Unsworth, D. G. (1) 1994/5 Everton

Vassell, D. (8) 2001/02 Aston Villa
Venables, T. (2) 1964/5 Chelsea
Venison, B. (2) 1994/5 Newcastle U
Viljoen, C. (2) 1974/5 Ipswich T
Viollet, D. (2) 1959/60 Manchester U

Waddle, C. R. (62) 1984/5 Newcastle U, Tottenham H, Marseille
Waiters, A. (5) 1963/4 Blackpool
Walker, D. S. (59) 1988/9 Nottingham F, Sampdoria, Sheffield W

Walker, I. M. (3) 1995/6 Tottenham H
Wallace, D. L. (1) 1985/6 Southampton
Walsh, P. (5) 1982/3 Luton T
Walters, K. M. (1) 1990/1 Rangers
Ward, P. (1) 1979/80 Brighton
Ward, T. (2) 1947/8 Derby C
Watson, D. (12) 1983/4 Norwich C,
  Everton
Watson, D. V. (65) 1973/4 Sunderland,
  Manchester C, Southampton,
  Werder Bremen, Southampton,
  Stoke C
Watson, W. (4) 1949/50 Sunderland
Webb, N. (26) 1987/8 Nottingham F,
  Manchester U
Weller, K. (4) 1973/4 Leicester C
West, G. (3) 1968/9 Everton
Wheeler, J. (1) 1954/5 Bolton W
White, D. (1) 1992/3 Manchester C
Whitworth, S. (7) 1974/5 Leicester C
Whymark, T. (1) 1977/8 Ipswich T
Wignall, F. (2) 1964/5 Nottingham F
Wilcox, J. M. (3) 1995/6 Blackburn R,
  Leeds U
Wilkins, R. (84) 1975/6 Chelsea,
  Manchester U, AC Milan
Williams, B. (24) 1948/9
  Wolverhampton W

Williams, S. (6) 1982/3 Southampton
Willis, A. (1) 1951/2 Tottenham H
Wilshaw, D. (12) 1953/4
  Wolverhampton W
Wilson, R. (63) 1959/60 Huddersfield
  T, Everton
Winterburn, N. (2) 1989/90 Arsenal
Wise, D. F. (21) 1990/1 Chelsea
Withe, P. (11) 1980/1 Aston Villa
Wood, R. (3) 1954/5 Manchester U
Woodcock, A. (42) 1977/8 Nottingham
  F, FC Cologne, Arsenal
Woodgate, J. S. (1) 1998/9 Leeds U
Woods, C. C. E. (43) 1984/5 Norwich
  C, Rangers, Sheffield W
Worthington, F. (8) 1973/4 Leicester C
Wright, I. E. (33) 1990/1 Crystal P,
  Arsenal, West Ham U
Wright, M. (45) 1983/4 Southampton,
  Derby C, Liverpool
Wright, R. I. (2) 1999/00 Ipswich T,
  Arsenal
Wright, T. (11) 1967/8 Everton
Wright, W. (105) 1946/7
  Wolverhampton W

Young, G. (1) 1964/5 Sheffield W

NORTHERN IRELAND

Aherne, T. (4) 1946/7 Belfast Celtic,
  Luton T
Anderson, T. (22) 1972/3 Manchester
  U, Swindon T, Peterborough U
Armstrong, G. (63) 1976/7 Tottenham
  H, Watford, Real Mallorca, WBA,
  Chesterfield
Barr, H. (3) 1961/2 Linfield, Coventry
  C
Best, G. (37) 1963/4 Manchester U,
  Fulham
Bingham, W. (56) 1950/1 Sunderland,
  Luton T, Everton, Port Vale
Black, K. (30) 1987/8 Luton T,
  Nottingham F
Blair, R. (5) 1974/5 Oldham Ath
Blanchflower, D. (54) 1949/50
  Barnsley, Aston Villa, Tottenham H
Blanchflower, J. (12) 1953/4
  Manchester U
Bowler, G. (3) 1949/50 Hull C
Braithwaite, R. (10) 1961/2 Linfield,
  Middlesbrough
Brennan, R. (5) 1948/9 Luton T,
  Birmingham C, Fulham
Briggs, R. (2) 1961/2 Manchester U,
  Swansea

Brotherston, N. (27) 1979/80
  Blackburn R
Bruce, W. (2) 1960/1 Glentoran

Campbell, A. (2) 1962/3 Crusaders
Campbell, D. A. (10) 1985/6
  Nottingham F, Charlton Ath
Campbell, J. (2) 1950/1 Fulham
Campbell, R. M. (2) 1981/2 Bradford C
Campbell, W. (6) 1967/8 Dundee
Carey, J. (7) 1946/7 Manchester U
Carroll, R. E. (11) 1996/7 Wigan Ath,
  Manchester U
Casey, T. (12) 1954/5 Newcastle U,
  Portsmouth
Caskey, A. (7) 1978/9 Derby C, Tulsa
  Roughnecks
Cassidy, T. (24) 1970/1 Newcastle U,
  Burnley
Caughey, M. (2) 1985/6 Linfield
Clarke, C. J. (38) 1985/6
  Bournemouth, Southampton,
  Portsmouth
Cleary, J. (5) 1981/2 Glentoran
Clements, D. (48) 1964/5 Coventry C,
  Sheffield W, Everton, New York
  Cosmos
Cochrane, D. (10) 1946/7 Leeds U

Cochrane, T. (26) 1975/6 Coleraine, Burnley, Middlesbrough, Gillingham
Coote, A. (6) 1998/9 Norwich C
Cowan, J. (1) 1969/70 Newcastle U
Coyle, F. (4) 1955/6 Coleraine, Nottingham F
Coyle, L. (1) 1988/9 Derry C
Coyle, R. (5) 1972/3 Sheffield W
Craig, D. (25) 1966/7 Newcastle U
Crossan, E. (3) 1949/50 Blackburn R
Crossan, J. (23) 1959/60 Sparta Rotterdam, Sunderland, Manchester C, Middlesbrough
Cunningham, W. (30) 1950/1 St Mirren, Leicester C, Dunfermline Ath
Cush, W. (26) 1950/1 Glentoran, Leeds U, Portadown

D'Arcy, S. (5) 1951/2 Chelsea, Brentford
Davison, A. J. (3) 1995/6 Bolton W, Bradford C, Grimsby T
Dennison, R. (18) 1987/8 Wolverhampton W
Devine, J. (1) 1989/90 Glentoran
Dickson, D. (4) 1969/70 Coleraine
Dickson, T. (1) 1956/7 Linfield
Dickson, W. (12) 1950/1 Chelsea, Arsenal
Doherty, L. (2) 1984/5 Linfield
Doherty, P. (6) 1946/7 Derby Co, Huddersfield T, Doncaster R
Donaghy, M. (91) 1979/80 Luton T, Manchester U, Chelsea
Dougan, D. (43) 1957/8 Portsmouth, Blackburn R, Aston Villa, Leicester C, Wolverhampton W
Douglas, J. P. (1) 1946/7 Belfast Celtic
Dowd, H. (3) 1972/3 Glentoran, Sheffield W
Dowie, I. (59) 1989/90 Luton T, Southampton, Crystal P, West Ham, QPR
Duff, M. J. (1) 2001/02 Cheltenham T
Dunlop, G. (4) 1984/5 Linfield

Eglington, T. (6) 1946/7 Everton
Elder, A. (40) 1959/60 Burnley, Stoke C
Elliott, S. (13) 2000/01 Motherwell

Farrell, P. (7) 1946/7 Everton
Feeney, J. (2) 1946/7 Linfield, Swansea C
Feeney, W. (1) 1975/6 Glentoran
Feeney, W. J. (2) 2001/02 Bournemouth
Ferguson, G. (5) 1998/9 Linfield
Ferguson, W. (2) 1965/6 Linfield

Ferris, R. (3) 1949/50 Birmingham C
Fettis, A. (25) 1991/2 Hull C, Nottingham F, Blackburn R
Finney, T. (14) 1974/5 Sunderland, Cambridge U
Fleming, J. G. (31) 1986/7 Nottingham F, Manchester C, Barnsley
Forde, T. (4) 1958/9 Ards

Gallogly, C. (2) 1950/1 Huddersfield T
Garton, R. (1) 1968/9 Oxford U
Gillespie, K. R. (41) 1994/5 Manchester U, Newcastle U, Blackburn R
Gorman, W. (4) 1946/7 Brentford
Graham, W. (14) 1950/1 Doncaster R
Gray, P. (26) 1992/3 Luton T, Sunderland, Nancy, Luton T, Burnley, Oxford U
Gregg, H. (25) 1953/4 Doncaster R, Manchester U
Griffin, D. J. (22) 1995/6 St Johnstone, Dundee U

Hamill, R. (1) 1998/9 Glentoran
Hamilton, B. (50) 1968/9 Linfield, Ipswich T, Everton, Millwall, Swindon T
Hamilton, W. (41) 1977/8 QPR, Burnley, Oxford U
Harkin, T. (5) 1967/8 Southport, Shrewsbury T
Harvey, M. (34) 1960/1 Sunderland
Hatton, S. (2) 1962/3 Linfield
Healy, D. J. (18) 1999/00 Manchester U, Preston NE
Healy, P. J. (4) 1981/2 Coleraine, Glentoran
Hegan, D. (7) 1969/70 WBA, Wolverhampton W
Hill, C. F. (27) 1989/90 Sheffield U, Leicester C, Trelleborg, Northampton T
Hill, J. (7) 1958/9 Norwich C, Everton
Hinton, E. (7) 1946/7 Fulham, Millwall
Holmes, S. P. (1) 2001/02 Wrexham
Horlock, K. (29) 1994/5 Swindon T, Manchester C
Hughes, A. W. (24) 1997/8 Newcastle U
Hughes, M. E. (63) 1991/2 Manchester C, Strasbourg, West Ham U, Wimbledon
Hughes, P. (3) 1986/7 Bury
Hughes, W. (1) 1950/1 Bolton W
Humphries, W. (14) 1961/2 Ards, Coventry C, Swansea T
Hunter, A. (53) 1969/70 Blackburn R, Ipswich T
Hunter, B. V. (15) 1994/5 Wrexham, Reading

Irvine, R. (8) 1961/2 Linfield, Stoke C
Irvine, W. (23) 1962/3 Burnley, Preston NE, Brighton & HA

Jackson, T. (35) 1968/9 Everton, Nottingham F, Manchester U
Jamison, A. (1) 1975/6 Glentoran
Jenkins, I. (6) 1996/7 Chester C, Dundee U
Jennings, P. (119) 1963/4 Watford, Tottenham H, Arsenal, Tottenham H, Everton, Tottenham H
Johnson, D. M. (16) 1998/9 Blackburn R, Birmingham C
Johnston, W. (1) 1961/2 Glentoran, Oldham Ath
Jones, J. (3) 1955/6 Glenavon

Keane, T. (1) 1948/9 Swansea T
Kee, P. V. (9) 1989/90 Oxford U, Ards
Keith, R. (23) 1957/8 Newcastle U
Kelly, H. (4) 1949/50 Fulham, Southampton
Kelly, P. (1) 1949/50 Barnsley
Kennedy, P. H. (13) 1998/9 Watford, Wigan Ath
Kirk, A. (2) 1999/00 Heart of Midlothian

Lawther, I. (4) 1959/60 Sunderland, Blackburn R
Lennon, N. F. (40) 1993/4 Crewe Alexandra, Leicester C, Celtic
Lockhart, N. (8) 1946/7 Linfield, Coventry C, Aston Villa
Lomas, S. M. (40) 1993/4 Manchester C, West Ham U
Lutton, B. (6) 1969/70 Wolverhampton W, West Ham U

Magill, E. (26) 1961/2 Arsenal, Brighton & HA
Magilton, J. (52) 1990/1 Oxford U, Southampton, Sheffield U, Ipswich T
Martin, C. (6) 1946/7 Glentoran, Leeds U, Aston Villa
McAdams, W. (15) 1953/4 Manchester C, Bolton W, Leeds U
McAlinden, J. (2) 1946/7 Portsmouth, Southend U
McBride, S. (4) 1990/1 Glenavon
McCabe, J. (6) 1948/9 Leeds U
McCann, G. S. (3) 2001/02 West Ham U
McCarthy, J. D. (18) 1995/6 Port Vale, Birmingham C
McCartney, G. S. (5) 2001/02 Sunderland
McCavana, T. (3) 1954/5 Coleraine
McCleary, J. W. (1) 1954/5 Cliftonville
McClelland, J. (6) 1960/1 Arsenal, Fulham

McClelland, J. (53) 1979/80 Mansfield T, Rangers, Watford, Leeds U
McCourt, F. (6) 1951/2 Manchester C
McCourt, P. J. (1) 2001/02 Rochdale
McCoy, R. (1) 1986/7 Coleraine
McCreery, D. (67) 1975/6 Manchester U, QPR, Tulsa Roughnecks, Newcastle U, Heart of Midlothian
McCrory, S. (1) 1957/8 Southend U
McCullough, W. (10) 1960/1 Arsenal, Millwall
McCurdy, C. (1) 1979/80 Linfield
McDonald, A. (52) 1985/6 QPR
McElhinney, G. (6) 1983/4 Bolton W
McEvilly, L. R. (1) 2001/02 Rochdale
McFaul, I. (6) 1966/7 Linfield, Newcastle U
McGarry, J. K. (3) 1950/1 Cliftonville
McGaughey, M. (1) 1984/5 Linfield
McGibbon, P. C. G. (7) 1994/5 Manchester U, Wigan Ath
McGrath, R. (21) 1973/4 Tottenham H, Manchester U
McIlroy, J. (55) 1951/2 Burnley, Stoke C
McIlroy, S. B. (88) 1971/2 Manchester U, Stoke C, Manchester C
McKeag, W. (2) 1967/8 Glentoran
McKenna, J. (7) 1949/50 Huddersfield T
McKenzie, R. (1) 1966/7 Airdrieonians
McKinney, W. (1) 1965/6 Falkirk
McKnight, A. (10) 1987/8 Celtic, West Ham U
McLaughlin, J. (12) 1961/2 Shrewsbury T, Swansea T
McMahon, G. J. (17) 1994/5 Tottenham H, Stoke C
McMichael, A. (39) 1949/50 Newcastle U
McMillan, S. (2) 1962/3 Manchester U
McMordie, E. (21) 1968/9 Middlesbrough
McMorran, E. (15) 1946/7 Belfast Celtic, Barnsley, Doncaster R
McNally, B. A. (5) 1985/6 Shrewsbury T
McParland, P. (34) 1953/4 Aston Villa, Wolverhampton W
McVeigh, P. (3) 1998/9 Tottenham H, Norwich C
Montgomery, F. J. (1) 1954/5 Coleraine
Moore, C. (1) 1948/9 Glentoran
Moreland, V. (6) 1978/9 Derby Co
Morgan, S. (18) 1971/2 Port Vale, Aston Villa, Brighton & HA, Sparta Rotterdam
Morrow, S. J. (39) 1989/90 Arsenal, QPR
Mullan, G. (4) 1982/3 Glentoran

Mulryne, P. P. (16) 1996/7 Manchester U, Norwich C
Murdock, C. J. (14) 1999/00 Preston NE

Napier, R. (1) 1965/6 Bolton W
Neill, T. (59) 1960/1 Arsenal, Hull C
Nelson, S. (51) 1969/70 Arsenal, Brighton & HA
Nicholl, C. (51) 1974/5 Aston Villa, Southampton, Grimsby T
Nicholl, J. M. (73) 1975/6 Manchester U, Toronto Blizzard, Sunderland, Rangers, WBA
Nicholson, J. (41) 1960/1 Manchester U, Huddersfield T
Nolan, I. R. (18) 1996/7 Sheffield W, Bradford C, Wigan Ath

O'Boyle, G. (13) 1993/4 Dunfermline Ath, St Johnstone
O'Doherty, A. (2) 1969/70 Coleraine
O'Driscoll, J. (3) 1948/9 Swansea T
O'Kane, L. (20) 1969/70 Nottingham F
O'Neill, C. (3) 1988/9 Motherwell
O'Neill, H. M. (64) 1971/2 Distillery, Nottingham F, Norwich C, Manchester C, Norwich C, Notts Co
O'Neill, J. (1) 1961/2 Sunderland
O'Neill, J. (39) 1979/80 Leicester C
O'Neill, M. A. (31) 1987/8 Newcastle U, Dundee U, Hibernian, Coventry C

Parke, J. (13) 1963/4 Linfield, Hibernian, Sunderland
Patterson, D. J. (17) 1993/4 Crystal P, Luton T, Dundee U
Peacock, R. (31) 1951/2 Celtic, Coleraine
Penney, S. (17) 1984/5 Brighton & HA
Platt, J. A. (23) 1975/6 Middlesbrough, Ballymena U, Coleraine

Quinn, J. M. (46) 1984/5 Blackburn R, Leicester, Bradford C, West Ham U, Bournemouth, Reading
Quinn, S. J. (25) 1995/6 Blackpool, WBA

Rafferty, P. (1) 1979/80 Linfield
Ramsey, P. (14) 1983/4 Leicester C
Rice, P. (49) 1968/9 Arsenal
Robinson, S. (5) 1996/7 Bournemouth
Rogan, A. (18) 1987/8 Celtic, Sunderland, Millwall
Ross, E. (1) 1968/9 Newcastle U
Rowland, K. (19) 1994/5 West Ham U
Russell, A. (1) 1946/7 Linfield
Ryan, R. (1) 1949/50 WBA

Sanchez, L. P. (3) 1986/7 Wimbledon

Scott, J. (2) 1957/8 Grimsby T
Scott, P. (10) 1974/5 Everton, York C, Aldershot
Sharkey, P. (1) 1975/6 Ipswich T
Shields, J. (1) 1956/7 Southampton
Simpson, W. (12) 1950/1 Rangers
Sloan, D. (2) 1968/9 Oxford
Sloan, T. (3) 1978/9 Manchester U
Sloan, W. (1) 1946/7 Arsenal
Smyth, S. (9) 1947/8 Wolverhampton W, Stoke C
Smyth, W. (4) 1948/9 Distillery
Sonner, D. J. (7) 1997/8 Ipswich T, Sheffield W, Birmingham C
Spence, D. (29) 1974/5 Bury, Blackpool, Southend U
Stevenson, A. (3) 1946/7 Everton
Stewart, A. (7) 1966/7 Glentoran, Derby
Stewart, D. (1) 1977/8 Hull C
Stewart, I. (31) 1981/2 QPR, Newcastle U
Stewart, T. (1) 1960/1 Linfield

Taggart, G. P. (50) 1989/90 Barnsley, Bolton W, Leicester C
Taylor, M. S. (21) 1998/9 Fulham
Todd, S. (11) 1965/6 Burnley, Sheffield W
Trainor, D. (1) 1966/7 Crusaders
Tully, C. (10) 1948/9 Celtic

Uprichard, N. (18) 1951/2 Swindon T, Portsmouth

Vernon, J. (17) 1946/7 Belfast Celtic, WBA

Walker, J. (1) 1954/5 Doncaster R
Walsh, D. (9) 1946/7 WBA
Walsh, W. (5) 1947/8 Manchester C
Watson, P. (1) 1970/1 Distillery
Welsh, S. (4) 1965/6 Carlisle U
Whiteside, N. (38) 1981/2 Manchester U, Everton
Whitley, Jeff (7) 1996/7 Manchester C
Whitley, Jim (3) 1997/8 Manchester C
Williams, M. S. (19) 1998/9 Chesterfield, Watford, Wimbledon
Williams, P. (1) 1990/1 WBA
Wilson, D. J. (24) 1986/7 Brighton & HA, Luton, Sheffield W
Wilson, K. J. (42) 1986/7 Ipswich T, Chelsea, Notts C, Walsall
Wilson, S. (12) 1961/2 Glenavon, Falkirk, Dundee
Wood, T. J. (1) 1995/6 Walsall
Worthington, N. (66) 1983/4 Sheffield W, Leeds U, Stoke C
Wright, T. J. (31) 1988/9 Newcastle U, Nottingham F, Manchester C

SCOTLAND

Aird, J. (4) 1953/4 Burnley

Aitken, G. G. (8) 1948/9 East Fife, Sunderland

Aitken, R. (57) 1979/80 Celtic, Newcastle U, St Mirren

Albiston, A. (14) 1981/2 Manchester U

Alexander, G. (4) 2001/02 Preston NE

Allan, T. (2) 1973/4 Dundee

Anderson, J. (1) 1953/4 Leicester C

Archibald, S. (27) 1979/80 Aberdeen, Tottenham H, Barcelona

Auld, B. (3) 1958/9 Celtic

Baird, H. (1) 1955/6 Airdrieonians

Baird, S. (7) 1956/7 Rangers

Bannon, E. (11) 1979/80 Dundee U

Bauld, W. (3) 1949/50 Heart of Midlothian

Baxter, J. (34) 1960/1 Rangers, Sunderland

Bell, W. (2) 1965/6 Leeds U

Bernard, P. R. (2) 1994/5 Oldham Ath

Bett, J. (25) 1981/2 Rangers, Lokeren, Aberdeen

Black, E. (2) 1987/8 Metz

Black, I. (1) 1947/8 Southampton

Blacklaw, A. (3) 1962/3 Burnley

Blackley, J. (7) 1973/4 Hibernian

Blair, J. (1) 1946/7 Blackpool

Blyth, J. (2) 1977/8 Coventry C

Bone, J. (2) 1971/2 Norwich C

Booth, S. (21) 1992/3 Aberdeen, Borussia Dortmund, Twente

Bowman, D. (6) 1991/2 Dundee U

Boyd, T. (72) 1990/1 Motherwell, Chelsea, Celtic

Brand, R. (8) 1960/1 Rangers

Brazil, A. (13) 1979/80 Ipswich T, Tottenham H

Bremner, D. (1) 1975/6 Hibernian

Bremner, W. (54) 1964/5 Leeds U

Brennan, F. (7) 1946/7 Newcastle U

Brogan, J. (4) 1970/1 Celtic

Brown, A. (14) 1949/50 East Fife, Blackpool

Brown, H. (3) 1946/7 Partick Thistle

Brown, J. (1) 1974/5 Sheffield U

Brown, R. (3) 1946/7 Rangers

Brown, W. (28) 1957/8 Dundee, Tottenham H

Brownlie, J. (7) 1970/1 Hibernian

Buchan, M. (34) 1971/2 Aberdeen, Manchester U

Buckley, P. (3) 1953/4 Aberdeen

Burchill, M. J. (6) 1999/00 Celtic

Burley, C. W. (45) 1994/5 Chelsea, Celtic, Derby Co

Burley, G. (11) 1978/9 Ipswich T

Burns, F. (1) 1969/70 Manchester U

Burns, K. (20) 1973/4 Birmingham C, Nottingham F

Burns, T. (8) 1980/1 Celtic

Calderwood, C. (36) 1994/5 Tottenham H, Aston Villa

Caldow, E. (40) 1956/7 Rangers

Caldwell, G. (4) 2001/02 Newcastle U

Caldwell, S. (1) 2000/01 Newcastle U

Callaghan, W. (2) 1969/70 Dunfermline

Cameron, C. (15) 1998/9 Heart of Midlothian, Wolverhampton W

Campbell, R. (5) 1946/7 Falkirk, Chelsea

Campbell, W. (5) 1946/7 Morton

Carr, W. (6) 1969/70 Coventry C

Chalmers, S. (5) 1964/5 Celtic

Clark, J. (4) 1965/6 Celtic

Clark, R. (17) 1967/8 Aberdeen

Clarke, S. (6) 1987/8 Chelsea

Collins, J. (58) 1987/8 Hibernian, Celtic, Monaco, Everton

Collins, R. (31) 1950/1 Celtic, Everton, Leeds U

Colquhoun, E. (9) 1971/2 Sheffield U

Colquhoun, J. (1) 1987/8 Heart of Midlothian

Combe, R. (3) 1947/8 Hibernian

Conn, A. (1) 1955/6 Heart of Midlothian

Conn, A. (2) 1974/5 Tottenham H

Connachan, E. (2) 1961/2 Dunfermline Ath

Connelly, G. (2) 1973/4 Celtic

Connolly, J. (1) 1972/3 Everton

Connor, R. (4) 1985/6 Dundee, Aberdeen

Cooke, C. (16) 1965/6 Dundee, Chelsea

Cooper, D. (22) 1979/80 Rangers, Motherwell

Cormack, P. (9) 1965/6 Hibernian, Nottingham F

Cowan, J. (25) 1947/8 Morton, Motherwell

Cowie, D. (20) 1952/3 Dundee

Cox, C. (1) 1947/8 Heart of Midlothian

Cox, S. (24) 1947/8 Rangers

Craig, J. (1) 1976/7 Celtic

Craig, J. P. (1) 1967/8 Celtic

Craig, T. (1) 1975/6 Newcastle U

Crainey, S. (2) 2001/02 Celtic

Crawford, S. (1) 1994/5 Raith R, Dunfermline Ath

Crerand, P. (16) 1960/1 Celtic, Manchester U

Cropley, A. (2) 1971/2 Hibernian
Cruickshank, J. (6) 1963/4 Heart of
  Midlothian
Cullen, M. (1) 1955/6 Luton T
Cumming, J. (9) 1954/5 Heart of
  Midlothian
Cummings. W. (1) 2001/02 Chelsea
Cunningham, W. (8) 1953/4 Preston
  NE
Curran, H. (5) 1969/70
  Wolverhampton W

Dailly, C. (35) 1996/7 Derby Co,
  Blackburn R, West Ham U
Dalglish, K. (102) 1971/2 Celtic,
  Liverpool
Davidson, C. I. (15) 1998/9 Blackburn
  R, Leicester C
Davidson, J. (8) 1953/4 Partick Thistle
Dawson, A. (5) 1979/80 Rangers
Deans, D. (2) 1974/5 Celtic
Delaney, J. (4) 1946/7 Manchester U
Dick, J. (1) 1958/9 West Ham U
Dickov, P. (3) 2000/01 Mancheser C
Dickson, W. (5) 1969/70 Kilmarnock
Docherty, T. (25) 1951/2 Preston NE,
  Arsenal
Dobie, R. S. (3) 2001/02 WBA
Dodds, D. (2) 1983/4 Dundee U
Dodds, W. (26) 1996/7 Aberdeen,
  Dundee U, Rangers
Donachie, W. (35) 1971/2 Manchester
  C
Donnelly, S. (10) 1996/7 Celtic
Dougall, C. (1) 1946/7 Birmingham C
Dougan, R. (1) 1949/50 Heart of
  Midlothian
Douglas, R. (3) 2001/02 Celtic
Doyle, J. (1) 1975/6 Ayr U
Duncan, A. (6) 1974/5 Hibernian
Duncan, D. (3) 1947/8 East Fife
Duncanson, J. (1) 1946/7 Rangers
Durie, G. S. (43) 1987/8 Chelsea,
  Tottenham H, Rangers
Durrant, I. (20) 1987/8 Rangers,
  Kilmarnock

Elliott, M. S. (18) 1997/8 Leicester C
Evans, A. (4) 1981/2 Aston Villa
Evans, R. (48) 1948/9 Celtic, Chelsea
Ewing, T. (2) 1957/8 Partick Thistle

Farm, G. (10) 1952/3 Blackpool
Ferguson, B. (10) 1998/9 Rangers
Ferguson, Derek (2) 1987/8 Rangers
Ferguson, Duncan (7) 1991/2 Dundee
  U, Everton
Ferguson, I. (9) 1988/9 Rangers
Ferguson, R. (7) 1965/6 Kilmarnock
Fernie, W. (12) 1953/4 Celtic

Flavell, R. (2) 1946/7 Airdrieonians
Fleck, R. (4) 1989/90 Norwich C
Fleming, C. (1) 1953/4 East Fife
Forbes, A. (14) 1946/7 Sheffield U,
  Arsenal
Ford, D. (3) 1973/4 Heart of
  Midlothian
Forrest, J. (1) 1957/8 Motherwell
Forrest, J. (5) 1965/6 Rangers,
  Aberdeen
Forsyth, A. (10) 1971/2 Partick Thistle,
  Manchester U
Forsyth, C. (4) 1963/4 Kilmarnock
Forsyth, T. (22) 1970/1 Motherwell,
  Rangers
Fraser, D. (2) 1967/8 WBA
Fraser, W. (2) 1954/5 Sunderland
Freedman, D. A. (2) 2001/02 Crystal P

Gabriel, J. (2) 1960/1 Everton
Gallacher, K. W. (53) 1987/8 Dundee
  U, Coventry C, Blackburn R,
  Newcastle U
Gallacher, P. (1) 2001/02 Dundee U
Galloway, M. (1) 1991/2 Celtic
Gardiner, W. (1) 1957/8 Motherwell
Gemmell, T. (2) 1954/5 St Mirren
Gemmell, T. (18) 1965/6 Celtic
Gemmill, A. (43) 1970/1 Derby Co,
  Nottingham F, Birmingham C
Gemmill, S. (23) 1994/5 Nottingham F,
  Everton
Gibson, D. (7) 1962/3 Leicester C
Gillespie, G. T. (13) 1987/8 Liverpool,
  Celtic
Gilzean, A. (22) 1963/4 Dundee,
  Tottenham H
Glass, S. (1) 1998/9 Newcastle U
Glavin, R. (1) 1976/7 Celtic
Glen, A. (2) 1955/6 Aberdeen
Goram, A. L. (43) 1985/6 Oldham Ath,
  Hibernian, Rangers
Gough, C. R. (61) 1982/3 Dundee U,
  Tottenham H, Rangers
Gould, J. (2) 1999/00 Celtic
Govan, J. (6) 1947/8 Hibernian
Graham, A. (10) 1977/8 Leeds U
Graham, G. (12) 1971/2 Arsenal,
  Manchester U
Grant, J. (2) 1958/9 Hibernian
Grant, P. (2) 1988/9 Celtic
Gray, A. (20) 1975/6 Aston Villa,
  Wolverhampton W, Everton
Gray, E. (12) 1968/9 Leeds U
Gray F. (32) 1975/6 Leeds U,
  Nottingham F, Leeds U
Green, A. (6) 1970/1 Blackpool,
  Newcastle U
Greig, J. (44) 1963/4 Rangers
Gunn, B. (6) 1989/90 Norwich C

Haddock, H. (6) 1954/5 Clyde
Haffey, F. (2) 1959/60 Celtic
Hamilton, A. (24) 1961/2 Dundee
Hamilton, G. (5) 1946/7 Aberdeen
Hamilton, W. (1) 1964/5 Hibernian
Hansen, A. (26) 1978/9 Liverpool
Hansen, J. (2) 1971/2 Partick Thistle
Harper, J. (4) 1972/3 Aberdeen
Hartford, A. (50) 1971/2 WBA,
    Manchester C, Everton, Manchester
    C
Harvey, D. (16) 1972/3 Leeds U
Haughney, M. (1) 1953/4 Celtic
Hay, D. (27) 1969/70 Celtic
Hegarty, P. (8) 1978/9 Dundee U
Henderson, J. (7) 1952/3 Portsmouth,
    Arsenal
Henderson, W. (29) 1962/3 Rangers
Hendry, E. C. J. (51) 1992/3 Blackburn
    R, Rangers, Coventry C, Bolton W
Herd, D, (5) 1958/9 Arsenal
Herd, G. (5) 1957/8 Clyde
Herriot, J. (8) 1968/9 Birmingham C
Hewie, J. (19) 1955/6 Charlton Ath
Holt, D. D. (5) 1962/3 Heart of
    Midlothian
Holt, G. J. (3) 2000/01 Kilmarnock,
    Norwich C
Holton, J. (15) 1972/3 Manchester U
Hope, R. (2) 1967/8 WBA
Hopkin, D. (7) 1996/7 Crystal P, Leeds
    U
Houliston, W. (3) 1948/9 Queen of the
    South
Houston, S. (1) 1975/6 Manchester U
Howie, H. (1) 1948/9 Hibernian
Hughes, J. (8) 1964/5 Celtic
Hughes, W. (1) 1974/5 Sunderland
Humphries, W. (1) 1951/2 Motherwell
Hunter, A. (4) 1971/2 Kilmarnock,
    Celtic
Hunter, W. (3) 1959/60 Motherwell
Husband, J. (1) 1946/7 Partick Thistle
Hutchison, D. (19) 1998/9 Everton,
    Sunderland, West Ham U
Hutchison, T. (17) 1973/4 Coventry C

Imlach, S. (4) 1957/8 Nottingham F
Irvine, B. (9) 1990/1 Aberdeen

Jackson, C. (8) 1974/5 Rangers
Jackson, D. (28) 1994/5 Hibernian,
    Celtic
Jardine, A. (38) 1970/1 Rangers
Jarvie, A. (3) 1970/1 Airdrieonians
Jess, E. (18) 1992/3 Aberdeen,
    Coventry C, Aberdeen
Johnston, A. (16) 1998/9 Sunderland,
    Rangers, Middlesbrough
Johnston, M. (38) 1983/4 Watford,
    Celtic, Nantes, Rangers

Johnston, W. (22) 1965/6 Rangers,
    WBA
Johnstone, D. (14) 1972/3 Rangers
Johnstone, J. (23) 1964/5 Celtic
Johnstone, L. (2) 1947/8 Clyde
Johnstone, R. (17) 1950/1 Hibernian,
    Manchester C
Jordan, J. (52) 1972/3 Leeds U,
    Manchester U, AC Milan

Kelly, H. (1) 1951/2 Blackpool
Kelly, J. (2) 1948/9 Barnsley
Kennedy, J. (6) 1963/4 Celtic
Kennedy, S. (2) 1974/5 Rangers
Kennedy, S. (8) 1977/8 Aberdeen
Kerr, A. (2) 1954/5 Partick Thistle
Kyle, K. (3) 2001/02 Sunderland

Lambert, P. (30) 1994/5 Motherwell,
    Borussia Dortmund, Celtic
Law, D. (55) 1958/9 Huddersfield T,
    Manchester C, Torino, Manchester
    U, Manchester C
Lawrence, T. (3) 1962/3 Liverpool
Leggat, G. (18) 1955/6 Aberdeen,
    Fulham
Leighton, J. (91) 1982/3 Aberdeen,
    Manchester U, Hibernian,
    Aberdeen
Lennox, R. (10) 1966/7 Celtic
Leslie, L. (5) 1960/1 Airdrieonians
Levein, C. (16) 1989/90 Heart of
    Midlothian
Liddell, W. (28) 1946/7 Liverpool
Linwood, A. (1) 1949/50 Clyde
Little, A. (1) 1952/3 Rangers
Logie, J. (1) 1952/3 Arsenal
Long, H. (1) 1946/7 Clyde
Lorimer, P. (21) 1969/70 Leeds U

Macari, L. (24) 1971/2 Celtic,
    Manchester U
Macaulay, A. (7) 1946/7 Brentford,
    Arsenal
MacDougall, E. (7) 1974/5 Norwich C
Mackay, D. (22) 1956/7 Heart of
    Midlothian, Tottenham H
Mackay, G. (4) 1987/8 Heart of
    Midlothian
Malpas, M. (55) 1983/4 Dundee U
Marshall, G. (1) 1991/2 Celtic
Martin, B. (2) 1994/5 Motherwell
Martin, F. (6) 1953/4 Aberdeen
Martin, N. (3) 1964/5 Hibernian,
    Sunderland
Martis, J. (1) 1960/1 Motherwell
Mason, J. (7) 1948/9 Third Lanark
Masson, D. (17) 1975/6 QPR, Derby C
Mathers, D. (1) 1953/4 Partick Thistle
Matteo, D. (6) 2000/01 Leeds U

315

McAllister, B. (3) 1996/7 Wimbledon

McAllister, G. (57) 1989/90 Leicester C, Leeds U, Coventry C

McAvennie, F. (5) 1985/6 West Ham U, Celtic

McBride, J. (2) 1966/7 Celtic

McCall, S. M. (40) 1989/90 Everton, Rangers

McCalliog, J. (5) 1966/7 Sheffield W, Wolverhampton W

McCann, N. D. (15) 1998/9 Heart of Midlothian, Rangers

McCann, R. (5) 1958/9 Motherwell

McClair, B. (30) 1986/7 Celtic, Manchester U

McCloy, P. (4) 1972/3 Rangers

McCoist, A. (61) 1985/6 Rangers, Kilmarnock

McColl, I. (14) 1949/50 Rangers

McCreadie, E. (23) 1964/5 Chelsea

MacDonald, A. (1) 1975/6 Rangers

MacDonald, J. (2) 1955/6 Sunderland

McFadden, J. (1) 2001/02 Motherwell

McFarlane, W. (1) 1946/7 Heart of Midlothian

McGarr, E. (2) 1969/70 Aberdeen

McGarvey, F. (7) 1978/9 Liverpool, Celtic

McGhee, M. (4) 1982/3 Aberdeen

McGinlay, J. (13) 1993/4 Bolton W

McGrain, D. (62) 1972/3 Celtic

McGrory, J. (3) 1964/5 Kilmarnock

McInally, A. (8) 1988/9 Aston Villa, Bayern Munich

McInally, J. (10) 1986/7 Dundee U

McKay, D. (14) 1958/9 Celtic

McKean, R. (1) 1975/6 Rangers

McKenzie, J. (9) 1953/4 Partick Thistle

McKimmie, S. (40) 1988/9 Aberdeen

McKinlay, T. (22) 1995/6 Celtic

McKinlay, W. (29) 1993/4 Dundee U, Blackburn R

McKinnon, R. (28) 1965/6 Rangers

McKinnon, R. (3) 1993/4 Motherwell

McLaren, A. (4) 1946/7 Preston NE

McLaren, A. (24) 1991/2 Heart of Midlothian, Rangers

McLaren, A. (1) 2000/01 Kilmarnock

McLean, G. (1) 1967/8 Dundee

McLean, T. (6) 1968/9 Kilmarnock

McLeish, A. (77) 1979/80 Aberdeen

McLeod, J. (4) 1960/1 Hibernian

MacLeod, M. (20) 1984/5 Celtic, Borussia Dortmund, Hibernian

McLintock, F. (9) 1962/3 Leicester C, Arsenal

McMillan, I. (6) 1951/2 Airdrieonians, Rangers

McNamara, J. (13) 1996/7 Celtic

McNaught, W. (5) 1950/1 Raith R

McNaughton, K. (1) 2001/02 Aberdeen

McNeill, W. (29) 1960/1 Celtic

McPhail, J. (5) 1949/50 Celtic

McPherson, D. (27) 1988/9 Heart of Midlothian, Rangers

McQueen, G. (30) 1973/4 Leeds U, Manchester U

McStay, P. (76) 1983/4 Celtic

McSwegan, G. (2) 1999/00 Heart of Midlothian

Millar, J. (2) 1962/3 Rangers

Miller, C. (1) 2000/01 Dundee U

Miller, K. (1) 2000/01 Rangers

Miller, W. (6) 1946/7 Celtic

Miller, W. (65) 1974/5 Aberdeen

Mitchell, R. (2) 1950/1 Newcastle U

Mochan, N. (3) 1953/4 Celtic

Moir, W. (1) 1949/50 Bolton W

Moncur, R. (16) 1967/8 Newcastle U

Morgan, W. (21) 1967/8 Burnley, Manchester U

Morris, H. (1) 1949/50 East Fife

Mudie, J. (17) 1956/7 Blackpool

Mulhall, G. (3) 1959/60 Aberdeen, Sunderland

Munro, F. (9) 1970/1 Wolverhampton W

Munro, I. (7) 1978/9 St Mirren

Murdoch, R. (12) 1965/6 Celtic

Murray, J. (5) 1957/8 Heart of Midlothian

Murray, S. (1) 1971/2 Aberdeen

Narey, D. (35) 1976/7 Dundee U

Naysmith, G. A. (6) 1999/00 Heart of Midlothian, Everton

Nevin, P. K. F. (28) 1985/6 Chelsea, Everton, Tranmere R

Nicholas, C. (20) 1982/3 Celtic, Arsenal, Aberdeen

Nicholson, B. (2) 2000/01 Dunfermline Ath

Nicol, S. (27) 1984/5 Liverpool

O'Connor, G. (3) 2001/02 Hibernian

O'Donnell, P. (1) 1993/4 Motherwell

O'Hare, J. (13) 1969/70 Derby Co

O'Neil, B. (6) 1995/6 Celtic, Wolfsburg, Derby Co

O'Neil, J. (1) 2000/01 Hibernian

Ormond, W. (6) 1953/4 Hibernian

Orr, T. (2) 1951/2 Morton

Parker, A. (15) 1954/5 Falkirk

Parlane, D. (12) 1972/3 Rangers

Paton, A. (2) 1951/2 Motherwell

Pearson, T. (2) 1946/7 Newcastle U

Penman, A. (1) 1965/6 Dundee

Pettigrew, W. (5) 1975/6 Motherwell

Plenderleith, J. (1) 1960/1 Manchester C

Pressley, S. J. (2) 1999/00 Heart of
  Midlothian
Provan, D. (5) 1963/4 Rangers
Provan, D. (10) 1979/80 Celtic

Quinn, P. (4) 1960/1 Motherwell

Rae, G. (2) 2000/01 Dundee
Redpath, W. (9) 1948/9 Motherwell
Reilly, L. (38) 1948/9 Hibernian
Ring, T. (12) 1952/3 Clydebank
Rioch, B. (24) 1974/5 Derby Co,
  Everton, Derby Co
Ritchie, P. S. (6) 1998/9 Heart of
  Midlothian, Bolton W
Robb, D. (5) 1970/1 Aberdeen
Robertson, A. (5) 1954/5 Clyde
Robertson, D. (3) 1991/2 Rangers
Robertson, H. (1) 1961/2 Dundee
Robertson, J. (16) 1990/1 Heart of
  Midlothian
Robertson, J. G. (1) 1964/5 Tottenham
  H
Robertson, J. N. (28) 1977/8
  Nottingham F, Derby Co
Robinson, B. (4) 1973/4 Dundee
Ross, M. (3) 2001/02 Rangers
Rough, A. (53) 1975/6 Partick Thistle,
  Hibernian
Rougvie, D. (1) 1983/4 Aberdeen
Rutherford, E. (1) 1947/8 Rangers

St John, I. (21) 1958/9 Motherwell,
  Liverpool
Schaedler, E. (1) 1973/4 Hibernian
Scott, A. (16) 1956/7 Rangers, Everton
Scott, J. (1) 1965/6 Hibernian
Scott, J. (2) 1970/1 Dundee
Scoular, J. (9) 1950/1 Portsmouth
Severin, S. (4) 2001/02 Heart of
  Midlothian
Sharp, G. M. (12) 1984/5 Everton
Shaw, D. (8) 1946/7 Hibernian
Shaw, J. (4) 1946/7 Rangers
Shearer, D. (7) 1993/4 Aberdeen
Shearer, R. (4) 1960/1 Rangers
Simpson, N. (4) 1982/3 Aberdeen
Simpson, R. (5) 1966/7 Celtic
Sinclair, J. (1) 1965/6 Leicester C
Smith, D. (2) 1965/6 Aberdeen,
  Rangers
Smith, E. (2) 1958/9 Celtic
Smith, G. (18) 1946/7 Hibernian
Smith, H. G. (3) 1987/8 Heart of
  Midlothian
Smith, J. (4) 1967/8 Aberdeen,
  Newcastle U
Souness, G. (54) 1974/5
  Middlesbrough, Liverpool,
  Sampdoria

Speedie, D. R. (10) 1984/5 Chelsea,
  Coventry C
Spencer, J. (14) 1994/5 Chelsea, QPR
Stanton, P. (16) 1965/6 Hibernian
Steel, W. (30) 1946/7 Morton, Derby
  C, Dundee
Stein, C. (21) 1968/9 Rangers,
  Coventry C
Stephen, J. (2) 1946/7 Bradford C
Stewart, D. (1) 1977/8 Leeds U
Stewart, J. (2) 1976/7 Kilmarnock,
  Middlesbrough
Stewart, M. J. (3) 2001/02 Manchester
  U
Stewart, R. (10) 1980/1 West Ham U
Stockdale, R. K. (4) 2001/02
  Middlesbrough
Strachan, G. (50) 1979/80 Aberdeen,
  Manchester U, Leeds U
Sturrock, P. (20) 1980/1 Dundee U
Sullivan, N. (27) 1996/7 Wimbledon,
  Tottenham H

Telfer, P. N. (1) 1999/00 Coventry C
Telfer, W. (1) 1953/4 St Mirren
Thompson, S. (3) 2001/02 Dundee U
Thomson, W. (7) 1979/80 St Mirren
Thornton, W. (7) 1946/7 Rangers
Toner, W. (2) 1958/9 Kilmarnock
Turnbull, E. (8) 1947/8 Hibernian

Ure, I. (11) 1961/2 Dundee, Arsenal

Waddell, W. (17) 1946/7 Rangers
Walker, A. (3) 1987/8 Celtic
Walker, J. N. (2) 1992/3 Heart of
  Midlothian, Partick Thistle
Wallace, L. A. (3) 1977/8 Coventry C
Wallace, W. S. B. (7) 1964/5 Heart of
  Midlothian, Celtic
Wardhaugh, J. (2) 1954/5 Heart of
  Midlothian
Wark, J. (29) 1978/9 Ipswich T,
  Liverpool
Watson, J. (2) 1947/8 Motherwell,
  Huddersfield T
Watson, R. (1) 1970/1 Motherwell
Weir, A. (6) 1958/9 Motherwell
Weir, D. G. (35) 1996/7 Heart of
  Midlothian, Everton
Weir, P. (6) 1979/80 St Mirren,
  Aberdeen
White, J. (22) 1958/9 Falkirk,
  Tottenham H
Whyte, D. (12) 1987/8 Celtic,
  Middlesbrough, Aberdeen
Wilkie, L. (2) 2001/02 Dundee
Williams, G. (4) 2001/02 Nottingham F
Wilson, A. (1) 1953/4 Portsmouth
Wilson, D. (22) 1960/1 Rangers

Wilson, I. A. (5) 1986/7 Leicester C, Everton
Wilson, P. (1) 1974/5 Celtic
Wilson, R. (2) 1971/2 Arsenal
Winters, R. (1) 1998/9 Aberdeen
Wood, G. (4) 1978/9 Everton, Arsenal
Woodburn, W. (24) 1946/7 Rangers
Wright, K. (1) 1991/2 Hibernian
Wright, S. (2) 1992/3 Aberdeen

Wright, T. (3) 1952/3 Sunderland

Yeats, R. (2) 1964/5 Liverpool
Yorston, H. (1) 1954/5 Aberdeen
Young, A. (9) 1959/60 Heart of Midlothian, Everton
Young, G. (53) 1946/7 Rangers
Younger, T. (24) 1954/5 Hibernian, Liverpool

WALES

Aizlewood, M. (39) 1985/6 Charlton Ath, Leeds U, Bradford C, Bristol C, Cardiff C
Allchurch, I. (68) 1950/1 Swansea T, Newcastle U, Cardiff C, Swansea T
Allchurch, L. (11) 1954/5 Swansea T, Sheffield U
Allen, B. (2) 1950/1 Coventry C
Allen, M. (14) 1985/6 Watford, Norwich C, Millwall, Newcastle U

Baker, C. (7) 1957/8 Cardiff C
Baker, W. (1) 1947/8 Cardiff C
Barnard, D. S. (16) 1997/8 Barnsley
Barnes, W. (22) 1947/8 Arsenal
Bellamy, C. D. (16) 1997/8 Norwich C, Coventry C, Newcastle U
Berry, G. (5) 1978/9 Wolverhampton W, Stoke C
Blackmore, C. G. (39) 1984/5 Manchester U, Middlesbrough
Blake, N. (22) 1993/4 Sheffield U, Bolton W, Blackburn R, Wolverhampton W
Bodin, P. J. (23) 1989/90 Swindon T, Crystal P, Swindon T
Bowen, D. (19) 1954/5 Arsenal
Bowen, J. P. (2) 1993/4 Swansea C, Birmingham C
Bowen, M. R. (41) 1985/6 Tottenham H, Norwich C, West Ham U
Boyle, T. (2) 1980/1 Crystal P
Browning, M. T. (5) 1995/6 Bristol R, Huddersfield T
Burgess, R. (32) 1946/7 Tottenham H
Burton, O. (9) 1962/3 Norwich C, Newcastle U

Cartwright, L. (7) 1973/4 Coventry C, Wrexham
Charles, J. (38) 1949/50 Leeds U, Juventus, Leeds U, Cardiff C
Charles, J. M. (19) 1980/1 Swansea C, QPR, Oxford U
Charles, M. (31) 1954/5 Swansea T, Arsenal, Cardiff C
Clarke, R. (22) 1948/9 Manchester C

Coleman, C. (32) 1991/2 Crystal P, Blackburn R, Fulham
Cornforth, J. M. (2) 1994/5 Swansea C
Coyne, D. (2) 1995/6 Tranmere R, Grimsby T
Crossley, M. G. (5) 1996/7 Nottingham F, Middlesbrough
Crowe, V. (16) 1958/9 Aston Villa
Curtis, A. (35) 1975/6 Swansea C, Southampton, Cardiff C

Daniel, R. (21) 1950/1 Arsenal, Sunderland
Davies, A. (13) 1982/3 Manchester U, Newcastle U, Swansea C, Bradford C
Davies, D. (52) 1974/5 Everton, Wrexham, Swansea C
Davies, G. (16) 1979/80 Fulham, Chelsea, Manchester C
Davies, R. Wyn (34) 1963/4 Bolton W, Newcastle U, Manchester C, Manchester U, Blackpool
Davies, Reg (6) 1952/3 Newcastle U
Davies, Ron (29) 1963/4 Norwich C, Southampton, Portsmouth
Davies, S. (8) 2000/01 Tottenham H
Davies, S. I. (1) 1995/6 Manchester U
Davis, C. (1) 1971/2 Charlton Ath
Davis, G. (4) 1977/8 Wrexham
Deacy, N. (11) 1976/7 PSV Eindhoven, Beringen
Delaney, M. A. (15) 1999/00 Aston Villa
Derrett, S. (4) 1968/9 Cardiff C
Dibble, A. (3) 1985/6 Luton T, Manchester C
Durban, A. (27) 1965/6 Derby C
Dwyer, P. (10) 1977/8 Cardiff C

Earnshaw, R. (1) 2001/02 Cardiff C
Edwards, C. N. H. (1) 1995/6 Swansea C
Edwards, G. (12) 1946/7 Birmingham C, Cardiff C
Edwards, I. (4) 1977/8 Chester
Edwards, R. W. (4) 1997/8 Bristol C

318

Edwards, T. (2) 1956/7 Charlton Ath
Emanuel, J. (2) 1972/3 Bristol C
England, M. (44) 1961/2 Blackburn R,
  Tottenham H
Evans, B. (7) 1971/2 Swansea C,
  Hereford U
Evans, I. (13) 1975/6 Crystal P
Evans, P. S. (1) 2001/02 Brentford
Evans, R. (1) 1963/4 Swansea T

Felgate, D. (1) 1983/4 Lincoln C
Flynn, B. (66) 1974/5 Burnley, Leeds
  U, Burnley
Ford, T. (38) 1946/7 Swansea T, Aston
  Villa, Sunderland, Cardiff C
Foulkes, W. (11) 1951/2 Newcastle U
Freestone, R. (1) 1999/00 Swansea C

Gabbidon, D. L. (1) 2001/02 Cardiff C
Giggs, R. J. (36) 1991/2 Manchester U
Giles, D. (12) 1979/80 Swansea C,
  Crystal P
Godfrey, B. (3) 1963/4 Preston NE
Goss, J. (9) 1990/1 Norwich C
Green, C. (15) 1964/5 Birmingham C
Green, R. M. (2) 1997/8
  Wolverhampton W
Griffiths, A. (17) 1970/1 Wrexham
Griffiths, H. (1) 1952/3 Swansea T
Griffiths, M. (11) 1946/7 Leicester C

Hall, G. D. (9) 1987/8 Chelsea
Harrington, A. (11) 1955/6 Cardiff C
Harris, C. (24) 1975/6 Leeds U
Harris, W. (6) 1953/4 Middlesbrough
Hartson, J. (29) 1994/5 Arsenal, West
  Ham U, Wimbledon, Coventry C,
  Celtic
Haworth, S. O. (3) 1996/7 Cardiff C,
  Coventry C
Hennessey, T. (39) 1961/2 Birmingham
  C, Nottingham F, Derby Co
Hewitt, R. (5) 1957/8 Cardiff C
Hill, M. (2) 1971/2 Ipswich T
Hockey, T. (9) 1971/2 Sheffield U,
  Norwich C, Aston Villa
Hodges, G. (18) 1983/4 Wimbledon,
  Newcastle U, Watford, Sheffield U
Holden, A. (1) 1983/4 Chester C
Hole, B. (30) 1962/3 Cardiff C,
  Blackburn R, Aston Villa, Swansea
  T
Hollins, D. (11) 1961/2 Newcastle U
Hopkins, J. (16) 1982/3 Fulham,
  Crystal P
Hopkins, M. (34) 1955/6 Tottenham H
Horne, B. (59) 1987/8 Portsmouth,
  Southampton, Everton, Birmingham
  C
Howells, R. (2) 1953/4 Cardiff C

Hughes, C. M. (8) 1991/2 Luton T,
  Wimbledon
Hughes, I. (4) 1950/1 Luton T
Hughes, L. M. (72) 1983/4 Manchester
  U, Barcelona, Manchester U,
  Chelsea, Southampton
Hughes, W. (3) 1946/7 Birmingham C
Hughes, W. A. (5) 1948/9 Blackburn R
Humphreys, J. (1) 1946/7 Everton

Jackett, K. (31) 1982/3 Watford
James, G. (9) 1965/6 Blackpool
James, L. (54) 1971/2 Burnley, Derby
  C, QPR, Burnley, Swansea C,
  Sunderland
James, R. M. (47) 1978/9 Swansea C,
  Stoke C, QPR, Leicester C, Swansea
  C
Jarvis, A. (3) 1966/7 Hull C
Jenkins, S. R. (16) 1995/6 Swansea C,
  Huddersfield T
Johnson, A. J. (7) 1998/9 Nottingham
  F
Johnson, M. (1) 1963/4 Swansea T
Jones, A. (6) 1986/7 Port Vale,
  Charlton Ath
Jones, Barrie (15) 1962/3 Swansea T,
  Plymouth Argyle, Cardiff C
Jones, Bryn (4) 1946/7 Arsenal
Jones, C. (59) 1953/4 Swansea T,
  Tottenham H, Fulham
Jones, D. (8) 1975/6 Norwich C
Jones, E. (4) 1947/8 Swansea T,
  Tottenham H
Jones, J. (72) 1975/6 Liverpool,
  Wrexham, Chelsea, Huddersfield T
Jones, K. (1) 1949/50 Aston Villa
Jones, M. G. (11) 1999/00 Leeds U,
  Leicester C
Jones, P. L. (2) 1996/7 Liverpool,
  Tranmere R
Jones, P. S. (25) 1996/7 Stockport Co,
  Southampton
Jones, R. (1) 1993/4 Sheffield W
Jones, T. G. (13) 1946/7 Everton
Jones, V. P. (9) 1994/5 Wimbledon
Jones, W. (1) 1970/1 Bristol C

Kelsey, A. (41) 1953/4 Arsenal
King, J. (1) 1954/5 Swansea T
Kinsey, N. (7) 1950/1 Norwich C,
  Birmingham C
Knill, A. R. (1) 1988/9 Swansea C
Koumas, J. (2) 2000/01 Tranmere R
Krzywicki, R. 1969/70 WBA,
  Huddersfield T

Lambert, R. (5) 1946/7 Liverpool
Law, B. J. (1) 1989/90 QPR
Lea, C. (2) 1964/5 Ipswich T

Leek, K. (13) 1960/1 Leicester C, Newcastle U, Birmingham C

Legg, A. (6) 1995/6 Birmingham C, Cardiff C

Lever, A. (1) 1952/3 Leicester C

Lewis, D. (1) 1982/3 Swansea C

Llewellyn, C. M. (2) 1997/8 Norwich C

Lloyd, B. (3) 1975/6 Wrexham

Lovell, S. (6) 1981/2 Crystal P, Millwall

Lowndes, S. (10) 1982/3 Newport Co, Millwall, Barnsley

Lowrie, G. (4) 1947/8 Coventry C, Newcastle U

Lucas, M. (4) 1961/2 Leyton Orient

Lucas, W. (7) 1948/9 Swansea T

Maguire, G. T. (7) 1989/90 Portsmouth

Mahoney, J. (51) 1967/8 Stoke C, Middlesbrough, Swansea C

Mardon, P. J. (1) 1995/6 WBA

Marriott, A. (5) 1995/6 Wrexham

Marustik, C. (6) 1981/2 Swansea C

Medwin, T. (30) 1952/3 Swansea T, Tottenham H

Melville, A. K. (51) 1989/90 Swansea C, Oxford U, Sunderland, Fulham

Mielczarek, R. (1) 1970/1 Rotherham U

Millington, A. (21) 1962/3 WBA, Crystal P, Peterborough U, Swansea C

Moore, G. (21) 1959/60 Cardiff C, Chelsea, Manchester U, Northampton T, Charlton Ath

Morris, W. (5) 1946/7 Burnley

Nardiello, D. (2) 1977/8 Coventry C

Neilson, A. B. (5) 1991/2 Newcastle U, Southampton

Nicholas, P. (73) 1978/9 Crystal P, Arsenal, Crystal P, Luton T, Aberdeen, Chelsea, Watford

Niedzwiecki, E. A. (2) 1984/5 Chelsea

Nogan, L. M. (2) 1991/2 Watford, Reading

Nurse, E. A. (2) 1984/5 Chelsea

Norman, A. J. (5) 1985/6 Hull C

Nurse, M. (12) 1959/60 Swansea T, Middlesbrough

O'Sullivan, P. (3) 1972/3 Brighton & HA

Oster, J. M. (4) 1997/8 Everton, Sunderland

Page, M. (28) 1970/1 Birmingham C

Page, R. J. (25) 1996/7 Watford, Sheffield U

Palmer, D. (3) 1956/7 Swansea T

Parry, J. (1) 1950/1 Swansea T

Pascoe, C. (10) 1983/4 Swansea C, Sunderland

Paul, R. (33) 1948/9 Swansea T, Manchester C

Pembridge, M. A. (42) 1991/2 Luton T, Derby C, Sheffield W, Benfica, Everton

Perry, J. (1) 1993/4 Cardiff C

Phillips, D. (62) 1983/4 Plymouth Argyle, Manchester C, Coventry C, Norwich C, Nottingham F

Phillips, J. (4) 1972/3 Chelsea

Phillips, L. (58) 1970/1 Cardiff C, Aston Villa, Swansea C, Charlton Ath

Pontin, K. (2) 1979/80 Cardiff C

Powell, A. (8) 1946/7 Leeds U, Everton, Birmingham C

Powell, D. (11) 1967/8 Wrexham, Sheffield U

Powell, I. (8) 1946/7 QPR, Aston Villa

Price, P. (25) 1979/80 Luton T, Tottenham H

Pring, K. (3) 1965/6 Rotherham U

Pritchard, H. K. (1) 1984/5 Bristol C

Rankmore, F. (1) 1965/6 Peterborough U

Ratcliffe, K. (59) 1980/1 Everton, Cardiff C

Ready, K. (5) 1996/7 QPR

Reece, G. (29) 1965/6 Sheffield U, Cardiff C

Reed, W. (2) 1954/5 Ipswich T

Rees, A. (1) 1983/4 Birmingham C

Rees, J. M. (1) 1991/2 Luton T

Rees, R. (39) 1964/5 Coventry C, WBA, Nottingham F

Rees, W. (4) 1948/9 Cardiff C, Tottenham H

Richards, S. (1) 1946/7 Cardiff C

Roberts, A. M. (2) 1992/3 QPR

Roberts, D. (17) 1972/3 Oxford U, Hull C

Roberts, G. W. (4) 1999/00 Tranmere R

Roberts, I. W. (15) 1989/90 Watford, Huddersfield T, Leicester C, Norwich C

Roberts, J. G. (22) 1970/1 Arsenal, Birmingham C

Roberts, J. H. (1) 1948/9 Bolton W

Roberts, N. W. (1) 1999/00 Wrexham

Roberts, P. (4) 1973/4 Portsmouth

Robinson, C. P. (8) 1999/00 Wolverhampton W

Robinson, J. R. C. (30) 1995/6 Charlton Ath

Rodrigues, P. (40) 1964/5 Cardiff C, Leicester C, Sheffield W

Rouse, V. (1) 1958/9 Crystal P

Rowley, T. (1) 1958/9 Tranmere R
Rush, I. (73) 1979/80 Liverpool, Juventus, Liverpool

Saunders, D. (75) 1985/6 Brighton & HA, Oxford U, Derby C, Liverpool, Aston Villa, Galatasaray, Nottingham F, Sheffield U, Benfica, Bradford C
Savage, R. W. (25) 1995/6 Crewe Alexandra, Leicester C
Sayer, P. (7) 1976/7 Cardiff C
Scrine, F. (2) 1949/50 Swansea T
Sear, C. (1) 1962/3 Manchester C
Sherwood, A. (41) 1946/7 Cardiff C, Newport C
Shortt, W. (12) 1946/7 Plymouth Argyle
Showers, D. (2) 1974/5 Cardiff C
Sidlow, C. (7) 1946/7 Liverpool
Slatter, N. (22) 1982/3 Bristol R, Oxford U
Smallman, D. (7) 1973/4 Wrexham, Everton
Southall, N. (92) 1981/2 Everton
Speed, G. A. (68) 1989/90 Leeds U, Everton, Newcastle U
Sprake, G. (37) 1963/4 Leeds U, Birmingham C
Stansfield, F. (1) 1948/9 Cardiff C
Stevenson, B. (15) 1977/8 Leeds U, Birmingham C
Stevenson, N. (4) 1981/2 Swansea C
Stitfall, R. (2) 1952/3 Cardiff C
Sullivan, D. (17) 1952/3 Cardiff C
Symons, C. J. (36) 1991/2 Portsmouth, Manchester C, Fulham

Tapscott, D. (14) 1953/4 Arsenal, Cardiff C
Taylor, G. K. (9) 1995/6 Crystal P, Sheffield U, Burnley
Thomas, D. (2) 1956/7 Swansea T
Thomas, M. (51) 1976/7 Wrexham, Manchester U, Everton, Brighton & HA, Stoke C, Chelsea, WBA
Thomas, M. R. (1) 1986/7 Newcastle U
Thomas, R. (50) 1966/7 Swindon T, Derby C, Cardiff C
Thomas, S. (4) 1947/8 Fulham

Toshack, J. (40) 1968/9 Cardiff C, Liverpool, Swansea C
Trollope, P. J. (6) 1996/7 Derby Co, Fulham, Coventry C

Van Den Hauwe, P. W. R. (13) 1984/5 Everton
Vaughan, N. (10) 1982/3 Newport Co, Cardiff C
Vearncombe, G. (2) 1957/8 Cardiff C
Vernon, R. (32) 1956/7 Blackburn R, Everton, Stoke C
Villars, A. (3) 1973/4 Cardiff C

Walley, T. (1) 1970/1 Watford
Walsh, I. (18) 1979/80 Crystal P, Swansea C
Ward, D. (2) 1958/9 Bristol R, Cardiff C
Ward, D. (2) 1999/00 Notts Co, Nottingham F
Webster, C. (4) 1956/7 Manchester U
Weston, R. D. (1) 1999/00 Arsenal
Williams, A. (12) 1993/4 Reading, Wolverhampton W
Williams, A. P. (2) 1997/8 Southampton
Williams, D. G. 1987/8 13, Derby Co, Ipswich T
Williams, D. M. (5) 1985/6 Norwich C
Williams, G. (1) 1950/1 Cardiff C
Williams, G. E. (26) 1959/60 WBA
Williams, G. G. (5) 1960/1 Swansea T
Williams, H. (4) 1948/9 Newport Co, Leeds U
Williams, Herbert (3) 1964/5 Swansea T
Williams, S. (43) 1953/4 WBA, Southampton
Witcomb, D. (3) 1946/7 WBA, Sheffield W
Woosnam, P. (17) 1958/9 Leyton Orient, West Ham U, Aston Villa

Yorath, T. (59) 1969/70 Leeds U, Coventry C, Tottenham H, Vancouver Whitecaps
Young, E. (21) 1989/90 Wimbledon, Crystal P, Wolverhampton W

EIRE

Aherne, T. (16) 1945/6 Belfast Celtic, Luton T
Aldridge, J. W. (69) 1985/6 Oxford U, Liverpool, Real Sociedad, Tranmere R
Ambrose, P. (5) 1954/5 Shamrock R

Anderson, J. (16) 1979/80 Preston NE, Newcastle U

Babb, P. (34) 1993/4 Coventry C, Liverpool
Bailham, E. (1) 1963/4 Shamrock R

Barber, E. (2) 1965/6 Shelbourne, Birmingham C
Beglin, J. (15) 1983/4 Liverpool
Bonner, P. (80) 1980/1 Celtic
Braddish, S. (1) 1977/8 Dundalk
Brady, T. R. (6) 1963/4 QPR
Brady, W. L. (72) 1974/5 Arsenal, Juventus, Sampdoria, Internazionale, Ascoli, West Ham U
Branagan, K. G. (1) 1996/7 Bolton W
Breen, B. (47) 1995/6 Birmingham C, Coventry C
Breen, T. (3) 1946/7 Shamrock R
Brennan, F. (1) 1964/5 Drumcondra
Brennan, S. A. (19) 1964/5 Manchester U, Waterford
Browne, W. (3) 1963/4 Bohemians
Buckley, L. (2) 1983/4 Shamrock R, Waregem
Burke, F. (1) 1951/2 Cork Ath
Butler, P. J. (1) 1999/00 Sunderland
Byrne, A. B. (14) 1969/70 Southampton
Byrne, J. (23) 1984/5 QPR, Le Havre, Brighton & HA, Sunderland, Millwall
Byrne, P. (8) 1983/4 Shamrock R

Campbell, A. (3) 1984/5 Santander
Campbell, N. (11) 1970/1 St Patrick's Ath, Fortuna Cologne
Cantwell, N. (36) 1953/4 West Ham U, Manchester U
Carey, B. P. (3) 1991/2 Manchester U, Leicester C
Carey, J. J. (21) 1945/6 Manchester U
Carolan, J. (2) 1959/60 Manchester U
Carr, S. (18) 1998/9 Tottenham H
Carroll, B. (2) 1948/9 Shelbourne
Carroll, T. R. (17) 1967/8 Ipswich T, Birmingham C
Carsley, L. K. (20) 1997/8 Derby Co, Blackburn R, Coventry C, Everton
Cascarino, A. G. (88) 1985/6 Gillingham, Millwall, Aston Villa, Celtic, Chelsea, Marseille, Nancy
Chandler, J. (2) 1979/80 Leeds U
Clarke, J. (1) 1977/8 Drogheda U
Clarke, K. (2) 1947/8 Drumcondra
Clarke, M. (1) 1949/50 Shamrock R
Clinton, T. J. (3) 1950/1 Everton
Coad, P. (11) 1946/7 Shamrock R
Coffey, J. (1) 1949/50 Drumcondra
Colfer, M. D. (2) 1949/50 Shelbourne
Colgan, N, (1) 2001/02 Hibernian
Conmy, O. M. (5) 1964/5 Peterborough U
Connolly, D. J. (34) 1995/6 Watford, Feyenoord, Wolverhampton W, Excelsior, Wimbledon
Conroy, G. A. (27) 1969/70 Stoke C

Conway, J. P. (20) 1966/7 Fulham, Manchester C
Corr, P. J. (4) 1948/9 Everton
Courtney, E. (1) 1945/6 Cork U
Coyle, O. (1) 1993/4 Bolton W
Coyne, T. (22) 1991/2 Celtic, Tranmere R, Motherwell
Cummins, G. P. (19) 1953/4 Luton T
Cuneen, T. (1) 1950/1 Limerick
Cunningham, K. (40) 1995/6 Wimbledon
Curtis, D. P. (17) 1956/7 Shelbourne, Bristol C, Ipswich T, Exeter C
Cusack, S. (1) 1952/3 Limerick

Daish, L. S. (5) 1991/2 Cambridge U, Coventry C
Daly, G. A. (48) 1972/3 Manchester U, Derby C, Coventry C, Birmingham C, Shrewsbury T
Daly, M. (2) 1977/8 Wolverhampton W
Daly, P. (1) 1949/50 Shamrock R
Delap, R. J. (7) 1997/8 Derby Co, Southampton
De Mange, K. J. P. P. (2) 1986/7 Liverpool, Hull C
Deacy, E. (4) 1981/2 Aston Villa
Dempsey, J. T. (19) 1966/7 Fulham, Chelsea
Dennehy, J. (11) 1971/2 Cork Hibernian, Nottingham F, Walsall
Desmond, P. (4) 1949/50 Middlesbrough
Devine, J. (12) 1979/80 Arsenal, Norwich C
Doherty, G. M. T. (9) 1999/00 Luton T, Tottenham H
Donovan, D. C. (5) 1954/5 Everton
Donovan, T. (1) 1979/80 Aston Villa
Doyle, C. (1) 1958/9 Shelbourne
Duff, D. A. (30) 1997/8 Blackburn R
Duffy, B. (1) 1949/50 Shamrock R
Dunne, A. P. (33) 1961/2 Manchester U, Bolton W
Dunne, J. C. (1) 1970/1 Fulham
Dunne, P. A. J. (5) 1964/5 Manchester U
Dunne, R. P. (14) 1999/00 Everton, Manchester C
Dunne, S. (15) 1952/3 Luton T
Dunne, T. (3) 1955/6 St Patrick's Ath
Dunning, P. (2) 1970/1 Shelbourne
Dunphy, E. M. (23) 1965/6 York C, Millwall
Dwyer, N. M. (14) 1959/60 West Ham U, Swansea C

Eccles, P. (1) 1985/6 Shamrock R
Eglington, T. J. (24) 1945/6 Shamrock R, Everton

Evans, M. J. (1) 1997/8 Southampton

Fagan, E. (1) 1972/3 Shamrock R
Fagan, F. (8) 1954/5 Manchester C,
   Derby C
Fairclough, M. (2) 1981/2 Dundalk
Fallon, S. (8) 1950/1 Celtic
Farrell, P. D. (28) 1945/6 Shamrock R,
   Everton
Farrelly, G. (6) 1995/6 Aston Villa,
   Everton, Bolton W
Finnan, S. (19) 1999/00 Fulham
Finucane, A. (11) 1966/7 Limerick
Fitzgerald, F. J. (2) 1954/5 Waterford
Fitzgerald, P. J. (5) 1960/1 Leeds U,
   Chester
Fitzpatrick, K. (1) 1969/70 Limerick
Fitzsimons, A. G. (26) 1949/50
   Middlesbrough, Lincoln C
Fleming, C. (10) 1995/6 Middlesbrough
Fogarty, A. (11) 1959/60 Sunderland,
   Hartlepool U
Foley, D. J. (6) 1999/00 Watford
Foley, T. C. (9) 1963/4 Northampton T
Fullam, J. 1960/1 Preston NE,
   Shamrock R

Gallagher, C. (2) 1966/7 Celtic
Gallagher, M. (1) 1953/4 Hibernian
Galvin, A. (29) 1982/3 Tottenham H,
   Sheffield W
Gannon, E. (14) 1948/9 Notts Co,
   Sheffield W, Shelbourne K
Gannon, M. (1) 1971/2 Shelbourne
Gavin, J. T. (7) 1949/50 Norwich C,
   Tottenham H, Norwich C
Gibbons, A. (4) 1951/2 St Patrick's Ath
Gilbert, R. (1) 1965/6 Shamrock R
Giles, C. (1) 1950/1 Doncaster R
Giles, M. J. (59) 1959/60 Manchester
   U, Leeds U, WBA, Shamrock R
Given, S. J. J. (43) 1995/6 Blackburn
   R, Newcastle U
Givens, D. J. (56) 1968/9 Manchester
   U, Luton T, QPR, Birmingham C,
   Neuchatel Xamax
Glynn, D. (2) 1951/2 Drumcondra
Godwin, T. F. (13) 1948/9 Shamrock R,
   Leicester C, Bournemouth
Goodman, J. (4) 1996/7 Wimbledon
Gorman, W. C. (2) 1946/7 Brentford
Grealish, A. (44) 1975/6 Orient, Luton
   T, Brighton & HA, WBA
Gregg, E. (8) 1977/8 Bohemians
Grimes, A. A. (17) 1977/8 Manchester
   U, Coventry C, Luton T

Hale, A. (13) 1961/2 Aston Villa,
   Doncaster R, Waterford
Hamilton, T. (2) 1958/9 Shamrock R

Hand, E. K. (20) 1968/9 Portsmouth
Harte, I. P. (44) 1995/6 Leeds U
Hartnett, J. B. (2) 1948/9
   Middlesbrough
Haverty, J. (32) 1955/6 Arsenal,
   Blackburn R, Millwall, Celtic,
   Bristol R, Shelbourne
Hayes, A. W. P. (1) 1978/9
   Southampton
Hayes, W. E. (2) 1946/7 Huddersfield
   T
Hayes, W. J. (1) 1948/9 Limerick
Healey, R. (2) 1976/7 Cardiff C
Healy, C. (3) 2001/02 Celtic
Heighway, S. D. (34) 1970/1 Liverpool,
   Minnesota Kicks
Henderson, B. (2) 1947/8 Drumcondra
Hennessy, J. (5) 1955/6 Shelbourne, St
   Patrick's Ath
Herrick, J. (3) 1971/2 Cork Hibernians,
   Shamrock R
Higgins, J. (1) 1950/1 Birmingham C
Holland, M. R. (23) 1999/00 Ipswich T
Holmes, J. 1970/1 Coventry C,
   Tottenham H, Vancouver Whitecaps
Houghton, R. J. (73) 1985/6 Oxford U,
   Liverpool, Aston Villa, Crystal P,
   Reading
Howlett, G. (1) 1983/4 Brighton & HA
Hughton, C. (53) 1979/80 Tottenham
   H, West Ham U
Hurley, C. J. (40) 1956/7 Millwall,
   Sunderland, Bolton W

Irwin, D. J. (56) 1990/1 Manchester U

Kavanagh, G. A. (3) 1997/8 Stoke C
Keane, R. D. (37) 1997/8
   Wolverhampton W, Coventry C,
   Internazionale, Leeds U
Keane, R. M. (58) 1990/1 Nottingham
   F, Manchester U
Keane, T. R. (4) 1948/9 Swansea T
Kearin, M. (1) 1971/2 Shamrock R
Kearns, F. T. (1) 1953/4 West Ham U
Kearns, M. (18) 1969/70 Oxford U,
   Walsall, Wolverhampton W
Kelly, A. T. (34) 1992/3 Sheffield U,
   Blackburn R
Kelly, D. T. (26) 1987/8 Walsall, West
   Ham U, Leicester C, Newcastle U,
   Wolverhampton W, Sunderland,
   Tranmere R
Kelly, G. (50) 1993/4 Leeds U
Kelly J. A. (48) 1956/7 Drumcondra,
   Preston NE
Kelly, J. P. V. (5) 1960/1
   Wolverhampton W
Kelly, M. J. (4) 1987/8 Portsmouth
Kelly, N. (1) 1953/4 Nottingham F

Kenna, J. J. (27) 1994/5 Blackburn R
Kennedy, M. (34) 1995/6 Liverpool,
  Wimbledon, Manchester C,
  Wolverhampton W
Kennedy, M. F. (2) 1985/6 Portsmouth
Keogh, J. (1) 1965/6 Shamrock R
Keogh, S. (1) 1958/9 Shamrock R
Kernaghan, A. N. (22) 1992/3
  Middlesbrough, Manchester C
Kiely, D. L. (6) 1999/00 Charlton Ath
Kiernan, F. W. (5) 1950/1 Shamrock R,
  Southampton
Kilbane, K. D. (37) 1997/8 WBA,
  Sunderland
Kinnear, J. P. (26) 1966/7 Tottenham
  H, Brighton & HA
Kinsella, M. A. (32) 1997/8 Charlton
  Ath

Langan, D. (25) 1977/8 Derby Co,
  Birmingham C, Oxford U
Lawler, J. F. (8) 1952/3 Fulham
Lawlor, J. C. (3) 1948/9 Drumcondra,
  Doncaster R
Lawlor, M. (5) 1970/1 Shamrock R
Lawrenson, M. (39) 1976/7 Preston
  NE, Brighton & HA, Liverpool
Leech, M. (8) 1968/9 Shamrock R
Lowry, D. (1) 1961/2 St Patrick's Ath

McAlinden, J. (2) 1945/6 Portsmouth
McAteer, J. W. (49) 1993/4 Bolton W,
  Liverpool, Blackburn R, Sunderland
McCann, J. (1) 1956/7 Shamrock R
McCarthy, M. (57) 1983/4 Manchester
  C, Celtic, Lyon, Millwall
McConville, T. (6) 1971/2 Dundalk,
  Waterford
McDonagh, J. (24) 1980/1 Everton,
  Bolton W, Notts C
McDonagh, Joe (3) 1983/4 Shamrock R
McEvoy, M. A. (17) 1960/1 Blackburn
  R
McGee, P. (15) 1977/8 QPR, Preston
  NE
McGoldrick, E. J. (15) 1991/2 Crystal
  P, Arsenal
McGowan, D. (3) 1948/9 West Ham U
McGowan, J. (1) 1946/7 Cork U
McGrath, M. (22) 1957/8 Blackburn R,
  Bradford Park Avenue
McGrath, P. (83) 1984/5 Manchester
  U, Aston Villa, Derby C
Macken, A. (1) 1976/7 Derby Co
Mackey, G. (3) 1956/7 Shamrock R
McLoughlin, A. F. (42) 1989/90
  Swindon T, Southampton,
  Portsmouth
McMillan, W. (2) 1945/6 Belfast Celtic
McNally, J. B. (3) 1958/9 Luton T

McPhail, S. (5) 1999/00 Leeds U
Mahon, A. J. (2) 1999/00 Tranmere R
Malone, G. (1) 1948/9 Shelbourne
Mancini, T. J. (5) 1973/4 QPR, Arsenal
Martin, C. J. (30) 1945/6 Glentoran,
  Leeds U, Aston Villa
Martin, M. P. (51) 1971/2 Bohemians,
  Manchester U, WBA, Newcastle U
Maybury, A. (2) 1997/8 Leeds U
Meagan, M. K. (17) 1960/1 Everton,
  Huddersfield T, Drogheda
Milligan, M. J. (1) 1991/2 Oldham Ath
Mooney, J. (2) 1964/5 Shamrock R
Moore, A. (8) 1995/6 Middlesbrough
Moran, K. (70) 1979/80 Manchester U,
  Sporting Gijon, Blackburn R
Moroney, T. (12) 1947/8 West Ham U
Morris, C. B. (35) 1987/8 Celtic,
  Middlesbrough
Morrison, C. H. (7) 2001/02 Crystal P
Moulson, G. B. (3) 1947/8 Lincoln C
Mucklan, C. (1) 1977/8 Drogheda
Mulligan, P. M. (50) 1968/9 Shamrock
  R, Chelsea, Crystal P, WBA,
  Shamrock R
Munroe, L. (1) 1953/4 Shamrock R
Murphy, A. (1) 1955/6 Clyde
Murphy, B. (1) 1985/6 Bohemians
Murphy, J. (1) 1979/80 Crystal P
Murray, T. (1) 1949/50 Dundalk

Newman, W. (1) 1968/9 Shelbourne
Nolan, R. (10) 1956/7 Shamrock R

O'Brien, A. J. (5) 2000/01 Newcastle U
O'Brien, F. (4) 1979/80 Philadelphia
  Fury
O'Brien, L. (16) 1985/6 Shamrock R,
  Manchester U, Newcastle U,
  Tranmere R
O'Brien, R. (4) 1975/6 Notts Co
O'Byrne, L. B. (1) 1948/9 Shamrock R
O'Callaghan, B. R. (6) 1978/9 Stoke C
O'Callaghan, K. (20) 1980/1 Ipswich T,
  Portsmouth
O'Connell, A. (2) 1966/7 Dundalk,
  Bohemians
O'Connor, T. (4) 1949/50 Shamrock R
O'Connor, T. (7) 1967/8 Fulham,
  Dundalk, Bohemians
O'Driscoll, J. F. (3) 1948/9 Swansea T
O'Driscoll, S. (3) 1981/2 Fulham
O'Farrell, F. (9) 1951/2 West Ham U,
  Preston NE
O'Flanagan, K. P. (3) 1946/7 Arsenal
O'Flanagan, M. (1) 1946/7 Bohemians
O'Hanlon, K. G. (1) 1987/8
  Rotherham U
O'Keefe, E. (5) 1980/1 Everton, Port
  Vale

324

O'Leary, D. (68) 1976/7 Arsenal
O'Leary, P. (7) 1979/80 Shamrock R
O'Neill, F. S. (20) 1961/2 Shamrock R
O'Neill, J. (17) 1951/2 Everton
O'Neill, J. (1) 1960/1 Preston NE
O'Neill, K. P. (13) 1995/6 Norwich C,
  Middlesbrough
O'Regan, K. (4) 1983/4 Brighton &
  HA
O'Reilly, J. (2) 1945/6 Cork U
O'Shea, J.F. (1) 2001/02 Manchester U

Peyton, G. (33) 1976/7 Fulham,
  Bournemouth, Everton
Peyton, N. (6) 1956/7 Shamrock R,
  Leeds U
Phelan, T. (42) 1991/2 Wimbledon,
  Manchester C, Chelsea, Everton,
  Fulham

Quinn, B. S. (4) 1999/00 Coventry C
Quinn, N. J. (91) 1985/6 Arsenal,
  Manchester C, Sunderland

Reid, S. J. (7) 2001/02 Millwall
Richardson, D. J. (3) 1971/2 Shamrock
  R, Gillingham
Ringstead, A. (20) 1950/1 Sheffield U
Robinson, M. (23) 1980/1 Brighton &
  HA, Liverpool, QPR
Roche, P. J. (8) 1971/2 Shelbourne,
  Manchester U
Rogers, E. (19) 1967/8 Blackburn R,
  Charlton Ath
Ryan, G. (16) 1977/8 Derby Co,
  Brighton & HA
Ryan, R. A. (16) 1949/50 WBA, Derby
  C

Sadlier, R.T. (1) 2001/02 Millwall
Savage, D. P. T. (5) 1995/6 Millwall
Saward, P. (18) 1953/4 Millwall, Aston
  Villa, Huddersfield T
Scannell, T. (1) 1953/4 Southend U
Scully, P. J. (1) 1988/9 Arsenal
Sheedy, K. (45) 1983/4 Everton,
  Newcastle U

Sheridan, J. J. (34) 1987/8 Leeds U,
  Sheffield W
Slaven, B. (7) 1989/90 Middlesbrough
Sloan, J. W. (2) 1945/6 Arsenal
Smyth, M. (1) 1968/9 Shamrock R
Stapleton, F. (70) 1976/7 Arsenal,
  Manchester U, Ajax, Derby Co, Le
  Havre, Blackburn R
Staunton, S. (102) 1988/9 Liverpool,
  Aston Villa, Liverpool, Aston Villa
Stevenson, A. E. (6) 1946/7 Everton
Strahan, F. (5) 1963/4 Shelbourne
Swan, M. M. G. (1) 1959/60
  Drumcondra
Synott, N. (3) 1977/8 Shamrock R

Thomas, P. (2) 1973/4 Waterford
Townsend, A. D. (70) 1988/9 Norwich
  C, Chelsea, Aston Villa,
  Middlesbrough
Traynor, T. J. (8) 1953/4 Southampton
Treacy, R. C. P. (42) 1965/6 WBA,
  Charlton Ath, Swindon T, Preston
  NE, WBA, Shamrock R
Tuohy, L. (8) 1955/6 Shamrock R,
  Newcastle U, Shamrock R
Turner, P. (2) 1962/3 Celtic

Vernon, J. (2) 1945/6 Belfast Celtic

Waddock, G. (20) 1979/80 QPR,
  Millwall
Walsh, D. J. (20) 1945/6 WBA, Aston
  Villa
Walsh, J. (1) 1981/2 Limerick
Walsh, M. (21) 1975/6 Blackpool,
  Everton, QPR, Porto
Walsh, M. (4) 1981/2 Everton, Norwich
  C
Walsh, W. (9) 1946/7 Manchester C
Waters, J. (2) 1976/7 Grimsby T
Whelan, R. (2) 1963/4 St Patrick's Ath
Whelan, R. (53) 1980/1 Liverpool,
  Southend U
Whelan, W. (4) 1955/6 Manchester U
Whittaker, R. (1) 1958/9 Chelsea

BRITISH ISLES INTERNATIONAL GOALSCORERS SINCE 1946

ENGLAND

A'Court, A.	1	Eastham, G.	2	Lee, S.	2
Adams, T.A.	5	Edwards, D.	5	Le Saux, G.P.	1
Allen, R.	2	Ehiogu, U.	1	Lineker, G.	48
Anderson, V.	2	Elliott, W.H.	3	Lofthouse, N.	30
Anderton, D.R.	7				
Astall, G.	1	Ferdinand, L.	5	Mabbutt, G.	1
Atyeo, P.J.W.	5	Ferdinand, R. G.	1	McDermott, T.	3
		Finney, T.	30	Macdonald, M.	6
Baily, E.F.	5	Flowers, R.	10	McManaman, S.	3
Baker, J.H.	3	Fowler, R.B.	7	Mannion, W.J.	11
Ball, A.J.	8	Francis, G.C.J.	3	Mariner, P.	13
Barnes, J.	11	Francis, T.	12	Marsh, R.W.	1
Barnes, P.S.	4	Froggatt, J.	2	Matthews, S.	3
Barmby, N.J.	4	Froggatt, R.	2	Medley, L.D.	1
Beardsley, P.A.	9			Melia, J.	1
Beattie, J.K.	1	Gascoigne, P.J.	10	Merson, P.C.	3
Beckham, D.R.J.	7	Gerrard, S. G.	1	Milburn, J.E.T.	10
Bell, C.	9	Goddard, P.	1	Moore, R.F.	2
Bentley, R.T.F.	9	Grainger, C.	3	Morris, J.	3
Blissett, L.	3	Greaves, J.	44	Mortensen, S.H.	23
Bowles, S.	1			Mullen, J.	6
Bradford, G.R.W.	1	Haines, J.T.W.	2	Mullery, A.P.	1
Bradley, W.	2	Hancocks, J.	2	Murphy, D. B.	1
Bridges, B.J.	1	Hassall, H.W.	4		
Broadbent, P.F.	2	Hateley, M.	9	Neal, P.G.	5
Broadis, I.A.	8	Haynes, J.N.	18	Nicholls, J.	1
Brooking, T.D.	5	Heskey, E.W.	4	Nicholson, W.E.	1
Brooks, J.	2	Hirst, D.E.	1		
Bull, S.G.	4	Hitchens, G.A.	5	O'Grady, M.	3
Butcher, T.	3	Hoddle, G.	8	Owen, M.J.	18
Byrne, J.J.	8	Hughes, E.W.	1	Own goals	24
		Hunt, R.	18		
Campbell, S. J.	1	Hunter, N.	2	Paine, T.L.	7
Carter, H.S.	5	Hurst, G.C.	24	Palmer, C.L.	1
Chamberlain, M.	1			Parry, R.A.	1
Channon, M.R.	21	Ince P.E.C.	2	Peacock, A.	3
Charlton, J.	6			Pearce, S.	5
Charlton, R.	49	Johnson, D.E.	6	Pearson, J.S.	5
Chivers, M.	13			Pearson, S.C.	5
Clarke, A.J.	10	Kay, A.H.	1	Perry, W.	2
Cole, A.	1	Keegan, J.K.	21	Peters, M.	20
Connelly, J.M.	7	Kennedy, R.	3	Pickering, F.	5
Coppell, S.J.	7	Keown, M.R.	2	Platt, D.	27
Cowans, G.	2	Kevan, D.T.	8	Pointer, R.	2
Crawford, R.	1	Kidd, B.	1		
Currie, A.W.	3			Ramsay, A.E.	3
		Langton, R.	1	Redknapp, J.F.	1
Dixon, L.M.	1	Latchford, R.D.	5	Revie, D.G.	4
Dixon, K.M.	4	Lawler, C.	1	Robson, B.	26
Douglas, B.	11	Lawton, T.	16	Robson, R.	4
		Lee, F.	10	Rowley, J.F.	6
		Lee, J.	1	Royle, J.	2
		Lee, R.M.	2		

Sansom, K.	1	Buckley, P.	1	Henderson, W.	5
Scholes, P.	13	Burley, C.W.	3	Hendry, E.C.J.	3
Sewell, J.	3	Burns, K.	1	Herd, D.G.	3
Shackleton, L.F.	1			Herd, G.	1
Shearer, A.	30	Calderwood, C.	1	Hewie, J.D.	2
Sheringham, E.P.	11	Caldow, E.	4	Holton, J.A.	2
Smith, A.M.	2	Cameron, C.	2	Hopkin, D.	2
Smith, R.	13	Campbell, R.	1	Houliston, W.	2
Southgate, G.	1	Chalmers, S.	3	Howie, H.	1
Steven, T.M.	4	Collins, J.	12	Hughes, J.	1
Stiles, N.P.	1	Collins, R.V.	10	Hunter, W.	1
Stone, S.B.	2	Combe, J.R.	1	Hutchison, D.	6
Summerbee, M.G.	1	Conn, A.	1	Hutchison, T.	1
		Cooper, D.	6		
Tambling, R.V.	1	Craig, J.	1	Jackson, C.	1
Taylor, P.J.	2	Crawford, S.	1	Jackson, D.	4
Taylor, T.	16	Curran, H.P.	1	Jardine, A.	1
Thompson, P.B.	1			Jess, E.	2
Tueart, D.	2	Dailly, C.	3	Johnston, A.	2
		Dalglish, K.	30	Johnston, L.H.	1
Vassell, D.	3	Davidson, J.A.	1	Johnston, M.	14
Viollet, D.S.	1	Dobie, R. S.	1	Johnstone, D.	2
		Docherty, T.H.	1	Johnstone, J.	4
Waddle, C.R.	6	Dodds, D.	1	Johnstone, R.	9
Wallace, D.L.	1	Dodds, W.	7	Jordan, J.	11
Walsh, P.	1	Duncan, D.M.	1		
Watson, D.V.	4	Durie, G.S.	7	Kyle, K.	1
Webb, N.	4				
Weller, K.	1	Elliott, M.S.	1	Law, D.	30
Wignall, F.	2			Leggat, G.	8
Wilkins, R.G.	3	Ferguson, B.	1	Lennox, R.	3
Wilshaw, D.J.	10	Fernie, W.	1	Liddell, W.	6
Wise, D.F.	1	Flavell, R.	2	Linwood, A.B.	1
Withe, P.	1	Fleming, C.	2	Lorimer, P.	4
Woodcock, T.	16	Freedman, D. A.	1		
Worthington, F.S.	2			Macari, L.	5
Wright, I.E.	9	Gallacher, K W	9	McAllister, G.	5
Wright, M.	1	Gemmell, T.K		MacDougall, E.J.	3
Wright, W.A.	3	*(St Mirren)*	1	MacKay, D.C.	4
		Gemmell, T.K		Mackay, G.	1
SCOTLAND		*(Celtic)*	1	MacKenzie, J.A.	1
		Gemmill, A.	8	MacLeod, M.	1
Aitken, R.	1	Gemmill, S.	1	McAvennie, F.	1
Archibald, S.	4	Gibson, D.W.	3	McCall, S.M.	1
		Gilzean, A.J.	12	McCalliog, J.	1
Baird, S.	2	Gough, C.R.	6	McCann, N.	1
Bannon, E.	1	Graham, A.	2	McClair, B.	2
Bauld, W.	2	Graham, G.	3	McCoist, A.	19
Baxter, J.C.	3	Gray, A.	5	McGhee, M.	2
Bett, J.	1	Gray, E.	3	McGinlay, J.	3
Bone, J.	1	Gray, F.	1	McInally, A.	3
Booth, S.	6	Greig, J.	3	McKimmie, S.I.	1
Boyd, T.	1			McKinlay, W.	4
Brand, R.	8	Hamilton, G.	4	McKinnon, R.	1
Brazil, A.	1	Harper, J.M.	3	McLaren, A.	4
Bremner, W.J.	3	Hartford, R.A.	4	McLean, T.	1
Brown, A.D.	6	Henderson, J.G.	1	McLintock, F.	1

McMillan, I.L.	2
McNeill, W.	3
McPhail, J.	3
McQueen, G.	5
McStay, P.	9
McSwegan, G.J.	1
Mason, J.	4
Masson, D.S.	5
Miller, W.	1
Mitchell, R.C.	1
Morgan, W.	1
Morris, H.	3
Mudie, J.K.	9
Mulhall, G.	1
Murdoch, R.	5
Murray, J.	1
Narey, D.	1
Nevin, P.K.F.	5
Nicholas, C.	5
O'Hare, J.	5
Ormond, W.E.	1
Orr, T.	1
Own goals	9
Parlane, D.	1
Pettigrew, W.	2
Provan, D.	1
Quinn, J.	7
Quinn, P.	1
Reilly, L.	22
Ring, T.	2
Rioch, B.D.	6
Ritchie, P.S.	1
Robertson, A.	2
Robertson, J.	2
Robertson, J.N.	9
St John, I.	9
Scott, A.S.	5
Sharp, G.	1
Shearer, D.	2
Smith, G.	4
Souness, G.J.	4
Steel, W.	12
Stein, C.	10
Stewart, R.	1
Strachan, G.	5
Sturrock, P.	3
Thompson, S.	1
Thornton, W.	1
Waddell, W.	6

Wallace, I.A.	1
Wark, J.	7
Weir, A.	1
Weir, D.	1
White, J.A.	3
Wilson, D.	9
Young, A.	2

WALES

Allchurch, I.J.	23
Allen, M.	3
Barnes, W.	1
Bellamy, C.D.	4
Blackmore, C.G.	1
Blake, N.A.	4
Bodin, P.J.	3
Bowen, D.I.	3
Bowen, M.	2
Boyle, T.	1
Burgess, W.A.R.	1
Charles, J.	1
Charles, M.	6
Charles, W.J.	15
Clarke, R.J.	5
Coleman, C.	4
Curtis, A.	6
Davies, G.	2
Davies, R.T.	9
Davies, R.W.	6
Deacy, N.	4
Durban, A.	2
Dwyer, P.	2
Earnshaw, R.	1
Edwards, G.	2
Edwards, R.I.	4
England, H.M.	4
Evans, I.	1
Flynn, B.	7
Ford, T.	23
Foulkes, W.J.	1
Giggs, R.J.	7
Giles, D.	2
Godfrey, B.C.	2
Griffiths, A.T.	6
Griffiths, M.W.	2
Harris, C.S.	1
Hartson, J.	6
Hewitt, R.	1
Hockey, T.	1

Hodges, G.	2
Horne, B.	2
Hughes, L.M.	16
James, L.	10
James, R.	7
Jones, A.	1
Jones, B.S.	2
Jones, Cliff	16
Jones, D.E.	1
Jones, J.P.	1
Kryzwicki, R.I.	1
Leek, K.	5
Lovell, S.	1
Lowrie, G.	2
Mahoney, J.F.	1
Medwin, T.C.	6
Melville, A.K.	3
Moore, G.	1
Nicholas, P.	2
O'Sullivan, P.A	1
Own goals	5
Palmer, D.	1
Paul, R.	1
Pembridge, M.A.	6
Phillips, D.	2
Powell, A.	1
Powell, D.	1
Price, P.	1
Reece, G.I.	2
Rees, R.R.	3
Roberts, P.S.	1
Robinson, J.R.C.	3
Rush, I.	28
Saunders, D.	22
Savage R.W.	2
Slatter, N.	2
Smallman, D.P.	1
Speed, G.A.	4
Symons, C.J.	2
Tapscott, D.R.	4
Thomas, M.	4
Toshack, J.B.	12
Vernon, T.R.	8
Walsh, I.	7
Williams, A.	1
Williams, G.E.	1

Williams, G.G. 1
Woosnam, A.P. 3

Yorath, T.C. 2
Young, E. 1

NORTHERN IRELAND

Anderson, T. 4
Armstrong, G. 12

Barr, H.H. 1
Best, G. 9
Bingham, W.L. 10
Black, K. 1
Blanchflower, D. 2
Blanchflower, J. 1
Brennan, R.A. 1
Brotherston, N. 3

Campbell, W.G. 1
Casey, T. 2
Caskey, W. 1
Cassidy, T. 1
Clarke, C.J. 13
Clements, D. 2
Cochrane, T. 1
Crossan, E. 1
Crossan, J.A. 10
Cush, W.W. 5

D'Arcy, S.D. 1
Doherty, I. 1
Doherty, P.D. 2
Dougan, A.D. 8
Dowie, I. 12

Elder, A.R. 1
Elliott, S. 1

Ferguson, W. 1
Ferris, R.O. 1
Finney, T. 2

Gillespie, K.R. 1
Gray, P. 6
Griffin, D.J. 1

Hamilton, B. 4
Hamilton, W. 5
Harkin, J.T. 2
Harvey, M. 3
Healy, D.J. 8
Hill, C.F. 1
Humphries, W. 1
Hughes, M.E. 5

Hunter, A. 1
Hunter, B.V. 1

Irvine, W.J. 8

Johnston, W.C. 1
Jones, J. 1

Lennon, N.F. 2
Lockhart, N. 3
Lomas, S.M. 3

Magilton, J. 5
McAdams, W.J. 7
McCartney, G. 1
McClelland, J. 1
McCrory, S. 1
McCurdy, C. 1
McDonald, A. 3
McGarry, J.K. 1
McGrath, R.C. 4
McIlroy, J. 10
McIlroy, S.B. 5
McLaughlin, J.C. 6
McMahon, G.J. 2
McMordie, A.S. 3
McMorran, E.J. 4
McParland, P.J. 10
Moreland, V. 1
Morgan, S. 3
Morrow, S.J. 1
Mulryne, P.P. 3

Neill, W.J.T. 2
Nelson, S. 1
Nicholl, C.J. 3
Nicholl, J.M. 1
Nicholson, J.J. 6

O'Boyle, G. 1
O'Kane, W.J. 1
O'Neill, J. 2
O'Neill, M.A. 4
O'Neill, M.H. 8
Own goals 5

Patterson, D.J. 1
Peacock, R. 2
Penney, S. 2

Quinn, J.M. 12
Quinn, S.J. 3

Rowland, K. 1

Simpson, W.J. 5
Smyth, S. 5

Spence, D.W. 3
Stewart, I. 2

Taggart, G.P. 7
Tully, C.P. 3

Walker, J. 1
Walsh, D.J. 5
Welsh, E. 1
Whiteside, N. 9
Whitley, Jeff 1
Williams, M.S. 1
Wilson, D.J. 1
Wilson, K.J. 6
Wilson, S.J. 7

EIRE

Aldridge, J. 19
Ambrose, P. 1
Anderson, J. 1

Brady, L. 9
Breen, G. 6
Byrne, J. *(QPR)* 4

Cantwell, J. 14
Carey, J. 3
Carroll, T. 1
Cascarino, A. 19
Coad, P. 3
Connolly, D.J. 8
Conroy, T. 2
Conway, J. 3
Coyne, T. 6
Cummings, G. 5
Curtis, D. 8

Daly, G. 13
Dempsey, J 1
Dennehy, M. 2
Doherty, G.M.T. 1
Duff, D.A. 2
Duffy, B. 1
Dunne, R.P. 3

Eglinton, T. 2

Fagan, F. 5
Fallon, S. 2
Farrell, P. 3
Finnan, S. 1
Fitzgerald, J. 1
Fitzgerald, P. 2
Fitzsimons, A. 7
Fogarty, A. 3
Foley, D. 2
Fullam, J. 1

Galvin, A.	1	Lawrenson, M.	5	Quinn, N.	21
Gavin, J.	2	Leech, M.	2		
Giles, J.	5			Reid, S.J.	2
Givens, D.	19	McAteer, J.W.	3	Ringstead, A.	7
Glynn, D.	1	McCann, J.	1	Robinson, M.	4
Grealish, T.	8	McCarthy, M.	2	Rogers, E.	5
Grimes, A.A.	1	McEvoy, A.	6	Ryan, G.	1
		McGee, P.	4	Ryan, R.	3
Hale, A.	2	McGrath, P.	8		
Hand, E.	2	McLoughlin, A.	2		
Harte, I.P.	8	McPhail, S.	1	Sheedy, K.	9
Haverty, J.	3	Mancini, T.	1	Sheridan, J.	5
Holland, M.R.	4	Martin, C.	6	Slaven, B.	1
Holmes, J.	1	Martin, M.	4	Sloan, W.	1
Houghton, R.	6	Mooney, J.	1	Stapleton, F.	20
Hughton, C.	1	Moran, K.	6	Staunton, S.	7
Hurley, C.	2	Moroney, T.	1	Strahan, F.	1
		Morrison, C.H.	2		
Irwin, D.	4	Mulligan, P.	1	Townsend, A.D.	7
				Treacy, R.	5
Kavanagh, G.A.	1	O'Callaghan, K.	1	Tuohy, L.	4
Keane, R.D.	13	O'Connor, T.	2		
Keane, R.M.	9	O'Farrell, F.	2	Waddock, G.	3
Kelly, D.	9	O'Keefe, E.	1	Walsh, D.	5
Kelly, G.	2	O'Leary, D.A.	1	Walsh, M.	3
Kennedy, M.	3	O'Neill, F.	1	Waters, J.	1
Kernaghan, A.	1	O'Neill, K.P.	4	Whelan, R.	3
Kilbane, K.D.	3	O'Reilly, J.	1		
Kinsella, M.A.	3	Own goals	8		

UEFA UNDER-21 CHAMPIONSHIP 2000–2002

GROUP 1
Switzerland 3, Russia 1
Luxembourg 0, Yugoslavia 3
Luxembourg 1, Slovenia 5
Slovenia 0, Switzerland 0
Russia 2, Luxembourg 0
Yugoslavia 3, Switzerland 3
Russia 0, Slovenia 0
Slovenia 1, Yugoslavia 2
Switzerland 6, Luxembourg 0
Yugoslavia 2, Russia 2
Slovenia 1, Luxembourg 0
Russia 2, Yugoslavia 0
Switzerland 2, Slovenia 1
Luxembourg 0, Russia 10
Switzerland 2, Yugoslavia 2
Slovenia 1, Russia 3
Luxembourg 0, Switzerland 3
Yugoslavia 2, Slovenia 1
Russia 3, Switzerland 3
Yugoslavia 8, Luxembourg 0

GROUP 2
Holland 2, Rep. of Ireland 0
Estonia 1, Portugal 3
Portugal 3, Rep. of Ireland 1
Cyprus 0, Holland 1

Holland 1, Portugal 1
Rep. of Ireland 1, Estonia 0
Cyprus 0, Rep. of Ireland 1
Cyprus 3, Estonia 1
Portugal 3, Holland 0
Holland 4, Cyprus 2
Estonia 0, Holland 5
Rep. of Ireland 0, Portugal 1
Estonia 0, Rep. of Ireland 3
Portugal 7, Cyprus 0
Estonia 0, Cyprus 3
Rep. of Ireland 1, Holland 1
Cyprus 1, Portugal 0
Holland 6, Estonia 0
Portugal 4, Estonia 0
Rep. of Ireland 3, Cyprus 0

GROUP 3
Bulgaria 1, Czech Republic 0
Iceland 0, Denmark 0
N Ireland 3, Malta 0
Czech Republic 2, Iceland 1
N Ireland 0, Denmark 3
Bulgaria 3, Malta 0
Iceland 2, N Ireland 5
Malta 0, Czech Republic 1
Denmark 2, Bulgaria 2

Bulgaria 1, Iceland 0
Malta 0, Denmark 0
N Ireland 0, Czech Republic 2
Bulgaria 2, N Ireland 0
Czech Republic 3, Denmark 0
Malta 1, Iceland 1
Iceland 3, Malta 0
Denmark 5, Czech Republic 4
N Ireland 1, Bulgaria 1
Denmark 3, Malta 0
Iceland 3, Bulgaria 2
Czech Republic 4, N Ireland 0
Iceland 0, Czech Republic 1
Denmark 2, N Ireland 0
Bulgaria 3, Denmark 1
Czech Republic 3, Malta 0
N Ireland 1, Iceland 3
Czech Republic 8, Bulgaria 0
Malta 2, N Ireland 2
Denmark 4, Iceland 0

GROUP 4
Turkey 1, Moldova 0
Azerbaijan 0, Sweden 5
Slovakia 2, Macedonia 0
Sweden 0, Turkey 0

Macedonia 1, Azerbaijan 2
Moldova 0, Slovakia 3
Slovakia 1, Sweden 1
Moldova 3, Macedonia 0
Azerbaijan 1, Turkey 2
Sweden 2, Macedonia 0
Turkey 0, Slovakia 1
Azerbaijan 0, Moldova 0
Macedonia 1, Turkey 4
Slovakia 5, Azerbaijan 0
Moldova 0, Sweden 2
Sweden 4, Slovakia 0
Turkey 3, Azerbaijan 0
Macedonia 2, Moldova 0
Azerbaijan 0, Slovakia 0
Sweden 3, Moldova 0
Turkey 2, Macedonia 0
Moldova 1, Azerbaijan 0
Slovakia 0, Turkey 1
Macedonia 1, Sweden 1
Azerbaijan 1, Macedonia 0
Slovakia 0, Moldova 0
Turkey 4, Sweden 1
Moldova 2, Turkey 2
Macedonia 1, Slovakia 1
Sweden 0, Azerbaijan 0

GROUP 5
Belarus 4, Wales 1
Norway 5, Armenia 1
Ukraine 2, Poland 2
Armenia 1, Ukraine 2
Poland 0, Belarus 4
Wales 0, Norway 2
Belarus 5, Armenia 0
Poland 2, Wales 1
Norway 3, Ukraine 1
Armenia 1, Wales 0
Ukraine 1, Belarus 0
Norway 1, Poland 2
Belarus 1, Norway 0
Poland 1, Armenia 1
Wales 0, Ukraine 3
Armenia 1, Belarus 0
Ukraine 1, Norway 3
Wales 0, Poland 4
Armenia 2, Poland 0
Ukraine 1, Wales 0
Norway 5, Belarus 0
Belarus 1, Ukraine 2
Poland 3, Norway 0
Wales 1, Armenia 1
Belarus 3, Poland 3
Norway 2, Wales 0
Ukraine 1, Armenia 0
Armenia 2, Norway 0
Poland 3, Ukraine 0
Wales 1, Belarus 2

GROUP 6
Latvia 1, Scotland 3
Belgium 2, Croatia 1

Latvia 0, Belgium 2
Croatia 3, Scotland 1
Croatia 2, Latvia 1
Scotland 0, Belgium 1
Belgium 3, Latvia 0
Latvia 1, Croatia 1
Scotland 1, Croatia 1
Belgium 0, Scotland 0
Croatia 1, Belgium 0
Scotland 1, Latvia 0

GROUP 7
France 3, Israel 0
Bosnia 0, Spain 2
France 2, Austria 1
Spain 1, Israel 0
Austria 2, Spain 1
Israel 2, Bosnia 1
Bosnia 0, France 1
Israel 3, France 4
Bosnia 0, Austria 0
Spain 1, France 1
Austria 0, Israel 2
Austria 1, France 1
Spain 5, Bosnia 1
Israel 0, Spain 1
Spain 2, Austria 0
Bosnia 2, Israel 4
Austria 2, Bosnia 1
France 3, Spain 0
France 1, Bosnia 0
Israel 5, Austria 1

GROUP 8
Romania 3, Lithuania 0
Hungary 0, Italy 3
Lithuania 2, Georgia 1
Italy 1, Romania 1
Lithuania 0, Hungary 1
Italy 3, Georgia 2
Hungary 4, Lithuania 1
Romania 0, Italy 1
Georgia 0, Romania 3
Italy 1, Lithuania 0
Romania 1, Hungary 0
Georgia 0, Italy 2
Lithuania 1, Romania 0
Hungary 2, Georgia 1
Georgia 0, Hungary 2
Lithuania 0, Italy 3
Georgia 4, Lithuania 1
Hungary 1, Romania 3
Italy 0, Hungary 2
Romania 2, Georgia 1

GROUP 9
Finland 3, Albania 0
Germany 2, Greece 1
Greece 3, Finland 1
England 1, Germany 1
Albania 0, Greece 1
Finland 2, England 2

Germany 8, Albania 0
England 4, Finland 0
Albania 0, England 1
Greece 2, Germany 0
Finland 1, Germany 3
Greece 0, Albania 0
Greece 3, England 1
Albania 0, Germany 1
Albania 3, Finland 0
Germany 1, England 2
England 5, Albania 0
Finland 0, Greece 3
England 2, Greece 1
Germany 2, Finland 0

PLAY-OFFS FIRST LEG
Croatia 1, Czech Republic 1
Greece 3, Turkey 0
Holland 2, England 2
Poland 2, Italy 5
Romania 0, France 1
Spain 2, Portugal 1
Sweden 3, Belgium 2
Ukraine 1, Switzerland 2

PLAY-OFFS SECOND LEG
Belgium 2, Sweden 0
Czech Republic 0, Croatia 0
England 1, Holland 0
France 4, Romania 0
Italy 0, Poland 0
Portugal 1, Spain 0
Switzerland 2, Ukraine 1
Turkey 2, Greece 1

FINALS (in Switzerland)
GROUP A
England 2, Switzerland 1
Italy 1, Portugal 1
Italy 2, England 1
Portugal 0, Switzerland 2
Portugal 3, Switzerland 2
Switzerland 0, Italy 0

GROUP B
Belgium 1, France 2
Czech Republic 1, Greece 1
France 2, Czech Republic 0
Greece 1, Belgium 2
Greece 1, France 3
Belgium 0, Czech Republic 1

SEMI-FINALS
Czech Republic 3, Italy 2
France 2, Switzerland 0

FINAL
Czech Republic 0, France 0
aet; Czech Republic won 3-1 on penalties.

331

WOMEN'S FOOTBALL 2001–2002

National Division	P	W	D	L	F	A	GD	Pts
Arsenal LFC	18	16	1	1	60	15	45	49
Doncaster Belles LFC	18	13	2	3	57	21	36	41
Charlton Athletic WFC	18	10	1	7	40	24	16	31
Leeds United	18	7	5	6	36	37	–1	26
Everton LFT	18	8	2	8	30	31	–1	26
Tranmere Rovers LFC	18	7	3	8	31	36	–5	24
Brighton & Hove Albion	18	7	3	8	19	33	–14	24
Southampton Saints WFC	18	5	3	10	19	34	–15	18
Barry Town LFC	18	2	3	13	19	49	–30	9
Sunderland AFC Women	18	1	5	12	15	46	–31	8

FA WOMEN'S CUP 2001–2002

FINAL (at Selhurst Park)

6 MAY

Doncaster Belles (0) 1 *(Handley 58)*

Fulham (0) 2 *(Yankey 55, Chapman 56)*   10,124

Doncaster Belles: Hall; Hunt C, Utley, Easton, Barr, Lowe, Burke, Exley, Walker, Handley, Hunt G.
Fulham: Johannessen; Jerray-Silver, Unitt, Haugenes (Mork 90), Terp, Phillip, McArthur, Chapman, Moore (Duncan 61), Pettersen, Yankey.
Referee: E. Evans.

ENGLAND WOMEN'S RECORD 2001–2002

Tournament	Date	Opponents	Score	Goalscorers
5th UEFA Finals, Group Stage	24.06.01	Russia	1-1	Banks
5th UEFA Finals, Group Stage	27.06.01	Sweden	0-4	–
5th UEFA Finals, Group Stage	30.06.01	Germany	0-3	–
Friendly	23.08.01	Denmark	0-3	–
World Cup qualifier	27.09.01	Germany	1-3	Yankey
World Cup qualifier	04.11.01	Holland	0-0	–
World Cup qualifier	24.11.01	Portugal	1-1	Karen Walker
Friendly	25.01.02	Sweden	0-5	–
World Cup qualifier	24.02.02	Portugal	3-0	Fara Williams, Kelly Smith 2
Friendly – Algarve Cup	01.03.02	Norway	1-3	Angie Banks
Friendly – Algarve Cup	03.03.02	USA	0-2	–
Friendly – Algarve Cup	05.03.02	Sweden	3-6	Walker 2, Amanda Barr
Friendly – Algarve Cup	07.03.02	Scotland	4-1	Walker, Williams, Exley, Burke
World Cup Qualificr	23.03.02	Holland	4-1	Chapman, Burke, Smith, Walker
World Cup Qualifer	19.05.02	Germany	0-1	

REPUBLIC OF IRELAND LEAGUE

	P	W	D	L	F	A	Pts
Shelbourne	33	19	6	8	50	28	63
Shamrock Rovers	33	17	6	10	54	32	57
St Patrick's Ath	33	20	8	5	59	29	53
Bohemians	33	14	10	9	57	32	52
Derry City	33	14	9	10	42	30	51
Cork City	33	14	7	12	48	39	49
UCD	33	12	12	9	40	39	48
Bray Wanderers	33	12	10	11	54	45	48
Longford Town	33	10	10	13	41	51	40
Dundalk	33	9	12	12	37	46	39
Galway United	33	5	4	24	28	73	19
Monaghan United	33	2	6	25	19	85	12

St. Patrick's Athletic had nine points deducted for fielding an ineligible player. The points were later reinstated. They then had a further 15 points deducted for fielding another ineligible player.

HIGHLAND LEAGUE

	P	W	D	L	F	A	GD	Pts
Fraserburgh	28	20	4	4	71	36	35	64
Deveronvale	28	19	4	5	68	27	41	61
Buckie Thistle	28	15	8	5	51	27	24	53
Clachnacuddin	28	13	10	5	60	39	21	49
Keith	28	14	5	9	57	37	20	47
Cove Rangers	28	12	7	9	72	60	12	43
Inverurie	28	12	4	12	48	43	5	40
Brora Rangers	28	12	4	12	47	55	-8	40
Huntly	28	11	6	11	46	36	10	39
Forres Mechanics	28	9	10	9	49	46	3	37
Lossiemouth	28	9	6	13	23	40	-17	33
Nairn County	28	6	8	14	44	61	-17	26
Fort William	28	7	2	19	30	61	-31	23
Wick Academy	28	5	4	19	20	59	-39	19
Rothes	28	2	6	20	24	83	-59	12

NATIONWIDE FOOTBALL CONFERENCE 2001–2002

		Home			Goals		Away			Goals			
	P	W	D	L	F	A	W	D	L	F	A	GD	Pts
Boston United	42	12	5	4	53	24	13	4	4	31	18	42	84
Dagenham & Redbridge	42	13	6	2	35	20	11	6	4	35	27	23	84
Yeovil Town	42	6	7	8	27	30	13	6	2	39	23	13	70
Doncaster Rovers	42	11	6	4	41	23	7	7	7	27	23	22	67
Barnet	42	10	4	7	30	19	9	6	6	34	29	16	67
Morecambe	42	12	5	4	30	27	5	6	10	33	40	–4	62
Farnborough Town	42	11	3	7	38	23	7	4	10	28	31	12	61
Margate	42	7	9	5	33	22	7	7	7	26	31	6	58
Telford United	42	8	6	7	34	31	6	9	6	29	27	5	57
Nuneaton Borough	42	9	3	9	33	27	7	6	8	24	30	0	57
Stevenage Borough	42	10	4	7	36	30	5	6	10	21	30	–3	55
Scarborough*	42	9	6	6	27	22	5	8	8	28	41	–8	55
Northwich Victoria	42	9	4	8	32	34	7	3	11	25	36	–13	55
Chester City	42	7	7	7	26	23	8	2	11	28	28	3	54
Southport	42	9	6	6	40	26	4	8	9	13	23	4	53
Leigh Railway Mechanics Institute	42	6	4	11	29	29	9	5	8	27	29	–2	53
Hereford United	42	9	6	6	28	15	5	4	12	22	38	3	52
Forest Green Rovers	42	7	7	7	28	32	5	8	8	26	44	–22	51
Woking	42	7	5	9	28	29	6	4	11	31	41	–11	48
Hayes	42	6	2	13	27	45	7	3	11	26	35	–27	44
Stalybridge Celtic	42	7	6	8	26	32	4	4	13	14	37	–29	43
Dover Athletic	42	6	5	10	20	25	5	1	15	21	40	–24	39

1 point deducted for breach of rule.

Leading Goalscorers 2001–02

	League	LDV	Total
Daryl Clare (Boston United)	24	0	24
Mark Stein (Dagenham & Redbridge)	24	0	24
Ken Charlery (Dagenham & Redbridge)	17	1	18
Mark Cooper (Forest Green Rovers)	17	0	17
Mark Beesley (Chester City)	16	0	16
(Including 8 League goals for Boston United)			
Gregg Blundell (Northwich Victoria)	16	0	16
Leon Braithwaite (Margate)	16	0	16
Simon Parke (Southport)	16	0	16
Lenny Piper (Farnborough Town)	15	0	15
Robbie Talbot (Morecambe)	15	0	15
Michael Twiss (Leigh RMI)	15	0	15
Jamie Paterson (Doncaster Rovers)	14	0	14
Dean Clark (Hayes)	13	0	13
Mark Quayle (Telford United)	13	0	13
Dino Maamria (Leigh RMI)	12	1	13
Ian Hodges (Hayes)	12	0	12
Darren Stamp (Scarborough)	12	0	12
Jeff Vansittart (Farnborough Town)	12	0	12
Simon Weatherstone (Boston United)	12	0	12
Warren Patmore (Woking)	11	0	11

NATIONWIDE FOOTBALL CONFERENCE RESULTS 2001-2002

Column key (away teams, left→right): Bar = Barnet, Bos = Boston United, Che = Chester City, Dag = Dagenham & Redbridge, Don = Doncaster Rovers, Dov = Dover Athletic, Far = Farnborough Town, FGR = Forest Green Rovers, Hay = Hayes, Her = Hereford United, Lei = Leigh RMI, Mar = Margate, Mor = Morecambe, Nor = Northwich Victoria, Nun = Nuneaton Borough, Sca = Scarborough, Sou = Southport, Sta = Stalybridge Celtic, Ste = Stevenage Borough, Tel = Telford United, Wok = Woking, Yeo = Yeovil Town

Home \ Away	Bar	Bos	Che	Dag	Don	Dov	Far	FGR	Hay	Her	Lei	Mar	Mor	Nor	Nun	Sca	Sou	Sta	Ste	Tel	Wok	Yeo
Barnet	—	0-1	3-1	4-0	2-0	2-0	0-3	0-3	3-1	2-0	2-0	0-1	4-1	1-0	1-0	1-1	0-0	0-0	0-0	0-0	0-0	2-3
Boston United	0-1	—	1-2	0-0	4-0	4-2	4-0	6-1	4-1	3-4	1-2	3-0	1-1	3-2	4-1	2-2	0-0	4-1	0-0	3-1	4-0	4-0
Chester City	1-0	1-2	—	3-0	1-0	2-0	0-1	3-0	1-2	0-0	2-1	2-4	2-1	1-1	2-0	0-2	0-2	0-0	5-1	2-2	0-2	1-1
Dagenham & Redbridge	1-0	1-2	1-1	—	1-1	2-1	1-1	2-3	3-1	2-0	0-0	3-0	3-2	2-2	2-0	4-2	1-1	1-0	2-0	3-1	3-1	1-2
Doncaster Rovers	2-3	2-2	1-0	1-1	—	0-0	5-1	3-0	5-2	2-0	2-0	1-0	3-3	2-2	2-2	0-2	1-0	0-1	1-0	1-0	1-1	1-1
Dover Athletic	2-2	0-1	2-0	2-1	0-0	—	1-1	1-0	3-1	1-0	0-0	1-0	2-1	4-1	1-2	0-1	2-1	2-0	6-1	0-0	0-1	1-2
Farnborough Town	2-1	0-3	0-1	1-1	5-1	1-1	—	1-0	1-2	2-2	1-0	0-0	2-1	2-1	1-1	4-2	2-1	0-2	0-2	1-1	0-1	1-2
Forest Green Rovers	2-2	0-2	3-0	2-3	3-0	1-0	1-0	—	3-0	1-1	2-4	0-3	0-2	1-2	1-2	1-2	1-0	0-0	1-2	0-1	2-1	1-1
Hayes	0-2	0-1	1-2	3-1	5-2	3-1	1-2	3-0	—	0-1	1-1	1-1	1-1	1-0	1-2	1-2	2-1	0-0	1-0	1-1	4-1	1-1
Hereford United	2-1	0-1	0-0	2-0	2-0	1-0	2-2	1-1	0-1	—	4-1	3-0	0-1	1-2	0-1	6-0	1-0	3-0	3-0	1-4	2-2	0-4
Leigh RMI	3-3	1-2	2-1	0-0	2-0	0-0	1-0	2-4	1-1	4-1	—	0-1	4-3	2-1	1-1	1-1	3-0	8-0	1-2	2-3	0-1	0-2
Margate	0-1	3-0	2-4	3-0	1-0	1-0	0-0	0-3	1-1	3-0	0-1	—	0-0	2-1	1-0	2-0	3-0	1-0	0-3	1-1	4-3	0-1
Morecambe	1-0	0-3	2-1	0-1	3-3	2-1	2-1	0-2	1-1	0-1	4-3	0-0	—	2-1	2-0	2-2	1-0	1-1	2-1	3-1	2-1	1-5
Northwich Victoria	0-3	1-1	1-1	2-2	2-2	4-1	2-1	1-2	1-0	1-2	2-1	2-1	0-2	—	3-0	1-2	2-0	1-0	1-0	3-1	0-3	1-3
Nuneaton Borough	2-3	1-1	2-0	2-0	2-2	1-2	1-1	1-2	1-2	0-1	1-1	1-0	2-0	3-0	—	1-0	1-0	1-1	4-2	2-2	1-2	1-2
Scarborough	3-0	1-3	0-2	4-2	0-2	0-1	4-2	1-2	1-2	6-0	1-1	2-0	4-1	1-2	1-2	—	1-0	1-0	2-3	2-1	1-0	3-0
Southport	0-1	2-3	0-2	1-1	1-0	2-1	2-1	1-0	2-1	1-0	3-0	3-0	1-3	1-2	1-0	1-0	—	3-1	2-0	3-1	1-0	0-0
Stalybridge Celtic	1-1	2-1	0-0	1-0	0-1	2-0	0-2	0-0	0-0	3-0	8-0	1-0	1-1	1-0	1-1	1-0	3-1	—	2-1	3-1	0-0	1-1
Stevenage Borough	3-2	2-2	5-1	2-0	1-0	6-1	0-2	1-2	1-0	3-0	1-2	0-3	2-1	1-0	4-2	2-3	2-0	2-1	—	0-0	0-2	2-3
Telford United	1-2	2-2	2-2	3-1	1-0	0-0	1-1	0-1	1-1	1-4	2-3	1-1	3-1	3-1	2-2	2-1	3-1	3-1	0-0	—	1-1	2-2
Woking	1-3	0-2	0-2	3-1	1-1	0-1	0-1	2-1	4-1	2-2	0-1	4-3	2-1	0-3	1-2	1-0	1-0	0-0	0-2	1-1	—	0-2
Yeovil Town	1-2	0-1	1-1	1-2	1-1	1-2	1-2	1-1	1-1	0-4	0-2	0-1	1-5	1-3	1-2	3-0	0-0	1-1	2-3	2-2	0-2	—

DR MARTENS LEAGUE 2001–2002

Premier Division

	P	Home			Away			Total			Goals			Pts
		W	D	L	W	D	L	W	D	L	F	A	GD	
Kettering Town	42	12	4	5	15	2	4	27	6	9	80	41	39	87
Tamworth	42	16	5	0	8	8	5	24	13	5	81	41	40	85
Havant & Waterlooville	42	14	4	3	8	5	8	22	9	11	74	50	24	75
Crawley Town	42	12	3	6	9	7	5	21	10	11	67	48	19	73
Newport County	42	10	6	5	9	3	9	19	9	14	61	48	13	66
Tiverton Town	42	10	4	7	7	6	8	17	10	15	70	63	7	61
Moor Green	42	10	6	5	8	1	12	18	7	17	64	62	2	61
Worcester City	42	9	7	5	7	5	9	16	12	14	65	54	11	60
Stafford Rangers	42	13	2	6	4	7	10	17	9	16	70	62	8	60
Ilkeston Town	42	8	8	5	6	8	7	14	16	12	58	61	–3	58
Weymouth	42	9	4	8	6	7	8	15	11	16	59	67	–8	56
Hinckley United	42	10	5	6	4	8	9	14	13	15	64	62	2	55
Folkestone Invicta	42	10	5	6	4	7	10	14	12	16	51	61	–10	54
Cambridge City	42	7	7	7	5	9	7	12	16	14	60	70	–10	52
Welling United	42	8	7	6	5	5	11	13	12	17	69	66	3	51
Hednesford Town	42	9	4	8	6	2	13	15	6	21	59	70	–11	51
Bath City	42	9	3	9	4	8	9	13	11	18	56	65	–9	50
Chelmsford City	42	8	6	7	5	5	11	13	11	18	63	75	–12	50
Newport (IW)	42	6	7	8	6	5	10	12	12	18	38	61	–23	48
King's Lynn	42	6	8	7	5	5	11	11	13	18	44	57	–13	46
Merthyr Tydfil	42	8	7	6	4	1	16	12	8	22	53	71	–18	44
Salisbury City	42	4	5	12	2	3	16	6	8	28	36	87	–51	26

Leading Goalscorers 2001–02

(League and Cup)

Premier Division

Paul Kiely (Stafford Rangers)	29
James Taylor (Havant & Waterlooville)	28
David Laws (Weymouth)	25
Nathan Lamey (Moor Green)	22
Ryan King (Salisbury City)	20
Lee Phillips (Weymouth)	20
Dale Watkins (Kettering Town)	20
Adrian Foster (Bath City)	19
Darren Roberts (Tamworth)	19
Gary Abbott (Welling United)	18
Glen Kirkwood (Ilkeston Town)	18
Adam Webster (Worcester City)	18
Jamie O'Rourke (Havant & Waterlooville)	17
Daniel Carroll (Crawley Town)	15
Timothy Hambley (Havant & Waterlooville)	15
Anthony Hemmings (Tamworth)	15
Daniel Hockton (Chelmsford City)	14
Jamie Lenton (Hinckley United)	14
Mark Owen (Worcester City)	14
Robert Collins (Crawley Town)	13
Neil Davis (Hednesford Town)	13
Darren Collins (Kettering Town)	12

DR MARTEN'S LEAGUE – PREMIER DIVISION RESULTS 2001-2002

Home \ Away	Bath City	Cambridge City	Chelmsford City	Crawley Town	Folkestone Invicta	Havant & Waterlooville	Hednesford Town	Hinckley United	Ilkeston Town	Kettering Town	King's Lynn	Merthyr Tydfil	Moor Green	Newport County	Newport (IoW)	Salisbury City	Stafford Rangers	Tamworth	Tiverton Town	Welling United	Weymouth	Worcester City
Bath City	—	1-1	1-3	3-0	1-1	3-0	1-0	2-2	3-3	0-0	1-1	3-1	0-0	1-0	2-1	0-1	2-1	1-1	3-1	4-0	0-0	0-1
Cambridge City	1-3	—	0-3	3-3	1-0	4-1	1-2	2-2	3-3	1-1	1-2	1-3	3-1	2-2	1-1	1-1	3-0	2-1	3-0	5-0	4-4	1-2
Chelmsford City	1-3	0-3	—	3-3	2-0	1-0	3-1	4-2	1-2	1-3	1-3	1-1	1-3	3-1	3-0	3-2	0-3	1-0	2-0	2-4	2-1	1-1
Crawley Town	3-0	4-3	2-2	—	1-1	4-1	1-0	1-0	0-2	1-2	2-0	3-1	1-2	0-3	3-0	0-1	1-4	0-1	1-3	1-2	0-0	1-0
Folkestone Invicta	1-1	1-0	2-0	1-1	—	1-1	0-1	1-2	0-2	2-3	4-0	1-0	2-1	2-2	1-4	2-0	1-2	0-2	3-3	1-2	3-2	2-1
Havant & Waterlooville	3-0	4-1	0-3	4-1	1-1	—	2-0	5-0	3-2	1-2	0-0	3-0	2-1	0-0	0-0	1-2	1-4	0-1	0-3	1-1	2-4	0-3
Hednesford Town	1-0	1-2	2-1	1-0	0-1	2-0	—	1-1	2-0	1-2	1-0	0-1	5-0	0-0	1-1	1-3	1-2	3-0	3-0	1-1	1-1	1-2
Hinckley United	2-2	2-2	4-2	1-0	1-2	5-0	1-1	—	1-1	2-1	2-2	2-0	3-4	1-1	0-0	0-1	3-1	1-0	1-0	3-2	2-2	0-0
Ilkeston Town	3-3	3-3	6-1	0-2	0-2	3-2	2-0	1-1	—	0-2	0-2	2-1	1-0	1-2	0-2	4-1	2-0	3-4	3-3	3-1	4-1	1-2
Kettering Town	0-0	1-1	1-3	1-2	2-3	1-2	1-2	2-1	0-2	—	2-1	2-0	1-2	4-2	0-0	0-1	1-1	0-1	0-0	0-2	0-0	4-1
King's Lynn	1-1	1-2	3-1	2-0	4-0	0-0	1-0	2-2	0-2	2-1	—	0-1	2-1	4-0	0-3	3-0	0-0	3-1	1-1	4-4	7-1	0-0
Merthyr Tydfil	3-1	1-3	1-1	3-1	1-0	3-0	0-1	2-0	2-1	2-0	0-1	—	2-1	1-0	2-1	1-1	2-2	1-3	0-1	2-1	1-2	0-1
Moor Green	0-0	3-1	1-3	1-2	2-1	2-1	5-0	3-4	1-0	1-2	2-1	2-1	—	2-1	5-0	3-4	2-0	2-0	1-1	2-1	0-0	0-2
Newport County	1-0	2-2	3-1	0-3	2-2	0-0	0-0	1-1	1-2	4-2	4-0	1-0	2-1	—	1-2	4-2	1-2	2-1	0-1	1-1	2-3	1-1
Newport (IoW)	2-1	1-1	3-0	3-0	1-4	0-0	1-1	0-0	0-2	0-0	0-3	2-1	5-0	1-2	—	0-0	1-1	5-1	2-1	1-2	2-1	0-1
Salisbury City	0-1	1-1	3-2	0-1	2-0	1-2	1-3	0-1	4-1	0-1	3-0	1-1	3-4	4-0	0-0	—	3-0	5-1	5-1	5-1	1-0	6-0
Stafford Rangers	2-1	3-0	0-3	1-4	1-2	1-4	1-2	3-1	2-0	1-1	0-0	2-2	2-0	1-4	1-1	3-0	—	1-0	3-3	1-0	0-2	1-2
Tamworth	1-1	2-1	1-0	0-1	0-2	0-1	3-0	1-0	3-4	0-1	3-1	1-3	2-0	2-1	5-1	5-1	1-0	—	1-1	2-2	1-0	4-2
Tiverton Town	3-1	3-0	2-0	1-3	3-3	0-3	3-0	1-0	3-3	0-0	1-1	0-1	1-1	0-1	2-1	5-1	3-3	1-1	—	0-2	0-1	0-3
Welling United	4-0	5-0	2-4	1-2	1-2	1-1	1-1	3-2	3-1	0-2	4-4	2-1	2-1	1-1	1-2	5-1	1-0	2-2	0-2	—	1-1	2-0
Weymouth	0-0	4-4	0-0	0-0	3-2	2-4	1-1	2-2	4-1	0-0	7-1	1-2	0-0	2-3	2-1	1-0	0-2	1-0	0-1	0-1	—	1-2
Worcester City	0-1	1-2	3-3	1-0	2-1	0-3	1-2	0-0	1-2	4-1	0-0	0-1	0-2	1-1	0-1	6-0	1-2	4-2	0-3	2-0	3-3	—

UNIBOND LEAGUE 2001–2002

Premier Division

	P	W	D	L	F	A	W	D	L	F	A	Pts
		Home			*Goals*		*Away*			*Goals*		
Burton Albion	44	17	5	0	59	12	14	6	2	47	18	104
Vauxhall Motors	44	16	3	3	50	26	11	5	6	36	29	89
Lancaster City	44	14	4	4	44	26	9	5	8	36	31	78
Worksop Town	44	13	4	5	40	22	10	5	7	34	29	78
Emley	44	15	4	3	43	24	7	5	10	26	30	75
Accrington Stanley	44	10	7	5	47	27	11	2	9	42	37	72
Runcorn FC Halton	44	11	2	9	36	26	10	6	6	40	27	71
Barrow	44	10	7	5	40	25	9	3	10	35	34	67
Altrincham	44	11	3	8	33	28	8	6	8	33	30	66
Bradford Park Avenue	44	11	2	9	45	37	7	3	12	32	39	59
Droylsden	44	11	3	8	32	34	6	5	11	33	44	59
Blyth Spartans	44	9	8	5	30	24	5	8	9	29	38	58
Frickley Athletic*	44	10	4	8	37	37	6	7	9	26	32	58
Gateshead	44	7	8	7	24	30	7	6	9	34	41	56
Whitby Town	44	7	5	10	33	39	8	3	11	28	37	53
Hucknall Town	44	6	5	11	25	35	8	4	10	24	33	51
Marine	44	7	7	8	36	38	4	10	8	26	33	50
Burscough	44	9	4	9	40	38	6	1	15	29	48	50
Gainsborough Trinity	44	9	5	8	36	30	4	5	13	25	46	49
Colwyn Bay	44	7	6	9	27	39	5	5	12	22	43	47
Bishop Auckland	44	5	5	12	22	34	7	3	12	24	34	44
Hyde United	44	5	7	10	29	37	5	3	14	32	50	40
Bamber Bridge*	44	5	4	13	23	40	2	6	14	15	48	30

* 1 point deducted for breach of rule

LEADING GOALSCORERS

(In order of League Goals)

Premier Division

Lge	Cup	Tot	
27	9	36	Terry Fearns (Vauxhall Motors)
26	6	32	Andy Whittaker (Lancaster City)
22	12	34	Paul Mullin (Accrington Stanley)
21	2	23	Lutel James (Accrington Stanley)
20	11	31	Andy Hayward (Bradford Park Avenue)
20	7	27	Glen Robson (Blyth Spartans)
17	16	33	Rod Thornley (Altrincham)
17	6	23	Darren Day (Emley)
16	8	24	Jason Maxwell (Bradford Park Avenue)
16	7	23	Steve Preen (Gateshead)
16	5	21	Paul McNally (Runcorn FC Halton)
16	4	20	Steve Housham (Barrow)
16	2	18	Richie Townsend (Marine)

ATTENDANCES
Premier Division
Highest Attendances: 2170 Burton Albion v Droylsden
2141 Burton Albion v Bradford
Park Avenue
2032 Barrow v Lancaster City

UNIBOND LEAGUE – PREMIER DIVISION RESULTS 2001-2002

	Accrington Stanley	Altrincham	Bamber Bridge	Barrow	Bishop Auckland	Blyth Spartans	Bradford Park Avenue	Burscough	Burton Albion	Colwyn Bay	Droylsden	Emley	Frickley Athletic	Gainsborough Trinity	Gateshead	Hucknall Town	Hyde United	Lancaster City	Marine	Runcorn FC Halton	Vauxhall Motors	Whitby Town	Worksop Town
Accrington Stanley	—	0-0	2-0	0-3	1-1	1-1	5-1	3-0	3-1	3-0	1-5	0-1	1-3	1-1	0-0	1-2	4-1	3-2	3-1	1-1	2-3	2-3	5-0
Altrincham	3-1	—	1-1	2-2	0-3	2-1	0-2	4-1	5-2	3-2	1-1	2-1	2-1	1-0	5-0	0-1	3-2	0-1	1-0	0-1	3-2	1-3	2-0
Bamber Bridge	0-1	1-1	—	1-0	0-2	0-1	2-1	0-3	3-0	1-2	2-3	0-2	0-2	1-0	1-4	4-1	1-3	1-1	0-1	1-6	1-3	3-0	0-0
Barrow	0-4	2-2	1-1	—	2-3	4-1	2-1	0-3	0-0	1-2	3-0	0-0	2-3	4-1	1-0	6-1	0-0	2-2	2-0	2-1	1-3	3-0	1-0
Bishop Auckland	1-2	0-3	3-1	2-3	—	1-0	4-1	1-0	0-1	1-2	1-2	0-0	0-0	0-1	4-1	6-1	0-0	0-0	1-3	2-1	3-4	1-0	1-2
Blyth Spartans	1-1	3-1	0-1	4-1	1-2	—	4-1	2-1	0-4	5-0	3-1	1-3	0-0	2-2	3-5	2-1	0-0	2-1	3-1	2-2	0-1	1-1	2-2
Bradford Park Avenue	1-2	0-3	2-1	2-3	4-1	0-0	—	1-4	0-2	4-0	6-2	2-1	4-0	3-1	2-2	0-1	3-1	0-2	2-0	1-3	3-4	1-1	1-5
Burscough	3-2	4-1	0-3	3-2	2-1	1-1	0-2	—	0-0	3-0	1-1	1-0	1-0	5-1	3-5	1-1	3-2	1-1	2-1	2-2	2-1	3-1	2-3
Burton Albion	3-1	5-2	0-1	5-0	1-1	4-0	0-2	0-0	—	3-2	1-1	4-0	4-2	2-2	4-1	1-3	4-4	2-3	2-1	1-3	2-3	5-1	1-0
Colwyn Bay	3-0	3-2	1-2	1-2	1-2	5-0	0-0	3-0	3-2	—	1-0	1-0	1-5	1-2	1-2	1-1	0-3	4-1	0-2	1-3	1-0	0-3	0-3
Droylsden	1-5	1-1	2-3	0-0	1-2	3-1	1-0	4-0	3-0	3-2	—	1-0	1-0	0-1	0-1	3-0	1-1	0-2	2-4	1-0	1-0	3-1	0-2
Emley	0-3	2-5	0-2	5-0	1-0	0-1	2-1	3-0	1-1	3-2	4-2	—	3-2	1-0	0-1	1-1	1-0	2-0	0-0	4-0	1-0	0-4	1-1
Frickley Athletic	1-3	2-1	1-0	2-3	1-0	0-0	1-0	3-0	2-2	1-0	1-3	3-2	—	3-1	0-0	0-0	2-2	0-4	3-1	2-1	3-1	0-1	4-0
Gainsborough Trinity	5-2	1-3	1-0	2-0	2-2	1-5	4-1	0-0	5-1	1-0	2-0	2-1	2-1	—	0-0	1-1	4-1	2-2	1-1	2-0	4-0	1-4	0-2
Gateshead	0-0	5-0	0-1	1-0	2-0	3-3	3-0	0-0	0-2	1-2	4-2	3-2	2-2	3-1	—	2-4	0-1	2-4	1-1	2-1	2-2	2-0	0-3
Hucknall Town	1-3	0-1	1-4	6-1	0-1	2-1	0-1	0-1	1-3	3-1	1-1	1-1	2-1	0-0	0-0	—	3-1	0-2	2-0	1-1	2-1	1-0	1-1
Hyde United	2-4	3-2	1-3	0-0	0-0	0-0	3-1	3-2	4-4	0-3	1-1	1-0	2-2	4-1	0-1	3-1	—	4-2	2-2	3-1	2-1	3-1	3-3
Lancaster City	1-0	0-1	1-1	2-2	0-0	2-1	0-2	1-1	2-3	4-1	0-2	2-0	0-4	2-2	2-4	0-2	4-2	—	2-1	2-0	1-2	2-1	2-1
Marine	2-5	1-0	0-1	2-0	1-3	3-1	2-0	2-1	2-1	0-2	2-4	0-0	3-1	1-1	1-1	2-0	2-2	4-2	—	1-1	2-3	5-1	1-1
Runcorn FC Halton	1-0	0-1	1-6	2-1	2-1	2-2	1-3	2-2	1-3	1-3	1-0	4-0	2-1	2-0	2-1	1-1	3-1	2-0	1-1	—	0-2	1-2	0-3
Vauxhall Motors	1-2	3-2	1-3	1-3	3-4	0-1	3-4	2-1	2-3	1-0	1-0	1-0	3-1	4-0	2-2	2-1	2-1	1-2	2-3	0-2	—	1-2	1-2
Whitby Town	2-1	2-3	3-0	3-0	1-0	1-1	1-1	3-1	5-1	0-3	3-1	0-4	0-1	1-4	2-0	1-0	3-1	2-1	5-1	1-2	2-3	—	0-2
Worksop Town	5-0	1-2	0-0	1-0	1-2	2-2	1-5	2-3	1-0	0-3	0-2	1-1	4-0	0-2	0-3	1-1	3-3	2-1	1-1	0-3	1-2	0-2	—

RYMAN FOOTBALL LEAGUE 2001–2002

Premier Division

	P	Home W	D	L	Goals F	A	Away W	D	L	Goals F	A	GD	Pts
Gravesend & Northfleet	42	14	4	3	43	18	17	2	2	47	15	57	99
Canvey Island	42	15	3	3	55	25	15	2	4	53	16	67	95
Aldershot Town	42	12	4	5	44	23	10	3	8	32	28	25	73
Braintree Town	42	15	2	4	37	20	8	2	11	29	41	5	73
Purfleet	42	11	8	2	39	20	8	7	6	28	24	23	72
Grays Athletic	42	12	5	4	33	21	8	5	8	32	34	10	70
Chesham United	42	11	7	3	40	27	8	3	10	29	26	16	67
Hendon	42	10	3	8	26	22	9	2	10	40	33	11	62
Billericay Town	42	8	6	7	32	34	8	7	6	27	26	–1	61
St Albans City	42	9	5	7	29	25	7	4	10	42	35	11	57
Hitchin Town	42	7	4	10	31	39	8	6	7	42	42	–8	55
Sutton United	42	8	9	4	33	26	5	6	10	29	37	–1	54
Heybridge Swifts	42	7	6	8	34	40	8	3	10	34	45	–17	54
Kingstonian	42	10	4	7	34	27	3	9	9	16	29	–6	52
Boreham Wood	42	6	4	11	24	36	9	2	10	26	26	–12	51
Maidenhead United	42	9	3	9	27	30	6	2	13	24	33	–12	50
Bedford Town	42	10	1	10	39	32	2	11	8	25	37	–5	48
Basingstoke Town	42	8	5	8	28	31	3	10	8	22	37	–18	48
Enfield	42	4	4	13	20	44	7	5	9	28	33	–29	42
Hampton & Richmond	42	5	8	8	26	32	4	5	12	25	39	–20	40
Harrow Borough	42	2	5	14	26	54	6	5	10	24	35	–39	34
Croydon	42	5	3	13	24	40	2	2	17	12	53	–57	26

LEADING GOALSCORERS

Premier Division		Lge	ILC
31	Lee Boylan (Canvey Island)	27	4
25	Nicky Simpson (Braintree Town)	18	7
24	Simon Martin (St Albans City)	24	
24	Craig Maskell (Hampton & Richmond B)	17	7
24	Kevin Slinn (Bedford Town)	24	
22	Stafford Browne (Aldershot Town)	19	3

Lge: Ryman League; ILC: Isthmian League Cup.

RYMAN FOOTBALL LEAGUE – PREMIER DIVISION RESULTS 2001–2002

Home \ Away	Aldershot Town	Basingstoke Town	Bedford Town	Billericay Town	Boreham Wood	Braintree Town	Canvey Island	Chesham United	Croydon	Enfield	Gravesend & Northfleet	Grays Athletic	Hampton & Richmond	Harrow Borough	Hendon	Heybridge Swifts	Hitchin Town	Kingstonian	Maidenhead United	Purfleet	St Albans City	Sutton United
Aldershot Town	—	1-1	1-2	2-0	1-3	2-0	1-3	2-1	1-1	3-1	2-1	1-1	2-3	0-1	1-2	0-3	2-1	1-2	2-1	2-1	1-1	1-0
Basingstoke Town	2-2	—	3-0	3-4	1-7	0-2	2-1	1-1	0-1	0-1	4-0	0-2	4-1	2-1	1-0	3-3	1-3	1-3	2-1	3-0	1-1	1-0
Bedford Town	1-1	3-0	—	3-4	0-1	2-0	1-3	0-1	3-2	3-2	4-1	4-0	3-4	2-1	4-6	5-2	1-1	2-2	1-2	1-0	0-1	0-1
Billericay Town	2-0	0-0	0-0	—	0-1	2-4	1-3	1-4	0-2	2-2	1-3	0-2	2-0	3-4	2-2	5-2	1-1	1-0	0-1	1-0	0-5	2-1
Boreham Wood	1-3	0-0	1-0	1-1	—	1-2	2-1	1-4	3-0	1-3	2-0	2-2	3-2	1-0	1-2	2-4	2-1	2-1	1-0	1-0	1-5	1-2
Braintree Town	2-0	3-2	0-1	1-1	2-0	—	2-1	2-1	2-1	2-3	3-2	2-3	1-2	3-0	0-1	2-4	2-1	1-3	2-0	2-2	3-2	3-0
Canvey Island	1-3	5-1	3-3	3-2	2-0	4-1	—	3-2	3-0	2-3	1-2	3-5	3-2	5-0	3-1	6-1	2-1	2-0	3-3	0-1	3-2	1-2
Chesham United	2-1	1-1	2-1	0-5	2-1	1-5	1-0	—	2-1	0-2	0-0	1-2	0-0	1-2	0-3	2-3	5-5	2-0	1-0	3-3	3-2	2-0
Croydon	1-2	1-1	3-3	0-0	0-5	0-4	2-1	1-2	—	0-2	2-4	1-0	0-0	1-2	2-3	2-3	5-0	4-0	0-2	0-1	0-0	2-0
Enfield	1-1	3-3	1-3	1-2	0-1	4-1	1-2	1-0	6-1	—	1-5	1-0	0-2	1-2	0-6	4-2	0-5	2-0	0-2	0-0	3-2	2-2
Gravesend & Northfleet	2-1	0-0	3-3	1-1	0-1	1-2	1-1	3-0	1-0	3-0	—	2-3	0-2	2-2	2-0	2-3	0-5	2-0	3-2	3-0	3-2	1-2
Grays Athletic	3-1	4-1	1-3	3-0	0-1	1-2	0-7	1-4	6-0	0-2	2-0	—	1-1	1-2	0-1	1-3	2-1	2-0	2-0	1-0	0-0	2-0
Hampton & Richmond	1-1	2-1	2-2	1-1	2-3	3-0	0-1	1-1	1-0	2-4	2-0	1-1	—	1-0	2-0	1-3	6-3	2-0	2-0	1-3	0-5	3-3
Harrow Borough	2-3	3-3	2-4	0-2	1-2	0-2	0-1	3-0	2-4	0-3	3-0	1-1	1-1	—	0-2	1-3	1-3	0-1	1-1	0-3	3-2	1-6
Hendon	0-1	1-2	3-1	1-5	0-2	3-0	0-1	2-1	0-1	0-0	1-0	1-0	1-0	0-1	—	1-3	2-1	2-0	0-3	2-0	2-6	4-3
Heybridge Swifts	1-2	5-1	3-1	0-7	0-2	0-2	1-2	2-3	1-2	4-2	1-3	1-1	1-3	1-0	1-6	—	0-0	2-0	1-1	3-3	2-6	2-1
Hitchin Town	0-3	2-0	1-2	1-1	4-1	3-0	2-3	4-1	3-0	1-2	0-4	1-1	2-4	3-0	3-0	1-0	—	1-0	1-0	0-3	2-4	4-0
Kingstonian	2-1	1-1	3-0	0-2	2-0	0-2	2-1	0-2	0-0	1-2	0-3	1-1	2-4	4-2	3-1	1-0	0-0	—	0-1	1-0	4-2	1-1
Maidenhead United	1-2	2-2	2-1	0-2	0-1	2-0	0-4	2-0	1-0	0-3	2-1	2-1	3-0	0-3	1-0	1-0	0-1	1-1	—	5-2	1-3	1-1
Purfleet	2-1	2-1	2-1	0-1	1-1	3-1	0-1	5-1	0-1	1-0	1-0	1-3	1-1	0-3	2-1	1-2	3-1	1-1	1-0	—	1-2	2-0
St Albans City	0-3	2-0	0-0	0-0	3-1	3-1	2-4	5-0	1-0	0-3	0-3	2-1	0-2	1-3	2-0	1-2	3-1	2-2	2-2	1-1	—	1-1
Sutton United	2-0	2-1	2-2	2-2	3-1	3-1	1-4	0-1	2-0	1-1	2-0	2-2	2-0	1-1	2-1	4-1	2-4	2-0	2-1	0-0	1-1	—

341

AVON LEAGUE

Premier Division

	P	W	D	L	F	A	GD	Pts
Preston NE	24	14	2	8	46	40	6	44
Barnsley	24	12	5	7	43	31	12	41
Tranmere R	24	12	5	7	40	32	8	41
Sheffield U	24	10	9	5	38	31	7	39
Burnley	24	11	6	7	43	40	3	39
Rotherham U	24	10	8	6	42	31	11	38
Wolverhampton W	24	11	4	9	25	22	3	37
Birmingham C	24	9	7	8	35	26	9	34
Huddersfield T	24	7	10	7	36	34	2	31
Oldham Ath	24	5	9	10	30	44	−14	24
WBA	24	5	8	11	20	29	−9	23
Wrexham	24	5	6	13	41	49	−8	21
Port Vale	24	3	5	16	19	49	−30	14

Division One

	P	W	D	L	F	A	GD	Pts
Walsall	22	14	3	5	52	22	30	45
Bury	22	13	2	7	45	34	11	41
Scunthorpe U	22	12	2	8	39	37	2	38
Grimsby T	22	11	3	8	42	34	8	36
Stoke C	22	10	3	9	52	27	25	33
Doncaster R	22	10	3	9	44	33	11	33
Shrewsbury T	22	9	3	10	35	35	0	30
Lincoln C	22	7	8	7	21	34	−13	29
Darlington	22	8	4	10	27	38	−11	28
Blackpool	22	5	6	11	28	48	−20	21
Stockport Co	22	5	6	11	26	51	−25	21
York C	22	5	3	14	19	37	−18	18

Division Two

	P	W	D	L	F	A	GD	Pts
Macclesfield T	20	14	3	3	37	13	24	45
Hull C	20	13	4	3	53	27	26	43
Kidderminster H	20	12	2	6	40	27	13	38
Notts Co	20	9	6	5	36	22	14	33
Mansfield T	20	9	4	7	31	31	0	31
Hartlepool U	20	9	1	10	39	32	7	28
Wigan Ath	20	7	4	9	36	34	2	25
Rochdale	20	6	4	10	29	35	−6	22
Chesterfield	20	5	2	13	22	58	−36	17
Halifax T	20	4	3	13	23	45	−22	15
Carlisle U	20	3	5	12	17	39	−22	14

AVON INSURANCE COMBINATION

Division One

	P	W	D	L	F	A	GD	Pts
QPR	24	14	6	4	52	22	30	48
Crystal P	24	14	5	5	50	26	24	47
Brentford	24	13	6	5	48	33	15	45
Portsmouth	24	12	6	6	36	22	14	38
Cardiff C	24	11	5	8	41	31	10	38
Peterborough U	24	12	2	10	41	39	2	38
Millwall	24	10	7	7	43	36	7	37
Luton T	24	10	7	7	39	30	9	37
Reading	24	10	6	8	35	25	10	36
Southend U	24	9	8	7	35	29	−6	35
Leyton Orient	24	11	2	11	37	53	−16	35
Norwich C	24	9	7	8	40	38	2	34
Oxford U	24	9	7	8	30	35	−5	34
Barnet	24	10	2	12	31	34	−3	32
Cheltenham T	24	9	5	10	30	43	−13	32
Gillingham	24	8	6	10	31	34	−3	30
Brighton & HA	24	7	11	6	30	27	3	32
Bristol R	24	9	4	11	31	34	−3	31
Bristol C	24	7	7	10	33	35	−2	28
Colchester U	24	7	5	12	32	38	−6	26
Cambridge U	24	7	4	13	29	43	−14	25
Wycombe W	24	7	3	14	31	44	−13	24
Bournemouth	24	6	5	13	26	47	−21	23
Northampton T	24	4	10	10	25	42	−17	22
Swindon T	24	4	6	14	22	38	−16	18

FA ACADEMY UNDER-17 LEAGUE

Group A

	P	W	D	L	F	A	GD	Pts
Tottenham H	24	13	7	4	38	20	+18	46
Arsenal	24	13	4	7	48	25	+23	43
Crystal Palace	24	11	4	9	43	44	−1	37
Charlton Ath	24	7	7	10	36	39	−3	28
Wimbledon	24	7	5	12	31	41	−10	26
Southampton	24	7	4	13	30	39	−9	25
Millwall	24	7	4	13	33	49	−16	25
Bristol C	24	6	5	13	32	51	−19	23
Reading	24	7	2	15	25	51	−26	23

Group B

	P	W	D	L	F	A	GD	Pts
Aston Villa	22	15	4	3	53	18	+35	49
Birmingham	22	13	3	7	45	23	+22	39
Leicester C	22	11	4	7	37	31	+6	37
West Ham U	22	10	5	7	28	25	+3	35
Ipswich T	22	10	3	9	43	38	+5	33
Watford	22	8	4	10	24	33	−9	28
Wolverhampton W	22	5	6	11	21	40	−19	21
Fulham	22	5	5	12	29	61	−32	20

Group C

	P	W	D	L	F	A	GD	Pts
Liverpool	24	19	5	0	75	16	+59	62
Blackburn R	24	13	8	3	53	21	+32	47
Manchester U	24	13	6	5	68	27	+41	45
Coventry C	24	10	6	8	37	38	−1	36
Crewe Alex	24	10	5	9	28	36	−8	35
Manchester C	24	7	9	8	37	40	−3	30
Bolton W	24	5	2	17	33	60	−27	17
Everton	24	4	4	16	18	47	−29	16
Wrexham	24	2	5	17	19	71	−52	11

Group D

	P	W	D	L	F	A	GD	Pts
Newcastle U	24	15	4	5	61	25	+36	49
Sunderland	24	12	10	2	49	24	+25	46
Leeds U	24	11	7	6	39	24	+15	40
Derby Co	24	9	9	5	52	38	+14	35
Sheffield U	24	10	5	9	36	39	−3	35
Nottingham F	24	11	2	11	33	44	−11	35
Barnsley	24	10	2	12	34	50	−16	32
Middlesbrough	24	9	2	13	24	32	−8	29
Sheffield W	24	3	5	16	29	61	−32	14

UNDER-17 PLAY-OFFS

Group 1

	P	W	D	L	F	A	GD	Pts
Tottenham H	2	1	1	0	3	2	+1	4
Coventry C	2	1	0	1	4	3	+1	3
Barnsley	2	0	1	1	2	4	−2	1

Group 2

	P	W	D	L	F	A	GD	Pts
Arsenal	3	3	0	0	7	2	+5	9
Nottingham F	3	1	1	1	5	3	+2	4
West Ham U	3	1	1	1	4	4	0	4
Everton	3	0	0	3	1	8	−7	0

Group 3

	P	W	D	L	F	A	GD	Pts
Aston Villa	3	2	1	0	8	4	+4	7
Middlesbrough	3	1	2	0	6	3	+3	5
Manchester C	3	1	1	1	5	5	0	4
Charlton Ath	3	0	0	3	3	10	−7	0

Group 4

	P	W	D	L	F	A	GD	Pts
Manchester U	3	2	1	0	9	1	+8	7
Birmingham C	3	1	1	1	3	3	0	4
Southampton	3	1	0	2	1	3	−2	3
Sheffield W	3	1	0	2	2	8	−6	3

Group 5

	P	W	D	L	F	A	GD	Pts
Sheffield U	3	2	0	1	4	2	+2	6
Liverpool	3	1	2	0	2	0	+2	5
Reading	3	1	1	1	2	4	−2	4
Leicester C	3	0	1	2	1	3	−2	1

Group 6

	P	W	D	L	F	A	GD	Pts
Blackburn R	3	2	1	0	6	2	+4	7
Wolverhampton W	3	2	0	1	4	2	+2	6
Derby Co	3	1	1	1	4	2	+2	4
Millwall	3	0	0	3	1	9	−8	0

Group 7

	P	W	D	L	F	A	GD	Pts
Newcastle U	3	3	0	0	12	1	+11	9
Crewe Alex	3	1	1	1	8	4	+4	4
Wimbledon	3	1	0	2	5	7	−2	3
Fulham	3	0	1	2	4	9	−5	1

Group 8

	P	W	D	L	F	A	GD	Pts
Ipswich T	3	2	1	0	6	2	+4	7
Bolton W	3	2	0	1	6	4	+2	6
Sunderland	3	1	0	2	5	5	−3	3
Bristol C	3	0	1	2	1	4	−3	1

Group 9

	P	W	D	L	F	A	GD	Pts
Leeds U	3	2	1	0	8	1	+7	7
Crystal Palace	3	1	2	0	9	5	+4	5
Watford	3	1	1	1	7	5	+2	4
Wrexham	3	0	0	3	0	13	−13	0

QUARTER-FINALS

Arsenal 1, Newcastle U 2
Tottenham H 1, Sheffield U 2
Aston Villa 1, Leeds U 2
Manchester U 2, Ipswich T 1

SEMI-FINALS

Sheffield U 2, Newcastle U 3
Leeds U 0, Manchester U 2

FINAL (two legs)

Manchester U 2, Newcastle U 3
Newcastle U 2, Manchester U 0

FA ACADEMY UNDER-19 LEAGUE

Group A	P	W	D	L	F	A	GD	Pts
Arsenal	27	17	7	3	63	22	+41	58
Chelsea	27	12	10	5	54	37	+17	46
Crystal Palace	27	11	7	9	45	35	+10	40
Tottenham H	27	10	9	8	43	28	+15	39
Charlton Ath	27	10	4	13	45	48	−3	34
Millwall	27	9	7	11	37	45	−8	34
Southampton	27	10	2	15	42	51	−9	32
Bristol C	27	9	5	13	39	59	−20	32
Wimbledon	27	6	9	12	28	39	−11	27
Reading	27	5	5	17	31	61	−30	20

Group B	P	W	D	L	F	A	GD	Pts
Ipswich T	26	17	7	2	69	38	+31	58
West Ham U	26	12	8	6	45	37	+8	44
Birmingham C	26	12	5	9	48	44	+4	41
Fulham	26	9	6	11	44	47	−3	33
Wolverhampton W	26	8	8	10	24	29	−5	32
Leicester C	26	8	7	11	33	37	−4	31
Norwich C	26	8	5	13	41	64	−23	29
Aston Villa	26	6	10	10	42	50	−8	28
Watford	26	7	7	12	28	44	−16	28

Group C	P	W	D	L	F	A	GD	Pts
Liverpool	28	18	7	3	74	37	+37	61
Manchester U	28	19	4	5	62	36	+26	61
Manchester C	28	15	5	8	53	38	+15	50
Crewe Alex	28	14	7	7	55	47	+8	49
Coventry C	28	12	6	10	49	37	+12	42
Everton	28	11	9	8	43	31	+12	42
Blackburn R	28	8	9	11	45	43	+2	33
Stoke C	28	7	6	15	40	46	−6	27
Bolton W	28	5	6	17	39	59	−20	21
Wrexham	28	1	2	25	25	103	−78	5

Group D	P	W	D	L	F	A	GD	Pts
Nottingham F	28	20	6	2	61	21	+40	66
Derby Co	28	16	2	10	58	33	+25	50
Newcastle U	28	14	5	9	72	42	+30	47
Middlesbrough	28	13	8	7	37	27	+10	47
Leeds U	28	13	6	9	52	45	+7	45
Sunderland	28	7	13	8	25	28	−3	34
Barnsley	28	10	3	15	36	56	−20	33
Sheffield U	28	6	8	14	36	55	−19	26
Huddersfield T	28	7	4	17	35	70	−35	25
Sheffield W	28	5	6	17	32	61	−29	21

UNDER-19 PLAY-OFFS

SEMI-FINALS
Ipswich T 1, Arsenal 2
Nottingham F 1, Liverpool 2

FINAL (two legs)
Liverpool 1, Arsenal 5
Arsenal 2, Liverpool 3

FA PREMIER RESERVE LEAGUES

NORTH FINAL TABLE

	P	W	D	L	F	A	GD	Pts
Manchester U	24	12	7	5	47	28	+19	43
Newcastle U	24	13	3	8	46	28	+18	42
Middlesbrough	24	12	6	6	39	28	+11	42
Sunderland	24	12	4	8	43	28	+15	40
Bolton W	24	12	3	9	45	40	+5	39
Manchester C	24	10	7	7	40	28	+12	37
Blackburn R	24	11	4	9	41	30	+11	37
Leeds U	24	10	4	10	25	33	–8	34
Liverpool	24	9	6	9	56	52	+4	33
Everton	24	8	8	8	30	30	0	32
Aston Villa	24	7	4	13	26	49	–23	25
Bradford C	24	5	6	13	27	56	–29	21
Sheffield W	24	2	4	18	26	61	–35	10

HIGHEST ATTENDANCE Sunderland v Newcastle U   9028

LEADING APPEARANCES

Bewers (Aston Villa)	24
Pilkington (Everton)	24
Greer (Blackburn R)	23
McLeod (Everton)	23
Hudson (Middlesbrough)	23
Bellion (Sunderland)	23
Smith (Aston Villa)	22
O'Brien (Blackburn R)	22
Shuker (Manchester C)	22
Kerr (Newcastle U)	22
Byrne (Sunderland)	22
Kyle (Sunderland)	22

LEADING GOALSCORERS

Mellor (Liverpool)	15
Kyle (Sunderland)	11
Windass (Middlesbrough)	10
Holdsworth (Bolton W)	9
Killen (Manchester C)	9
Lua-Lua (Newcastle U)	9
Chadwick (Everton)	8
Webber (Manchester U)	8
Ostenstad (Blackburn R)	7
Shuker (Manchester C)	7

SOUTH FINAL TABLE

	P	W	D	L	F	A	GD	Pts
Ipswich T	26	17	5	4	54	26	+28	56
Arsenal	26	15	5	6	49	27	+22	50
Derby Co	26	15	5	6	47	31	+16	50
Fulham	26	14	5	7	54	33	+21	47
Southampton	26	10	6	10	35	30	+5	36
West Ham U	26	9	7	10	39	32	+7	34
Charlton Ath	26	9	7	10	37	41	–4	34
Tottenham H	26	10	4	12	29	38	–9	34
Chelsea	26	9	7	10	28	40	–12	34
Nottingham F	26	9	5	12	28	40	–12	32
Leicester C	26	7	8	11	32	44	–12	29
Wimbledon	26	8	3	15	34	52	–18	27
Coventry C	26	6	7	13	29	42	–13	25
Watford	26	3	8	15	30	51	–21	17

HIGHEST ATTENDANCE Southampton v Arsenal   10,025

LEADING APPEARANCES

Collis (Charlton Ath)	26
Juan (Arsenal)	25
Bolder (Derby Co)	24
Godfrey (Watford)	24
Riza (West Ham U)	24
Heath (Leicester C)	23
MacDonald (Southampton)	23
Neill (Watford)	23
Pead (Coventry C)	23
Swonnell (Watford)	23
Willock (Fulham)	23

LEADING GOALSCORERS

Bent D (Ipswich T)	21
Cole (Chelsea)	10
Nowland (Wimbledon)	9
Aliadiere (Arsenal)	8
Bolder (Derby Co)	8
Willock (Fulham)	8
Ambrose (Ipswich T)	7
Foley (Watford)	7
Morris (Derby Co)	7
Riza (West Ham U)	7
Robinson (Wimbledon)	7

FA UMBRO TROPHY 2001–2002

FINAL (at Villa Park) – 12 May

Yeovil Town (1) 2 *(Alford 12, Stansfield 66)*
Stevenage Borough (0) 0   18,809

Yeovil Town: Weale; Lockwood, Tonkin, Skiverton, Pluck (White), Johnson, Crittenden (Lindegaard), Way, Alford (Giles), Stansfield, McIndoe.
Stevenage Borough: Wilkerson; Hamsher, Fraser, Goodliffe, Trott, Fisher, Evers (Williams), Sigere (Campbell D), Jackson, Clarke, Wormull (Sterling).
Referee: N. Barry (N. Lincolnshire).

FA CARLSBERG VASE 2001–2002

FINAL (at Villa Park) – 11 May

Tiptree United (0) 0
Whitley Bay (0) 1 *(Chandler 97)*   4742

Tiptree United: Haygreen; Battell, Brady, Houghton, Fish, Wall, Streetly (Gillespie), Wareham (Snow), Aransibia (Parnell), Barchfield, Daly.
Whitley Bay: Caffrey; Sunderland, Walmsley, Dixon (Neil), Anderson, Locker, Bowes (Carr), Walton, Chandler, Fenwick (Cuggy), Middleton.
aet.
Referee: A. Kaye (Wakefield).

THE AXA FA YOUTH CUP 2001–2002
(in association with *The Times*)

FINAL First Leg – 18 May

Everton (1) 1 *(Rooney 25)*
Aston Villa (1) 4 *(Moore S 37, 53, Hynes 68, Moore L 80)*   15,280

Everton: Pettinger; Moogan B, Crowder, Moogan A (Colbeck 74), Schumacher, Garside, Brown, Beck, Symes, Rooney, Carney.
Aston Villa: Henderson; Wells, Whittingham, Marshall, O'Connor (Amoo 83), Ridgewell, Davis, Hynes (Husbands 89), Moore L (Atkinson 90), Foley, Moore S.
Referee: B. Knight (Kent).

FINAL Second Leg – 22 May

Aston Villa (0) 0
Everton (0) 1 *(Brown 75)*   18,651

Aston Villa: Henderson; Wells, Whittingham, Marshall, Amoo, Ridgewell, Hynes (Scullion 87), Davis, Moore L (Husbands 90), Foley, Moore S.
Everton: Pettinger; Moogan B, Crowder, Moogan A, Schumacher, Garside, Brown, Beck (Hopkins 64), Symes, Rooney, Carney.
Referee: B. Knight (Kent).

FA UMBRO SUNDAY CUP 2001–2002

FINAL
Britannia v Little Paxton   2-0

FA COUNTY YOUTH CUP 2001–2002

FINAL
Birmingham v Durham   2-1

SOUTH AMERICAN CHAMPIONSHIP

(Copa America)

1916	Uruguay	1939	Peru	1967	Uruguay
1917	Uruguay	1941	Argentina	1975	Peru
1919	Brazil	1942	Uruguay	1979	Paraguay
1920	Uruguay	1945	Argentina	1983	Uruguay
1921	Argentina	1946	Argentina	1987	Uruguay
1922	Brazil	1947	Argentina	1989	Brazil
1923	Uruguay	1949	Brazil	1991	Argentina
1924	Uruguay	1953	Paraguay	1993	Argentina
1925	Argentina	1955	Argentina	1995	Uruguay
1926	Uruguay	1956	Uruguay	1997	Brazil
1927	Argentina	1957	Argentina	1999	Brazil
1929	Argentina	1959	Argentina	2001	Colombia
1935	Uruguay	1959	Uruguay		
1937	Argentina	1963	Bolivia		

SOUTH AMERICAN CUP

(Copa Libertadores)

1960	Penarol (Uruguay)	1982	Penarol
1961	Penarol	1983	Gremio Porto Alegre (Brazil)
1962	Santos (Brazil)	1984	Independiente
1963	Santos	1985	Argentinos Juniors (Argentina)
1964	Independiente (Argentina)	1986	River Plate (Argentina)
1965	Independiente	1987	Penarol
1966	Penarol	1988	Nacional (Uruguay)
1967	Racing Club (Argentina)	1989	Nacional (Colombia)
1968	Estudiantes (Argentina)	1990	Olimpia
1969	Estudiantes	1991	Colo Colo (Chile)
1970	Estudiantes	1992	São Paulo (Brazil)
1971	Nacional (Uruguay)	1993	São Paulo
1972	Independiente	1994	Velez Sarsfield (Argentina)
1973	Independiente	1995	Gremio Porto Alegre
1974	Independiente	1996	River Plate
1975	Independiente	1997	Cruzeiro
1976	Cruzeiro (Brazil)	1998	Vasco da Gama
1977	Boca Juniors (Argentina)	1999	Palmeiras
1978	Boca Juniors	2000	Boca Juniors
1979	Olimpia (Paraguay)	2001	Boca Juniors
1980	Nacional		
1981	Flamengo (Brazil)		

NATIONAL LIST OF REFEREES FOR SEASON 2002–2003

Indicates Select Group Referees

Baines, S.J. (Steve) Chesterfield
Barber, G.P. (Graham) Hertfordshire*
Barry, N.S. (Neale) N. Lincolnshire*
Bates, A. (Tony) Stoke-on-Trent
Beeby, R.J. (Richard) Northampton
Boyeson, C. (Carl) Hull
Bennett, S.G. (Steve) Kent*
Butler, A.N. (Alan) Nottinghamshire
Cable, L.E. (Lee) Woking
Cain, G. (George) Merseyside
Clattenburg, M. (Mark) Chester-le-Street
Cooper, M.A. (Mark) Walsall
Cowburn, M.G. (Mark) Blackpool
Crick, D.R. (David) Surrey
Crossley, P.T. (Phil) Kent
Curson, B. (Brian) Leicestershire
Danson, P.S. (Paul) Leicester
Dean, M.L. (Mike) Wirral*
Dowd, P. (Phil) Stoke-on-Trent*
Dunn, S.W. (Steve) Bristol*
Durkin, P.A. (Paul) Dorset*
D'Urso, A.P. (Andy) Essex*
Elleray, D.R. (David) Harrow-on-the-Hill*
Evans, EM (Eddie) Manchester
Fletcher, M. (Mick) Worcestershire
Foy, C.J. (Chris) Merseyside*
Frankland, G.B. (Graham) Middlesbrough
Gallagher, D.J. (Dermot) Oxfordshire*
Hall, A.R. (Andy) Birmingham*
Halsey, M.R. (Mark) Lancashire*
Hegley, G.K. (Grant) Bishops Stortford
Hill, K.D. (Keith) Hertfordshire
Ilderton, E.L. (Eddie) Tyne & Wear
Jones, M.J. (Michael) Chester
Jordan, W.M. (Bill) Hertfordshire
Joslin, P.J. (Phil) Nottinghamshire

Kaye, A. (Alan) Wakefield
Knight, B. (Barry) Kent*
Laws, D. (David) Newcastle upon Tyne
Laws, G. (Graham) Whitley Bay
Leake, A.R. (Tony) Lancashire
Mason, L.S. (Lee) Bolton
Mathieson, S.W. (Scott) Stockport
Messias, M.D. (Matt) York*
Olivier, R.J. (Ray) Sutton Coldfield
Parkes, T.A. (Trevor) Birmingham
Pearson, R. (Roy) Durham
Penn, A.M. (Andy) West Midlands
Penton, C. (Clive) Sussex
Pike, M.S. (Mike) Barrow-in-Furness
Poll, G. (Graham) Hertfordshire*
Prosser, P.J. (Phil) Tewkesbury
Pugh, D. (David) Merseyside*
Rejer, P. (Paul) Worcestershire
Rennie, U.D. (Uriah) Sheffield*
Riley, M.A. (Mike) Leeds*
Robinson, J.P. (Paul) Hull
Ross, J.J. (Joe) London
Ryan, M. (Michael) Preston
Salisbury, G. (Graham) Preston
Stretton, F.G. (Frazer) Nottingham
Styles, R. (Rob) Hampshire*
Taylor, P. (Paul) Hertfordshire
Thorpe, M. (Mike) Ipswich*
Tomlin, S.G. (Steve) East Sussex
Walton, P. (Peter) Northants
Warren, M.R. (Mark) Walsall
Webb, H.M. (Howard) Rotherham
Webster, C.H. (Colin) Gateshead
Wiley, A.G. (Alan) Burntwood*
Wilkes, C.R. (Clive) Gloucester*
Williamson, I.G. (Iain) Reading
Winter, J.T. (Jeff) Stockton-on-Tees*
Wolstenholme, E.K. (Eddie) Blackburn*

USEFUL ADDRESSES

The Football Association: The Secretary, 25 Soho Square, London W1D 4FA. *0207 745 4545*

Scotland: D. Taylor, Hampden Park, Glasgow G42 9AY. *0141 616 6000*

Northern Ireland (Irish FA): D. I. Bowen, 20 Windsor Avenue, Belfast BT9 6EG. *028 9066 9458*

Wales: D. Collins, 3 Westgate Street, Cardiff, South Glamorgan CF1 1DD. *029 2037 2325*

Republic of Ireland (FA of Ireland): B. O'Byrne, 80 Merrion Square South, Dublin 2. *00353-16766864*

International Federation (FIFA): M. Zen-Ruffinen, P. O. Box 85 8030 Zurich, Switzerland. *00 411 384 9595. Fax: 00 411 384 9696*

Union of European Football Associations: G. Aigner, Route de Geneve 46, Case Postale, CH-1260 Nyon, Switzerland. *0041 22 994 4444. Fax: 0041 22 994 4488*

The Premier League: M. Foster, 11 Connaught Place, London W2 2ET. *0207 298 1600*

The Football League: D Burns, The Football League, Unit 5, Edward VII Quay, Navigation Way, Preston, Lancashire PR2 2YF. *01772 325800. Fax 01772 325801*

Scottish Premier League: R. Mitchell, Hampden Park, Somerville Drive, Glasgow G42 9BA. *0141 646 6962*

The Scottish League: The Secretary, Hampden Park, Glasgow G42 9AY. *0141 616 6000*

The Irish League: H. Wallace, 96 University Street, Belfast BT7 1HE. *028 9024 2888*

Football League of Ireland: D Crowther, 80 Merrion Square, Dublin 2. *00353 167 65120*

The Nationwide Football Conference: J. A. Moules, Riverside House, 14b High Street, Crayford DA1 4HG. *01322 411021*

Northern Premier: R. D. Bayley, 22 Woburn Drive, Hale, Altrincham, Cheshire, WA15 8LZ. *0161-980 7007*

Isthmian League: N. Robinson, 226 Rye Lane, Peckham, SE15 4NL. *020 8409 1978. Fax 020 7639 5726*

English Schools FA: J. Read, 1/2 Eastgate Street, Stafford ST17 4RN. *01785 251142*

Southern League: D. J. Strudwick, PO Box 90, Worcester WR3 8RX. *01905-757509*

National Federation of Football Supporters' Clubs: Chairman: Ian D. Todd MBE, 8 Wyke Close, Wyke Gardens, Isleworth, Middlesex TW7 5PE. *020 8847 2905 (and fax). Mobile: 0961-558908.* National Secretary: Mark Agate, "The Stadium", 14 Coombe Close, Lordswood, Chatham, Kent ME5 8NU. *01634 319461 (and fax)*

Professional Footballers' Association: G. Taylor, 2 Oxford Court, Bishopsgate, Off Lower Mosley Street, Manchester M2 3WQ. *0161-236 0575*

Referees' Association: A. Smith, 1 Westhill Road, Coundon, Coventry CV6 2AD. *024 7660 1701*

Women's Football Alliance: The Football Association, 25 Soho Square, London W1D 4FA. *0207 745 4545*

The Football Programme Directory: David Stacey, 'The Beeches', 66 Southend Road, Wickford, Essex SS11 8EN. *01268 732041 (and fax)*

England Football Supporters Association: Publicity Officer, David Stacey, 66 Southend Road, Wickford, Essex SS11 8EN. *01268 732041 (and fax)*

World Cup (1966) Association: as above.

The Football Foundation Ltd: 25 Soho Square, London W1D 4FF. *0207 534 4210. Fax 0207 287 0459*

ENGLISH LEAGUE FIXTURES 2002–2003

Reproduced under Copyright/Database Licence No. PRINT/COUN/3013.

Copyright © The FA Premier League/The Football League Limited 2002

*Sky Sports; †Premiership Plus pay per view

Saturday, 10 August 2002
Nationwide Football League Division 1
Bradford C v Wolverhampton W
Burnley v Brighton & HA
Coventry C v Sheffield U
Derby Co v Reading
Leicester C v Watford
Millwall v Rotherham U
Norwich C v Grimsby T
Portsmouth v Nottingham F
Preston NE v Crystal P
Sheffield W v Stoke C
Walsall v Ipswich T
Wimbledon v Gillingham

Nationwide Football League Division 2
Bristol C v Blackpool
Cheltenham T v Wigan Ath
Colchester U v Stockport Co
Huddersfield T v Brentford
Luton T v Peterborough U
Mansfield T v Plymouth Arg
Northampton T v Crewe Alex
Notts Co v Wycombe W
Oldham Ath v Cardiff C
Port Vale v Tranmere R
QPR v Chesterfield
Swindon T v Barnsley

Nationwide Football League Division 3
Boston U v Bournemouth
Cambridge U v Darlington
Carlisle U v Hartlepool U
Hull C v Southend U
Kidderminster H v Lincoln C
Macclesfield T v York C
Oxford U v Bury
Rochdale v Leyton Orient
Scunthorpe U v Wrexham
Shrewsbury T v Exeter C
Swansea C v Rushden & D'monds
Torquay U v Bristol R

Tuesday, 13 August 2002
Nationwide Football League Division 1
Brighton & HA v Coventry C
Crystal P v Bradford C (8:00)
Gillingham v Derby Co
Grimsby T v Wimbledon
Reading v Sheffield W (8:00)
Rotherham U v Norwich C

Sheffield U v Portsmouth
Watford v Millwall
Wolverhampton W v Walsall

Nationwide Football League Division 2
Barnsley v Cheltenham T
Blackpool v Luton T
Brentford v Bristol C
Cardiff C v Port Vale
Chesterfield v Swindon T
Crewe Alex v Notts Co
Peterborough U v Oldham Ath
Plymouth Arg v Huddersfield T
Stockport Co v QPR
Tranmere R v Colchester U
Wigan Ath v Mansfield T
Wycombe W v Northampton T

Nationwide Football League Division 3
Bournemouth v Kidderminster H
Bristol R v Hull C
Bury v Cambridge U
Darlington v Swansea C (7:30)
Exeter C v Scunthorpe U
Hartlepool U v Boston U
Leyton Orient v Macclesfield T
Lincoln C v Rochdale
Rushden & D'monds v Torquay U
Southend U v Carlisle U
Wrexham v Oxford U
York C v Shrewsbury T

Wednesday, 14 August 2002
Nationwide Football League Division 1
Nottingham F v Preston NE
Stoke C v Leicester C

Saturday, 17 August 2002
FA Barclaycard Premiership
Blackburn R v Sunderland
Charlton Ath v Chelsea
Everton v Tottenham H
Fulham v Bolton W
Leeds U v Manchester C
Manchester U v WBA
Southampton v Middlesbrough

Nationwide Football League Division 1
Brighton & HA v Norwich C
Crystal P v Portsmouth

Gillingham v Millwall
Grimsby T v Derby Co
Nottingham F v Sheffield W
Reading v Coventry C
Rotherham U v Preston NE
Sheffield U v Walsall
Stoke C v Bradford C
Watford v Wimbledon
Wolverhampton W v Burnley

Nationwide Football League Division 2
Barnsley v QPR
Blackpool v Swindon T
Brentford v Oldham Ath
Cardiff C v Northampton T
Chesterfield v Port Vale
Crewe Alex v Colchester U
Peterborough U v Huddersfield T
Plymouth Arg v Luton T
Stockport Co v Notts Co
Tranmere R v Cheltenham T
Wigan Ath v Bristol C
Wycombe W v Mansfield T

Nationwide Football League Division 3
Bournemouth v Cambridge U
Bristol R v Rochdale
Bury v Swansea C
Darlington v Oxford U
Exeter C v Hull C
Hartlepool U v Macclesfield T
Leyton Orient v Scunthorpe U
Lincoln C v Carlisle U
Rushden & D'monds v
   Kidderminster H
Southend U v Shrewsbury T
Wrexham v Boston U
York C v Torquay U

Nationwide Conference
Burton Albion v Scarborough
Chester v Kettering
Dag & Red v Leigh RMI
Doncaster v Barnet
Halifax v Telford
Hereford v Farnborough
Margate v Morecambe
Southport v Nuneaton
Stevenage v Northwich
Woking v Forest Green
Yeovil v Gravesend

Sunday, 18 August 2002
FA Barclaycard Premiership
*Arsenal v Birmingham C (4:05)
†Aston Villa v Liverpool (2:00)

Nationwide Football League Division 1
Ipswich T v Leicester C

Monday, 19 August 2002
FA Barclaycard Premiership
*Newcastle U v West Ham U (8:00)

Nationwide Conference
Telford v Chester

Tuesday, 20 August 2002
Nationwide Conference
Barnet v Yeovil
Farnborough v Stevenage
Forest Green v Hereford
Gravesend v Dag & Red
Kettering v Margate
Leigh RMI v Doncaster
Morecambe v Halifax
Northwich v Burton Albion
Nuneaton v Woking
Scarborough v Southport

Friday, 23 August 2002
FA Barclaycard Premiership
*Chelsea v Manchester U (8:00)

Nationwide Football League Division 2
Northampton T v Blackpool

Saturday, 24 August 2002
FA Barclaycard Premiership
Birmingham C v Blackburn R
Bolton W v Charlton Ath
Liverpool v Southampton
*Manchester C v Newcastle U (12:15)
Middlesbrough v Fulham
Sunderland v Everton
Tottenham H v Aston Villa
†WBA v Leeds U (5:30)
West Ham U v Arsenal

Nationwide Football League Division 1
Bradford C v Grimsby T
Burnley v Sheffield U
Coventry C v Crystal P
Derby Co v Wolverhampton W
Leicester C v Reading
Millwall v Ipswich T
Norwich C v Gillingham
Portsmouth v Watford
Preston NE v Stoke C
Sheffield W v Rotherham U
Walsall v Nottingham F
Wimbledon v Brighton & HA

Nationwide Football League Division 2
Bristol C v Wycombe W
Cheltenham T v Plymouth Arg
Colchester U v Brentford
Huddersfield T v Crewe Alex
Luton T v Barnsley
Mansfield T v Chesterfield
Notts Co v Wigan Ath
Oldham Ath v Tranmere R
Port Vale v Stockport Co
QPR v Peterborough U
Swindon T v Cardiff C

Nationwide Football League Division 3
Boston U v Lincoln C
Cambridge U v Leyton Orient
Carlisle U v Bristol R
Hull C v Bury
Kidderminster H v Exeter C
Macclesfield T v Wrexham
Oxford U v Southend U
Rochdale v Darlington
Scunthorpe U v York C
Shrewsbury T v Rushden & D'monds
Swansea C v Bournemouth
Torquay U v Hartlepool U

Nationwide Conference
Barnet v Chester
Farnborough v Halifax
Forest Green v Southport
Gravesend v Hereford
Kettering v Woking
Leigh RMI v Burton Albion
Morecambe v Yeovil
Northwich v Margate
Nuneaton v Stevenage
Scarborough v Dag & Red
Telford v Doncaster

Monday, 26 August 2002
Nationwide Football League Division 1
Brighton & HA v Walsall (3:00)
Gillingham v Preston NE (3:00)
Grimsby T v Portsmouth (3:00)
Ipswich T v Bradford C
Rotherham U v Derby Co (3:00)
Sheffield U v Millwall (3:00)
Stoke C v Norwich C (3:00)
Watford v Coventry C (3:00)

Nationwide Football League Division 2
Barnsley v Notts Co (3:00)
Blackpool v Oldham Ath (3:00)
Brentford v Swindon T (3:00)
Cardiff C v Luton T (3:00)

Peterborough U v Colchester U (3:00)
Plymouth Arg v Bristol C (3:00)
Stockport Co v Mansfield T (3:00)
Tranmere R v Huddersfield T (3:00)
Wigan Ath v Port Vale (3:00)
Wycombe W v QPR (3:00)

Nationwide Football League Division 3
Bury v Shrewsbury T (3:00)
Exeter C v Torquay U (3:00)
Hartlepool U v Hull C (3:00)
Leyton Orient v Kidderminster H (3:00)
Lincoln C v Macclesfield T (3:00)
Rushden & D'monds v Scunthorpe U
  (3:00)
Southend U v Cambridge U (3:00)
Wrexham v Rochdale (3:00)
York C v Boston U (3:00)

Nationwide Conference
*Burton Albion v Barnet (7.45)
Chester v Scarborough
Dag & Red v Telford
Doncaster v Farnborough
Halifax v Northwich
Hereford v Morecambe
Margate v Forest Green
Southport v Kettering
Stevenage v Gravesend
Woking v Leigh RMI
Yeovil v Nuneaton

Tuesday, 27 August 2002
FA Barclaycard Premiership
†Arsenal v WBA (8:00)
Charlton Ath v Tottenham H

Nationwide Football League Division 1
Crystal P v Leicester C (8:00)
Reading v Burnley (8:00)
Wolverhampton W v Sheffield W

Nationwide Football League Division 2
Chesterfield v Northampton T
Crewe Alex v Cheltenham T

Nationwide Football League Division 3
Bournemouth v Oxford U
Bristol R v Swansea C
Darlington v Carlisle U (7:30)

Wednesday, 28 August 2002
FA Barclaycard Premiership
Aston Villa v Manchester C
Blackburn R v Liverpool (8:00)
Everton v Birmingham C (8:00)

*Fulham v West Ham U (8:00)
Leeds U v Sunderland
Newcastle U v Bolton W – postponed
*Alternative date required due to
European Cup Qualifier*
Southampton v Chelsea

Nationwide Football League Division 1
Nottingham F v Wimbledon

Saturday, 31 August 2002

FA Barclaycard Premiership
Birmingham C v Leeds U
Manchester C v Everton
Middlesbrough v Blackburn R
Sunderland v Manchester U
Tottenham H v Southampton
WBA v Fulham
West Ham U v Charlton Ath

Nationwide Football League Division 1
Bradford C v Rotherham U
Burnley v Crystal P
Coventry C v Nottingham F
Derby Co v Stoke C
Leicester C v Gillingham
Millwall v Grimsby T
Norwich C v Watford
Portsmouth v Brighton & HA
Walsall v Reading
Wimbledon v Wolverhampton W

Nationwide Football League Division 2
Bristol C v Tranmere R
Cheltenham T v Cardiff C
Colchester U v Wigan Ath
Huddersfield T v Blackpool
Luton T v Chesterfield
Mansfield T v Crewe Alex
Northampton T v Barnsley
Notts Co v Brentford
Oldham Ath v Wycombe W
Port Vale v Peterborough U
QPR v Plymouth Arg
Swindon T v Stockport Co

Nationwide Football League Division 3
Boston U v Bury
Cambridge U v Rushden & D'monds
Carlisle U v Exeter C
Hull C v Leyton Orient
Kidderminster H v Darlington
Macclesfield T v Bournemouth
Oxford U v Hartlepool U
Rochdale v Southend U
Scunthorpe U v Bristol R

Shrewsbury T v Lincoln C
Swansea C v York C
Torquay U v Wrexham

Nationwide Conference
Barnet v Halifax
Farnborough v Dag & Red
Forest Green v Chester
Gravesend v Southport
Kettering v Yeovil
Leigh RMI v Margate
Morecambe v Stevenage
Northwich v Doncaster
Nuneaton v Hereford
Scarborough v Woking
Telford v Burton Albion

Sunday, 1 September 2002

FA Barclaycard Premiership
†Bolton W v Aston Villa (2:00)
*Chelsea v Arsenal (4:05)

Nationwide Football League Division 1
Preston NE v Ipswich T (2:00)
Sheffield W v Sheffield U (1:00)

Monday, 2 September 2002

FA Barclaycard Premiership
*Liverpool v Newcastle U (8:00)

Nationwide Conference
Stevenage v Telford

Tuesday, 3 September 2002

FA Barclaycard Premiership
†Manchester U v Middlesbrough (8:00)

Nationwide Conference
Burton Albion v Forest Green
Chester v Morecambe
Dag & Red v Nuneaton
Doncaster v Kettering
Halifax v Scarborough
Hereford v Northwich
Margate v Barnet
Southport v Leigh RMI
Woking v Gravesend
Yeovil v Farnborough

Saturday, 7 September 2002
Nationwide Football League Division 1
Bradford C v Coventry C
Derby Co v Burnley
Gillingham v Portsmouth
Grimsby T v Ipswich T

Millwall v Brighton & HA
Norwich C v Sheffield U
Rotherham U v Reading
Sheffield W v Crystal P
Stoke C v Nottingham F
Watford v Walsall
Wimbledon v Leicester C
Wolverhampton W v Preston NE

Nationwide Football League Division 2
Blackpool v Tranmere R
Brentford v Luton T
Bristol C v Northampton T
Colchester U v Cheltenham T
Crewe Alex v Chesterfield
Huddersfield T v Barnsley
Mansfield T v QPR
Notts Co v Oldham Ath
Plymouth Arg v Cardiff C
Stockport Co v Peterborough U
Swindon T v Port Vale
Wigan Ath v Wycombe W

Nationwide Football League Division 3
Bury v York C
Cambridge U v Hull C
Carlisle U v Rochdale
Darlington v Wrexham
Exeter C v Bournemouth
Kidderminster H v Boston U
Lincoln C v Scunthorpe U
Macclesfield T v Bristol R
Oxford U v Torquay U
Rushden & D'monds v Southend U
Shrewsbury T v Leyton Orient
Swansea C v Hartlepool U

Nationwide Conference
Barnet v Telford
Burton Albion v Halifax
Chester v Leigh RMI
*Doncaster v Dag & Red (12:15)
Gravesend v Nuneaton
Margate v Stevenage
Morecambe v Forest Green
Scarborough v Kettering
Southport v Farnborough
Woking v Hereford
Yeovil v Northwich

Tuesday, 10 September 2002
FA Barclaycard Premiership
*Arsenal v Manchester C (8:00)
Middlesbrough v Sunderland

Wednesday, 11 September 2002
FA Barclaycard Premiership
Aston Villa v Charlton Ath
Blackburn R v Chelsea (8:00)
Fulham v Tottenham H
Liverpool v Birmingham C (8:00)
Manchester U v Bolton W (8:00)
†Newcastle U v Leeds U (8:00)
Southampton v Everton
West Ham U v WBA

Saturday, 14 September 2002
FA Barclaycard Premiership
Bolton W v Liverpool
Charlton Ath v Arsenal
Chelsea v Newcastle U
Everton v Middlesbrough
*Leeds U v Manchester U (12:00)
Sunderland v Fulham
WBA v Southampton

Nationwide Football League Division 1
Brighton & HA v Gillingham
Burnley v Stoke C
Coventry C v Grimsby T
Crystal P v Wolverhampton W
Leicester C v Derby Co
Nottingham F v Watford
Portsmouth v Millwall
Preston NE v Sheffield W
Reading v Wimbledon
Sheffield U v Rotherham U
Walsall v Bradford C

Nationwide Football League Division 2
Barnsley v Plymouth Arg
Cardiff C v Stockport Co
Cheltenham T v Bristol C
Chesterfield v Wigan Ath
Luton T v Notts Co
Northampton T v Huddersfield T
Oldham Ath v Mansfield T
Peterborough U v Crewe Alex
Port Vale v Colchester U
QPR v Swindon T
Tranmere R v Brentford
Wycombe W v Blackpool

Nationwide Football League Division 3
Boston U v Oxford U
Bournemouth v Bury
Bristol R v Exeter C
Hartlepool U v Darlington
Hull C v Carlisle U
Leyton Orient v Lincoln C

Rochdale v Shrewsbury T
Scunthorpe U v Kidderminster H
Southend U v Macclesfield T
Torquay U v Cambridge U
Wrexham v Swansea C
York C v Rushden & D'monds

Nationwide Conference
Dag & Red v Burton Albion
Farnborough v Scarborough
Forest Green v Gravesend
Halifax v Doncaster
Hereford v Chester
Kettering v Morecambe
Leigh RMI v Barnet
Northwich v Woking
Nuneaton v Margate
Stevenage v Yeovil
Telford v Southport

Sunday, 15 September 2002
FA Barclaycard Premiership
*Birmingham C v Aston Villa (4:05)
†Manchester C v Blackburn R (2:00)

Nationwide Football League Division 1
Ipswich T v Norwich C (1:00)

Monday, 16 September 2002
FA Barclaycard Premiership
*Tottenham H v West Ham U (8:00)

Nationwide Conference
Telford v Scarborough

Tuesday, 17 September 2002
Nationwide Football League Division 1
Brighton & HA v Stoke C
Burnley v Millwall
Crystal P v Derby Co (8:00)
Leicester C v Bradford C
Portsmouth v Wimbledon
Preston NE v Watford
Sheffield U v Grimsby T
Walsall v Rotherham U

Nationwide Football League Division 2
Barnsley v Blackpool
Cardiff C v Brentford
Cheltenham T v Swindon T
Chesterfield v Stockport Co
Luton T v Mansfield T
Northampton T v Colchester U
Oldham Ath v Bristol C
Peterborough U v Plymouth Arg

Port Vale v Notts Co
QPR v Huddersfield T
Tranmere R v Wigan Ath
Wycombe W v Crewe Alex

Nationwide Football League Division 3
Bournemouth v Rushden & D'monds
Bristol R v Bury
Hartlepool U v Lincoln C
Hull C v Macclesfield T
Leyton Orient v Oxford U
Rochdale v Cambridge U
Scunthorpe U v Carlisle U (7:30)
Southend U v Kidderminster H
Torquay U v Shrewsbury T
Wrexham v Exeter C
York C v Darlington

Nationwide Conference
Barnet v Farnborough
Burton Albion v Gravesend
Dag & Red v Kettering
Doncaster v Southport
Forest Green v Stevenage
Halifax v Chester
Hereford v Yeovil
Leigh RMI v Nuneaton
Northwich v Morecambe
Woking v Margate

Wednesday, 18 September 2002
Nationwide Football League Division 1
Coventry C v Sheffield W
Ipswich T v Wolverhampton W
Nottingham F v Gillingham
Reading v Norwich C (8:00)

Nationwide Football League Division 3
Boston U v Swansea C

Saturday, 21 September 2002
FA Barclaycard Premiership
Arsenal v Bolton W
Liverpool v WBA
Manchester U v Tottenham H
Middlesbrough v Birmingham C
Southampton v Charlton Ath
West Ham U v Manchester C

Nationwide Football League Division 1
Bradford C v Burnley
Derby Co v Preston NE
Gillingham v Sheffield U
Grimsby T v Nottingham F
Millwall v Walsall
Norwich C v Portsmouth

Rotherham U v Brighton & HA
Sheffield W v Leicester C
Stoke C v Ipswich T
Watford v Crystal P
Wimbledon v Coventry C
Wolverhampton W v Reading

Nationwide Football League Division 2
Blackpool v Port Vale
Brentford v Wycombe W
Bristol C v QPR
Colchester U v Oldham Ath
Crewe Alex v Tranmere R
Huddersfield T v Luton T
Mansfield T v Cheltenham T
Notts Co v Cardiff C
Plymouth Arg v Chesterfield
Stockport Co v Barnsley
Swindon T v Northampton T
Wigan Ath v Peterborough U

Nationwide Football League Division 3
Bury v Hartlepool U
Cambridge U v York C
Carlisle U v Boston U
Darlington v Bournemouth
Exeter C v Leyton Orient
Kidderminster H v Rochdale
Lincoln C v Southend U
Macclesfield T v Scunthorpe U
Oxford U v Hull C
Rushden & D'monds v Wrexham
Shrewsbury T v Bristol R
Swansea C v Torquay U

Nationwide Conference
Chester v Dag & Red
Farnborough v Leigh RMI
Gravesend v Telford
Kettering v Northwich
Margate v Doncaster
Morecambe v Woking
Nuneaton v Forest Green
Scarborough v Barnet
Southport v Burton Albion
Stevenage v Hereford
Yeovil v Halifax

Sunday, 22 September 2002
FA Barclaycard Premiership
†Aston Villa v Everton (2:00)
Blackburn R v Leeds U
*Newcastle U v Sunderland (4:05)

Monday, 23 September 2002
FA Barclaycard Premiership
*Fulham v Chelsea (8:00)

Nationwide Conference
Stevenage v Barnet

Tuesday, 24 September 2002
Nationwide Football League Division 1
Ipswich T v Burnley

Nationwide Conference
Chester v Burton Albion
Farnborough v Forest Green
Gravesend v Doncaster
Kettering v Hereford
Margate v Dag & Red
Morecambe v Telford
Nuneaton v Northwich
Scarborough v Leigh RMI
Southport v Halifax
*Yeovil v Woking (7:45)

Saturday, 28 September 2002
FA Barclaycard Premiership
†Birmingham C v Newcastle U (5:30)
Bolton W v Southampton
Charlton Ath v Manchester U
Chelsea v West Ham U
Everton v Fulham
*Leeds U v Arsenal (12:00)
Manchester C v Liverpool
Sunderland v Aston Villa
Tottenham H v Middlesbrough

Nationwide Football League Division 1
Brighton & HA v Grimsby T
Burnley v Wimbledon
Coventry C v Millwall
Crystal P v Gillingham
Ipswich T v Derby Co
Leicester C v Wolverhampton W
Nottingham F v Rotherham U
Portsmouth v Bradford C
Preston NE v Norwich C
Reading v Stoke C
Sheffield U v Watford
Walsall v Sheffield W

Nationwide Football League Division 2
Barnsley v Wigan Ath
Cardiff C v Crewe Alex
Cheltenham T v Notts Co
Chesterfield v Blackpool
Luton T v Swindon T

Northampton T v Mansfield T
Oldham Ath v Huddersfield T
Peterborough U v Brentford
Port Vale v Bristol C
QPR v Colchester U
Tranmere R v Stockport Co
Wycombe W v Plymouth Arg

Nationwide Football League Division 3
Boston U v Cambridge U
Bournemouth v Carlisle U
Bristol R v Kidderminster H
Hartlepool U v Rushden & D'monds
Hull C v Swansea C
Leyton Orient v Darlington
Rochdale v Macclesfield T
Scunthorpe U v Shrewsbury T
Southend U v Exeter C
Torquay U v Lincoln C
Wrexham v Bury
York C v Oxford U

Nationwide Conference
Barnet v Morecambe
Burton Albion v Margate
Dag & Red v Southport
Doncaster v Chester
Forest Green v Kettering
Halifax v Nuneaton
Hereford v Scarborough
Leigh RMI v Yeovil
Northwich v Gravesend
Telford v Farnborough
Woking v Stevenage

Monday, 30 September 2002

FA Barclaycard Premiership
*WBA v Blackburn R (8:00)

Saturday, 5 October 2002

FA Barclaycard Premiership
Fulham v Charlton Ath
Middlesbrough v Bolton W
Newcastle U v WBA
Southampton v Manchester C
West Ham U v Birmingham C

Nationwide Football League Division 1
Bradford C v Preston NE
Derby Co v Walsall
Gillingham v Coventry C
Grimsby T v Reading
Millwall v Nottingham F
Norwich C v Leicester C
Rotherham U v Portsmouth
Sheffield W v Burnley

Stoke C v Crystal P
Watford v Brighton & HA
Wimbledon v Ipswich T
Wolverhampton W v Sheffield U

Nationwide Football League Division 2
Blackpool v Cheltenham T
Brentford v Barnsley
Bristol C v Chesterfield
Colchester U v Wycombe W
Crewe Alex v QPR
Huddersfield T v Port Vale
Mansfield T v Tranmere R
Notts Co v Peterborough U
Plymouth Arg v Northampton T
Stockport Co v Luton T
Swindon T v Oldham Ath
Wigan Ath v Cardiff C

Nationwide Football League Division 3
Bury v Southend U
Cambridge U v Wrexham
Carlisle U v Torquay U
Darlington v Bristol R
Exeter C v York C
Kidderminster H v Hull C
Lincoln C v Bournemouth
Macclesfield T v Boston U
Oxford U v Scunthorpe U
Rushden & D'monds v Leyton Orient
Shrewsbury T v Hartlepool U
Swansea C v Rochdale

Nationwide Conference
Forest Green v Barnet
Gravesend v Scarborough
Hereford v Dag & Red
Kettering v Telford
Margate v Chester
Morecambe v Leigh RMI
Northwich v Farnborough
Nuneaton v Doncaster
Stevenage v Halifax
Woking v Burton Albion
Yeovil v Southport

Sunday, 6 October 2002

FA Barclaycard Premiership
†Arsenal v Sunderland (2:00)
Aston Villa v Leeds U
Blackburn R v Tottenham H
*Liverpool v Chelsea (4:05)

Monday, 7 October 2002

FA Barclaycard Premiership
*Manchester U v Everton (8:00)

Nationwide Conference
Telford v Forest Green

Tuesday, 8 October 2002
Nationwide Conference
Barnet v Gravesend
Burton Albion v Yeovil
Chester v Nuneaton
Dag & Red v Woking
Doncaster v Stevenage
Farnborough v Margate
Halifax v Kettering
Leigh RMI v Hereford
Scarborough v Morecambe
Southport v Northwich

Saturday, 12 October 2002
Nationwide Football League Division 1
Bradford C v Derby Co
Burnley v Walsall
Coventry C v Norwich C
Crystal P v Reading
Ipswich T v Sheffield W
Millwall v Wimbledon
Nottingham F v Brighton & HA
Preston NE v Leicester C
Rotherham U v Gillingham
Sheffield U v Stoke C
Watford v Grimsby T
Wolverhampton W v Portsmouth

Nationwide Football League Division 2
Barnsley v Bristol C
Cardiff C v Wycombe W
Chesterfield v Tranmere R
Huddersfield T v Notts Co
Luton T v Cheltenham T
Northampton T v Brentford
Peterborough U v Mansfield T
Plymouth Arg v Wigan Ath
Port Vale v Oldham Ath
QPR v Blackpool
Stockport Co v Crewe Alex
Swindon T v Colchester U

Nationwide Football League Division 3
Boston U v Torquay U
Bournemouth v Hartlepool U
Bristol R v Lincoln C
Bury v Darlington
Carlisle U v Shrewsbury T
Exeter C v Rushden & D'monds
Hull C v Rochdale
Kidderminster H v Macclesfield T
Oxford U v Swansea C

Scunthorpe U v Cambridge U
Southend U v York C
Wrexham v Leyton Orient

Nationwide Conference
Barnet v Nuneaton
Burton Albion v Hereford
Chester v Gravesend
Dag & Red v Morecambe
Doncaster v Forest Green
Farnborough v Kettering
Halifax v Margate
Leigh RMI v Stevenage
Scarborough v Northwich
Southport v Woking
Telford v Yeovil

Friday, 18 October 2002
Nationwide Football League Division 2
Colchester U v Chesterfield

Saturday, 19 October 2002
FA Barclaycard Premiership
Blackburn R v Newcastle U
Everton v Arsenal
Fulham v Manchester U
†Leeds U v Liverpool (12:00)
Manchester C v Chelsea
Sunderland v West Ham U
WBA v Birmingham C

Nationwide Football League Division 1
Derby Co v Nottingham F
Gillingham v Watford
Grimsby T v Rotherham U
Leicester C v Burnley
Norwich C v Millwall
Portsmouth v Coventry C
Reading v Ipswich T
Sheffield W v Bradford C
Stoke C v Wolverhampton W
Walsall v Preston NE
Wimbledon v Crystal P

Nationwide Football League Division 2
Blackpool v Cardiff C
Brentford v Port Vale
Bristol C v Swindon T
Cheltenham T v QPR
Crewe Alex v Plymouth Arg
Mansfield T v Huddersfield T
Notts Co v Northampton T
Oldham Ath v Luton T
Tranmere R v Barnsley
Wigan Ath v Stockport Co
Wycombe W v Peterborough U

Nationwide Football League Division 3
Cambridge U v Oxford U
Darlington v Boston U
Hartlepool U v Wrexham
Leyton Orient v Bournemouth
Lincoln C v Exeter C
Macclesfield T v Carlisle U
Rochdale v Scunthorpe U
Rushden & D'monds v Bury
Shrewsbury T v Kidderminster H
Swansea C v Southend U
Torquay U v Hull C
York C v Bristol R

Nationwide Conference
Forest Green v Scarborough
Gravesend v Leigh RMI
Hereford v Halifax
Kettering v Barnet
Margate v Southport
Morecambe v Farnborough
Northwich v Dag & Red
Nuneaton v Telford
Stevenage v Burton Albion
Woking v Chester
Yeovil v Doncaster

Sunday, 20 October 2002

FA Barclaycard Premiership
*Charlton Ath v Middlesbrough (4:05)
Tottenham H v Bolton W (4:05)

Nationwide Football League Division 1
Brighton & HA v Sheffield U

Monday, 21 October 2002

FA Barclaycard Premiership
*Aston Villa v Southampton (8:00)

Friday, 25 October 2002

Nationwide Football League Division 3
Southend U v Hartlepool U

Saturday, 26 October 2002

FA Barclaycard Premiership
Arsenal v Blackburn R
Birmingham C v Manchester C
Chelsea v WBA
Liverpool v Tottenham H
Manchester U v Aston Villa
Middlesbrough v Leeds U
Newcastle U v Charlton Ath

Nationwide Football League Division 1
Bradford C v Norwich C

Burnley v Portsmouth
Coventry C v Walsall
Crystal P v Brighton & HA
Ipswich T v Gillingham
Millwall v Derby Co
Nottingham F v Leicester C
Preston NE v Reading
Rotherham U v Stoke C
Sheffield U v Wimbledon
Watford v Sheffield W
Wolverhampton W v Grimsby T

Nationwide Football League Division 2
Barnsley v Wycombe W
Cardiff C v Tranmere R
Chesterfield v Notts Co
Huddersfield T v Colchester U
Luton T v Wigan Ath
Northampton T v Cheltenham T
Peterborough U v Bristol C
Plymouth Arg v Blackpool
Port Vale v Crewe Alex
QPR v Oldham Ath
Stockport Co v Brentford
Swindon T v Mansfield T

Nationwide Football League Division 3
Boston U v Rochdale
Bournemouth v York C
Bristol R v Leyton Orient
Bury v Macclesfield T
Carlisle U v Swansea C
Exeter C v Darlington
Hull C v Rushden & D'monds
Kidderminster H v Cambridge U
Oxford U v Shrewsbury T
Scunthorpe U v Torquay U
Wrexham v Lincoln C

Sunday, 27 October 2002

FA Barclaycard Premiership
†Southampton v Fulham (2:00)
*West Ham U v Everton (4:05)

Monday, 28 October 2002

FA Barclaycard Premiership
*Bolton W v Sunderland (8:00)

Tuesday, 29 October 2002

Nationwide Football League Division 1
Brighton & HA v Ipswich T
Gillingham v Wolverhampton W
Grimsby T v Burnley
Leicester C v Coventry C
Norwich C v Nottingham F

Portsmouth v Preston NE
Reading v Bradford C
Walsall v Crystal P
Wimbledon v Rotherham U

Nationwide Football League Division 2
Blackpool v Stockport Co
Brentford v Plymouth Arg
Bristol C v Huddersfield T
Cheltenham T v Port Vale
Colchester U v Barnsley
Crewe Alex v Luton T
Mansfield T v Cardiff C
Notts Co v Swindon T
Oldham Ath v Northampton T
Tranmere R v Peterborough U
Wigan Ath v QPR
Wycombe W v Chesterfield

Nationwide Football League Division 3
Cambridge U v Carlisle U
Darlington v Scunthorpe U
Hartlepool U v Bristol R
Leyton Orient v Southend U
Lincoln C v Bury
Macclesfield T v Oxford U
Rochdale v Exeter C
Rushden & D'monds v Boston U
Shrewsbury T v Hull C
Swansea C v Kidderminster H
Torquay U v Bournemouth
York C v Wrexham

Wednesday, 30 October 2002
Nationwide Football League Division 1
Derby Co v Sheffield U
Sheffield W v Millwall
Stoke C v Watford

Friday, 1 November 2002
Nationwide Football League Division 2
Mansfield T v Colchester U

Nationwide Football League Division 3
Hartlepool U v York C

Saturday, 2 November 2002
FA Barclaycard Premiership
Birmingham C v Bolton W
Blackburn R v Aston Villa
Fulham v Arsenal
Leeds U v Everton
Liverpool v West Ham U
Manchester U v Southampton
WBA v Manchester C

Nationwide Football League Division 1
Brighton & HA v Bradford C
Coventry C v Rotherham U
Grimsby T v Gillingham
Ipswich T v Crystal P
Nottingham F v Sheffield U
Portsmouth v Leicester C
Preston NE v Burnley
Reading v Millwall (12:00)
Sheffield W v Derby Co
Walsall v Stoke C
Watford v Wolverhampton W
Wimbledon v Norwich C

Nationwide Football League Division 2
Brentford v Blackpool
Bristol C v Notts Co
Cardiff C v Peterborough U
Cheltenham T v Huddersfield T
Chesterfield v Barnsley
Northampton T v Luton T
Oldham Ath v Stockport Co
Port Vale v QPR
Tranmere R v Plymouth Arg
Wigan Ath v Crewe Alex
Wycombe W v Swindon T

Nationwide Football League Division 3
Boston U v Exeter C
Bournemouth v Bristol R
Cambridge U v Swansea C
Carlisle U v Oxford U
Darlington v Lincoln C
Hull C v Scunthorpe U
Leyton Orient v Bury
Macclesfield T v Shrewsbury T
Rochdale v Rushden & D'monds
Southend U v Wrexham
Torquay U v Kidderminster H

Nationwide Conference
Barnet v Northwich
Burton Albion v Morecambe
Chester v Yeovil
Dag & Red v Forest Green
Doncaster v Hereford
Farnborough v Nuneaton
Halifax v Gravesend
Leigh RMI v Kettering
Scarborough v Margate
Southport v Stevenage
Telford v Woking

Sunday, 3 November 2002
FA Barclaycard Premiership
*Charlton Ath v Sunderland (4:05)
†Tottenham H v Chelsea (2:00)

Monday, 4 November 2002

FA Barclaycard Premiership
*Newcastle U v Middlesbrough (8:00)

Saturday, 9 November 2002

FA Barclaycard Premiership
Arsenal v Newcastle U
Aston Villa v Fulham
Bolton W v WBA
Chelsea v Birmingham C
Everton v Charlton Ath
*Manchester C v Manchester U (12:15)
Middlesbrough v Liverpool
Southampton v Blackburn R
West Ham U v Leeds U

Nationwide Football League Division 1
Bradford C v Wimbledon
Burnley v Coventry C
Crystal P v Nottingham F
Derby Co v Portsmouth
Gillingham v Reading
Leicester C v Walsall
Millwall v Preston NE
Norwich C v Sheffield W
Rotherham U v Watford
Sheffield U v Ipswich T
Stoke C v Grimsby T
Wolverhampton W v Brighton & HA

Nationwide Football League Division 2
Barnsley v Cardiff C
Blackpool v Wigan Ath
Colchester U v Bristol C
Crewe Alex v Brentford
Huddersfield T v Wycombe W
Luton T v Port Vale
Notts Co v Mansfield T
Peterborough U v Chesterfield
Plymouth Arg v Oldham Ath
QPR v Northampton T
Stockport Co v Cheltenham T
Swindon T v Tranmere R

Nationwide Football League Division 3
Bristol R v Southend U
Bury v Torquay U
Exeter C v Hartlepool U
Kidderminster H v Carlisle U
Lincoln C v Hull C
Oxford U v Rochdale
Rushden & D'monds v Darlington
Scunthorpe U v Boston U
Shrewsbury T v Cambridge U
Swansea C v Macclesfield T

Wrexham v Bournemouth
York C v Leyton Orient

Nationwide Conference
Forest Green v Halifax
Gravesend v Farnborough
Hereford v Southport
Kettering v Burton Albion
Margate v Telford
Morecambe v Doncaster
Northwich v Leigh RMI
Nuneaton v Scarborough
Stevenage v Chester
Woking v Barnet
Yeovil v Dag & Red

Sunday, 10 November 2002

FA Barclaycard Premiership
*Sunderland v Tottenham H (4:05)

Saturday, 16 November 2002

FA Barclaycard Premiership
Arsenal v Tottenham H
Birmingham C v Fulham
Blackburn R v Everton
Chelsea v Middlesbrough
Leeds U v Bolton W
Liverpool v Sunderland
Manchester C v Charlton Ath
Newcastle U v Southampton
WBA v Aston Villa

Nationwide Football League Division 1
Brighton & HA v Derby Co
Coventry C v Wolverhampton W
Gillingham v Sheffield W
Grimsby T v Preston NE
Millwall v Leicester C
Norwich C v Crystal P
Nottingham F v Bradford C
Portsmouth v Stoke C
Rotherham U v Burnley
Sheffield U v Reading
Watford v Ipswich T
Wimbledon v Walsall

Sunday, 17 November 2002

FA Barclaycard Premiership
*West Ham U v Manchester U (4:05)

Friday, 22 November 2002

Nationwide Football League Division 2
Cardiff C v Chesterfield

Saturday, 23 November 2002

FA Barclaycard Premiership
Aston Villa v West Ham U
Bolton W v Chelsea
Everton v WBA
Fulham v Liverpool
*Manchester U v Newcastle U (12:15)
Middlesbrough v Manchester C
Southampton v Arsenal
Sunderland v Birmingham C

Nationwide Football League Division 1
Bradford C v Sheffield U
Burnley v Norwich C
Crystal P v Grimsby T
Derby Co v Wimbledon
Ipswich T v Coventry C
Leicester C v Rotherham U
Preston NE v Brighton & HA
Reading v Watford
Sheffield W v Portsmouth
Stoke C v Millwall
Walsall v Gillingham
Wolverhampton W v Nottingham F

Nationwide Football League Division 2
Brentford v Wigan Ath
Crewe Alex v Blackpool
Huddersfield T v Swindon T
Luton T v QPR
Mansfield T v Bristol C
Northampton T v Port Vale
Notts Co v Colchester U
Oldham Ath v Cheltenham T
Peterborough U v Barnsley
Plymouth Arg v Stockport Co
Wycombe W v Tranmere R

Nationwide Football League Division 3
Bristol R v Wrexham
Carlisle U v Bury
Exeter C v Cambridge U
Hull C v Boston U
Kidderminster H v Oxford U
Leyton Orient v Hartlepool U
Lincoln C v Rushden & D'monds
Macclesfield T v Torquay U
Rochdale v York C
Scunthorpe U v Swansea C
Shrewsbury T v Darlington
Southend U v Bournemouth

Nationwide Conference
Barnet v Forest Green
Burton Albion v Woking
Chester v Margate

Dag & Red v Hereford
Doncaster v Nuneaton
Farnborough v Northwich
Halifax v Stevenage
Leigh RMI v Morecambe
Scarborough v Gravesend
Southport v Yeovil
Telford v Kettering

Sunday, 24 November 2002

FA Barclaycard Premiership
*Charlton Ath v Blackburn R (4:05)
Tottenham H v Leeds U

Saturday, 30 November 2002

FA Barclaycard Premiership
Arsenal v Aston Villa
Birmingham C v Tottenham H
Blackburn R v Fulham
Chelsea v Sunderland
Leeds U v Charlton Ath
Manchester C v Bolton W
Newcastle U v Everton
WBA v Middlesbrough

Nationwide Football League Division 1
Brighton & HA v Reading
Coventry C v Preston NE
Gillingham v Stoke C
Grimsby T v Leicester C
Millwall v Bradford C
Norwich C v Derby Co
Nottingham F v Ipswich T
Portsmouth v Walsall
Rotherham U v Wolverhampton W
Sheffield U v Crystal P
Watford v Burnley
Wimbledon v Sheffield W

Nationwide Football League Division 2
Barnsley v Oldham Ath
Blackpool v Notts Co
Bristol C v Crewe Alex
Cheltenham T v Brentford
Chesterfield v Huddersfield T
Colchester U v Plymouth Arg
Port Vale v Mansfield T
QPR v Cardiff C
Stockport Co v Wycombe W
Swindon T v Peterborough U
Tranmere R v Luton T
Wigan Ath v Northampton T

Nationwide Football League Division 3
Boston U v Leyton Orient
Bournemouth v Scunthorpe U

Bury v Exeter C
Cambridge U v Macclesfield T
Darlington v Southend U
Hartlepool U v Kidderminster H
Oxford U v Lincoln C
Rushden & D'monds v Bristol R
Swansea C v Shrewsbury T
Torquay U v Rochdale
Wrexham v Hull C
York C v Carlisle U

Nationwide Conference
Doncaster v Woking
Farnborough v Burton Albion
Halifax v Dag & Red
Hereford v Barnet
Kettering v Nuneaton
Leigh RMI v Telford
Morecambe v Gravesend
Northwich v Forest Green
Southport v Chester
Stevenage v Scarborough
Yeovil v Margate

Sunday, 1 December 2002
FA Barclaycard Premiership
*Liverpool v Manchester U (12:15)

Monday, 2 December 2002
FA Barclaycard Premiership
*West Ham U v Southampton (8:00)

Saturday, 7 December 2002
FA Barclaycard Premiership
Aston Villa v Newcastle U
Bolton W v Blackburn R
Charlton Ath v Liverpool
Everton v Chelsea
Fulham v Leeds U
*Manchester U v Arsenal (12:15)
Middlesbrough v West Ham U
Southampton v Birmingham C
Sunderland v Manchester C

Nationwide Football League Division 1
Bradford C v Gillingham
Burnley v Nottingham F
Crystal P v Millwall
Derby Co v Watford
Ipswich T v Rotherham U
Leicester C v Sheffield U
Preston NE v Wimbledon
Reading v Portsmouth
Sheffield W v Brighton & HA
Stoke C v Coventry C

Walsall v Grimsby T
Wolverhampton W v Norwich C

Nationwide Conference
Barnet v Southport
Burton Albion v Doncaster
Chester v Farnborough
Dag & Red v Stevenage
Forest Green v Leigh RMI
Gravesend v Kettering
Margate v Hereford
Nuneaton v Morecambe
Scarborough v Yeovil
Telford v Northwich
Woking v Halifax

Sunday, 8 December 2002
FA Barclaycard Premiership
*Tottenham H v WBA (4:05)

Saturday, 14 December 2002
FA Barclaycard Premiership
Aston Villa v WBA
Charlton Ath v Manchester C
Everton v Blackburn R
Fulham v Birmingham C
Manchester U v West Ham U
Middlesbrough v Chelsea
Southampton v Newcastle U
Tottenham H v Arsenal

Nationwide Football League Division 1
Bradford C v Nottingham F
Burnley v Rotherham U
Crystal P v Norwich C
Derby Co v Brighton & HA
Ipswich T v Watford
Leicester C v Millwall
Preston NE v Grimsby T
Reading v Sheffield U
Sheffield W v Gillingham
Stoke C v Portsmouth
Walsall v Wimbledon
Wolverhampton W v Coventry C

Nationwide Football League Division 2
Brentford v Chesterfield
Cardiff C v Bristol C
Crewe Alex v Barnsley
Huddersfield T v Stockport Co
Luton T v Colchester U
Mansfield T v Blackpool
Northampton T v Tranmere R
Notts Co v QPR
Oldham Ath v Wigan Ath
Peterborough U v Cheltenham T

Plymouth Arg v Swindon T
Wycombe W v Port Vale

Nationwide Football League Division 3
Bristol R v Oxford U
Carlisle U v Wrexham
Exeter C v Swansea C
Hull C v Darlington
Kidderminster H v York C
Leyton Orient v Torquay U
Lincoln C v Cambridge U
Macclesfield T v Rushden & D'monds
Rochdale v Hartlepool U
Scunthorpe U v Bury
Shrewsbury T v Bournemouth
Southend U v Boston U

Nationwide Conference
Dag & Red v Doncaster
Farnborough v Southport
Forest Green v Morecambe
Halifax v Burton Albion
Hereford v Woking
Kettering v Scarborough
Leigh RMI v Chester
Northwich v Yeovil
Nuneaton v Gravesend
Stevenage v Margate
Telford v Barnet

Sunday, 15 December 2002

FA Barclaycard Premiership
*Sunderland v Liverpool (4:05)

Monday, 16 December 2002

FA Barclaycard Premiership
*Bolton W v Leeds U (8:00)

Friday, 20 December 2002

Nationwide Football League Division 1
Brighton & HA v Leicester C

Nationwide Football League Division 2
Stockport Co v Northampton T

Nationwide Football League Division 3
Hartlepool U v Scunthorpe U
York C v Lincoln C

Saturday, 21 December 2002

FA Barclaycard Premiership
Arsenal v Middlesbrough
Birmingham C v Charlton Ath
Blackburn R v Manchester U
Chelsea v Aston Villa

Leeds U v Southampton
Newcastle U v Fulham
WBA v Sunderland
West Ham U v Bolton W

Nationwide Football League Division 1
Coventry C v Derby Co
Gillingham v Burnley
Grimsby T v Sheffield W
Millwall v Wolverhampton W
Norwich C v Walsall
Nottingham F v Reading
Portsmouth v Ipswich T
Rotherham U v Crystal P
Sheffield U v Preston NE
Watford v Bradford C
Wimbledon v Stoke C

Nationwide Football League Division 2
Barnsley v Mansfield T
Blackpool v Peterborough U
Bristol C v Luton T
Cheltenham T v Wycombe W
Chesterfield v Oldham Ath
Colchester U v Cardiff C
Port Vale v Plymouth Arg
QPR v Brentford
Swindon T v Crewe Alex
Tranmere R v Notts Co
Wigan Ath v Huddersfield T

Nationwide Football League Division 3
Boston U v Shrewsbury T
Bournemouth v Hull C
Bury v Rochdale
Cambridge U v Bristol R
Darlington v Macclesfield T
Oxford U v Exeter C
Rushden & D'monds v Carlisle U
Swansea C v Leyton Orient
Torquay U v Southend U
Wrexham v Kidderminster H

Nationwide Conference
Barnet v Leigh RMI
Burton Albion v Dag & Red
Chester v Hereford
Doncaster v Halifax
Gravesend v Forest Green
Margate v Nuneaton
Morecambe v Kettering
Scarborough v Farnborough
Southport v Telford
Woking v Northwich
Yeovil v Stevenage

Sunday, 22 December 2002

FA Barclaycard Premiership
*Liverpool v Everton (4:05)

Monday, 23 December 2002

FA Barclaycard Premiership
*Manchester C v Tottenham H (8:00)

Thursday, 26 December 2002

FA Barclaycard Premiership
Birmingham C v Everton (3:00)
Bolton W v Newcastle U (3:00)
Chelsea v Southampton (12:00)
Liverpool v Blackburn R (3:00)
Manchester C v Aston Villa (3:00)
*Middlesbrough v Manchester U (4:00)
Sunderland v Leeds U (3:00)
Tottenham H v Charlton Ath (12:00)
WBA v Arsenal (3:00)
West Ham U v Fulham (12:00)

Nationwide Football League Division 1
Bradford C v Stoke C (3:00)
Burnley v Wolverhampton W (3:00)
Coventry C v Reading (3:00)
Derby Co v Grimsby T (3:00)
Leicester C v Ipswich T (3:00)
Millwall v Gillingham (12:00)
Norwich C v Brighton & HA (3:00)
Portsmouth v Crystal P (3:00)
Preston NE v Rotherham U (3:00)
Sheffield W v Nottingham F (3:00)
Walsall v Sheffield U (3:00)
Wimbledon v Watford (12:00)

Nationwide Football League Division 2
Bristol C v Plymouth Arg (12:00)
Cheltenham T v Crewe Alex (3:00)
Colchester U v Peterborough U (3:00)
Huddersfield T v Tranmere R (3:00)
Luton T v Cardiff C (12:00)
Mansfield T v Stockport Co (3:00)
Northampton T v Chesterfield (3:00)
Notts Co v Barnsley (3:00)
Oldham Ath v Blackpool (3:00)
Port Vale v Wigan Ath (3:00)
QPR v Wycombe W (12:00)
Swindon T v Brentford (3:00)

Nationwide Football League Division 3
Boston U v York C (3:00)
Cambridge U v Southend U (3:00)
Carlisle U v Darlington (3:00)
Hull C v Hartlepool U (3:00)
Kidderminster H v Leyton Orient (3:00)

Macclesfield T v Lincoln C (3:00)
Oxford U v Bournemouth (3:00)
Rochdale v Wrexham
Scunthorpe U v Rushden & D'monds (3:00)
Shrewsbury T v Bury (3:00)
Swansea C v Bristol R (1:00)
Torquay U v Exeter C (11:00)

Nationwide Conference
Barnet v Dag & Red
Farnborough v Woking
Forest Green v Yeovil
Gravesend v Margate
Kettering v Stevenage
Leigh RMI v Halifax
Morecambe v Southport
Northwich v Chester
Nuneaton v Burton Albion
Scarborough v Doncaster
Telford v Hereford

Saturday, 28 December 2002

FA Barclaycard Premiership
Aston Villa v Middlesbrough
Blackburn R v West Ham U
Charlton Ath v WBA
Everton v Bolton W
Fulham v Manchester C
Leeds U v Chelsea
Manchester U v Birmingham C
Southampton v Sunderland

Nationwide Football League Division 1
Brighton & HA v Burnley
Crystal P v Preston NE
Gillingham v Wimbledon
Grimsby T v Norwich C
Ipswich T v Walsall
Nottingham F v Portsmouth
Reading v Derby Co
Rotherham U v Millwall
Sheffield U v Coventry C
Stoke C v Sheffield W
Watford v Leicester C
Wolverhampton W v Bradford C

Nationwide Football League Division 2
Barnsley v Port Vale
Blackpool v Colchester U
Brentford v Mansfield T
Chesterfield v Cheltenham T
Crewe Alex v Oldham Ath
Peterborough U v Northampton T (12:00)
Plymouth Arg v Notts Co
Stockport Co v Bristol C

Tranmere R v QPR
Wigan Ath v Swindon T
Wycombe W v Luton T

Nationwide Football League Division 3
Bournemouth v Rochdale
Bristol R v Boston U
Bury v Kidderminster H
Darlington v Torquay U
Exeter C v Macclesfield T
Hartlepool U v Cambridge U
Leyton Orient v Carlisle U
Lincoln C v Swansea C
Rushden & D'monds v Oxford U
Southend U v Scunthorpe U
Wrexham v Shrewsbury T (12:00)
York C v Hull C

Nationwide Conference
Burton Albion v Northwich
Chester v Telford
Dag & Red v Gravesend
Doncaster v Leigh RMI
Halifax v Morecambe
Hereford v Forest Green
Margate v Kettering
Southport v Scarborough
Stevenage v Farnborough
Woking v Nuneaton
Yeovil v Barnet

Sunday, 29 December 2002
FA Barclaycard Premiership
*Arsenal v Liverpool (4:05)
Newcastle U v Tottenham H

Nationwide Football League Division 2
Cardiff C v Huddersfield T

Wednesday, 1 January 2003
FA Barclaycard Premiership
Arsenal v Chelsea (3:00)
Aston Villa v Bolton W (3:00)
Blackburn R v Middlesbrough (3:00)
Charlton Ath v West Ham U (3:00)
Everton v Manchester C (3:00)
Fulham v WBA (3:00)
Leeds U v Birmingham C (3:00)
Manchester U v Sunderland (3:00)
*Newcastle U v Liverpool (7.45)
Southampton v Tottenham H (3:00)

Nationwide Football League Division 1
Brighton & HA v Wimbledon (3:00)
Crystal P v Coventry C (3:00)
Gillingham v Norwich C (3:00)

Grimsby T v Bradford C (3:00)
Ipswich T v Millwall (3:00)
Nottingham F v Walsall (3:00)
Reading v Leicester C (3:00)
Rotherham U v Sheffield W (3:00)
Sheffield U v Burnley (3:00)
Stoke C v Preston NE (3:00)
Watford v Portsmouth (3:00)
Wolverhampton W v Derby Co (3:00)

Nationwide Football League Division 2
Barnsley v Northampton T (3:00)
Blackpool v Huddersfield T (3:00)
Brentford v Colchester U (3:00)
Cardiff C v Swindon T (3:00)
Chesterfield v Luton T (3:00)
Crewe Alex v Mansfield T (3:00)
Peterborough U v QPR (3:00)
Plymouth Arg v Cheltenham T (3:00)
Stockport Co v Port Vale (3:00)
Tranmere R v Oldham Ath (3:00)
Wigan Ath v Notts Co (3:00)
Wycombe W v Bristol C (3:00)

Nationwide Football League Division 3
Bournemouth v Swansea C (3:00)
Bristol R v Torquay U (3:00)
Bury v Hull C (3:00)
Darlington v Rochdalev
Exeter C v Kidderminster H (3:00)
Hartlepool U v Carlisle U (3:00)
Leyton Orient v Cambridge U (3:00)
Lincoln C v Boston U (3:00)
Rushden & D'monds v Shrewsbury T (3:00)
Southend U v Oxford U (3:00)
Wrexham v Macclesfield T (3:00)
York C v Scunthorpe U (3:00)

Nationwide Conference
Burton Albion v Nuneaton
Chester v Northwich
Dag & Red v Barnet
Doncaster v Scarborough
Halifax v Leigh RMI
Hereford v Telford
Margate v Gravesend
Southport v Morecambe
Stevenage v Kettering
Woking v Farnborough
Yeovil v Forest Green

Saturday, 4 January 2003
Nationwide Football League Division 2
Bristol C v Brentford
Cheltenham T v Barnsley
Colchester U v Tranmere R

Huddersfield T v Plymouth Arg
Luton T v Blackpool
Mansfield T v Wigan Ath
Northampton T v Wycombe W
Notts Co v Crewe Alex
Oldham Ath v Peterborough U
Port Vale v Cardiff C
QPR v Stockport Co
Swindon T v Chesterfield

Nationwide Football League Division 3
Boston U v Hartlepool U
Cambridge U v Bury
Carlisle U v Southend U
Hull C v Bristol R
Kidderminster H v Bournemouth
Macclesfield T v Leyton Orient
Oxford U v Wrexham
Rochdale v Lincoln C
Scunthorpe U v Exeter C
Shrewsbury T v York C
Swansea C v Darlington
Torquay U v Rushden & D'monds

Nationwide Conference
Barnet v Doncaster
Farnborough v Hereford
Forest Green v Woking
Gravesend v Yeovil
Kettering v Chester
Leigh RMI v Dag & Red
Morecambe v Margate
Northwich v Stevenage
Nuneaton v Southport
Scarborough v Burton Albion
Telford v Halifax

Saturday, 11 January 2003

FA Barclaycard Premiership
Birmingham C v Arsenal
Bolton W v Fulham
Chelsea v Charlton Ath
Liverpool v Aston Villa
Manchester C v Leeds U
Middlesbrough v Southampton
Sunderland v Blackburn R
Tottenham H v Everton
WBA v Manchester U
West Ham U v Newcastle U

Nationwide Football League Division 1
Bradford C v Crystal P
Burnley v Ipswich T
Coventry C v Brighton & HA
Derby Co v Gillingham
Leicester C v Stoke C

Millwall v Watford
Norwich C v Rotherham U
Portsmouth v Sheffield U
Preston NE v Nottingham F
Sheffield W v Reading
Walsall v Wolverhampton W
Wimbledon v Grimsby T

Nationwide Football League Division 2
Bristol C v Wigan Ath
Cheltenham T v Tranmere R
Colchester U v Crewe Alex
Huddersfield T v Peterborough U
Luton T v Plymouth Arg
Mansfield T v Wycombe W
Northampton T v Cardiff C (12:00)
Notts Co v Stockport Co
Oldham Ath v Brentford
Port Vale v Chesterfield
QPR v Barnsley
Swindon T v Blackpool

Nationwide Football League Division 3
Boston U v Wrexham
Cambridge U v Bournemouth
Carlisle U v Lincoln C
Hull C v Exeter C
Kidderminster H v Rushden &
   D'monds
Macclesfield T v Hartlepool U
Oxford U v Darlington
Rochdale v Bristol R
Scunthorpe U v Leyton Orient
Shrewsbury T v Southend U
Swansea C v Bury
Torquay U v York C

Friday, 17 January 2003

Nationwide Football League Division 3
Bournemouth v Macclesfield T

Saturday, 18 January 2003

FA Barclaycard Premiership
Arsenal v West Ham U
Aston Villa v Tottenham H
Blackburn R v Birmingham C
Charlton Ath v Bolton W
Everton v Sunderland
Fulham v Middlesbrough
Leeds U v WBA
Manchester U v Chelsea
Newcastle U v Manchester C
Southampton v Liverpool

Nationwide Football League Division 1
Brighton & HA v Portsmouth

Crystal P v Burnley
Gillingham v Leicester C
Grimsby T v Millwall
Ipswich T v Preston NE
Nottingham F v Coventry C
Reading v Walsall
Rotherham U v Bradford C
Sheffield U v Sheffield W
Stoke C v Derby Co
Watford v Norwich C
Wolverhampton W v Wimbledon

Nationwide Football League Division 2
Barnsley v Luton T
Blackpool v Northampton T
Brentford v Notts Co
Cardiff C v Cheltenham T
Chesterfield v Mansfield T
Crewe Alex v Huddersfield T
Peterborough U v Port Vale
Plymouth Arg v QPR
Stockport Co v Swindon T
Tranmere R v Bristol C
Wigan Ath v Colchester U
Wycombe W v Oldham Ath

Nationwide Football League Division 3
Bristol R v Scunthorpe U
Bury v Boston U
Darlington v Kidderminster H
Exeter C v Carlisle U
Hartlepool U v Oxford U
Leyton Orient v Hull C
Lincoln C v Shrewsbury T
Rushden & D'monds v Cambridge U
Southend U v Rochdale
Wrexham v Torquay U
York C v Swansea C

Nationwide Conference
Burton Albion v Leigh RMI
Chester v Barnet
Dag & Red v Scarborough
Doncaster v Telford
Halifax v Farnborough
Hereford v Gravesend
Margate v Northwich
Southport v Forest Green
Stevenage v Nuneaton
Woking v Kettering
Yeovil v Morecambe

Saturday, 25 January 2003
Nationwide Football League Division 2
Bristol C v Stockport Co
Cheltenham T v Chesterfield

Colchester U v Blackpool
Huddersfield T v Cardiff C
Luton T v Wycombe W
Mansfield T v Brentford
Northampton T v Peterborough U
    (12:00)
Notts Co v Plymouth Arg
Oldham Ath v Crewe Alex
Port Vale v Barnsley
QPR v Tranmere R
Swindon T v Wigan Ath

Nationwide Football League Division 3
Boston U v Bristol R
Cambridge U v Hartlepool U
Carlisle U v Leyton Orient
Hull C v York C
Kidderminster H v Bury
Macclesfield T v Exeter C
Oxford U v Rushden & D'monds
Rochdale v Bournemouth
Scunthorpe U v Southend U
Swansea C v Lincoln C
Torquay U v Darlington

Nationwide Conference
Barnet v Burton Albion
Farnborough v Doncaster
Forest Green v Margate
Gravesend v Stevenage
Kettering v Southport
Leigh RMI v Woking
Morecambe v Hereford
Northwich v Halifax
Nuneaton v Yeovil
Scarborough v Chester
Telford v Dag & Red

Sunday, 26 January 2003
Nationwide Football League Division 3
Shrewsbury T v Wrexham (12.00)

Tuesday, 28 January 2003
FA Barclaycard Premiership
Birmingham C v Manchester U
Bolton W v Everton (8:00)
Middlesbrough v Aston Villa
Sunderland v Southampton (8:00)
WBA v Charlton Ath

Wednesday, 29 January 2003
FA Barclaycard Premiership
Chelsea v Leeds U
Liverpool v Arsenal (8:00)
Manchester C v Fulham

Tottenham H v Newcastle U
West Ham U v Blackburn R

Friday, 31 January 2003
Nationwide Football League Division 3
Bournemouth v Boston U

Saturday, 1 February 2003
FA Barclaycard Premiership
Arsenal v Fulham
Aston Villa v Blackburn R
Bolton W v Birmingham C
Chelsea v Tottenham H
Everton v Leeds U
Manchester C v WBA
Middlesbrough v Newcastle U
Southampton v Manchester U
Sunderland v Charlton Ath
West Ham U v Liverpool

Nationwide Football League Division 1
Bradford C v Ipswich T
Burnley v Reading
Coventry C v Watford
Derby Co v Rotherham U
Leicester C v Crystal P
Millwall v Sheffield U
Norwich C v Stoke C
Portsmouth v Grimsby T
Preston NE v Gillingham
Sheffield W v Wolverhampton W
Walsall v Brighton & HA
Wimbledon v Nottingham F

Nationwide Football League Division 2
Barnsley v Swindon T
Blackpool v Bristol C
Brentford v Huddersfield T
Cardiff C v Oldham Ath
Chesterfield v QPR
Crewe Alex v Northampton T
Peterborough U v Luton T (12:00)
Plymouth Arg v Mansfield T
Stockport Co v Colchester U
Tranmere R v Port Vale
Wigan Ath v Cheltenham T
Wycombe W v Notts Co

Nationwide Football League Division 3
Bristol R v Carlisle U
Bury v Oxford U
Darlington v Cambridge U
Exeter C v Shrewsbury T
Hartlepool U v Torquay U
Leyton Orient v Rochdale
Lincoln C v Kidderminster H

Rushden & D'monds v Swansea C
Southend U v Hull C
Wrexham v Scunthorpe U

Sunday, 2 February 2003
Nationwide Football League Division 3
York C v Macclesfield T

Saturday, 8 February 2003
FA Barclaycard Premiership
Birmingham C v Chelsea
Blackburn R v Southampton
Charlton Ath v Everton
Fulham v Aston Villa
Leeds U v West Ham U
Liverpool v Middlesbrough
Manchester U v Manchester C
Newcastle U v Arsenal
Tottenham H v Sunderland
WBA v Bolton W

Nationwide Football League Division 1
Brighton & HA v Wolverhampton W
Coventry C v Burnley
Grimsby T v Stoke C
Ipswich T v Sheffield U
Nottingham F v Crystal P
Portsmouth v Derby Co
Preston NE v Millwall
Reading v Gillingham
Sheffield W v Norwich C
Walsall v Leicester C
Watford v Rotherham U
Wimbledon v Bradford C

Nationwide Football League Division 2
Brentford v Crewe Alex
Bristol C v Colchester U
Cardiff C v Barnsley
Cheltenham T v Stockport Co
Chesterfield v Peterborough U
Mansfield T v Notts Co
Northampton T v QPR
Oldham Ath v Plymouth Arg
Port Vale v Luton T
Tranmere R v Swindon T
Wigan Ath v Blackpool
Wycombe W v Huddersfield T

Nationwide Football League Division 3
Boston U v Scunthorpe U
Bournemouth v Wrexham
Cambridge U v Shrewsbury T
Carlisle U v Kidderminster H
Darlington v Rushden & D'monds
Hartlepool U v Exeter C

Hull C v Lincoln C
Leyton Orient v York C
Macclesfield T v Swansea C
Rochdale v Oxford U
Southend U v Bristol R
Torquay U v Bury

Nationwide Conference
Burton Albion v Telford
Chester v Forest Green
Dag & Red v Farnborough
Doncaster v Northwich
Halifax v Barnet
Hereford v Nuneaton
Margate v Leigh RMI
Southport v Gravesend
Stevenage v Morecambe
Woking v Scarborough
Yeovil v Kettering

Friday, 14 February 2003
Nationwide Football League Division 2
Colchester U v Mansfield T

Saturday, 15 February 2003
Nationwide Football League Division 1
Bradford C v Brighton & HA
Burnley v Preston NE
Crystal P v Ipswich T
Derby Co v Sheffield W
Gillingham v Grimsby T
Leicester C v Portsmouth
Millwall v Reading (1:00)
Norwich C v Wimbledon
Rotherham U v Coventry C
Sheffield U v Nottingham F
Stoke C v Walsall
Wolverhampton W v Watford

Nationwide Football League Division 2
Barnsley v Chesterfield
Blackpool v Brentford
Crewe Alex v Wigan Ath
Huddersfield T v Cheltenham T
Luton T v Northampton T
Notts Co v Bristol C
Peterborough U v Cardiff C
Plymouth Arg v Tranmere R
QPR v Port Vale
Stockport Co v Oldham Ath
Swindon T v Wycombe W

Nationwide Football League Division 3
Bristol R v Bournemouth
Bury v Leyton Orient
Exeter C v Boston U

Kidderminster H v Torquay U
Lincoln C v Darlington
Oxford U v Carlisle U
Rushden & D'monds v Rochdale
Scunthorpe U v Hull C
Shrewsbury T v Macclesfield T
Swansea C v Cambridge U
Wrexham v Southend U
York C v Hartlepool U

Nationwide Conference
Barnet v Margate
Farnborough v Yeovil
Forest Green v Burton Albion
Gravesend v Woking
Kettering v Doncaster
Leigh RMI v Southport
Morecambe v Chester
Northwich v Hereford
Nuneaton v Dag & Red
Scarborough v Halifax
Telford v Stevenage

Friday, 21 February 2003
Nationwide Football League Division 2
Cardiff C v Plymouth Arg

Saturday, 22 February 2003
FA Barclaycard Premiership
Birmingham C v Liverpool
Bolton W v Manchester U
Charlton Ath v Aston Villa
Chelsea v Blackburn R
Everton v Southampton
Leeds U v Newcastle U
Manchester C v Arsenal
Sunderland v Middlesbrough
Tottenham H v Fulham
WBA v West Ham U

Nationwide Football League Division 1
Brighton & HA v Millwall
Burnley v Derby Co
Coventry C v Bradford C
Crystal P v Sheffield W
Ipswich T v Grimsby T
Leicester C v Wimbledon
Nottingham F v Stoke C
Portsmouth v Gillingham
Preston NE v Wolverhampton W
Reading v Rotherham U
Sheffield U v Norwich C
Walsall v Watford

Nationwide Football League Division 2
Barnsley v Huddersfield T

Cheltenham T v Colchester U
Chesterfield v Crewe Alex
Luton T v Brentford
Northampton T v Bristol C
Oldham Ath v Notts Co
Peterborough U v Stockport Co
Port Vale v Swindon T
QPR v Mansfield T
Tranmere R v Blackpool
Wycombe W v Wigan Ath

Nationwide Football League Division 3
Boston U v Kidderminster H
Bournemouth v Exeter C
Bristol R v Macclesfield S
Hartlepool U v Swansea C
Hull C v Cambridge U
Leyton Orient v Shrewsbury T
Rochdale v Carlisle U
Scunthorpe U v Lincoln C
Southend U v Rushden & D'monds
Torquay U v Oxford U
Wrexham v Darlington
York C v Bury

Nationwide Conference
Barnet v Scarborough
Burton Albion v Southport
Dag & Red v Chester
Doncaster v Margate
Forest Green v Nuneaton
Halifax v Yeovil
Hereford v Stevenage
Leigh RMI v Farnborough
Northwich v Kettering
Telford v Gravesend
Woking v Morecambe

Saturday, 1 March 2003
FA Barclaycard Premiership
Arsenal v Charlton Ath
Aston Villa v Birmingham C
Blackburn R v Manchester C
Fulham v Sunderland
Liverpool v Bolton W
Manchester U v Leeds U
Middlesbrough v Everton
Newcastle U v Chelsea
Southampton v WBA
West Ham U v Tottenham H

Nationwide Football League Division 1
Bradford C v Walsall
Derby Co v Leicester C
Gillingham v Brighton & HA
Grimsby T v Coventry C

Millwall v Portsmouth
Rotherham U v Sheffield U
Sheffield W v Preston NE
Stoke C v Burnley
Watford v Nottingham F
Wimbledon v Reading
Wolverhampton W v Crystal P

Nationwide Football League Division 2
Blackpool v Wycombe W
Brentford v Tranmere R
Bristol C v Cheltenham T
Colchester U v Port Vale
Crewe Alex v Peterborough U
Huddersfield T v Northampton T
Mansfield T v Oldham Ath
Notts Co v Luton T
Plymouth Arg v Barnsley
Stockport Co v Cardiff C
Swindon T v QPR
Wigan Ath v Chesterfield

Nationwide Football League Division 3
Bury v Bournemouth
Cambridge U v Torquay U
Carlisle U v Hull C
Darlington v Hartlepool U
Exeter C v Bristol R
Kidderminster H v Scunthorpe U
Lincoln C v Leyton Orient
Macclesfield T v Southend U
Oxford U v Boston U
Rushden & D'monds v York C
Shrewsbury T v Rochdale
Swansea C v Wrexham

Nationwide Conference
Chester v Halifax
Farnborough v Barnet
Gravesend v Burton Albion
Kettering v Dag & Red
Margate v Woking
Morecambe v Northwich
Nuneaton v Leigh RMI
Scarborough v Telford
Southport v Doncaster
Stevenage v Forest Green
Yeovil v Hereford

Sunday, 2 March 2003
Nationwide Football League Division 1
Norwich C v Ipswich T (1:00)

Tuesday, 4 March 2003
Nationwide Football League Division 1
Bradford C v Leicester C

Gillingham v Nottingham F
Grimsby T v Sheffield U
Millwall v Burnley
Rotherham U v Walsall
Watford v Preston NE
Wimbledon v Portsmouth
Wolverhampton W v Ipswich T

Nationwide Football League Division 2
Blackpool v Barnsley
Brentford v Cardiff C
Bristol C v Oldham Ath
Colchester U v Northampton T
Crewe Alex v Wycombe W
Huddersfield T v QPR
Mansfield T v Luton T
Notts Co v Port Vale
Plymouth Arg v Peterborough U
Stockport Co v Chesterfield
Wigan Ath v Tranmere R

Nationwide Football League Division 3
Bury v Bristol R
Cambridge U v Rochdale
Carlisle U v Scunthorpe U
Darlington v York C (7:30)
Exeter C v Wrexham
Kidderminster H v Southend U
Lincoln C v Hartlepool U
Macclesfield T v Hull C
Oxford U v Leyton Orient
Rushden & D'monds v Bournemouth
Shrewsbury T v Torquay U
Swansea C v Boston U

Wednesday, 5 March 2003
Nationwide Football League Division 1
Derby Co v Crystal P
Norwich C v Reading
Sheffield W v Coventry C
Stoke C v Brighton & HA

Nationwide Football League Division 2
Swindon T v Cheltenham T

Friday, 7 March 2003
Nationwide Football League Division 3
Hartlepool U v Bury

Saturday, 8 March 2003
Nationwide Football League Division 1
Brighton & HA v Rotherham U
Burnley v Bradford C
Coventry C v Wimbledon
Crystal P v Watford
Ipswich T v Stoke C

Leicester C v Sheffield W
Nottingham F v Grimsby T
Portsmouth v Norwich C
Preston NE v Derby Co
Reading v Wolverhampton W
Sheffield U v Gillingham
Walsall v Millwall

Nationwide Football League Division 2
Barnsley v Stockport Co
Cardiff C v Notts Co
Cheltenham T v Mansfield T
Chesterfield v Plymouth Arg
Luton T v Huddersfield T
Northampton T v Swindon T
Oldham Ath v Colchester U
Peterborough U v Wigan Ath
Port Vale v Blackpool
QPR v Bristol C
Tranmere R v Crewe Alex
Wycombe W v Brentford

Nationwide Football League Division 3
Boston U v Carlisle U
Bournemouth v Darlington
Bristol R v Shrewsbury T
Hull C v Oxford U
Leyton Orient v Exeter C
Rochdale v Kidderminster H
Scunthorpe U v Macclesfield T
Southend U v Lincoln C
Torquay U v Swansea C
Wrexham v Rushden & D'monds
York C v Cambridge U

Nationwide Conference
Barnet v Stevenage
Burton Albion v Chester
Dag & Red v Margate
Doncaster v Gravesend
Forest Green v Farnborough
Halifax v Southport
Hereford v Kettering
Leigh RMI v Scarborough
Northwich v Nuneaton
Telford v Morecambe
Woking v Yeovil

Friday, 14 March 2003

Nationwide Football League Division 2
Tranmere R v Cardiff C

Saturday, 15 March 2003

FA Barclaycard Premiership
Aston Villa v Manchester U
Blackburn R v Arsenal

Charlton Ath v Newcastle U
Everton v West Ham U
Fulham v Southampton
Leeds U v Middlesbrough
Manchester C v Birmingham C
Sunderland v Bolton W
Tottenham H v Liverpool
WBA v Chelsea

Nationwide Football League Division 1
Brighton & HA v Nottingham F
Derby Co v Bradford C
Gillingham v Rotherham U
Grimsby T v Watford
Leicester C v Preston NE
Norwich C v Coventry C
Portsmouth v Wolverhampton W
Reading v Crystal P
Sheffield W v Ipswich T
Stoke C v Sheffield U
Walsall v Burnley
Wimbledon v Millwall (12:00)

Nationwide Football League Division 2
Blackpool v Plymouth Arg
Brentford v Stockport Co
Bristol C v Peterborough U
Cheltenham T v Northampton T
Colchester U v Huddersfield T
Crewe Alex v Port Vale
Mansfield T v Swindon T
Notts Co v Chesterfield
Oldham Ath v QPR
Wigan Ath v Luton T
Wycombe W v Barnsley

Nationwide Football League Division 3
Cambridge U v Kidderminster H
Darlington v Exeter C
Hartlepool U v Southend U
Leyton Orient v Bristol R
Lincoln C v Wrexham
Macclesfield T v Bury
Rochdale v Boston U
Rushden & D'monds v Hull C
Shrewsbury T v Oxford U
Swansea C v Carlisle U
Torquay U v Scunthorpe U
York C v Bournemouth

Nationwide Conference
Chester v Doncaster
Farnborough v Telford
Gravesend v Northwich
Kettering v Forest Green
Margate v Burton Albion
Morecambe v Barnet

Nuneaton v Halifax
Scarborough v Hereford
Southport v Dag & Red
Stevenage v Woking
Yeovil v Leigh RMI

Tuesday, 18 March 2003
Nationwide Football League Division 1
Bradford C v Sheffield W
Burnley v Leicester C
Crystal P v Wimbledon (8:00)
Ipswich T v Reading
Millwall v Norwich C
Preston NE v Walsall
Rotherham U v Grimsby T
Sheffield U v Brighton & HA
Watford v Gillingham
Wolverhampton W v Stoke C

Nationwide Football League Division 2
Barnsley v Tranmere R
Cardiff C v Blackpool
Chesterfield v Colchester U
Huddersfield T v Mansfield T
Luton T v Oldham Ath
Northampton T v Notts Co
Peterborough U v Wycombe W
Plymouth Arg v Crewe Alex
Port Vale v Brentford
QPR v Cheltenham T
Stockport Co v Wigan Ath

Nationwide Football League Division 3
Bournemouth v Leyton Orient
Bristol R v York C
Bury v Rushden & D'monds
Carlisle U v Macclesfield T
Exeter C v Lincoln C
Hull C v Torquay U
Kidderminster H v Shrewsbury T
Oxford U v Cambridge U
Scunthorpe U v Rochdale (7:30)
Southend U v Swansea C
Wrexham v Hartlepool U

Wednesday, 19 March 2003
Nationwide Football League Division 1
Coventry C v Portsmouth
Nottingham F v Derby Co

Nationwide Football League Division 2
Swindon T v Bristol C

Nationwide Football League Division 3
Boston U v Darlington

Friday, 21 March 2003

Nationwide Football League Division 2
Cardiff C v Mansfield T

Saturday, 22 March 2003

FA Barclaycard Premiership
Arsenal v Everton
Birmingham C v WBA
Bolton W v Tottenham H
Chelsea v Manchester C
Liverpool v Leeds U
Manchester U v Fulham
Middlesbrough v Charlton Ath
Newcastle U v Blackburn R
Southampton v Aston Villa
West Ham U v Sunderland

Nationwide Football League Division 1
Bradford C v Reading
Burnley v Grimsby T
Coventry C v Leicester C
Crystal P v Walsall
Ipswich T v Brighton & HA
Millwall v Sheffield W
Nottingham F v Norwich C
Preston NE v Portsmouth
Rotherham U v Wimbledon
Sheffield U v Derby Co
Watford v Stoke C
Wolverhampton W v Gillingham

Nationwide Football League Division 2
Barnsley v Colchester U
Chesterfield v Wycombe W
Huddersfield T v Bristol C
Luton T v Crewe Alex
Northampton T v Oldham Ath
Peterborough U v Tranmere R
Plymouth Arg v Brentford
Port Vale v Cheltenham T
QPR v Wigan Ath
Stockport Co v Blackpool
Swindon T v Notts Co

Nationwide Football League Division 3
Boston U v Rushden & D'monds
Bournemouth v Torquay U
Bristol R v Hartlepool U
Bury v Lincoln C
Carlisle U v Cambridge U
Exeter C v Rochdale
Hull C v Shrewsbury T
Kidderminster H v Swansea C
Oxford U v Macclesfield T
Scunthorpe U v Darlington

Southend U v Leyton Orient
Wrexham v York C

Nationwide Conference
Barnet v Hereford
Burton Albion v Farnborough
Chester v Southport
Dag & Red v Halifax
Forest Green v Northwich
Gravesend v Morecambe
Margate v Yeovil
Nuneaton v Kettering
Scarborough v Stevenage
Telford v Leigh RMI
Woking v Doncaster

Friday, 28 March 2003

Nationwide Football League Division 3
Swansea C v Oxford U

Saturday, 29 March 2003

Nationwide Football League Division 1
Brighton & HA v Crystal P
Derby Co v Millwall
Gillingham v Ipswich T
Grimsby T v Wolverhampton W
Leicester C v Nottingham F
Norwich C v Bradford C
Portsmouth v Burnley
Reading v Preston NE
Sheffield W v Watford
Stoke C v Rotherham U
Walsall v Coventry C
Wimbledon v Sheffield U

Nationwide Football League Division 2
Blackpool v QPR
Brentford v Northampton T
Bristol C v Barnsley
Cheltenham T v Luton T
Colchester U v Swindon T
Crewe Alex v Stockport Co
Mansfield T v Peterborough U
Notts Co v Huddersfield T
Oldham Ath v Port Vale
Tranmere R v Chesterfield
Wigan Ath v Plymouth Arg
Wycombe W v Cardiff C

Nationwide Football League Division 3
Cambridge U v Scunthorpe U
Darlington v Bury
Hartlepool U v Bournemouth
Leyton Orient v Wrexham
Lincoln C v Bristol R
Macclesfield T v Kidderminster H

Rochdale v Hull C
Rushden & D'monds v Exeter C
Shrewsbury T v Carlisle U
Torquay U v Boston U
York C v Southend U

Nationwide Conference
Doncaster v Burton Albion
Farnborough v Chester
Halifax v Woking
Hereford v Margate
Kettering v Gravesend
Leigh RMI v Forest Green
Morecambe v Nuneaton
Northwich v Telford
Southport v Barnet
Stevenage v Dag & Red
Yeovil v Scarborough

Friday, 4 April 2003
Nationwide Football League Division 2
Northampton T v Wigan Ath

Saturday, 5 April 2003
FA Barclaycard Premiership
Aston Villa v Arsenal
Bolton W v Manchester C
Charlton Ath v Leeds U
Fulham v Blackburn R
Manchester U v Liverpool
Middlesbrough v WBA
Southampton v West Ham U
Sunderland v Chelsea
Tottenham H v Birmingham C

Nationwide Football League Division 1
Bradford C v Millwall
Burnley v Watford
Crystal P v Sheffield U
Derby Co v Norwich C
Ipswich T v Nottingham F
Leicester C v Grimsby T
Preston NE v Coventry C
Reading v Brighton & HA
Sheffield W v Wimbledon
Stoke C v Gillingham
Walsall v Portsmouth
Wolverhampton W v Rotherham U

Nationwide Football League Division 2
Brentford v Cheltenham T
Cardiff C v QPR
Crewe Alex v Bristol C
Huddersfield T v Chesterfield
Luton T v Tranmere R
Mansfield T v Port Vale

Notts Co v Blackpool
Oldham Ath v Barnsley
Peterborough U v Swindon T
Plymouth Arg v Colchester U
Wycombe W v Stockport Co

Nationwide Football League Division 3
Bristol R v Rushden & D'monds
Carlisle U v York C
Exeter C v Bury
Hull C v Wrexham
Kidderminster H v Hartlepool U
Leyton Orient v Boston U
Lincoln C v Oxford U
Macclesfield T v Cambridge U
Rochdale v Torquay U
Scunthorpe U v Bournemouth
Shrewsbury T v Swansea C
Southend U v Darlington

Nationwide Conference
Forest Green v Doncaster
Gravesend v Chester
Hereford v Burton Albion
Kettering v Farnborough
Margate v Halifax
Morecambe v Dag & Red
Northwich v Scarborough
Nuneaton v Barnet
Stevenage v Leigh RMI
Woking v Southport
Yeovil v Telford

Sunday, 6 April 2003

FA Barclaycard Premiership
Everton v Newcastle U

Saturday, 12 April 2003

FA Barclaycard Premiership
Arsenal v Southampton
Birmingham C v Sunderland
Blackburn R v Charlton Ath
Chelsea v Bolton W
Leeds U v Tottenham H
Liverpool v Fulham
Manchester C v Middlesbrough
Newcastle U v Manchester U
WBA v Everton
West Ham U v Aston Villa

Nationwide Football League Division 1
Brighton & HA v Preston NE
Coventry C v Ipswich T
Gillingham v Walsall
Grimsby T v Crystal P
Millwall v Stoke C

Norwich C v Burnley
Nottingham F v Wolverhampton W
Portsmouth v Sheffield W
Rotherham U v Leicester C
Sheffield U v Bradford C
Watford v Reading
Wimbledon v Derby Co

Nationwide Football League Division 2

Barnsley v Peterborough U
Blackpool v Crewe Alex
Bristol C v Mansfield T
Cheltenham T v Oldham Ath
Chesterfield v Cardiff C
Colchester U v Notts Co
Port Vale v Northampton T
QPR v Luton T
Stockport Co v Plymouth Arg
Swindon T v Huddersfield T
Tranmere R v Wycombe W
Wigan Ath v Brentford

Nationwide Football League Division 3

Boston U v Hull C
Bournemouth v Southend U
Bury v Carlisle U
Cambridge U v Exeter C
Darlington v Shrewsbury T
Hartlepool U v Leyton Orient
Oxford U v Kidderminster H
Rushden & D'monds v Lincoln C
Swansea C v Scunthorpe U
Torquay U v Macclesfield T
Wrexham v Bristol R
York C v Rochdale

Nationwide Conference

Barnet v Kettering
Burton Albion v Stevenage
Chester v Woking
Dag & Red v Northwich
Doncaster v Yeovil
Farnborough v Morecambe
Halifax v Hereford
Leigh RMI v Gravesend
Scarborough v Forest Green
Southport v Margate
Telford v Nuneaton

Friday, 18 April 2003

FA Barclaycard Premiership
Tottenham H v Manchester C (3:00)

Nationwide Football League Division 2
Northampton T v Stockport Co

Saturday, 19 April 2003

FA Barclaycard Premiership
Aston Villa v Chelsea
Bolton W v West Ham U
Charlton Ath v Birmingham C
Everton v Liverpool
Fulham v Newcastle U
Manchester U v Blackburn R
Middlesbrough v Arsenal
Southampton v Leeds U
Sunderland v WBA

Nationwide Football League Division 1

Bradford C v Watford
Burnley v Gillingham
Crystal P v Rotherham U
Derby Co v Coventry C
Ipswich T v Portsmouth
Leicester C v Brighton & HA
Preston NE v Sheffield U
Reading v Nottingham F
Sheffield W v Grimsby T
Stoke C v Wimbledon
Walsall v Norwich C
Wolverhampton W v Millwall

Nationwide Football League Division 2

Brentford v QPR
Cardiff C v Colchester U
Crewe Alex v Swindon T
Huddersfield T v Wigan Ath
Luton T v Bristol C
Mansfield T v Barnsley
Notts Co v Tranmere R
Oldham Ath v Chesterfield
Peterborough U v Blackpool
Plymouth Arg v Port Vale
Wycombe W v Cheltenham T

Nationwide Football League Division 3

Bristol R v Cambridge U
Carlisle U v Rushden & D'monds
Exeter C v Oxford U
Hull C v Bournemouth
Kidderminster H v Wrexham
Leyton Orient v Swansea C
Lincoln C v York C
Macclesfield T v Darlington
Rochdale v Bury
Scunthorpe U v Hartlepool U
Shrewsbury T v Boston U
Southend U v Torquay U

Nationwide Conference

Forest Green v Telford
Gravesend v Barnet

Hereford v Leigh RMI
Kettering v Halifax
Margate v Farnborough
Morecambe v Scarborough
Northwich v Southport
Nuneaton v Chester
Stevenage v Doncaster
Woking v Dag & Red
Yeovil v Burton Albion

Monday, 21 April 2003
FA Barclaycard Premiership
Arsenal v Manchester U (3:00)
Birmingham C v Southampton (3:00)
Blackburn R v Bolton W (3:00)
Chelsea v Everton (3:00)
Liverpool v Charlton Ath (3:00)
Manchester C v Sunderland (3:00)
Newcastle U v Aston Villa (3:00)
WBA v Tottenham H (3:00)
West Ham U v Middlesbrough (3:00)

Nationwide Football League Division 1
Brighton & HA v Sheffield W (3:00)
Coventry C v Stoke C (3:00)
Gillingham v Bradford C (3:00)
Grimsby T v Walsall (3:00)
Millwall v Crystal P (3:00)
Norwich C v Wolverhampton W (3:00)
Nottingham F v Burnley (3:00)
Portsmouth v Reading (3:00)
Rotherham U v Ipswich T (3:00)
Sheffield U v Leicester C (3:00)
Watford v Derby Co (3:00)

Nationwide Football League Division 2
Barnsley v Crewe Alex (3:00)
Blackpool v Mansfield T (3:00)
Cheltenham T v Peterborough U (3:00)
Chesterfield v Brentford (3:00)
Colchester U v Luton T (3:00)
Port Vale v Wycombe W (3:00)
QPR v Notts Co (3:00)
Stockport Co v Huddersfield T (3:00)
Swindon T v Plymouth Arg (3:00)
Tranmere R v Northampton T (3:00)
Wigan Ath v Oldham Ath (3:00)

Nationwide Football League Division 3
Boston U v Southend U (3:00)
Bury v Scunthorpe U (3:00)
Cambridge U v Lincoln C (3:00)
Darlington v Hull C (3:00)
Hartlepool U v Rochdale (3:00)
Oxford U v Bristol R (3:00)
Rushden & D'monds v Macclesfield T
  (3:00)

Swansea C v Exeter C (3:00)
Torquay U v Leyton Orient (3:00)
Wrexham v Carlisle U (3:00)
York C v Kidderminster H (3:00)

Nationwide Conference
Barnet v Woking
Burton Albion v Kettering
Chester v Stevenage
Dag & Red v Yeovil
Doncaster v Morecambe
Farnborough v Gravesend
Halifax v Forest Green
Leigh RMI v Northwich
Scarborough v Nuneaton
Southport v Hereford
Telford v Margate

Tuesday, 22 April 2003
FA Barclaycard Premiership
Leeds U v Fulham

Nationwide Football League Division 1
Wimbledon v Preston NE

Nationwide Football League Division 2
Bristol C v Cardiff C

Nationwide Football League Division 3
Bournemouth v Shrewsbury T

Saturday, 26 April 2003
FA Barclaycard Premiership
Birmingham C v Middlesbrough
Bolton W v Arsenal
Charlton Ath v Southampton
Chelsea v Fulham
Everton v Aston Villa
Leeds U v Blackburn R
Manchester C v West Ham U
Sunderland v Newcastle U
Tottenham H v Manchester U
WBA v Liverpool

Nationwide Football League Division 1
Brighton & HA v Watford
Burnley v Sheffield W
Coventry C v Gillingham
Crystal P v Stoke C
Ipswich T v Wimbledon
Leicester C v Norwich C
Nottingham F v Millwall
Portsmouth v Rotherham U
Preston NE v Bradford C
Reading v Grimsby T

378

Sheffield U v Wolverhampton W
Walsall v Derby Co

Nationwide Football League Division 2
Barnsley v Brentford
Cardiff C v Wigan Ath
Cheltenham T v Blackpool
Chesterfield v Bristol C
Luton T v Stockport Co
Northampton T v Plymouth Arg
Oldham Ath v Swindon T
Peterborough U v Notts Co
Port Vale v Huddersfield T
QPR v Crewe Alex
Tranmere R v Mansfield T
Wycombe W v Colchester U

Nationwide Football League Division 3
Boston U v Macclesfield T
Bournemouth v Lincoln C
Bristol R v Darlington
Hartlepool U v Shrewsbury T
Hull C v Kidderminster H
Leyton Orient v Rushden & D'monds
Rochdale v Swansea C
Scunthorpe U v Oxford U
Southend U v Bury
Torquay U v Carlisle U
Wrexham v Cambridge U
York C v Exeter C

Nationwide Conference
Forest Green v Dag & Red
Gravesend v Halifax
Hereford v Doncaster
Kettering v Leigh RMI
Margate v Scarborough
Morecambe v Burton Albion
Northwich v Barnet
Nuneaton v Farnborough
Stevenage v Southport
Woking v Telford
Yeovil v Chester

Saturday, 3 May 2003
FA Barclaycard Premiership
Arsenal v Leeds U
Aston Villa v Sunderland
Blackburn R v WBA
Fulham v Everton
Liverpool v Manchester C
Manchester U v Charlton Ath
Middlesbrough v Tottenham H
Newcastle U v Birmingham C
Southampton v Bolton W
West Ham U v Chelsea

Nationwide Football League Division 2
Blackpool v Chesterfield
Brentford v Peterborough U
Bristol C v Port Vale
Colchester U v QPR
Crewe Alex v Cardiff C
Huddersfield T v Oldham Ath
Mansfield T v Northampton T
Notts Co v Cheltenham T
Plymouth Arg v Wycombe W
Stockport Co v Tranmere R
Swindon T v Luton T
Wigan Ath v Barnsley

Nationwide Football League Division 3
Bury v Wrexham
Cambridge U v Boston U
Carlisle U v Bournemouth
Darlington v Leyton Orient
Exeter C v Southend U
Kidderminster H v Bristol R
Lincoln C v Torquay U
Macclesfield T v Rochdale
Oxford U v York C
Rushden & D'monds v Hartlepool U
Shrewsbury T v Scunthorpe U
Swansea C v Hull C

Sunday, 4 May 2003
Nationwide Football League Division 1
Bradford C v Portsmouth
Derby Co v Ipswich T
Gillingham v Crystal P
Grimsby T v Brighton & HA
Millwall v Coventry C
Norwich C v Preston NE
Rotherham U v Nottingham F
Sheffield W v Walsall
Stoke C v Reading
Watford v Sheffield U
Wimbledon v Burnley
Wolverhampton W v Leicester C

Sunday, 11 May 2003
FA Barclaycard Premiership
Birmingham C v West Ham U (4:00)
Bolton W v Middlesbrough (4:00)
Charlton Ath v Fulham (4:00)
Chelsea v Liverpool (4:00)
Everton v Manchester U (4:00)
Leeds U v Aston Villa (4:00)
Manchester C v Southampton (4:00)
Sunderland v Arsenal (4:00)
Tottenham H v Blackburn R (4:00)
WBA v Newcastle U (4:00)

OTHER FIXTURES — SEASON 2002–2003

July 2002

6/7 Sat/Sun UEFA Intertoto Cup 2 (1)

13/14 Sat/Sun UEFA Intertoto Cup 2 (2)

17 Wed UEFA Champions League 1Q (1)

20/21 Sat/Sun UEFA Intertoto Cup 3 (1)

24 Wed UEFA Champions League 1Q (2)

27 Sat UEFA Intertoto Cup 3 (2)

31 Wed UEFA Champions League 2Q (1)
UEFA Intertoto Cup Semi-Final (1)

August 2002

3 Sat

7 Wed UEFA Champions League 2Q (2)
UEFA Intertoto Cup Semi-Final (2)

10 Sat Football League Commences

11 Sun F.A. Community Shield
Arsenal v Liverpool at The Millennium Stadium, Cardiff – 2.00

13/14 Tues/Wed UEFA Champions League 3Q (1)
UEFA Intertoto Cup Final (1)

15 Thu UEFA Cup Q (1)

17 Sat F.A. Premier League Commences

18 Sun Start of F.A. Women's Premier League

21 Wed Friendly Internationals

23 Fri UEFA Super Cup

24 Sat F.A. Cup EP

26 Mon Bank Holiday

27 Tue UEFA Intertoto Cup Final (2)

27/28 Tue/Wed UEFA Champions League 3Q (2)

29 Thu UEFA Cup Q (2)

31 Sat F.A. Cup P

September 2002

7 Sat UEFA 2004 Qualifying Internationals
F.A. Vase 1Q
F.A. Youth Cup 1Q*

8 Sun F.A. Women's Cup 1Q
F.A. Women's Premier League Cup P

11 Wed F.L. Worthington Cup 1

14 Sat F.A. Cup 1Q

17/18 Tue/Wed UEFA Champions League Match Day (1)

19 Thu UEFA Cup 1 (1)

21 Sat F.A. Vase 2Q
F.A. Youth Cup 2Q*

22 Sun F.A. Women's Premier League Cup 1

24/25 Tue/Wed UEFA Champions League Match Day (2)

28 Sat F.A. Cup 2Q

29 Sun F.A. Women's Cup 2Q

October 2002

1/2 Tue/Wed UEFA Champions League Match Day (3)

2 Wed F.L. Worthington Cup 2

3 Thu UEFA Cup 1 (2)

5 Sat F.A. Trophy P
F.A. Youth Cup 3Q*
F.A. County Youth Cup 1*

6 Sun F.A. Sunday Cup 1

12 Sat Slovakia v England – UEFA 2004 Qualifying
F.A. Cup 3Q

16 Wed England v FYR Macedonia – UEFA 2004 Qualifying

19 Sat F.A. Vase 1P

22/23 Tue/Wed UEFA Champions League Match Day (4)

23 Wed F.L. LDV Vans Trophy 1

26 Sat F.A. Cup 4Q

27 Sun F.A. Women's Cup 1P
F.A. Youth Cup 1P*
F.A. Women's Premier League Cup 2

29/30 Tue/Wed UEFA Champions League Match Day (5)

31 Wed UEFA Cup 2 (1)

November 2002

2 Sat	F.A. Trophy 1	
3 Sun	F.A. Sunday Cup 2	
6 Wed	F.L. Worthington Cup 3	
9 Sat	F.A. Vase 2P	
	F.A. Youth Cup 2P*	
	F.A. County Youth Cup 2*	
10 Sun	F.A. Women's Cup 2P	
12/13 Tue/Wed	UEFA Champions League Match Day (6)	
13 Wed	F.L. LDV Vans Trophy 2	
14 Thu	UEFA Cup 2 (2)	
16 Sat	F.A. Cup 1P	
20 Wed	Friendly Internationals	
24 Sun	F.A. Women's Premier League Cup 3	
26/27 Tue/Wed	UEFA Champions League Match Day (7)	
27 Wed	F.A. Cup 1R	
28 Thu	UEFA Cup 3 (1)	
30 Sat	F.A. Trophy 2	

December 2002

1 Sun	F.A. Sunday Cup 3
3 Tue	Inter-Continental Cup
4 Wed	F.L. Worthington Cup 4
7 Sat	F.A. Cup 2P
	F.A. Vase 3P
	F.A. Youth Cup 3P*
8 Sun	F.A. Women's Cup 3P
10/11 Tue/Wed	UEFA Champions League Match Day (8)
11 Wed	F.L. LDV Vans Trophy QF
12 Thu	UEFA Cup 3 (2)
14 Sat	F.A. County Youth Cup 3*
18 Sat	F.A. Cup 2R
	F.L. Worthington Cup 5
24 Tue	Christmas Eve
25 Wed	Christmas Day
26 Thu	Boxing Day

January 2003

1 Wed	New Year's Day
4 Sat	F.A. Cup 3P
5 Sun	F.A. Women's Cup 4P
8 Wed	F.L. Worthington Cup SF1
11 Sat	F.A. Trophy 3
12 Sun	F.A. Sunday Cup 4
15 Wed	F.A. Cup 3R
18 Sat	F.A. Vase 4P

19 Sun	F.A. Women's Premier League Cup SF
22 Wed	F.L. Worthington Cup SF2
	F.L. LDV Vans Trophy SF
25 Sat	F.A. Cup 4P
	F.A. Youth Cup 4P*
26 Sun	F.A. Women's Cup 5P

February 2003

1 Sat	F.A. Trophy 4
	F.A. County Youth Cup 4*
2 Sun	F.A. Sunday Cup 5
5 Wed	F.A. Cup 4R
8 Sat	F.A. Vase 5P
9 Sun	F.A. Women's Cup 6P
12 Wed	International (Friendly)
15 Sat	F.A. Cup 5P
	F.A. Youth Cup 5P*
18/19 Tue/Wed	UEFA Champions League Match Day (9)
19 Wed	F.L. LDV Vans Trophy Area Final 1
20 Thu	UEFA Cup 4 (1)
22 Sat	F.A. Trophy 5
25/26 Tue/Wed	UEFA Champions League Match Day (10)
26 Wed	F.A. Cup 5R
	F.L. LDV Vans Trophy Area Final 2
27 Thu	UEFA Cup 4 (2)

March 2003

1 Sat	F.A. Vase 6P
2 Sun	F.L. Worthington Cup Final
8 Sat	F.A. Cup 6P
	F.A. Youth Cup 6P*
	F.A. County Youth Cup Semi Final*
11/12 Tue/Wed	UEFA Champions League Match Day (11)
13 Thu	UEFA Cup Quarter Final
15 Sat	F.A. Trophy 6
16 Sun	F.A. Sunday Cup Semi Final
	F.A. Women's Premier League Cup Final
18/19 Tue/Wed	UEFA Champions League Match Day (12)
19 Wed	F.A. Cup 6R
20 Thu	UEFA Cup Quarter Final (2)
22 Sat	F.A. Vase Semi Final (1)

29 Sat	Liechtenstein v England – UEFA 2004 Qualifying
	F.A. Vase Semi Final (2)
	F.A. Youth Cup Semi Final 1st Leg*
30 Sun	F.A. Women's Cup Semi Final

April 2003

2 Wed	England v Turkey – UEFA 2004 Qualifying
5 Sat	F.A. Trophy Semi Final (1)
6 Sun	F.L. LDV Vans Trophy Final
8/9 Tue/Wed	UEFA Champions League Quarter Final (1)
10 Thu	UEFA Cup Semi Final (1)
12 Sat	F.A. Trophy Semi Final (2)
	F.A. Youth Cup Semi Final 2nd Leg*
13 Sun	F.A. Cup Semi Finals
18 Fri	Good Friday
21 Mon	Easter Monday
22/23 Tue/Wed	UEFA Champions League Quarter Final (2)
24 Thu	UEFA Cup Semi Final (2)
26 Sat	F.A. County Youth Cup Final
27 Sun	F.A. Sunday Cup Final
30 Wed	International (Friendly)

May 2003

3 Sat	End of Football League
5 Mon	Bank Holiday
	F.A. Women's Cup Final
6/7 Tue/Wed	UEFA Champions League Semi Final (1)
10 Sat	End of Premier League
	F.A. Vase Final
11 Sun	F.A. Trophy Final (prov)
	F.L. Play-off Semi Final (1)
13/14 Tue/Wed	UEFA Champions League Semi Final (2)
14 Wed	F.L. Play-off Semi Final (2)

15 Thu	F.A. Youth Cup Cup Final 1 (prov)
17 Sat	F.A. Cup Final
18 Sun	F.A. Trophy Final (prov)
21 Wed	UEFA Cup Final
22 Thu	F.A. Youth Cup Final 2 (prov)
24 Sat	F.L. 3rd Division Play-off Final
25 Sun	F.L. 2nd Division Play-off Final
26 Mon	F.L. 1st Division Play-off Final
28 Wed	UEFA Champions League Final

June 2003

| 11 Wed | England v Slovakia – UEFA 2004 Qualifying |

* closing date of Round

Other UEFA 2004 Qualifying Ties

Sat 6 Sept 2003
FYR Macedonia v England

Wed 10 Sept 2003
England v Liechtenstein

Sat 11 Oct 2003
Turkey v England

Final Competition

Draw – 30 November 2003
Opening match, Porto – 12 June 2004
End of group stage – 23 June 2004
Quarter-Final 1 – 26 June 2004
Quarter-Final 2 – 27 June 2004
Semi-Final 1 – 30 June 2004
Semi-Final 2 – 1 July 2004
Final – 4 July 2004

CLUB AND OTHER RECORDS DURING 2001–2002

Arsenal
Premier League records: 13 consecutive wins; scored in every League match; unbeaten away

Aston Villa
Most capped player: Steve Staunton, Republic of Ireland.

Blackburn Rovers
League Cup winners 2002.
Most capped player: Henning Berg, Norway

Blackpool
LDV Vans Trophy winners 2002

Bristol Rovers
Most capped player: Vitalijs Astafjevs, Latvia

Cheltenham Town
Reached FA Cup 5th round

Crewe Alexandra
Most capped player: Clayton Ince, Trinidad & Tobago

Lincoln City
Most League appearances: Grant Brown

Luton Town
Most League points. 97 Div 3 2001-02

Manchester City
Most League points: 99 Div 1 2001-02
Most League goals: 108

Plymouth Argyle
Most League points: 102 Div 3 2001-02

Southampton
Record attendance: 31,973 v Newcastle United

West Bromwich Albion
Most League points: 89 Div 1 2001-02

Wycombe Wanderers
Most capped player: Mark Rogers, Canada.

International
Under-21 England v Holland substitute Jermain Defoe scored with first touch as a substitute 3.9 seconds.

Now you can buy any of these other bestselling sports titles
from your bookshop or *direct from the publisher*.

FREE P&P AND UK DELIVERY
(Overseas and Ireland £3.50 per book)

Rothmans Football Yearbook 2002–2003	Glenda Rollin and Jack Rollin	£19.99
1966 and All That	Geoff Hurst	£6.99
Psycho	Stuart Pearce	£6.99
The Autobiography	David Batty	£6.99
Priceless	Rodney Marsh	£7.99
The Autobiography	Gareth Edwards	£7.99
The Autobiography	John Barnes	£6.99
Ultra Nippon	Jonathan Birchall	£7.99
Barmy Army	Dougie Brimson	£6.99
Vinnie	Vinnie Jones	£6.99
Manchester United Ruined My Life	Colin Shindler	£6.99
God Save the Team	Eddy Brimson	£6.99
A Lot of Hard Yakka	Simon Hughes	£6.99
Left Foot Forward	Garry Nelson	£6.99

TO ORDER SIMPLY CALL THIS NUMBER

01235 400 414

or visit our website:
www.madaboutbooks.com

Prices and availability subject to change without notice.